Communications
in Computer and Information Science   304

De-Shuang Huang   Phalguni Gupta
Xiang Zhang   Prashan Premaratne (Eds.)

Emerging Intelligent Computing Technology and Applications

8th International Conference, ICIC 2012
Huangshan, China, July 25-29, 2012
Proceedings

 Springer

Volume Editors

De-Shuang Huang
Tongji University, Shanghai, China
E-mail: dshuang@tongji.edu.cn

Phalguni Gupta
Indian Institute of Technology Kanpur, India
E-mail: pg@cse.iitk.ac.in

Xiang Zhang
University of Louisville, KY, USA
E-mail: xiang.zhang@louisville.edu

Prashan Premaratne
University of Wollongong, NSW, Australia
E-mail: prashan@uow.edu.au

ISSN 1865-0929   e-ISSN 1865-0937
ISBN 978-3-642-31836-8   e-ISBN 978-3-642-31837-5
DOI 10.1007/978-3-642-31837-5
Springer Heidelberg Dordrecht London New York

Library of Congress Control Number: 2012941672

CR Subject Classification (1998): I.2, I.4, H.3, F.1, I.5, H.4

Typesetting: Camera-ready by author, data conversion by Scientific Publishing Services, Chennai, India

Printed on acid-free paper

Springer is part of Springer Science+Business Media (www.springer.com)

Preface

The International Conference on Intelligent Computing (ICIC) was started to provide an annual forum dedicated to the emerging and challenging topics in artificial intelligence, machine learning, pattern recognition, image processing, bioinformatics, and computational biology. It aims to bring together researchers and practitioners from both academia and industry to share ideas, problems, and solutions related to the multifaceted aspects of intelligent computing.

ICIC 2012, held in Huangshan, China, July 25–29, 2012, constituted the 8th International Conference on Intelligent Computing. It built upon the success of ICIC 2011, ICIC 2010, ICIC 2009, ICIC 2008, ICIC 2007, ICIC 2006, and ICIC 2005 that were held in Zhengzhou, Changsha, China, Ulsan, Korea, Shanghai, Qingdao, Kunming, and Hefei, China, respectively.

This year, the conference concentrated mainly on the theories and methodologies as well as the emerging applications of intelligent computing. Its aim was to unify the picture of contemporary intelligent computing techniques as an integral concept that highlights the trends in advanced computational intelligence and bridges theoretical research with applications. Therefore, the theme for this conference was "Emerging Intelligent Computing Technology and Applications." Papers focusing on this theme were solicited, addressing theories, methodologies, and applications in science and technology.

ICIC 2012 received 753 submissions from 28 countries and regions. All papers went through a rigorous peer-review procedure and each paper received at least three review reports. Based on the review reports, the Program Committee finally selected 242 high-quality papers for presentation at ICIC 2012, of which 242 papers are included in three volumes of proceedings published by Springer: one volume of *Lecture Notes in Computer Science* (LNCS), one volume of *Lecture Notes in Artificial Intelligence* (LNAI), and one volume of *Communications in Computer and Information Science* (CCIS).

This volume of *Communications in Computer and Information Science* (CCIS) includes 73 papers.

The organizers of ICIC 2012, including Tongji University, made an enormous effort to ensure the success of the conference. We hereby would like to thank the members of the Program Committee and the referees for their collective effort in reviewing and soliciting the papers. We would like to thank Alfred Hofmann, executive editor from Springer, for his frank and helpful advice and guidance throughout and for his continuous support in publishing the proceedings. In particular, we would like to thank all the authors for contributing their papers. Without the high-quality submissions from the authors, the success of the conference would not have been possible. Finally, we are especially grateful to the IEEE Computational Intelligence Society, the International Neural Network Society, and the National Science Foundation of China for their sponsorship.

May 2012

De-Shuang Huang
Phalguni Gupta
Xiang Zhang
Prashan Premaratne

ICIC 2012 Organization

General Co-chairs	Changjun Jiang, China
	Gary G. Yen, USA
Steering Committee Chair	De-Shuang Huang, China
Program Committee Co-chairs	Jianhua Ma, Japan
	Laurent Heutte, France
Organizing Committee Co-chairs	Duoqian Miao, China
	Yang Xiang, China
	Jihong Guan, China
Award Committee Chair	Kang-Hyun Jo, Korea
Publication Chair	Vitoantonio Bevilacqua, Italy
Workshop/Special Session Chair	Juan Carlos Figueroa, Colombia
Special Issue Chair	Michael Gromiha, India
Tutorial Chair	Phalguni Gupta, India
International Liaison Chair	Prashan Premaratne, Australia
Publicity Co-chairs	Kyungsook Han, Korea
	Ling Wang, China
	Xiang Zhang, USA
	Lei Zhang, China
Exhibition Chair	Qiong Wu, China
Organizing Committee	Zhijun Ding, China
	Hanli Wang, China
	Yan Wu, China
	Guo-Zheng Li, China
	Fanhuai Shi, China
Conference Secretary	Zhi-Yang Chen, China

Program Committee

Khalid Mahmood Aamir, Italy
Vasily Aristarkhov, Russian Federation
Costin Badica, Romania
Vitoantonio Bevilacqua, Italy
Shuhui Bi, China
Danail Bonchev, USA
Stefano Cagnoni, Italy
Chin-Chih Chang, Taiwan, China
Pei-Chann Chang, Taiwan, China
Jack Chen, Canada
Shih-Hsin Chen, Taiwan, China
Wen-Sheng Chen, China

Xiyuan Chen, China
Yang Chen, China
Ziping Chiang, Taiwan, China
Michal Choras, Poland
Angelo Ciaramella, Italy
Milan Cisty, Slovakia
Jose Alfredo F. Costa, Brazil
Loganathan D., India
Eng. Salvatore Distefano, Italy
Mariagrazia Dotoli, Italy
Karim Faez, Iran
Jianbo Fan, China

Minrui Fei, China
Wai-Keung Fung, Canada
Jun-Ying Gan, China
Xiao-Zhi Gao, Finland
Dunwei Gong, China
Valeriya Gribova, Russia
M. Michael Gromiha, Japan
Kayhan Gulez, Turkey
Anyuan Guo, China
Ping Guo, China
Phalguni Gupta, India
Fei Han, China
Kyungsook Han, Korea
Nojeong Heo, Korea
Laurent Heutte, France
Martin Holena, Czech Republic
Wei-Chiang Hong, Taiwan, China
Yuexian Hou, China
Sanqing Hu, China
Guangbin Huang, Singapore
Peter Hung, Ireland
Li Jia, China
Zhenran Jiang, China
Kang-Hyun Jo, Korea
Dah-Jing Jwo, Taiwan, China
Yoshiaki Kakuda, Japan
Vandana Dixit Kaushik, India
Muhammad Khurram Khan,
   Saudi Arabia
Bora Kumova, Turkey
Yoshinori Kuno, Japan
Takashi Kuremoto, Japan
Vincent C.S. Lee, Australia
Bo Li, China
Dalong Li, USA
Guo-Zheng Li, China
Shi-Hua Li, China
Xiaoou Li, Mexico
Hualou Liang, USA
Honghuang Lin, USA
Chunmei Liu, USA
Chun-Yu Liu, USA
Ju Liu, China
Ke Lv, China
Jinwen Ma, China

Igor V. Maslov, Japan
Xiandong Meng, USA
Filippo Menolascina, Italy
Pabitra Mitra, India
Ravi Monaragala, Sri Lanka
Tarik Veli Mumcu, Turkey
Primiano Di Nauta, Italy
Ben Niu, China
Sim-Heng Ong, Singapore
Vincenzo Pacelli, Italy
Shaoning Pang, New Zealand
Francesco Pappalardo, Italy
Young B. Park, Korea
Surya Prakash, India
Prashan Premaratne, Australia
Hong Qiao, China
Daowen Qiu, China
K.R. Seeja, India
Ajita Rattani, Italy
Angel D. Sappa, Spain
Simon See, Singapore
Akash K. Singh, USA
Jiatao Song, China
Qiankun Song, China
Zhan-Li Sun, Singapore
Stefano Squartini, Italy
Evi Syukur, Australia
Hao Tang, China
Chuan-Kang Ting, Taiwan, China
Jun Wan, USA
Bing Wang, USA
Jeen-Shing Wang, Taiwan, China
Ling Wang, China
Shitong Wang, China
Xuesong Wang, China
Yong Wang, China
Yufeng Wang, China
Zhi Wei, China
Xiaojun Wu, China
Junfeng Xia, USA
Shunren Xia, China
Bingji Xu, China
Shao Xu, Singapore
Zhenyu Xuan, USA
Yu Xue, China

Tao Ye, China
Jun-Heng Yeh, Taiwan, China
Myeong-Jae Yi, Korea
Zhi-Gang Zeng, China
Boyun Zhang, China
Chaoyang Joe Zhang, USA
Lei Zhang, Hong Kong, China
Rui Zhang, China

Xiaoguang Zhao, China
Xing-Ming Zhao, China
Zhongming Zhao, USA
Bo-Jin Zheng, China
Chun-Hou Zheng, China
Fengfeng Zhou, China
Waqas Haider Khan Bangyal, Pakistan
Yuhua Qian, China

Reviewers

Kezhi Mao
Xin Hao
Tarik Veli Mumcu
Muharrem Mercimek
Selin Ozcira
Ximo Torres
BinSong Cheng
Shihua Zhang
Yu Xue
Xiaoping Luo
Dingfei Ge
Jiayin Zhou
Mingyi Wang
Chung Chang Lien
Wei-Ling Hwang
Jian Jia
Jian Wang
Zhiliu Zuo
Sajid Bashir
Faisal Mufti
Hafiz Muhammad Farooq
Bilal Ahmed
Maryam Gul
Gurkan Tuna
Hajira Jabeen
Chandana Gamage
Prashan Premaratne
Chathura R. De Silva
Manodha Gamage
Kasun De Zoysa
Chesner Desir
Laksman Jayaratne
Francesco Camastra

Rémi Flamary
Antoninostaiano Alessio Ferone
Raffaele Montella
Nalin Karunasinghe
Vladislavs Dovgalecs
Pierrick Tranouez
Antonio Maratea
Giuseppe Vettigli
Ranga Rodrigo
Chyuan-Huei Yang
Rey-Sern Lin
Cheng-Hsiung Chiang
Jian-Shiun Hu
Yao-Hong Tsai
Hung-Chi Su
J.-H. Chen
Wen Ouyang
Chong Shen
Yuan Xu
Cucocris Tano
Tien-Dung Le
Hee-Jun Kang
Hong-Hee Lee
Ngoc-Tung Nguyen
Ju Kunru
Vladimir Brusic
Ping Zhang
Renjie Zhang
Alessandro Cincotti
Mojaharul Islam
Marzio Pennisi
Haili Wang
Santo Motta

Keun Ho Ryu
Alfredo Pulvirenti
Rosalba Giugno
Ge Guo
Chih-Min Lin
Yifeng Zhang
Xuefen Zhu
Lvzhou Li
Haozhen Situ
Qin Li
Nikola Paunkovic
Paulo Mateus
Jozef Gruska
Xiangfu Zou
Yasser Omar
Yin-Xiang Long
Bjoern Schuller
Erikcam Bria
Faundez-Zanuy Marcos
Rui Zhang
Yibin Ye
Qinglai Wei
Guangbin Huang
Lendasse Amaury
Michele Scarpiniti
Simone Bassis
Morabito Carlo
Amir Hussain
Li Zhang
Emilio Soria
Sanqing Hu
Hossein Javaherian
Veselin Stoyanov
Eric Fock
Yao-Nan Lien
Liangjun Xie
Nong Gu
Xuewei Wang
Shizhong Liao
Zheng Liu
Bingjun Sun
Yuexian Hou
Shiping Wen
Ailong Wu
Gang Bao

Takashi Kuremoto
Amin Yazdanpanah
Meng-Cheng Lau
Chi Tai Cheng
Jayanta Debnath
Raymond Ng
Baranyi Peter
Yongping Zhai
Baoquan Song
Weidi Dai
Jiangzhen Ran
Huiyu Jin
Guoping Lu
Xiaohua Qiao
Xuemei Ren
Mingxia Shen
Hao Tang
Zhong-Qiang Wu
Zhenhua Huang
Junlin Chang
Bin Ye
Yong Zhang
Yanzi Miao
Yindi Zhao
Jun Zhao
Mei-Qiang Zhu
Xue Xue
Yanjing Sun
Waqas Haider Khan Bangyal
Ming-Feng Yang
Guo-Feng Fan
Asma Nani
Xiangtao Li
Hongjun Jia
Yehu Shen
Tiantai Guo
Liya Ding
Dawen Xu
Jinhe Wang
Xiangyu Wang
Shihong Ding
Zhao Wang
Junyong Zhai
Haibo Du
Haibin Sun

Jun Yang
Chin-Sheng Yang
Jheng-Long Wu
Jyun-Jie Lin
Jun-Lin Lin
Liang-Chih Yu
S.H. Chen
Chien-Lung Chan
Eric Fan
X.H. Cloud
Yue Deng
Kun Yang
Badrinath Srinivas
Francesco Longo
Santo Motta
Giovanni Merlino
Shengjun Wen
Ni Bu
Changan Jiang
Caihong Zhang
Lihua Jiang
Aihui Wang
Cunchen Gao
Tianyu Liu
Pengfei Li
Jing Sun
Aimin Zhou
Ji-Hui Zhang
Xiufen Zou
Lianghong Wu
H. Chen
Jian Cheng
Zhihua Cui
Xiao-Zhi Gao
Guosheng Hao
Quan-Ke Pan
Bin Qian
Xiaoyan Sun
Byungjeong Lee
Woochang Shin
Jaewon Oh
Jong-Myon Kim
Yung-Keun Kwon
Mingjian Zhang
Xiai Yang

Lirong Wang
Xi Luo
Weidong Yang
Weiling Liu
Lanshen Guo
Yunxia Qu
Peng Kai
Song Yang
Xianxia Zhang
Min Zheng
Weiming Yu
Wangjun Xiang
Qing Liu
Xi Luo
Ali Ahmed Adam
Ibrahim Aliskan
Yusuf Altun
Kadir Erkan
Ilker Ustoglu
Levent Ucun
Janset Dasdemir
Xiai Yan
Stefano Ricciardi
Daniel Riccio
Marilena De Marsico
Fabio Narducci
Atsushi Yamashita
Kazunori Onoguchi
Ryuzo Okada
Naghmeh Garmsiri
Lockery Dan
Maddahi Yaser
Kurosh Zareinia
Ramhuzaini Abd Rahman
Xiaosong Li
Lei Song
Gang Chen
Yiming Peng
Fan Liu
Jun Zhang
Li Shang
Chunhou Zheng
Jayasudha John Suseela
Soniya Balram
K.J. Shanti

Aravindan Chandrabose
Parul Agarwal
Deepa Anand
Ranjit Biswas
Nobutaka Shimada
Hironobu Fujiyoshi
Giuseppe Vettigli
Francesco Napolitano
Xiao Zhang
Torres-Sospedra Joaquín
Kunikazu Kobayashi
Liangbing Feng
Fuhai Li
Yongsheng Dong
Shuyi Zhang
Yanqiao Zhu
Lei Huang
Yue Zhao
Yunsheng Jiang
Bin Xu
Wei Wang
Jin Wei
Kisha Ni
Yu-Liang Hsu
Che-Wei Lin
Jeen-Shing Wang
Yingke Lei
Jie Gui
Xiaoming Liu
Dong Yang
Jian Yu
Jin Gu
Chenghai Xue
Xiaowo Wang
Xin Feng
Bo Chen
Jianwei Yang
Chao Huang
Weixiang Liu
Qiang Huang
Yanjie Wei
Ao Li
Mingyuan Jiu
Dipankar Das
Gianluca Ippoliti

Lian Liu
Mohammad Bagher Bannae Sharifian
Hadi Afsharirad
S. Galvani
Chengdong Wu
Meiju Liu
Aamir Shahzad
Wei Xiong
Toshiaki Kondo
Andrea Prati
Bai Li
Domenico G. Sorrenti
Alessandro Rizzi
Raimondo Schettini
Mengjie Zhang
Gustavo Olague
Umarani Jayaraman
Aditya Nigam
Hunny Mehrotra
Gustavo Souza
Guilherme Barreto
Leandrodos Santos Coelho
Carlos Forster
Fernando Von Zuben
Anne Canuto
Jackson Souza
Carmelo Bastos Filho
Daniel Aloise
Sergio P. Santos
Ricardo Fabbri
Fábio Paiva
S.H. Chen
Tsung-Che Chiang
Cheng-Hung Chen
Shih-Hung Wu
Zhifeng Yun
Yanqing Ji
Kai Wang
Je-Ho Park
Junhong Wang
Jifang Pang
Thiran De Silva
Nalin Badara
Shaojing Fan
Chen Li

Qingfeng Li
Liangxu Liu
Rina Su
Hua Yu
Jie Sun
Linhua Zhou
Zhaohong Deng
Pengjiang Qian
Jun Wang
Puneet Gupta
Salim Flora
Jayaputera James
Sherchan Wanita
Helen Paik
Mohammed M. Gaber
Agustinus B. Waluyo
Dat Hoang
Hamid Motahari
Eric Pardede
Tim Ho
Jose A.F. Costa
Qiang Fan
Surya Prakash
Vandana Dixit K.
Saiful Islam
Kamlesh Tiwari
Sandesh Gupta
Zahid Akhtar
Min-Chih Chen
Andreas Konstantinidis
Quanming Zhao
Hongchun Li
Zhengjie Wang
Chong Meng
Lin Cai
Aiyu Zhang
Yang-Won Lee
Young Park
Chulantha Kulasekere
Akalanka Ranundeniya
Junfeng Xia
Min Zhao
Hamid Reza Rashidi Kanan
Mehdi Ezoji
Majid Ziaratban

Saeed Mozaffari
Javad Haddadnia
Peyman Moallem
Farzad Towhidkhah
Hamid Abrishamimoghaddam
Mohammad Reza Pourfard
M.J. Abdollahi Fard
Arana-Arexolaleiba Nestor
Carme Julià
Boris Vintimilla
Daniele Ranieri
Antonio De Giorgio
Vito Gallo
Leonarda Carnimeo
Paolo Pannarale
López-Chau Asdrúbal
Jair Cervantes
Debrup Chakraborty
Simon Dacey
Wei-Chiang Hong
Wenyong Dong
Lingling Wang
Hongrun Wu
Chien-Yuan Lai
Md.Kamrul Hasan
Mohammad Kaykobad
Young-Koo Lee
Sungyoung Lee
Chin-Chih Chang
Yuewang
Shinji Inoue
Tomoyuki Ohta
Eitaro Kohno
Alex Muscar
Sorin Ilie
Cosulschi Mirel
Min Chen
Wen Yu
Lopez-Arevalo Ivan
Sabooh Ajaz
Prashan Premaratne
Weimin Huang
Jingwen Wang
Kai Yin
Hong Wang

Yan Fan
Niu Qun
Youqing Wang
Dajun Du
Laurence T. Yang
Laurence Yang
Seng Loke
Syukur Evi
Luis Javier García Villalba
Tsutomu Terada
Tomas Sanchez Lopez
Eric Cheng
Battenfeld Oliver
Yokota Masao
Hanemann Sven
Yue Suo
Pao-Ann Hsiung
Kristiansen Lill
Callaghan Victor
Mzamudio Rodriguez Victor
Sherif Sakr
Rajiv Ranjan
Cheong Ghil Kim
Philip Chan
Wojtek Goscinski
Jefferson Tan
Bo Zhou
Huiwei Wang
Xiaofeng Chen
Bing Li
Wojtek Goscinski
Samar Zutshi
Rafal Kozik
Tomasz Andrysiak
Marian Cristian Mihaescu
Michal Choras
Yanwen Chong
Jinxing Liu
Miguel Gonzalez Mendoza
Ta-Yuan Chou
Hui Li
Chao Wu
Kyung DaeKo
Junhong Wang
Guoping Lin

Jiande Sun
Hui Yuan
Qiang Wu
Yannan Ren
Dianxing Liu
M. Sohel Rahman
Dengxin Li
Gerard J. Chang
Weidong Chang
Xulian Hua
Dan Tang
Sandesh Gupta
Uma Rani
Surya Prakash
Narendra Kohli
Meemee Ng
Olesya Kazakova
Vasily Aristarkhov
Ozgur Kaymakci
Xuesen Ma
Qiyue Li
Zhenchun Wei
Xin Wei
Xiangjuan Yao
Ling Wang
Shujuan Jiang
Changhai Nie
He Jiang
Fengfeng Zhou
Zexian Liu
Jian Ren
Xinjiao Gao
Tian-Shun Gao
Han Cheng
Yongbo Wang
Yuangen Yao
Juan Liu
Bing Luo
Zilu Ying
Junying Zeng
Guohui He
Yikui Zhai
Binyu Yi
Zhan Liu
Xiang Ji

Hongyuan Zha
Azzedine Boukerche
Horacio A.B.F. Oliveira
Eduardo F. Nakamura
Antonio A. F. Loureiro
Radhika Nagpal
Jonathan Bachrach
Daeyoung Choi
Woo Yul Kim
Amelia Badica
Fuqing Duan
Hui-Ping Tserng
Ren-Jye Dzeng
Machine Hsie
Milan Cisty
Muhammad Amjad
Muhammad Rashid
Waqas Bangyal
Bo Liu
Xueping Yu
Chenlong Liu
Jikui Shen
Julius Wan
Linlin Shen
Zhou Su
Weiyan Hou
Emil Vassev
Anuparp Boonsongsrikul
Paddy Nixon
Kyung-Suk Lhee
Man Pyo Hong
Vincent C.S. Lee
Yee-Wei Law
Touraj Banirostam
Ho-Quoc-Phuong Nguyen
Bin Ye
Huijun Li
Xue Sen
Mu Qiao
Xuesen Ma
Weizhen Chun
Qian Zhang
Baosheng Yang
Xuanfang Fei
Fanggao Cui

Xiaoning Song
Dongjun Yu
Bo Li
Huajiang Shao
Ke Gu
Helong Xiao
Wensheng Tang
Andrey Vavilin
Jong Eun Ha
Mun-Ho Jeong
Taeho Kim
Kaushik Deb
Daenyeong Kim
Dongjoong Kang
Hyun-Deok Kang
Hoang-Hon Trinh
Andrey Yakovenko
Dmitry Brazhkin
Sergey Ryabinin
Stanislav Efremov
Andrey Maslennikov
Oleg Sklyarov
Pabitra Mitra
Juan Li
Tiziano Politi
Vitoantonio Bevilacqua
Abdul Rauf
Yuting Yang
Lei Zhao
Shih-Wei Lin
Vincent Li
Chunlu Lai
Qian Wang
Liuzhao Chen
Xiaozhao Zhao
Plaban Bhowmick
Anupam Mandal
Biswajit Das
Pabitra Mitra
Tripti Swarnkar
Yang Dai
Chao Chen
Yi Ma
Emmanuel Camdes
Chenglei Sun

Yinying Wang
Jiangning Song
Ziping Chiang
Vincent Chiang
Xingming Zhao
Chenglei Sun
Francesca Nardone
Angelo Ciaramella
Alessia Albanese
Francesco Napolitano
Guo-Zheng Li
Xu-Ying Liu
Dalong Li
Jonathan Sun
Nan Wang
Yi Yang
Mingwei Li
Wierzbicki Adam
Marcin Czenko
Ha Tran
Jeroen Doumen
Sandro Etalle
Pieter Hartel
Jerryden Hartog
Hai Ren
Xiong Li
Ling Liu
Félix Gómez Mármol
Jih-Gau Juang
He-Sheng Wang
Xin Lu
Kyung-Suk Lhee
Sangyoon Oh
Chisa Takano
Sungwook S. Kim
Junichi Funasaka
Yoko Kamidoi
Dan Wu
Dah-Jing Jwo
Abdollah Shidfar
Reza Pourgholi
Xiujun Zhang
Yan Wang
Kun Yang
Iliya Slavutin

Ling Wang
Huizhong Yang
Ning Li
Tao Ye
Smile Gu
Phalguni Gupta
Guangxu Jin
Huijia Li
Xin Gao
Dan Liu
Zhenyu Xuan
Changbin Du
Mingkun Li
Haiyun Zhang
Baoli Wang
Giuseppe Pappalardo
Huisen Wang
Hai Min
Nalin Bandara
Lin Zhu
Wen Jiang
Can-Yi Lu
Lei Zhang
Jian Lu
Jian Lu
Hong-Jie Yu
Ke Gu
Hangjun Wang
Zhi-De Zhi
Xiaoming Ren
Ben Niu
Hua-Yun Chen
Fuqing Duan
Jing Xu
Marco Falagario
Fabio Sciancalepore
Nicola Epicoco
Wei Zhang
Mu-Chung Chen
Chinyuan Fan
Chun-Wei Lin
Chun-Hao Chen
Lien-Chin Chen
Seiki Inoue
K.R. Seeja

Gurkan Tuna
Cagri Gungor
Qian Zhang
Huanting Feng
Boyun Zhang
Jun Qin
Yang Zhao
Qinghua Cui
Hsiao Piau Ng
Qunfeng Dong
Hailei Zhang
Woochang Hwang
Joe Zhang
Marek Rodny
Bing-Nan Li
Yee-Wei Law

Lu Zhen
Bei Ye
Jl Xu
Pei-Chann Chang
Valeria Gribova
Xiandong Meng
Lasantha Meegahapola
Angel Sappa
Rajivmal Hotra
George Smith
Carlor Ossi
Lijing Tan
Antonio Puliafito
Nojeong Heo
Santosh Bbehera
Giuliana Rotunno

Table of Contents

Biology Inspired Computing and Optimization

Knowledge Discovery and Data Mining

Intelligent Computing in Bioinformatics

Intelligent Computing in Pattern Recognition

Intelligent Computing in Image Processing

Intelligent Computing in Computer Vision

Intelligent Control and Automation

Knowledge Representation/Reasoning and Expert Systems

Special Session on Advances in Information Security 2012

Special Session on Protein and Gene Bioinformatics: Analysis, Algorithms and Applications

Special Session on Soft Computing and Bio-inspired Techiques in Real-World Applications

Special Session on Bio-inspired Computing and Applications

Oscillation Analysis for a Recurrent Neural Network Model with Distributed Delays

Chunhua Feng[1] and Zhenkun Huang[2]

[1] College of Mathematical Science, Guangxi Normal University,
Guilin, Guangxi, China, 541004
[2] Department of Mathematics, Jimei University, Xiamen, Fujian, China, 361021
chfeng@mailbox.gxnu.edu.cn, hzk974226@jmu.edu.cn

Abstract. In this paper, oscillatory behavior of the solutions for a three-note recurrent neural network model with distributed delays and a strong kernel is investigated. Two simple and practical criteria to guarantee the oscillations of the solutions for the system are derived. Some numerical simulations are given to justify our theoretical analysis result.

Keywords: three-note network model, distributed delay, strong kernel, oscillation.

1   Introduction

It is known that recurrent neural networks have been used extensively in many areas. On the one hand, the stability problem of the networks has become very interesting and many sufficient conditions have been proposed to ensure the asymptotic or exponential stability for the networks with various time delays [1-4]. On the other hand, the oscillatory behavior including periodic solutions, almost periodic solutions for time delay systems have been the focus of many researchers in recent years [5-8]. Since bifurcation can induce periodic solutions, some researchers have discussed bifurcating periodic solutions for different neural networks [9-12]. In [11], Liao et al have studied two-neuron system with distributed delays as follows:

$$
\begin{cases}
\dfrac{dx_1(t)}{dt} = -x_1(t) + a_1 f\left[x_2(t) - b_2 \int_0^\infty F(r) x_2(t-r) dr - c_1 \right] \\
\dfrac{dx_2(t)}{dt} = -x_2(t) + a_2 f\left[x_1(t) - b_1 \int_0^\infty F(r) x_1(t-r) dr - c_2 \right]
\end{cases}
\tag{1}
$$

where $F(r) = \mu^2 r e^{-\mu r}, \mu > 0$ is strong kernel. By means of the frequency domain approach, the authors have shown that if the mean delay used as a bifurcation parameter, then Hopf bifurcation occurs for this model. A family of periodic solutions bifurcates from the equilibrium when the bifurcation parameter exceeds a critical

D.-S. Huang et al. (Eds.): ICIC 2012, CCIS 304, pp. 1–9, 2012.

value. In another paper, Hajihosseini et al have studied the following three-note system with distributed delays, strong kernel and activation function tanh(u) [12]:

$$\begin{cases} x_1'(t) = -x_1(t) + \tanh\left[\int_0^\infty F(r)x_2(t-r)dr\right] \\ x_2'(t) = -x_2(t) + \tanh\left[\int_0^\infty F(r)x_3(t-r)dr\right] \\ x_3'(t) = -x_3(t) + w_1\tanh\left[\int_0^\infty F(r)x_3(t-r)dr\right] + w_2\tanh\left[\int_0^\infty F(r)x_2(t-r)dr\right] \end{cases} \qquad (2)$$

where $F(\cdot)$ is the strong kernel and w_1, w_2 are parameters satisfying $|w_1 + w_2| < 1$. Also by using the frequency domain approach, the authors have proved that a Hopf bifurcation takes place in system (2) as the mean delay passes a critical value. In this paper, we shall discuss the following three-note system with distributed delays and general activation functions:

$$\begin{cases} x_1'(t) = -x_1(t) + f\left[\int_0^\infty F(r)x_2(t-r)dr\right] \\ x_2'(t) = -x_2(t) + f\left[\int_0^\infty F(r)x_3(t-r)dr\right] \\ x_3'(t) = -x_3(t) + w_1 f\left[\int_0^\infty F(r)x_3(t-r)dr\right] + w_2 f\left[\int_0^\infty F(r)x_2(t-r)dr\right] \end{cases} \qquad (3)$$

Based on Chafee's criterion, if system (3) has a unique equilibrium point which is unstable, and all solutions of system (3) are bounded, then this particular nonstability of equilibrium point with boundedness of the solutions will force system (3) to generate a limit cycle, namely, a periodic solution [13]. For the parameters w_1 and w_2, our condition to guarantee the oscillation of the system is $|w_1|\gamma_1\gamma_2\gamma_3 + |w_2|\gamma_2\gamma_3 > 1$. This condition is different from $|w_1 + w_2| < 1$.

2   Preliminaries

The same as [11], for system (3) with the strong kernel $F(r) = \mu^2 r e^{-\mu r}, \mu > 0$, we employ the following change of coordinates

$$\begin{cases} y_1(t) = \int_0^\infty F(r)x_1(t-r)dr \\ y_2(t) = \int_0^\infty F(r)x_2(t-r)dr \\ y_3(t) = \int_0^\infty F(r)x_3(t-r)dr \end{cases} \qquad (4)$$

Then in the new system of coordinates, system (3) becomes

$$
\begin{cases}
y_1'(t) = -y_1(t) + \int_{-\infty}^{0} F(-r)f(y_2(t+r))dr \\
y_2'(t) = -y_2(t) + \int_{-\infty}^{0} F(-r)f(y_3(t+r))dr \\
y_3'(t) = -y_3(t) + w_1\left[\int_{-\infty}^{0} F(-r)f(y_1(t+r))dr\right] + w_2\left[\int_{-\infty}^{0} F(-r)f(y_2(t+r))dr\right]
\end{cases}
\tag{5}
$$

Let $s = t + r$, by applying the strong kernel $F(r) = \mu^2 r e^{-\mu r}$ we have

$$
\int_{-\infty}^{0} F(-r)f(y_2(t+r))dr = \mu^2 e^{-\mu t}\left[t\int_{-\infty}^{t} e^{\mu s}f(y_2(s))ds - \int_{-\infty}^{t} se^{\mu s}f(y_2(s))ds\right]
\tag{6}
$$

Taking the derivative with respect to t on both sides of (5), and one more time, we get

$$
\begin{cases}
y_1''(t) = -\mu^2 y_1(t) - (\mu^2 + 2\mu)y_1(t) - (1+2\mu)y_1'(t) + \mu^2 f(y_2(t)) \\
y_2''(t) = -\mu^2 y_2(t) - (\mu^2 + 2\mu)y_2(t) - (1+2\mu)y_2'(t) + \mu^2 f(y_3(t)) \\
y_3''(t) = -\mu^2 y_3(t) - (\mu^2 + 2\mu)y_3(t) - (1+2\mu)y_3'(t) + w_1\mu^2 f(y_1(t)) + w_2\mu^2 f(y_2(t))
\end{cases}
\tag{7}
$$

Denoted $y_4(t) = -y_1'(t)$, $y_5(t) = -y_2'(t)$, $y_6(t) = -y_3'(t)$, $y_7(t) = -y_1''(t)$, $y_8(t) = -y_2''(t)$, $y_9(t) = -y_3''(t)$. Then we obtain the following equivalent system of (7):

$$
\begin{cases}
y_1'(t) = -y_4(t), \\
y_2'(t) = -y_5(t), \\
y_3'(t) = -y_6(t), \\
y_4'(t) = -y_7(t), \\
y_5'(t) = -y_8(t), \\
y_6'(t) = -y_9(t), \\
y_7'(t) = -\mu^2 y_1(t) + (\mu^2 + 2\mu)y_4(t) - (1+2\mu)y_7(t) + \mu^2 f(y_2(t)), \\
y_8'(t) = -\mu^2 y_2(t) + (\mu^2 + 2\mu)y_5(t) - (1+2\mu)y_8(t) + \mu^2 f(y_3(t)), \\
y_9'(t) = -\mu^2 y_3(t) + (\mu^2 + 2\mu)y_6(t) - (1+2\mu)y_9(t) + w_1\mu^2 f(y_1(t)) + w_2\mu^2 f(y_2(t))
\end{cases}
\tag{8}
$$

In this paper, we always assume that $f(y_i(t))$ is a continuous bounded activation function, satisfying

$$
\lim_{y_i \to 0} \frac{f(y_i(t))}{y_i(t)} = \gamma_i(>0), i = 1,2,3; \quad f(0) = 0
\tag{9}
$$

For example, activation functions tanh($y_i(t)$), arctan($y_i(t)$), and

$$
\frac{1}{2}\left(|y_i(t)+1| - |y_i(t)-1|\right)
$$

satisfy condition (9). From condition (9) we know that the linearized system of (8) is the following:

$$\begin{cases} y_1'(t) = -y_4(t), \\ y_2'(t) = -y_5(t), \\ y_3'(t) = -y_6(t), \\ y_4'(t) = -y_7(t), \\ y_5'(t) = -y_8(t), \\ y_6'(t) = -y_9(t), \\ y_7'(t) = -\mu^2 y_1(t) + \mu^2 \gamma_2 y_2(t) + (\mu^2 + 2\mu) y_4(t) - (1+2\mu) y_7(t), \\ y_8'(t) = -\mu^2 y_2(t) + \mu^2 \gamma_3 y_3(t) + (\mu^2 + 2\mu) y_5(t) - (1+2\mu) y_8(t), \\ y_9'(t) = -\mu^2 y_3(t) + w_1 \mu^2 \gamma_2 y_1(t) + w_2 \mu^2 \gamma_2 y_2(t) + (\mu^2 + 2\mu) y_6(t) - (1+2\mu) y_9(t) \end{cases} \tag{10}$$

A matrix form of (10) is follows:

$$Y'(t) = A(\mu)Y(t) \tag{11}$$

where $Y(t) = [y_1(t), y_2(t),..., y_9(t)]^T$ and $A(\mu)$ is a 9 by 9 matrix. According to [14], there is the same oscillatory behavior about system (10) (or (11)) and system (8) which is equivalent to system (5). Therefore, we only need to deal with system (10).

Lemma 1. If the coefficient matrix $A(\mu)$ is a nonsingular matrix, then system (10) has a unique equilibrium point.

Proof. The linearization of system (8) around x = 0 is (10). Hence, if system (10) has a unique equilibrium point, implying that system (8) also has a unique equilibrium point. An equilibrium point $y^* = \left[y_1^*, y_2^*,..., y_9^* \right]^T$ is the solution of the following algebraic equation

$$A(\mu)Y^* = 0 \tag{12}$$

Assume that Y^* and Z^* are equilibrium points of system (10), then we have

$$A(\mu)(Y^* - Z^*) = 0 \tag{13}$$

Since $A(\mu)$ is a nonsingular matrix, implying that $Y^* - Z^* = 0$ and $Y^* = Z^*$. Therefore, system (10) has a unique equilibrium point implying that system (8) also has a unique equilibrium point. Obviously, this equilibrium point exactly is the zero point.

Lemma 2. Each solution of system (3) is bounded, implying that each solution of system (5) is bounded.

Proof. Note that the activation functions are bounded continuous nonlinear functions. Therefore, there exist $N_i > 0$ such that $f[\int_0^\infty F(r)x_i(t-r)dr] \leq N_i(i=1,2,3)$.

Noting that for $x_i(t) \geq 0(i=1,2,3)$, then $|x_i(t)| = -x_i(t)$, while for $x_i(t) \leq 0(i=1,2,3)$, then $|x_i(t)| = -x_i(t)$, from (3) we get

$$\begin{cases} \dfrac{d|x_1(t)|}{dt} \leq -|x_1(t)| + N_2 \\ \dfrac{d|x_2(t)|}{dt} \leq -|x_2(t)| + N_3 \\ \dfrac{d|x_3(t)|}{dt} \leq -|x_3(t)| + |w_1|N_1 + |w_2|N_2 \end{cases} \quad (14)$$

Thus, when $t \geq 0$, we have

$$\begin{cases} |x_1(t)| \leq |x_1(0)|e^{-t} + N_2(1-e^{-t}) \\ |x_2(t)| \leq |x_2(0)|e^{-t} + N_3(1-e^{-t}) \\ |x_3(t)| \leq |x_3(0)|e^{-t} + (|w_1|N_1 + |w_2|N_2)(1-e^{-t}) \end{cases} \quad (15)$$

This means that each solution of system (3) is bounded. From (14), it is easily to know that each solution of system (5) is bounded.

3   Main Results

Theorem 1. Let $\alpha_1, \alpha_2, \alpha_3, ..., \alpha_9$ be the eigenvalues of the matrix $A(\mu)$. If linearized system (10) has a unique equilibrium point for given parameters values w_1, w_2 and μ. If each eigenvalue of $A(\mu)$ has negative real part, i.e., Re $\alpha_i > 0$ (i=1,2,..., 9), then the unique equilibrium point of system (10) is stable. All solutions of (10) converge to this equilibrium point, implying that the unique equilibrium point of system (10) is stable. If there is at least one Re $\alpha_i > 0(i \in 1,2,...,9)$, then the unique equilibrium point of system (10) is unstable, implying that system (8) or (5) generates periodic oscillations.

Proof. For given values of w_1, w_2 and μ, all eigenvalues have negative real part of system (10), the unique equilibrium point is stable according to the theory of ordinary differential equation, implying that all solutions of (8) converge to this equilibrium point. If there is at least one Re $\alpha_i > 0 (i \in 1, 2, ..., 9)$ then the unique equilibrium point of system (10) is unstable, based on the Chafee's criterion [14, Theorem 7.4], system (8) generates permanent oscillations, implying that there is a periodic solution of system (5) and therefore system (3).

Theorem 2. If system (10) has a unique equilibrium point, for given parameter values w_1, w_2 and μ, satisfying that there is at least one $w_i < 0 (i = 1, 2)$, and that

$$|w_1|\gamma_1\gamma_2\gamma_3 + |w_2|\gamma_2\gamma_3 > 1 \tag{16}$$

Then system (5) generates periodic oscillations, implying that system (3) has a periodic solution.

Proof. Since zero point is the unique equilibrium point, we only need to prove that the trivial solution of system (10) is unstable. So we consider a neighborhood of zero point $U(0, \varepsilon)$. From condition (9) and the Mean Value Theorem, in this neighborhood we have

$$f(y_i(t)) = \gamma_i y_i(t), i = 1, 2, 3. \tag{17}$$

Assume that

$$\limsup_{x \to \infty} |y_i(t)| = \sigma_i (\geq 0)(i = 1, 2, 3) \tag{18}$$

If zero solution is stable, then $\sigma_i (i = 1, 2, 3)$ must equal to zero. According to the definition of the superior limit, for a sufficiently small constant $\varepsilon > 0$ there exists a $t^* > 0$ such that for any large $t(t > t^*)$, $|y_i(t)| \leq (1 + \varepsilon)\sigma_i (i = 1, 2, 3)$ (i=1,2,3). Noting that

$$\int_{-\infty}^{0} F(-r)dr = -\int_{-\infty}^{0} \mu^2 r e^{\mu r} = 1 \tag{19}$$

From (5) as $t > t^*$ we have

$$\begin{cases} y_1'(t) \leq -y_1(t) + \gamma_2(1 + \varepsilon)\sigma_2 \\ y_2'(t) = -y_2(t) + \gamma_3(1 + \varepsilon)\sigma_3 \\ y_3'(t) = -y_3(t) + |w_1|\gamma_1(1 + \varepsilon)\sigma_1 + |w_2|\gamma_2(1 + \varepsilon)\sigma_2 \end{cases} \tag{20}$$

Therefore,

$$\begin{cases} |y_1(t)| \le \gamma_2(1+\varepsilon)(1-e^{-t})\sigma_2 \\ |y_2(t)| \le \gamma_3(1+\varepsilon)(1-e^{-t})\sigma_3 \\ |y_3(t)| \le |w_1|\gamma_1(1+\varepsilon)(1-e^{-t})\sigma_1 + |w_2|\gamma_2(1+\varepsilon)(1-e^{-t})\sigma_2 \end{cases} \qquad (21)$$

Letting $t \to \infty, \varepsilon \to 0$ we can get

$$\begin{cases} \sigma_1 \le \gamma_2\sigma_2 \\ \sigma_2 \le \gamma_2\sigma_3 \\ \sigma_3 \le |w_1|\gamma_1\sigma_1 + |w_2|\gamma_2\sigma_2 \end{cases} \qquad (22)$$

From (22) one can obtain

$$\sigma_3 \le \left(|w_1|r_1r_2r_3 + |w_2|r_2r_3 \right)\sigma_3 \qquad (23)$$

Since $|w_1|r_1r_2r_3 + |w_2|r_2r_3 > 1$, then (23) has a nontrivial positive solution. Thus, there exists $\sigma_3 > 0$ such that

$$\limsup_{t\to\infty} |y_3(t)| = \sigma_3(> 0) \qquad (24)$$

This means that the unique equilibrium point is unstable. Since all solutions of system (5) are bounded, the instability of the trivial solution implies that system (5) generates a permanent oscillation, means that system (3) has a periodic solution.

4   Numerical Simulations

We use system (8) as our simulation model. In figure 1 and figure 2, the activation function is tanh(u); in figure 3 and figure 4, the activation function is arctan(u). So $r_1 = r_2 = r_3 = 1$ We plot each solution of system (8). Indeed, $y_7(t), y_8(t), y_9(t)$ correspond to $x_1(t), x_2(t), x_3(t)$ of system (3) respectively. In figure 3, we select $w_1 = -3.5, w_2 = -4.5$, when $\mu = 2.5, 4.5$ and 6.5, system (3) has a periodic solution. In figure 4, we change the values of w_1 and w_2, such that $|w_1 + w_2| < 1$ we see that an oscillatory solution is appeared. However, figure 1 and figure 2 indicate when $|w_1 + w_2| > 1$, an oscillatory solution also occurs. Therefore, our result extended the criterion of [12] for bifurcating periodic solutions.

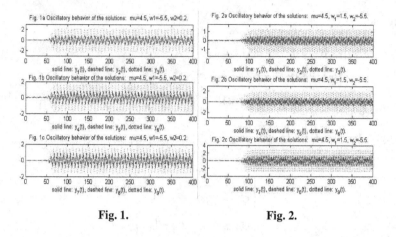

Fig. 1.

Fig. 2.

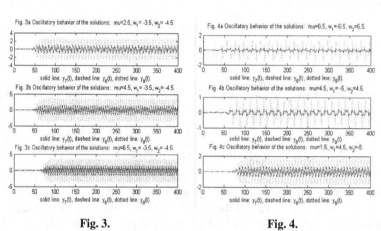

Fig. 3.

Fig. 4.

Acknowledgement. This work was supported by NNSF of China (10961005).

References

1. Chen, S., Zhang, Q., Wang, C.: Existence and Stability of Equilibria of the Continuous-Time Hopfield Neural Network. J. Comput. Appl. Math. 169, 117–125 (2004)
2. Shen, Y., Yu, H., Jian, J.: Delay-dependent Global Asymptotic Stability for Delayed Cellular Neural Networks. Commun. Nonlinear Sci. Numer. Simulat. 14, 1057–1063 (2009)
3. Zhang, Q., Wei, X., Xu, J.: Delay-dependent Global Stability Condition for Delayed Hopfield Neural Networks. Nonlinear Analysis, RWA 8, 997–1002 (2007)
4. Shen, Y., Wang, J.: An Improved Algebraic Criterion for Global Exponential Stability of Recurrent Neural Networks with Time-Varying Delays. IEEE Trans. Neural Networks 19, 528–531 (2008)

5. Cao, J., Wang, L.: Global Exponential Stability And Periodicity of Recurrent Neural Networks with Time Delays. IEEE Trans. Circuits Syst. 52, 920–931 (2005)
6. Liu, B., Huang, L.: Existence and Exponential Stability of Almost Periodic Solutions for Hopfield Neural Networks with Delays. Neurocomputing 68, 196–207 (2005)
7. Liu, Y., You, Z., Cao, L.: On the Almost Periodic Solution of Generalized Hopfield Neural Networks with Time-Varying Delays. Neurocomputing 69, 1760–1767 (2006)
8. Li, J., Yang, J., Wu, W.: Stability and Periodicity of Discrete Hopfield Neural Networks with Column Arbitrary-Magnitude-Dominant Weight Matrix. Neurocomputing 82, 52–61 (2012)
9. Liao, X., Wong, K., Wu, Z.: Bifurcation Analysis on A Two-Neuron System with Distributed Delays. Physica D 149, 123–141 (2001)
10. Zhao, H., Wang, L., Ma, C.: Hopf Bifurcation and Stability Analysis on Discrete-Time Hopfield Neural Network With Delay. Nonlinear Analysis: RWA 9, 103–113 (2008)
11. Liao, X., Li, S., Chen, G.: Bifurcation Analysis on A Two-Neuron System with Distributed Delays in The Frequency Domain. Neural Networks 17, 545–561 (2004)
12. Hajihosseini, A., Lamooki, G.R.R., Beheshti, B., Maleki, F.: The Hopf Bifurcation Analysis on A Time-Delayed Recurrent Neural Network in the Frequency Domain. Neurocomputing 73, 991–1005 (2010)
13. Chafee, N.: A Bifurcation Problem for A Functional Differential Equation of Finitely Retarded Type. J. Math. Anal. Appl. 35, 312–348 (1971)
14. Gyori, I., Lades, G.: Oscillation Theory of Delay Differential Equations with Applications. Clarendon Press, Oxford (1991)

Minimum Risk Neural Networks and Weight Decay Technique

I-Cheng Yeh[1], Pei-Yen Tseng[2], Kuan-Chieh Huang[3], and Yau-Hwang Kuo[4]

[1] Department of Civil Engineering, Tamkang University, Taiwan
[2] Department of Information Management, Chung Hua University, Taiwan
[3] Department of Computer Science and Information Engineering, National Cheng Kung University, Taiwan
[4] Department of Computer Science and Information Engineering, National Cheng Kung University, Taiwan
140910@mail.tku.edu.tw, lytetseng@gmail.com,
m9104041@chu.edu.tw, kuoyh@ismp.csie.ncku.edu.tw

Abstract. To enhance the generalization of neural network model, we proposed a novel neural network, Minimum Risk Neural Networks (MRNN), whose principle is the combination of minimizing the sum of squares of error and maximizing the classification margin, based on the principle of structural risk minimization. Therefore, the objective function of MRNN is the combination of the sum of squared error and the sum of squares of the slopes of the classification function. Besides, we derived a more sophisticated formula similar to the traditional weight decay technique from the MRNN, establishing a more rigorous theoretical basis for the technique. This study employed several real application examples to test the MRNN. The results led to the following conclusions. (1) As long as the penalty coefficient was in the appropriate range, MRNN performed better than pure MLP. (2) MRNN may perform better in difficult classification problems than MLP using weight decay technique.

Keywords: multi-layer perceptrons, weight decay, support vector machine, structural risk minimization.

1 Introduction

This study attempts to enhance the generalization of neural network model. Its basic principle is the combination of minimizing the sum of squares of errors and maximizing the classification margin based on principle of structural risk minimization. In this paper, the Minimum Risk Neural Networks (MRNN) is proposed. The objective function of MRNN is the combination of the sum of squares of errors and the sum of squares of the slopes (differential) of the classification function. This paper will prove that a more sophisticated formula similar to the traditional weight decay technique can be derived from the objective function of MRNN, resulting in a more rigorous theoretical basis for the technique. In Section 2, we will introduce the theoretical background of MRNN. Then we will derive the learning rules of MRNN in Section 3.

D.-S. Huang et al. (Eds.): ICIC 2012, CCIS 304, pp. 10–16, 2012.

We will demonstrate the performance of MRNN with several real application examples in the UCI databases in Section 4. Finally, in Section 5 we will make a summary of the testing results in the entire study.

2   Theoretical Background

2.1   Multi-layer Perceptrons with Weight Decay (MLPWD)

Although minimizing error function enables the neural network to build precise non-linear model fitting to the training examples, that is, the model possesses repetition. However, this model may not have the capacity to predict the testing samples, that is, the model may not possess generalization. This phenomenon is called over-learning. In order to overcome the phenomenon, some researchers have suggested weight decay technique, that is, the sum of squares of weights is added to the error function [1-5],

$$E = E_1 + E_2 = \frac{1}{2}\sum_j (T_j - Y_j)^2 + \frac{\lambda}{2}\sum_{k=1}^{N_W} W_k^2 \tag{1}$$

where W_k = the k-th weight in network; N_w = number of weights in network; λ = penalty coefficient of the sum of squares of weights, controlling the degree of weight decay, and its value is greater than or equal to 0.

2.2   Support Vector Machine (SVM) and Structural Risk Minimization

Support Vector Machine (SVM) is a new learning method proposed by Vapnik based on the statistical theory of Vapnik Chervonenks Dimension and Structural Risk Minimization Inductive Principle, and can better solve the practical problems like small amount of samples, high dimension, non-linear and local optimums. It has become one of the hottest topics in the study of machine learning, and is successfully used in classification, function approximation and time series prediction, etc. [6-10]. In SVM, the following objective function is used [6,7],

$$E = E_1 + E_2 = C\sum_{i=1}^{k} \xi_i + \frac{1}{p(w,b)} \tag{2}$$

where C = penalty coefficient, and $C \geq 0$. The greater C is, the greater the penalty of the classification error. ξ_i = the slack variable, and $\xi_i \geq 0$, on behalf of the degree of the classification error of i-th sample. $p(w,b)$ = margin of classification.

In the objective function of Eq. (2), the first item is to minimize the classification error to enable the model with the repetition; the second item is to maximize the classification margin of the hyper-plane to improve the generalization of the model. Compared with Eq. (1), the first item is equivalent to the sum of squares of errors and the second item is equivalent to the sum of squares of weights.

2.3   Minimum Risk Neural Network (MRNN)

Inspired by multi-layer perceptrons with weight decay (MLPWD) and SVM, in this paper, we proposed the Minimum Risk Neural Networks (MRNN). The objective function of MRNN is the combination of the sum of squares of errors and the sum of squares of the slopes (differential) of the classification function.

$$E = E_1 + \gamma \cdot E_2 = \frac{1}{2}\sum_j (T_j - Y_j)^2 + \frac{\gamma}{2}\sum_i \sum_j \left(\frac{\partial Y_j}{\partial X_i}\right)^2 \tag{3}$$

where T_j is the target value of the j-th output variable of the training examples; Y_j is the inference value of the j-th output unit in the output layers for the training examples; γ is the penalty coefficient controlling the proportion of the sum of square of the slopes in the objective function, and its value is greater than or equal to 0.

Comparisons of the objective functions of Multi-layer perceptrons with weight decay technique (MLPWD), support vector machine (SVM), and the minimum risk neural network (MRNN) are shown in Table 1.

Table 1. Comparisons of three kinds of objective function

Model	Error Term E_1	Generalization Term E_2	Principle of Regularization
MLP with weight decay (MLPWD)	$\frac{1}{2}\sum_j (T_j - Y_j)^2$	$\frac{\lambda}{2}\sum_{k=1}^{N_W} W_k^2$	Minimize the sum of square of weights
Support Vector Machine (SVM)	$c\sum_{i=1}^{k} \xi_i$	$\frac{1}{p(w,b)}$	Minimize the reciprocal of the classification margin
Minimum Risk Neural Network (MRNN)	$\frac{1}{2}\sum_j (T_j - Y_j)^2$	$\frac{\gamma}{2}\sum_i \sum_j \left(\frac{\partial Y_j}{\partial X_i}\right)^2$	Minimize the sum of squares of slopes of classification function

3   Theoretical Derivation

3.1   Minimum Risk Neural Network (MRNN)

The output of the hidden unit in MLP is as follows

$$H_k = f(net_k) = \frac{1}{1+\exp(-net_k)} = \frac{1}{1+\exp(-(\sum_i W_{ik} X_i - \theta_k))} \tag{4}$$

where H_k is the output of the k-th unit in the hidden layer; X_i is the i-th input variable; W_{ik} is the connection weight between the i-th unit in the input layer and the k-th unit in the hidden layer; θ_k is the threshold of the k-th unit in the hidden layer.

The output of the output unit in MLP is as follows

$$Y_j = f(net_j) = \frac{1}{1+\exp(-net_j)} = \frac{1}{1+\exp(-(\sum_k W_{kj}H_k - \theta_j))} \tag{5}$$

where W_{kj} is the connection weight between the k-th unit in the hidden layer and the j-th unit in the output layer; θ_j is the threshold of the j-th unit in the output layer.

In order to achieve the minimum of the objective function of MRNN in Eq. (3), we can use the steepest descent method to adjust the network parameters. The learning rules are derived in two steps as following.

(1) Connection weights between the hidden layer and the output layer

According to the chain rule in the partial differential, and let

$$\delta_j \equiv (T_j - Y_j) \cdot f'(net_j) \tag{6}$$

Then, we get

$$\Delta W_{kj} = \eta \cdot \left(\delta_j H_k - \gamma \cdot \sum_i \left(\sum_l f'(net_j) \cdot W_{lj} \cdot f'(net_l) \cdot W_{il} \right) \left(f'(net_j) \cdot f'(net_k) \cdot W_{ik} \right) \right) \tag{7}$$

(2) Connection weights between the input layer and the hidden layer

According to the chain rule in the partial differential, and let

$$\delta_k \equiv \left(\sum_j \delta_j W_{kj} \right) \cdot f'(net_k) \tag{8}$$

Then, we get

$$\Delta W_{ik} = \eta \cdot \left(\delta_k X_i - \gamma \cdot \sum_j \left(\sum_l f'(net_j) \cdot W_{lj} \cdot f'(net_l) \cdot W_{il} \right) \left(f'(net_j) \cdot W_{kj} \cdot f'(net_k) \right) \right) \tag{9}$$

3.2   The Relation between MRNN and Weight Decay Technique

In this section, we will simplify the above formula to derive formulas of weight decay technique. In Eq. (7), the first order partial derivatives of the transfer functions must be positive. Hence, they can be omitted so as to simplify the formula. Therefore,

$$\Delta W_{kj} = \eta \cdot \left(\delta_j H_k - \gamma \cdot \sum_i \left(\sum_l W_{il} \cdot W_{lj} \right) W_{ik} \right) \tag{10}$$

Similarly, Eq. (9) can be simplified as

$$\Delta W_{ik} = \eta \cdot \left(\delta_k X_i - \gamma \cdot \sum_j \left(\sum_l W_{il} \cdot W_{lj} \right) W_{kj} \right) \tag{11}$$

Comparing Eq. (10) and (11) with Eq. (1) of weigh decay technique, we can find that both of them imply the rule that "the modification of weigh is in reverse proportion to weight". Hence, conventional weight decay technique can be considered as the simplified version of MRNN. These formulas establish reasonable theoretical foundation for weight decay technique.

4   Application Examples

In this section, we tested three real data sets in the UCI Machine Learning Repository [11] compare the performance of MRNN, MLPDW and MLP, including (1) detection of spam mail (2) recognition of remote sensing image of Landsat satellite (3) classification of forest cover type. To evaluate the effectiveness of learning, we used the 10-fold cross-validation. We tried γ= 0.0001, 0.001, 0.01, 0.03, 0.1, 0.3, 1, 3, 5, and 10 for MRNN, and $\lambda=10^{-7}\sim10^{-1}$ for MLPWD. The results are shown in Figure 1. It can be found that as long as the parameter γ or λ is in the appropriate range, both of them perform better than pure MLP. We also experimented on other 12 practical data sets in UCI databases [11] listed in Table 2 to compare the performances of MRNN, MLPWD, and SVM. To evaluate the effectiveness of learning, we used the 10-fold cross-validation. In addition, to avoid the influence of the initial connection weights, the error rates are the average of the results of 30 sets of various initial connection weights. To evaluate whether the performance differences between the three kinds of

Table 2. Testing results of error rate of the 15 UCI data sets

UCI data sets	Benchmark			MRNN		MRNN vs. Benchmark t-test (Significance=5%)	
	MLPWD		SVM				
	Avg.	Std.		Avg.	Std.	MLPWD	SVM
SPAMBASE	0.0642	0.0027	0.0653	0.0631	0.0018	0.037 *	<0.001 *
Landsat	0.0981	0.0016	0.098	0.0974	0.0013	0.036 *	0.008 *
Forest cover	0.232	0.002	0.215	0.208	0.003	<0.001 *	<0.001 *
Iris	0.0270	0	0.027	0.0270	0	>0.5	>0.5
Insurance	0.3366	0.0131	0.3365	0.3363	0.0160	0.468	0.473
Glass	0.2675	0.0036	0.2665	0.2667	0.0047	0.248	>0.5
Shuttle	0.0049	0.0001	0.004	0.0040	0.0001	<0.001 *	>0.5
Vowel	0.4123	0.0091	0.4052	0.3983	0.0096	<0.001 *	<0.001 *
Wine	0.0116	0.0002	0.0115	0.0113	0.0002	<0.001 *	<0.001 *
Letter	0.3474	0.0071	0.3418	0.3315	0.0073	<0.001 *	<0.001 *
Image	0.0422	0.0008	0.0422	0.0421	0.0009	0.330	0.281
Vehicle	0.1240	0.0020	0.1232	0.1230	0.0015	0.025 *	0.294
German	0.2393	0.0071	0.2365	0.2362	0.0052	0.034 *	0.397
Heart	0.1430	0.0019	0.143	0.1430	0.0019	>0.5	>0.5
Thyroid	0.0241	0.0002	0.0231	0.0198	0.0002	<0.001 *	<0.001 *

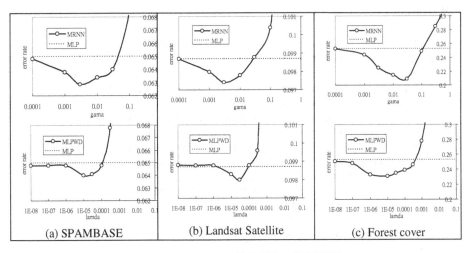

Fig. 1. The error rate of MRNN and MLPWD

neural networks are significant or not, the t-test was employed. From the experimental results listed in Table 2, we can see that there are 10 out of fifteen data sets whose error of MRNN is significantly smaller than that of MLPWD; however, there are only seven out of fifteen data sets whose error of MRNN is significantly smaller than that of SVM.

5   Conclusions

The generalization capability of a multilayer perceptron can be adjusted by adding a penalty (weight decay) term to the cost function used in the training process. To enhance the generalization of neural network model, inspired by SVM, we proposed the Minimum Risk Neural Networks, whose objective function is the combination of the sum of squares of errors and the sum of squares of the slopes of the classification function. Besides, this paper proved that a more sophisticated formula similar to the traditional weight decay technique can be derived from the MRNN, establishing a more rigorous theoretical foundation for the technique. This study employed fifteen real examples to test the MRNN. The results led to the following conclusions. (1) As long as the penalty coefficient was in the appropriate range, MRNN performed better than pure MLP. (2) MRNN may perform better in difficult classification problems than the MLP using weight decay technique.

Aknowledgements. This work was supported by the National Science Council, ROC, under Grant NSC-100-2221-E-032-070.

References

1. Wu, L.Z., Moody, J.: A Smoothing Regularizer for Feedforward and Recurrent Neural Networks. Neural Computation 8(3), 461–489 (1996)
2. Krogh, A., Hertz, J.A.: A Simple Weight Decay Can Improve Generalization. In: Moody, J.E., Hanson, S.J., Lippmann, R.P. (eds.) Advances in Neural Information Processing Systems, San Mateo, CA, pp. 450–957 (1992)
3. Krogh, A., Hertz, J.A.: A Simple Weight Decay Can Improve Generalization. In: Advances in Neural Information Processing Systems, vol. 4, pp. 950–957 (1992)
4. Hinton, G.E., Camp, D.: Keeping the Neural Networks Simple by Minimizing the Description Length of the Weights. In: Proceedings of the Sixth Annual Conference on Computational Learning Theory, pp. 5–13 (1993)
5. Treadgold, N.K., Gedeon, T.D.: Simulated Annealing and Weight Decay in Adaptive Learning: the SARPROP algorithm. IEEE Transactions on Neural Networks 9(4), 662–668 (1998)
6. Cortes, F., Vapnik, V.: Support Vector Networks. Machine Learning 20(3), 273–297 (1995)
7. Vapnik, V.N.: The Nature of Statistical Learning Theory. Springer, New York (1995)
8. Drucker, H., Wu, D., Vapink, V.: Support Vector Machines for Spam Categorization. IEEE Transactions on Neural Networks 10(5), 1048–1054 (1999)
9. Burges, C.: A Tutorial on Support Vector Machines for Pattern Recognitionl. Data Mining and Knowledge Discovery 2(2), 121–167 (1998)
10. Fan, R.E., Chen, P.H., Lin, C.J.: Working Set Selection using Second Order Information for Training Support Vector Machines. The Journal of Machine Learning Research 6, 1889–1918 (2005)
11. UCI Machine Learning Repository Content Summary (2008), http://archive.ics.uci.edu/ml/

Time Series Forecasting Using Restricted Boltzmann Machine

Takashi Kuremoto[1], Shinsuke Kimura[1],
Kunikazu Kobayashi[2], and Masanao Obayashi[1]

[1] Graduate School of Science and Engineering, Yamaguchi University, Tokiwadai 2-16-1, Ube,
Yamaguchi, 755-8611, Japan
{wu,m.obayas}@yamaguchi-u.ac.jp
[2] School of Information Science & Technology, Aichi Prefectural University, Ibaragabasama
1522-3, Nagakute, Aichi, 480-1198, Japan
kobayashi@ist.aichi-pu.ac.jp

Abstract. In this study, we propose a method for time series prediction using restricted Boltzmann machine (RBM), which is one of stochastic neural networks. The idea comes from Hinton & Salakhutdinov's multilayer "encoder" network which realized dimensionality reduction of data. A 3-layer deep network of RBMs is constructed and after pre-training RBMs using their energy functions, gradient descent training (error back propagation) is adopted to execute fine-tuning. Additionally, to deal with the problem of neural network structure determination, particle swarm optimization (PSO) is used to find the suitable number of units and parameters. Moreover, a preprocessing, "trend removal" to the original data, was also performed in the forecasting. To compare the proposed predictor with conventional neural network method, i.e., multi-layer perceptron (MLP), CATS benchmark data was used in the prediction experiments.

Keywords: time series forecasting, restricted Boltzmann machine, multilayer perceptron, CATS benchmark.

1   Introduction

Many time series forecasting models have been proposed since 1940s, and recently, artificial neural networks (ANN) becomes more and more popular in this field. As Crone and Nikolopoulos reported in 2007 [1], there have been over 5,000 publications on ANN for time series prediction after multi-layer perceptron (MLP) and its training method "error back propagation" (BP) were proposed in 1986 [2]. Also, for the complexity and difficulty of time series prediction, the art of this field is still attracting researchers to develop more efficient models and methods to yield more precise predictions.

In this paper, we propose a deep stochastic neural network using restricted Boltzmann machine (RBM) [2] to be a predictor. The idea comes from Hinton & Salakhutdinov's multilayer "encoder" network, i.e., deep belief network (DBN), which realized dimensionality reduction of data [3]. As shown in [3] and [4], the DBN with

D.-S. Huang et al. (Eds.): ICIC 2012, CCIS 304, pp. 17–22, 2012.

RBMs is successfully applied to image compression and reconstruction and data cluster-ing, however, still without any application to the time series forecasting. In fact, when the input data are accepted by the units of "visible layer" of RBM, then the units of "hidden layer" detect the feature of data according to the connection weights adjustment with a learning algorithm similar to BP [5] [6]. Meanwhile, when the hidden layer is used as another visible layer, a new hidden layer is able to estimate "the feature of fea-tures". So we consider to using this DBN to build a time series approximation model and apply it to be a predictor when untrained data are input. Furthermore, to decide the number units of input layer and hidden layer, and suitable learning rate, we adopt par-ticle swarm optimization (PSO) [7] into the design of DBN. Additionally, difference time series is adopted to meet the characteristic of neural network models.

To verify the effectiveness of our prediction model, CATS benchmark was used whereas it served as the problem of time series prediction competition since 2004 [8] [9]. The prediction results showed that the proposed method gave higher forecasting precision comparing with MLP and traditional prediction model autoregressive mov-ing average (ARMA or ARIMA) [10].

2   A Predictor Using DBN of RBMs

A predictor using DBN of RBMs is proposed and the learning algorithm is given in Section 2.1. Structure and parameter optimization using PSO will be stated in Section 2.2, and preprocessing to the original time series data is in Section 2.3.

2.1   Structure and Learning Algorithms of Proposed Predictor

A DBN with multiple RBMs as shown in Fig.1 is used as a model of time series pre-diction. The processing is as follows.

Step 1. Initialization. All binary units on each layer of RBMs are set as 0 or 1 ran-domly, and connection weights between units of different layers w_{ij} with random value in (0, 1). Units of the same layer of RBMs do not connect to each other.

Step 2. Repeat Step 2.1 to Step 2.6 until energy function E (v, h) decrease to be a convergent state.

$$E(v,h) = -\sum_{i=1}^{n} b_i v_i - \sum_{j=1}^{m} b_j h_j - \sum_{i=1}^{n} \sum_{j=1}^{m} v_i h_j w_{ij} \quad , \tag{1}$$

where v_i and h_j are the binary states of input x(t) and feature j, b_i and b_j are their biases. Convergence condition can be given by

$$\left| A'(v,h) - A(v,h) \right| < \alpha \, , \, A'(v,h) = \sum_{b=k-K}^{k-1} E_b(v,h)/K \, , \, A(v,h) = \sum_{a=k}^{K+k} E_a(v,h)/K \tag{2}$$

where αis a positive parameter and small enough, k is the iteration times and K is a constant indicates the length of evaluation period.

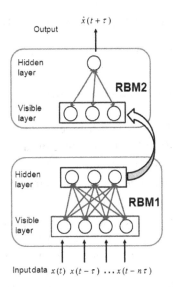

Fig. 1. A predictor constructed by a deep believe network (DBN) with two restricted Boltzmann machines (RBMs)

Step 2.1 Past data $x(t), x(t-\tau),...,x(t-n\tau)$ are input corresponding to the units v_i of visible layer of RBM1, where t is the current time, t=1, 2, ..., T, τ is a positive integer, n is the number of input data for forecasting.

Step 2.2 The value of a unit j, i.e., a feature detector, of hidden layer is set to 1 with probability:

$$p_j = (1+e^{-\Delta E_j})^{-1}, \Delta E_j = \sum_{i=1}^{n} w_{ij} v_i + b_j \quad , \tag{3}$$

where b_j is the bias of j, and $v_i = x(t-(i-1)\tau)$.

Step 2.3 Set v_i to 1 with probability:

$$p_i = (1+e^{-\Delta E_i})^{-1}, \Delta E_i = \sum_{j=1}^{m} w_{ij} h_j + b_i \quad , \tag{4}$$

where b_j is the bias of hidden unit j, and j=1, 2, ..., m.

Step 2.4 Fix the value of units on visible layer, and repeat Step 3 to change the state of the hidden layer to convergence, then calculate expectation (probability) $p_{ij} = <v_i h_j>_{data}$ of unit i and j are 1 at the same time.

Step 2.5 Fix the value of units on hidden layer, and repeat Step 4 to change the state of the visible layer to convergence, then calculate expectation (probability) $p_{ij}' = <v_i h_j>_{recon}$ of unit i and j are 1 at the same time.

Step 2.6 Change the weight w_{ij} as:

$$\Delta w_{ij} = \varepsilon(p_{ij} - p_{ij}') , \tag{5}$$

where ε is a learning rate.

Step 3. Let the hidden layer of RBM1 to be the visible layer of RBM2 as shown in Fig. 1. Repeat from Step 1 to Step 2 for RBM2.

Step 4. The output of the unit of RBM2 $\hat{x}(t+\tau)$ is the prediction value of unknown data $x(t+\tau)$.

Step 5. Using the difference between $x(t+\tau)$ and $\hat{x}(t+\tau)$, BP algorithm [2] is executed to tuning weights of each RBM again.

Step 6. Stop training if the difference between is little enough, i.e., converged as $(MSE(L-1)-MSE(L))/MSE(L-1)<\beta$, where β is a positive parameter and small enough, L is the iteration times of BP algorithm.

Step 7. Input unlearned time series data to the trained model and predict the future data (one-head or a long-term prediction).

The learning rule given by Eq. (5) is proved that it works well to train RBM to be an approximate model of the input in [7]. And for gradient descent training methods, e.g., BP [2], the initial weights are expected to be set closing to the global minimum, i.e., the optimal solution. So Eq. (5) serves as pre-training for BP learning algorithm, and these learning algorithms make DBN extract abstract features by their multiple output layers.

2.2   Optimization of the Model

The structure of a neural network is difficult to be designed. The number of layers, the number of units of every layer, learning rate and so on need to be decided when the model is applied to real problems. Here we adopt Kennedy & Eberhart's particle swarm optimization (PSO) [7] to find the optimal numbers of units and learning rate of RBM. Suppose the predictor is given as in Fig.1, i.e., 2 RBMs are used. The visible layer of RBM1 has n units, the hidden layer of RBM1 has m units as same as the visible layer of RBM2. The hidden layer of RBM1 has 1 unit, i.e., the output of the predictor. Considering the learning rate of RBM ε, a particle is designed to be a 3-dimension vector $\mathbf{y(n, m, \varepsilon)}$. Preparing population of this kind of particles with enough size P, and using the standard algorithm of PSO of [7], optimized predictor of DBN is able to be constructed.

2.3   Difference Time Series

Though artificial neural networks work well for nonlinear data prediction, they drop learning ability when linear factor exists strongly in the time series [11]. So Zhang proposed to combine the linear prediction model ARIMA [10] with MLP to raise the prediction precision [11]. Here we use Gardner & Mckenzie's smoothing method [12] to preprocessing the original time series data and yield difference time series data.

3   Forecasting Result

To evaluate prediction models for long-term prediction of time series, the CATS benchmark [8] gives artificial time series data in 5 blocks (t=1, 2, ..., 5000) and 20 are missing, 980 are known in each block. The evaluation functions are the mean square error E_1 and E_2 which computes on the 100 missing values of total 5 blocks and 80 missing values of the first 4-blocks respectively. Using a DBN composed with 2 RBMs, we performed prediction experiment with the CATS data. Table 1 shows the values of parameters used in the prediction. To compare with the conventional predictors, a 3-layer MLP was used and the numbers of input layer and hidden layer were also decided by PSO algorithm optimally. Table 2 compares the prediction precision of the proposed model RBM and conventional models, which includes typical neural network (MLP), traditional linear model ARIMA [10], the best model of IJCNN'04 prediction competition (Kalman Smoother for E_1 and Ensemble models for E_2) [8] [9], and the worst results of IJCNN'04 prediction competition [8] [9]. As a comparison result, we confirmed that the proposed prediction model, DBN with RBM, worked better than conventional MLP and ARIMA models in the case of using difference time series data for training, but worse than the best of IJCNN'04 competition models.

Table 1. Parameters used in the prediction

Description	Symbol	Quantity
The number of RBM	*RBM1, RBM2*	2
The number of input (visible) layer[*]	N	Given by PSO
The number of hidden layer[*]	M	Given by PSO
The number of output	-	1
Interval of input data	τ	1
Learning rate of RBM	ε	Given by PSO
Learning rate of BP	-	Given by PSO
Population of PSO	-	10
Convergence coefficient[**]	κ	0.5
Damping coefficient[**]	ω	0.95
Velocity coefficient[**]	c_1, c_2	1.0
Biases of units	b_i, b_j	0.0
Convergence parameter of RBM	α	0.05
Convergence parameter of BP	β	0.0005
Period of RBM convergence	K	50
Period of RBM convergence	L	$100 < L < 5000$
Delay of difference time series	-	6

[*]The exploration sizes of units were limited from 1 to 20 due to the computational cost.
[**]These parameters are described in standard PSO [7] and not appeared here.

Table 2. Prediction error (MSE) of different models

Evaluation/Model	RBMs (proposed)	MLP (with PSO)	ARIMA	The best of IJCNN'04	The worst of IJCNN'04
E_1 (original data)	1622	2655	1330	408	1156
E_1 (difference data)	**1215**	1317	1258	-	-
E_2 (original data)	1490	2694	1348	222	1229
E_2(difference data)	**979**	1137	1254	-	-

4   Conclusion

A novel neural network model for time series forecasting was proposed. The proposed model is a kind of deep believe network (DBN) composed by multiple restricted Boltzmann machines (RBMs). The structure of the model was optimized by particle swarm optimization (PSO) algorithm. Preprocessing to the original time series data were also used to obtain difference time series data for neural network models, i.e., DBN of RBMs and multilayer perceptron (MLP). Using CATS benchmark, the proposed model was confirmed its priority to conventional neural network model MLP, and mathematic model ARIMA. Though the prediction precision did not achieve the highest level of the best of IJCNN'04 prediction competition participant method, this work firstly shows that RBM is available to be used as a predictor for time series forecasting.

References

1. Crone, S., Nikolopoulos, K.: Results of the NN3 neural network forecasting competition. In: The 27 th International Symposium on Forecasting, Program, vol. 129 (2007)
2. Rumelhart, D.E., Hinton, G.E., Williams, R.J.: Learning Representation by Back-Propagating Errors. Nature 232(2), 533–536 (1986)
3. Hinton, G.E., Salakhutdinov, R.R.: Reducing the Dimensionality of Data with Neural Networks. Science 313(4), 504–507 (2006)
4. Roux, N.L., Bengio, Y.: Representational Power of Restricted Boltzmann Machines and Deep Belief Networks. Neural Computation 20(2), 1631–1649 (2008)
5. Hinton, G.E., Sejnowski, T.J.: Learning and Relearning in Boltzmann Machines. In: Parallel Distributed Processing: Explorations in the Microstructure of Cognition, Foundations, vol. 1. MIT Press, Cambridge (1986)
6. Ackley, D.H., Hinton, G.E., Sejnowski, T.J.: A Learning Algorithm for Boltzmann Machines. Cognitive Science 9(1), 147–169 (1985)
7. Kennedy, J., Eberhart, R.C.: Particle Swarm Optimization. In: IEEE International Conference on Neural Networks, pp. 1942–1948 (1995)
8. Lendasse, A., Oja, E., Simula, O., Verleysen, M.: Time Series Prediction Competition: The CATS Benchmark. In: International Joint Conference on Neural Networks, pp. 1615–1620 (2004)
9. Lendasse, A., Oja, E., Simula, O., Verleysen, M.: Time Series Prediction Competition: The CATS Benchmark. Neurocomputing 70(2), 2325–2329 (2007)
10. Box, G.E.P., Jenkins, G.: Time Series Analysis, Forecasting and Control. Cambridge University Press, Cambridge (1976)
11. Zhang, G.P.: Time Series Forecasting Using a Hybrid ARIMA and Neural Network Model. Neurocomputing 50(2), 159–175 (2003)
12. Gardner, E., McKenzie, E.: Seasonal Exponential Smoothing with Damped Trends. Management Science 35(3), 372–376 (1989)

Interactive Evolutionary Algorithms with Decision-Maker's Preferences for Solving Interval Multi-objective Optimization Problems

Dunwei Gong, Xinfang Ji, Jing Sun, and Xiaoyan Sun

School of Information and Electrical Engineering,
China University of Mining and Technology, Xuzhou, China

Abstract. Multi-objective optimization problems (MOPs) with interval parameters are considerably popular and important in real-world applications. A novel evolutionary algorithm incorporating with a decision-maker (DM)'s preferences is presented to obtain their Pareto subsets which meet the DM's preferences in this study. The proposed algorithm is applied to four MOPs with interval parameters and compared with other two algorithms. The experimental results confirm the advantages of the proposed algorithm.

Keywords. Multi-objective optimization, Evolutionary algorithm, Interval, Decision-maker's preferences, Relative importance.

1 Introduction

Various optimization problems with multiple objectives commonly exist in real-world applications. Due to the influence of subjective and objective factors, uncertain parameters, e.g., stochastic variables, fuzzy numbers and intervals, are often contained in these optimization problems. They are called optimization problems with uncertain parameters. Optimization problems with interval parameters [1] are focused on in this study since the values of these parameters are easy to be accessed.

As we all know, there is no solution which is optimal for all objectives in solving a MOP. What to be obtained is only its non-dominated solution set. The ultimate goal of solving a MOP, however, is to find one (or several) non-dominated solution(s) meeting the DM's preferences, so it is necessary to incorporate with the DM's preferences. Generally speaking, there are three means of embedding the DM's preferences [2]: (1) *a priori* methods; (2) *a posteriori* methods; and (3) interactive methods. Interactive methods have advantages of both *a priori* and *a posteriori* ones.

The expression of a DM's preferences is also important besides the means of embedding them. At present, there are many ways to express the preferences, e.g., reference points [3] and relative importance of objectives [4]. In the interactive methods based on relative importance of objectives, it is convenient for a DM to provide relative important relationship among objectives, so the way of expressing the preferences are thus used in this study.

D.-S. Huang et al. (Eds.): ICIC 2012, CCIS 304, pp. 23–29, 2012.

The remainder of this paper is organized as follows. Section 2 expounds the proposed algorithm. The application of the proposed method in typical MOPs with interval parameters and comparative experiments are given in Section 3. Finally, Section 4 concludes this paper.

2   Proposed Algorithm

In this algorithm, the DM is requested to input the relative important relationships among objectives before the evolution; and the DM's preference regions in the objective space and the corresponding mathematical models of the relative importance of objectives are deduced based on these relations described in subsection 2.1; a strategy is proposed to further distinguish the optimal solutions with the same Pareto rank based on the above region, elaborated in subsection 2.2, to guide the algorithm to the DM's real preference region. The DM can modify his/her preference during the evolution. The framework of NSGA-II is used in the proposed algorithm.

2.1   Mathematical Model of Relative Importance of Objectives

In this study, the notion of relative importance of objectives is adopted to qualitatively describe a DM's preferences. Three effective kinds of relative important relationships among objectives provided in reference [4] are: (1) $f_i P f_j$, implies that f_i is more important than f_j; (2) $f_i I f_j$ suggests that f_i and f_j are equally important; and (3) $f_j P f_i$, implies that f_j is more important than f_i.

The evolution process is divided into two phases in this study and the relationships above, called rough relative importance of objectives, are employed to express the DM's preferences in the first phase. Other more detailed relationships, called fine relative importance of objectives, are adopted in the second phase. The first phase mentioned here refers to the evolution when the number of generations, t, is smaller than or equal to αT, and the second phase refers to the evolution thereafter, where the value of α, in the range of [0, 1], is set by the DM.

Another relative important relationship among objectives is added to make the original relationships finer, and expressed as " PL ", whose preference degree is stronger than "P". Therefore, there are five kinds of relative important relationships among objectives in the fine relative importance of objectives: (1) $f_i I f_j$; (2) $f_i P f_j$; (3) $f_i PL f_j$; (4) $f_j P f_i$; and (5) $f_j PL f_i$.

To embed the preferences above into an algorithm, a novel method to transform the preferences described as languages into suitable mathematical models is presented in view of reference [4]. The method divides the normalized objective space w.r.t. identical angle, then the corresponding preference regions will be obtained and their corresponding mathematical models can thus be deduced.

Take an m-objective maximization problem as an example. The division of preference regions in the two-dimensional objective space formed by objectives f_i and f_j is shown as in Fig .1, where f_i and f_j are the objectives normalized in the range of $[0, 1]$. As can be seen, the objective space is divided into three and five regions with identical angle in Fig.1(a) and Fig.1(b), respectively, and each region is noted the corresponding preference.

In Fig .1(a), the equation of line b is $0.58f_i - f_j = 0$, then the region surrounded by f_i-axis and line b can be expressed by $0.58f_i > f_j$, the preference region noted by $f_i Pf_j$ is thus obtained, as depicted in inequality (1). Similarly, the mathematical models of the other preference regions in Fig.1(a) and Fig.1(b) can be constructed, and the specific inequalities of them are omitted for brevity.

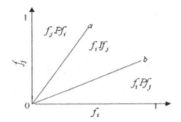 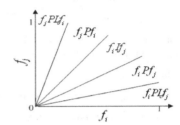

Fig. 1. (a) Rough relative importance   (b) Fine relative importance

$$f_i Pf_j \Leftrightarrow 0.58f_i > f_j. \tag{1}$$

All individuals in a population can get their corresponding Pareto ranks after the comparison of interval Pareto dominance [1]. The individuals with the same Pareto rank will further be distinguished based on the preference regions above in this study.

2.2   Rank of Evolutionary Individuals Based on Preference Regions

Consider two optimal solutions, say x_p and x_q, with the same rank, the following three cases imply that x_p is superior to x_q: (1) x_p is inside the preference region, whereas x_q is not; (2) both x_p and x_q are inside the preference region, and the crowding distance of x_p is larger than that of x_q; (3) both x_p and x_q are outside the preference region, or at least one of them intersects with the region, and the distance between x_p and the region is nearer than that between x_q and the region.

In order to discuss the quality of two optimal solutions with the same rank according to the three cases above, the optimal solution's location w.r.t the entire preference region of the optimization problem needs to be judged based on the mathematical models obtained in subsection 2.1. For the first case, their quality can be directly determined. For the second one, their quality can further be distinguished using the interval crowding measure proposed in reference [1]. For the third one, a measure method will be given in the following.

Consider the third case, for an optimal solution x, the following formula is suggested to calculate the distance between it and the preference region:

$$D(x) = d(x) \cdot (10^m V(x) + \rho), \tag{2}$$

$$d(x) = (\sum_{i=1}^{m-1} (\sum_{j=i+1}^{m} (\left| m(f_i(x,c)) - f_i(z_{i,j}) \right| + \left| m(f_j(x,c)) - f_j(z_{i,j}) \right|))) / C_m^2, \tag{3}$$

where $d(x)$ is the average of the distances between x and the nearest points of each two-dimensional preference region; $V(x)$ is the volume of x in the objective space; $\rho = 1$ to ensure that $10^m V(x) + \rho \neq 0$; $m(f_i(x,c))$ is the mid-point of $f_i(x,c)$; $z_{i,j}$ is the nearest point between a rectangle and a two-dimensional preference region, where the rectangle is composed of the i-th and the j-th normalized objectives of x and the region is formed by the relative important relationship between the i-th and the j-th objectives; $f_i(z_{i,j})$ is the i-th component of $z_{i,j}$; C_m^2 is the number of pair-wise combinations of objectives among m objectives.

It can be seen from formula (2) that, the smaller the average distance $d(x)$ and the volume $V(x)$, the smaller the distance $D(x)$, indicating that x meets the DM's preferences with a high degree; and vice versa.

3   Application in Typical MOPs with Interval Parameters

The effectiveness of the proposed method is validated by comparing it with other two methods. The first one was proposed in [1], and called an *a posteriori* method. The second one is that the DM's preferences are specified *a priori* and fixed during the evolution, i.e., the *a priori* method, and the method proposed in this study is used to solve the problem. The proposed method is compared with these two methods is to illustrate that the proposed one can obtain optimal solutions meeting the DM's real preferences, whereas the other two may not. The implementation environment is VB 6.0. Each method is run for 20 times independently, and the related results are recorded.

3.1   Optimization Problems and Parameter Settings

Two commonly used bi-objective optimization problems, i.e., ZDT1 and ZDT4 from [5], and two three-objective optimization problems, i.e., DTLZ1 and DTLZ2 from [6], are chosen to verify the performance of these algorithms. Since the objectives of all optimization problems above are deterministic, an imprecise factor, δ [7], is introduced to make them uncertain. Denote the corresponding optimization problems as *ZDT1'*, *ZDT4'*, *DTLZ1'* and *DTLZ2'* [1], respectively.

The three methods adopt the following parameter settings. The population size, N, is set to be 20. Tournament selection with size two, one-point crossover and uniform mutation are adopted, and the probabilities of crossover and mutation are 0.9 and 0.1, respectively. For bi-objective and three-objective optimization problems, the largest number of generations, T, is equal to 100 and 200, respectively. The preference settings of different methods are listed in Table 1. The data in the first row and the second row are the DM's preferences used in the *a priori* method and the *a posteriori* method, respectively, which are also the DM's initial preferences and anaphase preferences used in the proposed method, respectively.

Table 1. Preference settings

	ZDT1'	*ZDT4'*	*DTLZ1'*	*DTLZ2'*
initial preference	f_2Pf_1	f_1If_2	f_1If_2, f_1If_3	f_2Pf_1, f_2If_3
anaphase preference	f_1Pf_2	f_2PLf_1	f_1PLf_2, f_1Pf_3	f_2If_1, f_2PLf_3

3.2   Performance Indicators

The following two indicators are employed to compare the three methods.

(1) Approximation degree: The distance between the Pareto optimal solution set and the DM's preference regions, denoted as D, and it can be calculated by formula (2).

(2) Time consumption: The time required to get the Pareto optimal solution set, denoted as T. The smaller the value of T, the higher the efficiency of the method is.

3.3   Experimental Results and Analysis

In our experiments the value of α will be equal to 0.5, and the DM's preferences are assumed to change twice. Tables 2 and 3 list the averages and the variances of D and T obtained by different methods, respectively, where, *prop.*, *prio.*, and *post.* represent the proposed, *a priori* and *a posteriori* methods, respectively.

Table 2. D obtained by different methods

	ZDT1'		*ZDT4'*		*DTLZ1'*		*DTLZ2'*	
	average	variance	average	variance	average	variance	average	variance
prop.	0.3410	0.0884	0.4491	0.0767	0.2941	0.0688	0.4049	0.0788
prio.	0.7391	0.0930	0.7906	0.0494	0.3703	0.0516	1.0116	0.0742
post.	0.6121	0.1045	0.7652	0.0787	0.5005	0.0623	0.7080	0.0940

Table 3. T of different methods (unit: s)

	ZDT1'		ZDT4'		DTLZ1'		DTLZ2'	
	average	variance	average	variance	average	variance	average	variance
prop.	78.5	4.7	73.3	3.1	285.5	29.9	247.3	32.7
prio.	74.3	5.1	68.5	5.8	270.5	56.5	235.0	34.5
post.	128.3	11.8	131.9	6.7	429.6	53.1	380.7	56.3

As can be observed from Table 2, the averages of D obtained by the proposed method are obviously smaller than those obtained by the other two, indicating that the Pareto optimal solutions obtained by the proposed method are better than those obtained by the other two methods w.r.t. reflecting the DM's preferences.

As can be observed from Table 3, (1) the averages of T of the proposed method are slightly more than those of the *a priori* one, but significantly smaller than those of the *a posteriori* one; (2) the averages of T of *a priori* method are also significantly smaller than those of the *a posteriori* one.

It can be concluded from the experimental results and analysis above that compared with the other two methods, the proposed one can spend less time in obtaining Pareto optimal solutions which more fit the DM's preferences.

4   Conclusions

An evolutionary algorithm incorporating with a DM's preferences is proposed in this study to solve MOPs with interval parameters. The DM's preferences are represented by relative importance relationships of objectives, and the DM can interactively modify his/her preferences during the evolution. Furthermore, the DM's preferences are employed to further distinguish different optimal solutions with the same Pareto rank to guide the population to evolve towards the DM's real preference regions.

Acknowledgments. This work was jointly supported by National Natural Science Foundation of China, grant No. 60775044 and 61105063, and Program for New Century Excellent Talents in Universities, grant No. NCET-07-0802.

References

1. Gong, D.W., Qin, N.N., Sun, X.Y.: Evolutionary Algorithms for Multi-objective Optimization Problems with Interval Parameters. In: 5th IEEE International Conference on Bio-Inspired Computing: Theories and Applications, pp. 411–420 (2010)
2. Yang, D.D., Jiao, L.C., Gong, M.G., Yu, H.: Clone Selection Algorithm to Solve Prefer-ence Multi-objective Optimization. Journal of Software 21, 14–33 (2010)
3. Luque, M., Miettinen, K., Eskelinen, P., Ruiz, F.: Incorporating Preference Information in Interactive Reference Point Methods for Multiobjective Optimization. Omega 37, 450–462 (2009)

4. Rachmawati, L., Srinivasan, D.: Incorporating the Notion of Relative Importance of Ob-jectives in Evolutionary Multiobjective Optimization. IEEE Transactions on Evolu-tion-ary Computation 14, 530–546 (2010)
5. Zitzler, E., Deb, K., Thiele, L.: Comparison of Multiobjective Evolutionary Algorithms: Empirical Results. Evolutionary Computation 8, 173–195 (2000)
6. Deb, K., Thiele, L., Laumanns, M., Zitzler, E.: Scalable Test Problems for Evolutionary Multiobjective Optimization. In: Abraham, A., Jain, L., Goldberg, R. (eds.) Evolution-ary Mul-tiobjective Optimization: Theoretical Advances and Applications, pp. 105–145. Sprin-ger, New York (2005)
7. Limbourg, P., Aponte, D.E.: An Optimization Algorithm for Imprecise Multi-objective Problem Functions. In: Proceedings of IEEE Congress on Evolutionary Computation, pp. 459–466. IEEE Press, New York (2005)

Precipitation Control for Mixed Solution Based on Fuzzy Adaptive Robust Algorithm

Hongjun Duan[1], Fengwen Wang[1], and Silong Peng[2]

[1] Department of Automation Engineering, Northeastern University at Qinhuangdao, Qinhuangdao, China
[2] Institute of Automation, Chinese Academy of Sciences, Beijing, China
dhj@mail.neuq.edu.cn, wfw0335@126.com, Silong.peng@ia.ac.cn

Abstract. Fuzzy adaptive robust control algorithm was proposed for a class of uncertain nonlinear systems based on Lyapunov's stability theory. The system was divided into nominal model and lumped disturbance term which embodies modeling error, parameter uncertainties, disturbances and unmodeled dynamics. Fuzzy adaptive control was adopted to approach uncertain parameters of the system in real time; the impact of external disturbances was eliminated by robust control. The on-line calculation amount of fuzzy logic system is relatively less, the dynamic performance of system is better, and the output of system tracks the expectation well. The stability was proved and the algorithm was applied to the precipitation control of sucrose-glucose mixed solution. Simulation result supported the validity of the proposed algorithm.

Keywords: batch processes, precipitation of mixed solution, nonlinearity, fuzzy adaptive robust, Chinese medicine.

1 Introduction

Precipitation of mixed solution is a batch process. In recent years, there has been a growing interest in the optimization control of batch processes, which are suitable for responsive manufacturing of low volume and high value-added products [1-2]. However, it is usually very difficult to obtain the accurate models due to the complexity of the processes, and it is also difficult to implement them for on-line optimization since optimization based on mechanistic models is usually very time-consuming [3]. The repetitive nature of batch process operations allows that the information of previous batch runs can be used to improve the operation of the next batch. Of late, the relative algorithms are mainly iterative learning control (ILC) [4-6] and nonlinear model-based predictive control (NMPC) [7-8]. However, the batch numbers of some industry processes are restricted, in other words, the cycle of each batch process is very long, so the above-mentioned algorithms are inapplicable. For example, it claims almost seven days for one batch Chinese medicine produce. The content of effective components is discrepant for the medicinal materials from different producing areas. These come into being tremendous challenge for the steady productions of different batch processes.

D.-S. Huang et al. (Eds.): ICIC 2012, CCIS 304, pp. 30–37, 2012.
© Springer-Verlag Berlin Heidelberg 2012

In recent years, Fuzzy control has become very popular and enjoys a wide variety of application areas [9-12]. However, the tracking errors of most fuzzy control systems can be merely converged to a global field of residual errors, the global field would augment along with system uncertainty [13], so fuzzy control is not robust for system uncertainty. In paper [14], an effectual fuzzy adaptive controller was contrived for a class of nth-order single-input single-output (SISO) nonlinear systems, but the calculation quantum is too great. For nth-order multi-input multi-output (MIMO) nonlinear systems, the precision is very difficult to obtain. In this paper, a designed method of fuzzy adaptive robust controller was studied for a class of MIMO nonlinear systems. The uncertain parameters are approached by fuzzy adaptive control in real time and the impact of external disturbances is eliminated by robust feedback control. The on-line calculation amount is decreased correspondingly and the control precision is improved. The fuzzy adaptive robust algorithm was simulated for the precipitation control of sucrose-glucose mixed solution. The sugars were all precipitated according to their respective crystal rates, and sucrose and glucose track their respective concentration setpoints in real time.

2   Problem formulation

A class of MIMO uncertain nonlinear systems is of the following form

$$\begin{cases} x^{(n)} = f\left(x, \dot{x}, \cdots, x^{(n-1)}\right) + \tilde{f} + b(x)u + d \\ y = x \end{cases} \tag{1}$$

where $x \in R^m$, $u \in R^m$, $y \in R^m$ are the state vector, system input and output, respectively; $b(x) \in R^{m \times m}$ is the coefficient matrix; $f\left(x, \dot{x}, \cdots, x^{(n-1)}\right) \in R^m$ is the function vector; $\tilde{f} \in R^m$ is the uncertain vector; $d \in R^m$ is the disturb vector. The objective is to enable the output y to follow a desired trajectory y_d.

There exists a known positive constant η or η_i $(i = 1, 2, \cdots, m)$, such that

$$\|d\| \leq \eta \text{ or } |d_i| \leq \eta_i \tag{2}$$

where, $\|\cdot\|$ denotes the standard Euclidean norm. Define the error vector as follows

$$e := \left[x - x_d, \dot{x} - \dot{x}_d, \cdots, x^{(n-1)} - x_d^{(n-1)}\right]^T = \left[e_1, e_2, \cdots, e_n\right]^T \tag{3}$$

where, x_d is the desired vector of x, $e_1 = \left[x_1 - x_{1d}, x_2 - x_{2d}, \cdots, x_m - x_{md}\right]^T$

$$=[e_1,e_2,\cdots,e_m]^{\mathrm{T}}, \quad e_2=[\dot{e}_1,\dot{e}_2,\cdots,\dot{e}_m]^{\mathrm{T}}, \quad \cdots, \quad e_n=[e_1^{(n-1)},e_2^{(n-1)},\cdots,e_m^{(n-1)}]^{\mathrm{T}}.$$

Again define filter tracking error vector $s \in R^m$ as follows

$$s:=(p+\lambda)^{(n-1)}e_1 \tag{4}$$

where, $p=\mathrm{d}/\mathrm{d}t$ denotes a differential operator, $\lambda>0$ is a known positive constant. From (4), we know that $e_1 \to 0$ as $s \to 0$. Rewrite the coefficient matrix

$$b(x)=\mathrm{diag}\{b_{01}+\tilde{b}_1,b_{02}+\tilde{b}_2,\cdots,b_{0i}+\tilde{b}_i,\cdots,b_{0m}+\tilde{b}_m\} \tag{5}$$

where $b_{0i}>0, \tilde{b}_i\,(i=1,2,\cdots,m)$ are the nominal values and uncertain values of coefficient matrix, respectively, $b_{0i}+\tilde{b}_i=b_i$. Substitute the derivative of (4) into (1)

$$\dot{s}=p(p+\lambda)^{n-1}e_1=-\lambda s+f+\tilde{f}+(b_0+\tilde{b})u+d-x_\mathrm{d}^{(n)}+\sum_{j=1}^{n}C_n^j\lambda^j e_{n-j+1} \tag{6}$$

In (6), the uncertainties $\tilde{b}$ with $\tilde{f}$, and disturbance d are all unknown, a fuzzy adaptive controller and a robust controller will be designed for them.

3   Design of Fuzzy Logic System

Assume that a fuzzy logic controller with q inputs ($v_1,v_2,\cdots,v_q$), single output (w), and the number of fuzzy rules is r. IF-THEN rule is introduced

R^r: If v_1 is $A_1^r(v_1)$ and ... and v_q is $A_q^r(v_q)$ then $w=\theta^r$

The output of fuzzy logic system can be represented as

$$w=\sum_{l=1}^{r}\left(\frac{\prod_{j=1}^{q}\mu_{A_j^l}(v_j)}{\sum_{l=1}^{r}\prod_{j=1}^{q}\mu_{A_j^l}(v_j)}\right)\theta_l \tag{7}$$

where, A_j^l is the j-th fuzzy set corresponding to the l-th fuzzy rule, $\mu_{A_j^l}$ is the membership function for A_j^l, and θ_l is can be taken as a center of the l-th fuzzy set corresponding to the controller's output w.

$$\mu_{A_j^l}(v_j) = \exp(-(v_j - c_j^l)^2 / (\sigma_j^l)^2) \tag{8}$$

where, c_j^l, σ_j^l are the median and width for Gauss member function. Let

$$\boldsymbol{\theta} = [\theta_1, \theta_2, \cdots, \theta_r]^T, \boldsymbol{\xi} = \left[\frac{\prod_{j=1}^q \mu_{A_j^1}(v_j)}{\sum_{l=1}^r \prod_{j=1}^q \mu_{A_j^l}(v_j)}, \cdots, \frac{\prod_{j=1}^q \mu_{A_j^r}(v_j)}{\sum_{l=1}^r \prod_{j=1}^q \mu_{A_j^l}(v_j)} \right]^T.$$

Then, we can represent (7) as

$$w = \boldsymbol{\theta}^T \boldsymbol{\xi} \tag{9}$$

We approximate $\tilde{b}$ and $\tilde{f}$ with fuzzy logic systems

$$\tilde{\boldsymbol{b}}(x \mid \boldsymbol{\theta}_{\tilde{b}}) = \mathrm{diag}\left\{ \boldsymbol{\theta}_{\tilde{b}_1}^T \boldsymbol{\xi}_{\tilde{b}_1}, \boldsymbol{\theta}_{\tilde{b}_2}^T \boldsymbol{\xi}_{\tilde{b}_2}, \cdots, \boldsymbol{\theta}_{\tilde{b}_m}^T \boldsymbol{\xi}_{\tilde{b}_m} \right\} \tag{10}$$

$$\tilde{\boldsymbol{f}}\left((x, \dot{x}, \cdots, x^{(n-1)}) \mid \boldsymbol{\theta}_{\tilde{f}}\right) = \left[\boldsymbol{\theta}_{\tilde{f}_1}^T \boldsymbol{\xi}_{\tilde{f}_1}, \boldsymbol{\theta}_{\tilde{f}_2}^T \boldsymbol{\xi}_{\tilde{f}_2}, \cdots, \boldsymbol{\theta}_{\tilde{f}_m}^T \boldsymbol{\xi}_{\tilde{f}_m} \right]^T \tag{11}$$

4   Design of Fuzzy Adaptive Controller

We denote optimal vectors by $\boldsymbol{\theta}_{\tilde{b}_i}^*$, $\boldsymbol{\theta}_{\tilde{f}_i}^*$ ($i = 1, 2, \cdots, m$) such that

$$\boldsymbol{\theta}_{\tilde{b}_i}^* = \arg \min_{\boldsymbol{\theta}_{\tilde{b}_i}} \left(\sup_{x \in X} \left| \tilde{b}_i(x) - \boldsymbol{\theta}_{\tilde{b}_i}^T \boldsymbol{\xi}_{\tilde{b}_i}(x) \right| \right) \tag{12}$$

$$\boldsymbol{\theta}_{\tilde{f}_i}^* = \arg \min_{\boldsymbol{\theta}_{\tilde{f}_i}} \left(\sup_{x, \dot{x}, \cdots, x^{(n-1)} \in X} \left(\left| \tilde{f}_i(x, \dot{x}, \cdots, x^{(n-1)}) - \boldsymbol{\theta}_{\tilde{f}_i}^T \boldsymbol{\xi}_{\tilde{f}_i}(x, \dot{x}, \cdots, x^{(n-1)}) \right| \right) \right) \tag{13}$$

where, $X \subseteq R^{mn}$ is a region in which the state $x, \dot{x}, \cdots, x^{(n-1)}$ are constrained to reside. We define the adaptive parameter errors as

$$\boldsymbol{\phi}_{\tilde{b}_i} := \boldsymbol{\theta}_{\tilde{b}_i} - \boldsymbol{\theta}_{\tilde{b}_i}^* \qquad\qquad \boldsymbol{\phi}_{\tilde{f}_i} := \boldsymbol{\theta}_{\tilde{f}_i} - \boldsymbol{\theta}_{\tilde{f}_i}^* \tag{14}$$

We will use the adaptive law

$$\dot{\boldsymbol{\phi}}_{\tilde{b}_i}(t) = \dot{\boldsymbol{\theta}}_{\tilde{b}_i}(t) = \boldsymbol{\Gamma}_{\tilde{b}_i} s_i \boldsymbol{\xi}_{\tilde{b}_i}(x) u_i \tag{15}$$

$$\dot{\phi}_{\tilde{f}_i}(t) = \dot{\theta}_{\tilde{f}_i}(t) = \Gamma_{\tilde{f}_i} s_i \xi_{\tilde{f}_i}\left(x, \dot{x}, \cdots, x^{(n-1)}\right) \tag{16}$$

where, $\Gamma_{\tilde{b}_i}, \Gamma_{\tilde{f}_i} \in R^{m \times m}$ are diagonal symmetric positive definite matrices whose elements are adaptive rates. s_i is i-th element of s. From (6), we can contrive the control law as follows

$$u_i = \left(b_{0i} + \theta_{\tilde{b}_i}^{\mathrm{T}} \xi_{\tilde{b}_i}\right)^{-1}\left(-f_i - \theta_{\tilde{f}_i}^{\mathrm{T}} \xi_{\tilde{f}_i} - u_{si} + x_{di}^{(n)} - \sum_{j=1}^{n} C_n^j \lambda^j e_{(n-j+1),i}\right) \tag{17}$$

where, u_{si} is a robust controller to manage disturbances

$$u_{si} = \begin{cases} \eta_i s_i / |s_i|, & |s_i| \ge \varepsilon_i \\ \eta_i s_i / \varepsilon_i, & |s_i| < \varepsilon_i \end{cases} \tag{18}$$

where, ε_i is positive constant, and $\varepsilon = \sum_{i=1}^{m} \varepsilon_i$.

Theorem 1: Given the uncertain nonlinear system (1), if there exist $\theta_{\tilde{f}_i}^*$ and $\theta_{\tilde{b}_i}^*$, the following condition is satisfied

$$\tilde{f}_i\left(x, \dot{x}, \cdots, x^{(n-1)}\right) = \theta_{\tilde{f}_i}^{*\mathrm{T}} \xi_{\tilde{f}_i}\left(x, \dot{x}, \cdots, x^{(n-1)}\right) \qquad \tilde{b}_i(x) = \theta_{\tilde{b}_i}^{*\mathrm{T}} \xi_{\tilde{b}_i}(x) \tag{19}$$

Then the system (1) can be stable under the controller (17) ~ (18) with the adaptive laws (15) ~ (16). Moreover, $e(t) \to 0$ as $t \to \infty$.

Proof: Define a positive Lyapunov function by

$$V := \sum_{i=1}^{m} V_i\left(s_i, \phi_{\tilde{f}_i}, \phi_{\tilde{b}_i}\right) \tag{20}$$

where

$$V_i\left(s_i, \phi_{\tilde{f}_i}, \phi_{\tilde{b}_i}\right) = \frac{1}{2}s_i^2 + \frac{1}{2}\phi_{\tilde{f}_i}^{\mathrm{T}} \Gamma_{\tilde{f}_i}^{-1} \phi_{\tilde{f}_i} + \frac{1}{2}\phi_{\tilde{b}_i}^{\mathrm{T}} \Gamma_{\tilde{b}_i}^{-1} \phi_{\tilde{b}_i} \tag{21}$$

Substitute (6), (14) ~ (17), (19), and (2) into the time derivative of (21), we obtain

$$\dot{V}_i = s_i \dot{s}_i + \phi_{\tilde{f}_i}^{\mathrm{T}} \Gamma_{\tilde{f}_i}^{-1} \dot{\phi}_{\tilde{f}_i} + \phi_{\tilde{b}_i}^{\mathrm{T}} \Gamma_{\tilde{b}_i}^{-1} \dot{\phi}_{\tilde{b}_i} \le -\lambda s_i^2 + s_i(d_i - u_{si}) - s_i \phi_{\tilde{f}_i}^{\mathrm{T}} \xi_{\tilde{f}_i} - s_i \phi_{\tilde{b}_i}^{\mathrm{T}} \xi_{\tilde{b}_i} u_i$$

$$+ \phi_{\tilde{f}_i}^{\mathrm{T}} \Gamma_{\tilde{f}_i}^{-1}\left(\Gamma_{\tilde{f}_i} s_i \xi_{\tilde{f}_i}\right) + \phi_{\tilde{b}_i}^{\mathrm{T}} \Gamma_{\tilde{b}_i}^{-1}\left(\Gamma_{\tilde{b}_i} s_i \xi_{\tilde{b}_i} u_i\right) \le -\lambda s_i^2 + s_i(\eta_i - u_{si}) \tag{22}$$

Substitute (22) into the result the time derivative of (20), we obtain

$$\dot{V} \le \sum_{i=1}^{m} \left(-\lambda s_i^2 + s_i \left(\eta_i - u_{si} \right) \right) = -\lambda s^{\mathrm{T}} s + \|s\| \eta - s^{\mathrm{T}} u_s \tag{23}$$

Substitute (18) into (23) with $\|s\| \ge \varepsilon$

$$\dot{V} \le -\lambda \|s\|^2 < 0 \tag{24}$$

Substitute (18) into (23) with $\|s\| < \varepsilon$

$$\dot{V} \le -\lambda \|s\|^2 + \|s\| \eta \left(1 - \|s\| / \varepsilon \right) \tag{25}$$

when $\|s\| = \varepsilon / 2$, there exists the maximum $\varepsilon \eta / 4$ for the second item in (25). If $\|s\| > \sqrt{\varepsilon \eta / 4 \lambda}$, (25) is negative. This implies that the tracking error is congruously bounded, i.e. $e(t) \to 0$ as $t \to \infty$.

5   Precipitation Control Simulation of Mixed Solution

In order to verify the proposed control algorithm, precipitation control simulation for sucrose-glucose mixed solution is performed. The model is as follows

$$\begin{cases} \dot{x} = f(x) + \tilde{f} + b(x)u + d \\ y = x \end{cases} \tag{19}$$

where $x = \left[m_{\mathrm{s}}, m_{\mathrm{g}}, m_{\mathrm{w}} \right]^{\mathrm{T}}$; $b(x) = \begin{bmatrix} \rho_{\mathrm{f}} F_{\mathrm{f}} Bx_{\mathrm{fs}} Pte_{\mathrm{fs}} & 0 & 0 \\ \rho_{\mathrm{f}} F_{\mathrm{f}} Bx_{\mathrm{fg}} Pte_{\mathrm{fg}} & 0 & 0 \\ \rho_{\mathrm{f}} \left(\dfrac{h_1}{\vartheta} - Bx_{\mathrm{fs}} - Bx_{\mathrm{fg}} \right) & \rho_{\mathrm{w}} \dfrac{h_2}{\vartheta} & -\dfrac{1}{\vartheta} \end{bmatrix}$;

$f = \left[-\alpha_{\mathrm{cryst}} m_{\mathrm{s}}, -\beta_{\mathrm{cryst}} m_{\mathrm{g}}, \lambda_{\mathrm{cryst}} \left(\alpha_{\mathrm{cryst}} m_{\mathrm{sc}} + \beta_{\mathrm{cryst}} m_{\mathrm{gc}} \right) / \vartheta \right]^{\mathrm{T}}$; $u = \left[F_{\mathrm{f}}, F_{\mathrm{w}}, \dot{Q} \right]^{\mathrm{T}}$;

All the thermal and physical parameters are issued from literature or estimated from available correlations [15]. The controller parameters are as follows

$\tilde{f} = \left[2\cos t, 1.5\cos t, \cos t \right]^{\mathrm{T}}$, $d = \left[3\sin t, 2\sin t, \cdots, \sin t \right]^{\mathrm{T}}$, $k_s = \left[4, 3, 1.5 \right]^{\mathrm{T}}$,

$\varepsilon = \left[2, 1.5, 0.8 \right]^{\mathrm{T}}$, $\eta = \left[0.5, 0.5, 0.5 \right]^{\mathrm{T}}$, $\lambda = 2$, $\Gamma_{\tilde{f}_1} = \mathrm{diag}\{25, 25, 25\}$,

$$\boldsymbol{\Gamma}_{\tilde{f}_2} = \mathrm{diag}\{20,20,20\} \ , \ \boldsymbol{\Gamma}_{\tilde{f}_3} = \mathrm{diag}\{16,16,16\} \ , \ \boldsymbol{\Gamma}_{\tilde{b}_1} = \mathrm{diag}\{12,12,12\} \ ,$$
$$\boldsymbol{\Gamma}_{\tilde{b}_2} = \mathrm{diag}\{10,10,10\}, \boldsymbol{\Gamma}_{\tilde{b}_3} = \mathrm{diag}\{8,8,8\} \ .$$

There are five fuzzy sets for every input of the fuzzy logic system: NB, NS, ZE, PS, PB. In simulation, let $e_{\tilde{b}_i}$ be -0.5, -0.3, 0, 0.3, 0.5; let $e_{\tilde{f}_i}$ be -1.0, -0.5, 0, 0.5, 1.0; let $\dot{e}_{\tilde{b}_i}$ and $\dot{e}_{\tilde{f}_i}$ all be -0.8, -0.4, 0, 0.4, 0.8.

The precipitation tracking curves of sucrose-glucose solution are illustrated in Fig.1, where M_{scd} , M_{sc} are the setpoints and tracking results of sucrose crystal masses; $M_{\mathrm{gcd}}, M_{\mathrm{gc}}$ are the setpoints and tracking results of glucose crystal masses. The concentration tracking curves of sucrose-glucose solution are illustrated in Fig.2, where, C_{sd} , C_{s} are the setpoints and tracking results of sucrose concentration; C_{gd} , C_{g} are the setpoints and tracking results of glucose concentration.

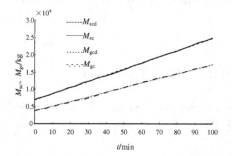

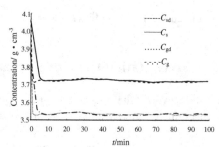

Fig. 1. Precipitation tracking curves   **Fig. 2.** Concentration tracking curves

From the simulation results in figure 1, we get to know that the crystal masses of sucrose-glucose track their respective setpoints commendably. From the simulation results in figure 2, we get to know that the concentrations of sucrose-glucose track their respective setpoints commendably. The sucrose and glucose are all crystalline state. As a result, the uncertainties are approximated, the control precision and robustness are improved. Furthermore, the impact of disturbance is restrained by a robust controller.

6   Conclusion

For a class of uncertain nonlinear systems with disturbance, a design method of fuzzy adaptive robust controller was proposed. The uncertain parameters were approached by fuzzy adaptive control in real time and the external disturbances were eliminated by robust feedback control. The scheme manifests good control precision, strong robustness, less on-line computation. The validity was supported by the precipitation simulations of sucrose-glucose mixed solution.

References

1. Bonvin, D.: Optimal Operation of Batch Reactors: A Personal View. Journal of Process Control 8, 355–368 (1998)
2. Chen, Z.G., Xu, C., Shao, H.H.: Batch Processes Optimization and Advanced Control—A Survey. Control and Instruments in Chemical Industry 30(3), 1–6 (2003) (in Chinese)
3. Xiong, Z.H., Zhang, J.: Neural network Model-based On-line Re-optimization Control of Fed-batch Processes using a Modified Iterative Dynamic Programming Algorithm. Chemical Engineering and Processing 44, 477–484 (2005)
4. Xiong, Z.H., Zhang, J., Dong, J.: Optimal Iterative Learning Control for Batch Processes based on Linear Time-varying Perturbation Model. Chinese Journal of Chemical Engineering 16(2), 235–240 (2008) (in Chinese)
5. Zhang, J., Nguyen, J., Xiong, Z.H.: Iterative Learning Control of Batch Processes based on Time Varying Perturbation Models. Journal of Tsinghua University (Sci. &Tech.) 48(S2), 1771–1774 (2008) (in Chinese)
6. Jia, L., Shi, J.P., Qiu, M.S., et al.: Nonrestraint-Iterative Learning-based Optimal Control for Batch Processes. CIESC Journal 61(8), 1889–1893 (2010)
7. Damour, C., Benne, M., Boillereaux, L., et al.: NMPC of an Industrial Crystallization Process using Model-based Observers. Journal of Industrial and Engineering Chemistry 16, 708–716 (2010) (in Chinese)
8. Fan, L., Wang, H.Q., Song, Z.H., et al.: Iterative Optimal Control for Batch Process based on Generalized Predictive Control. Control and Instruments in Chemical Industry 33(2), 25–28 (2006)
9. Mendes, J., Araujo, R., Sousa, P.: An Architecture for Adaptive Fuzzy Control in Industrial Environments. Computers in Industry 62, 364–373 (2011)
10. Liu, Y.J., Tong, S.C., Li, T.S.: Observer-based Adaptive Fuzzy Tracking Control for a Class of Uncertain Nonlinear MIMO systems. Fuzzy Sets and Systems 164, 25–44 (2011)
11. Shi, W.X., Zhang, M., Guo, W.C., et al.: Stable Adaptive Fuzzy Control for MIMO Nonlinear Systems. Computers and Mathematics with Applications 62, 2843–2853 (2011)
12. Wang, Y.F., Chai, T.Y., Zhang, Y.M.: State Observer-based Adaptive Fuzzy Output-Feedback Control for a Class of Uncertain Nonlinear Systems. Information Sciences 180, 5029–5040 (2010)
13. Yu, W.S.: Adaptive Fuzzy PID Control for Nonlinear Systems with H^{∞} Tracking Performance. In: 2006 IEEE International Conference on Fuzzy Systems, Vancouver, BC Canada, pp. 1010–1015 (2006)
14. Lee, Y.G., Gong, J.Q., Yao, B.: Fuzzy Adaptive Robust Control of a Class of Nonlinear Systems. In: Proceedings of the American Control Conference, Arlington, VA, pp. 4040–4045 (2001)
15. Damour, C., Benne, M., Boillereaux, L., et al.: Multivariable Linearizing Control of an Industrial Sugar Crystallization Process. Journal of Process Control 21, 46–54 (2011)

B-Spline Neural Networks Based PID Controller for Hammerstein Systems

Xia Hong[1], Serdar Iplikci[2], Sheng Chen[3], and Kevin Warwick[1]

[1] School of Systems Engineering, University of Reading, UK
[2] Pamukkale University, Department of Electrical and Electronics Engineering,
Kinikli Campus, 20040, Denizli, Turkey
[3] School of Electronics and Computer Science, University of Southampton, UK
and Faculty of Engineering, King Abdulaziz University, Jeddah 21589, Saudi Arabia

Abstract. A new PID tuning and controller approach is introduced for Hammerstein systems based on input/output data. A B-spline neural network is used to model the nonlinear static function in the Hammerstein system. The control signal is composed of a PID controller together with a correction term. In order to update the control signal, the multistep ahead predictions of the Hammerstein system based on the B-spline neural networks and the associated Jacobians matrix are calculated using the De Boor algorithms including both the functional and derivative recursions. A numerical example is utilized to demonstrate the efficacy of the proposed approaches.

Keywords: Hammerstein model, PID controller, system identification.

1 Introduction

The proportional–integral–derivative (PID) controllers have been the most popular controller structures. Neural networks have been widely applied to model unknown dynamical processes and then used for PID parameter tuning [10,4,12]. Recently a novel predictive model-based PID tuning and control approach has been proposed for unknown nonlinear systems that are modelled using neural networks and support vector machines (SVMs) [8]. The work introduces a useful technique both for PID parameter tuning and for the correction of the PID output during control, which yields superior tracking and parameter convergence performance.

The Hammerstein model, comprising a nonlinear static functional transformation followed by a linear dynamical model, has been applied to nonlinear plant/process modelling in a wide range of biological/engineering problems [7,2]. Model based control for the Hammerstein system has been well studied [1,2]. The implementation of model based control for an *a priori* unknown Hammerstein model requires system identification including modelling and identification of the nonlinear static function. In this work a new PID controller is introduced for Hammerstein systems that are identified based on observational input/output

D.-S. Huang et al. (Eds.): ICIC 2012, CCIS 304, pp. 38–46, 2012.

data, in which the nonlinear static function in the Hammerstein system is modelled using a B-spline neural network. For system identification we used the Gauss-Newton algorithm subject to constraints as proposed in [6]. The predictive model-based PID tuning and controller approach in [8] was combined with the B-spline neural network based Hammerstein model. For this purpose, multistep ahead predictions of the B-spline neural networks based Hammerstein model are generated as well as the essential Jacobian matrix for updating the control signal, based on the De Boor recursion including both the functional and derivative recursions. The proposed model based on B-spline neural networks has a significant advantage in that this enables stable and efficient evaluations of functional and derivative values based on De Boor recursion, which is used for updating the PID control signals.

2   Modelling of the Hammerstein System Based on B-Spline Functions

The Hammerstein system consists of a cascade of two subsystems, a nonlinear memoryless function $\Psi(\bullet)$ as the first subsystem, followed by a linear dynamic part as the second subsystem. The system can be represented by

$$y(t) = -a_1 y(t-1) - a_2 y(t-2) - ... - a_{n_a} y(t-n_a)$$
$$+ b_1 v(t-1) + ... + b_{n_b} v(t-n_b) + \xi(t) \qquad (1)$$
$$v(t-j) = \Psi(u(t-j)), \qquad j = 1, ..., n_b \qquad (2)$$

where $y(t)$ is the system output and $u(t)$ is the system input. $\xi(t)$ is assumed to be a white noise sequence independent of $u(t)$ with zero mean and variance of σ^2. $v(t)$ is the output of nonlinear subsystem and the input to the linear subsystem. a_j's, b_j's are parameters of the linear subsystem. n_a and n_b are assumed known system output and input lags. Denote $\mathbf{a} = [a_1, ..., a_{n_a}]^T \in \Re^{n_a}$ and $\mathbf{b} = [b_1, ..., b_{n_b}]^T \in \Re^{n_b}$. It is assumed that $A(q^{-1}) = 1 + a_1 q^{-1} + ... + a_{n_a} q^{-n_a}$ and $B(q^{-1}) = b_1 q^{-1} + ... + b_{n_b} q^{-n_b}$ are coprime polynomials of q^{-1}, where q^{-1} denotes the backward shift operator.

Without significantly loss of generality the following assumptions are initially made about the problem.

Assumption 1: The gain of the linear subsystem is given by

$$G = \lim_{q \to 1} \frac{B(q^{-1})}{A(q^{-1})} = \frac{\sum_{j=1}^{n_b} b_j}{1 + \sum_{j=1}^{n_a} a_j} = 1 \qquad (3)$$

Assumption 2: $\Psi(\bullet)$ is a one to one mapping, i.e. it is an invertible and continuous function.

Assumption 3: $u(t)$ is bounded by $U_{min} < u(t) < U_{max}$, where U_{min} and U_{max} are assumed known finite real values.

The objective of the work is controller design for the system based on observational data. The objective of system identification for the above Hammerstein model is that, given an observational input/output data set $D_N = \{y(t), u(t)\}_{t=1}^{N}$, to identify $\Psi(\bullet)$ and to estimate the parameters a_j, b_j in the linear subsystems. In this work B-spline basis functions are adopted in order to model $\Psi(\bullet)$. Specifically, the B-spline basis functions are initially formed by using the De-Boor algorithm [3] for the input data sets.

Univariate B-spline basis functions are parameterized using a piecewise polynomial of order k, and also by a knot vector which is a set of values defined on the real line that break it up into a number of intervals. Supposing that there are d basis functions, the knot vector is specified by $(d + k)$ knot values, $\{U_1, U_2, \cdots, U_{d+k}\}$. At each end there are k knots satisfying the condition of being external to the input region, and as a result the number of internal knots is $(d - k)$. Specifically

$$U_1 < U_2 < U_k = U_{min} < U_{k+1} < U_{k+2} < \cdots < U_d < U_{max} = U_{d+1} < \cdots < U_{d+k}. \quad (4)$$

Given these predetermined knots, a set of d B-spline basis functions can be formed by using the De Boor recursion [3], given by

$$\mathcal{B}_j^{(0)}(u) = \begin{cases} 1 \text{ if } U_j \leq u < U_{j+1} \\ 0 \quad \text{otherwise} \end{cases} \quad (5)$$
$$j = 1, \cdots, (d + k)$$

$$\left. \mathcal{B}_j^{(i)}(u) = \frac{u - U_j}{U_{i+j} - U_j} \mathcal{B}_i^{(i-1)}(u) + \frac{U_{i+j+1} - u}{U_{i+j+1} - U_{j+1}} \mathcal{B}_{j+1}^{(i-1)}(u), \atop j = 1, \cdots, (d + k - i) \right\} \ i = 1, \cdots, k \quad (6)$$

The first order derivatives of the B-spline function have a similar recursion

$$\frac{d}{du} \mathcal{B}_j^{(k)}(u) = \frac{k}{U_{k+j} - U_j} \mathcal{B}_j^{(k-1)}(u) - \frac{k}{U_{k+j+1} - U_{j+1}} \mathcal{B}_{j+1}^{(k-1)}(u), \ j = 1, \cdots, d \quad (7)$$

We model $\Psi(\bullet)$ as a B-spline neural network [5], in the form of

$$\Psi(u) = \sum_{j=1}^{d} \mathcal{B}_j^{(k)}(u) \omega_j \quad (8)$$

where ω_j's are weights to be determined. Denote $\boldsymbol{\omega} = [\omega_1, \cdots, \omega_d]^T \in \Re^d$.

The model predicted output $\hat{y}(t)$ in (1) can be written as

$$\hat{y}(t) = -a_1 y(t - 1) - a_2 y(t - 2) - \ldots - a_{n_a} y(t - n_a) +$$
$$b_1 \sum_{j=1}^{d} \omega_j \mathcal{B}_j^{(k)}(t - 1) + \ldots + b_{n_b} \sum_{j=1}^{d} \omega_j \mathcal{B}_j^{(k)}(t - n_b). \quad (9)$$

Let the modelling error be $\varepsilon(t) = y(t) - \hat{y}(t)$. Over the estimation data set $D_N = \{y(t), u(t)\}_{t=1}^{N}$, (1) can be rewritten in a linear regression form

$$y(t) = [\mathbf{p}(\mathbf{x}(t))]^T \boldsymbol{\vartheta} + \varepsilon(t) \quad (10)$$

where $\mathbf{x}(t) = [-y(t-1), ..., -y(t-n_a), u(t-1), ..., u(t-n_b)]^T$ is system input vector of observables with assumed known dimension of $(n_a + n_b)$, $\boldsymbol{\vartheta} = [\mathbf{a}^T, (b_1\omega_1), ..., (b_1\omega_d), ...(b_{n_b}\omega_1), ..., (b_{n_b}\omega_{n_b})]^T \in \Re^{n_a + d \cdot n_b}$,

$$\mathbf{p}(\mathbf{x}(t)) = [-y(t-1), ..., -y(t-n_a), \mathcal{B}_1^{(k)}(t-1), ...$$
$$..., \mathcal{B}_d^{(k)}(t-1), ...\mathcal{B}_1^{(k)}(t-n_b), ..., \mathcal{B}_d^{(k)}(t-n_b)]^T \quad (11)$$

(10) can be rewritten in the matrix form as

$$\mathbf{y} = \mathbf{P}\boldsymbol{\vartheta} + \boldsymbol{\varepsilon} \quad (12)$$

where $\mathbf{y} = [y(1), \cdots, y(N)]^T$ is the output vector. $\boldsymbol{\varepsilon} = [\varepsilon(1), ..., \varepsilon(N)]^T$, and $\mathbf{P}$ is the regression matrix

$$\mathbf{P} = \begin{bmatrix} p_1(\mathbf{x}(1)) & p_2(\mathbf{x}(1)) & \cdots & p_{n_a+d\cdot n_b}(\mathbf{x}(1)) \\ p_1(\mathbf{x}(2)) & p_2(\mathbf{x}(2)) & \cdots & p_{n_a+d\cdot n_b}(\mathbf{x}(2)) \\ \cdots\cdots\cdots\cdots\cdots\cdots\cdots\cdots\cdots\cdots\cdots\cdots \\ p_1(\mathbf{x}(N)) & p_2(\mathbf{x}(N)) & \cdots & p_{n_a+d\cdot n_b}(\mathbf{x}(N)) \end{bmatrix} \quad (13)$$

Let $\mathbf{B} = \mathbf{P}^T\mathbf{P}$ and perform the singular value decomposition (SVD) $\mathbf{BQ} = \mathbf{Q}\boldsymbol{\Sigma}$, where $\boldsymbol{\Sigma} = \text{diag}[\sigma_1, ...\sigma_r, 0, \cdots, 0]$. $\mathbf{Q} = [\mathbf{q}_1, \cdots, \mathbf{q}_1, \cdots, \mathbf{q}_{n_a+d\cdot n_b}]$ to yield

$$\boldsymbol{\vartheta}_{LS}^{svd} = \sum_{i=1}^{r} \frac{\mathbf{y}^T\mathbf{Pq}_i}{\sigma_i}\mathbf{q}_i \quad (14)$$

This procedure produces our final estimate of â, which is simply taken as the subvector of the resultant $\boldsymbol{\vartheta}_{LS}^{svd}$, consisting of its first n_a elements. The parameter estimation for $\mathbf{b}$ and $\boldsymbol{\omega}$ can be obtained using our previous work [6].

3   The Model Based PID Controller

Figure 1 illustrates the proposed model based PID controller for Hammerstein systems using B-spline neural networks where $r(t)$ is the desired reference trajectory to be followed by the plant output $y(t)$, and $e(t)$ is the error between

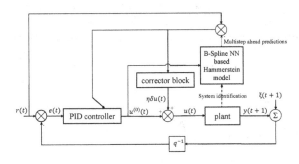

Fig. 1. Diagram of the model based PID controller

the desired and measured output at time index t. Both the PID controller parameters and the control signal are derived using the concept of predictive control, explained as follows. At each sampling time, consider that the control signal $u(t)$ is repeatedly applied to the plant exactly for consecutive K time steps and the resultant predictive output trajectory vector is denoted as $[\hat{y}(t+1|t), \hat{y}(t+2|t), \ldots, \hat{y}(t+K|t)]$. The optimal $u(t)$ is then derived such that the sum of the squared K-step ahead prediction errors are minimized with minimum deviation in the control action. In other words, it is obtained by minimizing the objective function J given by

$$J(u(t)) = \frac{1}{2} \sum_{\kappa=1}^{K} [e(t + \kappa|t)]^2 + \frac{1}{2}\lambda\left(u(t) - u(t-1)\right)^2, \tag{15}$$

where $e(t + \kappa|t) = r(t + \kappa) - \hat{y}(t + \kappa|t)$ is the κ-step ahead prediction error, $\kappa = 1, \cdots, K$, K is the predetermined prediction horizon and $\lambda > 0$ is a predetermined penalty term. The control signal $u(t)$ is designed to be composed of the PID output $u^{(0)}(t)$ plus a correction term $\eta\delta u(t)$, with η as an optimum step-length, given by

$$u(t) = u^{(0)}(t) + \eta\delta u(t), \tag{16}$$

which is obtained by a two step procedure; (i) the PID controller parameters are initially optimized based on minimizing (15) without the correction term ($\eta = 0$), followed by (ii) obtaining $\eta\delta u(t)$ minimizing (15) subject to the PID controller as derived in (i).

Initially consider that the output of the PID controller $u^{(0)}(t)$ in response to error $e(t)$ according to the formula given below:

$$u^{(0)}(t) = u(t-1) + K_P[e(t) - e(t-1)] + K_I e(t) + K_D[e(t) - 2e(t-1) + e(t-2)], \tag{17}$$

is applied to the Hammerstein system, where K_P, K_I and K_D are the PID parameters to be optimized based on the objective function $J(u^{(0)}(t))$. At the beginning of the control sequence, the PID parameters are set to zero. In the proposed scheme, we adopt the Levenberg-Marquardt (LM) rule (18) as the minimization algorithm, such that the PID parameters are updated at every time step according to

$$\begin{bmatrix} K_P^{new} \\ K_I^{new} \\ K_D^{new} \end{bmatrix} = \begin{bmatrix} K_P^{old} \\ K_I^{old} \\ K_D^{old} \end{bmatrix} - \alpha(\mathbf{J}^T\mathbf{J} + \mu\mathbf{I})^{-1}\mathbf{J}^T\hat{\mathbf{e}}, \tag{18}$$

where α is a small predetermined positive number. $\mu > 0$ is a small positive parameter. $\mathbf{I}$ is the 3×3 identity matrix, $\mathbf{J}$ is the $(K+1) \times 3$ Jacobian matrix given by,

$$
\mathbf{J} = - \begin{bmatrix}
\frac{\partial \hat{y}(t+1|t)}{\partial K_P} & \frac{\partial \hat{y}(t+1|t)}{\partial K_I} & \frac{\partial \hat{y}(t+1|t)}{\partial K_D} \\
\frac{\partial \hat{y}(t+2|t)}{\partial K_P} & \frac{\partial \hat{y}(t+2|t)}{\partial K_I} & \frac{\partial \hat{y}(t+2|t)}{\partial K_D} \\
\vdots & \vdots & \vdots \\
\frac{\partial \hat{y}(t+K|t)}{\partial K_P} & \frac{\partial \hat{y}(t+K|t)}{\partial K_I} & \frac{\partial \hat{y}(t+K|t)}{\partial K_D} \\
\sqrt{\lambda}\frac{\partial u(t)}{\partial K_P} & \sqrt{\lambda}\frac{\partial u(t)}{\partial K_I} & \sqrt{\lambda}\frac{\partial u(t)}{\partial K_D}
\end{bmatrix}_{|u(t)=u^{(0)}(t)}, \tag{19}
$$

and $\hat{\mathbf{e}}$ is the vector of prediction errors and input slew given by,

$$
\hat{\mathbf{e}} = \begin{bmatrix}
e(t+1|t) \\
\vdots \\
e(t+K|t) \\
\sqrt{\lambda}(u(t)-u(t-1))
\end{bmatrix}_{|u(t)=u^{(0)}(t)} = \begin{bmatrix}
r(t+1|t)-\hat{y}(t+1|t) \\
\vdots \\
r(t+K|t)-\hat{y}(t+\kappa|t) \\
\sqrt{\lambda}(u(t)-u(t-1))
\end{bmatrix}_{|u(t)=u^{(0)}(t)}. \tag{20}
$$

It can be seen that the Jacobian matrix (19) can be decomposed as the product of two different matrices by using the chain rule as $\mathbf{J} = \mathbf{J}_m\mathbf{J}_c$, with

$$
\mathbf{J}_m = - \begin{bmatrix} \frac{\partial \hat{y}(t+1|t)}{\partial u(t)} & \frac{\partial \hat{y}(t+2|t)}{\partial u(t)} & \cdots & \frac{\partial \hat{y}(t+K|t)}{\partial u(t)} & \sqrt{\lambda} \end{bmatrix}^T_{|u(t)=u^{(0)}(t)}, \tag{21}
$$

and

$$
\mathbf{J}_c = \begin{bmatrix} \frac{\partial u(t)}{\partial K_P} & \frac{\partial u(t)}{\partial K_I} & \frac{\partial u(t)}{\partial K_D} \end{bmatrix} = \begin{bmatrix} e(t)-e(t-1) \\ e(t) \\ e(t)-2e(t-1)+e(t-2) \end{bmatrix}^T \tag{22}
$$

The aim of the corrector block is to produce a suboptimal correction term $\delta u(t)$ used in (16) by minimizing the objective function $J(u(t))$ given by (15). More specifically, the corrector block tries to minimize the objective function J with respect to $\delta u(t)$ based on the second-order Taylor approximation of the objective function J as follows:

$$
\begin{aligned}
J(u(t)) &= J\left(u^{(0)}(t)+\delta u(t)\right) \\
&\approx J(u^{(0)}(t)) + \frac{\partial J(u(t))}{\partial u(t)}\bigg|_{|u(t)=u^{(0)}(t)} \delta u(t) \\
&\quad + \frac{1}{2}\frac{\partial^2 J(u(t))}{\partial u(t)^2}\bigg|_{|u(t)=u^{(0)}(t)} (\delta u(t))^2.
\end{aligned} \tag{23}
$$

Since we wish to find the $\delta u(t)$ that minimizes the objective function, if we take the derivative of the approximate J with respect to $\delta u(t)$ and equate it to zero, we obtain,

$$
\frac{\partial J(u(t))}{\partial u(t)}\bigg|_{|u(t)=u^{(0)}(t)} + \frac{\partial^2 J(u(t))}{\partial u(t)^2}\bigg|_{|u(t)=u^{(0)}(t)} \delta u(t) = 0 \tag{24}
$$

so

$$\delta u(t) = -\frac{\frac{\partial J}{\partial u(t)}|_{u(t)=u^{(0)}(t)}}{\frac{\partial^2 J}{\partial u(t)^2}|_{u(t)=u^{(0)}(t)}} = -\mathbf{J}_m^T \hat{\mathbf{e}} / \mathbf{J}_m^T \mathbf{J}_m, \qquad (25)$$

by making use of

$$\frac{\partial J(u(t))}{\partial u(t)}\bigg|_{u(t)=u^{(0)}(t)} = 2\mathbf{J}_m^T \hat{\mathbf{e}} \quad \text{and} \quad \frac{\partial^2 J(u(t))}{\partial u(t)^2}\bigg|_{u(t)=u^{(0)}(t)} \approx 2\mathbf{J}_m^T \mathbf{J}_m. \qquad (26)$$

Finally, once $\delta u(t)$ is determined, a line search is used to search for the optimum step-length η to further minimize the objective function. This is a typical one-dimensional optimization problem and can be solved by the golden section algorithm [11]. This algorithm directly evaluates $J(u^{(n)}(t))$ for a sequence of control signals $u^{(n)}(t)$, $n = 1, 2, \cdots$, until this converges to the optimal $u(t)$ which is associated with the optimum step-length η.

Note that the PID controller parameter updating formula (18) requires the calculation of multistep ahead predictions and the Jacobian $\mathbf{J}_m$. Moreover the subsequent control signal correction term given by (16)&(??) via the golden section algorithm not only requires the Jacobian $\mathbf{J}_m$, but also the *iterative* calculation of multistep ahead predictions for the objective functional evaluations. The κ-step ahead predictions ($\kappa = 1, \cdots, K$) using the B-spline neural network based Hammerstein model are given by

$$\hat{y}(t + \kappa|t) = -a_1 \hat{y}(t + \kappa - 1|t) - a_2 \hat{y}(t + \kappa - 2|t) - \ldots - a_{n_a} \hat{y}(t + \kappa - n_a|t)$$
$$+ b_1 v(t + k - 1) + \ldots + b_{n_b} v(t + k - n_b) \qquad (27)$$

in which each term in the right hand side of (27) is computed by

$$\hat{y}(t + \kappa - i|t) = \begin{cases} \hat{y}(t + \kappa - i|t) & \text{if } (\kappa - i) > 0 \\ y(t + \kappa - i) & \text{otherwise} \end{cases}$$
$$i = 1, \cdots, n_a, \quad \kappa = 1, \cdots, K \qquad (28)$$

and

$$v(t + \kappa - i) = \begin{cases} \sum_{j=1}^{d} \mathcal{B}_j^{(k)}(u(t))\omega_j & \text{if } (\kappa - i) \geq 0 \\ \sum_{j=1}^{d} \mathcal{B}_j^{(k)}(u(t + k - i))\omega_j & \text{otherwise} \end{cases}$$
$$i = 1, \cdots, n_b, \quad \kappa = 1, \cdots, K \qquad (29)$$

Similarly the elements in $\mathbf{J}_m$, $\frac{\partial \hat{y}(t+\kappa|t)}{\partial u(t)}$, $\kappa = 1, \cdots, K$ are also computed recursively from

$$\frac{\partial \hat{y}(t + \kappa|t)}{\partial u(t)} = -a_1 \frac{\partial \hat{y}(t + \kappa - 1|t)}{\partial u(t)} - a_2 \frac{\partial \hat{y}(t + \kappa - 2|t)}{\partial u(t)} - \ldots - a_{n_a} \frac{\partial \hat{y}(t + \kappa - n_a|t)}{\partial u(t)}$$
$$+ b_1 \frac{\partial v(t + \kappa - 1|t)}{\partial u(t)} + \ldots + b_{n_b} \frac{\partial v(t + \kappa - n_b|t)}{\partial u(t)} \qquad (30)$$

in which each term in the right hand side of (30) is computed by

$$\frac{\partial \hat{y}(t+\kappa-1|t)}{\partial u(t)} = \begin{cases} \frac{\partial \hat{y}(t+\kappa-1|t)}{\partial u(t)} & \text{if } (\kappa-i) > 0 \\ 0 & \text{otherwise} \end{cases}$$

$$i = 1, \cdots, n_a, \quad \kappa = 1, \cdots, K \qquad (31)$$

and

$$\frac{\partial v(t+\kappa-i|t)}{\partial u(t)} = \begin{cases} \sum_{j=1}^{d} \omega_j \frac{d}{du(t)} \mathcal{B}_j^{(k)}(u(t)) & \text{if } (\kappa-i) \geq 0 \\ 0 & \text{otherwise} \end{cases}$$

$$i = 1, \cdots, n_b, \quad \kappa = 1, \cdots, K \qquad (32)$$

Note that in calculating (27)-(32), the De Boor algorithm (5)-(7) is applied in evaluating the associated entries. In particular we point out the term $\frac{d}{du(t)}\mathcal{B}_j^{(k)}$ $(u(t))$ in (32) is evaluated using (7) and gives exact derivative values at minimum extra computational cost.

4   An Illustrative Example

An illustrative Hammerstein system is simulated, in which the linear subsystem is given by $A(q^{-1}) = 1 - 1.2q^{-1} + 0.9q^{-2}$, $B(q^{-1}) = 1.7q^{-1} - q^{-2}$. The nonlinear subsystem, $\Psi(\bullet)$ is given by $\Psi(u) = -2\text{sign}(u)u^2$. The variances of the additive noise to the system output are set as $\sigma^2 = 0.0001$. 1000 training data samples $y(t)$ were generated by using (1) and (2), where $u(t)$ was a uniformly distributed random variable $u(t) \in [-1.5, 1.5]$. The polynomial degree of B-spline basis functions was set as $k = 2$ (piecewise quadratic). The knots sequence U_j was set as $[-3, -2.5, -2, -1, -0.3, 0, 0.3, 1, 2, 2.5, 3]$. Initially system identification was carried out. The parameters were empirically set at $\alpha = 0.2$, $\mu = 10^{-3}$, $K = 15$, $\lambda = 10$ for illustration only because it was found that the proposed approach is robust for a wide range of parameters. The reference signal $r(t)$ was generated

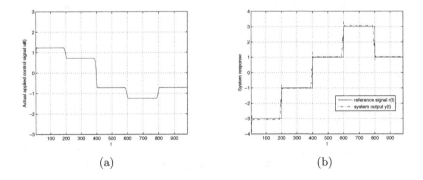

(a)   (b)

Fig. 2. Results of the proposed PID controller

as a series of square waves resembling a staircase. Figure 2(a) plot the applied computed control signal. Figure 2(b) plot the system output $y(t)$ together with the corresponding reference signal $r(t)$ with a small noise ($\sigma^2 = 9 \times 10^{-6}$). It is shown that the proposed method exhibits excellent result.

5 Conclusions

This paper has introduced a new effective PID control method for Hammerstein systems based on observational input/output data. By minimizing the multistep ahead prediction errors the PID controller parameters are updated and then corrected to generate the control signal. The multistep ahead predictions of the B-spline neural networks based Hammerstein system and the associated Jacobians matrix are very efficiently computed based on the De Boor algorithms.

References

1. Anbumani, K., Patnaik, L.M., Sarma, I.G.: Self-tuning minimum variance control of nonlinear systems of the Hammerstein model. IEEE Transactions on Automatic Control AC-26(4), 959–961 (1981)
2. Bloemen, H.H.J., Boom, T.J.V.D., Verbruggen, H.B.: Model-based predictive control for Hammerstein-Wiener systems. International Journal of Control 74(5), 482–295 (2001)
3. de Boor, A.: Practical Guide to Splines. Springer, New York (1978)
4. Chen, J., Huang, T.: Applying neural networks to on-line updated PID controllers for nonlnear process control. Journal of Process Control 14, 211–230 (2004)
5. Harris, C.J., Hong, X., Gan, Q.: Adaptive Modelling, Estimation and Fusion from Data: A Neurofuzzy Approach. Springer (2002)
6. Hong, X., Mitchell, R.J.: A Hammerstein model identification algorithm using bezier-bernstein approximation. IET Proc. Control Theory and Applications 1(4), 1149–1159 (2007)
7. Hunter, I.W., Korenberg, M.J.: The identification of nonlinear biological systems: Wiener and Hammerstein cascade models. Biological Cybernetics 55(2-3), 135–144 (1986)
8. Iplikci, S.: A comparative study on a novel model-based PID tuning and control mechanism for nonlinear systems. International Journal of Robust and Nonlinear Control 20(13), 1483–1501 (2010)
9. Nocedal, J., Wright, S.J.: Numerical Optimization. Springer, New York (1999)
10. Parlos, A.G., Parthasarathy, S., Atiya, A.F.: Neuro-predicitive process control using on-line controller adaptation. IEEE Transactions on Control Systems Technology 9, 741–755 (2001)
11. Venkataraman, P.: Applied Optimization with MATLAB Programming. Wiley Interscience, New York (2002)
12. Zhang, M., Li, W., Liu, M.: Adaptive PID control strategy based on RBF neural network identification. In: Proceedings of the ICNNB International Conference on Neural Networks and Brain, Beijing, China, pp. 1854–1857 (2005)

Constrained Multi-objective Particle Swarm Optimization Algorithm

Yue-lin Gao and Min Qu

Institute of Information & System Science of North Ethnic University,
Yinchuan, Ningxia, China
gaoyuelin@263.net, victoryqumin@163.com

Abstract. A particle swarm optimization for solving constrained multi-objective optimization problem was proposed (CMPSO). In this paper, the main idea is the use of penalty function to handle the constraints. CMPSO employs particle swarm optimization algorithm and Pareto neighborhood crossover operation to generate new population. Numerical experiments are compared with NSGA-II and MOPSO on three benchmark problems. The numerical results show the effectiveness of the proposed CMPSO algorithm.

Keywords: particle swarm optimization algorithm, constrained multi-objective optimization, Pareto neighborhood crossover operation, penalty function method.

1   Introduction

Constrained multi-objective optimization problems are very common in engineering design, science study and engineering optimization, however, the present study is the most focus on unconstrained multi-objective optimization, for dealing with constrained multi-objective evolutionary algorithm few papers. Thus the study of constrained multi-objective optimization problem has important theoretical and practical significance. In recent years, with the evolutionary algorithm for solving constrained optimization problem has become a hot research [1-3].

Particle swarm optimization(PSO)[4,5] algorithm is a based on the population evolutionary algorithm, which has gained wide attentions in a variety of fields for solving constrained multi-objective optimization problem because of its simplicity to implement and its high convergence speed. For example, Harada et al[6] proposed constraint-handling method for multi-objective function optimization: Pareto descent repair operator. Chunhua Yang, Zhixun Mo, Yonggang Li [7] proposed constrained multi-objective optimization based on improved particle swarm optimization algorithm. Shengyu Pei, Yongquan[8] proposed using hybrid particle swarm algorithm for solving constrained multi-objective optimization problem. In this paper, constrained multi-objective particle swarm optimization algorithm (CMPSO) is proposed.

D.-S. Huang et al. (Eds.): ICIC 2012, CCIS 304, pp. 47–55, 2012.

2   Constrained Multi-Objective Optimization Problem

Without any loss of generality, an n-dimensional decision variable, m- dimensional sub-objective optimization of constrained multi-objective optimization problem can be described as follows[9]:

$$
\begin{cases}
\min & y = [f_1(x), f_2(x), \cdots, f_m(x)] \\
s.t. & g_i(x) \leq 0, \ i = 1, 2, \cdots, q. \\
& h_j(x) = 0, \ j = 1, 2, \cdots, p.
\end{cases}
\tag{1}
$$

Where $x = (x_1, x_2, \cdots, x_n) \in X \subset R^n$ is an n-dimensional decision variable, X are decision space, $y = (y_1, y_2, \cdots, y_m) \in X \subset R^m$ are m-dimensional vector of target, Y are m-dimensional objective space. The objective function $F(x)$ is defined by the m decision space to the target space of the mapping function; $g_i(x) \leq 0 \ (i = 1, 2, \cdots, q)$ define q inequality constraints; $h_j(x) = 0 \ (j = 1, 2, \cdots, p)$ define p equality constraints.

In the later, the paper will introduce several basic concepts of constrained multi-objective optimization

Definition 1[9] (Feasible Solution). For one $x \in X$, if x satisfies the constraints $g_i(x) \leq 0 \ (i = 1, 2, \cdots, q)$ 和 $h_j(x) = 0 \ (j = 1, 2, \cdots, p)$, so x is called feasible solutions.

Definition 2[9] (Feasible Solution Set). By X the set consisting of all feasible solution is called a feasible solution set, denote X_f and $X_f \subset X$.

Definition 3[9] (Pareto dominance). Let $x^1, x^2 \in X_f$, a solution x^1 is said to dominate the other solution x^2 ($x^1 \succ x^2$), if both statement below are satisfied.

1. The solution x^0 is no worse than x^1 in all objectives, or $f_i(x^1) \leq f_i(x^2)$ for all $i = 1, 2, \cdots, m$.
2. The solution x^1 is strictly better than x^2 in at least one objective, or $f_{i_0}(x^1) < f_{i_0}(x^2)$ for at least one $i_0 \in \{1, 2, \cdots, m\}$.

Definition 4[9] (Pareto optimality). A point $x^* \in X_f$ is Pareto optimal if and only if there is not exist another x to satisfy $x \succ x^*$.

Definition 5[9] (Pareto optimal set or non-inferior optimal set). The Pareto optimal set (P^*) is defined as $P^* = \{x^* \mid \neg \exists x \in X_f : x \succ x^*\}$.

Definition 6[9] (Pareto-optimal front). P_F is all Pareto optimal solutions corresponding formed by the objective function values, the Pareto-optimal front (P_F) is defined as $P_F = \{f(x) = (f_1(x), f_2(x), \cdots, f_m(x)) \mid x \in P^*\}$.

Definition 7[10]. Let set $A \subseteq X$:

1. Set A is called local Pareto optimal set if and only if
   $\forall a \in A, \neg \exists x \in X, x \succ a \wedge \| x - a \| < \varepsilon \wedge \| f(x) - f(a) \| < \delta$.
2. Set A is called global Pareto optimal set if and only if
   $\forall a \in A, \neg \exists x \in X, x \succ a$.

3 Particle Swarm Optimization Algorithm

Particle swarm optimization (PSO) is an optimization algorithm simulates the behaviour of birds flocking foraging flight, which is through the collective collaboration between birds that groups achieve their goals. In particle swarm optimization algorithm, each individual is called a particle and each particle represents a potential solution. Each particle update its position and velocity according to personal best (pbest) and global best (gbest).

Let N denote the swarm size, D denote search space , x_{ij}^t is the jth dimension position of particle i in cycle t; v_{ij}^t is the jth dimension velocity of particle i in cycle t; $pbest_i^t$ is the jth dimension of personal best of particle i in cycle t; $gbest^t$ is global best of the whole population in cycle t. The new velocity and position of every particle x_{ij}^t are updated by(2)and (3)

$$v_{ij}^{t+1} = w v_{ij}^t + c_1 r_1 (pbest_{ij}^t - x_{ij}^t) + c_2 r_2 (gbest_{1j}^t - x_{ij}^t) \tag{2}$$

$$x_{ij}^{t+1} = x_{ij}^t + v_{ij}^{t+1} \tag{3}$$

Where c_1 and c_2 denote constant, which was called the acceleration coefficients, r_1 and r_2 are elements from two uniform random sequences in the range of [0, 1], w is the inertia weight which descent by linear decrease.

4   Constrained Multi-objective Particle Swarm Optimization Algorithm

4.1   Constrained Approach

When handling multi-objective constrained optimization problem, the key is to design a reasonable constrained handling techniques. At present, a variety of ways for solving constrained multi-objective optimization problem become hot research in intelligence research community. For constrained optimization, the penalty function method has been regarded as one of the most popular constraint-handling technique so far, which method has good convergence properties and simplicity. Penalty function method require less demanding for objective function and constraint, which has been gained wide applications in a variety of fields. This paper take advantage of penalty function method to deal with constrained multi-objective optimization problem based on above merits. This paper considers only inequality constraints of multi-objective optimization problem, which employ penalty function method[11] to deal with constrained multi-objective optimization problem, the constraint violation degree is defined for each particle x as follows:

$$G(x) = \sum_{i=1}^{q} \max\left\{0, g_i(x)\right\} \tag{4}$$

Thus a penalty function of problem (1) can be formulated as follows:

$$T(x,\sigma) = f(x) + \sigma G(x) \tag{5}$$

Where $f(x)$ is the objective function; σ denotes the penalty factor and $\sigma > 0$.

4.2   Choose Pbest and Gbest

In multi-objective particle swarm optimization algorithm, the choosing gbest is very important, which directly affect the convergence speed and capabilities. In CMPSO, not only the size of particle swarm is fixed and it is not be replaced, but also adjust their pbest and gbest. In multi-objective condition, gbest normally exists a group of non-inferior solution and is not single gbest position. When each other is not dominated, each particle may be more than one pbest. Therefore, it is necessary to choose pbest and gbest by appropriate method.

1)   Choose Pbest

Specific process as follows if particle x dominate pbest, then $pbest = x$; if particle pbest dominate x, remain unchanged; if each other is not dominated, then at random generated a random number r in the range of [0,1], if $r < 0.5$, then $pbest = x$, if $r \geq 0.5$, otherwise unchanged.

2) Choose Gbest

Specific process as follows[12]:When CMPSO deal with multi-objective optimization problems, gbest position is a group of non-inferior solution rather than a single solution. CMPSO choose a solution as the particle gbest taken from the optimal set and independently choose gbest for each particle by adopt dual tournament, each particle attain different gbest, this means that particles will along different directions to fly in order to enhance exploring ability of algorithm .

4.3   Pareto Neighborhood Crossover Operation

Particle swarm optimization (PSO) has good global search capability, but easily lost in the Pareto local optimality arising tendency of premature convergence. So in this paper introduces Pareto neighbourhood crossover operation in order to avoid premature convergence, specific process as follows [10]:

Let Pop denote the current evolutionary population, Opti denote Pareto optimal set, $(x_1, x_2, \cdots, x_n) \in$ Pop. Random choosing an individual $(r_1, r_2, \cdots, r_n)$ from Opti, following below formula generate a new individual $(z_1, z_2, \cdots, z_n)$.

$$z_i = r_i + U(-1,1) \times (r_i - x_i) \quad (i = 1, 2, \cdots, n) \tag{6}$$

Where $U(-1,1)$ represent uniformly distributed random number the range of [0, 1] .By definition 7, we can know in the vicinity of Pareto optimal solution to may exist a better solution in Pop. The role of (6) equal to local climbing operation for the Pareto optimal solution and sufficient play local search ability. Taking into account the good powerful global search capabilities of the particle swarm optimization and the good powerful local search of Pareto neighbourhood crossover operation, so introduced a scale factor $p_r \in [0,1]$ in order to achieve mutual advantage of both. At beginning random generate a number in the range of [0, 1], when $r < p_r$, taking advantage of particle swarm optimization generate a new population; when $r \geq p_r$, taking advantage of Pareto neighbourhood crossover operation generate a new population. Scale factor [13] defined as follows:

$$\begin{cases} p_r^0 = p_r^{max}; \\ p_r^{G+1} = p_r^{min} + \beta(p_r^G - p_r^{min}). \end{cases} \tag{7}$$

Where p_r^{max} and p_r^{min} are respectively maximum and minimum value of disturbance rate, β is annealing factor in the range of [0, 1] .

5   The Specific Steps of CMPSO Algorithm

Step 1. Let algorithms parameters D, N, w_{min} , w_{max} , p_r^{max} , p_r^{min} , c_1, c_2, σ, T_{max} and so on;

Step 2. Initial population Pop is randomly generated in decision space and randomly updating position and velocity of each particle of initial population;

Step 3. Each particle update its position and its velocity according to (2) and (3);

Step 4. When $r < p_r$, taking advantage of particle swarm optimization generate a new population; when $r \geq p_r$, taking advantage of Pareto neighbourhood crossover operation generate a new population.

Step 5. Non-dominated individual of double population is added to Pareto optimal set, with selecting non-dominated personal from Pareto optimal set, when non-dominated personal is more than NP, using crowded degree distance from large to small sorting of NSGA-II for non-dominated personal, while select before NP non-dominated personal and left it in Pareto optimal set, the rest personal will be deleted;

Step 6. If algorithm achieves maximum iterating, then stop and output Pareto optimal set, otherwise returns Step3.

6   Experimental Results

6.1   The Performance Indicators

The quality evaluation mainly focus on distance between the solution produced by the algorithms and the Pareto optimal solution for multi-objective optimization problems, and the extent covered by the solution produced of the algorithms, in this paper two performance indicators are adopted.

1) Convergence Indicators

The metric of generational distance (GD)[14] gives a good indication of the gap between non-dominated solution produced by the algorithms and the Pareto optimal solution. It is defined as the following:

$$GD = \frac{\sqrt{\sum_{i=1}^{n} d_i^2}}{n} \qquad (8)$$

Where n is the number of members in the set of optimal solution found so far and d_i is the minimum Euclidean distance between the ith personal and the theory Pareto optimal front in objective space. A low value of GD is desirable, which reflects a small deviation between the evolved and the true Pareto front, if the value of GD=0, it indicates that all solution produced by the algorithms are in the Pareto optimal set.

2) Spread Indicators

The spread indicators[15]: reflect uniform degree between non-dominated solution produced by the algorithms and the Pareto front, with adopting modified spread to evaluate solution of indicators, it is defined as the following:

$$\Delta = \frac{\displaystyle\sum_{i=1}^{m} d(E_i,\Omega) + \sum_{x\in\Omega} \mid d(X,\Omega) - \bar{d} \mid}{\displaystyle\sum_{i=1}^{m} d(E_i,\Omega) + (\mid\Omega\mid - m)\,\bar{d}} \tag{9}$$

Where Ω is a set of solution produced by the algorithms, $E_i(i=1,2,\ldots,m)$ are m extreme solutions in the set of Pareto optimal solutions, m is the number of objectives, d and $\bar{d}$ are respectively defined as

$$d(X,\Omega) = \min_{Y\in\Omega,Y\neq X} \parallel F(X) - F(Y) \parallel, \quad \bar{d} = \frac{1}{\mid\Omega\mid} \sum_{x\in\Omega} d(X,\Omega).$$

A low value of Δ is desirable, which reflects solution produced by algorithms uniform distribution well in Pareto front, if the value of $\Delta = 0$, it indicates that non-dominated set produced by algorithms and Pareto front attain good fit.

6.2   Experimental Results and Analysis

In order to verify CMPSO performance of the algorithms, which numerical experiments chosen three benchmark problems [9] and compared with NSGA-II[9] and MOPSO[16]. Pareto candidate solution set up is 100. The parameter of CMPSO algorithm give $\sigma = 1\times10^8$; $c_1 = c_2 = 0.5$; $w_{min} = 0.2$, $w_{max} = 0.9$; $p_r^{max} = 0.9$, $p_r^{min} = 0.2$, $\beta = 0.95$. Table 1 and Table 2 get the convergence of the index of the mean value(uplink) and standard deviations(downlink), and spread index of the mean value(uplink) and standard deviations(downlink),which all the algorithms independently run 30 times on each problem, the population size is 100, maximum iterating 250 times. Figure 1 to figure 3 is simulation diagram of CMPSO algorithms.

Table 1 shows that CMPSO algorithm get convergence indicator of CONSTR and TNK are superior to NSGA-II and MOPSO, but convergence indicator of SRN are inferior to NSGA-II and MOPSO. Table 2 shows that CMPSO algorithm get spread

Table 1. Statistical results of convergence index of four algorithms for 3 test functions

Algorithm	NSGA-II	MOPSO	CMPSO
	5. 1349E-3	4. 5437E-3	2. 9894E-3
CONSTR	2. 4753E-4	6. 8558E-4	8. 3111E-3
	3. 7069E-3	2. 7623E-3	2. 5331E-2
SRN	5. 1034E-4	2. 0794E-4	5. 2561E-3
	4. 0488E-3	5. 0877E-3	5. 4811E-4
TNK	4. 3465E-4	4. 5564E-4	7. 9634E-5

Table 2. Statistical results of spread index of four algorithms for 3 test functions

Algorithm	NSGA-II	MOPSO	CMPSO
	0.54863	0.94312	0.57586
CONSTR	2.7171E-2	3.6719E-1	2.2894E-2
	0.3869	0.6655	0.19659
SRN	2.5115E-2	7.2196E-2	2.4527E-2
	0.82286	0.79363	0.25871
TNK	2.8678E-4	5.1029E-2	2.7272E-2

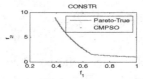

Fig. 1.

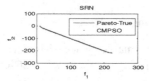

Fig. 2.

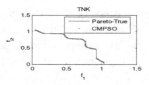

Fig. 3.

indicator of SRN and TNK are superior to NSGA-II and MOPSO; The spread indicator of CONSTR are superior to MOPSO, but spread indicator of CONSTR are inferior to NSGA-II. From figure 1 to figure 3 simulation experiments can see, experiment Pareto curve produced by CMPSO algorithm are good fit to real Pareto curve.

7   Conclusion

This paper convert constrained multi-objective optimization problem into unconstrained multi-objective optimization problem by penalty function method. Meanwhile, this paper will introduce Pareto neighbourhood crossover operation to enhance the local search abilities of particle swarm optimization. A scaling factor used to balance contributions of particle swarm optimization algorithm and Pareto neighbourhood crossover operation.

Thus constrained multi-objective particle swarm optimization algorithm (CMPSO) is proposed. Experimental results and simulation results show that CMPSO can be an effective method for solving constrained multi-objective particle swarm optimization.

Acknowledgments. The work is supported by the National Natural Science Foundation of China under Grant No. 60962006.

References

1. Gen, M., Cheng, R.W.: Genetic Algorithms & Engineering Design. John Wiley & Sons, Inc., New York (1997)
2. Glover, F.: Heuristics for Integer Programming Using Surrogate Constraints. Decision Sciences 8(1), 156–166 (1977)
3. Goldberg, D.E.: Genetic in Search, Optimization and Machine Learning. Addison Wesley, Reading (1989)
4. Kennedy, J., Eberhart, R.: Particle Swarm Optimization. In: IEEE International Conference on Neural Networks, pp. 1942–1948 (1995)
5. Shi, Y., Eberhart, R.: A Modified Particle Swarm Optimizer. In: Proceeging of the IEEE World Congress on Computational Intelligence, pp. 69–73 (1998)
6. Harada, K., Sakuma, J., Ono, I., Kobayashi, S.: Constraint-handling. Method for Multi-Objective Function Optimization: Pareto Descent Repair Operator. In: Int. Conf. Evol. Multi-Criterion Opt., Matshushima, Japan, pp. 156–170 (2007)
7. Yang, C.H., Mo, Z.X., Li, Y.G.: Constrained Multi-Objective Optimization Based on Improved Particle. Swarm Optimization Algorithm 36(20), 203–205 (2010)
8. Pei, S.Y.: Using Hybrid Particle Swarm Algorithm for Solving Constrained Multi-Objective Optimization Problem. Computer Engineering and Applications 47(15), 49–52 (2011)
9. Deb, K., Pratap, A., Agarwal, S., Meyarivan, T.: A Fast And Elitist Multi-Objective Genetic Algorithm: NSGA-II. IEEE Transactions on Evolutionary Computation 6(2), 182–197 (2002)
10. Jiao, L.Q., Liu, J., Zhong, W.C.: Co-evolutionary Algorithms and Multi-Agent System, pp. 22–25. Science Press, Beijing (2007)
11. Bazaraa, M.S., Sherali, H.D., Shetty, C.M.: Nonlinear Programming, Theory and Algorithm. Academic Press, New York (1979)
12. Liu, D., Tan, K.C., Coh, C.K., et al.: A Multi-Objective Memetic Algorithm Based On Particle Swarm Optimization. IEEE Transactions on Systems, Man and Cybernetics, Part B 37(1), 42–50 (2007)
13. Wang, X.S., Hao, M.L., Cheng, Y.H., et al.: A Multi-Objective Optimization Problems with a Hybrid Algorithms. Journal of System Simulation 21(16), 4980–4985 (2009)
14. Van, V., David, A., Lamont, G.B.: Evolutionary Computation and Convergence to a Pareto Front. In: Koza, J.R. (ed.) Late Breaking Papers at the Genetic Programming 1998 Conference, pp. 221–228. Stanford Bookstore, Stanford University, California (1998)
15. Zhou, A., Jin, Y., Zhang, Q., et al.: Combing Model-Based And Generics-Based Offspring Generation For Multi-Objective Optimization Using A Convergence Criterion. In: 2006 Congress on Evolutionary Computation, pp. 3234–3241 (2006)
16. Coello, C.A., Pulido, G.T., Lechuga, M.S.: Handling Multiple Objectives with Particle Swarm Optimization. IEEE Trans. on Evolutionary Computations 8(3), 256–279 (2004)

A Particle Swarm Optimization Using Local Stochastic Search for Continuous Optimization

Jianli Ding[1], Jin Liu[1,2], Yun Wang[3], Wensheng Zhang[2], and Wenyong Dong[1,2]

[1] Computer School, Wuhan University, Wuhan, China 430072, PR China
[2] State Key Lab. of Management and Control for Complex Systems, Institute of Automation, Chinese Academy of Science, Beijing, China 100190, PR China
[3] Computer Science and Information Systems, Bradley University, Illinois, USA
mailjinliu@yahoo.com

Abstract. The particle swarm optimizer (PSO) is a swarm intelligence based heuristic optimization technique that can be applied to a wide range of problems. After analyzing the dynamics of tranditioal PSO, this paper presents a new PSO variant based on local stochastic search strategy (LSSPSO) for performance enhancement. This is inspired by a social phenomenon that everyone wants to first exceed the nearest superior and then all superior. Specifically, LSSPSO adopts a local stochastic search to adjust inertia weight in terms of keeping a balance between the diversity and the convergence speed, aiming to improve the performance of tranditioal PSO. Experiments conducted on unimodal and multimodal test functions demonstrate the effectiveness of LSSPSO in solving multiple benchmark problems as compared to several other PSO variants.

Keywords: particle swarm optimization, continuous optimization, local stochastic search.

1 Introduction

Particle swarm optimization (PSO) was motivated from the study of simplified social behavior of birds [1, 2]. It has already been applied successfully in many application areas [3-5]. However, the tranditioal PSO has difficulties in keeping the balance between exploration and exploitation when the application environment is dynamic [6-8]. In other words, the tranditioal PSO cannot adapt to the changing environment and converge to an optimum in an early period of iteration [9, 10]. Another main drawback of the tranditioal PSO is that it may get stuck at a local-optimal solution region [11]. In view of this, we propose a new PSO variant algorithm using local stochastic search strategy (LSSPSO), inspired by a social phenomenon that each individual first wants to stand out among its neighbors and then stand out among the whole community. The proposed LSSPSO algorithm regulates inertia weight in such a way that it does not decrease the diversity rapidly and at the same time prevents early convergence to local optima. More specifically, LSSPSO introduces a new direction to the particle trajectory model to increase the diversity of the particle swarm without

D.-S. Huang et al. (Eds.): ICIC 2012, CCIS 304, pp. 56–61, 2012.

decreasing the convegence speed. Experimental results demonstrate the effectiveness of LSSPSO in solving multiple benchmark problems.

The rest of the paper is organized as follows: Section 2 briefly overviews the basic particle optimization paradigm and describes the proposed LSSPSO algorithm. Section 3 presents the experimental results and show the effectiveness and efficiency of the proposed LSSPSO algorithm through comparing to several other well-known PSO variants. Finally, this work is concluded in Section 4.

2   The Proposed LSSPSO Algorithm

2.1   Overview of the PSO Algorithms

The tranditioal PSO performs well for continuous optimization problems [2]. By introducing a new inertial weight w into the updating rules of tranditioal PSO, the canonical PSO (CPSO) [13] is described as:

$$v_{i,d}^{t+1} = w \cdot v_{i,d}^{t} + c_1 \cdot rand_1 \cdot (P_{i,d} - x_{i,d}^{t}) + c_2 \cdot rand_2 \cdot (G_{i,d} - x_{i,d}^{t}) \tag{1}$$

$$x_{i,d}^{t+1} = x_{i,d}^{t} + v_{i,d}^{t+1} \quad 1 \le i \le n, 1 \le d \le N \tag{2}$$

where X is a volume-less particle (a point) in the N-dimensional search space; n is the total number of particles; $x_i = (x_{i,1}, ..., x_{i,N})$ is the current position of the i_{th} particle ; $v_i = (v_{i,1}, ..., v_{i,N})$ is the velocity of the i_{th} particle ; $P_i = (P_{i,1}, ..., P_{i,N})$ is the best position of the i_{th} particle by the current iteration; $G = (G_{,1}, ..., G_{,N})$ is the best position of total particle swarm. $rand_1$ and $rand_2$ are random numbers uniformly distributed in (0,1). c_1 and c_2 are the acceleration coefficients that determine the relative cognition and social influence on the particle's velocity. The parameter w reduces gradually as the generation increases. After adjusting the parameters w and V_{max}, the CPSO can achieve the best search ability [12].

2.2   Local Stochastic Search PSO

Premature convergence occurs when most particles in the swarm stop updating their positions over successive iterations while the global optimum remains undiscovered. In order to alleviate the early convergence problem, LSSPSO untilizes a local stochastic search strategy in which each particle tries to discover a local optima along a direction and then keeps moving in the same direction instead of changing the moving direction according to other factors such as neighbor particles or random vector etc. To be specific, the i_{th} particle velocity v_i^{t+1} is updated by:

$$v_i^{t+1} = \begin{cases} w \cdot rand_1 \cdot v_i^{t} & x_i = G_{best} \\ w \cdot rand_1 \cdot v_i^{t} + r * randV & otherwise \end{cases} \tag{3}$$

where r is a small constant and $randV$ is an random unit vector.

Finally, $x_i^{t+1,LSS}$ is updated by:

$$x_i^{t+1,LSS} = x_i^t + v_i^{t+1} \tag{4}$$

$x_i^{t+1,LSS}$ is compared with x_i^{t+1} (the result from Equation 1, 2). If the fitness of $x_i^{t+1,LSS}$ is better than x_i^{t+1}, namely, $x_i^{t+1,LSS}$ supersedes x_i^{t+1}, then the ith particle keeps moving in the same direction again until the local resolution can't improve along the same direction. In this way, the ith particle can quickly converge to the local optima while retaining the chance to find a globe optima according to a nearby particle. In addition, we employ the exponential function in updating the inertia weight such that it decreases quickly at the initial stage and decrements gradually at the later period. This helps keeping the diversity of swarm at an early period of evolvement and at the same time ensuring the convergence of the algorithm.

3   Experiments and Discussion

We conduct extensive experiments in MATLAB 7.0 environment using a Intel Core2 Duo 2.10 GHz CPU. We set the population size as 50, accoridng to [14]. The performance of our proposed LSSPSO is compared with CPSO algorithm, PSO-W algorithm [7], and CPSO-H algorithm [8] on five benchmark functions as shown in Table 1. Table 2 lists the parameters of the four PSO algorithms.

Table 1. Benchmark functions

Name	F	Search Range	Min position
F1=Sphere	$f_1(X) = \sum_{i=1}^{N} X_i^2$	$[-100,100]^N$	$[0,...,0]$
F2=Rosenbrock	$f_2(X) = \sum_{i=1}^{N}[100(X_{i+1} - X_i)^2 + (X_i - 1)^2]$	$[-30,30]^N$	$[1,..,1]$
F3=Ackley	$f_3(X) = -20\,exp\,(-0.2\sqrt{\frac{1}{N}\sum_{i=1}^{N} X_i^2})$ $- exp\,(\frac{1}{N}\sum_{i=1}^{N} cos\,(2\cdot\pi\cdot X_i)) + 0 + e$	$[-32,32]^N$	$[1,..,1]$
F4=Griewank	$f_4(X) = \frac{1}{4000}\sum_{i=1}^{N} X_i^2 - \prod_{i=1}^{N} cos(\frac{X_i}{\sqrt{i}}) + 1$	$[-600,600]^N$	$[0,...,0]$
F5=Rastrigin	$f_5(X) = \sum_{i=1}^{N}[X_i^2 - 10\cdot cos(2\cdot\pi\cdot X_i) + 10]$	$[-5,12,5.12]^N$	$[0,...,0]$

The performance of the four algorithms in terms of convergence over all four multimodel test functions in 30 dimensions is shown in Fig.1. The results indicate that LSSPSO converges to optima quicker as it arrives at the global optima at a earlier period, comparing to the other three PSO variants. Note that LSSPSO should be restarted during the excution to avoid converging to local optima solution.

Table 2. Parameters of PSO algorithms

Parameter	Meaning	CPSO	PSO-W	PSO-H	LSSPSO
N	Dimension number	30	30	30	30
M	Particle number	50	50	50	50
T	Number of iterations	5000	5000	5000	5000
w	Weight of velocity	linear	linear	linear	exponent
C_1	Constant value	1.49445	1.49445	1.49445	1.49445
C_2	Constant value	1.49445	1.49445	1.49445	1.49445
r	small constant	N/A	N/A	N/A	0.1

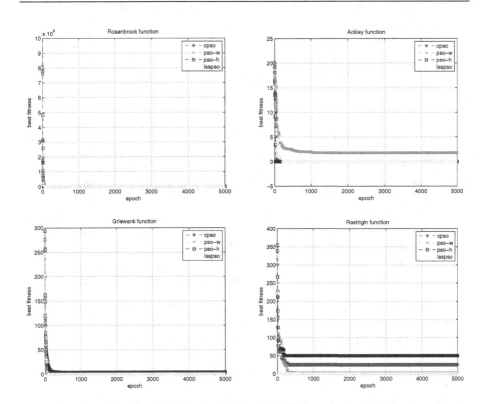

Fig. 1. Performance of CPSO, PSO-W, PSO-H and LSSPSO on the four benchmark problems

The best solutions, average/mean values, and standard deviation for all the four studied algorithms are presented in Table 3. Table 3 also shows the standard deviation of the best fitness of all algorithms. It can be observed from the table that LSSPSO performs better than the other three algorithms on all test functions. As an instance, the standard deviation resulting from LSSPSO algorithms is the smallest, which reflects the effectiveness of LSSPSO in solving multimodal function problems.

Table 3. Performance comparison of LSSPSO with other PSOs

Algorithm		Sphere	Rosenbrock	Ackleys	Griewank's	Rastrigin's
CPSO	min	0	28.7402	-8.8818e-16	0	25
	Mean	620	2.4066e+05	11.63	48.8225	160
	SD	107.0216	3.0477e+05	7.2482	52.3115	56.9192
PSO-W	Min	0	16.8021	-8.8818e-16	0	0
	Mean	1.0265e-09	2.1649e+05	0.2645	1.9845	153.4975
	SD	2.8111e-09	1.4315e+03	7.1104	1.3880	40.0609
PSO-H	Min	0	28.5397	-8.8818e-16	0	50
	Mean	105.8815	1.8012e+05	1.0402	54.1872	153.4975
	SD	2.3938	4.3107e+05	3.3859	48.2582	45.4585
LSSPSO	Min	1.9148e-09	28.3787	-8.8818e-16	0	0
	Mean	2.2163e-09	283.8949	0.2645	0.0162	53.9882
	SD	5.8851e-09	3.8804e+05	0.7444	0.0519	35.5494

4   Conclusions

This paper presents a new PSO algorithm (LSSPSO) in which each particle can find a better local position using local stochastic search strategy. In addition, LSSPSO employs an exponential function to update the inertia weight so that the balance between the diversity of the swarm and the algorithm convergence is maintained. The peformance of the proposed LSSPSO algorithm is compared with three other well-known PSO-variants using a five-function test suite. Experimental results demonstrate that LSSPOS outperforms others for a majority of the test cases and hence support its effectiveness from a statistical standpoint. Note that the improved performance of LSSPSO does not lead to the conclusion that it may outperform all other PSO variants over every possible objective function as we utilized the limited test-suite for algorithm evaluation and comparison.

Acknowledgement. This work was supported by the grants of the National Natural Science Foundation of China (61070013, U1135005, 61170305,61070009), Research on the Mechanism of Distributed Data Storage & Processing for Real-time GIS, the Open Fund Project of Key Lab. of Shanghai Information Security Management and Technology Research, the knowledge innovation program of the Chinese academy of sciences under grant No.Y1W1031PB1, the Project for the National Basic Research 12th Five Program under Grant No.0101050302 and the Science and Technology Commission of Wuhan Municipality "Chenguang Jihua"(201050231058).and China Postdoctoral Science Foundation (No.20080440073). The Open Fund Project of State Key Lab. of Software Engineering.

References

1. Kennedy, J., Eberhart, R.: Particle Swarm Optimization. In: IEEE International Conference on Proceeding, vol. 4, pp. 1942–1948 (1995)
2. Eberhart, R., Kennedy, J.: A New Optimizer Using Particle Swarm Theory. In: Proceedings of the Sixth International Symposium on Micro Machine and Human Science, pp. 39–43 (1995)

3. Poli, R.: Analysis of the Publications on the Applications of Particle Swarm Optimisation. Journal of Artificial Evolution and Applications 13(1), 1–10 (2008)
4. Panduro, M.A., Brizuela, C.A.: A Comparison of Genetic Algorithms, Particle Swarm Optimization and the Differential Evolution Method for the Design of Scannable Circular Antenna Arrays. Progress in Electromagnetics Research 13(2), 171–186 (2009)
5. Khan, S.A., Engelbrecht, A.P.: A Fuzzy Particle Swarm Optimization Algorithm for Computer Communication Network Topology Design. Applied Intelligence 36(1), 161–177 (2012)
6. Kang, Q., Wang, L.: A Novel Ecological Particle Swarm Optimization Algorithm and Its Population Dynamics Analysis. Applied Mathematics and Computation 205(1), 61–72 (2008)
7. Xin, Z.: A Perturbed Particle Swarm Algorithm for Numerical Optimization. Applied Soft Computing 10(1), 119–124 (2010)
8. Li, M., Kou, J.: A Hybrid Niching Pso Enhanced with Recombination Replacement Crowding Strategy for Multimodal Function Optimization. Applied Soft Computing 12(3), 975–987 (2012)
9. Engelbrecht, A.P.: A Cooperative Approach to Particle Swarm Optimization. IEEE Transactions on Evolutionary Computation 8(3), 225–239 (2004)
10. Liang, J.J., Qin, A.K.: Comprehensive Learning Particle Swarm Optimizer for Global Optimization of Multimodal Functions. IEEE Transactions on Evolutionary Computation 10(3), 281–295 (2006)
11. Clerc, M., Kennedy, J.: The Particle Swarm-explosion, Stability, and Convergence in a Multidimensional Complex Space. IEEE Transactions on Evolutionary Computation 6(1), 58–73 (2002)
12. Poli, R., Kennedy, J., Blackwell, T.: Particle Swarm Optimization. Swarm Intelligence 1(1), 33–57 (2007)
13. Shi, Y., Eberhart, R.: A Modified Particle Swarm Optimizer. In: IEEE World Congress on Computational Intelligence, pp. 69–73 (1998)
14. Engelbrecht, A.P.: Effects of Swarm Size on Cooperative Particle Swarm Optimizers. South African Computer Journal 26(3), 84–90 (2001)

Component Random Walk

Xiaohua Xu[*], Ping He, Lin Lu, Zhoujin Pan, and Ling Chen

Department of Computer Science, Yangzhou University, Yangzhou 225009, China
{arterx,angeletx,linklu60,pprivulet,yzulchen}@gmail.com

Abstract. Label propagation has become a successful method for transductive learning. In this paper, we propose a unified label propagation model named Component Random Walk. We demonstrate that besides most of the existing label propagation algorithms, a novel Multilevel Component Propagation (MCP) algorithm can be derived from this Component Random Walk model as well. Promising experimental results are provided for MCP algorithm.

Keywords: Transductive Learning, Label Propagation, Random Walk.

1   Introduction

In many real world applications, there are classification problems with only a few labeled instances and a great many unlabeled instances. The research of making full use of both labeled and unlabeled instances for classification is called Transductive Learning. Various algorithms have been proposed for approaching transductive learning. They can be mainly divided into two categories: (1) methods based on cluster assumption [1,2,3]; (2) methods based on smoothness assumption [4,5,6]. Under the smoothness assumption, Label Propagation algorithms, in which class information is propagated from the labeled instances to the unlabeled or all the instances with Markov Random Walk, have been proposed recently[7,8,9,10,11]. Despite the various ideas and methods of these label propagation algorithms, their final solutions turn to take the similar forms. However, as far as we know, there is not any model yet that can explains the existing label propagation algorithms in a unified manner.

In this paper, we propose a general label propagation model, named Component Random Walk. It treats the labeled instances and the unlabeled instances as different components and dealing with their transition properly in different ways. Besides most of the well-known label propagation algorithms, a novel Multilevel Component Propagation (MCP) algorithm is also derived from this Component Random Walk model. Experimental results on real-world data sets illustrate that MCP algorithm is superior to other label propagation algorithms.

---

[*] Corresponding author.

D.-S. Huang et al. (Eds.): ICIC 2012, CCIS 304, pp. 62–66, 2012.

2   Prerequisite

Transductive Learning on graph G is usually defined as follows. Given a data set $X = X_m \cup X_u = \{x_1, ..., x_m, x_{m+1}, ..., x_n\}$, where $X_m = (x_i)_{i=1..m}$ is labeled, corresponding to the known label subset $Y_m = (y_i)_{i=1..m}$, and $X_u = (x_i)_{m+1..n}$ is unlabeled, corresponding to the unknown label subset $Y_u = (y_i)_{m+1..n}$. Map X to the vertex set V of graph $G = (V, E, W)$, where $V = V_m \cup V_u = \{v_1, ..., v_m, v_{m+1}, ..., v_n\}$, V_m is the vertex subset with labels Y_m, V_u is the vertex subset without labels, E is the edge set, and W is the pairwise similarity set with $w_{ij} = \text{sim}(v_i, v_j)$. The goal of Transductive Learning is to predict the label subset Y_u for the unlabeled instances subset X_u.

Usually, an $n \times c$ label indicating matrix c is constructed, where F_m and F_u respectively denote the state of the known label Y_m and the unknown label Y_u. In the initialization, F is set $f_{ij} = 1$ if and only if $y_i = j$, $f_{ij} = 0$ if $y_i \neq j$ or y_i is unknown. The evolution of F (or rather the label propagation process) depends on a $n \times n$ transition matrix P with $F^{t+1} = PF^t$, where F^t represents the state of F at time step t, similarly F^{t+1} represents the state of F at time step $(t + 1)$. Each element of P, $p_{ij} \in [0, 1]$, contains the possibility of propagating the class information from vertex j to vertex i. The construction of P involves a normalized similarity matrix $P = D^{-1}W$ where $D = \text{diag}(W\mathbf{1}_n)$.

After the convergence of sequence $\{F^t\}$, the elements in F usually become real values between 0 and 1. To get the final prediction of the unlabeled instances Y_u, we retrieve $y_i = \arg \max_j \{f_{ij}\}$.

A similar concept to the transition matrix P is the affinity matrix

$$A = D^{-\frac{1}{2}} W D^{-\frac{1}{2}} \tag{1}$$

whose element $a_{ij} \in [0, 1]$ represents the pairwise affinity between vertex i and vertex j. Because of the symmetry of A, P is usually replaced with A in the analysis of the regularization framework of label propagation algorithms.

3   Component Random Walk Model

We start from viewing the whole vertex set V as a single component, with F indicating its state and P indicating the transition matrix. In such a setting, the traditional random walk defined on independent vertices is reduced to a simple component random walk of F with P (Fig. 1(a)).

In the context of transductive learning, since labeled instances bear discriminative information while unlabeled instances do not, the transition probabilities of labeled instances are distinct from those of unlabeled instances. Consequently, the single component V is split into two sub-components V_m and V_u, in correspondence to the known state F_m and the to-be-predicted state F_u (Fig.1 (b)). The transition matrix P is also decomposed into

$$P = \begin{bmatrix} P_{mm} & P_{mu} \\ P_{um} & P_{uu} \end{bmatrix} \tag{2}$$

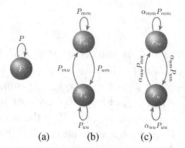

Fig. 1. Three different views of transductive learning

where P_{mm} is the transition submatrix from F_m to F_m, P_{uu} is the transition submatrix from F_u to F_u, P_{mu} and P_{um} are the transition submatrices from F_m and F_u to each other.

A more refined way to deal with the transductive learning problems is to take into account the different importance of the transition from labeled instances and the transition from unlabeled instances. It means that different weight α_{mm}, α_{mu}, α_{um} and α_{uu} need to be imposed on the transition matrices P_{mm}, P_{mu}, P_{um} and P_{uu} (Fig.1(c)). This forms the basis of our unified Component Random Walk model for label propagation. A reasonable component division combined with proper transition matrices design plus appropriate transition weight setting can give rise to a good label propagation algorithm.

3.1   Deriving Multilevel Component Propagation Algorithm

Based on Component Random Walk model, a novel Multilevel Component Propagation (MCP) algorithm can be derived as illustrated in Fig. 2.There are two specifications that MCP makes on the Component Random Walk mode. First, MCP keeps the state of the labeled instances unchanged. Second, the states of the unlabeled instances F_u^{t+1} only receive the information propagated from its previous state F_u^t and the previous state of the labeled instances F_m^t. Its state transition equation is described in eq. (3). When $\alpha_{uu} = 1$, the solution to MCP is the same as that to Gaussian Field, which means MCP is a generalization of Gaussian Field.

$$\begin{cases} F_m^{t+1} = F_m^0 \\ F_u^{t+1} = \alpha_{uu} P_{uu} F_u^t + \alpha_{um} P_{um} F_m^t \end{cases} \tag{3}$$

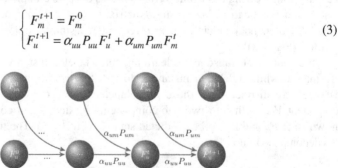

Fig. 2. Multilevel Component Propagation

4 Experiments

To investigate the classification performance of MCP algorithm on real-world data sets, we compare its mean error ratios with another two well-known label propagation algorithms on six real-world data sets. We adopt six UCI data sets from UCI data base and the two well-known label propagation algorithms include Gaussian Field and Consistency Method. Fig. 3 illustrates the comparison result on increasing labeled data ratios. The parameters α_{uu} in MCP and α in Consistency Method are both set 0.99 for all the data sets.

In Fig. 3, the mean error ratios of MCP are lower than those of Gaussian Field and Consistency Method on each test data set. With the increase of the labeled data ratio, the mean error ratio curves of Gaussian Field and MCP exhibit similar decreasing trend, while that of Consistency Method shows much slower decreasing speed and sometimes even keeps at the same level.

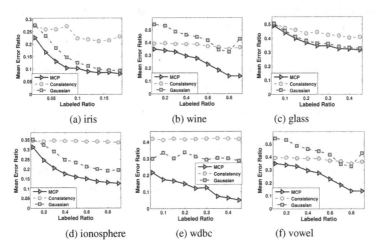

Fig. 3. Performance comparison of MCP with Gaussian Field and Consistency Method on six UCI data sets (average over 100 runs)

5 Conclusions

Label propagation is an effective approach for transductive learning. This paper proposes a generalized Component Random Walk model. Based on this model, a novel Multi-level Component Propagation (MCP) algorithm is presented with its classification performance compared well with another two well-known label propagation algorithms.

Acknowledgement. This work is supported by the National Natural Science Foundation of China under grant No.61003180, No.61070047 and No.61103018; Natural Science Foundation of Education Department of Jiangsu Province under contract

09KJB20013; Natural Science Foundation of Jiangsu Province under contract BK2010318 and BK2011442.

References

1. Chapelle, A.Z.: Semi-supervised Classification by Low Density Separation. In: Proceedings of the Tenth International Workshop on Artificial Intelligence and Statistics (2005)
2. Joachims, T.: Transductive Inference for Text Classification using Support Vector Machines. In: Proc. 16th International Conf. on Machine Learning, pp. 200–209 (1999)
3. Weston, J., Leslie, C.S., Ie, E., Zhou, D., Elisseeff, A., Noble, W.S.: Semi-supervised Protein Classification using Cluster Kernels. Bioinformatics
4. Joachims, T.: Transductive Learning via Spectral Graph Partitioning. In: Proceedings of ICML 2003, 20th International Conference on Machine Learning (2003)
5. Kemp, C., Griffiths, T., Stromsten, S., Tenenbaum, J.: Semi-supervised Learning with Trees. In: Advances in Neural Information Processing System 16 (2003)
6. Belkin, M., Niyogi, P., Sindhwani, V.: Manifold Regularization: A Geometric Framework for Learning from Examples. Tech. rep., University of Chicago (2004)
7. Szummer, M., Jaakkola, T.: Partially Labeled Classification with Markov Random Walks. In: Advances in Neural Information Processing Systems 14 (2001)
8. Zhu, X., Ghahramani, Z., Lafferty, J.: Semi-supervised Learning using Gaussian Fields and Harmonic Functions. In: The 20th International Conference on Machine Learning, ICML (2003)
9. Zhou, D., Bousquet, O., Lal, T., Weston, J., Schöelkopf, B.: Learning with Local and Global Consistency. In: Advances in Neural Information Processing System 16 (2004)
10. (A) Azran: The rendezvous algorithm: Multiclass Semi-supervised Learning with Markov Random Walks. In: The 24th International Conference on Machine Learning (2007)
11. Wang, J., Jebara, T., Chang, S.-F.: Graph Transduction via Alternating Minimization. In: ICML 2008: Proceedings of the 25th International Conference on Machine Learning, pp. 1144–1151. ACM, New York (2008)

Regularized Complete Linear Discriminant Analysis for Small Sample Size Problems

Wuyi Yang

Key Laboratory of Underwater Acoustic Communication and Marine Information Technology
of the Minister of Education, Xiamen University, Xiamen, China
wyyang@xmu.edu.cn

Abstract. In small sample size (SSS) problems, the number of available training samples is smaller than the dimensionality of the sample space. Since linear discriminant analysis (LDA) requires the within-class scatter matrix to be nonsigular, LDA cannot be directly applied to SSS problems. In this paper, regularized complete linear discriminant analysis (RCLDA) is proposed to solve SSS problems. RCLDA uses two regularized criterion to derive "regular" discriminant vectors in the range space of the within-class scatter matrix and "irregular" discriminant vectors in the null space of the within-class scatter matrix. Extensive experiments on the SSS problem of face recognition are carried out to evaluate the proposed algorithm in terms of classification accuracy and demonstrate the effectiveness of the proposed algorithm.

Keywords: Complete linear discriminant analysis, regularization, small sample size problems.

1   Introduction

Linear discriminant analysis (LDA) [1] is a very popular algorithm for dimensionality reduction. LDA tries to find a linear transformation that maximizes the ratio of the between-class scatter to the within-class scatter in the reduced dimensional space. LDA requires the within-class scatter matrix to be non-singular, and the linear transformation can be found by applying an eigen-decomposition on the scatter matrices of the given training data set. Many interesting machine learning and data mining problems are known as small sample size (SSS) problems in which the number of available training samples in general is smaller than the dimensionality of the sample space. Since the within-class scatter matrices in SSS problems are singular, LDA cannot be directly applied.

Several extensions of LDA were proposed to deal with SSS problems. In the two-stage principle component analysis (PCA) plus LDA framework, an intermediate dimension reduction stage using PCA is applied to reduce the dimension of the original data before LDA is applied. Chen et al. [2] projected the original space to the null space of the within-class scatter matrix, and then obtained the optimal discriminant vectors by finding the eigenvectors corresponding to the largest nonzero eigenvalues

D.-S. Huang et al. (Eds.): ICIC 2012, CCIS 304, pp. 67–73, 2012.

of the "reduced" between-class scatter. Yu and Yang [3] suggested extracting the optimal discriminant vectors within the range space of the between-class scatter matrix and proposed the direct LDA (DLDA) algorithm. Complete linear discriminant analysis (CLDA) [4, 5] finds "regular" discriminant vectors in the range space of the within-class scatter matrix and "irregular" discriminant vectors in the null space of the within-class scatter matrix, and these two kinds of discriminant feature vectors are fused in the classification level [4, 5].

For SSS problems, a variant of CLDA is developed by using regularized criterions to derive "regular" discriminant vectors and "irregular" discriminant vectors. The proposed regularized complete linear discriminant analysis (RCLDA) is introduced and analyzed in section 2. In section 3, experiments are conducted to demonstrate the effectiveness of the proposed algorithm. A conclusion is drawn in section 4.

2   Regularized Complete Linear Discriminant Analysis

Given a set of n data samples $x_1, \dots , x_n \in \mathbf{R}^m$ that belong to c classes, $n = \sum_{k=1}^c n_k$, where n_k is the number of samples in the k-th class, linear dimensionality reduction focuses on finding a linear transformation $A = (a_1, \dots , a_d)$ that maps each data sample in the m-dimensional space to a vector in the d-dimensional space ($d \ll m$). For a sample x in the m-dimensional space, the embedded sample y is given by $y = A^T x$.

Yu and Yang [4] proved that all optimal discriminant vectors can be derived from the range space of the total scatter matrix without any loss of the discriminatory information with respect to the criterion

$$J_1(a) = \frac{a^T S_b a}{a^T S_t a},$$

where S_b is the between-class scatter matrix, and S_t is the total scatter matrix. So, all discriminatory information can be derived from the range space of the total scatter matrix, and LDA can be performed in the PCA transformed space [4].

In the PCA transformed space, RCLDA derives "regular" discriminant vectors in the range space of the within-class scatter matrix and derives "irregular" discriminant vectors in the null space of the within-class scatter matrix. Suppose $p_1,\dots,p_m$ are m orthonormal eigenvectors of S_t, and the first s ($s = \text{rank}(S_t)$) ones are corresponding to the nonzero eigenvalues. Let $q_1,\dots,q_s$ be s orthonormal eigenvectors of $P^T S_w P$, and the first t ($t = \text{rank}(P^T S_w P)$) ones are corresponding to nonzero eigenvalues, where S_w is the within-class scatter matrix, and $P = (p_1,\dots,p_s)$. Regular discriminant vectors are found with respect to the criterion

$$J_2(u) = \frac{u^T (PQ_1)^T S_b PQ_1 u}{u^T (PQ_1)^T (S_w + \sigma I) PQ_1 u}, \tag{1}$$

where $\sigma > 0$ is a regularization parameter, and $Q_1 = (q_1,\dots,q_t)$. With respect to the above criterion, we can derive vectors $u_1,\dots,u_d$ ($d \le c-1$), which are the generalized eigenvectors of $(PQ_1)^T S_b (PQ_1) u = \lambda (PQ_1)^T (S_w + \sigma I)(PQ_1) u$ corresponding to the d largest positive eigenvalues, and $u_i^T (PQ_1)^T (S_w + \sigma I)(PQ_1) u_i = 1$, $i = 1,\ldots,d$. Generally, $d = c - 1$. Then, $PQ_1 u_1,\ldots, PQ_1 u_d$ are the optimal regular discriminant vectors. To derive irregular discriminant vectors, the regularized criterion can be expressed as follows:

$$J_3(v) = \frac{v^T (PQ_2)^T S_b PQ_2 v}{v^T (\sigma I) v} \tag{2}$$

where $Q_2 = (q_{t+1},\ldots,q_s)$. With respect to the above criterion, we can derive vectors $v_1,\ldots,v_l$ ($l \le c-1$), which are the eigenvectors of $(PQ_2)^T S_b PQ_2 v = \lambda \sigma v$ corresponding to the l largest positive eigenvalues, and $\sigma v_i^T v_i = 1$, $i = 1,\ldots,l$. Generally, $l = c - 1$. Then, $PQ_2 v_1,\ldots, PQ_2 v_l$ are the optimal irregular discriminant vectors.

The discriminant feature vector of a sample x can be obtained by projecting the sample onto the regular and the irregular discriminant vectors:

$$y = \begin{pmatrix} U^T (PQ_1)^T \\ V^T (PQ_2)^T \end{pmatrix} x = (PQ_1 U, PQ_2 V)^T x = A^T x, \tag{3}$$

where $U=(u_1,\ldots,u_d)$, $V=(v_1,\ldots,v_l)$, and $A = P(Q_1 U, Q_2 V)$.

The distance between sample y and the training sample $y_i = A x_i$ is defined by

$$g(y, y_i) = \|y - y_i\|,$$

where $\| \cdot \|$ is the notation of norm. The norm determines what measure is used and the Euclidean distance is adopted in this paper.

3 Experiments

In this section, we first present the data sets for our performance study in section 3.1. In section 3.2, we compare RCLAD with other algorithms in terms of classification accuracy. Section 3.3 evaluates the effect of regularization parameter in RCLDA.

3.1 Datasets

We carry out experiments on the following three face databases: the PIE (pose, illumination, and expression) database from CMU, the Yale database, and the ORL database. The PIE database from CMU contains more than 40,000 facial images of 68 people. 20 persons and 80 images for each person are randomly selected from the dataset that contains five near frontal poses (C05, C07, C09, C27, and C29) in the experiments. The Yale face database contains 165 facial images of 15 people. The ORL face database contains 400 facial images of 40 people. The original images were normalized in scale and orientation so that the two eyes were aligned at the same position. Then, the facial areas were cropped into the final images for experiments. In all the experiments, the size of each face image is 32×32 pixels, with 256 gray levels per pixel. Each face image is represented by a 1024-dimensional vector in image space.

3.2   Classification performance

In terms of classification accuracy, we evaluate the performance of RCLDA and compare it with other algorithms including PCA+LDA (PCA followed by LDA), NLDA [2], DLDA [3], and CLDA [5]. In the PCA step of PCA+LDA, we kept 99.5% information in the sense of reconstruction error to deal with the SSS problem. In CLDA, we search for the best coefficient to fuse regular and irregular discriminant feature vectors in the classification level and report the best classification accuracies. In RCLDA, we set the regularization parameter as $\sigma = 0.005$. The face image set is partitioned into training and testing sets with different numbers. For ease of representation, Gm/Pn means m images per person are randomly selected for training and the remaining n images are for testing. Testing images are classified by the nearest neighbor criterion, and the Euclidean distance is adopted. For each Gm/Pn, we average the results over 30 random splits and report the mean as well as the standard deviation. Table 1 shows the classification accuracies of different algorithms.

Table 1. Recognition accuracies (%) of different LDA algorithms

Method	PIE				
	G5/P75	G8/P72	G10/P70	G12/P68	G15/P65
PCA+LDA	76.25(6.05)	84.72(3.42)	86.69(4.86)	90.58(2.60)	91.93(2.09)
DLDA	73.91(5.75)	81.75(3.48)	84.16(6.18)	88.16(2.67)	89.92(2.38)
NLDA	80.55(6.09)	87.77(3.18)	88.53(4.84)	92.08(2.47)	93.02(1.98)
CLDA	80.93(6.03)	88.20(3.17)	88.95(4.61)	92.40(2.35)	93.25(1.90)
RCLDA	**81.00(5.83)**	**88.68(2.97)**	**89.81(4.12)**	**93.12(2.00)**	**94.21(1.73)**
Method	Yale				
	G3/P8	G4/P7	G5/P6	G6/P5	G7/P4
PCA+LDA	67.47(4.07)	73.49(5.03)	77.81(3.72)	80.00(4.05)	81.67(4.53)
DLDA	58.53(5.00)	65.11(4.72)	71.37(3.39)	72.44(4.96)	73.06(5.45)
NLDA	**70.31(3.36)**	**77.56(4.26)**	**82.44(3.49)**	84.53(3.94)	86.78(3.69)
CLDA	69.03(3.49)	76.83(4.91)	82.00(3.43)	84.62(3.34)	**87.11(3.66)**
RCLDA	70.11(3.47)	77.49(4.27)	82.30(3.50)	**84.71(3.75)**	**87.11(3.42)**
Method	ORL				
	G3/P7	G4/P6	G5/P5	G6/P4	G7/P3
PCA+LDA	84.55(1.56)	89.26(1.91)	92.48(1.73)	93.69(2.37)	94.89(2.24)
DLDA	82.90(2.53)	90.89(1.82)	94.17(1.61)	95.54(2.04)	96.53(1.78)
NLDA	88.57(1.61)	93.26(1.75)	95.88(1.47)	96.58(2.05)	96.97(1.93)
CLDA	**88.95(1.48)**	**93.69(1.57)**	96.17(1.41)	96.79(1.86)	97.31(1.94)
RCLDA	88.87(1.58)	93.67(1.74)	**96.45(1.21)**	**97.35(1.82)**	**97.64(1.55)**

From the results in Table 1, we observe that: (1) NLDA achieved better performance than PCA+LDA. The underlying reason may be that the PCA step in PCA+LDA removes some important discriminative information in the null space of the within-class scatter matrix. (2) DLDA achieved poorer performance than NLDA. The underlying reason may be that DLDA discards the discriminatory information in the null space of the between-class scatter matrix, which includes some discriminative information in the null space of the within-class scatter matrix. (3) CLDA achieved better performance than PCA+LDA and DLDA. CLDA achieved better performance than NLDA except for G3/P8, G4/P7, and G5/P6 on Yale. The underlying reason may be that it is difficult to fuse regular and irregular discriminative vectors for classification in some cases. (4) For most cases, RCLDA achieved better performance than CLDA, which show that RCLDA can more efficiently use two kinds of discriminative information in the null and the range space of the within-class scatter matrix.

3.3   RCLDA Performance with Varying Regularization Parameter

The experiment is designed to test the performance of RCLDA with varying regularization parameter. In the experiment, we let $\sigma = 2^r$, where r varies from -15 to 0 incremented by 1. Fig. 1 shows the performance of RCLDA with different values of r ranging from -15 to 0 incremented by 1 on PIE, Yale, and ORL. As can be seen from Fig.1, when $\sigma = 2^r$ and $r \leq -6$, RCLDA achieved similar face recognition results. In order to fuse two kinds of discriminative information in the null and the range space of the within-class scatter matrix for classification, the value of σ should be set to a small value.

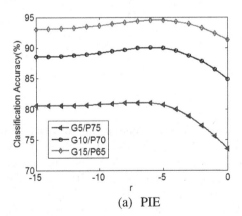

(a) PIE

Fig. 1. Classification accuracies of RCLDA with respect to different values of the regularization parameter $\sigma = 2^r$

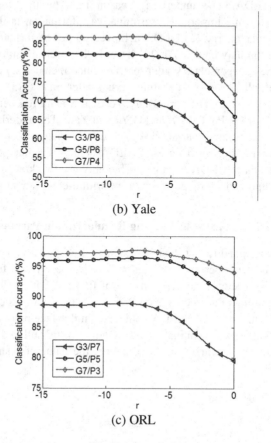

(b) Yale

(c) ORL

Fig. 1. *(continued)*

4   Conclusion

RCLDA is proposed to address SSS problems arising from the small number of available training samples compared to the dimensionality of the sample space. In terms of classification accuracy, experiments on the SSS problem of face recognition were conducted to evaluate the proposed algorithm. RCLDA can efficiently fuse two kinds of discriminative information in the null and the range space of the within-class scatter matrix and finds optimal discriminative vectors for classification.

Acknowledgments. This study is supported by the Fundamental Research Funds for the Central Universities under the grant (No. 2011121010).

References

1. Fukunaga, K.: Introduction to Statistical Pattern Recognition, 2nd edn. Academic Press, New York (1990)
2. Chen, L.F., Liao, H.Y.M., Lin, J.C., Kao, M.D., Yu, G.J.: A New LDA-Based Face Recognition System which Can Solve the Small Sample Size Problem. Pattern Recognition 33(10), 1713–1726 (2000)
3. Yu, H., Yang, J.: A Direct LDA Algorithm for High-Dimensional Data-With Application to Face Recognition. Pattern Recognition 34(10), 2067–2070 (2001)
4. Yang, J., Yang, J.Y.: Why Can LDA Be Performed in PCA Transformed Space? Pattern Recognition 36(2), 563–566 (2003)
5. Yang, J., Frangi, A.F., Yang, J.Y., Zhang, D., Jin, Z.: KPCA plus LDA: A Complete Kernel Fisher Discriminant Framework for Feature Extraction and Recognition. IEEE Trans. Pattern Analysis and Machine Intelligence 27(2), 230–244 (2005)

Unsupervised Feature Selection for Multi-cluster Data via Smooth Distributed Score

Furui Liu and Xiyan Liu

State Key Lab of CAD&CG
College of Computer Science, Zhejiang University
College of Computer Science and Information Engineering
Chongqing Technology and Business University
furuiliu210@gmail.com, lxyan@ctbu.edu.cn

Abstract. Unsupervised feature selection is one of the key topics in data engineering. Previous studies usually use a score vector which has the same length as the feature number to measure the discriminating power of each feature, and the top ranked features are considered to represent the intrinsic multi-cluster structure of the original data. Among different algorithms, Multi-Cluster Feature Selection(MCFS) is one well designed algorithm for its superior performance in feature selection tasks. However, in practice the score vector of MCFS is often sparse, and it brings a problem that only few features are well evaluated about the discriminating power while most others' are still ambiguous. In this paper, by simultaneously solving one L1-regularized regression and one L2-regularized regression, we propose a novel Multi-Cluster Feature Selection via Smooth Distributed Score(MCFS-SDS), which combines the two results to clearly evaluate the discriminating power of most features via smooth distributed score vector. It is extremely efficient when cluster number is small. Experimental results over various real-life data demonstrate the effectiveness of the proposed algorithm.

Keywords: Unsupervised feature selection, clustering, spectral regression.

1   Introduction

In real world applications about computer vision and data mining, we often need to cope with very large scale data. The high dimensionality and complex structure of data makes data processing both time and space cost [1]. Various studies show that irrelevant features can be removed without performance deterioration. Thus we can get a proper subset of the original features to perform conventional data analytic techniques to get computational advantage.

There are many methods for unsupervised learning. The early maximum variance criteria finds a useful representation of data, while its discrimination power also needs disgussing. LaplacianScore and its extensions [2] take advantage of the spectral thoery [5] and use a nearest graph to model the intrinsic locality relation of the underlying manifold structure, for each feature, it labels a score to measure its discrimination power

D.-S. Huang et al. (Eds.): ICIC 2012, CCIS 304, pp. 74–79, 2012.

and intuitively, a higher score means a better representation efficiency. Q-α algorithm [6] optimizes over a least-squares criterion function which measures the clusterability of the data points projected onto a special coordinates. It aims to maximize the cluster coherence, which can be measured by the spectral gap of affinity matrix. It is worth attention that this method always yields sparse solutions.

Multi-Cluster Feature Selection(MCFS) [7] is recently proposed to form a direct interpretation of the original data in a subset of features. For p feature candidates, it uses a score matrix $S \in R^{p \times k}$ to generate a score vector MCFS to evaluate the discriminating power of each feature. It will be discussed in detail in the next section. However, just as MCFS follows the work of sparse subplace learning [7], in practice MCFS comes with the problem that the k score vectors are sparse and their values often concentrate on the same r positions and the value on other positions is too small to form a meaningful evaluation. Thus, if d>r the selected ones after the first r features are almost as randomly selected. To overcome this defect and form a wide scale evaluation, we propose a novel **Multi-Cluster Feature Selection via Smooth Distributed Score**(MCFS-SDS), which controls the score vectors with a proper smooth degree, and get a meaningful evaluation of most feature candidates. It can be viewed as properly "split down" the value in the r concentrated positions to other positions, and it will make a more efficient ranking of all features.

2   Spectral Embedding and Regression

In this section, we will give a brief review of the key related knowledge of our algorithm, and a profile of our algorithm can also be presented. We start with the spectral embedding anf regression.

Given n vertices in p dimensional space $\{x_i\}$ i from 1 to n,, the data matrix can be recorded as X=[$x_1, \ldots ,x_n$]. To begin with, we want to find an linear projection of the original data matrix X to the real line $y= [y_1, \ldots , y_n]^T$, we first find a nearest graph W, let W be a symmetric n square matrix. For each vertice $\{x_i\}$, if it is among t nearest neighbors of x_j then $W_{ij} = 1$, (W is symmetric), otherwise $W_{ij} = 0$. Let L= D - W, it is the *graph Laplacian* [4] and D is a diagnoal matrix whose entries are column (or row) sums of W, $D_{ii} = \Sigma_j W_{ji}$ The optimal **y** is given by minimizing the follows:

$$y^* = \arg\min_{y^T Dy=1} y^T Ly = \arg\min \frac{y^T Ly}{y^T Dy}$$

Thus this **y** can be found by solving the generalized eigen-problem to find a minimum eigenvalue [5]:

$$Ly = \lambda Dy \tag{1}$$

Suppose we want to cluster the original data into k clusters, then we solve (1) and find k eigenvectors with respect to the smallest eigen-value. The k vectors form a matrix Y= [$y_1, \ldots ,y_k$]∈$R^{n \times k}$, here each **y** stands for a vector. Each row of Y is the "flat" embedding for each data point in the eigen-subspace and each y_i reflects the data distribution along the corresponding dimension (topic, concept, etc) [7]. That is why we choose the number of engin-vectors the same as cluster number k .

Then we want to learn a score matrix $S \in R^{p \times k}$, each vector $s_i=[S_{1i}, \ldots, S_{pi}]$ can be viewed as the measure of fitting degree of each feature candidate of X, if we shape the L2-norm regularized optimization problem to:

$$\min_{S} \| Y - X^T S \|^2 + \alpha \| S \|^2 \qquad (2)$$

α is a regularization parameter to avoid over-fitting [1], in statistics, this model is called *Ridge Regression* [3], by taking the deriviate of (2) with respect to S and setting it to 0, we get

$$S^* = (XX^T + \alpha I)^{-1} XY \qquad (3)$$

where $I \in R^{p \times p}$ is an identity matrix.in real world it is often computational expensive to inverse $XX^T + \alpha I$, so we can use some iterative algorithm to solve the regression problem such as LSQR [9].

If we change the cost function and set a linear constraint of the score matrix S, we will get

$$\min_{s_i} \| y_i - X^T s_i \|^2 + \beta | s_i | \qquad (4)$$

x_i and s_i are the *ith* column of X and S respectively. This L1-norm regularized problem can force the sparseness of s_i, and it is called *Lasso Regression* in statistics [3]. It can be solved by Least Angle Regression(LARs) algorithm [10] after some proper formula changing.

Ridge regression often makes a result vector smoother than lasso regression [10]. MCFS uses LARs to solve the L1-regularized lasso regression problem (4) and gets a score matrix S_{lasso}. As its nature states, the S_{lasso} is often sparse because informations are over-concentrated. A combined evaluation using both ridge and lasso may give more complete information.

3   Multi-cluster Feature Selection via Smooth Distributed Score(MCFS-SDS)

As mentioned in the first section, in practice the score matrix S_{lasso} is often sparse and the final MCFS score also concentrates on the r positions. So only few features of the r positions are well evaluated, others' discriminating power is still ambiguous. To overcome this defect, in MCFS-SDS we seperately solve a ridge regression and a lasso regression problem to get two score matrix S_{ridge} and S_{lasso}, and combine them to get the final score matrix S. The S is defined as:

$$S_{ij} = \max\{| S_{ridge,ij} |, | S_{lasso,ij} |\} \qquad (5)$$

The final S is smoothed by S_{ridge} with the highest score of S_{lasso} kept. Solving the L2-regularized problem (2) can get smooth distributed vectors s_i with some concentrated parts "split down", and solving the L1-regularized problem (4) can select out the most powerful features. So it can clearly evaluate most features. The final MCFS-SDS score can be calculated from the S using the same max-selection way as (5). We give the main steps of our algorithm.

1. **Learning eigen-subspace Y.** By constructing a nearest graph $W \in R^{n \times n}$ for data matrix $X \in R^{p \times n}$ and solving the problem in (1), we select k eigen-vectors with respect to the smallest eigenvalue and form a eigenspace $Y \in R^{n \times k}$

2. **Learning score matrix S.** By solving the ridge regression problems in (2) for k vectors $s_{ridge,i}$, we get a properly smoothed score matrix $S_{ridge} = [s_{ridge,1}, s_{ridge,2}, \ldots, s_{ridge,k}]$. By solving the lasso regression problems in (4) for k vectors $s_{lasso,i}$, we get a sparse score matrix $S_{lasso} = [s_{lasso,1}, s_{lasso,2}, \ldots, s_{lasso,k}]$. Then we combine the two matrix and generate the final score matrix S as (6), denoted as:

$$S_{ij} = \max\{ | S_{ridge} |, | S_{lasso} | \} \tag{6}$$

that is to select the max element of S_{ridge} and S_{lasso} in each position and form the final S.

3. **Calculating MCFS-SDS score.** Using the same method as (5), we set

$$MCFS - SDS(a) = \max_{j \in \{1,\ldots,k\}} S_{aj} \tag{7}$$

a from 1 to p and get the final score vector $MCFS\text{-}SDS \in R^p$.

4. **Selecting top ranked d features.** We use the final MCFS-SDS score to measure the discriminating power of all p feature candidates and select d features with highest MCFS-SDS score out to form the final feature subset.

With the combination of L1 and L2 regularization, the score vector got by MCFS-SDS is less sparse than the original one and it makes the dicriminating power information of more features available. Notice that the degree of smooth is very important, over-smooth will lead to the result that the S_{ridge} is meaningless. A proper setting of regularization parameters can make a good result.

4   Experimental Results

In this section, we compare clustering performance of our proposed algorithm with previous MCFS and other related methods, we perform k-means clustering by using selected features via different algorithms and the results are reported and compared.

4.1   Compared Algorithms and Data Sets

We compare our algorithm with some state-of-the-art unsupervised feature selection algorithms, all participants are **MCFS-SDS, MCFS** [7], **Q- α algorithm** [6].

LaplacianScore [2] and **Max-Variance**. The well-known algorithm selects the features of maximum variances for obtaining the best expressive power.

We use some popular real-life benchmark data sets to test the efficiency of the proposed algorithm, two big data sets are selected to evaluate these algorithms. The are Isolet spoken[1] letter recognition data and COIL20 image library[2]. Normalized Mutual Information (NMI) [7] is used to measure the efficiency of the result.

4.2   Clustering Results

To show a general fitting, we evaluate the performance of our algorithm with different number of clusters (K = 5, 10, 15 ,20 on COIL20 and K = 10, 15, 20, 26 on Isolet). We select d features and apply k-means for clustering on the selected features. For each cluster number K excluding when the entire set is used, 20 tests were run on different randomly chosen clusters, and the average performance and standard deviation was computed. Figure 1 and 2 show the plots of the clustering results on COIL20 and Isolet, Table 1 show the clustering results using 50 features on COIL20. The last line of tables are the results of using all features to perform clustering methods as K-means.

We summarize the advantages of MCFS-SDS as: Excellent performance when cluster number is small. Nearly consistent better performance with selected feature number more than 50. Feature number is more than 50, MCFS-SDS has achieved better performance than MCFS.

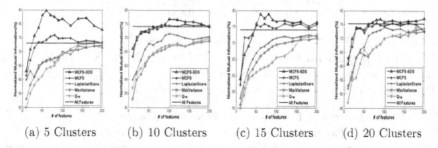

| (a) 5 Clusters | (b) 10 Clusters | (c) 15 Clusters | (d) 20 Clusters |

Fig. 1. Clustering performance vs. Feature Numbers on COIL20

Table 1. Clustering performance(%) using 50 features on COIL20

	5 Clusters	*10 Clusters*	*15 Clusters*	*20 Clusters*	*Average*
MCFS-SDS	**83.0±11.9**	72.1±8.2	**75.9±4.5**	**73.0**	**76.0**
MCFS	73.4±12.4	**73.1±9.8**	75.4±4.1	71.9	73.4
Q-α	61.4±11.9	63.2±7.9	61.1±5.2	65.9	62.9
Laplacianscore	66.1±13.1	67.9±7.8	67.1±3.9	66.9	67.0
MaxVariance	65.8±11.7	63.2±8.8	64.0±5.4	63.9	64.2
All features	73.1±12.4	74.0±8.7	74.6±2.9	75.2	74.2

---

[1] http://www.ics.uci.edu/~mlearn/MLSummary.html
[2] http://www.cs.columbia.edu/CAVE/software/softlib/coil-20.php

5   Conclusion

This paper proposes a novel method for unsupervised feature selection, named Multi-Cluster Feature Selection via Smooth Distributed Score(MCFS-SDS) which can clearly evaluates the discriminating power of most features. MCFS-SDS simultanouslys solve one L1-regularized lasso regression problem and one L2-regularized ridge regression problem, and combines their result to get a properly smoothed score matrix.Thus it clearly evaluates most features. Experimental results show that MCFS-SDS outperforms most state-of-the-art unsupervised feature selection algorithms as MCFS, LaplacianScore, Max-variance, and Q-α, and MCFS-SDS achieves consistent better performance than MCFS when selected feature number is more than 50.

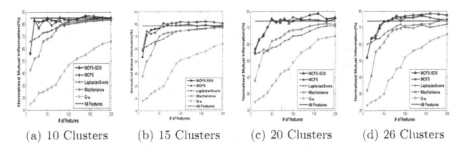

(a) 10 Clusters   (b) 15 Clusters   (c) 20 Clusters   (d) 26 Clusters

Fig. 2. Clustering performance vs. Feature Numbers on Isolet

References

1. Duda, R.O., Hart, P.E., Stork, D.G.: Pattern Classification, 2nd edn. Wiley-Interscience, Hoboken (2000)
2. He, X., Cai, D., Niyogi, P.: Laplacian Score for Feature Selection. In: Advances in Neural Information Processing Systems 18 (NIPS 2005) (2005)
3. Hastie, T., Tibshirani, R., Friedman, J.: The Elements of Statistical Learning: Data Mining, Inference, and Prediction. Springer, New York (2001)
4. Stewart, G.W.: Matrix Algorithms: Eigensystems, vol. II. SIAM, Philadelphia (2001)
5. Chung, F.R.K.: Spectral Graph Theory. Regional Conference Series in Mathematics, vol. 92. AMS (1997)
6. Wolf, L., Shashua, A.: Feature Selection for Unsupervised and Supervised Infe-rence: The Emergence of Sparsity in A Weight-Based Approach. Journal of Machine Learning Research 6, 1855–1887 (2005)
7. Cai, D., Zhang, C., He, X.: Unsupervised Feature Selection for Multi-Cluster Data. In: 16th ACM SIGKDD International Conference on Knowledge Discovery and Data Mining (KDD 2010), pp. 333–342 (2010)
8. Tenenbaum, J., Silva, V.D.: A Global Geometric Framework for Nonlinear Dimensionality Reduction. Science 290(5500), 2319–2323 (2000)
9. Paige, C.C., Saunders, M.A.: LSQR: An Algorithm for Sparse Linear Equations And Sparse Least Squares. ACM Transactions on Mathematical Software 8(1), 43–71 (1982)

Reinforcement Learning Based on Extreme Learning Machine

Jie Pan, Xuesong Wang, Yuhu Cheng, and Ge Cao

School of Information and Electrical Engineering
China University of Mining and Technology, Xuzhou, Jiangsu 221116, P.R. China
Panjie1616@126.com, {wangxuesongcumt,chengyuhu}@163.com

Abstract. Extreme learning machine not only has the best generalization performance but also has simple structure and convenient calculation. In this paper, its merits are used for reinforcement learning. The use of extreme learning machine on Q function approximation can improve the speed of reinforcement learning. As the number of hidden layer nodes is equal to that of samples, the larger sample size will seriously affect the learning speed. To solve this problem, a rolling time-window mechanism is introduced to the algorithm, which can reduce the size of the sample space to a certain extent. Finally, our algorithm is compared with a reinforcement learning based on a traditional BP neural network using a boat problem. Simulation results show that the proposed algorithm is faster and more effective.

Keywords: Extreme learning machine, Neural network, Q learning, Rolling time-window, Boat problem.

1 Introduction

Reinforcement learning is a computational method containing comprehension, directive property and decision-making [1]. Combined with bionics, reinforcement learning has great intelligence and general application in the field of control and optimization. It has been paid attention to by many researchers.

Conventional reinforcement learning can be further subdivided into the value iteration and the policy gradient algorithm [2]. Although each of two algorithms has its own advantages, inherent deficiencies still exist in varying degrees. The curse of dimensionality makes the value iteration methods difficult to converge in solving the problems of continuous domain [3]. The policy gradient algorithm can ensure convergence, but its complicated network structure will reduce the convergence speed. These deficiencies restrict the development of reinforcement learning [4].

In order to solve the above problems, an extreme learning machine (ELM) is introduced to the reinforcement learning system. ELM has simple structure, fast learning speed and good generalization, which can greatly approximate the Q function and improve the efficiency of reinforcement learning [5]. Compared with the

D.-S. Huang et al. (Eds.): ICIC 2012, CCIS 304, pp. 80–86, 2012.

reinforcement learning based on a conventional BP neural network [6], the proposed algorithm is analyzed in the simulation of a boat problem.

2   Overview of ELM

Extreme learning machine, a new type of single hidden layer feed-forward neural network, can provide a good generalization performance [7]. The approximation of feed-forward neural network is often concerned about two aspects: the overall approximation based on the unlimited input set and the local approximation based on the limited set. ELM is used to approximate Q-function of reinforcement learning in this paper, which belongs to the latter.

Given a training set $S = \{(x_k, t_k) \mid x_k \in R^n, t_k \in R^m, k = 1, 2, ..., M\}$, activation function f, and the number of hidden nodes N, the process of ELM algorithm consists of the following three steps [5]:

1) Randomly assign input weight vectors or centers and hidden node bias or impact factor α_i and a hidden node bias or impact factor β_i where $i = 1, 2, \cdots, N$;
2) Calculate the output matrix H of the hidden layer;
3) Calculate the output weight $T = H'Y$.

where H' is the Moore-Penrose generalized inverse of the output matrix H.

3   Reinforcement Learning Based on Extreme Learning Machine

Q-learning, the most important algorithm in the field of reinforcement learning, is essentially an extension of TD control algorithm, which was proposed by Watkins in 1989. The basic iterative formula of the algorithm is [1]:

$$Q_{t+1}(s,a) = (1-\eta)Q_t(s,a) + \eta[r_t + \gamma \max_{a_{t+1}} Q_t(s_{t+1}, a_{t+1})] \qquad (1)$$

where $0 < \eta < 1$ is a learning factor controlling the learning rate, $0 < \gamma < 1$ is a discount factor affecting the degree of hyperopia when the decision is made, s indicates the current state, and a indicates an action. The basic framework of reinforcement learning based on ELM is shown in Fig. 1. The top half of Fig. 1 is Q-learning system, and the lower half is environment of system.

In the step of training, given N arbitrary different samples (s_t, a_t, Q_t), $(s_t, a_t) = [x_{t1}, x_{t2}, ..., x_{tn}]^T \in R^n$ is the input samples, and $Q_t = Y_t = [y_{t1}, y_{t2}, ..., y_{tm}]^T \in R^m$ is the output samples. ELM can approach sample function with zero-error $\sum_{t=1}^{N}\|O_t - Q_t\| = 0$, if only input weights α_i, bias values β_i, and output weight matrix T meet the formula shown as follows:

$$\sum_{i=1}^{N} T \cdot g(\alpha_i x_{tj} + \beta_i) = Q_{tj} \ (j = 1, 2, ..., N) \tag{2}$$

The above N equations can be simplified as:

$$HT = Y \tag{3}$$

where

$$H(\alpha_1, ..., \alpha_N, \beta_1, ..., \beta_N, x_1, ..., x_N)$$
$$= \begin{bmatrix} g(\alpha_1 x_1 + \beta_1) & \cdots & g(\alpha_N x_1 + \beta_N) \\ \vdots & \cdots & \vdots \\ g(\alpha_1 x_N + \beta_1) & \cdots & g(\alpha_N x_N + \beta_N) \end{bmatrix}_{N \times N} \tag{4}$$

$$T = \begin{bmatrix} t_1^T \\ \vdots \\ t_N^T \end{bmatrix}_{N \times m}, \quad Y = \begin{bmatrix} y_1^T \\ \vdots \\ y_N^T \end{bmatrix}_{N \times m}. \tag{5}$$

Therefore, the output weight matrix T is calculated as

$$T = H'Y \tag{6}$$

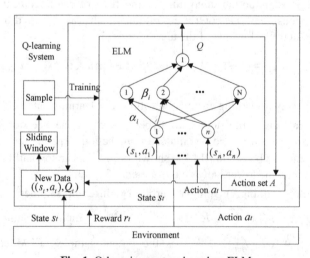

Fig. 1. Q-learning system based on ELM

The algorithm steps of Q-learning based on ELM can be summarized as follows.

Step 1. Generate initialization parameters of reinforcement learning and ELM.
Step 2. Detect the current state of the Q-learning system.
Step 3. Construct the training samples SAM at time t, and calculate the output matrix H of the hidden layer according to equation (4).
Step 4. Calculate the output weight matrix T according to equation (6) so as to complete the training of ELM.
Step 5. Obtain Q values corresponding to different actions a_t at the current state s_t, and select an optimal action a_t by Gibbs strategy.
Step 6. Take the action a_t so as to get the next state s_{t+1} and the immediate reward r_{t+1}.
Step 7. Update the Q value by equation (1).
Step 8. Add new data (s_t, a_t, Q_t) into the training sample set SAM, and scroll the rolling time window forward to discard the oldest samples.
Step 9. Finish the algorithm if the terminal condition of Q-learning is satisfied, otherwise go to Step 2.

4   Simulation Study

As shown in Fig. 2, a boat problem is used for simulations [8]. The boat starts out from the left side of river to the right side. Under the influence of the river flow marked on the figure, the boat need to select a series of reasonable actions to reach the pier in the center of the right side of the river. The problem can be modeled by the deterministic MDP consisting of five elements (S, A, p, r, Q) [9]. In the algorithm model, the state set $S = \{(x, y) \mid 0 \le x \le 200, 0 \le y \le 200\}$, expresses the positions of boat. The action set $A = \{-100^0, -90^0, -80^0, -70^0, -60^0, -45^0, -30^0, -15^0, 0^0, 15^0, 30^0, 40^0, 50^0, 65^0, 80^0, 90^0\}$, a total of 16 discrete actions, expresses the deflection angle of the boat rudder. $p(s_1, a, s_2)$ is the state transfer probability, where $s_1, s_2 \in S$, $a \in A$. Q indicates the value function.

Given a set of 16 discrete actions $A = \{-100^0, -90^0, -80^0, -70^0, -60^0, -45^0, -30^0, -15^0, 0^0, 15^0, 30^0, 40^0, 50^0, 65^0, 80^0, 90^0\}$, Fig. 3 shows the trajectory curve of successful landing when the boat is in the different states $s_1 = \{(x, y) \mid x = 10, y = 40\}$, $s_2 = \{(x, y) \mid x = 10, y = 120\}$ and $s_3 = \{(x, y) \mid x = 10, y = 180\}$. In every experiment, the number of hidden layer nodes $N = 100$.

In order to examine the precision, ELM-based Q learning (ELM-Q) is compared with a BP neural network-based Q learning (BP-Q). Table 1 shows the statistical data of two algorithms when the boat lands successfully ten times. In the table, $n = n_{trial} / n_s$ represents the average number of training, where n_{trial} is the total

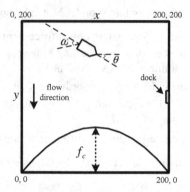

Fig. 2. Sketch map of the boat problem

number of trials, and $n_s = 10$ is the number of successful landing. $t = t_{train} / n_{trial}$ represents the average training time   in which t_{train} is the total time. The accuracy of the i th successful landing is $d_i = | y_i - 100 |$, in which y_i indicates the longitudinal coordinates of the boat landing successfully at the i th time, and $d = (1/n_s) \sum d_i$ shows the average accuracy of landing.

Table 1. Comparison of BP-based and ELM-based Q learning algorithms

Algorithm	Average number of training n	Average time of training t	Precision of landing d
BP-Q	57.8	25.7211	2.0124
ELM-Q	33.6	11.0789	1.9855

The two Q learning algorithms have almost the same accuracy, but in training times and training time, ELM-based is better than BP-based, which demonstrates the advantages of simple structure and convenient calculation of ELM.

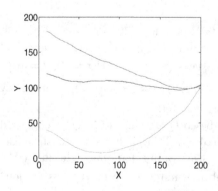

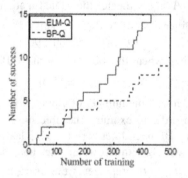

Fig. 3. Boat trajectory curve   **Fig. 4.** Training curve

In the condition of 500 training times, we compared BP-Q with ELM-Q in Fig. 4. It can be seen that the first 100 training is still in the learning stage. Q learner collects samples and trains the weights. We cannot identify the performance of BP-Q and the ELM-Q algorithm in this stage. Once the learning is completed in test phase at last 400 times, ELM-Q makes the boat land 13 times, while the BP-Q only 7 times.

5   Conclusions

The approximation for Q-value in reinforcement learning is changed into regression forecasting in this paper. With simple structures, short calculation steps, and fast learning speed, ELM can produce good results and overcome the shortcoming of both value iteration algorithms and policy gradient algorithms. However, there are still areas for improvement. The following points are the research priorities in future.

(1) As the accuracy and speed of ELM can be affected by the number of hidden nodes, too many hidden nodes will decrease the learning speed, and too few reduce the learning accuracy.

(2) The sample set will be updated online. New data are absorbed during each training process, with sliding time window reducing sample space, which can be expected to improve the learning speed further more and avoid the frequent sample updating with the assurance of high accuracy.

(3) A reinforcement learning system does not have prior knowledge. The initial sample is got in the environment which interacts with the agent. For the case of priori knowledge, the algorithm should be improved to reduce or remove the process of the samples construction.

Acknowledgements. This work was supported by National Nature Science Foundation of China (60804022, 60974050, 61072094), Program for New Century Excellent Talents in University (NCET-08-0836, NCET-10-0765), Specialized Research Fund for the Doctoral Program of Higher Education of China (20110095110016).

References

1. Sutton, R.S., Barto, A.G.: Reinforcement Learning: An Introduction. MIT Press (1998)
2. Abe, K.: Reinforcement Learning-Value Function Estimation and Policy Search. Society of Instrument and Control Engineers 41(9), 680–685 (2002)
3. Wang, X.S., Tian, X.L., Cheng, Y.H.: Value Approximation with Least Squares Support Vector Machine in Reinforcement Learning System. Journal of Computational and Theoretical Nanoscience 4(7/8), 1290–1294 (2007)
4. Vien, N.A., Yu, H., Chung, T.C.: Hessian Matrix Distribution for Bayesian Policy Gradient Reinforcement Learning. Information Sciences 181(9), 1671–1685 (2011)
5. Huang, G.B., Zhu, Q.Y., Siew, C.K.: Extreme Learning Machine: A New Learning Scheme of Feedforward Neural Networks. In: Proceedings of the International Joint Conference on Neural Networks, pp. 25–29. The MIT Press, Budapest (2004)

6. Ding, S., Su, C.Y.: Application of Optimizing Bp Neural Networks Algorithm Based on Genetic Algorithm. In: Proceedings of the 29th Chinese Control Conference, pp. 2425–2428. The MIT Press, Beijing (2010)
7. Wang, G., Li, P.: Dynamic Adaboost Ensemble Extreme Learning Machine. In: Proceedings of the International Conference on Advanced Computer Theory and Engineering, pp. 54–58. The MIT Press, Chengdu (2010)
8. Jouffe, L.: Fuzzy Inference System Learning By Reinforcement Methods. IEEE Transactions on Systems, Man and Cybernetics 28(3), 338–355 (1998)
9. Thomas, A., Marcus, S.I.: Reinforcement Learning for MDPs Using Temporal Difference Schemes. In: Proceedings of the IEEE Conference on Decision and Control, pp. 577–583. The MIT Press, San Diego (1997)

A Novel Multiple Kernel Clustering Method

Lujiang Zhang[1] and Xiaohui Hu[1,2]

[1] School of Automation Science and Electrical Engineering,
Beijing University of Aeronautics & Astronautics, Beijing, China
zhang.lujiang@hotmail.com
[2] Institute of Software,
Chinese Academy of Sciences, Beijing, China

Abstract. Recently *Multiple Kernel Learning* (MKL) has gained increasing attention in constructing a combinational kernel from a number of basis kernels. In this paper, we proposed a novel approach of multiple kernel learning for clustering based on the kernel k-means algorithm. Rather than using a convex combination of multiple kernels over the whole input space, our method associates to each cluster a localized kernel. We assign to each cluster a weight vector for feature selection and combine it with a Gaussian kernel to form a unique kernel for the corresponding cluster. A locally adaptive strategy is used to localize the kernel for each cluster with the aim of minimizing the within-cluster variance of the corresponding cluster. We experimentally compared our methods to kernel k-means and spectral clustering on several data sets. Empirical results demonstrate the effectiveness of our method.

Keywords: kernel methods, kernel k-means, multiple kernel clustering, localized kernel.

1   Introduction

Recently, a variety of kernel clustering methods have been proposed to handle the data sets that are not linearly separable. The use of kernels allows to map implicitly the input data into a high-dimensional feature space [1] so that the data sets that are not linearly separable in input space become linearly separable in feature space. Kernel clustering methods can be roughly divided into three categories [2], including kernelization of the metric [3-5], clustering in feature space [6-9] and description via support vectors [10-11]. Besides, Dhillon et al. [12] have proved that spectral clustering including ratio cut, normalized cut and ratio association is mathematically equivalent to the weighted kernel k-means.

Usually, data sets have varying local distributions for different regions in input space, and different kernels will be appropriate for different regions. Thus, instead of using a single kernel, recently Multiple Kernel Learning (MKL) has gained increasing attention in constructing a combinational kernel from a number of homogeneous or even heterogeneous kernels [13-14]. In this paper, we propose an unsupervised multiple kernel learning method for clustering based on the kernel k-means algorithm [6], called locally adaptive multiple kernel clustering (LAMKC). Rather than using a convex combination

D.-S. Huang et al. (Eds.): ICIC 2012, CCIS 304, pp. 87–92, 2012.
© Springer-Verlag Berlin Heidelberg 2012

of multiple kernels for the whole input space, we associate to each cluster a localized kernel. The basic idea is that the data distribution within a cluster tends to be uniform while the data distribution across different clusters may present diversity, so the kernels for the same cluster can be uniform while the kernels for different clusters are allowed to vary. We assign to each cluster a weight vector for feature selection by weighting the points within the corresponding cluster in input space. Then each weight vector is combined with a Gaussian kernel to form a unique kernel for the corresponding cluster. Every kernel is localized to fit for the data distribution of the corresponding cluster by optimizing its weight vector and kernel parameter jointly. A locally adaptive strategy is used to localize the kernels. That is, at every iteration we optimize the parameters of each kernel respectively with the aim of minimizing the within-cluster variance of the corresponding cluster, and then refeeding the kernel into clustering algorithm to perform the next iteration until convergence.

2   Multiple Kernel Learning

It is often not easy to choose an appropriate kernel for a particular task. In recent years, Multiple Kernel Learning (MKL) [13-15] has been proposed to address this problem, which aims at learning a convex combination of multiple kernels to obtain a good target kernel. It has gained increasing attention and a lot of extended MKL techniques have been proposed [16-19]. Besides the supervised MKL methods, Zhao et al. [20] proposed an unsupervised multiple kernel clustering method based on maximum margin clustering [9]. Usually multiple kernel learning methods use a global combination formulation which assigns the same weight to a kernel over the whole input space. However, if a data set has varying local distributions in input space, localized multiple kernel learning which assigns different weights to a kernel in different regions can match the complexity of data distribution better. Lewis et al. [21] proposed a method for combining multiple kernels in a nonstationary fashion by using a large-margin latent variable generative model. Gönen and Alpaydin [22] developed a localized multiple kernel learning algorithm which uses a gating model to assign data-dependent weights to kernels for selecting the appropriate kernel locally.

3   Locally Adaptive Multiple Kernel Clustering (LAMKC)

Given a data set $X = \{\mathbf{x_n}\}_{n=1}^{N}$ ($\mathbf{x_n} = (x_n^1, x_n^2, ..., x_n^d)$) to be partitioned into k clusters $\{c_i\}_{i=1}^{k}$, we assign a set of weight vectors $\{\mathbf{w_i}\}_{i=1}^{k}$ ($\mathbf{w_i} = (w_i^1, w_i^2, ..., w_i^d)$) to the k clusters, where the weight vector $\mathbf{w_i}$ is associated to the cluster c_i for feature selection by weighting the feature components of points in c_i. Every weight vector $\mathbf{w_i}$ ($i = 1, 2, ..., k$) is combined with a Gaussian kernel $G(\mathbf{x}, \mathbf{y}) = \exp(-\dfrac{\|\mathbf{x} - \mathbf{y}\|^2}{2\sigma^2})$ to form a unique kernel $K_i(\mathbf{x}, \mathbf{y})$ for cluster c_i :

$$K_i(\mathbf{x},\mathbf{y}) = \exp(-\frac{\left\|\mathbf{x}^T diag(\mathbf{w}_1) - \mathbf{y}^T diag(\mathbf{w}_1)\right\|^2}{2\sigma^2}) = \exp(-\frac{\sum_{j=1}^{d}(w_i^j)^2(x^j - y^j)^2}{2\sigma^2}) \tag{1}$$

$diag(\mathbf{w}_1)$ denotes the diagonal matrix with the diagonal elements equal to the corresponding elements of $\mathbf{w}_1$. Let $\mathbf{s}_i = (s_i^1, s_i^2,..., s_i^d)$ and $s_i^j = \frac{\sigma}{w_i^j}$ ($j = 1, 2,..., d$), then $K_i(\mathbf{x},\mathbf{y})$ ($i = 1, 2,..., k$) can be rewritten as:

$$K_i(\mathbf{x},\mathbf{y}) = \exp(-\frac{1}{2}\left\|\mathbf{x}^T diag(\mathbf{s}_i)^{-1} - \mathbf{y}^T diag(\mathbf{s}_i)^{-1}\right\|^2) = \exp(-\frac{1}{2}\sum_{j=1}^{d}\frac{(x^j - y^j)^2}{(s_i^j)^2}) \tag{2}$$

Let $K_i(\mathbf{x},\mathbf{y}) = <\Phi_i(\mathbf{x}), \Phi_i(\mathbf{y})>$, then the centroid of cluster c_i in feature space is given by $\mathbf{m_i} = \frac{\sum_{\mathbf{x} \in c_i}\Phi_i(\mathbf{x})}{|c_i|}$. The distance $d_i(\mathbf{x_1},\mathbf{x_j})$ and $d_i(\mathbf{x},\mathbf{m_i})$ for cluster c_i in feature space can be extended as follows using the so called kernel trick:

$$d_i^2(\mathbf{x_1},\mathbf{x_j}) = \left\|\Phi_i(\mathbf{x_1}) - \Phi_i(\mathbf{x_j})\right\|^2 = 2(1 - K_i(\mathbf{x_1},\mathbf{x_j})) \tag{3}$$

$$d_i^2(\mathbf{x},\mathbf{m_i}) = \left\|\Phi_i(\mathbf{x}) - \mathbf{m_i}\right\|^2 = 1 - \frac{2\sum_{\mathbf{x_m} \in c_i}K_i(\mathbf{x},\mathbf{x_m})}{|c_i|} + \frac{\sum_{\mathbf{x_m},\mathbf{x_n} \in c_i}K_i(\mathbf{x_m},\mathbf{x_n})}{|c_i|^2} \tag{4}$$

Our method seeks to find clusters $\{c_i\}_{i=1}^{k}$ that minimize the objective function:

$$J(\{c_i\}_{i=1}^{k}) = \sum_{i=1}^{k}\sum_{\mathbf{x} \in c_i}\left\|\Phi_i(\mathbf{x}) - \mathbf{m_i}\right\|^2 \tag{5}$$

As the kernel k-means, our method also assigns each point to the closest cluster. Each kernel K_i ($i = 1, 2,..., k$) has a parameter $\mathbf{s}_i$. The learning problem is how to optimize the parameters of kernels. To address this problem, we solve the within-cluster variance minimization problem for each cluster:

$$\min_{\mathbf{s}_i} J(c_i) = \frac{1}{|c_i|^2}\sum_{\mathbf{x_m} \in c_i}\sum_{\mathbf{x_n} \in c_i}\left\|\Phi_i(\mathbf{x_m}) - \Phi_i(\mathbf{x_n})\right\|^2 = \frac{2}{|c_i|^2}\sum_{\mathbf{x_m} \in c_i}\sum_{\mathbf{x_n} \in c_i}(1 - K_i(\mathbf{x_m},\mathbf{x_n})) \tag{6}$$

When s_i^j ($j = 1, 2,..., d$) approaches infinity, $J(c_i)$ approaches zero. So we add a regularization penalty term $\left\|\mathbf{s}_i\right\|^2$ to (6):

$$\min_{\mathbf{s}_i} J(c_i) = \frac{2}{|c_i|^2}\sum_{\mathbf{x_m} \in c_i}\sum_{\mathbf{x_n} \in c_i}(1 - K_i(\mathbf{x_m},\mathbf{x_n})) + \lambda\left\|\mathbf{s}_i\right\|^2 \tag{7}$$

λ is a regularization parameter. The objective function (7) has no closed form solution with respect to $\mathbf{s}_i$. We use the gradient descent method to compute $\mathbf{s}_i$:

$$(s_i^j)^{New} = (s_i^j)^{Old} - \rho \frac{\partial J(c_i)}{\partial s_i^j} \quad {}^{(j=1,2,...,d)} \tag{8}$$

$$\frac{\partial J(c_i)}{\partial s_i^j} = -\frac{2}{|c_i|^2} \sum_{x_m \in c_i} \sum_{x_n \in c_i} \frac{(x_m^j - x_n^j)^2}{(s_i^j)^3} \exp(-\frac{1}{2}\sum_{j=1}^{d} \frac{(x_m^j - x_n^j)^2}{(s_i^j)^2}) + 2\lambda s_i^j \tag{9}$$

ρ is a scalar parameter which can be optimized via the line-search method.

We select the well-scattered points as the initial k centroids: first choosing a centroid at random, and then selecting the next centroid in turn so that it is far from the previous centroids. We denote by σ_0 the mean square error of all points in a data set X in input space, and by $\sigma_{i,0}$ the mean square error of points in cluster c_i.

Algorithm: Locally adaptive multiple kernel clustering (LAMKC).
Input: $X = \{\mathbf{x_n}\}_{n=1}^N$: Data set, k : Number of clusters, λ : Regularization parameter;
Output: $\{c_i\}_{i=1}^k$: Final partition of the data set X ;
Procedure:

1: Initialize the kernel K_i $(i=1,2,...,k)$ with $\mathbf{s_i} = (\sigma_0, \sigma_0,...,\sigma_0)$;

2: Initialize the k centroids $\{\mathbf{m_1}, \mathbf{m_2},...,\mathbf{m_k}\}$ of clusters $\{c_1, c_2,...,c_k\}$;

3: For each point $\mathbf{x} \in X$ and each cluster c_i , compute $d_i(\mathbf{x}, \mathbf{m_i})$ using equation (4) ;

4: For each cluster c_i , update cluster $c_i = \{\mathbf{x} \in X \mid i = \arg \min_{j=1,...,k} d_j(\mathbf{x}, \mathbf{m_j})\}$;

5: For each cluster $c_i \in \{c_1, c_2,...,c_k\}$

    Set $\mathbf{s_i} = (\sigma_{i,0}, \sigma_{i,0},...,\sigma_{i,0})$;

    Repeat:

        Updating $\mathbf{s_i}$ using (8) and (9);

    Until $|J(c_i)^{New} - J(c_i)^{Old}| < \varepsilon$;

6: Repeat steps 3, 4 and 5 until there is no change for each cluster.

With the running of LAMKC, each kernel is optimized to fit for the data distribution of the corresponding cluster. The algorithm can compute the Euclidean distance between points and centroids in feature space without knowing the explicit representations of centroids due to the equation (4). The convergence of this algorithm is quite obvious. As the kernel k-means, at each iteration the objective function (5) of the algorithm decreases, and finally it converges to a local minimum.

4   Experimental Results

In this section, we conducted experiments to demonstrate the effectiveness of our method. We use the kernel k-means [6] and spectral clustering [23] as the baselines for comparison. The experiments were performed on six data sets from the UCI machine learning repository, including Iris, Breast (Diagnostic), Spambase, mfeat-fou, mfeat-fac, mfeat-pix. We evaluated performance with the clustering accuracy. The kernel matrices of kernel k-means and spectral clustering are both computed with Gaussian kernel $K(\mathbf{x},\mathbf{y}) = \exp(-\frac{\|\mathbf{x}-\mathbf{y}\|^2}{2\sigma^2})$. The parameter σ is searched from $\{\sigma_0/8, \sigma_0/4, \sigma_0/2, \sigma_0, 2\sigma_0, 4\sigma_0, 8\sigma_0\}$, where σ_0 is the mean square error of all points in input space. The regularization parameter λ of our method is selected from $\{0.1, 0.5, 1, 2, 10\}$.

Clustering results are displayed in Table 1. The results of our method and kernel k-means are averaged over 10 runs. We use the boldface to mark the best result for each data set. From the Table 1, we can see that our method obtained encouraging results on the six data sets. It obtained three best results for the six data sets. Furthermore, the performance of our method is consistently better than that of the kernel k-means on the six data sets, and is roughly comparable to that of the spectral clustering. The outcome demonstrates the effectiveness of our method.

Table 1. Clustering accuracies (%) on the six data sets

Dataset	Our method	Kernel k-means	Spectral clustering
Iris	**91.6**	89.3	87.5
Breast	86.4	85.9	**88.7**
Spambase	**72.1**	71.3	64.6
mfeat-fou	**63.8**	63.5	60.9
mfeat-fac	72.2	71.0	**74.7**
mfeat-pix	69.8	68.3	**70.1**

5   Conclusion

In this paper, we proposed a novel multiple kernel clustering method based on the kernel k-means. Instead of using a convex combination of multiple kernels, our method associates to each cluster a unique kernel which is localized to fit for the data distribution of the corresponding cluster. This allows better adaptability for kernels to each cluster. We use a locally adaptive strategy to localize the kernel for each cluster, and use the gradient descent method to solve the parameter of each kernel. Experiments show encouraging results of our method compared to the kernel k-means and spectral clustering.

References

1. Schölkopf, B., Smola, A.J.: Learning with Kernels: Support Vector Machines, Regularization, Optimization, and Beyond. MIT Press (2002)
2. Filippone, M., Camastra, F., Masulli, F., Rovetta, S.: A Survey of Kernel and Spectral Methods for Clustering. Pattern Recognition 41(1), 176–190 (2008)

3. Wu, Z.D., Xie, W.X., Yu, J.P.: Fuzzy C-means Clustering Algorithm Based on Kernel Method. In: Proceedings of the International Conference on Computational Intelligence and Multimedia Applications, pp. 49–54 (2003)
4. Yu, K., Ji, L., Zhang, X.: Kernel Nearest-Neighbor Algorithm. Neural Processing Letters 15(2), 147–156 (2002)
5. Zhang, D.Q., Chen, S.C.: Kernel Based Fuzzy and Possibilistic C-means Clustering. In: Proceedings of the International Conference Artificial Neural Network, Turkey, pp. 122–125 (2003)
6. Schölkopf, B., Smola, A.J., Müller, K.R.: Nonlinear Component Analysis as a Kernel Eigenvalue Problem. Neural Computation 10, 1299–1319 (1998)
7. Inokuchi, R., Miyamoto, S.: LVQ Clustering and SOM Using a Kernel Function. In: Proceedings of IEEE International Conference on Fuzzy Systems, vol. 3, pp. 1497–1500 (2004)
8. Qinand, A.K., Suganthan, P.N.: Kernel Neural Gas Algorithms with Application to Cluster Analysis. In: 17th International Conference on Pattern Recognition (ICPR 2004), vol. 4, pp. 617–620 (2004)
9. Xu, L., Neufeld, J., Larson, B., Schuurmans, D.: Maximum Margin Clustering. In: Advances in Neural Information Processing Systems, vol. 17, pp. 1537–1544 (2005)
10. Camastra, F., Verri, A.: A Novel Kernel Method for Clustering. IEEE Transactions on Pattern Analysis and Machine Intelligence 27(5), 801–804 (2005)
11. Hur, A.B., Horn, D., Siegelmann, H.T., Vapnik, V.: Support vector clustering. Journal of Machine Learning Research 2, 125–137 (2001)
12. Dhillon, I.S., Guan, Y., Kulis, B.: A Unified View of Kernel K-means. Spectral Clustering and Graph Cuts. Computational Complexity, 1–20 (2005)
13. Lanckriet, G., Cristianini, N., Ghaoui, L., Bartlett, P., Jordan, M.: Learning the Kernel Matrix with Semidefinite Programming. Journal of Machine Learning Research 5, 27–72 (2004)
14. Sonnenburg, S., Rätsch, G., Schäfer, C., Schölkopf, B.: Large Scale Multiple Kernel Learning. Journal of Machine Learning Research 7, 1531–1565 (2006)
15. Bach, F., Lanckriet, G., Jordan, M.: Multiple Kernel Learning, Conic Duality, and the SMO Algorithm. In: Proceedings of the 21th International Conference on Machine Learning, pp. 6–13 (2004)
16. Gehler, P.V., Nowozin, S.: Infinite Kernel Learning. Technical Report No. TR-178, Max Planck Institute for Biological Cybernetics (2008)
17. Rakotomamonjy, A., Bach, F., Canu, S., Grandvalet, Y.: Simple MKL. Journal of Machine Learning Research 9, 2491–2521 (2008)
18. Kloft, M., Brefeld, U., Sonnenburg, S., Laskov, P., Müller, K.R., Zien, A.: Efficient and Accurate l_p-norm Multiple Kernel Learning. In: Advances in Neural Information Processing Systems, vol. 22, pp. 997–1005 (2009)
19. Jin, R., Hoi, S.C.H., Yang, T.: Online Multiple Kernel Learning: Algorithms and Mistake Bounds. In: Hutter, M., Stephan, F., Vovk, V., Zeugmann, T. (eds.) ALT 2010. LNCS, vol. 6331, pp. 390–404. Springer, Heidelberg (2010)
20. Zhao, B., Kwok, J.T., Zhang, C.: Multiple Kernel Clustering. In: Proceedings of the 9th SIAM International Conference on Data Mining (SDM 2009), pp. 638–649 (2009)
21. Lewis, D.P., Jebara, T., Noble, W.S.: Nonstationary Kernel Combination. In: Proceedings of the 23th International Conference on Machine Learning, pp. 553–560 (2006)
22. Gönen, M., Alpaydin, E.: Localized multiple kernel learning. In: Proceedings of the 25th International Conference on Machine Learning, pp. 352–359 (2008)
23. Ng, A.Y., Jordan, M.I., Weiss, Y.: On Spectral Clustering: Analysis and an Algorithm. In: Advances in Neural Information Processing Systems, vol. 14, pp. 849–856 (2001)

A Comparative Study of Two Independent Component Analysis Using Reference Signal Methods

Jian-Xun Mi[1,2] and Yanxin Yang[3]

[1] Bio-Computing Research Center, Shenzhen Graduate School,
Harbin Institute of Technology, Shenzhen, Guangdong Province, China
[2] Key Laboratory of Network Oriented Intelligent Computation, Shenzhen,
Guangdong Province, China
[3] Faculty of Engineering and Technology, Yunnan Agriculture University,
Kunming, Yunnan Province, China
cookiexdy@126.com, mijianxun@gmail.com

Abstract. Independent Component Analysis (ICA) using reference signal is a useful tool for extracting a desired independent component (IC). Reference signal is served as *a priori information* to conduct ICA to converge to the local extreme point related to a desired IC. There are two methods can perform ICA using reference signal, namely ICA with reference (ICA-R) and fast ICA with reference signal (FICAR). In this paper, we present a comparative assessment of the two methods to highlight their respective characteristics.

Keywords: Independent component analysis, ICA-R, FICAR.

1   Introduction

ICA is a popular statistical technique for revealing hidden independent sources that underlie observed multichannel signals. In some practical applications, only a small subset of ICs is required. A convenient method is to use available a priori knowledge to extract only interesting sources, whereas classical ICA methods have to recovery all ICs. However, for classical ICA, uninteresting ICs will be calculated at first and then be discarded, which is consumptive.

A framework called constrained ICA (cICA) was proposed by Lu and Rajapakse in [1]. Then ICA with reference (ICA-R) [2] was proposed under cICA which incorporates the reference signal, which carries priori knowledge on desired IC, into the ICA contrast function.

Another famous ICA method using a priori information, called fast ICA with Reference signal (FICAR), was proposed by Barros, et al. [3] which was used to cancel cardiac artifacts from a magnetoencephalogram (MEG) originally. FICAR is a two-stage method which first uses reference signal to construct a Wiener vector as an initial weight vector and then implements one-unit Fast ICA to extract desired IC with the predesigned initial weight vector.

Compared with classical ICA methods, both ICA-R and FICAR take advantage of reference signal to avoid computing uninteresting ICs and have many applications[8][9].

D.-S. Huang et al. (Eds.): ICIC 2012, CCIS 304, pp. 93–99, 2012.
© Springer-Verlag Berlin Heidelberg 2012

For ICA-R, reference signal is added into ICA-R as an inequality constraint so as to form an augmented Lagrangian function, and it works during search of the function's global minimum. FICAR uses the reference signal only in its first stage to construct initial weight vector. Although the reference signal is used differently, both methods are capable of extract the desired IC directly. However, there is no study to compare ICA-R and FICAR theoretically and experimentally. In this paper, we present a comparative study of the mentioned two ICA using reference signal methods.

The paper is organized as follows. Section 2 introduces ICA problem and the second-order method of extraction of underlying source. Section 3 presents FICAR and ICA-R respectively and then their differences are summarized. We compare two methods experimentally in Section 4. Section 5 provides conclusions.

2   ICA and Extraction by the Second-Order Approach

To introduce ICA problem, we assume the observed signal $\mathbf{x} = (x_1, x_2, \cdots, x_n)^T$ is an instantaneous linear mixture of ICs $\mathbf{s} = (s_1, s_2, \cdots, s_m)^T$ by a $n \times m$ matrix $\mathbf{A}$. Therefore ICA problem can be expressed as:

$$\mathbf{x} = \mathbf{As} \qquad (1)$$

For simplicity, we address the problem of complete ICA, so that $n = m$. Without loss of generality, we whiten $\mathbf{x}$ to have:

$$\mathbf{z} = \mathbf{Vx} \qquad (2)$$

where $\mathbf{V}$ is an $n \times n$ whitening matrix, so that $E\{\mathbf{zz}^T\} = \mathbf{I}$. In practice, the pre-whitening operation simplifies and speeds up the algorithm. Therefore, we can rewrite :

$$\mathbf{z} = \mathbf{VAs} = \mathbf{Bs} \qquad (3)$$

which is treated as input signals. It is easy to derive that $\mathbf{B}^T \mathbf{B} = \mathbf{I}$. The aim of ICA is to find a demixing matrix $\mathbf{W}$ so as to uncover ICs, i.e. $\mathbf{s} = \mathbf{Wz}$.

In general, an output can be produced by projecting $\mathbf{x}$ onto a weight vector, i.e. $y = \mathbf{w}^T \mathbf{z}$, where $\mathbf{w} = (w_1, w_2, \cdots, w_n)^T$. As mentioned before, a priori information of desired IC is carried by a reference signal denoted by r. Using normalization, $s_i (i = 1, 2, \cdots, n)$, r and $x_i (i = 1, 2, \cdots, n)$ have zero mean and unit variance, respectively. Wiener filer is an early approach which uses the second-order method to find a optimum weight $\mathbf{w}^*$ to produce an output $y^* = \mathbf{w}^* \mathbf{z}$ minimizing the mean square error (MSE) given by $E\{(r - y^*)^2\}$. By straightforward algebra calculation, the optimum weight is given by [3]

$$\mathbf{w}^* = E\{\mathbf{zr}\} / \|E\{\mathbf{zr}\}\| \qquad (4)$$

where $\|\cdot\|$ is the Frobenius norm. Therefore, if $\mathbf{x}$ satisfies ICA model, we should have

$$y^* = E\{\mathbf{zr}\}\mathbf{z}/\|E\{\mathbf{zr}\}\| = E\{s^T r\}\mathbf{s}/\|E\{sr\}\| \tag{5}$$

The second-order method could produce correct IC, only if desired IC is the only source which has non-zero correlation with the reference signal, which is, however, too rigorous for reference signal. It is concluded in [2] that second-order statistics is insufficient to recover ICs.

ICA methods uncover independent sources using high-order statistics. Generally speaking, a method of ICA includes two aspects: objective function and optimization algorithm. Several independent measurements or independent source separating criterion functions have been proposed [4]. Some ICA algorithms using Kurtosis or Negentropy as objective function can extract one independent component at a time, namely one-unit ICA algorithm. However, the order of extracted ICs is arbitrary.

3   Two ICA Using the Reference Signal Methods

In the sense of semi-blind source extraction, the available a priori information should be combined with objective function so that the post-selection process and calculation of uninteresting ICs can be avoided. Therefore, the ICA using the reference signal technique is described as: a one-unit ICA algorithm which is capable of extracting a desired IC directly with the assistance of the reference signal.

3.1   Objective Function

In [5], negentropy is introduced as independent measurement that unmixed ICs should maximize such measurement. Both methods compared in this paper use Negentropy as ICA objective function. A flexible and reliable approximation of negentropy is given by:

$$J(y) \approx (E\{f(y_{Gaus})\} - E\{f(y)\})^2 \tag{6}$$

where $f(\cdot)$ is a non-quadratic function and there are two functions of $f(\cdot)$ used in this paper:

$$f_1(y) = \log \cosh(ay)/a \tag{7}$$

$$f_2(y) = by^4/4 \tag{8}$$

where $a, b \in R^+$.

3.2   FICAR

In FICAR, the Wiener vector is used as a predesigned initial weight vector $\mathbf{w}_0$ which should not be far from the optimum vector $\mathbf{w}^+$ for extracting desired IC. FICAR uses Eqn. (8) ($b = 1$) to construct the learning rule [3]

$$\mathbf{w} \leftarrow E\{\mathbf{z}(\mathbf{w}^T\mathbf{z})^3\} - 3\mathbf{w} \qquad (9)$$

which is the same weight vector update rule as one-unit FastICA [5]. FICAR algorithm is summarized as follows:

1. Whiten the observed signals $\mathbf{x}$ to obtain $\mathbf{z} = \mathbf{Vx}$.
2. Compute the initial vector $\mathbf{w}_0 = E\{\mathbf{zr}\}/\|E\{\mathbf{zr}\}\|$.
3. Update the weight vector by Eqn.(9) and let $\mathbf{w} \leftarrow \mathbf{w}/\|\mathbf{w}\|$.
4. Test if $\min\{\|\mathbf{w} - \mathbf{w}_0\|, \|\mathbf{w} + \mathbf{w}_0\|\} \le \varsigma$, otherwise, change the current weight to $\mathbf{w}_0$ and add random deviation.
5. Repeat step 3 and 4 until $\mathbf{w}$ converges.

The convergence speed of FICAR is determined by two aspects: the algorithm of one-unit FastICA and the location of $\mathbf{w}_0$. It is proven that the convergence of one-unit FastICA is quadratic (at least) or cubic when the densities of independent sources are symmetric [6]. Since there is not enough information about the location of $\mathbf{w}_0$, $\mathbf{w}_0$ may be out of the attraction region of the correct solution $\mathbf{w}^+$, which causes the weight vector converges to an incorrect solution. If incorrect convergence happens, the algorithm has to stop the current updating process and randomly select a new initial weight vector near $\mathbf{w}_0$ and operate one-unit FastICA again. This procedure will repeat until an initial vector is in the attraction basin of desired IC. Hence the location of $\mathbf{w}_0$ has great impact on the convergence speed.

3.3   ICA-R

In contrast to FICAR, ICA-R method is a single step optimization algorithm in which the uncovered IC is the closest to the reference signal according to some distance criteria, denoted by $\varepsilon(y,r)$. In [6], three typical distance criterions were compared and we choose negative correlation as distance criteria for simplicity, which is

$$\varepsilon(y,r) = -E\{yr\} \cdot \qquad (10)$$

A threshold parameter ξ is used to restrict the distance

$$g(y) = \varepsilon(y,r) - \xi \le 0 \qquad (11)$$

To incorporate the restriction of Eqn. (11) into the ICA contrast function, ICA-R is modeled under the cICA framework as a constrained optimization problem:

$$\text{minimize } -J(y) \text{ subject to } g(y) \leq 0 \text{ and } h(y) = E\{y^2\} - 1 = 0 \tag{12}$$

where the equality constraint compels the output to have a unit covariance. We use improved ICA-R algorithm proposed in [7] to learn $\mathbf{w}$ which is given by:

$$\Delta\mathbf{w} = -\frac{\eta}{8\lambda - E\{\hat{\rho}f''(y)\}}(-E\{J'(y)\mathbf{x}\} - \mu E\{r\mathbf{x}\} + 4\lambda(E\{y^2\} - 1)E\{y\mathbf{x}\})$$

$$\Delta\mu = \max\{-\mu, \gamma g(\mathbf{w}^T\mathbf{x})\} \text{ and } \Delta\lambda = \gamma h(\mathbf{w}^T\mathbf{x}) \tag{13}$$

where η and γ are learning rates. For more details, please refer to [7]. The ICA-R use Eqn. (8) for sub-Gaussian signal and Eqn.(7) for super-Gaussian signal. It is proven in [1] that the distribution type of output IC is determined by non-quadratic functions. Therefore the distribution type of IC extracted by ICA-R can be preassigned. We refer to this characteristic of ICA-R as the distribution selectivity. ICA-R algorithm is summarized as follows:

1. Whiten the observed signals $\mathbf{x}$ to obtain $\mathbf{z} = \mathbf{V}\mathbf{x}$.
2. Give an initial $\mathbf{w}$ with random direction and small length, and set initial μ and λ to 0, respectively.
3. Update $\mathbf{w}$, μ, and λ according to Eqn. (13), respectively.
4. If not converge, go back to step 3.

We compare FICAR with ICA-R in 7 aspects summarized in Table 1.

Table 1. Differences between FICAR and ICA-R

	FICAR	ICA-R
Number of operating stages	Two-stage method	One-stage method
Optimization objective function	Correlation (stage 1) Kurtosis (stage2)	Negentropy
The critical parameter and its selection method	ς and no selection principle (An empirical guess value is $\varsigma = 0.8$.)	ξ and parameter selection depends on empirical experience.
Optimization method	Fixed-point optimization	Newton-like optimization
Distribution type of output	Not specified	Controlled by choice of non-quadratic function
Convergence speed in one iteration of weight updating	At least quadratic (cubic, if ICs are symmetric distributed).	Quadratic in theory

Although the two methods differ with each other in many aspects, essentially both of them are aim to search the local minimum of approximated negentropy function corresponding to the desired IC. Hence, the estimated IC should be the same when FICA and ICA-R use an appropriate parameter respectively.

4   Experimental Results

In the following experiment, we produced observed data by four synthetic sources (see Fig. 1 (a)), which are independent with each other. Sources 1 and 3 are sub-Gaussian distributed, and the rests are super-Gaussian distributed. For ICA-R, we set $\eta = 1$, $\gamma = 0.2$, and $\xi = -0.5$. And let $\varsigma = 0.8$ for FICAR. We ran each algorithm 10 times to obtain average CPU times shown in Table 2.

Since using fix-point algorithm, FICAR is more than 50 times as fast as ICA-R. Therefore, FICAR is with high efficiency. At the mean time, we would like to point out the unique characteristic of ICA-R. In some applications, such as EEG analysis, desired ICs are of super-Gaussian distribution usually. It is convenient to use ICA-R to extract the ICs of super-Gaussian distribution.

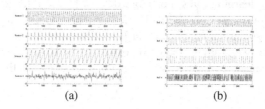

(a)   (b)

Fig. 1. (a) Four synthetic independent sources. (b) Four reference signals associated with four ICs respectively.

Table 2. Average CPU time (s) to extract ICs

IC number	IC 1	IC 2	IC 3	IC 4
ICA-R	0.184	0.586	0.239	1.016
FICAR	3.12×10^{-3}	3.74×10^{-3}	2.81×10^{-3}	2.03×10^{-3}

5   Conclusions

In this paper, we compare the differences between ICA-R and FICAR. Both methods use reference signal to extract IC from observed data. According to the experiment, FICAR is much more efficient than ICA-R. ICA-R has characteristic of distribution selectivity, therefore distribution type of its output can be specified by users.

References

1. Lu, W., Rajapakse, J.C.: Approach and Applications of Constrained ICA. IEEE Transactions on Neural Networks 16, 203–212 (2005)
2. Lu, W., Rajapakse, J.C.: ICA with Reference. Neurocomputing 69, 2244–2257 (2006)

3. Barros, A.K., Vigario, R., Jousmaki, V., et al.: Extraction of Event-related Signals from Multichannel Bioelectrical Measurements. IEEE Transactions on Bio-Medical Engineering 475, 583–588 (2000)
4. Barros, A.K., Principe, J.C., Erdogmus, D.: Independent Component Analysis and Blind Source Separation. Signal Processing 87, 1817–1818 (2007)
5. Hyvarinen, A., Oja, E.: A Fast Fixed-point Algorithm for Independent Compo-nent Analysis. Neural Computation 9, 1483–1492 (1997)
6. Hyvarinen, A.: Fast and Robust Fixed-point Algorithms for Independent Com-ponent Analysis. IEEE Transactions on Neural Networks 10, 626–634 (1999)
7. Huang, D.S., Mi, J.X.: A new constrained independent component analysis method. IEEE Transactions on Neural Networks 18, 1532–1535 (2007)
8. Khan, O.I., Farooq, F., Akram, F., Choi, M.T., Han, S.M., Kim, T.S.: Robust extraction of P300 using constrained ICA for BCI applications. Med. Biol. Eng. Comput. 50, 231–241 (2012)
9. Spasić, S., Nikolić, L., Mutavdžić, D., Šaponjić, J.: Independent Complexity Patterns in Single Neuron Activity Induced by Static Magnetic Field. Computer Methods and Programs in Biomedicine 104, 212–218 (2011)

A Novel Hybrid ACO/SA Approach to Solve Stochastic Dynamic Facility Layout Problem (SDFLP)

T.S. Lee[1], Ghorbanali Moslemipour[1], T.O. Ting[2,*], and Dirk Rilling[1]

[1] Faculty of Engineering and Technology, Multimedia University, 75450 Malacca, Malaysia
[2] Department of Electrical and Electronic Engineering, Xi'an Jiaotong-Liverpool University, Suzhou, Jiangsu Province, P.R. China
{tslee,dirk.rilling}@mmu.edu.my, ghmoslemipour@yahoo.com, toting@xjtlu.edu.cn

Abstract. This paper proposes a new hybrid algorithm using ant colony optimization and simulated annealing intelligent approaches to solve a stochastic dynamic facility layout problem in which product demands are normally distributed random variables with known probability density function that changes from period to period in a random manner. Finally, the performance of the proposed algorithm is compared with the simulated annealing and another approach using data taken from the literature.

Keywords: Ant colony optimization, dynamic layout problem, simulated annealing, stochastic environment.

1 Introduction

Facility layout is the problem of determining the relative locations of facilities on the shop floor. The optimal arrangement of these facilities leads to minimizing the total manufacturing cost and maximizing the productivity. Considering stochastic product demands in the dynamic (multi-period) facility layout problem (FLP) leads to the stochastic dynamic FLP (SDFLP).

Since the facility layout is a non-deterministic polynomial (NP)-complete and hard combinatorial optimization problem, it should be solved using intelligent approaches. Simulated annealing (SA) algorithm is one of the intelligent approaches, which has been widely used to solve the FLP. It is a simulation of physical annealing process of solids in statistical mechanics, which starts with a known or randomly generated initial solution and a high initial value of temperature. It is formed by two loops namely, the inner loop to search for a neighboring solution, and the outer loop for decrease the temperature to reduce the probability of accepting the non-improving neighboring solutions in the inner loop. Selecting a good initial solution for this algorithm leads to improvement in both the obtained solution quality and execution time [1].

Ant colony optimization (ACO) algorithm takes inspiration from the social behavior of real ants to find the shortest path from the nest to the food source. As the ant

---

* Corresponding author.

D.-S. Huang et al. (Eds.): ICIC 2012, CCIS 304, pp. 100–108, 2012.
© Springer-Verlag Berlin Heidelberg 2012

moves along a randomly selected path, it lays a volatile value of a chemical substance named pheromone on the path. Using the smell of the pheromone the other ants follow the path and thereby the amount of pheromone on the path is increased. Finally, the ants find the shortest path from the nest to the food source. Huntley and Brown [2] combined a high-level genetic algorithm (GA) with SA to obtain a hybrid algorithm. Mahdi et al. [3] proposed a hybrid algorithm by combining SA, GA, and Hitchcock's exact method to solve the FLP. Gambardella et al. [4] proposed a hybrid ant system (HAS) algorithm to solve the quadratic assignment problem (QAP). Mir and Imam [5] solved an unequal-sized FLP by using SA to generate an initial solution and an analytical search method to determine the optimal location of facilities.

Lee and Lee [6] proposed a hybrid algorithm by combining SA, tabu search (TS), and GA to find the global solution for a layout problem with fixed shape and unequal-sized facilities. McKendall and Shang [7] introduced three different types of ACO approaches including HAS I, II, and III to solve the dynamic FLP. Ramkumar and Ponnambalam [8] developed a population-based hybrid ant-colony system (PHAS) to solve the FLP. Teo and Ponnambalam [9] proposed a hybrid meta-heuristic approach for solving a single row FLP by using ACO and particle swarm optimization (PSO). Chen and Rogers [10] proposed a hybrid ant system (HAS) algorithm to solve the QAP. Yuying et al. [11] developed a hybrid chaotic ant swarm optimization (HCASO) approach by proposing pre-selection and discrete recombination operators in the CASO to improve the computational time, solution accuracy and stability. In this paper, a new hybrid resolution approach, in which ant colony optimization (ACO) algorithm is used to construct the initial solution for SA, is proposed to solve the SDFLP.

In general, the FLP with discrete representation and equal-sized facilities, which are assigned to the same number of locations, can be formulated as the QAP. Koopmans and Beckman [12] proposed the first QAP model as shown in Eq. (1). In this equation, $C(\pi)$ represents the total material handling cost for a given layout π and f_{ij} denotes the flow of materials between facilities i and j. The distance between locations l and q is denoted by d_{lq}. The 0-1 integer decision variable x_{il} is equal to 1 if the facility i is assigned to location l.

$$C(\pi) = \sum_{i=1}^{M}\sum_{j=1}^{M}\sum_{l=1}^{M}\sum_{q=1}^{M} f_{ij} d_{lq} x_{il} x_{jq} \tag{1}$$

Moslemipour and Lee [13] proposed a new QAP-based mathematical model as given in equations (2) to (5) for designing an optimal machine layout for each period of the SDFLP, in which the product demands are independent normally distributed random variables with known probability density function that changes from period to period at random. In Eq. (2), M is number of machines and T is number of periods.

Eq. (2) represents the total cost function in which $E(D_{tk})$ and $Var(D_{tk})$ are expected value and variance of demand of part k in period t, respectively. B_k is the transfer batch size for part k, C_{tk} is the cost of movement for part k in period t, and Z_p is the standard normal Z value for percentile p.

$$f_{min}(X) = \left\{ \begin{array}{l} \sum_{t=1}^{T}\sum_{i=1}^{M}\sum_{j=1}^{M}\sum_{k=1}^{K}\frac{E(D_{tk})}{B_k}C_{tk}\sum_{l=1}^{M}\sum_{q=1}^{M}d_{lq}x_{til}x_{tjq} + \sum_{t=2}^{T}\sum_{i=1}^{M}\sum_{l=1}^{M}\sum_{q=1}^{M}a_{tilq}x_{(t-1)il}x_{tiq} + \\ Z_p\sqrt{\sum_{t=1}^{T}\sum_{i=1}^{M}\sum_{j=1}^{M}\sum_{k=1}^{K}\frac{Var(D_{tk})}{B_k^{2}}C_{tk}^{2}\left(\sum_{l=1}^{M}\sum_{q=1}^{M}d_{lq}x_{til}x_{tjq}\right)^2} \end{array} \right\} \tag{2}$$

Subject to:

$$\sum_{i=1}^{M}x_{til} = 1 \quad \forall t,l; \quad \sum_{l=1}^{M}x_{til} = 1 \quad \forall t,i \tag{3}$$

$$x_{til} = \begin{cases} 1 & \text{if machine } i \text{ is assigned to location } l \text{ in period } t \\ 0 & \text{otherwise} \end{cases} \tag{4}$$

$$\left|N_{ki} - N_{kj}\right| = 1 \tag{5}$$

Constraint (3) ensures assigning each facility in each period to exactly one location and vice versa. Equation (4) represents the decision variables that are the solution of the problem so that they determine the location of each facility in each period. Eq. (5) refers to two consecutive operations, which are done on part k by machines i and j.

2   Proposed ACO/SA Algorithm

The proposed hybrid algorithm contains two stages namely, construction of a feasible initial solution using ACO approach and improving the initial solution using SA algorithm.

2.1   Stage 1: Initial Solution Construction

In the first stage, the ACO approach is used to construct a good feasible initial solution required for the SA algorithm as shown in Fig. 1. Each ant is assigned to one period of a multi-period (dynamic) layout problem. It is necessary to mention that a solution of the SDFLP is represented as a two dimensional matrix where each row represents a period, each column represents a location, and each element represents a machine number. The probability of selecting machine j after machine i by ant t is given in Eq. (6).

$$P_{ij}^{t} = \begin{cases} \dfrac{[\tau_{ij}]^{\alpha}[\eta_{ij}]^{\beta}}{\sum_{t}[\tau_{ij}]^{\alpha}[\eta_{ij}]^{\beta}} & \text{if } j,t \in \{N - tabu_t\} \\ \\ 0 & \text{otherwise} \end{cases} \tag{6}$$

where, N is the set of machines, and the parameters α and β indicate the significance of trail against selectivity. The set $\{N - tabu_t\}$ contains the machines, which have not been selected yet. The trail intensity is updated according to the Eq. (7) in which the coefficient $1-\rho$ stands for the amount of trail after evaporation. $f(X)$ is given in Eq.(2).

$$\tau_{ij} \leftarrow (1-\rho).\tau_{ij} + \frac{1}{f(X)} \tag{7}$$

Figure 1: The proposed ACO/SA algorithm

Initialization,

$\alpha = 5, \beta = 1, \tau_{ij}(0) = 10^{-4}, \rho = 0.1, \theta = 0.95, il_{max} = M \times T, il = 0, el = 0$

$el_{max} = \log_\theta \left(\ln \dfrac{P_{in}}{P_f} \right), P_{in} = 0.95, P_f = 10^{-15}, T_{in} = -0.1f(s^0) / \ln(0.25)$

Stage 1: for $t = 1 : T$

        Place the randomly selected machine at the first location

        for $i = 1 : M$

          Select next machine with probability in (6) to locate at next location

        end

        Update the pheromone trail using (7).

    end

Stage 2: while outer-loop criterion not satisfied (i.e. $el \leq el_{max}$)

      while inner-loop criterion not satisfied (i.e. $il \leq il_{max}$)

         $s = s^0$

         If $f(s) \leq f(s')$ %better solution is accepted

         $s = s'$

         end

        if $f(s) > f(s')$

         if randomly generated $x \in (0,1) \leq P_{el} = \exp((f(s) - f(s'))/T_{el})$

          $s = s'$

         end

        end

        $il = il + 1$

      end

      $T_{el} = T_{in}\theta^{el}$ % Update Temp T_{el} , % Cooling ratio $\theta \in (0.80, 0.99)$;

      $el = el + 1$

    end   Hybrid ACO/SA

The selectivity, which is the desirability of selecting machine j after machine i denoted by η_{ij}, is calculated using Eq. (8).

$$\eta_{ij} = \frac{1}{c_{ij}}, \; c_{ij} = \left(\sum_{u=1}^{M} d_{\pi(i)\pi(u)}\right)\left(\sum_{v=1}^{M} f_{vj}\right) \tag{8}$$

where, c_{ij} represents the total part handling cost between machines i and j, $\pi(i)$ represents the location containing the machine i, $d_{\pi(i)\pi(u)}$ denotes the distance between the locations where machines i and j are placed, and f_{vj} shows the flow of parts between machines v and j.

In the SDFLP, the part demands are assumed to be normally distributed random variables. Therefore, the flow of parts is a normally distributed random variable. As a result, c_{ij} is also a random variable with the expected value $E(C_{ij})$ and variance $Var(C_{ij})$ shown in Eq. (9).

$$E(c_{ij}) = \left(\sum_{u=1}^{M} d_{\pi(i)\pi(u)}\right)\left(\sum_{v=1}^{M} E(f_{vj})\right), \; Var(c_{ij}) = \left(\sum_{u=1}^{M} d_{\pi(i)\pi(u)}\right)^2\left(\sum_{v=1}^{M} Var(f_{vj})\right) \tag{9}$$

Considering u_{ij} as the upper bound of c_{ij} and the confidence level p leads to using u_{ij} rather than c_{ij} [3]. By doing so, u_{ij} and η_{ij} are written as in equation (10).

$$u_{ij} = E(c_{ij}) + Z_p\sqrt{Var(c_{ij})}, \; \eta_{ij} = \frac{1}{u_{ij}} \tag{10}$$

2.2   Stage2: Initial Solution Improvement

As shown in Figure 1, in this stage, the local search SA method is used to improve the initial solution s_0 generated by the ACO approach in the first stage. It starts with the high initial temperature T_{in}.

3   Computational Results

To evaluate the performance of the proposed hybrid ACO/SA algorithm for solving the SDFLP with the mathematical model given in equations (2) to (5), two randomly generated test problems obtained from Moslemipour and Lee [13] (Problem I with M=12; T=5 and Problem II with M=12; T=10) are solved by this algorithm, which is programmed in Matlab. The data on machine sequence, transfer batch size (=50), part movement cost (=5), distance between machine locations, facility rearrangement costs (=1000), and normally distributed product demands with known expected value and variance for each period, as the inputs of the model are given in Tables A.1 to A.4 in the appendix. A personal computer with Intel 2.10 GHZ CPU and 3 GB RAM is used to run the hybrid algorithm. The results, including objective function value $f(x)$, and elapsed computational time for three different confidence levels are obtained by running this algorithm ten times. These results along with the results obtained from the SA are shown in Table 1. According to the results, the proposed hybrid algorithm has better performance than the SA.

According to Krishnan et al. [14], Raytheon Aircraft Company is a real world case study in which six parts are processed by using 21 equal-sized machines (35' X 35'). Part movement cost and machine rearrangement cost are presumed to be $3.75/foot and zero respectively.

Table 1. The objective function value (10 trails)

Problem	I	II	I	II
Confidence level (p)	SA		ACO/SA	
0.75	1265500	2155600	1246800	2124100
0.85	1274300	2173000	1270300	2157300
0.95	1301100	2241200	1300400	2229300
Computational time [s]	4.855082	16.329078	4.901165	16.228156

An aisle space of 10 feet is assumed to be considered around each machine. Euclidean distance between centers of machines is considered in the case study. The data on yearly part demands, which are not shown here, are considered as the expectation of the part demands. Since there is no data on variance of part demands, fifty percent percentile p equivalent of $z_p = 0$ is regarded. The problem is applied to the model given in equations (2) to (6). Then, it is solved by using the proposed hybrid AC/SA algorithm. Table 2 shows the results of our method and that of the best previous one (*i.e.* Krishnan et al.) including the cost associated with each period and the total cost over the whole time planning horizon. According to the results, a 4.73 percent improvement is resulted in the total cost.

Table 2. The results of the real case study

Period \ Approach	Krishnan et al	ACO/SA	Percentage Savings
1	$194,638.76	$174,438	10.38 %
2	$211,428.07	$200,103	5.36 %
3	$347,675.62	$339,793	2.27 %
4	$464,675.32	$459,835	1.04 %
5	$560,878.42	$521,021	7.11 %
Total Cost	$1,779,296.19	$1,695,190	4.73 %

4   Conclusion

In this paper, the hybrid ACO/SA algorithm was proposed to solve the SDFLP with better results than SA algorithm. An outstanding performance of the proposed algorithm was also concluded by solving a real world case study taken from literature. Finally, the following works can be taken into consideration in the future researches. Firstly is the consideration of the selectivity of the next machine as a function of time periods by regarding the parts flow of each period rather than the average flow. Secondly is the use of fuzzy logic to update trail intensity and temperature.

References

1. Ram, D.J., Sreenivas, T.H., Subramaniam, G.: Parallel Simulated Annealing Algorithms. Journal of Parallel and Distributed Computing 37, 207–212 (1996)
2. Huntley, C., Brown, D.: A Parallel Heuristic for Quadratic Assignment Problems. Computers Ops. Res. 18(3), 275–289 (1991)
3. Mahdi, A.H., Amet, H., Portman, M.C.: Physical Layout with Minimization of The Transport Cost (Research Internal Report). LORIA, Nancy (1998)
4. Gambardella, L.M., Taillard, E.D., Dorigo, M.: Ant Colonies for the Quadratic Assignment Problem. Journal of Operational Research Society 50, 167–176 (1999)
5. Mir, M., Imam, M.H.: A Hybrid Optimization Approach for Layout Design Of Unequal-Area Facilities. Computers & Industrial Engineering 39(1–2), 49–63 (2001)
6. Lee, Y.H., Lee, M.H.: A Shape-Based Block Layout Approach to Facility Layout Problems Using Hybrid Genetic Algorithm. Computers & Industrial Engineering 42, 237–248 (2002)
7. McKendall, A.R., Shang, J.: Hybrid Ant Systems for The Dynamic Facility Layout Problem. Computers and Operations Research 33, 790–803 (2006)
8. Ramkumar, A.S., Ponnambalam, S.G.: Hybrid Ant Colony System for Solving Quadratic Assignment Formulation of Machine Layout Problems. IEEE (2006)
9. Teo, Y.T., Ponnambalam, S.G.: A Hybrid ACO/PSO Heuristic to Solve Single Row Layout Problem. In: 4th IEEE Conference on Automation Science and Engineering Key Bridge Marriott, Washington DC, USA, pp. 597–602 (2008)
10. Chen, G., Rogers, J.: Managing Dynamic Facility Layout with Multiple Objectives. In: PICMET Proceedings, Portland, Oregon USA, August 2-6, pp. 1175–1184 (2009)
11. Yuying, L., Qiaoyan, W., Lixiang, L., Haipeng, P.: Hybrid Chaotic Ant Swarm Optimization. Chaos, Solitons and Fractals 42, 880–889 (2009)
12. Koopmans, T.C., Beckman, M.: Assignment Problems and the Location of Economic Activities. Econometric 25, 53–76 (1957)
13. Moslemipour, G., Lee, T.S.: Intelligent Design of A Dynamic Machine Layout in Uncertain Environment of Flexible Manufacturing Systems. J. Intell. Manuf. (2011), doi:10.1007/s10845-010-0499-8
14. Krishnan, K.K., Cheraghi, S.H., Nayak, C.N.: Dynamic From-Between Chart: A New Tool for Solving Dynamic Facility Layout Problems. Int. J. Industrial and Systems Engineering 1(1/2), 182–200 (2006)

Table A.1.   Input Data

Parts	Machine sequence
1	5→3→10→9→11
2	11→10→3→9→5
3	1→12→8
4	12→8→1
5	8→1→12
6	7→2→6
7	2→4→7→6
8	6→7→4→2
9	2→6
10	5→10→3

Table A.2.   Distance between machine lotions

To From	1	2	3	4	5	6	7	8	9	10	11	12
1	0	10	20	30	40	50	70	60	50	40	30	20
2	10	0	10	20	30	40	60	50	40	30	20	30
3	20	10	0	10	20	30	50	40	30	20	30	40
4	30	20	10	0	10	20	40	30	20	30	40	50
5	40	30	20	10	0	10	30	20	30	40	50	60
6	50	40	30	20	10	0	20	30	40	50	60	70
7	70	60	50	40	30	20	0	10	20	30	40	50
8	60	50	40	30	20	30	10	0	10	20	30	40
9	50	40	30	20	30	40	20	10	0	10	20	30
10	40	30	20	30	40	50	03	20	10	0	10	20
11	30	20	30	40	50	60	40	30	20	10	0	10
12	20	30	40	50	60	70	50	40	30	20	10	0

Table A.3.   Input data for part demands for periods 1 to 5

	Period 1		Period 2		Period 3		Period 4		Period 5	
Part	Mean	Variance	Mean	Variance	Mean	Variance	Mean	Variance	Mean	Variance
1	6220	1073	5656	1118	3764	2584	6503	2629	6503	1553
2	2565	2824	8863	2442	6636	1609	9101	1344	7589	2940
3	7623	1893	9120	2318	3543	1372	4554	1668	5948	1388
4	2067	1573	4347	2578	2646	2986	9746	2262	8496	1812
5	8965	1283	2358	2251	2720	1909	7540	1898	8085	1663
6	8736	2892	9998	1190	7804	1045	3677	1417	2066	2998
7	6823	1373	8104	2493	6861	2062	4910	2499	8772	1856
8	6088	1030	9696	2751	3116	1195	9253	1052	8257	2355
9	6907	1641	7493	2087	4458	1854	5141	1384	6664	2676
10	4093	2316	5496	1447	1606	1177	7172	2648	5258	1236

Table A.4. Input data for part demands for periods 6 to 10

Part	Period 6 Mean	Variance	Period 7 Mean	Variance	Period 8 Mean	Variance	Period 9 Mean	Variance	Period 10 Mean	Variance
1	5468	1713	6510	1464	1060	2562	7409	2923	2132	2190
2	7614	1907	2045	2356	1231	2389	2802	1073	4250	2045
3	7543	2469	8514	2561	6809	1738	3857	1720	1380	2752
4	3220	2587	1847	1439	6784	2841	4097	1464	1386	2403
5	3502	1871	7706	2098	6153	1587	9746	1673	5346	2680
6	1784	2296	3538	1882	8842	2395	2321	2437	4873	2881
7	2627	1332	2278	2642	2833	2193	1311	2632	6757	2135
8	1487	2122	6682	1391	1104	2158	3767	1999	6488	2999
9	8362	2277	9602	2681	5478	1933	7343	1850	6680	2676
10	4417	2322	2105	2501	2384	1881	8405	2703	4007	2499

ACO with Fuzzy Pheromone Laying Mechanism

Liu Yu[1,*], Jian-Feng Yan[2], Guang-Rong Yan[1], and Lei Yi[1]

[1] School of Mechanical Engineering and Automation Beihang University,
Beijing 100191, China
[2] School of Computer Science & Technology, Soochow University, Soochow 215006, China
buaa_liuyu@163.com

Abstract. Pheromone laying mechanism is an important aspect to affect performance of ant colony optimization (ACO) algorithms. In most existing ACO algorithms, either only one best ant is allowed to release pheromone, or all the ants are allowed to lay pheromone in the same way. To make full use of ants to explore high quality routes, a fuzzy pheromone laying mechanism is proposed in the paper. The amount of ants that are allowed to lay pheromone varies at each iteration to differentiate different contributions of the ants. The experimental results show that the proposed algorithm possesses high searching ability and excellent convergence performance in comparison with the classic ACO algorithm.

Keywords: ant colony optimization (ACO), fuzzy, pheromone laying.

1 Introduction

Swarm intelligence is a kind of population-based artificial intelligence inspired by social animals or insects, such as ants, fish schools, and bird flocks. By mimicking the behaviors of such animals or insects, many intelligent algorithms have been proposed to solve the real-world problems. Ant colony optimization (ACO) is one of the most famous swarm intelligence algorithms that mimics the real ant system[1]. The ant system can be regarded as a distributed system where each ant possesses very limited abilities. However, the whole colony can accomplish very complex tasks such as foraging, cooperative transport and brood sorting. This is because that there exists an underlying mechanism making the individual ant exchange information with others to reach consensus on complex tasks. In the complex behaviors such as foraging, pheromone is found by biologists to act as stigmergy to coordinate the ants' behavior to find the shortest route from nest to food source[2]. Because of high performance in solving combination problems, ACO has been successfully applied in many fields, such as topology design [3], vehicle routing problem[4], classification[5], optimizing discounted cash flows[6], distributed image retrieval[7], and grid workflow scheduling problem[8].

---

* Corresponding author.

D.-S. Huang et al. (Eds.): ICIC 2012, CCIS 304, pp. 109–117, 2012.
© Springer-Verlag Berlin Heidelberg 2012

Ants deposit pheromone when they move. In the real foraging behavior, ants create a trail of pheromone between nest and food source by laying pheromone. When facing choice of routes, following ants can observe such pheromone trail and is more likely to choose the route with higher pheromone. In this simple way, the pheromone on the route will get enforced to finally form a positive feedback. That is the mechanism that a path attracts more and more ants and the path is reinforced. Based on the pheromone laying mechanism, the first ACO algorithm called Ant System is proposed. Although the initial Ant System is inferior in some aspects, many improved ACO algorithms have been proposed, such as Ant Colony System[9], Elitist Ant System[10] and Max-Min ant system[11].

Inspired by the pheromone laying phenomenon in real ant colony, all kinds of ACO algorithms adopt several artificial pheromone laying mechanisms. Different pheromone laying mechanisms used in these ACO methods affect the performance of the ACO in a complex way. It is often difficult to select the proper mechanisms. Hence, there are three main questions to be answered:

1) How many (artificial) ants should we use to construct an effective and efficient artificial ant colony according to the different problem scale?

2) How many ants can lay pheromone to achieve an optimal solution?

3) What mechanism should we select to make each ant lay pheromone in order to reach an acceptable consensus?

To answer the questions above, this paper reviews the main pheromone laying methods used in the main ACO algorithms and proposes a new fuzzy pheromone laying mechanism.

The initial ACO, i.e., Ant System was first applied to solving the Travelling Salesman Problem (TSP), which is one of the most famous combinatorial optimization problems. TSP has been tackled with many meta-heuristic methods, such as simulated annealing, genetic algorithms, tabu search and neural networks. Hence, TSP is a natural choice to compare performance of all kinds of algorithms with existing mature meta-heuristic methods. In this paper, we will validate the proposed fuzzy pheromone laying mechanism in three representative TSP instances, i.e., small-scale, medium-scale and large-scale.

In this paper, we will introduce a new fuzzy pheromone laying mechanism and use it in the Max-Min ant system called FuzAS. Performance of FuzAS is demonstrated by extensive comparison with the original Max-Min ant system and Ant Colony System on three TSP instances of different sizes, respectively. The remainder of the paper is organized as follows. Section 2 reviews several pheromone laying mechanisms in existing ACO algorithms. In Section 3, we propose a new fuzzy pheromone laying mechanism. Section 4 shows experimental results and analysis of the proposed algorithm. In Section 5, we briefly summarize our main results and envision future research.

2   Pheromone Deposit Mechanism in ACO

Many problems can be classified or transferred into TSP problems. In swam intelligence filed, TSP problems are used as benchmark to validate performance of given algorithms, especially for ACO algorithms. To explicit the present pheromone depositing mechanism in ACO, in this section all the algorithms are discussed on TSP problems.

Pheromone deposit mechanism is an important factor to affect performance of ACO. In the original ACO algorithms, all ants deposit pheromone in the same way. However, with the development of ACO, different pheromone deposit mechanism are put forth to achieve higher performance. Different pheromone laying affect performance of the ACO algorithms put forward. To explicit and compare the different pheromone deposit mechanism, amount of ants to deposit pheromone and whether or not the pheromone are deposited in the same way will be considered.

In ACO, the pheromone update process can be divided into two steps: the evaporating process and the releasing process. In the evaporating process, pheromone of all the routes decreases by a constant quality. The evaporating process functions to prevent unlimited accumulation of pheromone. Each ant deposits pheromone when it finishes the route exploring process. In ACO, the evaporating process functions according to the following formula:

$$\tau_{ij} \leftarrow (1-\rho)\tau_{ij} \tag{1}$$

Where ρ denotes a evaporating constant.

In the releasing process, the routes passed by the ants get reinforced according to a given formula according to different algorithms. By this two-step pheromone updating process, pheromone of the routes that never get chosen by ants will get less and less and the routes that get chosen by more ants will get more pheromone.

Ant System (AS) is the first ACO algorithm. After the pheromone evaporating process in all routes, the pheromone releasing process executes followed by the formula:

$$\tau_{ij} \leftarrow \tau_{ij} + \sum_{k=1}^{m} \Delta\tau_{ij}^{k} \tag{2}$$

Where $\Delta\tau_{ij}^{k}$ denotes pheromone released by ant k on the routes it passed.

Elitist strategy for ant system (EAS) is the first improvement on the Ant System. Its main idea is to strengthen the pheromone of the best route T^{bs} that is ever found so far. In EAS, the best route so far will get additional pheromone with a given amount at the end of each iteration. Hence, pheromone updating rule is as follows:

$$\tau_{ij} \leftarrow \tau_{ij} + \sum_{k=1}^{m} \Delta\tau_{ij}^{k} + e\Delta\tau_{ij}^{bs} \tag{3}$$

Where e denotes the weigh assigned to route T^{bs} and $\Delta\tau_{ij}^{bs}$ denotes the additional pheromone given to route T^{bs}.

Ant system with elitist strategy and ranking (AS_rank) is another improved ACO algorithm. The ants will be ranked according to the quality of the routes they find in AS_rank. Only the ant finding the best route so far and the best w ants can release pheromone. The ants lay pheromone according to the following formula:

$$\tau_{ij} \leftarrow \tau_{ij} + \sum_{r=1}^{w-1} (w-r)\Delta\tau_{ij}^{r} + w\Delta\tau_{ij}^{bs} \tag{4}$$

MAX-MIN Ant System (MMAS) has improved the original ant algorithm in several ways. Only one ant finding the best route in the present iteration or the best route so far can lay pheromone. The quantity of pheromone in the route is limited within an interval $[\tau_{min}, \tau_{max}]$ to avoid unlimited accumulation or evaporation of pheromone. Pheromone deposit in the routes according to the following formula:

$$\tau_{ij} \leftarrow \tau_{ij} + \Delta\tau_{ij}^{bs} \tag{5}$$

Where $\Delta\tau_{ij}^{bs}$ denotes pheromone released by the best ant so far or best ant in the present iteration.

3   Fuzzy Pheromone Laying Mechanism

In ACO, different algorithms allow different amount of ants to lay pheromone. In the original AS, all the ants are allowed to release pheromone and these ants lay pheromone in the same way. In AS_rank, the best w ants can lay pheromone but each ant is assigned a weight, indicating the pheromone proportion it releases. While in EAS and MMAS, only one best ant is allowed to lay pheromone. Detailed comparison of the pheromone laying mechanism in different ACO algorithms are illustrated in table 1. From the search study of the algorithms above, it can be told that different amount of ants laying pheromone have consequence on performance of the algorithms. Based on the data of the given algorithm, it seems that the less amount of ants laying pheromone, the better performance. However, there isn't a strict computational study to validate this assumption.

Table 1. Comparison of different pheromone laying mechanism

Ants laying pheromone	ACO Algorithms			
	AS	EAS	AS_rank	MMAS
Quantity	all	1	w	1
Weighted	No	No	Yes	No

To find out effect of amount of ants laying pheromone on the quality of the results, experiments are designed using different size of TSP problem. To illustrate the generality of the phenomenon, we carry out experiments on the middle-scale TSP instance with 101 cities and the large-scale TSP instance with 200 cities, respectively.

The two pieces of curve in fig1 and fig2 denote the average length and the minimum length, respectively. The abscissa indicates the amount of ants laying pheromone in the end of iteration and the ordinate indicates the length of tour. From the experiments shown in fig 1 and fig 2, the best result (shortest route) doesn't turn up when only one ant is allowed to lay pheromone. When amount of the ants laying pheromone is from 10% to 30% of the total ants, we get the best result.

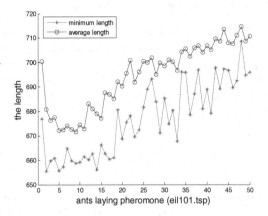

Fig. 1. Result of TSP eil101

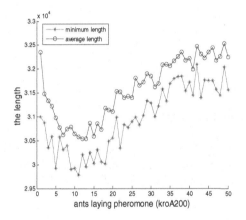

Fig. 2. Result of TSP kroA200

Because the best amount of ants laying pheromone is within an interval, it's hard to tell what exact amount of ants should be chosen to get the best result. To solve this problem, we introduce a fuzzy pheromone laying method in this paper.

3.1 Variable Ants to Lay Pheromone

Different from the existing ACO algorithms that the amount of ant laying pheromone is set as crisp number, amount of ants to release pheromone in this paper is a fuzzy quantity. At each iteration, the amount of ants that explore new routes is set to a constant N, usually equal to the amount of cities. However, the amount of ant laying pheromone varies with iterations. According to the experimental results shown in fig 1 and fig 3, the interval is set as [0.1, 0.3] and the ants varies from 0.1N to 0.3N at each iteration.

3.2   Variable Weight for Each Ant Laying Pheromone

Assume that there are M ants that are allowed to lay pheromone at one cycle and M is within interval [0.1N, 0.3N]. These M ants find routes with different length, i.e., results with different quality. However, traditional ACO algorithms didn't notice this important characteristic. To make full use of this feature, we differentiate the weight of the ants laying pheromone. Each ant gets a weight according to the tour length it finds. Weight w_k for ant k is calculated as follows:

$$w_k = L_k / \sum_{r=1}^{M} L_M \qquad (6)$$

The effect of the best route so far on performance of the algorithm has been proven by many studies. To utilize the best route so far, we assume that ant finding the best route always functions and has a weigh w_k =1. Hence, the ants lay pheromone according to the following formula:

$$\tau_{ij} \leftarrow \tau_{ij} + \sum_{r=1}^{M} w_M \Delta \tau_{ij}^{r} + \Delta \tau_{ij}^{bs} \qquad (7)$$

4   Experiment and Discussion

We implemented the fuzzy pheromone laying mechanism on AS. To illustrate the strength and weakness ofthe proposed algorithm, we carried out several experiments. The default value of the parameters was α=1, β=5, ρ=0.5. Ants' amount is equal to quantity of cities.

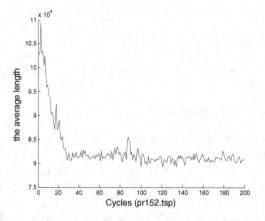

Fig. 3. Result of TSP pr152

Figs. 3-4 show performance of the proposed algorithm within 200 cycles. Fig. 3 shows the average length found by ants with evolution of cycles. We note that the algorithm can achieve good quality at early stage of the iteration. This fast convergence is caused by the variable ants to lay pheromone. By allowing part of the good ants to lay pheromone, the fuzzy pheromone laying mechanism ensures that the pheromone accumulates in a proper manner based on performance of ants.

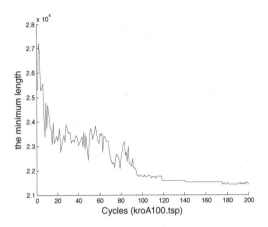

Fig. 4. Result of TSP kroA100

Fig. 4 shows the best length of the found tour at each iteration. Although good results are achieved at early stage as illustrated in fig. 3, the results are refined by the algorithm continuously. The fuzzy pheromone laying mechanism ensures that the algorithm will not exhibit stagnation behavior.

To validate performance of the proposed algorithm, we compare its performance with other four famous ACO algorithms including AS, AS-rank, MMAS and ACS. To have a comprehensive comparison, three TSP instances (eil51, kroA100 and pr152) are tested.

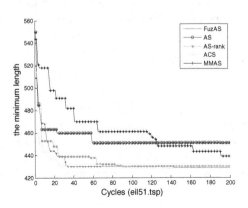

Fig. 5. Comparison on eil51

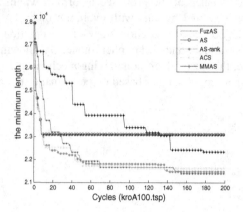

Fig. 6. Comparison on kroA100

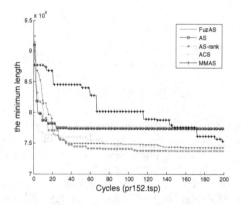

Fig. 7. Comparison on pr152

Figs. 5-7 show that our algorithm exhibits high performance in these instance. Among the five algorithms, AS and AS-rank can't achieve the shortest route while FuzAS, MMAS and ACS always achieve the best result. Moreover, FuzAS can get the best result much earlier that the other two algorithms.

5   Conclusions

Different from the classic ACO algorithms allowing crisp amount of ants to lay pheromone, we have introduced a new fuzzy pheromone mechanism in this paper. The fuzzy pheromone allows that the amount of ants laying pheromone varies at each iteration to find the best route faster. In addition, each ant is assigned a weight according to the route quality it found to emphasize the different contribution of each ant.

References

1. Dorigo, M., Birattari, M., Stutzle, T.: Ant Colony Optimization. IEEE Computational Intelligence Magazine 1(4), 28–39 (2006)
2. Deneubourg, J.L., et al.: The Self-organizing Exploratory Pattern of the Argentine ant. Journal of Insect Behavior 3(2), 159–168 (1990)
3. Khan, S., Engelbrecht, A.: A Fuzzy Ant Colony Optimization Algorithm for Topology Design of Distributed Local Area Networks. In: 2008 IEEE Swarm Intelligence Symposium. IEEE, St. Louis (2008)
4. Donati, A.V., et al.: Time Dependent Vehicle Routing Problem with a Multi Ant Colony System. European Journal of Operational Research 185(3), 1174–1191 (2008)
5. Martens, D., et al.: Classification with Ant Colony Optimization. IEEE Transactions on Evolutionary Computation 11(5), 651–665 (2007)
6. Chen, W.N., et al.: Optimizing Discounted Cash Flows in Project Scheduling–An Ant Colony Optimization Approach. IEEE Transactions on Systems, Man, and Cybernetics, Part C: Applications and Reviews 40(1), 64–77 (2010)
7. Picard, D., Revel, A., Cord, M.: An Application of Swarm Intelligence to Distributed Image Retrieval. Information Sciences (2010)
8. Chen, W.N., Zhang, J.: An Ant Colony Optimization Approach to a Grid Workflow Scheduling Problem with Various QoS Requirements. IEEE Transactions on Systems, Man, and Cybernetics, Part C: Applications and Reviews 39(1), 29–43 (2009)

Locating Tandem Repeats in Weighted Biological Sequences[*]

Hui Zhang[1], Qing Guo[2], and Costas S. Iliopoulos[3]

[1] College of Computer Science and Technology, Zhejiang University of Technology,
Hangzhou, 310023, China
zhangh@zjut.edu.cn
[2] College of Computer Science, Zhejiang University, Hangzhou, 310027, China
13385718936@189.cn
[3] Department of Computer Science, King's College London Strand,
London WC2R 2LS, England
csi@dcs.kcl.ac.uk

Abstract. A weighted biological sequence is a string in which a set of characters may appear at each position with respective probabilities of occurrence. We attempt to locate all the tandem repeats in a weighted sequence. By introducing the idea of equivalence classes in weighted sequences, we identify the tandem repeats of every possible length using an iterative partitioning technique, and present the $O(n^2)$ time algorithm.

Keywords: Weighted sequence, tandem repeat, equivalence class, equivalence relation.

1   Introduction

A weighted biological sequence, called for short a weighted sequence, is a special string that allows a set of characters to occur at each position of the sequence with respective probability. Weighted sequences are apt at summarizing poorly defined short sequences, e.g. transcription factor binding sites and the profiles of protein families and complete chromosome sequences [5]. With this model, one can attempt to locate the biological important motifs, and to estimate the binding energy of the proteins. It thus exhibits theoretical and practical significance to design powerful algorithms on weighted sequences.

This paper concentrates on locating those tandem repeats in a weighted sequence. Tandem repeats occur in a string when a substring is repeated for two or more times and the repetitions are directly adjacent to each other. For example, the substring ATT occurs in string X = CATTATTATTG for three times, and each occurrence of ATT is consecutive, one after the other. Then ATT is a tandem repeat of length 3 of X.

---

[*] Corresponding author: Qing Guo, College of Computer Science, Zhejiang University, Hangzhou, China. Tel: 0086-571-88939701. Fax: 0086-571-88867185.

D.-S. Huang et al. (Eds.): ICIC 2012, CCIS 304, pp. 118–123, 2012.

The motivation for investigating tandem repeats in weighted sequences comes from the striking feature of DNA that vast quantities of tandemly repetitive segments occur in the genome, with high proportion of more than 50 percent in fact [13]. Some examples are Microsatellite, minisatellite, and satellite DNA [10].

Large amount of work has been done to find all tandem repeats in non-weighted strings. These solutions can be divided into two categories: One employs traditional string comparison and searching method, the most famous algorithms are Crochemore's partitioning[3], and LZ decomposition[8] with time complexity O(nlogn) respectively. The other computes tandem repeats by constructing suffix tree and suffix array. By limiting the number of output, these algorithms can also reach O(nlogn) time[1, 4, 9, 11].

However, relatively less work has been studied in weighted sequences circumstance. Iliopoulos et al. [6, 7] were the first to touch this field, and extract repeats and other types of repetitive motifs in weighted sequences by constructing weighted suffix tree. Another solution [2] finds tandem repeats of length d in O(nlogd) time.

The paper is organized as follows. Section 2 gives the necessary theoretical preliminaries used. Section 3 introduces the all-tandem-repeats problem and presents an O(n2) algorithm. Finally Section 4 concludes.

2   Preliminaries

A biological sequence used throughout the paper is a string either over the 4-character DNA alphabet $\Sigma=\{A,C,G,T\}$ of nucleotides or the 20-character alphabet of amino acids. Assume that readers have essential knowledge of the basic concepts of strings, now we extend parts of it to weighted sequences. Formally speaking:

Definition 1. *Let an alphabet be* $\Sigma = \{\sigma_1, \sigma_2, \ldots, \sigma_l\}$. *A weighted sequence X over Σ, denoted by* $X[1, n] = X[1]X[2]\ldots X[n]$, *is a sequence of n sets X[i] for* $1\le i\le n$, *such that:*

$$X[i] = \{(\sigma_j, \pi_i(\sigma_j)) \mid 1 \le j \le l, \pi_i(\sigma_j) \ge 0, and \sum_{j=1}^{l} \pi_i(\sigma_j) = 1\}$$

Each X[i] is a set of couples $(\sigma_j, \pi_i(\sigma_i))$, *where* $\pi_i(\sigma_i)$ *is the non-negative weight of σj at position i, representing the probability of having character σ_j at position i of X.*

Let X be a weighted sequence of length n, σ be a character in Σ. We say that σ occurs at position i of X if and only $\pi i (\sigma)> 0$, written as $\sigma \in X[i]$. A nonempty non-weighted string f [1, m] ($m\in[1, n]$) occurs at position i of X if and only if position i + j − 1 is an occurrence of the character f [j] in X, for all $1\le j\le m$. Then f is said to be a factor of X, and i is an occurrence of f in X.

The probability of the presence of f at position i of X is called the weight of f at i, written as $\pi i(f)$, which can be obtained by using the cumulative weight, defined as the product of the weight of the character at every position of f, that is, $\pi_i(f) = \prod_{j=1}^{m} \pi_{i+j-1}(f[j])$.

Considering the following weighted sequence:

$$X = \begin{Bmatrix} (A,0.5) \\ (C,0.25) \\ (G,0.25) \end{Bmatrix} G \begin{Bmatrix} (A,0.6) \\ (C,0.4) \end{Bmatrix} \begin{Bmatrix} (A,0.25) \\ (C,0.25) \\ (G,0.25) \\ (T,0.25) \end{Bmatrix} C \qquad (1)$$

the weight of f =CGAT at position 1 of X is: $\pi_1(f) = 0.25 \times 1 \times 0.6 \times 0.25 = 0.0375$. That is, CGAT occurs at position 1 of X with probability 0.0375.

Definition 2. *A factor f of length p of a weighted sequence X is called a tandem repeat in X if there exists a triple (i, f, l) such that for each $0 \le j < l-1$, position $i + jp$ is an occurrence of the factor of f in X.*

As scientists pay more attention to the pieces with high probabilities in DNA sequences, we fix a constant threshold for the presence probability of the motif, that is, only those occurrences with probability not less than this threshold are counted.

Definition 3. *Let f be a factor of length d of a weighted sequence X that occurs at position i, a real constant threshold $k \ge 1$. We say that f is a real factor of X if and only if the weight of f at i, $\pi_i(f)$, is at least $1/k$. Exactly,* $\prod_{j=1}^{d} \pi_{i+j-1}(f[j]) \ge 1/k$.

In the above example, set $1/k = 0.3$, then AGA is a real factor of X that occurs at position 1 since $\pi_1(AGA) = 0.5 \times 1 \times 0.6 = 0.3 \ge 0.3$, while CAC is not a real factor of X at position 3 since $\pi_3(CAC) = 0.1 < 0.3$.

3   The All-Tandem-Repeats Problem

Now we introduce the all-tandem-repeats problem in weighted sequences as below:

Problem 1. Given a weighted sequence $X[1, n]$ and a real constant $k \ge 1$, the all-tandem-repeats problem identifies the set S of all triples (i, f, l), where $1 \le |f| \le n/2$ and f is a real factor of X.

Our algorithm for picking all the tandem repeats is based on the following idea of equivalence relation on positions of a string.

Definition 4. *Given a string x of length n over Σ, an integer $p \in \{1, 2, \ldots, n\}$, S be a set of positions of x: $\{1, 2, \ldots, n - p + 1\}$, then E_p is defined to be an equivalence relation on S such that: for two i, $j \in S$, $(i, j) \in E_p$ if $x[i, i + p - 1] = x[j, j + p - 1]$.*

In other words, two positions i and j of x are said to be p-equivalent when two substrings of length p starting at i and j in x are identical. It is clear that each E_p-class of cardinality not less than two records the occurrences of a repetitive substring of length p in x. Hence, the problem of computing all the repeated substrings of length p can be rephrased as finding the corresponding E_p-classes.

By improving the method for computing repeated patterns in weighted sequences we proposed in [12], we first simulate the definition for E_p-classes of non-weighted strings, and give the following weighted version:

Definition 5. *Consider a factor f of length p in a weighted sequence X* [1, *n*]. *An E_p-class associated with f is the set $C_f(p)$ of all position-probability pairs (i, $\pi_i(f)$), such that f occurs at position i with probability $\pi_i(f) \geq 1/k$.*

$C_f(p)$ is an ordered list that contains all the positions of X where f occurs. Note that only the occurrences of those real factors are considered. For this reason, the probability of each appearance of a factor should be recorded and kept for the next iteration. In this case, a position i is allowed to go to several but no more than $|\Sigma|$ different E_p-classes, due to the uncertainty of weighted sequences. The process of building E_p-classes from E_{p-1}-classes can be computed based upon the following corollary:

Corollary 1. *Let $p \in \{1, 2, \ldots, n\}$, $i, j \in \{1, 2, \ldots, n - p\}$. Then:*

$$((i, \pi_i(f)), (j, \pi_j(f))) \in C_f(p) \quad iff ((i, \pi_i(f')), (j, \pi_j(f'))) \in C_{f'}(p\text{-}1) \quad and$$
$$((i + p - 1, \pi_{i+p-1}(\sigma)), (j + p - 1, \pi_{i+p-1}(\sigma))) \in C_\sigma(1)$$

Where $\sigma \in \Sigma$, f and f' are two factors of length p and p-1 respectively, such that $f = f'\sigma$ and $\pi_j(f) \geq 1/k$, $\pi_j(f) \geq 1/k$.

Our algorithm for picking all the tandem repeats of X then operates as follows:

1. "Partition" all the n positions of X to build E_1 and detect all the tandem repeats of length 1: For every character $\sigma \in \Sigma$, create a class $C_\sigma(1)$ that is an ordered list of couples $(i, \pi_i(\sigma))$, where i is an occurrence of σ in X with probability not less than $1/k$. Each class composed of more than one element forms E_1. Those $C_\sigma(1)$s in which the distance between two or more adjacent position i is 1 report the tandem repeat of length 1.
2. Iteratively compute E_p-classes from E_{p-1}-classes using the above corollary for $p \geq 2$, and find all the tandem repeats of length p: Take each class $C(p\text{-}1)$ of E_{p-1}, partition $C(p\text{-}1)$ so that any two positions $i, j \in C(p\text{-}1)$ go to the same E_p-class if positions $i+p-1$, $j+p-1$ belongs to a same E_1-class, and this E_p-class represents a real factor of X.
3. For each E_p-class $C(p)$ partitioned by $C(p\text{-}1)$, if the cardinality of $C(p)$ is at least two and any distance between two or more adjacent positions in $C(p)$ equals p, add the corresponding triple into the tandem repeat set S. Eliminate those $C(p)$ s who are singletons, and keep the rest to proceed the iterative computation at stage $p + 1$.
4. The computation stops at stage L, once no new E_{L+1}-classes can be created or each E_L-class is a singleton.

We use a doubly linked list to store each equivalence class, which needs $O(n)$ space for a bounded-size alphabet. Algorithm 1 depicts the procedure to construct all possible E_p-classes from a certain E_{p-1}-class, and report those tandem repeats of length p. The running time of Algorithm 1 is proportional to the size of the given E_{p-1}-class, since tandem repeats of length p are reported along with the partitioning of the given

E_{p-1}-class. Taking all the E_{p-1}-classes into account, stage p requires $O(n)$ time and $O(n)$ extra space to report all the tandem repeats of length p.

As stated above, our algorithm for computing all tandem repeats repeatedly calls function Create-Equiv-Class. It is easy to see that it takes $O(n^2)$ time for a constant-size alphabet, since each refinement of E_p from E_{p-1} costs linear time, and there are $O(n)$ stages in total. Thus the overall time complexity of finding all tandem repeats of every possible length amounts to $O(n^2)$.

Theorem 1. The all-tandem-repeats problem can be solved in $O(n^2)$ time.

Algorithm 1. Identify tandem repeats of length p
Input: An E_{p-1}-pair $(C_f(p-1), f)$: class $C_f(p-1)$, a factor f corresponding to C_{p-1}
Output: All the E_p-pairs derived from the input
1: **Function** Create-Equiv-Class$(C_f(p-1), f)$
2: for each $(i, _i(f)) \in C_f(p-1)$ do
3:      $l \leftarrow 0$
4:      for each $_j \in X[i+p-1]$ do
5:          $f_j \leftarrow f _j$
6:          $_i(f_j) \leftarrow _i(f) * _{i+p-1}(_j)$
7:          while $_{i+1}(f_j) \geq 1/k$ do
8:              add $(i+1, _{i+1}(j))$ to $C_{f_j}(p)$
9:              $l \leftarrow l + 1$
10:         if $l > 1$ then
11:             $S \leftarrow S \cup (i, f_j, l)$
12: for each j do
13:     if $|C_{f_j}(p)| = 1$ then
14:         delete $C_{f_j}(p)$
15:     else
16:         add $(C_{f_j}(p), f_j)$ to E_p
17: return E_p

4   Conclusions

The paper investigated the tandem repeats arisen in weighted sequences. As opposed to the non-weighted version, the uncertainty of weighted sequences and the presence probability of every character in the sequence must be considered. We devised efficient algorithm for identify all the tandem repeats in a weighted sequence, which operates in $O(n^2)$ time.

Acknowledgments. This work was partially supported by Zhejiang Provincial Natural Science Foundation under Grant No: Y1101043 and Foundation of Zhejiang Provincial Education Department under Grant No: Y201018240 of China.

References

1. Apostolico, A., Prepamta, F.P.: Optimal Off-line Detection of Repetitions in a string. Theoretical Computer Science 22, 297–315 (1983)
2. Christodoulakis, M., Iliopoulos, C.S., Mouchard, L., Perdikuri, K., Tsakalidis, A., Tsichlas, K.: Computation of Repetitions and Regularities on Biological Weighted Sequences. Journal of Computational Biology 13(6), 1214–1231 (2006)
3. Crochemore, M.: An Optimal Algorithm for Computing the Repetitions in a Word. Information Processing Letter 12(5), 244–250 (1981)
4. Franêk, F., Smyth, W.F., Tang, Y.: Computing All Repeats Using Suffix Arrays. Journal of Automata, Languages and Combinatorics 8(4), 579–591 (2003)
5. Gusfield, D.: Algorithms on Strings, Trees and Sequences: Computer Science and Computational Biology. Cambridge University Press (1997)
6. Iliopoulos, C.S., Makris, C., Panagis, Y., Perdikuri, K., Theodoridis, E., Tsakalidis, A.: Efficient Algorithms for Handling Molecular Weighted Sequences. IFIP Theoretical Computer Science 147, 265–278 (2004)
7. Iliopoulos, C.S., Mouchard, L., Perdikuri, K., Tsakalidis, A.: Computing the Repetitions in a Weighted Sequence. In: Proc. of the 8th Prague Stringology Conference (PSC 2003), pp. 91–98 (2003)
8. Main, M.G., Lorentz, R.J.: An $O(nlngn)$ Algorithm for Finding All Repetitions in a String. Journal of Algorithms 5, 422–432 (1984)
9. Manber, U., Myers, G.: Suffix Arrays: A New Method for On-Line String Searches. SIAM Journal on Computing 22(5), 935–948 (1993)
10. Ohno, S.: Repeats of Base Oligomers as the Primordial Coding Sequences of the Primeval Earth and Their Vestiges in Modern Genes. Journal of Molecular Evolution 20, 313–321 (1984)
11. Stoye, J., Gusfield, D.: Simple and Flexible Detection of Contiguous Repeats Using a Suffix Tree. In: Farach-Colton, M. (ed.) CPM 1998. LNCS, vol. 1448, pp. 140–152. Springer, Heidelberg (1998)
12. Zhang, H., Guo, Q., Iliopoulos, C.S.: Loose and Strict Repeats in Weighted Sequences. Protein and Peptide Letters 17(9), 1136–1142 (2010)
13. The Human Genome Project(HGP), http://www.nbgri.nih.gov/HGP/

Analysis of Flow Field in the Cylinder of Gasoline Engine before and after Being Turbocharged

Hongjuan Ren[1,2], Yongxiang Tian[3], Qihua Ma[1], and Jiao Luo[1]

[1] College of Automotive, Shanghai University of Engineering Science
[2] College of Automotive, Tongji University, Shanghai 201804, China
[3] Scientific Research Center, Shanghai Fire Research Institute of Ministry of Public Security
ren-hongjuan@163.com

Abstract. Turbocharged gasoline engine can effectively improve engine performance, but it is more easy to lead to deflagration and other abnormal combustion phenomenon. In this paper, flow field in the cylinder of gasoline engine before and after being turbocharged is simulated instantaneously by numerical simulation. The results show that when the gasoline engine is turbocharged, the air flow in the cylinder is unchanged, which provide the visualization of the reason for deflagration of turbocharged gasoline engine. And the results provide the theoretical reference for the design and improvement of turbocharged gasoline engine.

Keywords: Gasoline Engine, Turbocharging, Numerical Simulation, Flow Field.

1   Introduction

Supercharging technology plays a very important role on reducing emissions, increasing power, improving the engine power density and recovering power at an altitude[1]. Supercharging technology was first used in diesel engines, supercharging technology has been used in all high and middle power diesel engine, and 70% of small vehicle diesel engines has also used supercharging technology [2]. Practice has proved that the gasoline engine with supercharging technology maybe be affected by detonation, cooling difficulty and difficult match to turbocharger size [3], thus it is the fundamental premise for promoting the supercharging technology on gasoline engines to solve knock of turbocharged gasoline engines. The reason of gasoline engine detonation can be found by comparing the work process of gasoline engine before and after be turbocharged, which will provide theoretical guidance for avoiding gasoline engine detonation. At present, the methods of researching gasoline engine working process are experiment and numerical simulation. Numerical simulation is not affected by environment and conditions, and it can obtain data quickly and simply, and save a large amount of manpower, material and financial resources. At the same time, numerical simulation can reveal the deeper layer of the physical phenomena, such as flow rate, structure, temperature and pressure distribution and so on [4-6]. So in this paper, work process of the gasoline engine before and after being turbocharged is researched by numerical simulation.

D.-S. Huang et al. (Eds.): ICIC 2012, CCIS 304, pp. 124–131, 2012.

2   Simulation Principle

Fluid control equations are mathematical models reflecting fluid nature, especially the control equations are differential equations reflecting the relationship of the various physical quantities of fluid and corresponding boundary conditions, and they are the starting points for numerical simulation. If there is no perfect mathematical model, numerical simulation will be useless. The basic controlling equations of fluid usually include mass conservation equation (continuity equation), momentum conservation equation (Navier-Stokes equation), energy conservation equation and the corresponding boundary conditions for these equations. The continuity equation, the momentum equation and the energy equation can be derived separately from the basic control equations of fluid, and the Navier-Stokes differential equations are gained, which are referred to as N-S equations. N-S equations are the common law that must be abided by fluid flow. If the flow is at turbulent state, besides the conservation equations of fluid flow, the turbulence model (i.e., turbulent transport control equation) reflecting the special nature of fluid flow, the boundary conditions and the initial conditions should be added. All these equations form a closed group of equations. This group of equations can describe the law of a flow field of fluid.

The basic model and algorithm used in this paper are: simulation calculations are done when the gas flow in the engine inlet port-valve-cylinder is believed as a 3-D viscous, compressible and turbulent gas flow. The k-εmodel is applied during the turbulent flow calculation, control equations were discretized using finite volume method, and algebraic equations gained form control equations were solved with SIMPLE algorithm.

3   Simulation Calculation

3.1   Geometric Model

Geometry models are the and the cylinder. The intake ports include the valve seats, the valves and intake ports. The cylinder include the combustion chamber, the wall and the crown of the cylinder. The models were built with ProE software, which included opening the intake valves, closing the exhaust valves and closing the intake valves and the exhaust valves, as shown in Figure 1. These models were transformed into STL files and introduced into Fire software.

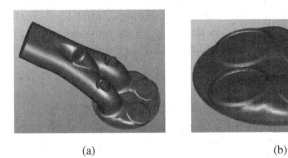

(a)   (b)

Fig. 1. Geometric Model

3.2   Division of Grids

In order to describe the working process of a gasoline engine accurately, the transient numerical simulation method was used. The transient simulation is actually the super-position of multiple steady state simulation, that is the last simulation results is the next boundary conditions of the simulation, so the model should be divided by moving grids. Before the moving grids were divided, fixed grids should be given with FAH automatic mesh generator for the model imported into FIRE [7], and save it as a fip file. The moving grids were divided with FEP in Fire during 379-863°CA for the fip file. According to the open state of the inlet valve, when the intake valve and the exhaust valve were closed, and the intake valve was opened, the exhaust valve was closed, two models were built. Then the transient simulation was done for the engine during the intake, compression and power stroke. Some related parameters of the engine were used when the moving grids were divided, such as the diameter of the cylinder, stroke, the length of the connecting rod, the lift curve of the intake, exhaust valve and the angle between the valve axis and the cylinder axis. The part of the moving grids divided is shown in Fig.2.

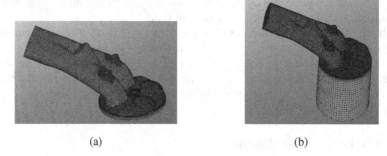

(a)   (b)

Fig. 2. Division of Moving Grids

3.3   Calculating Conditions

The pressure ratio of the gasoline engine is 1.4. The thermodynamic cycles of the engine before and after being turbocharged were calculated with AVL BOOST soft-ware, and the results can provide the initial conditions for the transient simulation of the gasoline engine. Before calculating, the boundary conditions for the intake ports, chamber, the wall of the chamber, piston, the intake valve, the exhaust valve and the valve seats should be set. When the calculation was done, a fixed crankshaft angle can be the calculating step, the fluid flow depended on the movement of the piston, and the open state of the valves is controlled by the files of the valve lift.

4   Calculating Results

4.1   Comparison of the Fluid Flow during Intake Stroke

The fluid flow distribution in the intake ports and cylinder is shown as Fig.3 and Fig.4. Fig.3 is the fluid flow distribution in the naturally aspirated engine, and Fig.4 is that in the turbocharged engine.

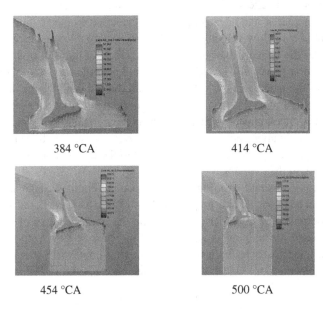

384 °CA   414 °CA

454 °CA   500 °CA

Fig. 3. Fluid Flow Distribution during Intake Stroke

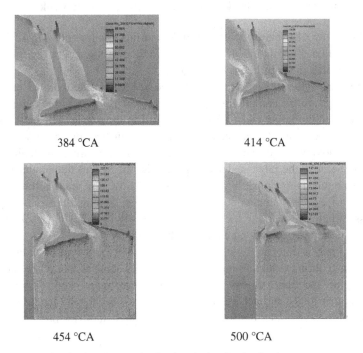

384 °CA   414 °CA

454 °CA   500 °CA

Fig. 4. Fluid Flow Distribution during Intake Stroke

From Fig.3, the inlet flow is relatively smooth, and there is no vortex structure at the beginning of the intake stroke. With the lift of the inlet valves increasing, the cylinder volume increases, and negative pressure is generated in the cylinder, which will increase the intake air flow velocity. At 454°CA, the tumble prototype has begun to be formed under the intake valves because of the effect of the wall of the cylinder. At this time the piston moves downward, and the fluid near the surface of the piston flow downward. But the intake airflow velocity is high, inertia is also large, and forming a vortex in the cylinder generate tumble flow with the wall surface resistance function. The tumble flow phenomenon still exists during the intake valve closure process. With the piston and valves moving, the vortex formed by tumble become evenly, and have detachment sign. At this time, velocity field in the cylinder become uniform, and the flow velocity in the intake ports decrease.

When Fig.4 is compared with Fig.3, to the gasoline engine turbocharged, because the pressure between the intake ports and the cylinder is bigger, the flow velocity between the ports and the cylinder increase. And the initial velocity of the inlet grow larger, with the piston moving downward, the increase of flow velocity is reduced gradually, the main reason is with the piston moving downward, the increase of the pressure between the ports and the cylinder decrease for the turbocharged gasoline engine.

4.2   Comparison of the Fluid Flow during Compression Stroke

The fluid flow distribution in the cylinder during compression stroke is shown as Fig.5 and Fig.6. Fig.5 is the fluid flow distribution in the naturally aspirated engine, and Fig.6 is that in the turbocharged engine.

From Fig.5, after closing the intake valve, the gas in the cylinder enter the compression stage. In the compression process, the small vortex in the cylinder attenuate gradually, and the larger eddy motion is formed in the whole cylinder. Gas flow area reduces, and tumble intensity increases gradually in the compression process. With the piston moving to the TDC, the tumble is broken into numerous small scale vortex, which is because the large scale rolling flow is forced into the combustion chamber whose structure is incompatible with the rolling flow, the great deformation and the shear is formed. The tumble develops through strengthening, decay and fragmentation process, which will increase the turbulence intensity in the cylinder, and improve the velocity of flame propagation and the combustion process.

When Fig.6 is compared with Fig.5, to the turbocharged gasoline engine, the gas flow formed during compression stroke is basically same as that of the naturally aspirated engine, the flow velocity is higher, but the increase extent is limit. The main reason is that to the turbocharged gasoline engine, during the intake stroke the gas movement in the cylinder is stronger than that in the naturally aspirated engine.

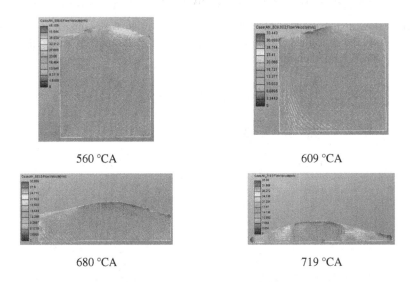

560 °CA   609 °CA

680 °CA   719 °CA

Fig. 5. Fluid Flow Distribution during Compression Stroke

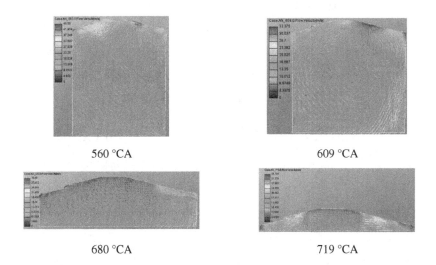

560 °CA   609 °CA

680 °CA   719 °CA

Fig. 6. Fluid Flow Distribution during Compression Stroke

4.3   Comparison of the Fluid Flow during Power Stroke

The fluid flow distribution in the cylinder during power stroke is shown as Fig.7 and Fig.8. Fig.7 is the fluid flow distribution in the naturally aspirated engine, and Fig.8 is that in the turbocharged engine.

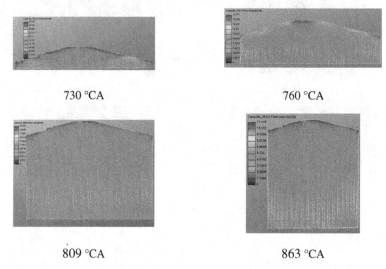

730 °CA   760 °CA

809 °CA   863 °CA

Fig. 7. Fluid Flow Distribution during Power Stroke

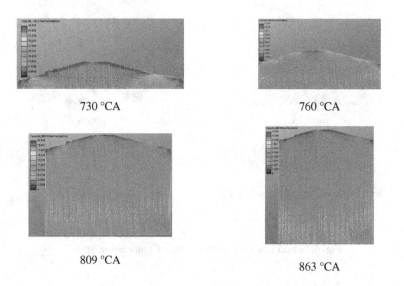

730 °CA   760 °CA

809 °CA   863 °CA

Fig. 8. Fluid Flow Distribution during Power Stroke

At the initial stage of the power stroke, the fluid flow velocity distribution is not uniform, and it is quite disorder. With the piston moving downward, the fluid flow distribution in the cylinder is driven by the piston, the gas flow velocity at the top of the piston is obviously higher, and that near the wall of the cylinder is lower, which is because there is the friction between the gas flow and the wall. But the whole flow is smooth, and there is no vortex formation.

When Fig.8 is compared with Fig.7, to the turbocharged gasoline engine, the gas flow formed during power stroke is basically same as that of the naturally aspirated engine, the numerical value is basically same too. That is to say, compared with the naturally aspirated engine, the change of the flame propagation speed in the turbo-charged engine will be very small.

5   Conclusion

1) Transient simulation calculation for gasoline engines can be done by AVL Fire software, and the results provide the visualization of reason for deflagration of turbo-charged gasoline engine, which will provide theoretical reference for the structure improvement of turbocharged engines.

2) For the turbocharged engine, the flow velocity is bigger than that of the naturally aspirated engine during intake stroke, which is because the pressure between the ports and the cylinder increase.

3) During compression stroke and power stroke, the flow field in the cylinder of the turbocharged engine is basically same as that of the naturally aspirated engine, which show that the flame propagation speed is unchanged basically.

Acknowledgements. This work is supported by Shanghai excellent young teacher fund (gjd-09014).

References

1. Shi, X., Ma, C.C., Wang, Q.: Design and Simulation of Turbocharging System for 491QE Gasoline Engine. Vehicle Engine, 8–10
2. Zhu, D.X.: Tubocharging Turbo-charger. Machinery Industry Press, Beijing (1997)
3. Hou, L.B.: Study of Internal Combustion Engine. Machinery Industry Press, Beijing (2005)
4. Li, Y.Q., Liu, B., Wang, H.X.: Numerical Calculation on Tumble Flows in Gasoline Engine Based on AVL-Fire Code. Design and Manufacture of Diesel Engine 15(3), 6–9 (2007)
5. Liu, S.J., Jia, H.K., Wang, J.: CFD Numerical Simulation and Research on the Intake Port of Non-road Small Spark-ignition Engines. Small Internal Combustion Engine and Motor-cycle 38(5), 45–46 (2009)
6. Liu, D.X., Li, D., Feng, H.Q., et al.: Study of Three-Dimensional Numerical Simulation for Air Flows in Intake Port of Four-Valve Gasoline Engine. Chinese Internal Combustion Engine Engineering (4), 36–38 (2006)
7. AVL. CFD WM Users Guide, Fire v2008 (2008)

Spectrum Sensing Algorithms in the Cognitive Radio Network

Yanbin Shi[1], Jian Guo[2], and Yuanfang Jian[3]

[1] Aviation University of Air force, Changchun, 130022, China
[2] Information Engineering Institute, Urumqi Vocational University, Urumqi 830001, China
[3] 94170 troop of PLA, Xian, 710082, China
{shiyanbin_80,sbbe}@163.com, 605664836@qq.com

Abstract. Detecting the unused spectrum and sharing it without harmful interference with other users is an important requirement of the Cognitive Radio network to sense spectrum holes. This paper focused on the spectrum sensing models and some kinds of spectrum sensing algorithms and their improved algorithms. And attention is concentrated on the performance compare of the different algorithms.

Keywords: spectrum sensing, algorithm, cognitive radio, spectrum holes, wavelet transform.

1 Introduction

As a kind of intellectual frequency spectrum share technology, cognitive radio has offered the wireless communication equipment has the shared and utilized spectrum means according to the way of waiting for an opportunity, which enable the has the ability to find the "spectrum holes" and rational utilization[1].

Spectrum sensing is the key technology of the cognitive radio, its purpose is to sense the wireless spectrum environment dynamically. Compare with other traditional radio systems, the difference is the primary users have priority to use the spectrum than the cognitive users. The cognitive users can use the spectrum band only when the primary users not to take up this frequency band, and keep sensing the state of the primary users, ensure to authorize the primary users to use this band again and the cognitive users quit this channel when the primary users appear.

2 Spectrum Sensing Models

The primary mission of the spectrum sensing is to find the "spectrum holes" accurately. Compare with the demodulation, spectrum sensing needs to judge if there are the primary users, and does not need to extract the original information-bearing signal from a modulated carrier wave[2]. In practice, in order to guarantee not to interfere normal communication of the authorizing primary users, the spectrum

D.-S. Huang et al. (Eds.): ICIC 2012, CCIS 304, pp. 132–138, 2012.

sensing sensitivity need beyond primary users receiver 30~40dB because the cognitive users unable to detect the channel situation between primary users and the transmitters directly, and at the same time, the wireless spectrum environment have many disadvantage factor such as the multi-path transmission effect, fading, noise and so on, so the judgment of the spectrum sensing only can based on the cognitive users detect to the transmitter of the   primary users.

On the AWGN (Additive White Gaussian Noise) channels, the simplest spectrum sensing model is the binary hypothesis detect model.

$$H_0 : Y[n] = W[N], H_1 : Y[n] = X[n] + W[N], \qquad n = 1, \cdots, N \tag{1}$$

Where H_0 and H_1 express the different hypotheses of the primary users signal exist or not in the AWGN channels; $Y[n]$ is the signals received by the unlicensed users(cognitive users); $X[n]$ is the signals transmitted by the licensed users (primary users); $W[N]$ is the White Gaussian Noise.

According to the sensing algorithms, the statistic T can be gotten by $Y[n]$, and the sensing results can be gotten based on the decision theorem.

$$H_0 : T < \lambda, \ H_1 : T > \lambda \tag{2}$$

Where λ is the decision threshold. The detailed process is shown as Figure1.

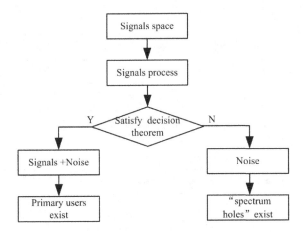

Fig. 1. The flowchart of binary hypothesis detect model

Usually use these two criteria to evaluate the spectrum detection's performance: the probability of detection $P_d = P\{Y > \lambda | H_1\}$ and the probability of false alarm $P_f = P\{Y > \lambda | H_0\}$. While the threshold increases, P_d and P_f will both decrease, when P_d is small, will think by mistake that authorize primary users not to exist, which will increase the interference to primary users. When P_f is big, will make the cognitive users lost some access chances, which will reduce the spectrum utilization ratio. In the cognitive radio, in order to protect the primary users when the cognitive users enter the authorized spectrum, the P_d is more important than P_f, and IEEE802.22 working group demands $P_d \geq 0.9$, $P_f \leq 0.1$.

3   Spectrum Sensing Algorithms

Spectrum sensing is detecting the unused spectrum and sharing it without harmful interference with other users [3]. It is an important requirement of the cognitive radio network to sense spectrum holes. Detecting primary users is the most efficient way to detect "spectrum holes".

3.1   Energy Detection

Though detect one observation section of the received signal to judge whether the primary users are present, it is not require too much to the phase synchronization, and it is one kind of the noncorrelated sensing method. According to the different of the observation section, the energy detection sensing algorithm can be divided into the tradition time domain method and the cyclegraph technique frequency domain method, the each realization block diagram is shown as Fig. 2 and Fig. 3.

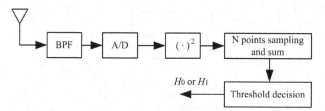

Fig. 2. The tradition time domain method

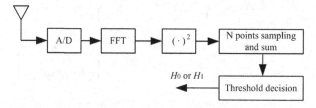

Fig. 3. The cyclegraph technique frequency domain method

The tradition time domain method need filter to the every detect signal through the low pass filter matching with the signal's bandwidth, the filter is   not easy to change, especially while directing the narrowband signal and sinusoidal signal, it is relatively bad to realize the flexibility. The cyclegraph technique frequency domain method through choose one corresponding frequency sub-signal carrier, signals with the arbitrary bandwidth can all use this method to deal with, and through increasing the point of the FFT operation, it can improve the sensing performance in a certain degree on the premise of not increasing detection time.

3.2   Cyclostationary Feature Detection

For the demodulation of receiver, it is redundant that there are certain spectrums after modulating in most communication signals, thus enable it or its mean value has circulation cycle characteristic with its self-correlation. This algorithm utilizes the generalized stationary no-relativity and the signal's cyclic stationary spectrum to distinguish the primary users' signal from noise, and get rid of the influence of the background noise. Even under the low SNR condition, it has better sensing performance.

The different type modulating signal, even their power spectral density is same, but their frequency correlation function is different, so the cyclostationary feature detection algorithm not only can appears the characteristics of the different kinds of modulation signals, distinguishs primary users' signal from the interference range. But also can works on the energy detection state, so long as makes circulation frequency is zero, that is $S_x^{\alpha}(f)$ ($\alpha = 0$). So the cyclostationary feature detection algorithm has better flexibility. In the environment of unknown noise or stronger interfere, it is more excellent than energy detection algorithm, but it also has some shortages, such as relatively great calculating complexity and long observation time. The realization block diagram is shown as Fig. 4.

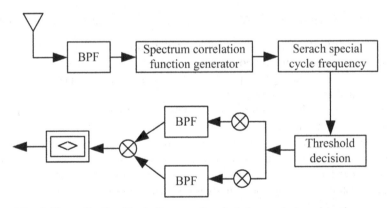

Fig. 4. The realization block diagram of cyclostationary feature detection

3.3   Matched Filter Detection

Under the AWGN environment, if the priori information of the primary users' signal is known, the matched filter detection diagram has best performance[4], it can get maximize SNR and fast rate of convergence, reaches higher gain and less necessary time. This method belongs to relevant detection method, and has high requirement to the phase synchronization, must through time synchronization, carrier synchronization and channel equalization to safeguard the performance at the demodulation.

3.4   Multi-resolution Spectrum Sensing Algorithms

In the cyclostationary feature detection spectrum sensing algorithms, the resolution in frequency domain of FFT is fixed, it is unable to dynamically adjust the pace and quality. The key of the multi-resolution spectrum sensing algorithm use the wavelet transform to estimate the signal's power spectrum[5], and dynamically adjust the resolution. Through the continuous wavelet transform to calculate the power of the sensing spectrum, and make decision the primary users are exist or not.

The multi-resolution spectrum sensing algorithm get the received signal's correlation coefficient based on the special wavelet primary function, through change the carry frequency and impulse duration, the wavelet transform coefficient of the received signal on the different frequency and different resolution, then calculate the sum of square of the wavelet transform coefficient on same frequency, the sum is energy estimation value.

Because the multi-resolution spectrum sensing algorithm use the continuous wavelet transform to estimate the power of the sensing spectrum, it has higher resolution in low frequency part, but the resolution in high frequency part is relatively low, through reducing the impulse duration of the wavelet transform primary function, the resolution can be promoted.

3.5   The Spectrum Sensing Algorithm Based on Wavelet Packet Transform

In order to modify the demerit of the multi-resolution spectrum sensing algorithm, the spectrum sensing algorithm based on wavelet take segment treatment to the frequency band[6], subdivide the high-frequency part to many pieces; make the whole goal frequency band have same resolutions.

The essence of this algorithm is take numerous orthogonal decomposition to the received signals using the wavelet packet transform, each time the orthogonal decomposition rate is improved until the low frequency and the high-frequency parts all get the necessary resolution, then calculate the sum of square of the wavelet transform coefficient on same frequency, get the energy estimation value, compare with the threshold can judge the primary users are exist or not.

3.6   Cyclic Spectrum Detection Algorithm Based on Spectrum Correlation Coefficient

The classical steady characteristic of circulation sensing algorithm can distinguish the authorized primary users and the noise in theory, but in case of low SNR in practical application, the peak value differences of the noise and signal are fuzzier in the circulation, it is very difficult in quantization effectively of the peak value judgment.

In order to modify this defect, the cyclic spectrum detection algorithm based on spectrum correlation coefficient is suggested[7]. For convenience this algorithm to deal with the spectrum correlation function get by the classical steady characteristic of circulation sensing algorithms, get the conduct judgment amount of spectrum coefficient correlation in normalization form:

$$T = C_x^\alpha = \frac{S_x^\alpha(f)}{[S(f + \alpha/2)S(f - \alpha/2)]^{1/2}} \tag{3}$$

Under the low SNR condition, the detection time of the cyclic spectrum detection algorithm based on spectrum correlation coefficient is short than the detection time of classical steady characteristic of circulation sensing algorithm; And under the better SNR condition, the performance of these two different algorithms is similar. Under the same channel condition, when SNR=-10dB, P_f =0.1, P_d of the cyclic spectrum detection algorithm based on spectrum correlation coefficient is 0.9, and P_d of the classical steady characteristic of circulation sensing algorithm is 0.2. When SNR=10dB, the P_d of the two algorithms is basically same.

4   Conclusion

How to fast and accurate confirms the "spectrum holes" is the key issue in cognitive radio. At present, there are many kinds' spectrum sensing algorithms, and they have respective merits and demerits. How to combine these detection or sensing methods in practical application, and give attention to the sensing rate and detection quality is the emphasis in future research.

References

1. Ariananda, D.D., Lakshmanan, M.K., Nikoo, H.: A Survey on Spectrum Sensing Techniques for Cognitive Radio. In: Second International Workshop on Cognitive Radio and Advanced Spectrum Management, pp. 74–79. IEEE Press, New York (2009)
2. Chen, H., Tse, C.K., Zhao, F.: Optimal Quantisation Bit Budget For A Spectrum Sensing Scheme In Bandwidth-Constrained Cognitive Sensor Networks. IET Wireless Sensor Systems 1, 144–150 (2011)
3. Yi, Z., Xianzhong, X., Lili, Y.: Cooperative Spectrum Sensing Based On Blind Source Separation for Cognitive Radio. In: First International Conference on Future Information Networks, pp. 398–402. IEEE Press, New York (2009)
4. Kapoor, S., Rao, S.V.R.K., Singh, G.: Opportunistic Spectrum Sensing by Employing Matched Filter in Cognitive Radio Network. In: 2011 International Conference on Communication Systems and Network Technologies, pp. 580–583. IEEE Press, New York (2011)
5. Zhu, J., Xu, Z., Wang, F., Huang, B., Zhang, B.: Double Threshold Energy Detection of Cooperative Spectrum Sensing in Cognitive Radio. In: International Conference on Cognitive Radio Oriented Wireless Networks and Communications, pp. 1–5. IEEE Press, New York (2008)

6. Jiang, Z.-L., Zhang, Q.-Y., Wang, Y., Shang, X.-Q.: Wavelet Packet Entropy Based Spectrum Sensing In Cognitive Radio. In: 2011 IEEE 3rd International Conference on Communication Software and Networks, pp. 293–298. IEEE Press, New York (2011)
7. Chien, W.-B., Yang, C.-K., Huang, Y.-H.: Energy-Saving Cooperative Spectrum Sensing. In: Processor for Cognitive Radio System, vol. 58, pp. 711–723. IEEE Press, New York (2011)

Research on Information Fusion Method
Based on sFlow and Netflow in Network Security Situation

Yanbo Wang[1], Huiqiang Wang[1], Chengqin Han[1], Baoyu Ge[1], and Ming Yu[2]

[1] College of Computer Science and Technology Harbin Engineering University, Harbin 150001
[2] Information and computer engineering college Northeast Forestry University, Harbin 150040
Heu_wangyanbo@126.com

Abstract. This paper firstly analyses the characteristic of sFlow and Netflow data as situation awareness data source, then introduces the current common used information fusion methods, and researches the applicability of various methods in the network safety situation awareness system based on sFlow and Netflow. Finally, an improved fusion algorithm is proposed which is combined Bayes estimation and fuzzy clustering method. This method can effectively integrate the information from different data source, and fused data is more credible and comprehensive. It provides important data basis and theoretical guidance for analysis and realization of the network security situation.

Keywords: sFlow, netflow, data fusion, bayes, fuzzy clustering.

1 Introduction

Network security situation awareness research is a hot spot at home and abroad, through the real-time monitoring on network security situation, the network situation awareness system can identify, defense, response, warn and provide the corresponding solutions before malicious attack happened, which aims at solving the severe situation that current network security fields faces with. This paper proposes a fusion technology of network security situation information based on the sFlow and Netflow as a new data fusion method in the safety situation field, which can effectively improve the shortage of monophyletic data information, and provide the necessary basic information to accurately judge the current network security situation status and predict the future development trend.

2 Analysis of Data Characteristic

SFlow data is network flow information based on certain sampling probability. The network flow mainly covers all the communication elements in the network. But because of sampling granularity, namely there are the geneogenous sampling errors during the process of gaining small flow data by sFlow owing to the limitation of sampling time interval.

D.-S. Huang et al. (Eds.): ICIC 2012, CCIS 304, pp. 139–145, 2012.
© Springer-Verlag Berlin Heidelberg 2012

Netflow data is a kind of sampling method based on the content, it continuously extracts several fields information from the switch data packet. Because of continuously extracting information, part of important information in the network communication (such as the MAC address, etc.) were filtered out ，which leads to hard to effectively develop for analysis methods who can recognize the corresponding information. In addition, because Netflow gains the data by the continuous sampling, which greatly depends on the network traffic, when the traffic is too large to keep up with transition rate for the sampling rate, which results in higher packet loss rate, it is difficult to effectively satisfy efficient and real-time requirements in large-scale network.

It is notable that there is crossover and similar information gained by two kinds of situation awareness data source, such as the source and destination address, the inflow and outflow port, communication protocol and TCP mark bits, etc. And both are complementary on the different network traffic information. The fusion data based on the sFlow and Netflow can satisfy the requirement of representativeness, real-time, and reliability, comprehensiveness and multi-element for the situation awareness data source. Through reasonable usage and fusion of information, it will reduce information missing during the process of data acquisition, and expand the amount of network information, improve the accuracy of data acquisition, which provides reliable and comprehensive data information for the analysis of security situation events even network situation prediction.

3   Analysis of Common Data Fusion Methods

3.1   D-S Evidence Theory

D-S Evidence Theory, also called trust function theory, is an expansion study on classical probability theory, which has strong theory foundation. Through the evidence theory we can solve the uncertainty problems caused by the random and fuzzy information. D-S Evidence Theory uses the axiom weaker than probability theory, and makes decision through introducing the different trust functions, thus it can be used to distinguish uncertain and unknown fuzzy concept. But the evidence theory has potential exponential order complexity, which makes it hard to guarantee real-time data fusion system requirement.

3.2   Bayes Method

Bayes method is a kind of way to carry on probability inferences by actual observed value of binomial distribution of the parameters that method. The fundamental principle of Bayesian method is through the combination of prior information and sample getting event posterior information. By this method during the process of the experiment parameter estimation, we can get more accurate estimation results to guide the practice. Compared with the frequency method, the bayes method can give more comprehensive description for the estimation event. But by the method can only gain the network situation data closed to the truth, it is difficult to be directly applied into fusion of similar data information.

3.3   Fuzzy Clustering

Fuzzy clustering method is used to classify data from the fuzzy angle, and fuse similar data together. Due to adopting a kind of fuzzy method, which makes this method in the process of integration not according to the uniform fusion rules or fusion direction to conduct, the random or experience factors frequently play a dominant role, and lacking of effective integration mechanism. So in the application it is hard to find reasonable fusion standards and fusion direction, that either due to the broader fusion rules makes information redundancy bigger, or due to stricter fusion rules makes data difficult to be fused effectively.

4   Research on Data Fusion Method Based sFlow and Netflow

Based on analysis and comparison of applicability of the above several common data fusion method, we find that every method is difficult to effectively satisfy data fusion based on sFlow and Netflow. Therefore, On the basis of characteristics of the sFlow and Netflow, this paper converts prior probability into posterior probability (fusion factor) by bayes estimation, and uses posteriori probability to guide fuzzy clustering data fusion rules and fusion direction, and proposes a new fusion algorithm based on the bayes and fuzzy clustering used to solve data fusion.

4.1   B-F Algorithm

B-F Algorithm mainly consists of three steps: Firstly, calculate fusion granularity parameters λ, by comparing the accuracy of two sampling method to determine information fusion direction, that is when the accuracy of sFlow data is higher and amount of information is larger, the fused data information should take more account of sFlow data to ensure the comprehensiveness and effectiveness of data, vice versa. At the same time, when fusing the same data information, λ can provide a reasonable fusion granularity, which improves the disadvantage of the traditional method that fuses data in random granularity by experience. Secondly, quantify the fused data, by the quantified processing algorithm convert the original data into the one used to calculate directly. Finally, handle the quantized data with fuzzy clustering, and confirm the fusion information and direction according to the granularity parameter, and generate the fusion information at last.

Firstly, ascertain fusion granularity parameter λ, according to the characteristics of sFlow data, assume that sample N data packets, and at the same time analyze n samples, there are c certain kind of data packets designated to obtain, since the sampling probability of each packet is same, so the average sampling probability of designated packets is $P = c/n$, among the value of P can be obtained by switch configuration sampling information, and often assume that when the sampling packet is enough more, the error formula can be simplified as:

$$\text{error}_{\text{sFlow}} \leq 1.96\sqrt{1/c} \tag{1}$$

Therefore, the error rate of sFlow sampling data is only correlated with specific certain types of data packets, therefore only related to the amount of sampling. Due to during the process of data collection using two data sources, and the way of data collection is not same, the data packets sampling used by sFlow is suitable for large amount data, and the information sampling used by Netflow reduces the data information, sequentially ensure data collection continuous, it is more suitable for less data volume, both are complementary for each other on data information collection. When the network traffic is less, the error rate of sFlow data acquisitions will be very high and Netflow is low, when network traffic is greater, sFlow data gains more sample data so as to reduce the error rate, and meanwhile data packet loss rate of Netflow data increases, which result in the reliability of the information decreasing, obviously data measurement error rate between sFlow and Netflow exists the following relationships: $\text{error}_{\text{sFlow}} + \text{error}_{\text{Netflow}} = 1$.

With bayese theory we regard the error rate of sFlow data sampling as prior probability of data fusion probability θ, and because during the process of sFlow packet sampling data sampling rate P is known, then $C = N / P$. So the prior probability formula:

$$\text{error}_{\text{sFlow}} = 1.96\sqrt{P / N} \tag{2}$$

N is the total amount of captured packets, because the amount of collected data packets can be directly acquired by network traffic, so select sFlow and Netflow traffic data information during the same time period as sample in the sample space $\{X1 , X2 ; \cdots , Xn\}$, thereby calculate data sampling information. Calculate the posterior error rate of sFlow data sampling recorded λ by the formula, namely fusion granularity parameters.

The second step: quantization and fuzzy clustering on fusion information. Because monitoring the same part of network with sFlow and Netflow, and there are much similar information in both detection method such as the source and destination IP, source and destination Port, TCP sign, IP protocol, IP service type and time information, etc, but the data types are different in kinds of information, frequently not in $[0,1]$, which makes it difficult to be effective clustered, so the data should be quantified prior to application. Each of data information from sFlow or Netflow contains eight characteristic elements Mentioned above, where each characteristic element is set as x_k. Assume that there are n raw data extracted during the same period of time, namely each characteristic x_k has n raw data, recorded $x'_{1k} , x'_{2k} ; \cdots , x'_{nk}$, and called each element of the feature. In order to convert these raw data into the available data by fuzzy clustering, which need to be quantified, firstly calculate average value and variance of data:

$$\overline{x}'_k = \frac{1}{n}\sum_{i=1}^{n} x'_{ik} \ , \quad S_k^2 = \frac{1}{n}\sum_{i=1}^{n}(x'_{ik} - \overline{x}'_k)^2 \tag{3}$$

And then according to the formula (4) solve each data quantization value x''_{ik} :

$$x''_{ik} = \frac{x'_{ik} - \overline{x}'_k}{S_k} \tag{4}$$

Through the above method we still can't guarantee that all data is in $[0,1]$ region. In order to compress the quantization data into $[0,1]$ interval, adopting the linear scaling transformation algorithm ensure the attribute value before and after the transformation, the transformation formula is:

$$x_{ik} = \frac{x''_{ik}}{\max x''_{ik}} \quad (\max x''_{ik} \neq 0) \tag{5}$$

Among, $\max x''_{ik}$ is the maximum value in x''_{1k} , x''_{2k} ;$\cdots$, x''_{nk} . Through the formula (5) quantify the raw data information to the data who can be used directly in fuzzy clustering compute, provide effective support for data clustering.

The third step: combine fusion granularity parameter λ with quantitative data to carry out data clustering. Firstly, establish fuzzy similar matrix, assume that in a period of time extracting n data information, namely the sample space $X = \{x_1 , x_2 ;\cdots , x_n\}$, each of data sample x_i contains eight characteristic data $(x_{i1} , x_{i2} ;\cdots , x_{i8})$, respectively indicates the source/destination IP, source and destination Port, TCP sign, IP Protocol, IP service type and time information. Taking the quantization data into formula (5), we can get the similar coefficient r_{ij} which is the similar degree of two pieces of data, and establish similar matrix $R = [r_{ij}]$. Then, we use transitive closure method to cluster on the similar matrix R , and gain transitive closure $R^k = t_{ij}$ recorder $t(R)$, the cut matrix can be modified as :

$$R_\lambda = \begin{cases} 1 & t_{ij} \geq t' \\ 0 & t_{ij} < t' \end{cases} \quad (i,j = 1,2 ,\ldots,n) \tag{6}$$

t' is obtained by the following method: assume that t_{ij} has w value from small to large

in $t(R)$, λ is fusion granularity parameter, t' is the $\lfloor \lambda * w \rfloor$ value.

The column in cut matrix R_λ corresponds to data information in the sample space, when the value of column vector in cut matrix is the same as others, which means that the corresponding data information is the same kind of information so that they can be merged, during the procedure refer to fusion parameter λ again to judge the integration direction. If $\lambda > 0.5$, it means the error rate of sFlow data information is higher, the Netflow is lower, so the Netflow data information acts as the main part, the information from sFlow due to discrete and unreliability is eliminated; if $\lambda \leq 0.5$ SFlow data information is more accurate, with the increase of data traffic, Netflow data will appear higher package loss rate, which causes information distortion, during the data fusion process tend to sFlow data information.

5   Performance Analysis of B-F Algorithm

B-F algorithm combines the superiorities of bayes estimation and fuzzy clustering. The process fully considers of the influence that because sampling frequency is different, the data distribution is not uniform. The fusion factor a certain extent reflects the proportion two kinds of information taken up during the information fusion process. And network traffic packet information are directly acquired from the analytical packets, so that reduce the influence of information acquisition efficiency on the algorithm.

Meanwhile, B-F algorithm adopts the reasonable quantitative treatment method, and converts complex disorder data into available data information in unified interval, and ensures the data of the linear correlation between information. And the quantitative treatment algorithm is simple; whose time complexity is low, the influence on the situation analysis efficiency of the real-time system is very small.

In addition, the introduction of the fusion factor makes fuzzy clustering method free from the original random model, makes information fusion based on sFlow and Netflow according to their actual distribution develop. Compared with the previous clustering method, fusion conditions are more reasonable, which can effectively integrate the same information from different data source; fusion data is more credible, which avoids a large amount of data fused randomly makes anomaly information maintained; fusion information is more comprehensive.

The algorithm complexity of the improved algorithm is superior to rough set theory and D-S evidence method, and the accuracy of the algorithm is significantly better than gray system theory. Therefore, it can be used to guide data fusion based on sFlow and Netflow, which provides the reliable data base for safety situation analysis.

Acknowledgement. This paper is supported by the National Natural Science Foundation of China (60973027), the Specialized Research Fund for the Doctoral Program of Higher Education of China (20102304120012) and the Natural Science Foundation of Heilongjiang Province of China(F201037).

References

1. Liu, X., Wang, H., Lai, J., Ye, H.: Network Security Situation Generation and Evaluation Based on Heterogeneous Multi-sensor Fusion. Journal of System Simulation 22(6), 133–142 (2010)
2. Ronald, P.S.: Statistical Multisource-multitarget Information Fusion. Artech House (2007)
3. Goodman, I.R., Nguyen, H.T.: Mathemtics of Data Fusion. Kluwer Academic Publishers (1997)
4. Varshney, P.K.: Distributed Detection and Data Fusion. Springer (1996)
5. Bass, T.: Intrusion Systems and Multisensor Data Fusion. Communications of the ACM 43(4), 99–105 (2009)

Discrete Exponential Bayesian Networks Structure Learning for Density Estimation

Aida Jarraya[1,2], Philippe Leray[2], and Afif Masmoudi[1]

[1] Laboratory of Probability and Statistics
Faculty of Sciences of Sfax, University of Sfax, Tunisia
[2] LINA Computer Science Lab UMR 6241
Knowledge and Decision Team, University of Nantes, France
aidajarraya@yahoo.fr, afif.masmoudi@fss.rnu.tn,
philippe.leray@univ-nantes.fr

Abstract. Our work aims at developing or expliciting bridges between Bayesian Networks and Natural Exponential Families, by proposing discrete exponential Bayesian networks as a generalization of usual discrete ones. In this paper, we illustrate the use of discrete exponential Bayesian networks for Bayesian structure learning and density estimation. Our goal is to empirically determine in which contexts these models can be a good alternative to usual Bayesian networks for density estimation.

1   Introduction

Bayesian networks (BNs) are probabilistic graphical models used to model com- plex systems with variables of different natures. In the literature we find many works about discrete Bayesian network where the conditional distribution of each variable given its parents is a multinomial distribution. As initially proposed by [5], we are interested in extending this conditional distribution to natural exponential families (NEF) [1][9]. This idea has been used by [2] for instance with conjugate-exponential models, for Bayesian networks with latent variables. They concentrate their work on variational EM estimation needed because of latent variables, but they don't explicit the Bayesian estimators used and restrict their experiments to usual multinomial distributions. [12] also propose one great study of graphical models as exponential families, showing that very specific structures of directed or undirected probabilistic graphical models can be interpreted as an element of exponential family. Our work deals with the same general idea, developing or expliciting bridges between BNs and NEFs, dealing with discrete exponential BNs instead of usual discrete ones. We formally introduced in [6] discrete exponential Bayesian networks (deBNs) with a specific prior family proposed by [4] and demonstrated that this prior is a generalization of Dirichlet priors usually considered with discrete BNs. We illustrate now the use of deBNs for Bayesian structure learning and density estimation. Our goal is to empirically determine in which contexts deBNs can be a good alternative to usual BNs for density estimation. The present paper is structured as follows. In section 2, we summarized our theoretical results concerning structure and parameter learning for discrete exponential BNs. Section 3 then describes our experimental protocol, evaluation criteria, and finally

D.-S. Huang et al. (Eds.): ICIC 2012, CCIS 304, pp. 146–151, 2012.

gives interpretations of results obtained in this context. Section 4 concludes our paper by giving some perspectives for future work.

2   Discrete Exponential Bayesian Network

Usually, the statistical model of a discrete BN is a multinomial distribution [11]. We described in [6] how to use discrete exponential families in a more general way. We summarized here the main points concerning the definition of discrete exponential BNs (deBNs), our proposal of Bayesian scoring function and parameter estimator.

2.1   Notations

A Bayesian network (BN) is defined as a set of variables $X = \{X_1, ...,X_n\}$ with a network structure G that encodes a set of conditional independence assertions about variables in X, and a set P of local probability distributions associated with each variable. Together, these components define the joint probability distribution for X. The network structure G is a directed acyclic graph (DAG). Each X_i denotes both the variable and its corresponding node in G, and $Pa(X_i)$ the parents of node X_i in G. For BN learning, we assume that we have one dataset $d = \{x^{(1)},..., x^{(M)}\}$ of size M where $x^{(l)} = \{x_1^{(l)}, ..., x_n^{(l)}\}$ is the lth sample and $x_i^{(l)}$ is the value of variable X_i for this sample.

2.2   DeBN Definition

A discrete exponential Bayesian network is defined as a Bayesian network where conditional probability distributions are discrete natural exponential families (NEF). Let F be a NEF, usually described by its parameters $\upsilon, k_\upsilon = k$ and $\Psi_\upsilon = \Psi$. These general parameters allow us to describe any discrete exponential distribution (Poisson, Negative Binomial, ...).

We suppose that $X_i|Pa_i = j \sim P(\mu_{ij}, F)$. This conditional probability distribution can be expressed in an "exponential" way, where μ_{ij} parameters are mutually independent

$$P(x_i|Pa_i = j) = e^{<\psi(\mu_{ij}), x_i> - k(\psi(\mu_{ij}))} \upsilon\{x_i\}. \tag{1}$$

For Bayesian estimation or structure learning, we also need to define a prior distribution for parameters μ_{ij}. In [6], we propose to choose the $\tilde{\Pi}$ prior family introduced by [4] and demonstrated that this prior was a generalization of Dirichlet priors usually considered with discrete BNs. So $\mu_{ij} \sim \tilde{\Pi}_{t_{ij},m_{ij}}$ with

$$\tilde{\Pi}_{t_{ij},m_{ij}}(\mu_{ij}) = \tilde{K}_{t_{ij},m_{ij}} e^{t_{ij}<\psi(\mu_{ij}), m_{ij}> - t_{ij} k(\psi(\mu_{ij}))} \tag{2}$$

where $\tilde{K}_{t_{ij},m_{ij}}$ is a normalizing constant depending on the considered NEF.

2.3 DeBN learning

As for their usual counterpart, deBN structure learning can be performed by using any heuristic method whose objective is the optimization of the marginal likelihood or one of its approximations. In the Bayesian estimation framework, we described in [6] the computation of this marginal likelihood for discrete exponential BN and a generalized scoring function gBD extending the Bayesian Dirichlet (BD) score to any NEF distribution.

$$gBD(d,G) = P(G) \prod_{i=1}^{n} \prod_{j=1}^{q_i} \frac{\tilde{K}_{t_{ij},m_{ij}}}{\tilde{K}_{\frac{N_{ij}+t_{ij},\frac{\sum_{h \in M_{ij}} x_i^{(h)} + t_{ij}m_{ij}}{N_{ij}+t_{ij}}}}} \tag{3}$$

where $M_{ij} = \left\{ h \in \{1,...,M\} | Pa_i^{(h)} = j \right\}$ and $N_{ij} = |M_{ij}|$.

We also demonstrated that the Maximum a Posteriori (MAP) estimator of parameter μ_{ij} is given by the following closed form : $\hat{\mu}_{ij}^{MAP} = \left(\frac{\overline{X}_i + t_{ij}m_{ij}}{(t_{ij}/N_{ij})+1} \right)$ \tag{4}

where $\overline{X}_i = \frac{1}{N_{ij}} \sum_{h \in M_{ij}} x_i^{(h)}$.

2.4 DeBN Examples: Poisson and Negative Binomial BNs

Let us apply these previous results to Poisson and Negative Binomial distributions. For the Poisson distribution, the normalizing constant is

$$\tilde{K}_{t_{ij},m_{ij}} = \frac{t_{ij}^{t_{ij}m_{ij}+1}}{\Gamma(t_{ij}m_{ij}+1)} . \tag{5}$$

The score function $gBD(d,G)$ is given by

$$P(G) \prod_{i=1}^{n} \prod_{j=1}^{q_i} \frac{t_{ij}^{t_{ij}m_{ij}+1}}{(N_{ij}+t_{ij})^{\sum_{h \in M_{ij}} x_i^{(h)} + t_{ij}m_{ij}+1}} \frac{\Gamma(t_{ij}m_{ij} + \sum_{h \in M_{ij}} x_i^{(h)} + 1)}{\Gamma(t_{ij}m_{ij}+1)} \tag{6}$$

For the *Negative Binomial Model*, we get the following normalizing constant:

$$\tilde{K}_{t_{ij},m_{ij}} = \frac{\Gamma(t_{ij}m_{ij}+t_{ij})}{\Gamma(t_{ij}m_{ij}+1)\Gamma(t_{ij}-1)}, \quad t_{ij} > 1 . \tag{7}$$

The score function $gBD(d,G)$ is given by

$$P(G)\prod_{i=1}^{n}\prod_{j=1}^{q_i}\frac{\Gamma(t_{ij}m_{ij}+t_{ij})\Gamma(t_{ij}m_{ij}+\sum_{h\in M_{ij}}x_i^{(h)}+1)\Gamma(N_{ij}+t_{ij}-1)}{\Gamma(t_{ij}m_{ij}+1)\Gamma(t_{ij}m_{ij}+\sum_{h\in M_{ij}}x_i^{(h)})\Gamma(t_{ij}-1)} \tag{8}$$

3 Experimentations

3.1 Data

In order to evaluate the interest of using deBNs instead of usual BNs for density estimation, we carried out repetitive experiments in several contexts. In the first context, data are generated from distributions described by usual BNs (dist=multi). In the second context, data are generated from distributions described by Poisson deBNs (dist=poisson). In these contexts, we are able to control several parameters such as the number n of variables (n = 10, 20, 50) and the size M of generated datasets (M = 100, 1.000, 10.000). The maximal cardinality K of our discrete variables is also controlled for usual BNs (K = 2, 3, 5) but measured in the generated samples for Poisson deBNs.

Every dataset generation in such conditions is iterated 10x10 times, with 10 randomly generated DAGs, and 10 random parameter values for each of these DAGs.

3.2 Models and Algorithms

Our goal is comparing performances of usual discrete BN models (model=multi) versus Poisson deBN (model=poisson) learnt with the previous datasets. Prior parameters are chosen in their simplest form, $\alpha_{ij}=1$, uniform Dirichlet coefficient, for discrete BNs and $t_{ij}=1$, $m_{ij}=0$ for Poisson deBNs.

Structure learning procedure used for optimizing the Bayesian scoring function is an usual greedy search procedure as proposed in [3]. In order to obtain more robust results, this greedy search is performed 10 times with different random initializations and the best result of the 10 runs is kept. Maximum A Posteriori estimation is used for parameter learning. Our various models and algorithms have been implemented in Matlab with BNT [10] and BNT Structure Learning Package [8].

3.3 Evaluation Criteria

Accuracy evaluation of each model is estimated by the Kullback-Leibler (KL) divergence between the "original" distribution described by the model used for generating a given dataset and the "final" distribution obtained by the model learnt from this dataset. For large numbers of variable configurations (greater than 10^5), an MCMC approximation is used with 10^5 random configurations.

Comparison of both models is illustrated by plotting absolute values of KL obtained by deBNs versus usual BNs for the same datasets. The fact that one model is better than the other can be observed with respect to the first diagonal (upper triangle : deBN is better, versus lower triangle : usual BN is better). In order to determine whether the observed differences are statistically significant, we use the Wilcoxon paired signed rank test, with a significance level equal to 0.05, for the 100 experiments performed for one given context (dist, n, M, K).

3.4   Results and Interpretations

Our preliminary results described in Figure 1 concern n = 10. As we can see, when data are generated from Poisson distributions (results in magenta), our Poisson deBNs are logically better models than usual BNs. When data are generated from multinomial distributions (results in blue), results depend on the sample size M. When M is high (M = 10.000, third figure on the right), usual BNs are better models than Poisson deBNs. When the sample size decreases (M = 1000), usual BNs and deBNs give similar results. With a small sample size (M = 100), deBNs are better than usual BNs. All these results are confirmed by Wilcoxon tests. By comparing results for M = 1.000 with respect to the maximum variable cardinality K (not described right now in the figure), we can observe than deBNs and usual BNs give similar results for K = 3 but the situation changes if K increases. For K = 6, deBN give better results than BNs.

These intermediate results need to be completed with other values of n and K, but we can already observe than deBNs seems to be a good alternative to usual BNs in several contexts. If we compare Poisson deBNs and usual BNs, the first ones have less free parameters than the others and this number of parameters is less dependent of the value of K. So when the sample size M is low or when the value of K is high, deBN are a good compromise for density estimation.

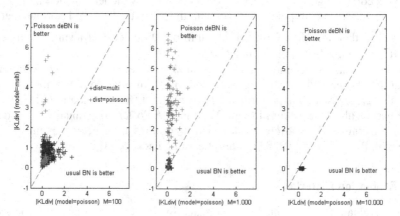

Fig. 1. Comparison of KL divergence obtained by Poisson deBNs versus usual BNs for the same datasets (upper triangle : deBN is better, versus lower triangle : usual BN is better) with respect to dataset size ($M = 100 < 1 > 000 < 10 > 000$) and data original distribution (*dist=poisson vs. multinomial*) for $n = 10$

4   Conclusion and Perspectives

In this paper, we have developed the concept of discrete exponential Bayesian network (deBN) previously, described in [6], for Bayesian structure learning and density estimation. Experiments described here show us that Poisson deBNs can be a good alternative to usual BNs for density estimation when the sample size is low or when the maximum variable cardinality is high, because of the reduced number of parameters used by deBNs. These experiments could be extended to other discrete NEF distributions such as the Negative Binomial one, or continuous distributions. For each distribution, we need to propose a better way to deal with a priori parameters such as t_{ij} and m_{ij} for Poisson distribution, in order to obtain Bayesian scoring functions verifying the Markov equivalence property (like BDe scoring function for usual discrete BNs). Probabilistic inference algorithms also have to be extended for these distributions, which seems to be not so difficult for any exponential distribution as shown in [7] for hybrid BNs with conditional Gaussian distributions.

References

1. Barndorff-Nielsen, O.: Information and Exponential families in Statistical Theory. John Wiley (1978)
2. Beal, M., Ghahramani, Z.: The Variational Bayesian EM Algorithm for Incomplete Data:with Application to Scoring Graphical Model Structures. Bayesian Statistics 7, 453–464 (2003)
3. Chickering, D., Geiger, D., Heckerman, D.: Learning Bayesian Networks: Search Methods and Experimental Results. In: Conference on Artificial Intelligence and Statistics, pp. 112–128 (1995)
4. Consonni, G., Veronese, P.: Conjugate Priors for Exponential Families Having Quadratic Variance Functions. J. Amer. Statist. Assoc. 87, 1123–1127 (1992)
5. Geiger, D., Heckerman, D., King, H., Meek, C.: Stratified Exponential Families: Graphical Models and Model Selection. Annals of Statistics 29, 505–529 (2001)
6. Jarraya, A., Leray, P., Masmoudi, A.: Discrete Exponential Bayesian Networks: an Extension of Bayesian Networks to Discrete Natural Exponential Families. In: International Conference on Tools with Artificial Intelligence, pp. 205–208 (2011)
7. Lauritzen, S.L., Jensen, F.: Stable Local Computation with Conditional Gaussian Distributions. Statistics and Computing 11(2), 191–203 (2001)
8. Leray, P., Francois, O.: BNT Structure Learning Package: Documentation and Experiments. Tech. rep., Laboratoire PSI (2004)
9. Letac, G.: Lectures on Natural Exponential Families and their Variance Functions. No. 50 in Monograph. Math., Inst. Mat. Pura Aplic. Rio (1992)
10. Murphy, K.: The Bayesnet Toolbox for Matlab. In: Computing Science and Statistics: Proceedings of Interface, vol. 33 (2001)
11. Studeny, M.: Mathematical Aspects of Learning Bayesian Networks: Bayesian Quality Criteria. Research Report 2234, Institute of Information Theory and Automation (2008)
12. Wainwright, M.J., Jordan, M.I.: Graphical models, Exponential Families, and Variational Inference. Foundations and Trends in Machine Learning 1(1-2), 1–305 (2008)

A New Adaptive Signal Segmentation Approach Based on Hiaguchi's Fractal Dimension

Hamed Azami[1], Alireza Khosravi[2], Milad Malekzadeh[2], and Saeid Sanei[3]

[1] Department of Electrical Engineering, Iran University of Science and Technology
[2] Department of Electrical and Computer Engineering, Babol Industrial University
[3] Department of Computing, University of Surrey, UK
hamed_azami@ieee.org, akhosravi@nit.ac.ir,
m.malekzade@stu.nit.ac.ir, s.sanei@surrey.ac.uk

Abstract. In many non-stationary signal processing applications such as electroencephalogram (EEG), it is better to divide the signal into smaller segments during which the signals are pseudo-stationary. Therefore, they can be considered stationary and analyzed separately. In this paper a new segmentation method based on discrete wavelet transform (DWT) and Hiaguchi's fractal dimension (FD) is proposed. Although the Hiaguchi's algorithm is the most accurate algorithms to obtain an FD for EEG signals, the algorithm is very sensitive to the inherent existing noise. To overcome the problem, we use the DWT to reduce the artifacts such as electrooculogram (EOG) and electromyogram (EMG) which often occur in higher frequency bands. In order to evaluate the performance of the proposed method, it is applied to a synthetic and real EEG signals. The simulation results show the Hiaguchi's FD with DWT can accurately detect the signal segments.

Keywords: Non-stationary signal, adaptive segmentation, discrete wavelet transform, Hiaguchi's fractal dimension.

1 Introduction

Non-stationary data originate from the sources of time-varing statistics. These include most of physiological recordings such as electroencephalogram (EEG), electrocardiogram (ECG) and electromyogram (EMG) data that are called non-stationary signals. In such cases the signals are often segmented into smaller epochs during which the signal remains approximately stationary. The segmentation may be fixed or adaptive. Dividing the non-stationary signals into fixed size segments is easy and fast. However, it can't precisely follow the epoch boundaries [1-3]. In adaptive segmentation, on the other hand, the boundaries are accurately and automatically followed [1]. Many adaptive segmentation methods have been suggested by researchers in the field such as those in [4-10].

Fractal dimension (FD) is a useful method to indicate varies in both amplitude and frequency of a signal. Katz's and Hiaguchi's algorithms are well-known techniques to achieve a FD of a signal. Although the Hiaguchi's method computes the FD more

D.-S. Huang et al. (Eds.): ICIC 2012, CCIS 304, pp. 152–159, 2012.

precise than Katz's method, due to Hiaguchi's method is very sensitive to noises, in all researches about the signal segmentation, especially electroencephalogram (EEG), the Katz's method was used [2]. To overcome the problem, in this paper we use the discrete wavelet transform (DWT) as a pre-processing step to reduce noises [11].

The other sections of this paper are organized as follows. In section 2.1 DWT is briefly explained. In section 2.2 the Hiaguchi's method as a technique to calculate the FD has been introduced. The proposed adaptive method is explained in section 3. The performance of the proposed method is evaluated in sections 4. The last section concludes the paper.

2   Background Knowledge for Proposed Method

2.1   Discrete Wavelet Transform

DWT is a powerful tool which is widely used to analyze a signal in the time series such as diagnosis of various central nervous system abnormalities like seizures, epilepsy, and brain damage. [12-14]. DWT can remove destructive noises like electrooculogram (EOG), electrocardiogram (ECG), electromyogram (EMG) which these often occurred in higher frequencies of EEG signal [15,16].

The DWT decomposes a signal into different scales with different level of resolution. Majority of signal information is in low frequency which is the most important part of the signal and the information in high frequency indicates details of the signal. Because of this, DWT utilizes low-pass and high-pass filters that like in Figure 1 [17].

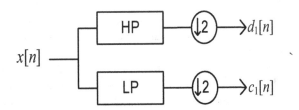

Fig. 1. Decomposition of $x[n]$ into one-level

Where x[n] is the input data and d1(n) and c1(n) describe the sub-bands signal components. After filtering, because each of the two outputs has the same length with the input signal, these outputs are downsampled by a factor of two. Thus, both d1(n) and c1(n) have half the length of the input signal [18].

2.2   Fractal Dimension

The FD of a signal depicts a powerful tool for transient detection and is widely used for image segmentation [17], analysis of audio signals [19], and analysis of biomedical signals such as EEG and ECG [20]. FD is a useful method to indicate varies in both amplitude and frequency of signal. In Figure 2 it is shown how FD changes when frequency or amplitude of a signal is changed.

The original signal includes four segments. The first and second segments have the same amplitude. The frequency of the first part is however different from that of the second part. In the third segment the amplitude becomes different from that of the second segment. Amplitude and frequency in the 4th segment are different from those of the third segment. The reason for creating this signal is to show that if two adjacent epochs of a signal have different amplitudes or frequencies the FD will vary.

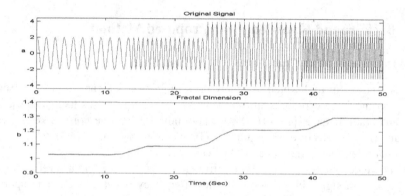

Fig. 2. Variation of FD when amplitude or frequency changes

There are several specific FD algorithms such as Hiaguchi's, Petrosian's, and Katz's. All of these algorithms have advantages and disadvantages and using them depends on the application [21].

Katz's algorithm compared with Petrosian's algorithm is slightly slower. In this algorithm, unlike the Petrosian's algorithm, it doesn't exist any pre-processing level for creating binary sequence. This algorithm, however, can be implemented directly on the analyzed signal [22].

Consider X (1), X (2). . . X (N) the time series to be analyzed, Construct k new time series x_m^k should as:

$$X_m^k = \left\{ X(m), X(m+k), X(m+2k), ..., X\left(m + \left[\frac{N-m}{k}\right]k\right) \right\} \quad m = 1, 2, \ldots, k \quad (1)$$

Where m and k indicate the initial value of the time series and the discrete time interval between points, respectively, N is the number of samples in the time series and [a] means integer part of a. For each time series shown as xmk, the average length $L_m(k)$ is computed as:

$$L_m(k) = \frac{\sum_{i=1}^{\left[\frac{N-m}{k}\right]} |X(m+ik) - X(m+(i-1)k)|(N-1)}{\left[\frac{N-m}{k}\right]k} \tag{2}$$

Where $(N-1)/\left[\frac{N-m}{k}\right]k$ is a normalization factor. $L_m(k)$ is computed for

m=1,…,k. This procedure is repeated for each k ranging from 1 to kmax, yielding an sum of average lengths L(k) for each k as indicated in (2)

$$L(k) = \sum_{i=1}^{k} L_m(k) \tag{3}$$

In the curve of $\ln(L(k))$ versus $\ln(1/k)$, the slope of the least-squares linear best fit, is the fractal dimension estimate by Hiaguchi's method.

3   Proposed Adaptive Segmentation

In this section the proposed method is explained briefly in three steps as follows:

1. The original signal is initially decomposed using Daubechies wavelet of order 8. The decomposed signal can indicate the slowly changing features of the signal in the lower frequency bands. Also, as mentioned before, for real signals such as EEG, DWT can be used as a time frequency filtering approach to remove the undesired signals such as EMG.
2. After reducing noises of the signal by the DWT, two successive windows are slid along the signal. For each window, the FD is computed by the Hiagochi's method. The FD variation is used to obtain the segment boundaries as follows:

$$G_t = |FD_{t+1} - FD_t| \qquad t = 1, 2, …, L-1 . \tag{4}$$

Where t and L are the number of analyzed windows, the total number of   analyzed windows is respective. It should be noted that for the proposed method G is normalized to 0 to 1.
3. Mean value of G ($\overline{G}$) is chosen as the threshold level, meaning that when the local maximum is bigger than this threshold, the current time sample is chosen as a boundary of the segment.

4   Simulation Data and Results

In order to evaluate the performance of the suggested method, we use two kind signals, namely, the synthetic data and real EEG signal. The synthetic signal includes the following seven epochs:

Epoch 1: 5.5cos (2πt) + 3.5cos (6πt),
Epoch 2: 3.5cos (3πt) + 7cos (11πt),
Epoch 3: 5cos (πt) + 5.5cos (7πt),
Epoch 4: 2.5cos (3πt) + 4.5cos (5πt) + 3cos (7πt),
Epoch 5: 2cos (2.5πt) + 2cos (7πt) + 8cos (10πt),
Epoch 6: 4.8cos (3πt) + 7.4cos (8πt),
Epoch 7: 7cos (2.5πt) + 3.8cos (5πt) + 4.5cos (8πt).

Fig. 1.a and 1.b show 50 seconds of the original signal and the decomposed signal using DWT, respectively. In this paper we have used the DWT with Daubechies wavelet of order 8. As can be seen in Figure 1.b, the filtered signal has lesser short-term variations compared with original signal. The output of the FD and changes of the G are shown in Figure 1.c and 1.d, respectively. As can be seen the boundaries for all seven segments accurately discerned.

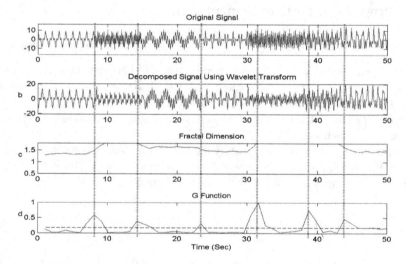

Fig. 3. Results of the proposed technique with Bee algorithm; (a) original signal, (b) decomposed signal by one-level DWT, (c) output of FD, and (d) *G* function result. As can be seen the boundaries for all seven segments can be accurately detected.

Second data that we use in this paper is EEG signal. Registration of electrical activity of the neurons in the brain is called EEG and it is an important tool in identifying and treating some neurological disorders like epilepsy. In this paper one EEG signal recorded from the scalp was used. The length of signals and the sampling frequency were 30 seconds and 256 Hz, respectively. The result of applying the proposed method is shown in Figure 4. In Figure 4.d can be seen that all four segments are accurately segmented. Figure 5.a shows the original signal as in Figure 4.a. The output of segmentation using proposed method without DWT is shown in Figure 5.c. As can be seen in Figure 5.c, the proposed method without DWT cannot indicate the boundaries of the EEG signal properly. One segment is not indicated (miss boundary) and two segment are indicated as boundaries of segments while they are not the boundaries of segments (false boundaries). By comparing Figures 4 and 5, we can notice the effect of the DWT in suggested method.

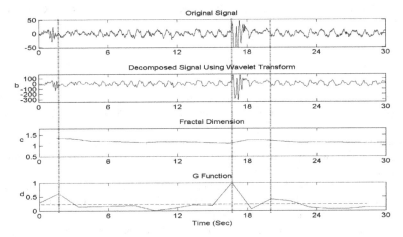

Fig. 4. Signal segmentation in real EEG data using proposed method; (a) original signal, (b) decomposed signal after applying five-level DWT, (c) output of FD, and (d) G function result. It can be seen that all four segments can be accurately segmented.

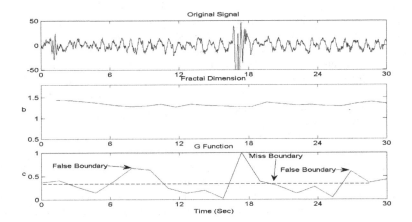

Fig. 5. Signal segmentation in real EEG data using proposed method without DWT; (a) original signal, (b) output of FD, and (c) G function result

5   Conclusions

In this paper a new adaptive signal segmentation approach using DWT and Hiaguchi's FD has been proposed. In order to obtain a better multiresolution representation of a signal which is vary valuable in detection of abrupt changes within that signal, the DWT is used. The changes in the Hiaguchi's FD refer to the underlying statistical variations of the signals and time series including the transients and sharp changes in both amplitude and frequency. The results of applying the proposed method on both the synthetic and real EEG signals show the clear advantages of the suggested method.

References

1. Azami, H., Sanei, S., Mohammadi, K.: A Novel Signal Segmentation Method Based on Standard Deviation and Variable Threshold. Journal of Computer Applications 34(2), 27–34 (2011)
2. Azami, H., Bozorgtabar, B., Shiroie, M.: Automatic signal segmentation using the fractal dimension and weighted moving average filter. Journal of Electrical & Computer science 11(6), 8–15 (2011)
3. Agarwal, R., Gotman, J.: Adaptive Segmentation of Electroencephalographic Data Using a Nonlinear Energy Operator. In: IEEE International Symposium on Circuits and Systems (ISCAS 1999), vol. 4, pp. 199–202 (1999)
4. Hassanpour, H., Mesbah, M., Boashash, B.: Time-Frequency Based Newborn EEG Seizure Detection Using Low and High Frequency Signatures. Physiological Measurement 25, 935–944 (2004)
5. Hassanpour, H., Mesbah, M., Boashash, B.: Time-Frequency Feature Extraction of Newborn EEG Seizure Using SVD-based Techniques. EURASIP Journal on Applied Signal Processing 16, 2544–2554 (2004)
6. Kosar, K., Lhotská, L., Krajca, V.: Classification of Long-Term EEG Recordings. In: Barreiro, J.M., Martín-Sánchez, F., Maojo, V., Sanz, F. (eds.) ISBMDA 2004. LNCS, vol. 3337, pp. 322–332. Springer, Heidelberg (2004)
7. Kirlangic, M.E., Perez, D., Kudryavtseva, S., Griessbach, G., Henning, G., Ivanova, G.: Fractal Dimension as a Feature for Adaptive Electroencephalogram Segmentation in Epilepsy. In: IEEE International EMBS Conference, vol. 2, pp. 1573–1576 (2001)
8. Azami, H., Mohammadi, K., Bozorgtabar, B.: An Improved Signal Segmentation Using Moving Average and Savitzky-Golay Filter. Journal of Signal and Information Processing 3(1), 39–44 (2012)
9. Azami, H., Mohammadi, K., Hassanpour, H.: An Improved Signal Segmentation Method Using Genetic Algorithm. Journal of Computer Applications 29(8), 5–9 (2011)
10. Hassanpour, H., Shahiri, M.: Adaptive Segmentation Using Wavelet Transform. In: International Conference on Electrical Engineering, pp. 1–5 (April 2007)
11. Gao, J., Sultan, H., Hu, J., Tung, W.W.: Denoising Nonlinear Time Series by Adaptive Filtering and Wavelet Shrinkage: a Comparison. IEEE Signal Processing Letters 17(3), 237–240 (2010)
12. Hsu, W.Y., Lin, C.C., Ju, M.S., Sun, Y.N.: Wavelet-Based Fractal Features with Active Segment Selection: Application to Single-Trial EEG Data. Elsevier Journal of Neuroscience Methods 163(1), 145–160 (2007)

13. Asaduzzaman, K., Reaz, M.B.I., Mohd-Yasin, F., Sim, K.S., Hussain, M.S.: A Study on Discrete Wavelet-Based Noise Removal from EEG Signals. Journal of Advances in Experimental Medicine and Biology 680, 593–599 (2010)
14. Estrada, E., Nazeran, H., Sierra, G., Ebrahimi, F., Setarehdan, S.K.: Wavelet-Based EEG Denoising for Automatic Sleep Stage Classification. In: International Conference on Electrical Communications and Computers (CONIELECOMP), pp. 295–298 (2011)
15. Geetha, G., Geethalakshmi, S.N.: EEG De-noising Using Sure Thresholding Based on Wavelet Transforms. International Journal of Computer Applications 24(6) (2011)
16. Easwaramoorthy, D., Uthayakumar, R.: Analysis of Biomedical EEG Signals Using Wavelet Transforms and Multifractal Analysis. In: IEEE International Conference on Communication Control and Computing Technologies (ICCCCT), pp. 545–549 (2010)
17. Tao, Y., Lam, E.C.M., Tang, Y.Y.: Feature Extraction Using Wavelet and Fractal. Elsevier Journal of Pattern Recognition 22(3-4), 271–287 (2001)
18. Rajagopalan, S., Aller, J.M., Restrepo, J.A., Habetler, T.G., Harley, R.G.: Analytic-Wavelet-Ridge-Based Detection of Dynamic Eccentricity in Brushless Direct Current (BLDC) Motors Functioning Under Dynamic Operating Conditions. IEEE Transaction on Industrial Electronics 54(3), 1410–1419 (2007)
19. Gunasekaran, S., Revathy, K.: Fractal Dimension Analysis of Audio Signals for Indian Musical Instrument Recognition. In: International Conference on Audio, Language and Image Processing (ICALIP), pp. 257–261 (2008)
20. Acharya, U.R., Faust, O., Kannathal, N., Chua, T., Laxminarayan, S.: Non-Linear Analysis of EEG Signals at Various Sleep Stages. Computer Methods and Programs in Biomedicine 80(1), 37–45 (2005)
21. Esteller, R., Vachtsevanos, G., Echauz, J., Litt, B.: A Comparison of Fractal Dimension Algorithms Using Synthetic and Experimental Data. In: IEEE International Symposium on Circuits and Systems (ISCAS 1999), vol. 3, pp. 199–202 (1999)
22. Esteller, R., Vachtsevanos, G., Echauz, J., Litt, B.: A Comparison of Waveform Fractal Dimension Algorithms. IEEE Transaction on Circuits and Systems 48(2), 177–183 (2001)

Predicting Binding-Peptide of HLA-I on Unknown Alleles by Integrating Sequence Information and Energies of Contact Residues

Fei Luo, Yangyang Gao, Yongqiong Zhu, and Juan Liu

School of Computer, Wuhan University, Wuhan, Hubei, China
{Luofei,liujuan}@whu.edu.cn, yangygao@yahoo.com.cn,
zhuyongqiong@hotmail.com

Abstract. The human MHC class I system is extremely polymorphic and now the registered number of HLA-I molecules has exceeded 3000. These HLAs have slightly different amino acid sequences, which makes them potentially bind to different sets of peptides. In order to overcome the problems existing in current methods and take into account the MHC sequence and energies of contact residues information, in this paper a method based on artificial neural network is proposed to predict peptides binding to HLAs on unknown alleles with limited or even no prior experimental data. The super-type experiments are implemented to validate our method. In the experiment, we collected 14 HLA-A and 14 HLA-B molecules on Bjoern Peters dataset and did leave-one-out cross-validation on MHC-peptide binding data with different alleles but sharing the same super-type, our method got the best average AUC value as 0.846 compared to gold standard methods such as NetMHC and NetMHCpan.

Keywords: peptide, HLA, artificial neural network.

1   Introduction

In the cellular immune system, binding of peptides to MHC (Major Histocompatibility Complex) is the most selective step in recognition of pathogens. Large amount of research experiments on binding of the peptides to MHC show that their binding sites have specificities. These specificities are usually decided by molecular weight, electric charges, pH value and other attributes, and these attributes could help predict which peptides will bind to the given MHC. From the binding fragments of peptide binding to MHC, Rudensky [1] purified and detected their amino acid sequences. After analyzing these amino acid sequences they proposed I-As, I-Ab, and I-Eb three binding motifs. According to these three motifs, Cole [2] successfully predicted MHC class II-restricted epitopes in the Sendai virus M protein. In the past decades, a large number of prediction methods have been proposed to identify which peptides could bind to the given MHC. These prediction methods could be divided into several types. The first one is motif matching based methods [3-5]. This kind of methods is simple and easy to understand but the prediction accuracy is not high. The second type is

D.-S. Huang et al. (Eds.): ICIC 2012, CCIS 304, pp. 160–165, 2012.

based on scoring matrix. Typical methods include ProPred [6], ARB[7], SMM [8]. They usually have higher accuracy than the motif based methods, but their shortcomings lie in they assumed that each amino acid residue independently contributes to the binding process of peptide and MHC, and ignored the interactions among the residues. In order to further improve the accuracy of prediction, some methods tried to consider the whole peptide sequence and establish more complex models to reflect the real situation. This kind of method includes the Bayesian method (Bayesian) [9], HMM (Hidden Markov Model) [10], SVM (Support Vector Machine) [11], ANN (Artificial Neural Network) [12] and so on. In fact, the human MHC class I system (HLA-I) is extremely polymorphic and the registered number of HLA-I molecules has now surpassed 3000. These HLAs with slightly different amino acid sequences have their own binding specificities, so they can potentially bind to different sets of peptides. Thus, these sequence-based prediction methods have been biased towards the known alleles and may have over-fitting problem. On the other hand, structure-based methods could jump over the polymorphic sequence and binding specificity problem by directly using 3D structure of the MHC molecule and their empirical force fields to estimate the peptide and HLA-I binding affinity. However, the available 3D structure data is few. Only 17 HLA-I molecules' 3D structures are resolved, therefore the accuracy of structure-based methods is usually lower than sequence-based methods due to the insufficiency of data.

In order to overcome the existing problems and meanwhile guarantee the prediction accuracy, we still take machine learning strategy. A method based on artificial neural network is proposed to predict peptides binding to HLAs on unknown alleles in the case that there are limited or even no prior experimental data. Different from other sequence-based methods using ANN technologies, our method not only takes peptide sequence information into account but also the energies of contact residues information. With more information involvement, our method is expected to predict the binding affinity between peptide and HLA-I with high accuracy.

2   Method

2.1   Calculate the Interacting Residues of HLA and Peptide

The peptide and HLA-I binding prediction on unknown Alleles is still an important and difficult job. According to the above analysis, we adopt ANN (Artificial Neural Network) classifier to predict the peptide and HLA-1 binding. The ANN model has the advantages of self-learning, self-adaptive and non-linear modeling. More important, different from other methods which just consider the peptides sequence information, we not only consider the MHC molecules sequence information but also the amino acids' interaction between peptide and MHC.

Inspired by Madden's work [13], we calculated and got the residues of peptide and HLA interaction from the existing peptide-HLA binding complexes structure data. The statistical results show when different HLAs with the same gene loci bind to peptides, the sites of HLAs' amino acid residue interacting with peptide are similar, which is consistent with the result of Madden. Obviously, not all interaction residue sites are the same, so we neglected those residues of HLAs which interacted with peptides less than 5 times. Finally, we got 59 interaction residues in HLA-A and peptide and 75 interaction residues in HLA-B and peptide. All the peptide and HLA structure data comes from the PDB (protein Data Base). In total there're 111 peptide-HLA-A binding complexes data and 87 peptide-HLA-B binding complexes data. When the residues' distance of HLA and peptide is less than 4 Å, we thought they interacted.

2.2   Affinity of Amino Acid Residues

The interaction strength could be calculated by the electromagnetic theory. If the attracting strength between two residues is greater, their position will have more chance to be near. Therefore, if there are enough protein structure data, the mutual attracting strength could be obtained by computing their position distance. In the structure biology, Miyazawa and Jernigan [14] matrix has been widely used for computing the protein sequence energy in different structure template. In order to take into account the interaction function between MHC and water molecule, we will use the B matrix [15] to get the interacting energy of amino acid residues.

2.3   Encoding the Peptide and HLA

In this paper, HLA sequence is coded by the affinity of residues which interact with peptide (B matrix). Therefore the coding length for the HLA-A and peptide is 239 dimensions, in which 180 dimension is coding for peptide by BLOSUM matrix and 59 dimensions is coding for HLA-A residues interacting with the peptides by the B matrix. The coding length for the HLA-B and peptide is 255 dimensions, in which 180 dimension is coding for peptide by BLOSUM matrix and 75 dimensions is coding for HLA-B residues interacting with the peptides by the B matrix. In order to better measure the difference of affinity and facilitate the artificial neural network training. The affinity will be transformed to log value (affinity = 1 - log (IC50)/log50000)

2.4   ANNBM Building and Training

There're many subtypes in the ANN. In this paper we use error back propagation neural network. It consists of three layers including an input layer, a hidden layer and an output layer. Neural network's input layer has 239 nodes for predicting peptide-HLA-A binding, while neural network's input layer has 255 nodes for predicting peptide-HLA-B binding. The output layer has only one node. It is the logarithmic value of affinity between MHC molecules and peptide. There is no golden criterion to decide the number of hidden layers. So we test the number of hidden nodes varying from 2 to 12. Hidden layer with 9 nodes has gotten the minimum mean square error.

3   Experiments on unknown Alleles Dataset

If there is no prior binding dataset for the HLA molecules, we make use of the Sette and Sidney work[16] to indirectly solve this obstacle. Sette and Sidney discovered that HLA-I class molecules could be divided into several super classes based on their

Table 1. Prediction Result Comparison

Allele	Supertype	ANNBM	NetMHC	NetMHCpan	peptides
A*0101	A1	0.854	0.671	0.873	1157
A*0201	A2	0.905	0.886	0.911	3089
A*0202	A2	0.840	0.783	0.815	1447
A*0203	A2	0.835	0.818	0.831	1443
A*0206	A2	0.883	0.826	0.846	1436
A*0301	A3	0.866	0.819	0.849	2094
A*1101	A3	0.878	0.850	0.865	1985
A*2301	A24	0.916	0.876	0.863	104
A*2402	A24	0.863	0.848	0.821	197
A*2403	A24	0.922	0.893	0.911	254
A*2601	A1	0.771	0.631	0.733	672
A*2902	A3	0.832	0.602	0.749	160
A*3001	A3	0.863	0.845	0.838	669
A*3002	A1	0.671	0.711	0.721	92
A*3101	A3	0.852	0.821	0.877	1869
A*3301	A3	0.838	0.699	0.762	1140
A*6801	A3	0.767	0.743	0.759	1141
A*6802	A2	0.811	0.663	0.669	1434
A*6901	A2	0.901	0.811	0.823	833
B*0702	B7	0.919	0.863	0.901	1262
B*1501	B62	0.687	0.536	0.749	978
B*1801	B62	0.823	0.775	0.728	969
B*3501	B7	0.805	0.737	0.761	736
B*4001	B44	0.851	0.817	0.869	1078
B*4002	B44	0.883	0.802	0.806	118
B*4402	B44	0.824	0.771	0.839	119
B*4403	B44	0.835	0.800	0.841	119
B*4501	B44	0.822	0.804	0.809	114
B*5101	B7	0.887	0.878	0.904	244
B*5301	B7	0.827	0.818	0.838	254
B*5401	B7	0.880	0.846	0.844	255
B*5701	B58	0.945	0.652	0.918	59
B*5801	B58	0.868	0.625	0.841	988
AVG		0.846	0.773	0.823	

binding specificity. MHC molecules belonging to the same super class have similar binding site structure. Sette and Sidney divided allele genes of HLA-A into 5 super classes: A1、A2、A3、A24 and A26，and divided allele genes of HLA-B into 7 super classes: B7、B8、B27、B39、B44、B58 and B62. In this part, we will validate ANNBM prediction without direct binding data. Besides the Bjoern Peters' dataset, another 6 HLA molecules were added from the IEDB. We used the leave-one-out method to do validation. Finally we got the result table 1, in which the first column is the name of allele gene, the second column is the super class that the HLA molecule belongs to, the columns from 3 to 5 are the AUC value of ANNBM, NetMHC and NetMHCpan and the last column is the number of binding peptides to the corresponding HLA molecule. Methods NetMHC and NetMHCpan come from the works [17, 18].

From table 1, we can see that ANNBM method has the greater AUC value than NetMHCpan and NetMHC methods by 0.023 and 0.073. NetMHC encoding method doesn't take into account the HLA molecules information, although the training data comes from the same super-type. The HLA differences in the same super class are not reflected, so the NetMHC prediction accuracy less than those of ANNBM and NetMHCpan which encoded HLA molecules information is not difficult to understand. Comparing the encoding method between ANNBM and NetMHCpan, When ANNBM encoding the HLA molecules, ANNBM uses the B matrix and each amino acid that could interact with peptide is denoted by a numerical value, while NetMHCpan uses the BLOSUM matrix and each amino acid is denoted by a 20 dimensions vector. For each super class, the AUC of ANNBM is greater than that of NetMHCpan

4   Conclusion

We have developed ANNBM method that can well predict peptide binding to HLAs with limited or even no experimental data. This method takes both peptide sequence information and potential energies of contact residues between peptide and HLA into account, and gives out the quantitative binding affinity. Super-type experimental validations on benchmark datasets successfully validate this method.

Acknowledgements. This work is supported by National Natural Science Foundation of China (No. 60970063) ，Doctoral Fund of Ministry of Education of China (No. 20110141120031) and Central University Scientific Research Fund (No.211275701).

References

1. Rudensky, A., Preston-Hurlburt, P., Al-Ramadi, B.K., Rothbard, J., Janeway, C.A.: Truncation Variants of Peptides Isolated From Mhc Class Ii Molecules Suggest Sequence Motifs. Nature 359, 429–431 (1992)
2. Cole, G.A., Tao, T., Hogg, T.L., Ryan, K.W., Woodland, D.L.: Binding Motifs Predict Major Histo-Com Patibility Complex Class Ii-Restricted Epitopes in The Sendai Virus M Protein. J. Virol. 69, 8057–8060 (1995)

3. Rammensee, H., Bachmann, J., Emmerich, N.P., Stevanovic, S.: SYFPEITHI: Database for Mhc Ligands And Peptide Motif. Immunogenetics 50, 213–219 (1999)

4. Doytchinova, I.A., Blythe, M.J., Flower, D.R.: Additive Methods for the Prediction of Protein-Peptide Binding Affinity. Application to the mhc class i Molecules hla-a*0201. J. Proteome Res. 1, 263–272 (2002)

5. Jain, A.K., Mao, J., Mohiuddin, K.M.: Atificial Neural Networks: A Turorial. IEEE Computer 29, 31–44; [55] Rudy, G., Harrison, L.C., Brusic, V.: MHCPEP: a database of MHC-binding peptides. Nucleic Acids Res. 25, 269–271 (1997)

6. Zhu, S., Udaka, K., Sidney, J., Sette, A., Aoki-Kinoshita, K.F., et al.: Improving MHC Binding Peptide Prediction By Incorporating Binding Data of Auxiliary Mhc Molecules. Bioinformatics 22, 1648–1655 (2006)

7. Bui, H.H., Sidney, J., Peters, B., Sathiamurthy, M., Sinichi, A., Purton, K.A., Mothe, B.R., Chisari, F.V., Watkins, D.I., Sette, A.: Automated Generation and Evaluation of Specific Mhc Binding Predictive Tools: ARB Matrix Applications. Immunogenetics 57, 304–314 (2005)

8. Peters, B., Tong, W., Sette, A., Weng, Z.: Examining the Independent Binding Assumption for Binding of Peptide Epitopes to MHC-I Molecules. Bioinformatics 19, 1765–1772 (2003)

9. Wen, Z., Juan, L., Yan, Q., Lian, W., Xihao, H.: Bayesian Regression Approach To The Prediction of Mhc-Ii Binding Affinity. Computer Methods and Programs in Biomedicine 92, 1–7 (2008)

10. Zhang, C., Bickis, M.G., Wu, F.X., Kusalik, A.J.: Optimally Connected Hidden Markov Models For Predicting Mhc-Binding Peptides. J. Bioinform. Comput. Biol. 4, 959–980 (2006)

11. Liu, W., Meng, X., Xu, Q., Flower, D.R., Li, T.: Quantitative Prediction Of Mouse Class I Mhc Peptide Binding Affinity Using Support Vector Machine Regression (Svr) Models. BMC Bioinformatics 7, 182–189 (2006)

12. Buus, S., Lauemøller, S.L., Worning, P., Kesmir, C., Frimurer, T., et al.: Sensitive Quantitative Predictions Of Peptide-Mhc Binding By A Query By Committee Artificial Neural Network Approach. Tissue Antigens 62, 378–384 (2003)

13. Madden, D.R.: The Three-Dimensional Structure of Peptide-Mhc Complexes. Annu. Rev. Immunol. 13, 587–622 (1995)

14. Miyazawa, S., Jernigan, R.L.: Estimation of Effective Interresidue Contact Energiesfrom Protein Crystal Structures: Quasi-Chemical Approximation Macromolecules 18534 (1985)

15. Betancourt, M.R., Thirumalai, D.: air Potentials For Protein Folding: Choice of Referencestates and Sensitivity of Predicted Native Statesto Variations In The Interaction Schemes. Protein Sci. 8, 361–369 (1999)

16. Sette, A., Sidney, J.: Ninemajor HLA Class I Supertypesaccount for the Vast Preponderance of HLA-A and-B Polymorphism. Immunogenetics 50, 201–212 (1999)

17. Nielsen, M.: NetMHCpan, A Method For Quantitative Predictionsof Peptide Bindingto Any Hla-A And -B Locus Protein of Known Sequence. PLoS ONE, 2, e796 (2007)

18. Nielsen, M., Lundegaard, C., Worning, P., Lauemoller, S.L., Lamberth, K., Buus, S., Brunak, S., Lund, O.: Reliable Prediction of T-Cell Epitopes Using Neural Networks With Novel Sequence Representations. Protein Sci 12, 1007–1017 (2003)

As³p: A Fast Algorithm to Search Structurally Similar Proteins

Satish Rohit, Ravichandran Akshaya, Radhakrishnan Sabarinathan,
Marthandan Kirti Vaishnavi, Durairaj Sherlin,
Manickam Gurusaran, and Kanagaraj Sekar

Supercomputer Education and Research Centre
Indian Institute of Science
Bangalore 560 012
sekar@physics.iisc.ernet.in

Abstract. Protein structure comparison is essential for understanding various aspects of protein structure, function and evolution. It can be used to explore the structural diversity and evolutionary patterns of protein families. In view of the above, a new algorithm is proposed which performs faster protein structure comparison using the peptide backbone torsional angles. It is fast, robust, computationally less expensive and efficient in finding structural similarities between two different protein structures and is also capable of identifying structural repeats within the same protein molecule.

Keywords: protein structure comparison, protein structural fragments, Cα angle, structural repeats.

1 Introduction

Protein structure alignment is of great biological significance and it can be used to identify functional and distant evolutionary relationships. The number of protein structures being added to the Protein Data Bank (PDB) [1] is increasing exponentially with recent technological advances such as high power tunable synchrotron radiation, high end digital computers and large scale structural genomics initiatives etc. These abundant resources demand the need for an accurate and automatic tool for identifying structurally similar protein structures. However, protein structure comparison is computationally expensive and time consuming [2]. Therefore, a new algorithm has been created which is capable of identifying structurally similar proteins (available in the PDB) using the peptide backbone Cα angles.

It is a well known fact that the structure of a protein molecule is closely related to its biological function and is more conserved than its amino acid sequence. Two protein structures with high sequence similarity almost (always) share the same fold. However, the reverse is not true because a pair of protein molecules with similar three-dimensional structures possess on an average 3 to 10% sequence similarity [3-5]. In addition, the function of a protein molecule is directly related to its three-dimensional structure. Thus, it is imperative to identify structural similarities between protein structures [6].

D.-S. Huang et al. (Eds.): ICIC 2012, CCIS 304, pp. 166–173, 2012.

It has been established that the study of protein fragments is vital for investigating sequence-structure relationship. Compared to amino acid sequence alignment, protein structure alignment is complicated, as it involves detecting geometric relationship between protein structures [7]. An efficient way to achieve an accurate structure comparison is to translate the protein structure into a string of alphabets. The comparison becomes easier and less time consuming if the protein structure is represented in a one dimensional format [4,7,8]. Thus, one dimensional representation of the protein structure can be used for alignment based similarity scoring in a way analogous to amino acid sequence alignment [9].

There are structure comparison tools available online which are capable of performing pairwise structure comparison. However, only a few tools like DALI [10] and SALAMI [11] are available for comparing a given structure against all the three-dimensional structures present in its archive, the protein data bank. However, the existing tools do not find structural similarities (see case study 2 for details) within the same protein structure. Further, the above mentioned structure comparison tools take a long time for computing the results which are at times sent via email to the users. Thus, to address the above short comings, an efficient algorithm has been developed and the details are discussed below.

2   Methodology

2.1   Representation of a Protein Structure

The algorithm has been designed to perform structure comparison based on similarities in the protein Cα angle, which is a torsion angle calculated by considering four consecutive Cα atoms. The use of Cα angles in protein structure comparison was first employed by Usha and Murphy [12] and since then this method has been implemented in several programs like, SWELFE [13], ProSTRIP [14] and SSM [15] etc. The following methodology, however, describes the effective utilization of Cα angles in protein structure comparison as well as internal structural repeats. The computed angles are stored as alphabets to speed-up the search process, wherein, the angles with positive values are denoted in capital letters and the angles with negative values are denoted in small letters. For example, the positive angles (0° to 180°) are equally divided (10° interval) and assigned the alphabets "A to R". The same procedure is followed for the negative angles which are assigned the alphabets "a to r" accordingly. All the protein structures present in the 90% non-homologous protein chains [16] were downloaded. The necessary Cα angles were calculated and the one dimensional array was created as mentioned above.

2.2   Proposed Algorithm

The algorithm has been developed using dynamic programming [17]. By the same method used to create the subject/reference database, the input query protein structure is also converted to a one dimensional array and stored in the variable q_pro. The string of alphabets from the database is stored in the variable db_pro. Now, the translated query structure is compared with each structure from the subject/reference database in a pair wise manner. The match scores from the comparison are stored in four vectors –variant, hold, mis1 and mis2. It is to note that these vectors are used in place of N x N matrix, which is generally used to store the match scores of pairwise comparison. The vectors variant and hold are used to store the current and previous match scores, respectively. The details of the comparison are described below.

Each alphabet i of the string in variable q_pro is compared with each alphabet j of the string in variable db_pro. If a match is found at the jth position, the vector element hold [j-1] is incremented by one and assigned to variant [j].   At the end of this iteration, the vector variant is copied into hold and variant is set to zero. This process is repeated for all the characters in the variable q_pro. Tolerance value is used by allowing the appropriate deviations in the ASCII values of the query characters. The program is, to a certain extent, tolerant of mismatches as it allows a maximum of two consecutive mismatched characters in the variable db_pro. This is done by using the vectors mis1 and mis2.

Pseudo code for finding match and allowing mismatches

```
WHILE i < length of q_pro
  set j to zero
  WHILE j < length of db_pro
IF (q_pro[i] equals db_pro[j]) or (q_pro[i] equals
db_pro[j]-1) or (q_pro[i] equals db_pro[j]+1) THEN
  set variant[j] to hold[j-1]+1
  IF hold[j-1] equals 0 THEN
  IF mis1[j-1] not equal to 0 THEN
            variant[j]=mis1[j-1]+2
ELSE mis2[j-1] not equal to 0
            variant[j]=mis2[j-1]+3
  ENDIF
ENDIF
    ENDIF
    ENDWHILE
  set hold to variant
    set variant to null vector
    set i to i+1
ENDWHILE
```

2.3   Filtering Hits

When mismatches are tolerated in a fragment which is considered as a 'hit', several false hits may be encountered. In order to filter out the unrelated fragments, only alignments with a minimum of 85% similarity (by default) are considered. This is done by using four vectors – *gap, gap1, gap2* and *gap3*.

Pseudo code for filtering hits

```
IF hold[j-1] equals 0 THEN
IF mis1[j-1] is not equal to 0 and j is greater than 1
THEN
    SET variant[j]=mis1[j-1]+2
    SET  gap[j]=gap2[j-1]+1
    ELSE IF mis2[j-1] is not equal to 0 and j is
greater than 2 THEN
        SET variant[j]=mis2[j-1]+3
        SET gap[j]=gap3[j-1]+2
            END IF
    ELSE
        gap[j]=gap1[j-1]
    END IF
```

The number of gaps allowed is used to determine the percentage of mismatches in the fragment. If this percentage is less than 15%, the fragment is considered a valid hit and the corresponding subject fragments (with similarity greater than or equal to 85%) are displayed in the output. The hits obtained may include small fragments which are subsets of larger hits, leading to redundancy in the hits. In such cases, the redundant fragments are removed and only non-redundant fragments are displayed.

To better understand the algorithm, let us consider two one dimensional arrays "ASDGHFGGSERHDJT" and "HDHERRDPGGGFEGD" in the form of a matrix (Figure 1). Each row of the matrix represents the "hold" vector and the blank cells denote zero. The two cells filled with tiny squares represent the matched regions. Here, the algorithm identifies a match of H and D at the 12th and the 13th positions respectively. When the algorithm encounters a match, it assigns a value 1 to the first match and during the next iteration; the algorithm adds 1 to the previous cell's value for every consecutive match encountered. Thus, when a hit occurs at the 13th position (at D) during the second iteration, the value stored in "variant [13]" and "hold [13]" is "hold [13-1] + 1", which is 2. A typical case of a mismatch encountered by the algorithm is denoted by the cells filled with diagonals. Here again, a match "R" is recorded at the 11th position, five rows down the matrix. However, the algorithm encounters a mismatch during the next iteration for which it introduces a gap (grey colored cell) and proceeds with the next iteration. This way, the algorithm identifies all possible matches (cells colored in black and filled with stripes) and stores them. After this, significant matches are filtered based on the tolerance value. For instance, if the tolerance is 10° and the percentage of mismatches allowed is 15%, the match denoted in the striped cells will be filtered out as "loose" hit, because it contains two mismatches and the percentage mismatch is greater than 15. Hence, only the match colored in black is considered a significant hit.

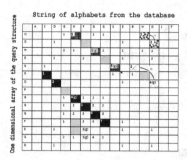

Fig. 1. One dimensional array of alphabets of a particular structure from the database (X-axis) and the query structure (Y-axis) are represented in the form of a matrix. The gradient cells denote the matched hits obtained and the grey cells denote mismatched regions.

2.4   Percentage Similarity

The end of a match is determined by comparing the values of *variant[j]* and *hold[j-1]*. If the value of *hold[j-1]* is greater than that of *variant[j]*, the end of the match is reached at position (j-1). Value of *hold[j-1]* gives the length of the match. The length of the match is compared to the cutoff given by the user (or to the default cutoff). If the length is greater than the cutoff, the start and the end positions of the match are stored. The total number of residues in the query protein for which a hit is encountered by the algorithm is divided by the size of query protein. This provides the structural similarity in percentage and is denoted as match percent.

The exact similarity of a fragment is determined by calculating the fraction of exact matches by excluding the number of mismatches that have been allowed in the total length of the fragment. This value is considered as the gap percent. Higher the gap percent, better the match. The final similarity score is calculated by giving equal weightage to the structural similarity percent and the product of the gap percent with a ratio of the length of the largest fragment to the size of the query. Without this ratio, a match of a large fragment would be considered same as match between several small fragments, other constraints being the same.

Similarity score= 0.5 (matchpercent) + 0.5 (gap percent * ratio of the largest fragment length to the query length)

The results obtained are sorted based on the similarity score.

3   Results and Discussion

3.1   Case Study: 1

The crystal structure of a heavy chain variable domain (FV) fragment from mouse (PDB-id: 1MFA) was given as the input. The proposed algorithm identified 286 similar protein chains (Figure 2) in 0.08 seconds and this result was further analyzed based on the classification given in SCOP. If a protein is similar to the query in three parameters (class, fold and superfamily) it is given a high rank. Based on this the protein 1MFA_H is classified under the class "all beta" and belongs to the "immunog-lobulin" superfamily. Similarly, the results obtained also fall under the same catego-ries and it is interesting to note that similar results were obtained when the query fragment was submitted in the DALI and SALAMI servers.

Query ID: 1mfa H
Length of the query: 120

Number of matches found=281

(a)	(b)	(c)	(d)	(e)
1mfa_H	100%	123	1	5	92	IGG1-LAMBDA 8E152-4 FAB (LIGHT CHAIN);
1oaq_H	96%	124	0.515	12	80	HEAVY CHAIN;
3nc8_H	76%	226	0.4068	21	151	NATIVIDNAB FAB LIGHT CHAIN;
3 hc4_H	81%	216	0.3989	16	181	IMMUNOGLOBULIN IGG1 FAB, HEAVY CHAIN;
1e6o_H	77%	222	0.39	15	108	IMMUNOGLOBULIN HEAVY CHAIN;
1eam_H	78%	216	0.3892	17	191	IGG ANTIBODY (LIGHT CHAIN);
1iqw_K	78%	233	0.3892	17	138	ANTIBODY N-EF67A, LIGHT CHAIN;
1yni_H	80%	222	0.3906	21	113	IG GAMMA LIGHT CHAIN;
1t3f_B	79%	223	0.3452	25	148	BH2AF ANTIBODY LIGHT CHAIN;
3n8g_H	76%	233	0.3342	21	149	FAB FRAGMENT OF MAB CR4354, HEAVY CHAIN;
1iy0_H	52%	123	0.321	14	78	FAB 14, LIGHT DOMAIN;
1lK9_H	76%	222	0.3306	27	187	INTERLEUKIN-10;
1k6q_H	76%	219	0.3303	27	125	IMMUNOGLOBULIN FAB 59, LIGHT CHAIN;
2d7t_H	76%	142	0.3136	17	71	ANTI POLYHYDROXYBUTYRATE ANTIBODY FV, HEAVY CHAIN;
3ec8_H	69%	222	0.3128	29	156	EFALIZUMAB FAB FRAGMENT, LIGHT CHAIN;
1jfq_H	70%	215	0.3102	17	159	ANTIGEN-BINDING FRAGMENT OF ANTI-PHENYLARBONATE ANTIBODY;
1f11_D	70%	216	0.306	21	125	HYBRIDOMA ANTIBODY LA2 (LIGHT CHAIN);
3d1f_D	76%	232	0.3041	16	182	FAB0K117 LIGHT CHAIN FRAGMENT;
3uu0_B	68%	228	0.3031	18	180	GC-1008 FAB LIGHT CHAIN;
1yqv_H	49%	218	0.3005	24	133	HYHEL-5 ANTIBODY LIGHT CHAIN;
3mrw_H	64%	223	0.2948	27	146	SONIC HEDGEHOG PROTEIN;
3mni_M	68%	231	0.289	24	159	C706 MONOCLONAL LIGHT CHAIN;
1h16_D	64%	216	0.281	23	134	IGG1A KAPPA ANTIBODY CD41 (LIGHT CHAIN);
1nsm_H	64%	218	0.2801	17	98	CHIMERIC 8D1 CHIX21;
1jpt_H	45%	228	0.2786	25	162	IMMUNOGLOBULIN FAB D3N44, LIGHT CHAIN;
1qkz_H	64%	224	0.2784	21	187	FAB 981, LIGHT CHAIN;
1vj3_D	45%	230	0.2707	16	180	190 FAB LIGHT CHAIN;
2hh0_H	45%	233	0.2681	23	131	LIGHT CHAIN, F-CLONE FAB, CHIMERA;
1dzb_A	45%	256	0.2655	19	106	SCFV FRAGMENT 1F9;
1mvu_D	45%	124	0.2655	12	86	IG KAPPA-CHAIN VJ-REGION (LIGHT CHAIN);

(a) -> PDB-id_chain name

(b) -> Percentage similarity

(c) -> No. of residues

(d) -> Similarity score

(e) -> Name of the protein molecule

Fig. 2. Results obtained when a heavy chain FV fragment from mouse (PDB-id: 1MFA, chain H) was given as the input query structure. The output (only part of the result is shown) given by the algorithm is shown here.

3.2 Case Study: 2

The fact that the algorithm can effectively recognize structurally similar fragments within the protein molecule is a major advantage. One such protein molecule is the three-dimensional structure of human gamma B crystalline (PDB-id: 2JDF_A) which contains two sequentially dissimilar and structurally similar domains (Figure 3). These domains extend from residue numbers 2-81 and 89-170. When the atomic coordinates corresponding to the domain from 2-81 was given to the proposed

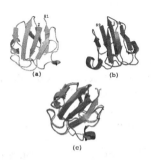

Fig. 3. (a) and (b) The sequentially dissimilar and structurally similar domains of the human gamma-B crystalline (PDB-id: 2JDF_A) is shown and (c) superposition of the two domains

algorithm, it identified several fragments (Figure 4) from within the domain 89-170. The algorithm took 0.17 seconds to display the results. Thus, the proposed algorithm is capable of recognizing both the regions as individual fragments. However, this is not the case with DALI and SALAMI which identified several structurally similar fragments from other protein molecules but not structurally similar fragments from within the 2JDF molecule.

FRAGMENT RESULT

>2jdf_A

Number of fragments found=6

2jdf_A	2jdf_A	Length
2-81	2-81	80
2-22	89-109	21
39-56	128-145	18
41-54	89-102	14
3-15	131-143	13
60-71	149-160	12

Fig. 4. Structurally similar but sequentially dissimilar fragments obtained when the Beta/Gamma crystallin domain 2JDF_A was given as the input query structure

3.3   Confusion Matrix

In order to analyze the biological relevance of the proposed algorithm, a confusion matrix was constructed for the results obtained by searching PDB-ids 1TLK, 2ACT and 1MDC against the reference database, SCOP. The above three protein structures fall under three different super-families, namely, "Immunoglobin", "Cysteine protease" and "Lipocalin" respectively. From the confusion matrix, precision and recall were calculated which provided a more detailed analysis than measuring the algorithm's accuracy (proportion of correct predictions) as measuring accuracy may mislead if the data set was unbalanced. The precision and recall values were calculated to be one (Maximum). Thus, a high recall means that the algorithm computed most of the relevant results and a high precision means that the algorithm computed more relevant than irrelevant results.

4   Conclusions

The proposed algorithm allows three-dimensional structure comparison of the query protein structure with other protein structures available in the subject/reference database. From the above, it can be concluded that the proposed algorithm is fast and more efficient when compare to other structure comparison tools available online and will be of immense use to structural biologists and bioinformaticians worldwide.

Acknowledgements. The work reported in the manuscript is fully supported by the Department of Information Technology (DIT), Government of India. The authors gratefully acknowledge the facilities offered by the Bioinformatics Centre and the Interactive graphics facility.

References

1. Berman, H.M., Westbrook, J., Feng, Z., Gilliland, G., Bhat, T.N., Weissig, H., Shindyalov, I.N., Bourne, P.E.: The Protein Data Bank. Nucleic Acids Res. 28, 235–242 (2000)
2. Zotenko, E., Gogan, R.I., Wilbur, W.J., O'Leary, D.P., Przytycka, T.M.: Structural Footprinting In Protein Structure Comparison: the Impact of Structural Fragments. BMC Struct. Biol. 7, 53–66 (2007)
3. Rost, B.: Protein Structures Sustain Evolutionary Drift. Fold Des. 24, S19–S24 (1997)
4. Balaji, S., Srinivasan, N.: Comparison of Sequence-Based and Structure-Based Phylogenetic Trees of Homologous Proteins: Inferences on Protein Evolution. J. Biosci. 32, 83–96 (2007)
5. Illergard, K., Ardell, D.H., Elofsson, A.: Structure is Three To Ten Times More Conserved Than Sequence–A Study Of Structural Response In Protein Cores. Protein 77, 499–508 (2009)
6. Le, Q., Pollastri, G., Koehl, P.: Structural Alphabets for Protein Structure Classification: A Comparison Study. J. Mol. Biol. 387, 431–450 (2009)
7. Kolodny, R., Petrey, D., Honig, B.: Protein Structure Comparison: Implications For The Nature of 'Fold Space', And Structure And Function Prediction. Curr. Opin. Struct. Biol. 16, 393–398 (2006)
8. Zheng, W.M.: The Use of A Conformational Alphabet for Fast Alignment of Protein Structures. In: Măndoiu, I., Wang, S.-L., Zelikovsky, A. (eds.) ISBRA 2008. LNCS (LNBI), vol. 4983, pp. 331–342. Springer, Heidelberg (2008)
9. Friedberg, I., Harder, T., Kolodny, R., Sitbon, E., Li, Z., Godzik, A.: Using An Alignment of Fragment Strings for Comparing Protein Structures. Bioinformatics 23, 219–224 (2007)
10. Holm, L., Kaariainen, S., Rosenstrom, P., Schenkel, A.: Searching Protein Structure Databases with DaliLite v.3. Bioinformatics 24, 2780–2781 (2008)
11. Margraf, T., Schenk, G., Torda, A.E.: The SALAMI Protein Structure Search Server. Nucleic. Acids. Res. 37, 480–484 (2009)
12. Usha, R., Murthy, M.R.: Protein Structural Homology: A Metric Approach. Int. J. Pept. Protein Res. 28(4), 364–369 (1986)
13. Abraham, A.L., Rocha, E.P., Pothier, J.: Swelfe: A Detector of Internal Repeats in Sequences and Structures. Bioinformatics 24(13), 1536–1537 (2008)
14. Sabarinathan, R., Basu, R., Sekar, K.: ProSTRIP: A Method to Find Similar Structural Repeats In Three-Dimensional Protein Structures. Comput. Biol. Chem. 34(2), 126–130 (2010)
15. Krissinel, E., Henrick, K.: Secondary-structure Matching (Ssm), A New Tool for Fast Protein Structure Alignment in Three Dimensions. Acta Cryst. D60, 2256–2268 (2004)
16. Wang, G., Dunbrack Jr., R.L.: PISCES: A Protein Sequence Culling Server. Bioinformatics 19(12), 1589–1591 (2003)
17. Eddy, S.R.: What Is Dynamic Programming? Nat. Biotechnol. 22, 909–910 (2004)

Identifying Characteristic Genes Based on Robust Principal Component Analysis

Chun-Hou Zheng[1], Jin-Xing Liu[2,3], Jian-Xun Mi[2], and Yong Xu[2]

[1] College of Electrical Engineering and Automation, Anhui University, Hefei, China
[2] Bio-Computing Research Center, Shenzhen Graduate School,
Harbin Institute of Technology, Shenzhen, China
[3] College of Information and Communication Technology,
Qufu Normal University, Rizhao, China
{zhengch99,JXL:sdcavell}@126.com,
JXM:mijianxun@gmail.com, YX:laterfall2@yahoo.com.cn

Abstract. In this paper, based on robust PCA, a novel method of characteristic genes identification is proposed. In our method, the differentially expressed genes and non-differentially expressed genes are treated as perturbation signals S_0 and low-rank matrix A_0, respectively, which can be recovered from the gene expression data using robust PCA. The scheme to identify the characteristic genes is as following. Firstly, the matrix S_0 of perturbation signals is discovered from gene expression data matrix D by using robust PCA. Secondly, the characteristic genes are selected according to matrix S_0. Finally, the characteristic genes are checked by the tool of Gene Ontology. The experimental results show that our method is efficient and effective.

Keywords: robust PCA, gene identification, gene expression data.

1 Introduction

DNA microarray technology has enabled high-throughput genome-wide measurements of gene transcript levels, which is promising in providing insight into biological processes involved in gene regulation [1, 2]. Although thousands of genes are experimented simultaneously, only a small number of genes are relevant to a biological process. Therefore, it is important how to find these genes associated with a special biological process.

So far, many mathematical methods, such as principal component analysis (PCA) and panelized matrix decomposition (PMD), have been devised to analyze gene expression data. For example, PCA was used to analyze gene expression data by Nyamundanda *et al.* [3]. In [4], Witten *et al.* proposed a method, based on penalized matrix decomposition (PMD), which was used to extract plant core genes by Liu *et al.* [5]. However, the brittleness of these methods with respect to grossly corrupted observations often puts its validity in jeopardy.

D.-S. Huang et al. (Eds.): ICIC 2012, CCIS 304, pp. 174–179, 2012.

A new method, namely robust PCA proposed by Candes *et al.* [6], can recover a low-rank matrix $\mathbf{A}_0$ from highly corrupted measurements $\mathbf{D}$. Although the method has been successfully applied to model background from surveillance video and to remove shadows from face images [6], it's validity in gene expression data analysis is still need to be studied.

In this paper, based on robust PCA, a novel method is proposed to identify characteristic genes. The differentially expressed genes are treated as perturbation signals $\mathbf{S}_0$ and the non-differentially expressed genes are treated as the low-rank matrix $\mathbf{A}_0$. Firstly, the matrix $\mathbf{D}$ of expression data is decomposed into two adding matrix $\mathbf{A}_0$ and $\mathbf{S}_0$ by using RPCA. Secondly, the characteristic genes are selected according to matrix $\mathbf{S}_0$. Finally, the characteristic genes are checked by the tool of Gene Ontology.

2   Robust Principal Component Analysis (RPCA)

2.1   The Algorithm of RPCA

This subsection simply introduces robust principal component analysis (RPCA) proposed by Candes *et al.* [6]. Let $\|\mathbf{A}\|_* := \sum_i \sigma_i(\mathbf{A})$ denote the nuclear norm of the matrix $\mathbf{A}$, that is, the sum of its singular values, and let $\|\mathbf{S}\|_1 := \sum_{ij} |S_{ij}|$ denote the l_1-norm of $\mathbf{S}$. Supposing that $\mathbf{D}$ denotes the observation matrix, RPCA solves the following optimization problem:

$$\begin{aligned} \text{minimize} \quad & \|\mathbf{A}\|_* + \lambda\|\mathbf{S}\|_1 \\ \text{subject to} \quad & \mathbf{D} = \mathbf{A} + \mathbf{S} \end{aligned} \tag{1}$$

where λ is a positive regulation parameter. For the RPCA problem Eq.(1), Lin *et al.* gave a method for solving it, which is referred to as the inexact ALM (IALM) method [7]. The details of this algorithm can be seen in [7].

2.2   The RPCA Model of Gene Expression Data

Considering the matrix $\mathbf{D}$ of gene expression data with size $m \times n$, each row of $\mathbf{D}$ represents the transcriptional responses of a gene in all the n samples, and each column of $\mathbf{D}$ represents the expression levels of all the m genes in one sample. Without loss of generality, $m \gg n$, so it is a classical small-sample-size problem.

Our goal of using RPCA to model the microarray data is to identify these significant genes. Suppose the matrix decomposition $\mathbf{D} = \mathbf{A} + \mathbf{S}$ has been done by using RPCA. By choosing the appropriate parameter λ, the sparse perturbation matrix $\mathbf{S}$ can be obtained, i.e. most of entries in $\mathbf{S}$ are zero. The genes corresponding to non-zero entries in $\mathbf{S}$ can be considered as ones of different expression.

The sparse matrix $\mathbf{S}$ can be denoted as:

$$\mathbf{S} = \begin{bmatrix} s_{11} & s_{12} & \cdots & s_{1n} \\ s_{21} & s_{22} & \cdots & s_{2n} \\ \vdots & \vdots & \ddots & \vdots \\ s_{m1} & s_{m2} & \cdots & s_{mn} \end{bmatrix}. \tag{2}$$

Then the following two steps are executed: firstly, the absolute values of entries in the sparse matrix $\mathbf{S}$ are find out; secondly, to get the evaluating vector, the matrix is summed by row. Consequently, the evaluating vector $\hat{S}$ is sorted in descending order. Without loss of generality, suppose that the first c_1 entries in $\hat{S}$ are non-zero, that is,

$$\hat{S} = \begin{bmatrix} \hat{s}_1, & \cdots, & \hat{s}_{c_1}, & \underbrace{0, \cdots, 0}_{m-c_1} \end{bmatrix}^T. \tag{3}$$

Generally, the larger the element in $\hat{S}$ is, the more different the gene is in expression data. So, the genes associated with only the first num ($num \le c_1$) entries in $\hat{S}$ can be picked out as characteristic ones.

3   Experimental Results

In this section, our method is compared with the following methods on the real gene expression data: (a) PMD method using the left singular vectors $\{\mathbf{u}_k\}$ to identify the characteristic genes (proposed by Witten et al. [4]); (b) SPCA method using all the PCs of SPCA (proposed by Journée et al. [8]) to identify the characteristic genes.

Table 1. The number of each stress type in the raw data

Stress Type	cold	drought	salt	UV-B	heat	osmotic	control
Reference No. (NASCArrays-)	138	141	140	144	146	139	137
Number of Samples	6	7	6	7	8	6	8

3.1   Data Source

The raw data were downloaded from NASCArrays [http://affy.arabidopsis.info/], which include two classes: roots and shoots in each stress. Table 1 lists the reference numbers and sample number of each stress type. There are 22810 genes in each sample. The data are adjusted for background of optical noise using the GC-RMA software and normalized using quartile normalization. The results of GC-RMA are gathered in a matrix for further processed.

3.2   Selection of the Parameters

In this paper, for PMD method, the l_1-norm of **u** is taken as the penalty function, i.e. $\|\mathbf{u}\|_{l_1} \le \alpha_1$. Because of $1 \le \alpha_1 \le \sqrt{m}$, let $\alpha_1 = \alpha * \sqrt{m}$, where $1/\sqrt{m} \le \alpha \le 1$. For simplicity, let $p = 1$, that is, only one factor is used. l_0-norm penalty and the parameter γ are taken in SPCA. For a fair comparison, 500 genes are roughly selected by these methods via choosing appropriate parameters. According to [7], in RPCA, the regulation parameter $\lambda = \left(0.3 * \max(m, n)\right)^{-\frac{1}{2}}$.

3.3   Gene Ontology (GO) Analysis

In this subsection, our proposed method will be evaluated by GOTermFinder [9], which is publicly available at http://go.princeton.edu/cgi-bin/GOTermFinder. The analysis of GOTermFinder provides significant information for the biological inter-pretation of high-throughput experiments.

Fig. 1 shows the sample frequency of response to abiotic stimulus (GO:0009628) given by the three methods, whose back sample frequency in TAIR set is 1539/29556 (5.2%). From Fig. 1(a), RPCA method outperforms others in all the data sets of shoot samples with six different stresses. Fig. 1(b) shows that only in cold-stress data set of root samples, PMD is equal to our method and they are superior to SPCA. In other data sets, our method is superior to the others.

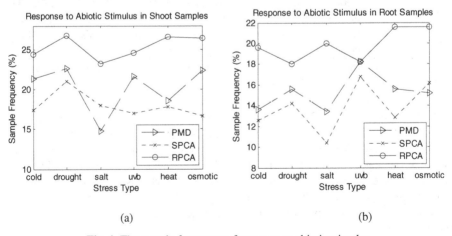

(a)   (b)

Fig. 1. The sample frequency of response to abiotic stimulus

The characteristic terms are listed in Table 2, in which the superior results are in bold type.

Table 2. Characteristic terms selected from GO by algorithms

Stress type		GO Terms	Back-ground frequency	Sample frequency		
				PMD	SPCA	RPCA
drought	s	GO:0009414 response to water deprivation	207/29887 (0.7%)	**47/500** **(9.4%)**	23/500 (4.6%)	34/500 (6.8%)
drought	r	GO:0009415 response to water deprivation	207/29887 (0.7%)	26/500 (5.2%)	24/500 (4.8%)	**30/500** **(6.0%)**
salt	s	GO:0009651 response to salt stress	395/29887 (1.3%)	41/500 (8.2%)	28/500 (5.6%)	**48/500** **(9.8%)**
salt	r	GO:0009651 response to salt stress	395/29887 (1.3%)	**33/500** **(6.6%)**	22/500 (4.4%)	31/500 (6.2%)
UV-B	s	GO:0009416Response to light stimulus	557/29887 (1.9%)	23/500 (4.6%)	30/500 (6.0%)	**42/500** **(8.4%)**
UV-B	r	GO:0009416Response to light stimulus	557/29887 (1.9%)	24/500 (4.8%)	none	**36/500** **(7.2%)**
cold	s	GO:0009409 response to cold	276/29887 (0.9%)	44/500 (8.8%)	34/500 (6.8%)	**58/500** **(11.6%)**
cold	r	GO:0009410 response to cold	276/29887 (0.9%)	**43/500** **(8.6%)**	33/500 (6.6%)	38/500 (7.6%)
heat	s	GO:0009408 response to heat	140/29887 (0.5%)	45/500 (9.0%)	30/500 (6.0%)	**47/500** **(9.4%)**
heat	r	GO:0009409 response to heat	140/29887 (0.5%)	43/500 (8.6%)	28/500 (5.6%)	**48/500** **(9.6%)**
osmotic	s	GO:0006970 response to osmotic stress	474/29887 (1.6%)	**55/500** **(11.0%)**	29/500 (5.8%)	**55/500** **(11.0%)**
osmotic	r	GO:0006970 response to osmotic stress	474/29887 (1.6%)	39/500 (7.8%)	27/500 (5.4%)	**41/500** **(8.2%)**

In this table, 's' denotes the shoot samples; 'r' denotes the root samples; 'none' denotes that the algorithm cannot give the GO terms.

As listed in Table 2, PMD method outperforms SPCA and our method in three items, such as drought in shoot, salt in root and cold in root, among the whole items. However, it shows that, on one of the twelve items (osmotic in shoot), our method has the same competitive result as PMD, while both methods are superior to SPCA. In other eight items, our method excels PMD and SPCA methods. In addition, on all the characteristic items, our method has superiority over SPCA.

From the results of experiments, it can be concluded that our method is efficient and effective.

4   Conclusion

In this paper, a novel RPCA-based method was proposed for indentifying characteristic genes. It combined RPCA and sparsity of gene different expression to provide an efficient and effective approach for gene identification. Our method mainly includes the following two steps: firstly, the matrix S of different expression is discovered from gene expression data matrix by using robust PCA; secondly, the different expressed genes are selected according to matrix S. The experimental results on real gene data show that our method outperforms the other state-of-the-art methods. In future, we will focus on the biological meaning of the characteristic genes.

Acknowledgements. This work was supported by fund for Program for New Century Excellent Talents in University (No.NCET-08-0156), NSFC under grant No. 61071179; Provincial Natural Science Research Program of Higher Education Institutions of Anhui Province, No. KJ2012A005.

References

1. Wang, L., Li, P.C.H.: Microfluidic DNA Microarray Analysis: A Review. Analytica Chimica Acta 687, 12–27 (2011)
2. Heller, M.J.: DNA Microarray Technology: Devices, Systems, and Applications. Annual Review of Biomedical Engineering 4, 129–153 (2002)
3. Nyamundanda, G., Brennan, L., Gormley, I.C.: Probabilistic Principal Component Analysis for Metabolomic Data. BMC Bioinformatics 11, 571 (2010)
4. Witten, D.M., Tibshirani, R., Hastie, T.: A Penalized Matrix Decomposition, with Applications to Sparse Principal Components and Canonical Correlation Analysis. Biostatistics 10, 515–534 (2009)
5. Liu, J.X., Zheng, C.H., Xu, Y.: Extracting Plants Core Genes Responding to Abiotic Stresses by Penalized Matrix Decomposition. Comput. Biol. Med. (2012), doi:10.1016 /j.compbiomed.2012.1002.1002
6. Candes, E.J., Li, X., Ma, Y., Wright, J.: Robust Principal Component Analysis? Journal of the ACM 58, 11 (2011)
7. Lin, Z., Chen, M., Wu, L., Ma, Y.: The Augmented Lagrange Multiplier Method for Exact Recovery of Corrupted Low-rank Matrices (2010), http://Arxiv.org/abs/1009.5055v2
8. Journée, M., Nesterov, Y., Richtarik, P., Sepulchre, R.: Generalized Power Method for Sparse Principal Component Analysis. The Journal of Machine Learning Research 11, 517–553 (2010)
9. Boyle, E.I., Weng, S.A., Gollub, J., Jin, H., Botstein, D., Cherry, J.M., Sherlock, G.: GO:TermFinder - Open Source Software for Accessing Gene Ontology Information and Finding Significantly Enriched Gene Ontology Terms Associated with a list of Genes. Bioinformatics 20, 3710–3715 (2004)

Protein Classification Using Random Walk on Graph

Xiaohua Xu[*], Lin Lu, Ping He, Zhoujin Pan, and Cheng Jing

Department of Computer Science, Yangzhou University, Yangzhou 225009, China
{arterx,LinLu60,angeletx,pprivulet,jingc1989}@gmail.com

Abstract. Inspired by the label propagation based on random walk, a basic classifier is proposed for biological computation. We apply this model to predict the localization of proteins, specifically the yeast and gram-negative bacteria protein data. A series of evaluations and comparisons are conducted to prove its excellent performance as an effectively independent classifier.

Keywords: random walk, classification, protein classification.

1 Introduction

Random walk on graph [1] is a powerful tool in semi-supervised learning or transductive learning. It is closely related to label propagation when applied to classification fields. Hence the traditional classification problems turn out to predict the labels of missing nodes, given an input graph with some nodes being labeled. Several approaches have been proposed to tackle node classification on graph. In 2001, Szummer and Jaakkola [2] first used random walk to uncover the low-dimensional manifold structure of data thus solving the classification of partially labeled data. The following contributive work was the kernel methods [3,4] that embed the nodes of the input graph into a Euclidean feature space so that the decision margin could be estimated. Bhagat et al. [5] also present a brief summarization about label types, graph formulation and random walk based methods.

Recently, random walk is gradually combined into biological computation for the classification of proteins into functional or structural classes, given their amino acid sequences. Min et al. [6] put forward a method using the random-walk kernel with optimal random steps and applied this approach to classify protein sequence. Freschi et al. [7] proposed a random walk ranking algorithm aiming at the protein function prediction from interaction networks. However, there still remains a host of protein-related issues waiting for better classification methods.

This paper, standing on the shoulder of our past theoretical work [8], concerns the implementation of a basic model for node classification on graph. We present an intuitive interpretation about the graph presentation, label propagation and model formulation. Later we analyze in detail their performances on predicting the (sub-)cellular localization of proteins considering several respects. The tests have showed competitive and promising results when compared with the conventional support vector machine(SVM) method.

---

[*] Corresponding author.

D.-S. Huang et al. (Eds.): ICIC 2012, CCIS 304, pp. 180–184, 2012.
© Springer-Verlag Berlin Heidelberg 2012

2   Random Walk Classifier Model

Usually, a training set (X, C) is given to specify the set of labeled data and the set of their classes, n is the number of tuples in X, and the traditional task is to predict the classes of a test set. While we consider an initial graph of the form $G(V, E, W)$ constructed over the training set. So V is the set of nodes with its member v_i only responds to (x_i, c_i). This graph is assumed to be complete; hence the edge set E is trivial. W is the edge weight matrix sized $n \times n$ indicating the pairwise similarities, $w_{ij} = \text{sim}(v_i, v_j) = \text{sim}(x_i, x_j)$. Normally, $w_{ij} = \exp(-\|x_i - x_j\|^2 / 2\sigma^2)$, where $\|\cdot\|$ represents Euclidean norm. We also let Y be a set of m labels that can be applied to nodes of the graph. After that, a state transition matrix $P=[P_{ij}]_{n \times n}$ should be defined inferring the probability p_{ij} that one node v_i transits to the state of node v_j. P is normally computed as $P = D^{-1}W$, where the diagonal matrix $D = \text{diag}(W\mathbf{1}_n)$. Besides, we convert the y_i into an indicating vector of labels, i.e., $Y = [y_1, y_2, ..., y_n]_{m \times n}$ and $y_i = [y_{1i}, y_{2i}, ..., y_{mi}]^T$. Therefore, the label or state of v_i is c_j if and only if $y_{ji} = 1$, otherwise $y_{ji} = 0$.

Provided the state matrix and transition matrix, the simple random walk on V is described as the process that the state y_i of any node v_i transfers with the probability p_{ij} to the state y_j of node v_j. Yet, random walks on readily labeled nodes are meaningless since we address employing the information already encoded in the partially labeled graph to help us predict labels of missing data. Thus the solution of node classification relies on a random walk originates at the unlabeled node v_j and ends at one labeled node v_i after several steps, in this way v_j obtains its label from v_i. Here we assume $p(v_i, v)$ to be the state-transition probability with which a walk proceeds from node v_i in V to the new node v represented by unlabeled data x. In that way, the state y of new node v is $y = \sum_{v_i \in V} p(v_i, v) y_i = Yp_v$.

We define $p_v = p(V, v)$ to be a column vector, then for the node v_i in V, $p(V, v_i) = D^{-1}w_i$. On the other hand, for the new node v not in V, $p(V, v) = D^{-1}w(V, v)$. Thus, the state y of v can be achieved by $y = Yp(V, v) = YD^{-1}WW^+w(V, v) = YPW^+w(V, v)$, where W^+ denotes the pseudo-reverse matrix of W, and $w(V, v)$ is a column vector indicates the similarity between new node v and nodes in V. When considering the multi-step random walk, say t steps, we just need to replace P with P^t. Therefore after t steps, the state of new node v or new data x is $y=YP^tW^+w(V, v)$, where $P^t = (\alpha I + (1-\alpha)P)P^{t-1}$ and the parameter $\alpha \in (0,1)$ implying the nodes may stay at the current positions with the possibility α.

3   Tests and Results

In this section, we will test our classifier on two real data sets, in comparison with SVM utilizing the radial basis function (RBF) kernel. In our tests, the parameter α ranges between (0, 1) and the $-1/2\sigma^2$ is limited over the interval $\{2^{-15}, 2^{-11}, \ldots, 2^{13}, 2^{15}\}$. All the optimal parameter selections are done by n-fold cross-validation so as to produce the lowest average error ratio, computed by dividing the number of misclassified data with the size of the whole unlabeled data.

3.1   Predict the (Sub-)Cellular Localization Sites of Protein

The YEAST data, including 1484 items with 9 attributes, is used to predict the cellular localization sites of proteins and has been categorized into 10 classes. The second data is for the prediction of Gram-negative bacteria protein sub-cellular location. This dataset contains 653 Gram-negative bacterial proteins classified into 8 sub-cellular locations according to the experimental annotations. It contains 69 features that are extracted by generating pseudo amino acid composition (PseAA).

- **Influence of α and t**

First in our experiment, we investigate the influence of random-walk steps with respect to different values of α. This parameter rises from 0.05 to 0.95 as we can see from Fig. 1 and the maximum random-walk step is set to 30. Fig. 1 is the result on YEAST data, where each line, corresponding each α, illustrates the trend of error ratios with the increase of steps. The error ratios are the average results from 10-fold cross-validation. Regardless of the minor local vibrations, in Fig. 1, nearly all lines start at lower error ratios before climbing up with the growth of steps t. Among all the different parameters, the lowest error ratio lies on the curve when $\alpha = 0.95$ and $t = 8$. What is more, all curves do not give sharp ups and downs. This situation is quite obvious in Fig. 2, where the line has the least error ratio when $\alpha = 0.95$ and remains more or less a straight line. Therefore, the random walk method distinguishes itself with the traditional iterative methods which produce better results after each iteration.

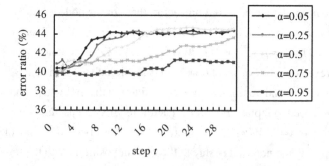

Fig. 1. The influence of α and t when tested by YEAST data

Since Former work [1] has already guaranteed the convergence of random walks on graph, so it is unnecessary to precede a great number of steps before our algorithm RaWa achieves the best result. As we can see from Fig. 3 and 4, the best one is always chosen within 10 steps. Szummer and Jaakola [2] also found in their experiments that a small constant values of t to be effective, around $t = 8$ on a dataset with a few thousand examples.

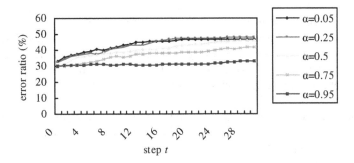

Fig. 2. The influence of α and t when tested by Gram-negative bacteria proteins data

• Influence of the Training Data Size

Next we look into the performance of our classifier under varied partitions (n=2,4,6,8,10) in the n-cross validation. Actually, the influences of different partitions imply the impacts posed by the changing size of training data on the performance of our classifier. The results are summarized in Table 1 for YEAST data and Table 2 for Gram-negative bacteria both including the comparison of RBF-SVM.

Table 1. The error ratios (%) given by the test on YEAST data

	n=2	n=4	n=6	n=8	n=10
RaWa(α=0.95)	39.99	39.22	39.28	38.75	38.82
RaWa (α=0.50)	42.39	41.44	40.90	40.64	39.57
RaWa (α=0.05)	41.31	40.16	40.15	39.95	39.02
RBF-SVM	41.09	40.73	40.73	40.31	39.94

Table 2. The error ratios (%) given by the test on Gram-negative Bacteria Proteins

	n=2	n=4	n=6	n=8	n=10
RaWa(α=0.95)	33. 54	32.48	31.24	30.12	30.31
RaWa (α=0.50)	35.22	32.62	31.39	31.70	31.03
RaWa (α=0.05)	33.54	34.00	33.85	34.31	33.21
RBF-SVM	33.55	33.07	33.54	32.76	33.70

Given the appropriate parameters, RaWa can make the best of limited training data. Our classifier, as is shown in Table 1 and 2, produces the best results on both data sets when α equals 0.95. While this model seems a little sensitive to the size of training data compared to RBF-SVM.

4   Conclusions

Label propagation through random walk on graph is the foundation of our proposed classification model. We successfully established a classification model so that any node can start a random walk and propagate its label to any unlabeled data after simple steps of walk. Our basic classification model reveals potentials in promoting the accuracy and effectiveness in data classification.

Acknowledgement. This work is supported by the National Natural Science Foundation of China under grant No.61003180, No.61070047 and No.61103018; Natural Science Foundation of Education Department of Jiangsu Province under contract 09KJB20013; Natural Science Foundation of Jiangsu Province under contract BK2010318 and BK2011442.

References

1. Lovász, L.: Random Walks on Graphs: A Survey. Combinatorics. In: Paul Erdös is Eighty, vol. 2, pp. 1–46. Keszthely, Hungary (1993)
2. Szummer, M., Jaakkola, T.: Patially Labeled Classification with Markov Random Walk. In: Advances in Neural Information Processing Systems 14, pp. 945–952 (2002)
3. Zhu, X.J., Ghahramani, Z.B., John, L.: Semi-supervised Learning using Gaussian Fields and Harmonic Functions. In: The 20th International Conference on Machine Learning, pp. 912–919 (2003)
4. Zhu, X.J., John, L., Zoubin, G.: Combining Active Learning and Semi-supervised Learning using Gaussian Fields and Harmonic Functions. In: ICML 2003 Workshop on The Continuum from Labeled to Unlabeled Data in Machine Learning and Data Mining, pp. 58–65 (2003)
5. Smriti, B., Graham, C., Muthukrishnan, S.: Node Classification in Social Networks (2011), Arxiv preprint arXiv: 1101. 3291
6. Min, R., Bonner, A., Li, J., Zhang, Z.: Learned Random-Walk Kernels and Empirical-map Kernels for Protein Sequence Classification. J. Comput Biol. 16(3), 457–474 (2009)
7. Freschi, V.: Protein Function Prediction from Interaction Networks using a Random Walk Ranking Algorithm. In: Proceedings of the 7th IEEE International Conference on Bioinformatics and Bioengineering BIBE 2007, pp. 42–48 (2007)
8. Xu, X.H. (ed.): Random Walk Learning on Graph. Nanjing University of Aeronautics and Astronautics, Nanjing (2008)

Protein Molecular Function Prediction Based on the Phylogenetic Tree

Lu Jian[1,2]

[1] School of Information Science and Technology,
University of Science and Technology of China,
Hefei, Anhui 230027, China
[2] Intelligent Computing Laboratory, Institute of Intelligent Machines,
Chinese Academy of Sciences, Hefei, Anhui 230031, China
lujianbubi@gmail.com

Abstract. We employ a novel method to construct a phylogenetic tree based on distance matrix among different protein molecular sequences, and present a statistical model to infer specific molecular function for unannotated protein sequences within the phylogenetic tree. Our method produced specific and consistent molecular function prediction across the P-falciparum family. For the P-falciparum family, it achieves 91.2% precision and 76.9% recall, outperforms the related method GOtcha and BLAST. Finally, we intend to improve our method through adopting a more appropriate feature extraction approach from the sequence or a better statistical inference model in the future.

Keywords: distance matrix, phylogenetic tree, GO term.

1 Introduction

The post-genomic era has revealed the nucleic and amino acid sequences for large numbers of genes and proteins, but the rate of sequence acquisition far surpasses the rate of accurate protein function determination. Sequences that lack molecular function annotation cause a large restriction to the researchers in the fields of protein function prediction. Therefore, one important role of computational biology is to make exact prediction for these additional properties based on sequence alone.

Phylogenomics is a methodology for annotating the specific molecular function of a protein using the evolutionary history of the protein as captured by a phylogenetic tree, which dues to the observation that protein function and protein sequence tend to evolve in parallel [1]. Recently, in a number of sequenced genomes, phylogenomics has acquitted itself admirably in assigning precise functional annotations to proteins and specific protein families [4]. Phylogenomics applies knowledge about how molecular function evolves to boost the protein function prediction. The phylogenomics methodology implies that a phylogeny based on protein sequences accurately represents how molecular function evolved for that particular set of proteins. In this paper, we describe a method to predict the function of the proteins using the phylogeny based on the distance of the sequences, which is called IPFDMP (Infer Protein

D.-S. Huang et al. (Eds.): ICIC 2012, CCIS 304, pp. 185–190, 2012.
© Springer-Verlag Berlin Heidelberg 2012

Function from the Distance Matrix Phylogeny), and we combine a statistical inference to acquire the function terms.

The remainder of this paper is organized as follows: Section 2 gives details of our method. In Section 3, we present the experiment results of IPFDMP and a comparison with other related method. Conclusion and future directions are depicted in Section 4.

2   Methodology

Our approach based on the phylogeny has the following two steps, the first step contains five sub-steps to construct a tree from the protein sequences using the phylip-3.69. It is more specific to IPFDMP and will be described in Section 2.1. We will briefly describe Step 2 in Section 2.3.

3   Distance Matrix of the Sequences

Given a protein family which contains a small fraction of proteins without annotation, while the others have specific function annotation terms, we attempt a method to produce a distance matrix according to the amino acid sequences alignment results, followed by constructing a phylogenetic tree based on the distance information. From the obtained phylogenetic tree, we use a function evolution model and a statistical inference approach to inferring the unannotated function items.

We used Clustal X [6] to align the sequences, by setting the output "*.phy" file, for the subsequent management, where phylip-3.69 was used for phylogeny reconstruction. In the implementation of the phylip-3.69, program "seqboot" is firstly executed to analyze the input aligned sequences, the replicated number is set to 1000. And we chose program "protdist" to compute distance matrix from protein sequences. There are five models of amino acid substitution and we implement "the categories distance" with the "ease" parameter being set to 0.457 which is approximately the value implied by the empirical rates in the Dayhoff PAM matrix, followed by the Neighbor-Joining method to give out the relationships among the proteins. The output of "Neighbor" is used as an input for "consense" program, so we can expediently read the tree of the phylogeny of the proteins.

4   Molecular Function: Terms and Data

We make use of the well-curated molecular function ontology from GO to provide a basic set of terms that capture these concepts. In our algorithm, GO not only provides a vocabulary of basic terms for IPFDMP, but also organizes these terms into a directed acyclic graph (DAG), a feature that IPFDMP exploits.

Another character of GO makes it acquire widely application is that it is accompanied by a database (the GOA database [7]) of function annotations. We gather a list of candidate molecular functions for the corresponding family of proteins by taking the union of all experimental GO annotations associated with the proteins in the

P-falciparum family (e.g., the subgraph in Figure 1). We prune the list so that as much as possible function terms at the leaves or as the direct ancestors of the leaves of the DAG are left, they are called the candidate functions. This choice of terms will give a more specific protein molecular function terms which is of the greatest utility for the biology researchers, and it is generally hard to predict by the computational biology.

5   Statistical Inference

In the following implementation of IPFDMP, having assembled a list of candidate molecular function terms for the P-falciparum protein family, we form a Boolean state vector based on the list. Note in particular that the representation of function as a Boolean vector implies that multiple functions can be asserted as present in a single protein. And then apply a model similar to Jukes-Cantor [8] but appropriate for molecular function evolution to acquire the function terms of these unannotated proteins.

After the phylogenetic tree has been derived from the "phylip" (the subtree shown in Figure 1), we retain these structural elements of the phylogeny, and replace the amino acid characters with vectors of function annotations that is described above. At last, we place a model of protein molecular function evolution on the branches of the phylogeny.

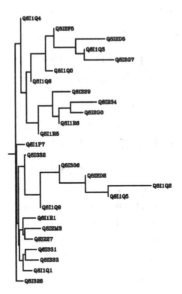

Fig. 1. The topology of the phylogenetic tree from the subset of the P-falciparum protein

Now, we give a briefly description for the model which simulates the evolution of the protein molecular function that IPFDMP associates with the branches of the phylogeny. For each node in the phylogeny that represents a single particular protein, this model defines the conditional probability for the Boolean vector of molecular function annotations at the node conditioning on the value of the vector of molecular function terms at the ancestor of the node. Here we use Noisy-OR [8] as a simple phylogeny graphical model.

A log-linear model is applied here as a statistical model to simulate the molecular function evolution. It is a simply phenomenological model that captures in broad outlines some of the desiderata of a simulation for function evolution.

In the model, Xi denotes the Boolean vector of candidate molecular function annotations for node i and let Xim be the mth component of this vector. Let α_i indicates the immediate ancestor of the ith node in the phylogeny, and X_{α_i} denotes the annotation vector at the ancestor. Then the transition probability associated with the branch from the ancestor to the child can be written as follows:

$$p(X_i^n = 0 \mid X_{\alpha_i} = x_{\alpha_i}) = \prod_{m=1}^{M} (1 - g_{m,n})^{d_i x_{\alpha_i}^m} \tag{1}$$

where d_i and $g_{m,n}$ are parametric functions of branch length in the phylogeny and path lengths in GO, respectively. This functional form is known as a Noisy-OR function [9], and the multiplication in Eq. (1) implies an assumption of independence of the different function components between the ancestor and the descendant.

Parameter $g_{m,n}$ is a decreasing function of the path length $l_{m,n}$ in GO to capture the notion that a transition should be less possibly happen the less "similar" two function are. The formula is $g_{m,n} = 1 / l_{m,n}^s$, where s is a free parameter. In our implement of IPFDMP for the P-falciparum protein family, we set s=3. In the situation, $g_{m,m} = (1/r)^{s/2}$, this normalizes the self-transitions probability with respect to the number of components of the annotation vector. Parameter d_i is a function of the branch length in the phylogeny as a transition rate. It is a decreasing nonlinear function of the branch length. In $d_i = 1.5 - 1/(1 + e^{-b_i})$, b_i denotes the most parsimonious number of amino acid mutations along the branch from α_i to i.

A standard probabilistic propagation algorithm is applied to compute the posterior probability of the unobserved functions in the tree. By the classical pruning algorithm, also known as (a special case of) the junction tree algorithm [10], all posterior probabilities can be obtained in linear time.

6   Experiments

We implement the IPFDMP on 2570 proteins with 1860 function terms of P-falciparum protein family. The cross-validation method is used, where TP is the total number of proteins for which we correctly predict a function term for the query proteins, FP is the total number of proteins for which we incorrectly predict a final function term that the protein doesn't have, and FN is the total number of proteins for which we incorrectly predict a function term that the protein does have (we compute these numbers by summing over all of the functions). Then the "precision" of our procedure is TP/(TP+FP), and the "recall", or sensitivity, of our approach is TP/(TP+FN).

In addition, we ran the GOtcha [12] software and BLAST [13] on our protein family to make a comparison. GOtcha predicts protein function using a statistical model, which is applied to BLAST searches on a manually-constructed database containing complete GO annotation of seven genomes, including GO evidence codes.

For each query protein in the selected family we searched the BLAST output with the most significant E-value (probability of the alignment score based on an extreme value distribution for aligning protein sequences at random).

The ROC analysis in Figure 2 uses a cutoff to determine the correct functions. The purpose of the ROC plot here is to show that a user-specified cutoff value may be used to identify when a functional prediction should not be made for a particular protein. With such a cutoff, we can identify proteins for which the posterior probability of every molecular function is too low to support a prediction.

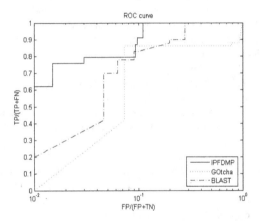

Fig. 2. ROC figure comparing the three different methods on the P-falciparum protein family. There are 43 proteins annotated, with a total of 51 annotations (multiple function terms).

The IPFDMP achieves 91.2% precision and 76.9% recall over the P-falciparum protein family, which performs better than GOthca and BLAST method. These results are shown in Table 1.

Table 1. Comparison of our proposed approach (IPFDMP) with the existing GOtcha and BLAST method

	IPFDMP	GOtcha	BLAST
precision	91.2%	87.2%	83.4%
recall	76.9%	68.7%	62.8%

7   Conclusion

At present, protein function prediction by computation method is challenge. Based on the pairwise distance among the protein sequences, the IPFDMP combines the evolution information with the statistic inference method to predict the function terms of proteins, and we are glad to pin our hope on finding an informative feature extraction method to construct the distance matrix or a powerful inference approach to infer the function from the phylogeny in the future.

Acknowledgments. This work was supported by the grant of the National Science Foundation of China, Nos. 61133010 & 31071168.

References

1. Eisen, J.A.: Phylogenomics: Improving Functional Predictions for Uncharacterized Genes by Evolutionary Analysis. Genome Research (8), 163–167 (1998)
2. Barbara, E.E., Michael, I.J., Kathryn, E.M.: Protein Molecular Function Prediction by Bayesian Phylogenomics. PLoS Computational Biology 1(5), e45 (2005)
3. Barbara, E.E., Michael, I.J., Kathryn, E.M.: A Graphical Model for Predicting Protein Molecular Function. In: ICML, Pittsburgh (2006)
4. Eisen, J.A., Hanawalt, P.C.: A Phylogenomics Study of DNA Repair Genes, proteins, and Processes. Mutation Research (3), 171–213 (1999)
5. Shen, J., Zhang, J., Luo, X.: Predicting Protein–protein Interactions Based Only on Sequences Information. Proceedings of the National Academy of Sciences 104(11), 4337–4341 (2007)
6. http://www.softpedia.com/get/Science-CAD/Clustal-X.shtml
7. Camon, E.: The Gene Ontology Annotation (GOA) Database: Sharing Knowledge in Uniprot with Gene Ontology. Nucleic Acids Research (32), 262–266 (2004)
8. Jukes, T.H., Cantor, C.R.: Evolution of Protein Molecules. Mammalian protein metabolism, pp. 21–132. Academic Press, New York (1969)
9. Pearl, J.: Probabilistic Reasoning in Intelligent Systems: Networks of Plausible Inference, p. 531. Morgan Kaufmann (1988)
10. Cowell, R.G., Dawid, A.P., Lauritzen, S.L.: Probabilistic Networks and Expert System, 321 p. Springer, New York (2003)
11. Karaoz, U., Murail, T.M., Letovsky, S.: Whole-genome Annotation by Using Evidence Intergration in Functional-linkage Networks. Proceedings of the National Academy of Sciences 101, 2888–2893 (2004)
12. Martin, D.M.A.: GOtcha: A New Method for Prediction of Protein Function Assessed by the Annotation of Seven Genomes. BMC Bioinformatics (5), 178–195 (2004)
13. Altschul, S.F.: Basic Local Alignment Search Tool. J. Mol. Biol. (215), 403–410 (1990)

Efficient Mode of Action Identification by Support Vector Machine Regression

Vitoantonio Bevilacqua[1,2] and Paolo Pannarale[1]

[1] Dipartimento di Elettrotecnica ed Elettronica, Politecnico di Bari,
Via E. Orabona 4, 70125 Bari, Italy
[2] eBis, Via Pavoncelli 139, 70100 Bari, Italy
bevilacqua@poliba.it

Abstract. Abstract. Discovering the molecular targets of compounds or the cause of physiological conditions, among the multitude of known genes, is one of the major challenges of bioinformatics. Our approach has the advantage of not needing control samples, libraries or numerous assays. The so far proposed implementations of this strategy are computationally demanding. Our solution, while performing comparably to state of the art algorithms in terms of discovered targets, is more efficient in terms of memory and time consumption.

1   Introduction

The algorithms that identify the MoA of existing molecules, using quantitative gene network models, assume that training profiles are obtained in steady state following a variety of treatments, including compounds, RNAi, and gene-specific mutations. The quantitative gene network reverse engineering algorithms can be devided in two categories [1]: those requiring knowledge of the gene targeted in each training experiment and those, like MNI [3] and Ssem-lasso [2], that improve flexibility not requiring this additional information. This improved flexibility enables their application to higher model organisms, where gene-specific perturbations are more difficult to implement. For both approaches, once the regulatory model is trained, the expression profile of a test compound is filtered, in essence, checking the expression level of each gene in the cell (relative to the level of all other genes in the cell) for consistency with regulatory influences embodied in the trained regulatory model. The genes are then ranked by a measure of their level of consistency with the expected behaviour, based on the model. The inconsistency is attributed to the external influence of the compound on those genes. Our mode of action identification procedure is based on Support Vector Machine Regression. The method has been tested on simulated datasets and on the combination of two publicly available, whole-genome yeast expression data sets: a compendium of 300 profiles of gene deletions, titratable promoter insertions and drug compound treatments from Hughes et al. [5] and a second set of 215 titratable promoter insertions in essential genes from Mnaimneh et al. [7].

D.-S. Huang et al. (Eds.): ICIC 2012, CCIS 304, pp. 191–196, 2012.

2   Material and Methods

2.1   Attribute Selection and Regression

The attribute selection was performed in two steps. First the attributes were discretized using equal frequency bins, with a fixed number of 10 bins. After that the information gain (IG) for each attribute a was computed. The attributes were sorted according to their information gain and only the more informative n   attributes were retained. In the second step a correlation based feature selection [4] gave the list of regressors for the gene expression model. The support vector machine for regression has been used to build the regression model. The parameters could be learned using an improvement of the SMO Algorithm for SVM Regression, developed by Keerthi et al. [6] The complexity parameter has been set to 0.8, the data has been normalized, the tolerance parameter has been set to 0.001, the epsilon to 1.0E-12 and the kernel polynomial of the first order.

2.2   Filtering and Target Identification

The residual estimation has been performed via a bootstrap procedure. N   subsamples were created and each subsample has been 60/40 splitted into training and test set. The models for each gene were created on the training set and evaluated on the test set. The residuals were computed as difference of the predicted and real values. The normal density function for each gene of the treated sample was computed, with mean and standard deviation computed from the residuals. The genes having a probability of belonging to the residual distribution below a given threshold were returned to the user. If the list contained more than 100 genes only the first 100 genes were returned. The threshold was adapted to the number of genes in order to control the rate of false positives.

2.3   Pathway Analysis

The list of genes filtered by our algorithm was subsequently used for pathway analysis. Hypergeomtric p-values for over or under-representation of each GO term in the specified ontology among the GO annotations for the interesting genes were comuted. The computations were done conditionally based on the structure of the GO graph. For this analysis was used the hyperGTest function from the Bioconductor GOStats package. The p-value cutoff was set to 0.01.

3   Results

A lognormal noise with expected value equal to 10% of the raw expression value has been added to the simulated datasets. In each experiment one gene has been randomly selected and its value has been modified by adding or subtracting a quantity proportional, with a given ratio to the experimental noise. In this way we obtained datasets with different values of Signal to Noise Ratio. The SNR has been set to 16, 4 and 2, which led to 100%, 99% and 98% AUC for a 200 genes network and 100%, 98% and 97% AUC for a 2000 genes network.

In analyzing the microarray compendia predictions for compound treatments, we considered as targets both the pathways that are significantly overrepresented among the perturbed genes and the genes themselves. Pathways are identified as significantly overrepresented Gene Ontology processes among the highly ranked genes. The results for the promoter insertions are reported in table 1.

Our algorithm has also been tested on real compound treated experiments. The compounds used were lovastatin, terbinafine, itraconazole, hydroxyurea and tunicamycin. For the drug treated samples our algorithm identified the target genes for only 3/7 of the compound targets, while the competing methods performed better with 5/7 of correctly identified genes. The results are showed on table 2. Even if the performance of mode of action identification of our algorithm were worse than those of MNI or SSEM-LASSO in the identification of targeted genes, surprisingly it was more effective in the identification of the involved pathways (table 3).

Table 1. Results for genetic perturbations. SSEM-LASSO ranks are sensitively worse than MNI.

Promoter Mutant	Target	MNI		SSEM-LASSO		SVM		N° Attributes
		Rank	Results	Rank	Results	Rank	Results	
tet-CMD1	CMD1	1	100	>MNI	100	2	100	29
tet-AUR1	AUR1	1	100	>MNI	100	1	100	40
tet-CDC42	CDC42	1	100	>MNI	100	1	100	26
tet-ERG11	ERG11	42	100	>MNI	100	10	100	15
tet-FKS1	FKS1	1	100	>MNI	100	2	17	21
tet-HMG2	HMG2	1	100	>MNI	100	10	100	34
tet-IDI1	IDI1	1	100	>MNI	100	1	16	28
tet-KAR2	KAR2	1	100	>MNI	100	1	100	29
tet-PMA1	PMA1	6	100	>MNI	100	5	100	23
tet-RHO1	RHO1	4	100	>MNI	100	1	10	32
tet-YEF3	YEF3	1	100	>MNI	100	1	36	44

Performance results are summarized in figure 1. The SVM regression algorithm is markedly more demanding than MNI, but, over both, SSEM-LASSO requires several orders of magnitude more CPU. It is heavily affected by both the number of genes and the number of experiments. The use of SSEM-LASSO on an ordinary computer is actually unfeasible and this makes its use prohibitive.

The memory test results were unaffected by the number of experiments and the results showed refer to 500 experiments dataset (figure 1). The tests show that MNI, while beeing favorable in terms of time, requires an amount of memory which rises rapidly with the number of genes in the chip. This makes the MNI execution prohibitive for a common desktop PC given that the number of probe sets on microarray chips is rapidly increasing and is well above the 40 thousands probe sets since the begin of the past decade.

Our algorithm scales well if considering both the time and memory consumption.

Table 2. Results for drug perturbations

Promoter Mutant	Target	MNI		SSEM-LASSO		SVM		N° Attributes
		Rank	Results	Rank	Results	Rank	Results	
Terbinafine	ERG1	5	100	-	100	-	57	20
Lovastatin	HMG2	30	100	31	100	-	59	34
Lovastatin	HMG1	-	100	89	100	-	59	33
Itraconazole	ERG11	2	100	17	100	27	100	15
Hydroxyurea	RNR2	2	100	20	100	26	83	22
Hydroxyurea	RNR4	6	100	4	100	7	83	30
Tunicamycin	ALG7	-	100	-	100	-	59	10

Table 3. Pathway analysis

Drug	SVM Pathways	MNI Pathways	Known MoA
Terbinafine	Ergosterol biosynthetic process (27)	Steroid metabolism (2130)	Inhibition of squalene monooxygenase, thus blocking the biosynthesis of ergosterol
Lovastatin	-	Lipid metabolism (16244)	Inhibition of HMG-CoA reductase
Itraconazole	Ergosterol biosynthetic process (256)	Steroid metabolism (2130)	Interaction with 14-α demethylase an enzyme necessary to convert lanosterol to ergosterol.
Hydroxyurea	Deoxyribonucleotide biosynthetic process (704)	Dna replication (5480)	Inhibition of ribonucleotide reductase and consequently of DNA synthesis
Tunicamycin	Cellular nitrogen compound catabolic process (6678), Protein targeting to ER (585)	Protein-ER targeting (585)	N-linked glycosylation

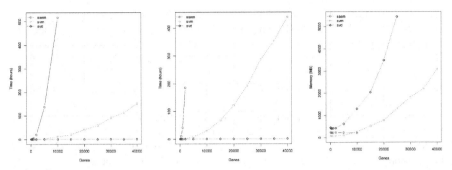

Fig. 1. Time performance comparison for 1500 (left) and 500 (center) experiments and memory performance comparison (right). SSEM is reported with continuous line, SVM is dashed, MNI is dotted.

4   Discussion

Gene network filtering of expression profiles has been demonstrated to be a valuable tool for the identification of compound mode of action. In particular these tools can destinguish the direct target of the compounds better than simply detecting the gene expression ratio with respect to some reference sample. MNI and SSEM-LASSO have showed good rates of target identification and anyway an improvement over the tested null methods. While SSEM-LASSO perfomed better than MNI on simulated datasets, it has been outperfomed by the latter on real yeast two-color array datasets. Our approach demostrated very good performances on synthetic datasets, and results comparable to MNI on promoter insertion samples. Unfortunately the SVM based algorithm obtained a lower rate of success on compound trated samples. Nevertheless when it comes to the pathway identification we showed that we identified more specific pathways than MNI did. One of the major drawbacks of MNI and SSEM-LASSO is their poor scalability both in terms of memory and elaboration time. They can't be applied to contemporary gene expression microarrays, given the number of probe sets in each chip, by means of common desktop computers. On the contrary the behaviour of our strategy is acceptable also in the absence of more powerfull means.

References

1. Mukesh, B., Vincenzo, B., Alberto, A.I., Diego, d.B.: How to Infer Gene Networks from Expression Profiles. Mol. Syst. Biol. 3, 78 (2007)
2. Elissa, J.C., Zhou, Y.C., Timothy, S.G., Eric, D.K.: Predicting Gene Targets of Perturbations via Network-based Filtering of MRNA Expression Compendia. Bioinformatics (Oxford, England) 24(21), 2482–2490 (2008)
3. Diego, d.B., Michael, J.T., Timothy, S.G., Sarah, E.C., Erin, L.E., Andrew, P.W., Sean, J.E., Scott, E.S., James, J.C.: Chemogenomic Profiling on a Genome-wide Scale Using Reverse-Engineered Gene Networks. Nature Biotechnology 23(3), 377–383 (2005)
4. Hall, M.A.: Correlation-based Feature Selection for Machine Learning. PhD thesis. The University of Waikato (1999)

5. Hughes, T.R., Marton, M.J., Jones, A.R., Roberts, C.J., Stoughton, R., Armour, C.D., Bennett, H.A., Coffey, E., Dai, H., He, Y.D., Kidd, M.J., King, A.M., Meyer, M.R., Slade, D., Lum, P.Y., Stepaniants, S.B., Sho Emaker, D.D., Gachotte, D., Chakraburtty, K., Simon, J., Bard, M., Friend, S.H.: Functional discovery via a compendium of expression profiles. Cell 102(1), 109–126 (2000)
6. Keerthi, S.S., Shevade, S.K., Bhattacharyya, C., Murthy, K.R.K.: Improvements to platt's smo algorithm for svm classifier design. Neural Computation 13(3), 637–649 (2001)
7. Mnaimneh, S., Davierwala, A.P., Haynes, J., Maffat, J., Peng, W.-T., Zhang, W., Yang, X., Pootoolal, J., Chua, G., Lopez, A., Trochesset, M., Morse, D., Krogan, N.J., Hiley, S.L., Li, Z., Morris, Q., Grigull, J., Mitsakakis, N., Roberts, C.J., Greenblatt, J.F., Boone, C., Kaiser, C.A., Andrews, B.J., Hughes, T.R.: Exploration of essential gene functions via titratable promoter alleles. Cell 118(1), 31–44 (2004)

A New De-noising Method for Infrared Spectrum

Qingwei Gao, De Zhu, Yixiang Lu, and Dong Sun

College of Electrical Engineering and Automation, Anhui University, Hefei, 230601, China
qingweigao@ahu.edu.cn

Abstract. Selecting the most appropriate algorithms for reducing the noise component in infrared spectrum is very necessary, since the infrared signal is often corrupted by noise. To solve this problem, a novel de-noising method based on the null space pursuit (NSP) is proposed in this paper. The NSP is the adaptive operator-based signal separation approach, which can decompose the signal into sub-band components and the residue according to their characteristics. We consider the residue as noise, because it basically dose not contain any useful information. Then, the sub-band components are used to reconstructing the ideal signal. Experimental results show that the proposed de-noising method is effective in suppressing noise while protecting signal characteristics.

Keywords: infrared spectrum, de-noising, null space pursuit.

1   Introduction

Infrared spectroscopy is being increasingly used to measure, both directly and indirectly, of small molecules in chemical and physical properties [1-3]. The high information content in an infrared spectrum is often corrupted by noise [4]. Therefore, to achieve a high sensitivity and accuracy, the de-noising of the infrared spectrum is necessary before the further processing of the data.

In order to improve the signal-to-noise ratio (SNR) of the infrared spectrum, many effective approaches, such as least squares smoothing [5], Gabor filtering [6] and wavelet transform (WT) [7], have been introduced to remove the noise. However, the infrared signal that spans wide ranges in both time and frequency contains peaks of various shapes. Thus, those traditional smoothing and filtering techniques are not efficient for de-noising of infrared signal.

The null space pursuit (NSP) proposed by Peng and Hwang [8-12] is an operator-based signal decomposition algorithm, which uses several adaptive operators derived from a signal to separate the signal into additive subcomponents according to their characteristics. This algorithm estimate the parameters of the operators according to the tested signal during execution. NSP performs better both in suppressing noise and separating signal.

In this paper, we propose a novel method based on NSP for de-noising infrared signal. NSP is first utilized to separate infrared signal into additive sub-components. Then, various sub-components are correspondingly filtered according to their characteristics. Finally, the de-noised infrared signal is obtained through the sum of each filtered sub-component.

D.-S. Huang et al. (Eds.): ICIC 2012, CCIS 304, pp. 197–202, 2012.

2   NSP Theory and Algorithm

To decompose a signal, Peng and Hwang have proposed a method using several operators to extract the local narrow band sub-components from signal [9]. Moreover, some
improved algorithms have been published [8, 10-12].

It is known that a narrow band signal can be approximated as $A(t)\cos(\omega t + \Phi(t))$,
where $A(t)$ is a band-limited signal whose maximal frequency is much smaller that ω,
and $\Phi(t)$ is a slow-varying phase function [9]. In short, a narrow band signal is a concentrated energy region in the frequency domain. For instance, $S(t)$ is a narrow band
signal and a linear operator T from $L_2(R)$ to $L_2(R)$ is call a singular local linear
operator. If there exists a neighborhood for each t such that

$$T(S)(t) = 0, a.e. \tag{1}$$

we say that $S(t)$ is in the null space of the operator T.

If a sequence of operators is applied to a signal, the part of signal in the null spaces
will be removed by the operators, and the residual signal will not contain any information about the null spaces of the operators. So the signal S is expressed as

$$S = \sum_{i=1}^{k} V_i + U_k \tag{2}$$

where V_i are the subcomponents in the null space of the operator T_{i-1} derived from
$S - \sum_{k=1}^{i-1} V_k$, U_k is the residue after k iteration.

There are two types of singular local linear operator, the integral operator and the
differential operator, which can be used by NSP. In this paper, we choose the following
differential operator in order to demonstrate the proposed approach,

$$T = \frac{d^2}{dt^2} + \alpha(t) \tag{3}$$

where d^2/dt^2 is the second differential operator, $\alpha(t)$ is the square of the instantaneous frequency of the signal.

Here, the step-by-step of NSP algorithm is summarized as follows.

1. Input: the original signal S, the ending threshold ε, and the initial values of λ_1^0,
   λ_2 and γ^0.
2. Let $j = 0$, $\hat{U}_j = 0$, $\lambda_1^j = \lambda_1^0$ and $\gamma^j = \gamma^0$.
3. Compute $\hat{\alpha}_j$ as follows

$$\hat{\alpha}_j(t) = -\left(c_i^T D(S - \hat{U}_j)\right)/\left(c_i^T c_i + \lambda_2\right) \tag{4}$$

where c_t is the restriction of $S - \hat{U}_j$ on the interval B_t, which is 31 points for any t, D is the second order differential operator.

4. Compute λ_1^{j+1} as

$$\lambda_1^{j+1} = \frac{S^T M(Q_j, \lambda_1^j, \gamma^j)^T S}{(1+\gamma^j) S^T M(Q_j, \lambda_1^j, \gamma^j)^T M(Q_j, \lambda_1^j, \gamma^j) S} \tag{5}$$

where $M(Q_j, \lambda_1^j, \gamma^j) = (Q_j^T Q_j + (1+\gamma^j)\lambda_1^j I)^{-1}$ and $Q_j = D + P_{\hat{\alpha}_j}$, $P_{\hat{\alpha}_j}$ is a diagonal matrix whose diagonal elements are equal to $\hat{\alpha}_j$.

5. Compute $\hat{U}_{j+1}$ as

$$\hat{U}_{j+1} = \left(Q_j^T Q_j + (1+\gamma^j)\lambda_1^{j+1} I\right)^{-1} * \left(Q_j^T Q_j S + \gamma^j \lambda_1^{j+1} S\right) \tag{6}$$

6. Compute γ^{j+1} as

$$\gamma^{j+1} = \frac{(S-\hat{U}_{j+1})^T S}{\left\|S-\hat{U}_{j+1}\right\|^2} - 1. \tag{7}$$

7. If $\left\|\hat{U}_{j+1} - \hat{U}_j\right\| > \varepsilon\|S\|$, then set $j = j+1$ and go to step iii. Otherwise: the parameter $\hat{\lambda}_1 = \hat{\lambda}_1^{j+1}$, the leakage parameter $\hat{\gamma} = \gamma^{j+1}$ and the operator parameter $\hat{\alpha} = \hat{\alpha}_j$.

8. Output signal as follows

$$\hat{V} = (S - \hat{U}_{j+1}) * (1 + \hat{\gamma}) \tag{8}$$

$$\hat{U} = S - \hat{V}. \tag{9}$$

At step 6, in order to obtain the modified spectrum of $S - \hat{U}$, we only extract the same range of the spectrum of $S - \hat{U}$ as the spectrum of S. And the threshold ε can be set lower $1e-4$ for most noisy signals, the initial value of λ_1 is set from 0.01 to 0.0000001, $\hat{\lambda}_2$ and γ^0 are set as 0.0001 and 1 respectively.

3   De-noising Method Based on NSP

The infrared signal with noise can be written as

$$y_i = f(t_i) + e_i \tag{10}$$

where $t_i = i/n$, e_i is independently distributed as $N(0, \sigma^2)$ and $f(.)$ is an unknown signal which we would like to recover.

With regard to the noisy signal y_i, a series of local narrow band subcomponents will be obtained by using NSP.

$$y_i = \sum_{i=1}^{k} V_i + U_k \tag{11}$$

where V_i is extracted signal which has a strong correlation with the ideal signal, the residue U_k mainly contain the component of noise and few components of the ideal signal. So the estimate signal $\hat{f}$ can be written as

$$\hat{f} = \sum_{i=1}^{k} V_i \tag{12}$$

4   Simulation Experiments

In the experiments, the threshold ε in the proposed algorithm is set less than $1e-4$. The other parameters are set as follows: $\lambda_1 = 1e-5$, $\lambda_2 = 1e-5$ and $\gamma = 1$ for initialization. A synthetic infrared signal and the real infrared signal, where the signal-to-nose ratio (SNR) is 20, are used to evaluate the performance of the proposed algorithm. In order to assess the performance of proposed de-noising method, we compare the proposed algorithm with the WT de-noising method with various wavelets belonging to different families, such as Haar, Daubechies, Coiflet, and Symmlet. The de-noising effect is determined by computing the signal-to-noise ratio (SNR) and the root-mean-square error (RMSE).

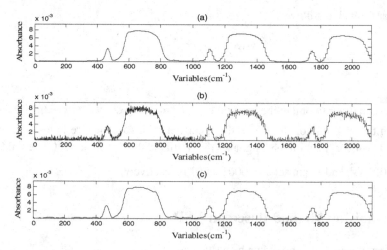

Fig. 1. De-noising of the simulated infrared signal ($SNR = 20$): (a) original pure infrared signal; (b) noisy infrared signal; (c) the de-noising result by using NSP method

The given original pure infrared signal is shown in Fig.1a, and the noisy infrared signal, where SNR is 20, is shown in Fig.1b, Fig.1c shows the de-noising results obtained by using the proposed method; Table1 shows the de-noising results of SNR and RMSE by using those methods. From Table1, it can be seen that the proposed de-noising method yields a higher SNR and a lower RMSE than the WT-based de-noising method with different wavelet families. Thus the proposed method performs better than traditional WT filtering method.

Table 1. SNR and RMSE of de-noising results by using NSP method and WT method with various wavelet families

Algorithm		SNR	RMSE
NSP		20.3455	1.0109e-4
WT	Haar	18.9345	2.5599e-4
	Dauechies2	19.8983	1.4641e-4
	Dauechies4	20.0810	1.1424e-4
	Dauechies6	20.1409	1.0734e-4
	Coiflet1	19.9456	1.4629e-4
	Coiflet2	20.0908	1.1214e-4
	Coiflet3	20.1263	1.1044e-4
	Symmlet2	19.8983	1.4641e-4
	Symmlet4	20.1182	1.1398e-4
	Symmlet6	20.1423	1.0670e-4

5   Conclusions

In this paper, a new de-noising method based on NSP is proposed to remove noise from the noisy infrared signal. We compare the proposed method with the wavelet de-noising algorithm in terms of SNR and RMSE. The experimental results show that the proposed method provides a stronger de-noising ability than WT de-noising method.

Acknowledgements. This work was supported by the National Science Foundation of China (grant NO. 61032007 and 51177002).

References

1. Ho, L.T.: Infrared Absorption Spectrum of Magnesium Double Donors in Silicon. In: Infrared and Millimeter Waves and 13th International Conference on Terahertz Electronics, IRMMW-THz 2005, vol. 1, pp. 170–171 (2005)

2. Yang, H., Xie, S.S., Hu, X.L., Chen, L., Lu, Z.K.: Infrared Spectrum Visualizing Human Acupoints And Meridian-Like Structure. In: International Symposium on Metamaterial, pp. 54–56 (2006)
3. Barth, A.: Infrared Spectroscopy of Proteins. Elsevier Biochimica et Biophysica Acta (BBA)-Bioenergetics 1767(9), 1073–1101 (2007)
4. Guo, Q., Pan, J., Jiang, B., Yi, Z.: Astronomical Spectra Denoising based on Simplified SURE-LET Wavelet Thresholding. In: IEEE International Conference on Information and Automation, Zhangjiajie, China (2008)
5. Qu, J.S., Wang, J.Y.: Theory of Multi-channel Pulse Analysis System, pp. 206–214. Atomic Energy Press, Beijing (1987)
6. Zhao, Y.N., Yang, J.Y.: Weighted Features For Infrared Vehicle Verification Based On Gabor Filters. control, automation. In: Robotics and Vision Conference (ICARCV), vol. 1, pp. 671–675 (2004)
7. Peng, D., Li, X., Dong, K.N.: A Wavelet Component Selection Method for Multivariate Alibration of Near-Infrared Spectra Based on Information Entropy Theory. In: International Conference on ICBECS 2010. Wuhan, pp. 1–4 (2010)
8. Peng, S.L., Hwang, W.L.: Null Space Pursuit: an Operator-based Approach to Adaptive Signal Separation. IEEE Trans. Signal Process. 58, 2475–2483 (2010)
9. Peng, S.L., Hwang, W.L.: Adaptive Signal Decomposition based on Local Narrow Band Signals. IEEE Trans. Signal Process. 56, 2669–2676 (2008)
10. Hu, X.Y., Peng, S.L., Hwang, W.L.: Estimation of Instantaneous Frequency Parameters of the Operator-based Signal Separation Method. Advance in Adaptive Data Analysis 1(4), 573–586 (2009)
11. Xiao, Z.Y., Shen, L.J., Peng, S.L.: Image Super-resolution based on Null Space Pursuit. In: 2010 3rd International Congress Image and Signal Processing (CISP), Yantai, vol. 3, pp. 1200–1203 (2010)
12. Hu, X.Y., Peng, S.L., Hwang, W.L.: Operator based Multicomponent AM-FM Signal Separation Approach. In: IEEE International Workshop on Machine Learning for Signal Processing, Santander, pp. 1–6 (2011)

A Novel Segmentation Algorithm of Fingerprint Images Based on Mean Shift

Zhe Xue[1], Tong Zhao[2], Min Wu[1], and Tiande Guo[2]

[1] School of information Sciences and Engineering, Graduate University of Chinese Academy of Sciences, Beijing, China
[2] School of mathematical Sciences, Graduate University of Chinese Academy of Sciences, Beijing, China
{zhaotong,tdguo}@gucas.ac.cn,
{xuezhe10,wumin0109}@mails.gucas.ac.cn

Abstract. The segmentation of fingerprint images is an important step in an automatic fingerprint identification system (AFIS). It is used to identify the foreground of a fingerprint image. Existing methods are usually based on some point features such as average gray level, variance, Gabor response, etc, while they ignored the local information of foreground regions. In this paper, a novel segmentation approach is proposed based on the mean shift algorithm, which not only take advantage of the traditional features, but also use the local information. In order to segment the fingerprint image better, we modified the original mean shift segmentation algorithm. First we calculate some effective features of fingerprint images and determine the parameters adaptively, and then we process the image based on the mean shift algorithm and get some divided regions, finally the foreground are selected from these regions. The accuracy and effectiveness of our method are validated by experiments performed on FVC database.

Keywords: mean shift, fingerprint image segmentation, image processing.

1   Introduction

An important preprocessing step in an AFIS is the segmentation of fingerprint images. A fingerprint image usually consists of two components, which are called the foreground and the background. The area originated from the contact of a fingertip with the sensor is called the foreground, and the noisy area at the borders of the image is called the background. The task of the fingerprint segmentation is to distinguish between the foregrounds from the background. If we can't segment the fingerprint image correctly, it will result in a lot of false minutiae which can influence the recognition accuracy badly. Therefore, the main goal of the segmentation algorithm is to discard the background, and thus reduce the number of false features. An accurate segmentation algorithm is very helpful in improving the performance of AFIS.

Several approaches to fingerprint image segmentation are known from literature. In [1], fingerprint area is isolated according to local histograms of ridge orientations.

D.-S. Huang et al. (Eds.): ICIC 2012, CCIS 304, pp. 203–211, 2012.

Ridge orientation is estimated at each pixel and a histogram is computed for each 16*16 block. Then, each block is classified according to the distribution of the orientation in that block. In [2], the variance of gray-levels in the orthogonal direction to the ridge orientation in each 16*16 block is computed. The foreground exhibits a very high variance in direction orthogonal to orientation of ridges and very low variance along ridges. In [3], the variance of the Gabor filter responses is used for fingerprint segmentation. An improved version of this Gabor-based method was introduced in [4]. Some learning-based techniques are also used in fingerprint segmentation. In [5], a linear classifier is trained to select foreground pixels based on three features. In [6], An AdaBoost classifier is designed to discriminate between foreground and background blocks based on two new features and five commonly used features.

In this paper, we propose a novel fingerprint segmentation algorithm based on mean shift. We use the modified mean shift algorithm instead of the original algorithm for fingerprint image segmentation. We first calculate the features of the fingerprint image and determine the parameters of the mean shift algorithm. Then, we use the modified mean shift algorithm to process the fingerprint images. Finally, the foreground region is selected from the alternative region. Because the Mean shift method takes into account spatial information, it is not affected by background noise during fingerprint segmentation. This paper is organized as follows. First, Section 2 introduces the original mean shift algorithm. Then, Section 3 proposes the modified algorithm, and the experiment results are shown in Section 4. Finally, Section 5 presents some conclusions.

2   Original Mean Shift Algorithm

Mean shift is proposed in 1975 by Fukunaga and Hostetler [7] and largely forgotten till Cheng's paper [8] rekindled the interest in it. Then, Comaniciu and Meer introduced the algorithm to image processing [9, 10], making it can be well used for image filtering and segmentation. We briefly introduce the mean shift algorithm here.

Given n data points x_i, i=1... n in the d-dimensional space R^d. The *mean shift* is proposed in [10] as follow:

$$m_{h,G}(x) = \frac{\sum_{i=1}^{n} x_i g\left(\left\|\frac{x-x_i}{h}\right\|^2\right)}{\sum_{i=1}^{n} g\left(\left\|\frac{x-x_i}{h}\right\|^2\right)} - x \tag{1}$$

Where g(x) is the kernel function, continue to calculate the mean shift, we will get a series of iterative points. Denote by $\{y_j\}_{j=1,2...}$ the sequence of successive locations of the iterative points, where from (1)

$$y_{j+1} = \frac{\sum_{i=1}^{n} x_i g\left(\left\|\frac{y_j - x_i}{h}\right\|^2\right)}{\sum_{i=1}^{n} g\left(\left\|\frac{y_j - x_i}{h}\right\|^2\right)} \quad j = 1, 2, \ldots \tag{2}$$

Is the weighted mean at y_j and y_1 is the center of the initial position of the kernel. Through iteration, we will eventually find the modes in a feature space.

The mean shift can be used in image segmentation. An image is typically represented as a two-dimensional lattice of p-dimensional vectors, where p=1 in the gray level case, 3 for color images. The space of the lattice is known as the spatial domain, and the gray level, color information is represented in the range domain. Because the nature of the two vectors is different, the multivariate kernel is defined as the product of two radially symmetric kernels

$$K_{hs,hr}(x) = \frac{C}{h_s^2 h_r^2} k\left(\left\|\frac{x^s}{h^s}\right\|^2\right) k\left(\left\|\frac{x^r}{h^r}\right\|^2\right) \tag{3}$$

Where x^s is the spatial part, x^r is the range part of a feature vector, k(x) is the profile used in both two domains, h_s and h_r are the employed kernel bandwidth, and C is the corresponding normalization constant. An Epanechnikov kernel always provides satisfactory performance, so we only has to set the bandwidth parameters h_s and h_r.

In [10], the Mean Shift Image Segmentation Algorithm is proposed as follow:

Let x_i and z_i, $i = 1, \ldots, n$, be the d-dimensional input and filtered image pixels in the joint spatial-range domain, and L_i the label of the i-th pixel in the segmented image.

1. For each pixel, initialize j=1 and $y_{i,1} = x_i$.
2. Compute $y_{i, j+1}$ according to (2) until convergence, $y = y_{i,c}$, assign $z_i = (x_i^s, y_{i,c}^r)$.
3. Repeat step2 until all pixels have been processed. Delineate in the joint domain the clusters $\{C_p\}_{p=1\ldots m}$ by grouping together all z_i which arc closcr than h_s in the spatial domain and h_r in the range domain.
4. For each $i = 1, \ldots, n$, assign $L_i = \{p \mid z_i \in C_p\}$.
5. Optional: Eliminate spatial regions containing less than M pixels.

3   Modified Mean Shift Segmentation Algorithm for Fingerprint Image Segmentation

Although mean shift algorithm is a good method for image segmentation, it has to be modified for the fingerprint image segmentation because of the special nature of fingerprint images. In this paper, the following three aspects are proposed to modify the algorithm. First, we extract some fingerprint features instead of the original features used in [10]. To improve the speed of the algorithm, we divide the image into small blocks, and then each block is treated as a basic unit for operation. Second, to make the algorithm applicable to different situations, we use adaptive method to obtain parameters. Finally, because the mean shift image segmentation algorithm is a clustering method, we have to select the foreground class from all the classes, and the other classes are set to the background.

3.1   Feature Extraction

The original mean shift algorithm for image segmentation using color or gray-value as the feature, but it does not make sense for fingerprint images. The foreground is made up of interleaved ridges and valleys, and the pixel gray-values in this region change a lot. So the gray-value isn't a good characterization of foreground, and it can't be used in the algorithm directly. Therefore, we extract some fingerprint features from the fingerprint image, and the mean shift algorithm is based on these features.

For fingerprint images, there are a lot of features can be used. We have selected three features that may contain useful information for segmentation. These features are the local variance, the local mean and the coherence of the fingerprint image.

The variance and average of the gray-value are two features that might be useful for the segmentation of fingerprint images. In general, the variance of the ridge-valley structures in the foreground is higher than the variance of the noise in the background, and the average gray-value in the foreground is lower than it is in the background. So we use $Var / Mean$ as the first feature. Let I denote the intensity of the image, in a window W around a pixel, the variance and the mean for each pixel is given by:

$$Var = \frac{1}{w \cdot w} \sum_W (I - mean)^2 \qquad Mean = \frac{1}{w \cdot w} \sum_W I \qquad (4)$$

The coherence is another useful feature for fingerprint images. It gives a measure how well the gradients are pointing in the same direction. Since a fingerprint mainly consists of parallel line structures, the coherence will be considerably higher in the foreground than in the background. The coherence in a window W is defined as:

$$Coh = \frac{\sqrt{\left(G_{xx} - G_{yy}\right)^2 + 4G_{xy}^2}}{G_{xx} + G_{yy}} \qquad (5)$$

Where $G_{xx} = \sum_w G_x^2, G_{yy} = \sum_w G_y^2, G_{xy} = \sum_w G_x G_y$ and (G_x, G_y) is the local gradient.

We hope that the feature has a high response value in the foreground, and the value is relatively low in the background. The above two features have their own advantages and disadvantages. Generally, $Var / Mean$ has a high response in the foreground (Fig. a, Fig. b, Fig. c). But for some noise areas (Fig. 1e), the response is also high.

The feature *Coh* has a high response in the region with good quality (Fig. 1a), and it has a low response in the background (Fig. 1d, Fig. 1e) and the foreground which the ridges are broken (Fig. 1b) or with creases (Fig. 1c).

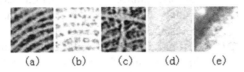

(a)   (b)   (c)   (d)   (e)

Fig. 1. Some Regions of Fingerprint Images (a) Good Quality Foreground Region (b) Foreground Region Which the Ridges are Broken. (c) Foreground Region with Creases. (d) Background Region with Low Noise. (e) Background Region with High Noise.

In order to obtain a better feature, we propose a new one. The new feature is defined as:

$$Fea = \lambda \frac{Var}{Mean} + (1 - \lambda)Coh \qquad (6)$$

Where λ is $(0,1)$. Both $Var/Mean$ and Coh have been normalized before summation. It was found that $\lambda = 0.5$ always provides satisfactory performance.

By adding these two features, the value of the new feature in the foreground and the background has greater differences. Through experiments we found the new feature to can distinguish between foreground and background regions better than using the two features alone.

To speed up the algorithm, we don't calculate the feature for every pixel. We divide the image into blocks of size r*r and calculate the feature of every block. The mean shift segmentation algorithm is based on these blocks. This will not only improve the speed of the segmentation, but also segment the image better. According to our empirical experimental experience, the algorithm with r=15 performs well for most fingerprint images.

3.2   Determine the Parameters

The choice of parameters in (3) is very important for the mean shift algorithm. In general image segmentation, it can be seen that the spatial bandwidth has a distinct effect on the output when compared to the range (color) bandwidth. As h_s increases, the regions with large spatial support are retained while the small ones are discarded in the segmented image. On the other hand, only the regions with large difference in features survive when h_r is large.

For fingerprint images, hs doesn't affect the segmentation results greatly, we can generally take a fixed value. Through experiments, we found the general case can take hs=15. But the requirement is different for selecting hr. The value of hr reflects the difference in features between different classes (foreground and background). For different fingerprint images, the difference of features between the classes varies largely. If the value of hr is too large, regions belong to both foreground and background will merge together. If the value is small, regions that should merge in the same class will be separated and lead to over-segmentation. We can get the feature differences between different classes through the feature distribution histogram. The distribution of features in fingerprint images is roughly bimodal structure (Fig. 2). Some distribution has large distance between the two peaks, others small. It can be seen from the figure that the distance between two peaks are about 0.7(Fig. 2a), 0.4(Fig. 2b), 0.3(Fig. 2c), 0.25(Fig. 2d). So the value of hr should not be fixed. Its value must be adjusted according to the specific circumstances of the image.

Therefore, we propose a simple and effective adaptive method to determine hr. Because the distribution of fingerprint image features focused on two peaks, we think hr should be associated with the distance between the two peaks. If the distance is relatively large, hr should be large, while if the distance is small, hr should be small. So we first find the values of the two peaks u1 and u2, then take $h_r = \alpha |u1 - u2|$ ($0 < \alpha < 1$). We use k-means algorithm to find the two clustering center points of the feature distribution, and the two center points are considered as the peaks approximatively. Through this method of selecting parameters, making the algorithm automatically adapts to the different images with different distribution of features, improving the adaptability of the algorithm and the results of segmentation.

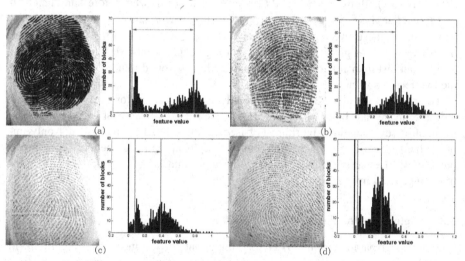

Fig. 2. Some fingerprint images and their feature distributions

3.3   Foreground Selection

After running the mean shift segmentation algorithm, the image is divided into several regions of interest. Some of them are composed by foreground blocks and some are composed by background blocks. To get the foreground, we need to pick out the desired regions from all the regions. Generally, the foreground has the following characteristics: first, the area of the foreground is relatively large; second, the feature of foreground is larger than the feature of the other region; third, the center of the foreground is generally located in the central location of the image and not too close to the edge. Based on the above three characteristics, we designed the following method to select the foreground:

(1) Arrange the regions according to their size in decreasing order, denoted by R_1, R_2,..., R_n,

(2) **for** k: 1 to n

(3)   **if** the distance between the center of R_k and the edge < D

(4)   **if** the feature of R_k > threshold

(5)   **then** R_k is selected as the foreground

(6)   **return**

(7)   **end**

(8)   **end**

(9) **end**

The center of Rk is the average spatial position of the block. In practice, the parameter D takes 0.2*(Image_Width+Image_Height) and the threshold takes 0.5(u1+u2), where u1 and u2 is computed from 3.2. Experiments have shown that the proposed method can select the foreground effectively.

3.4   The Proposed Algorithm

By modifying the original mean shift algorithm, we propose the following algorithm for fingerprint segmentation.

(1) Divide the image into blocks at size of r*r.

(2) Compute the new feature *Fea* for every block.

(3) Determine the parameters: h_s and h_r.

(4) Run the modified mean shift algorithm and get some candidate regions.

(5) Pick out the foreground regions from the candidate regions.

4   Experimental Results

The segmentation algorithm was tested on some images from FVC 2000 database [11]. First, segmentation results of our method compared with the traditional Mean and Variance based method are shown in Fig. 3.

The results of traditional techniques are unsatisfied beacuse they cann't remove the background with high noise correctly. And the foreground is usually composed by a number of isolated areas. These foreground regions are not continuous and it doesn't accord with the real characteristics of fingerprint. Our method can remove the background effectively and the foreground area is accurate and complete.

To further confirm the effectiveness of our method, the results are compared with VeriFinger 6.4 published by Neurotechnology (hereinafter abbreviated as Neuro) [12] in Fig. 4. In some images, some remaining ridges which are caused by the previously scanned fingers are expected to be removed as background. We can see that the Neuro's results usually contain many remaining ridges which should be removed and some noise regions are regarded as foreground. The proposed algorithm can segment the images accurately and effectively even if the image contains a lot of noise. Compared to Neuro, our algorithm also reduces the spurious minutiae (Fig. 4).

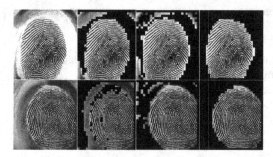

Fig. 3. Comparison of proposed algorithm with traditional techniques, the 1st column shows fingerprint images from FVC2000. The 2nd and 3rd columns show the results of the Mean and Variance based techniques respectively. The 4th column shows the results of our method.

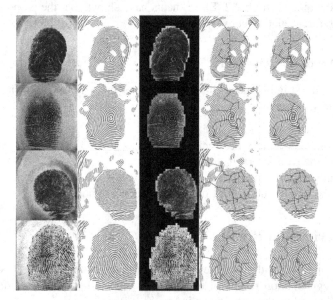

Fig. 4. Comparison of the proposed algorithm with Neuro's method, the 1st column shows the original images from FVC 2000. The 2nd column shows the segmentation results by Neuro. The 3rd column shows the results by the proposed algorithm. The 4th and 5th column show the minutiae extraction results of Neuro's method and the proposed algorithm respectively.

5   Conclusion

In this paper, an algorithm for segmentation of fingerprints is proposed. We modified the original mean shift segmentation algorithm to make it better applied to fingerprint image segmentation. The proposed method can segment the image accurately even if the image contains much noise. The experiments show that the proposed method is able to remove the remaining ridges and noise background regions effectively and leads to an improvement of minutiae extraction.

Acknowledgments. This work was supported by Innovation Program of CAS, under Grants kjcx-yw-s7, National Natural Science Foundation of P.R. China, under Grant 10831006 and 11101420.

References

1. Mehtre, B.M., Murthy, N.N., Kapoor, S., Chatterjee, B.: Segmentation of Fingerprint Images Using Directional Image. Pattern Recognition 20(4), 429–435 (1987)
2. Ratha, N.K., Chen, S., Jain, A.K.: Adaptive Flow Orientation-Based Feature Extraction in Fingerprint Images. Pattern Recognition 28(11), 1657–1672 (1995)
3. Shen, L., Kot, A.C., Koo, W.M.: Quality Measures of Fingerprint Images. In: Bigun, J., Smeraldi, F. (eds.) AVBPA 2001. LNCS, vol. 2091, pp. 266–271. Springer, Heidelberg (2001)
4. Fernando, A.F., Julian, F.A., Javier, O.G.: An Enhanced Gabor Filter-Based Segmentation Algorithm for Fingerprint Recognition Systems. In: Proceedings of the 4th International Symposium on Image and Signal Processing and Analysis, pp. 239–244 (2005)
5. Asker, M., Bazen, S.H.: Gerez: Segmentation of Fingerprint Images. In: ProRISC 2001 Workshop on Circuits, Systems and Signal Processing, Veldhoven, The Netherlands (2001)
6. Liu, E., Zhao, H., Guo, F.F., Liang, J.M., Tian, J.: Fingerprint segmentation based on an AdaBoost classifier. Frontiers of Computer Science in China 5(2), 148–157
7. Fukunaga, K., Hostetler, L.D.: The Estimation of the Gradient of a Density Functions with Applications in Pattern Recognition. IEEE Trans. on Information Theory 21(1), 32–40 (1975)
8. Cheng, Y.Z.: Mean Shift, mode seeking, and clustering. IEEE Trans. on Pattern Analysis and Machine Intelligence 17(8), 790–799 (1995)
9. Comaniciu, D., Meer, P.: Robust Analysis of Feature Spaces: Color Image Segmentation. In: Proceedings of the IEEE Computer Society Conference on Computer Vision and Pattern Recognition (CVPR 1997), San Juan, PR, USA, pp. 750–755 (1997)
10. Comaniciu, D., Meer, P.: Mean Shift: A Robust Approach toward Feature Space Analysis. IEEE Transactions on Pattern Analysis and Machine Intelligence 24(5), 603–619 (2002)
11. http://bias.csr.unibo.it/fvc2000/default.asp
12. http://www.neurotechnology.com

A New Hybrid Method with Biomimetic Pattern Recognition and Sparse Representation for EEG Classification

Yanbin Ge and Yan Wu[*]

Department of Computer Science and Technology, Tongji University,
201804, Shanghai, China
yanwu@tongji.edu.cn

Abstract. This paper presents a novel classification framework combining Biomimetic Pattern Recognition (BPR) with Sparse Representation (SR) for Brain Computer Interface based on motor imagery. This framework can work well when encountering the overlap coverage problem of BPR by introducing the idea of SR. Using Common Spatial Pattern to extract the rhythm features of EEG data, we evaluate the performance of the proposed method in the datasets from previous BCI Competitions. By making comparison with those of LDA, SVM and original BPR, our proposed method shows the better classification accuracy.

Keywords: biomimetic pattern recognition, hyper sausage neuron, sparse representation, brain-computer interface, motor imagery.

1   Introduction

The research of brain-computer interfaces (BCI) initially aimed at designing an Electroencephalogram (EEG) – based device to help the patients with severe disabilities to control the external environment without via the traditional muscle-dependent pathway [1]. With the constant deepening of studies on BCI, the BCI applications have played an important role in the field of rehabilitation engineering, military, entertainment etc. The most significant phase of BCI is the EEG classification that determines the final recognition accuracy of the EEG signal. The state of art classifiers which have been successfully applied into the EEG classification includes various classical linear or nonlinear classifiers such as linear discriminant analysis (LDA) [2], support vector machine (SVM) [3], artificial neural network (ANN) [4] etc.

For achieving higher classification accuracy of MI-EEG, some novel classifiers were proposed recently. Biomimetic pattern recognition (BPR), first introduced into the EEG classification in 2010 [5], proven its clear advantages over the traditional classifiers. But, a problem cannot be ignored in the classification of BPR – the overlap coverage problem. A traditional method to solve this embarrass is the distance method

---

[*] Corresponding author.

D.-S. Huang et al. (Eds.): ICIC 2012, CCIS 304, pp. 212–217, 2012.

that we named. The main idea is computing the Euclid-distance between this sample and associated neuron models, and then the sample belongs to the neuron model closest to it [5, 6]. However, some experiment results have shown that the classification accuracy of distance method is generally not so high, may lead to BPR degenerate.

In this paper, we are interested in developing a new method to solve the overlap problem based on the Sparse Representation (SR). The idea of SR derived from the classical Compressed Sensing (CS) theory [7], which has increasingly become recognized as providing extremely high performance for applications as diverse as: noise reduction, compression, feature extraction and pattern classification, especially in the field of image processing [8]. In BCI area, some researchers have also attempted to introduce SR into the EEG classification in recent years. The work [9] employed SR to the EEG based driver's vigilance detection problem and the literation [10] showed the SR method works better in MI-EEG classification compared with LDA, another common classifier.

In this paper, a new classification method is proposed combined BPR with SR for the motor imagery based BCI application. We use Common Spatial Pattern (CSP) for extracting the features of EEG and apply our novel classifier to the datasets collected from 2005 BCI Competition to evaluate its performance. For comparison, other classifiers are also made to test classification accuracy.

The rest of this paper is organized as follows: Section 2 introduces the proposed method and Section 3 presents the experiments and results. Finally, conclusions and future work are discussed in Section 4.

2   Methods

2.1   Construction of BPR

For using the BPR algorithm into classification, the construction of covering neuron is the key point. Hyper-Sausage Neuron (HSN) [11] is used in this paper to cover the training set. HSN's coverage in the n-dimensional space can be seen as a topological product of a one-dimensional line segment and an n-dimensional hypersphere. HSN is a kind of frequently used neuron model in BPR, which has better generalize ability and wide applicable scope. The main construction process as follows:

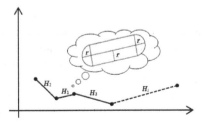

Fig. 1. An approximate diagram of BPR construction: the subscript of H_1, H_2, ... H_i shows the build sequence of every HSN. The quasi-ellipsoid denotes the approximate two-dimensional drawing of HSN coverage; r denotes the radius of the hypersphere.

Firstly, for the training set T, we need calculate the Euclid-distance between any two points of the same class and choose the shortest pair to build the first HSN H_1. Secondly, filter remaining points in T which are covered by H_1. Find another point in the remaining samples which is closest to H_1, build H_2. And next, repeat the last step, delete the remaining points which are covered by $H_1, H_2, \ldots H_i$. Find the point which is closest to these neurons and build a new HSN $H_{(i+1)}$ to cover it. Finally, if all the points in T have been covered, the construction process is terminated. n HSNs are produced and so are the BPR classifier. A brief construction diagram is shown in Fig. 1.

2.2   Classification with Sparse Representation

An important part of SR is the over-complete dictionary [12] in which the signal represents. Generally speaking, there are two methods to build a suitable dictionary [13]: (1) analytic dictionary method which based on the mathematical model of signal; (2) trained dictionary method which learning from large sets of training samples. In this paper, we choose trained dictionary method to linear represent the test signal in an over-complete dictionary which constructed by training sample set.

Suppose that training samples matrix $T = [A_1, A_2, ..., A_n] \in R^{m \times N}$, where m denotes the dimension of sample and N denotes the number of class. We define $A_i = [a_1, a_2, ..., a_t]$ as the samples belong to class A_i and t denotes the total number of samples which belong to class A_i. For a test signal $y \in A_i$, it can be represented as a linear combination of the samples of A_i:

$$y = \beta_1 a_1 + \beta_2 a_2 + ... + \beta_t a_t \tag{1}$$

where β_i ($i=1,2,...,t$) is the scalar coefficients of the linear combination.

Considering the real label of test signal is unknown in advance, so we can use all classes' samples to linear represent this signal.

$$y = Tx_0 \in R^m \tag{2}$$

where $x_0 = [0, ..., 0, \beta_1, ..., \beta_t, 0, ..., 0]^T \in R^N$ denotes the coefficients of the linear combination that most of are equal to or close to zero except the samples associated with A_i.

To declare that, for equation (2), it is meaningful in SR when the samples size larger than the dimensions of the sample, that is, m<N*t. The solution process of above equation is actually an optimization problem called ell-0 minimization. Yet, ell-0 minimization is an NP-hard problem. Recent studies in the CS theory have shown that if signal x_0 is sparse enough, the ell-0 minimization problem is equivalent to ell-1 minimization problem [14]. Thus, equation (2) is transformed into the optimization problem of ell-1 and can be computed within the linear time-cost via the linear programming algorithm:

$$(\ell^1): x_{1opt} = \arg\min \| x \|_1 \;.\; \text{Subject to} \;\; y = Tx_0 \tag{3}$$

Actually the solve process of above equation is named sparse coding, another major research direction in SR. There have been many sparse coding algorithms presently and in this paper, we adopt the Orthogonal Matching Pursuit (OMP) method [15]. After solving the ell-1 minimization problem, we can get the nonzero elements of y; the residuals $r_i(y) := \| y - T\delta_i(x) \|$ also can be obtained. Then, the classification rule is given by:

$$class(y) = \arg \min_i r_i(y) \quad \cdot \tag{4}$$

2.3   The Algorithm of BPR-SR

When employing BPR into the classification of MI-EEG, we cannot directly use BPR coverage to classify the samples which fall into the overlap area. The previous solution is the distance method, easy to implement but with higher error rate, restricts the whole classification performance of BPR classifier. Since SR works well in mining the elementary features and internal structures of signals, and plus the time-cost also be acceptable, we replace the traditional distance method with SR method in the classification of BPR. The specific classification algorithm as follows:

- **Step1.** Input: Training Set $T \in R^{m \times Ni}$ for i classes, a test signal $y \in R^{m \times 1}$.
- **Step2.** Construct the BPR classifier with the training set as mentioned in Section 2.1.
- **Step3.** Judge whether the test signal falls into the normal coverage of BPR, if so, then classified via BPR.
- **Step4.** If the test signal falls into the overlap coverage of BPR, and then we employ SR method.
  - Step4.1. Solve the minimization optimization problem (as shown in equation 3) with OMP, x_0 denotes the SR coefficients.
  - Step4.2. Compute the residuals and make the classification by finding the minimum according equation (4).
- **Step5.** Output the predict label of signal y
- **Step6.** Repeat the 3-5 steps, until there are no new test samples.

3   Experiments and Results

We have analyzed an open EEG datasets to conduct the experiments of our new method, which come from 2005 BCI Competition. It includes the 'aa', 'al' and 'aw' three subsets, which was provided by Berlin BCI group. Each subset contains a total of 280 groups of right hand and foot MI EEG data.

For each dataset, we compare the performance of the proposed BPR-SR with the LDA, SVM, SR and BPR with distance method. To make a fair comparison, in the other classifiers, we use the CSP filtering and choose 8-12Hz as our filter bank. In our experiments, we make use of 5-cross validation to determine the value of all necessary parameters of all classifiers.

Fig. 2 compares the classification accuracy rate of each traditional method with the BPR-SR classifier. Sub graph (a) for subject '*al*', (b) for subject '*aa*' and (c) for subject '*aw*'. We set different number of training samples, which is 84, 140, 190, 210 and 224, accounted for 30%, 50%, 68%, 75% and 80% of the whole dataset, be in accordance with the requirement of BCIC. Inspecting each sub graph, we see that the BPR-SR generally outperforms the other four classifiers, about 7%~ 10% average higher.

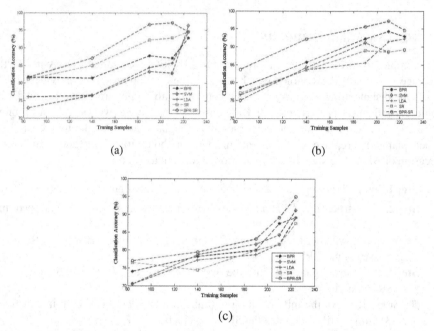

Fig. 2. Comparison of five classifiers using classification accuracy in the three different datasets ('*al*' for '*a*', '*aa*' for '*b*', '*aw*' for '*c*') from EEG dataset. The classification accuracy on the y-axis while the number of training samples on the x-axis.

4   Conclusion

A new hybrid BCI classifier has been proposed based BPR and SR in this paper. To our knowledge, this is the first attempt to implement SR to solve the overlap problem in BPR. We have conducted some experiments to compare the performance of different classifiers in the datasets of previous BCIC. The results demonstrate that our new algorithm is efficiency and robust compared with the other classifiers. Future experiments can be conducted on more datasets of three or more classes. And we also continue to investigate another way to combine BPR with SR, for example in the co-training scheme under the frame of semi-supervised learning.

References

1. Walpaw, J.R., Birbaumer, N., Heetderks, W.J.: Brain-Computer Interface Technology: A Review of the First International Meeting. IEEE Trans. Rehab. Eng. 8(2), 164–173 (2000)
2. Graimann, B., Huggins, J.E., Schlogl, A.: Detection of Movement-related Desynchronization Patterns in Ongoing Single-channel Electrocorticogram. IEEE Trans. Neural Syst. Rehabil. Eng. 11(3), 276–281 (2003)
3. Schlogl, A., Lee, F., Pfurtscheller, G.: Characterization of Four-class Motor Imagery EEG Data for the BCI-competition 2005. Journal of Neural Engineering 2(4), 14–22 (2005)
4. Lotte, F., Congedo, M., Arnaldi, B.: A Review of Classification Algorithms for EEG-based Brain–Computer Interfaces. Journal of Neural Engineering 4(2), 1–13 (2007)
5. Xu, K., Wu, Y.: Motor Imagery EEG Recognition Based on Biomimetic Pattern Recognition. In: The 3rd International Conference on Biomedical Engineering and Informatics (BMEI), pp. 955–959 (2010)
6. Wu, Y., Yao, X., Wang, S.J.: Relative Division of Overlapping Space Based Biomimetic Pattern Recognition. Pattern Recognition & Artificial Intelligence 21(3), 346–350 (2008)
7. Candes, E.J., Wakin, M.B.: An Introduction to Compressive Sampling. IEEE Signal Proc. Magazine 25(21), 21–30 (2008)
8. Deng, Y., Dai, Q.H., Zhang, Z.K.: Graph Laplace for Occluded Face Completion and Recognition. IEEE Trans. on Image Processing 20(8), 2329–2338 (2011)
9. Yu, H.B., Lu, H.T., Ouyang, T., Liu, H.J., Lu, B.L.: Vigilance Detection Based on Sparse Representation of EEG. In: 32nd International Conference- IEEE/EMBS, pp. 2439–2442 (2010)
10. Younghak, S., Seungchan, L., Minkyu, A., Sung, C.J., Heung, L.: Motor Imagery based BCI Classification via Sparse Representation of EEG Signals. In: NFSI & ICBEM, Banff, Canada, pp. 93–97 (2011)
11. Wang, S.J., Lai, J.L.: Geometrical Learning, Descriptive Geometry, and Biomimetic Pattern Recognition. Neurocomputing 67(3), 9–28 (2005)
12. Yang, M., Zhang, L., Feng, X.C.: Fisher Discrimination on Dictionary Learning for Sparse Representation. In: 2011 IEEE ICCV, pp. 543–550 (2011)
13. Rubinstein, R., Bruckstein, A.M., Elad, M.: Dictionaries for Sparse Representation Modeling. Proceedings of the IEEE 98(6), 1045–1057 (2010)
14. Cande's, E., Romberg, J., Tao, T.: Stable Signal Recovery from Incomplete and Inaccurate Measurements. Comm. Pure and Applied Math 59(8), 1207–1223 (2006)
15. Tropp, J.A., Gilbert, A.C.: Signal Recovery From Partial Information Via Orthogonal Matching Pursuit. IEEE Trans. Inf. Theory 53(12), 4655–4666 (2007)

Recognizing Complex Events in Real Movies
by Audio Features

Ji-Xiang Du, Yi-Lan Guo, and Chuan-Min Zhai

Department of Computer Science and Technology, Huaqiao University, Xiamen 361021
{jxdu77,gylwerlove,cmzhai}@gmail.com

Abstract. This paper proposes a novel approach to taking audio feature into account for better event recognition performance in recognizing complex events in real movies. Firstly, local-space time feature and audio feature are extracted, and then an individual video sequence is represented as a SOFM density map, finally we integrate such density map with SVM for recognition events. Using the public Hollywood dataset, the presented result justify the proposed method explicitly improve the average accuracy and average precision compared to other relative approaches.

Keywords: local space-time features, audio feature, self-organization feature map, event recognition.

1   Introduction

Video event recognition has been an active research in computer vision due to its wide range of applications such as behavioral biometrics, content-based video analysis, and surveillance [1]. In the study of event recognition, there are many common datasets, such as KTH dataset, Weizmann dataset, UCF dataset and Hollywood dataset. Comparing to the other datasets, Hollywood dataset is from the real movie scenes, and there are great changes in events apparent in both of space and time. Obscured, camera movement and dynamic background make this dataset very challenging. This dataset has been adopted in our experiments.

Local space-time features have become a popular video representation for event recognition. Many different space-time feature detectors [2][3][4] and descriptors [5][6][7] have been proposed in the past few years. Local space-time features capture characteristic shape and motion in video and provide relatively independent representation of events with respect to their spatio-temporal shifts and scales as well as background clutter and multiple motions in the scene.

Meanwhile, audio, another very important modality of movies, can also provide helpful evidence on videos scenes for event recognition. Research outcomes have demonstrated strong evidence that auditory information can enhance human perception [8]. There also exist a large number of research works fusing audio with visual information for multi-modal video content analysis [9] and various successful applications including event detection in sports video and real movies and so on.

D.-S. Huang et al. (Eds.): ICIC 2012, CCIS 304, pp. 218–223, 2012.
© Springer-Verlag Berlin Heidelberg 2012

Therefore, we propose to exploit audio feature in movies for event recognition. Firstly, visual features are extracted based on spatial-temporal interest points and self-organizing feature map (SOM) is utilized for feature representation. Secondly, Mel Frequency Cepstrum Coefficient (MFCC) is extracted, and SOM is also adopted for audio feature representation. Finally, SVM classifier is trained for classification. The extraction of the visual feature has been introduced in [10], so it's not to be described in this paper and the details of the SOM can also read from [10].

The presented result justify the proposed method explicitly improve the average accuracy and average precision compared to other relative approaches.

2   Feature Representation and Classification

2.1   Audio Feature

The one commonly used in voice recognition speech features is Mel Frequency Cepstrum Coefficient (MFCC)[11]. MFCC considers fully the characteristics of the human ear, highlighting low-frequency information which is helpful for identifying and shielding the noise comes from high frequency. MFCC parameters have high recognition performance and anti-noise ability. Therefore in our experimental MFCC parameters are adopted as audio features.

MFCC can only reflect the static characteristic of sound, while first order differentials of MFCC ($\Delta MFCC$), a kind of dynamic parameter, can reflect dynamic characteristic of sound and has better robustness. So, MFCC and $\Delta MFCC$ are combined as audio feature. And then we also use the speech endpoint detection algorithm. The following section of this part will describe the process in detail.

Normalization: the sound signal is normalized by diving the maximum value of the magnitude, i.e.:

$$\tilde{x}(i) = x(i) / \max_{0 \le i < n-1} x(i) \tag{1}$$

Pre-emphasis: this step is to boost the signal's high-frequency components, while leaving the low-frequency components in their original state. The transfer function of the pre-emphasis factor α is

$$H(z) = 1 - \alpha z^{-1} \tag{2}$$

Segmentation: the segmentation is based on the detector of acoustic activity, which estimates the pre-emphasis energy for a frame of K successive samples as:

$$E(k) = \sum_{i=1}^{K} (x(kL+i-ax(kL+i-1))^2$$
$$k = 0, \cdots M - 1 \tag{3}$$

where L is a predefined step size which defines the degree of overlapping between two successive frames

Hamming windowed: in order to minimize the signal discontinuities at the boundaries of each frame, we multiply each frame with a raised cosine windowing function — Hamming window:

$$
\omega_H = \begin{cases} 0.54 - 0.46\cos(\dfrac{2\pi n}{n-1}) &, n = 0,1,\cdots N-1 \\ 0 & \text{other} \end{cases}
$$

(4)

Fast fourier transform: we set frame length N to 256 , take Fast Fourier Transform (FFT) of each frame, then the spectrum of the mth frame is:

$$
S(k,m) = \sum_{n=0}^{255} s(n,m)\exp(-f\frac{2\pi nk}{256})
$$

(5)

Triangular window filtering: map the powers of above obtained spectrum to mel scale, filtered with M Mel bandpass filters (in our experiment M is 24), resulting in a group of coefficients $m_1, m_2, \cdots\cdots$. The Mel filters are actually triangular overlapping windows in mel scale.

Log: take the logs of the powers at each of the mel frequencies.

DCT: the purpose of this step is to remove the correlation between each dimensional of signal, the signal is mapped to a low-dimensional space.

$$
C_n = \sum_{k=1}^{M} \ln x'(k)\cos[\pi(k-0.5)n/M] \quad n = 1,2,\cdots,L
$$

(6)

where x'(k) is input power spectrum of the kth filter. M is the number of Mel filters, L is the number of frames.

Window normalization: MFCC parameters have been obtained and then multiplied by a normalized cepstrum upgrade window.

$$
\begin{aligned}
w &= 1 + 6*\sin(pi*[1:12]./12); \\
w &= w/\max(w); \\
C_i &= C_i.*w;
\end{aligned}
$$

(7)

Differential: first order differential of MFCC($\Delta MFCC$) can be calculated as:

$$
d(n) = \frac{1}{\sqrt{\sum_{i=-k}^{k} i^2}} \sum_{i=k}^{k} i \times C(n+i)
$$

(8)

Endpoint detection: the purpose of the endpoint detection of speech signals is to determine accurately the start and the end of the voice signal. In speech recognition systems endpoint detection can not only reduce the amount of data collection, saving processing time, but also to reduce the interference of noise or silence, to improve the performance of speech recognition. There are many way of speech endpoint detection. In our experiments we adopt the method based on shot-time average zero crossing rate and short-time energy.

Shot-time energy can be calculated as:

$$E_n = \sum_{m=-\infty}^{\infty} [x(m) \cdot w(n-m)]^2 \qquad (9)$$

Short-time average zero crossing rate can be calculated as:

$$Zn = \frac{1}{2} \sum_{m=-\infty}^{\infty} |\text{sgn}[x(m)] - \text{sgn}[x(m-1)]| \, w(n-m) \qquad (10)$$

where sgn is sign function.

So, finally take the MFCC and $\Delta MFCC$ between the two endpoints as feature parameters.

2.2   Self-organization Feature Map and SOFM Analysis

The number of features of each video clip is different, so in order to unify the representation of video sequence, we adopt the idea of Self-Organizing Feature Map[12].

For a given video sequence sample $S = (j_1, j_2, \cdots, j_m)$, it contains m features, namely m space-time interest points. If cell i responds to input vector j_i, we call cell i or the location of cell i on the map as the image of vector j_i. Every feature vector j_i in the input set has and only has one image on the neural map, but one cell can be the image of many vectors. If we use a plane with a lattice on it to represent the neural map, one square representing one neuron, and write the number h_i of input features whose image is this cell in the corresponding square, we get a map $H = (h_1, h_2, \cdots, h_n)$. This map tells us how many images of input patterns are distributed on the neural map, thus we call it SOFM density map or SOFM image distribution map.

Statistics the number of features of all the nodes in the density map $sum = h_1 + h_2 + \cdots + h_n$ and normalization the density map $H' = (h_1, h_2, \cdots, h_n) / sum$, every video sequence has the density map of audio feature and visual feature respectively, finally we merge these two feature vectors as the total feature vector of each video sequence $H = (H_{visual}, H_{audio})$.

3   Experiment

Support Vector Machines are state-of-the art large margin classifiers which have recently gained popularity within visual pattern recognition, so our experience uses SVM as a classifier.

The Hollywood dataset used in our experiment is the subset of samples originates from 32 movies, where the training samples come from 12 movies and the testing samples are from another 20 movies. There are 8 event classes: answering the phone, getting out of the car, hand shaking, hugging, kissing, sitting down, sitting up and standing up. In our experiments, we used the clean training dataset.

For each event classes, we use the positive training samples to get neural map respectively. The number of neurons of map layer is 10*10. Because the number of samples for audio experiments reduces obviously, we use cross-validation. The experiment is divided into 10 groups, and each group was extracted 2, 1, 2, 2, 5, 5, 1, 5 samples from samples of each category for testing. For each of 10 groups there are also 7 group tests in every event class, the samples of every group come from the positive samples and one of another seven kind of negative samples. By these tests, we obtain mean average accuracy, mean average precision and mean average recall is 0.615, 0.510 and 0.550. The result is show in Table.1, and this table also lists the recognition rate of simple using visual features or audio feature.

By comparing our result with the result of papers [7] and [13] was show in Table.2, we can get conclusion that the average precision improved. In [14] author adopted four local features detector and six descriptors for recognizing events, and the best average accuracy is only 45.8%.

Table 1. The result of our experiments

	Fusion of two features	Visual Feature	Audio Feature
Average Accuracy	0. 615	0. 586	0. 592
Average Precision	0. 510	0. 498	0. 485
Average Recall	0. 550	0. 550	0. 527

Table 2. The result of contrastive papers compared with different methods

event	SIFT	HoG+HoF	SIFT+HoG+HoF	Literature [7]
Answerphone	0.105	0.088	0.107	0.321
Getoutcar	0.191	0.090	0.116	0.415
Handshake	0.123	0.116	0.141	0.323
Hugperson	0.129	0.135	0.138	0.406
Kiss	0.348	0.496	0.556	0.533
Sitdown	0.161	0.316	0.278	0.386
Situp	0.142	0.072	0.078	0.182
Standup	0.262	0.350	0.325	0.505
Total precision	0.183	0.208	0.0.217	0.384

4   Conclusion

The presented result justify the proposed framework explicitly improve the average accuracy and average precision compared to other relative approaches. According to the experiments, we can also obtain relatively good results by simply using the audio feature. In contrast, although the recognition rate of audio feature is slightly lower than visual feature, however in terms of time, the use of audio feature is much faster than the use of local space-time feature.

Acknowledgement. This work was supported by the grants of the National Science Foundation of China (Nos. 60805021, 61175121, 61102163), the Program for New Century Excellent Talents in University (No.NCET-10-0117), Natural Science Foundation of Fujian Province of China (No. 2011J01349), the Program for Excellent Youth Talents in University of Fujian Province (No.JA10006), the Fundamental Research Funds for the Central Universities (No.JB-SJ1003, 11QZR05).

References

1. Turaga, P., Chellappa, R., Subrahmanian, V.S., Udrea, O.: Machine Recognition of Human Activities: A Survey. IEEE Transactions on Circuits and Systems for Video Technology, 1473–1488 (2008)
2. Laptev, I., Lindeberg, T.: Space-time interest points. In: ICCV, pp. 432–439 (2003)
3. Dollar, P., Rabaud, V., Cottrell, G., Belongie, S.: Behavior recognition via Sparse spatio-temporal Features. In: Joint IEEE International Workshop on Visual Surveillance and Performance Evaluation of Tracking and Surveillance, pp. 65–72 (2005)
4. Willems, G., Tuytelaars, T., Van Gool, L.: An Efficient Dense and Scale-Invariant Spatio-Temporal Interest Point Detector. In: Forsyth, D., Torr, P., Zisserman, A. (eds.) ECCV 2008, Part II. LNCS, vol. 5303, pp. 650–663. Springer, Heidelberg (2008)
5. Kläser, A., Marszałek, M., Schmid, C.: A Spatio-temporal Descriptor Based on 3D-gradients. In: BMVC (2008)
6. Laptev, I., Marszałek, M., Schmid, C., Rozenfeld, B.: Learning Realistic Human Actions from Movies. In: CVPR, pp. 1–8 (2008)
7. Arrighi, R., Marini, F., Burr, D.: Meaningful Auditory in Formation Enhances Perception of Visual Biological Motion. Journal of Vision, 1–7 (2009)
8. Snoek, C.G., Worring, M.: Multimodal Video Indexing: A Review of the State-of-the-art. Multimedia Tools and Applications, 5–35 (2005)
9. Kim, H.-G., Jeong, J., Kim, J.-H., Kim, J.: Real-time Highlight Detection in Baseball Video for TVs with Time-shift Function. IEEE Transactions on Consumer Electronics, 831–838 (2008)
10. Guo, Y.-L., Du, J.-X., Zhai, C.-M.: Event Recognition Based on a Local Space-Time Interest Points and Self-Organization Feature Map Method. In: Huang, D.-S., Gan, Y., Bevilacqua, V., Figueroa, J.C. (eds.) ICIC 2011. LNCS, vol. 6838, pp. 242–249. Springer, Heidelberg (2011)
11. Zhu, L.: Insect Sound Recognition Based on MFCC and PNN. In: 2011 International Conference on Multimedia and Signal Processing, pp. 42–46 (2011)
12. Xue, Z., Yan, L.: Self-organizing Map as a New Method for Clustering and Data Analysis. In: Proceeding of 1993 International Joint Conference on Neural Networks, pp. 2448–2451 (1993)
13. Marszalek, M., Laptev, I., Schmid, C.: Actions in Context. In: CVPR 2009, pp. 2929–2936 (2009)
14. Wang, H., Muneeb Ullah, M., Klaser, A., Laptev, I., Schmid, C.: Evaluation of Local Spatio-temporal Features for Action Recognition. In: BMVC 2009 (2009)

Finger-Knuckle-Print Recognition Using Local Orientation Feature Based on Steerable Filter[*]

Zichao Li, Kuanquan Wang, and Wangmeng Zuo

Biocomputing Research Center, School of Computer Science and Technology
Harbin Institute of Technology, Harbin, China
wangkq@hit.edu.cn

Abstract. Automatic personal identification based on finger-knuckle-print (FKP) has been considered as a promising technology in biometrics family in recent years. Previous work indicates that local orientation analysis supplies an efficient framework for FKP representation. In this paper, we propose a novel FKP recognition method using the Adaptive Steerable Orientation Coding (ASOC). High order steerable filters are first employed to extract the continuous orientation feature map, then we use multilevel histogram thresholding method to quantize the feature map adaptively and the discrete orientations are used for coding a FKP image. Furthermore, we measure the similarity between two coded FKP images by designing an effective angular matching function. Experimental results on the PolyU FKP database demonstrate the accuracy of the proposed method.

Keywords: Biometrics, finger-knuckle-print, steerable filter, local orientation.

1 Introduction

Finger-knuckle-print (FKP) recognition, as a new branch of biometric technology, has attracted increasing attention by researchers in recent years. Bending line patterns from the FKP surface are highly rich and unique between individuals, which provides a novel but promising way for personal identification.

Woodard and Flynn [1] pioneered the work of FKP recognition. They examined the fine feature of finger back surface as a distinctive biometric identifier. This work uses Minolta 900/910 sensor to capture 3D finger back surface and extracts the curvature future for identification. However, the 3D sensor is quite expensive and the 3D data processing is computationally costly, which limits its application in civil systems.

To overcome the limits, Zhang et al. [2] developed a 2D acquisition device equipped with LED and CCD camera to capture the FKP image. Local convex direction map is developed to extract the region of interest, then real Gabor filters based competitive coding scheme [2] and band-limited phase-correlation technique [3] are

---

[*] The work is partially supported by the NSFC funds of China under Contract No.s 61173086, 60902099, and 61179009, and Harbin special funds for innovative talents of science and technology research project.

D.-S. Huang et al. (Eds.): ICIC 2012, CCIS 304, pp. 224–230, 2012.
© Springer-Verlag Berlin Heidelberg 2012

proposed for feature extraction and matching, respectively. In their most recent study [4], local phase and phase congruency are integrated for more accurate recognition.

Recently, Yue et al. [5] proposed a palmprint descriptor using steerable filter, which could extract continuous palm line orientation by minimizing the steerable filter response of palmprint image. Motivated by the work in [5], we propose a novel FKP recognition method using adaptive steerable orientation coding (ASOC). Continuous local orientations map is extracted using high order steerable filters, and then multilevel histogram thresholding based method is employed to discretize the feature map for an efficient and robust FKP matching. Extensive experiments conducted on the PolyU FKP database [6] show that the proposed method is robust and accurate.

The rest of this paper is organized as follows. Section 2 introduces the local orientation feature extraction method using high order steerable filters. Section 3 describes the ASOC framework. Section 4 demonstrates performances of the approaches on the PolyU FKP database. Section 5 concludes the whole paper.

2   Local Orientation Extraction Using Steerable Filter

The steerable filter [7] enables us to obtain the response at a distinct orientation as a linear combination of the responses to a bank of basis filters, which has following form [8]:

$$h(x, y) = \sum_{k=1}^{M} \sum_{i=0}^{k} \alpha_{k,i} \underbrace{\frac{\partial^{k-i}}{\partial x^{k-i}} \frac{\partial^{i}}{\partial y^{i}} g(x, y)}_{g_{k,i}(x,y)}, \tag{1}$$

where $g(x, y)$ is an arbitrary isotropic window function, $g_{k,i}(x, y)$ is a basic filter, $\alpha_{k,i}$ is the interpolation coefficient, and M is the order of steerable filter. The convolution of a 2D signal $f(x, y)$ with any rotated version of $h(x, y)$ can be expressed as

$$f(\mathbf{x}) * h(\mathbf{R}_\theta \mathbf{x}) = \sum_{k=1}^{M} \sum_{i=0}^{k} b_{k,i}(\theta) f_{k,i}(\mathbf{x}), \tag{2}$$

where $\mathbf{x} = (x, y)$, $\mathbf{R}_\theta$ is the rotation matrix, and $f_{k,i}(x, y) = f(x, y) * g_{k,i}(x, y)$ are filtered versions of the signal $f(x, y)$. The weights $b_{k,i}(\theta)$ are given by

$$b_{k,i}(\theta) = \sum_{j=0}^{k} \alpha_{k,i} \sum_{l,m \in S(k,j,i)} \binom{k-j}{l}\binom{j}{m}(-1)^m \cos(\theta)^{j+(l-m)} \sin(\theta)^{(k-j)-(l-m)}, \tag{3}$$

where $S(k, j, i) = \{l, m \mid 0 \le l \le k - j; 0 \le m \le j; k - (l + m) = i\}$.

Once the $f_{k,i}(x, y)$ are available, $f(\mathbf{x}) * h(\mathbf{R}_\theta \mathbf{x})$ can be evaluated very efficiently via a weighted sum with its coefficients that are trigonometric polynomials of θ [8]. The steerable filter's response at an arbitrary orientation can be expressed as

$$f * h_\theta = q_0 \cos(\theta)^M + q_1 \cos(\theta)^{M-1} \sin(\theta) + \cdots + q_M \sin(\theta)^M, \tag{4}$$

where h_θ is the rotate version of filter $h(x, y)$, and $q_0, q_1, \cdots, q_M$ can be determined by the basic filters' response $f_{k,i}(x, y)$.

Eq. 4 shows that steerable filter response $f * h_\theta$ is a function only with respect to the orientation θ. Bending line on the FKP surface is a kind of dark line, so the dominate orientation of a line can be derived by minimizing its response:

$$\theta^* = \arg \min_\theta (f * h_\theta). \tag{5}$$

This optimization can be easily solved using the equation $\partial(f * h_\theta) / \partial\theta = 0$.

To design a suitable steerable filer for FKP line feature extraction, we need to choose the isotropic windows function $g(x, y)$, the interpolation coefficient $\alpha_{k,i}$, and the steerable filter order M in Eq. 1. For the isotropic windows function $g(x, y)$, we choose Gaussian and the coefficient $\alpha_{k,i}$ can be calculated based on the Canny-like optimal criterion [8]. Here, if we choose the idealized FKP line model as $L(x, y) = \delta(x)$, where δ denotes the Dirac delta function, the optimal filter for $L(x, y)$ can be derived by maximizing the Canny-like optimal criterion defined in [8]. Since the detector becomes more orientation selective as M increases, the number of basic filters as well as the computational loads increases. In this paper, we choose M as 4 and use follow as optimal steerable filter for feature extraction:

$$h = -0.392\sigma g_{2,2} + 0.113\sigma g_{2,0} + 0.034\sigma^3 g_{4,4} - 0.184\sigma^3 g_{4,2} + 0.025\sigma^3 g_{4,0}, \tag{6}$$

where σ is the scale of Gaussian function, we choose it as 4.0 in our experiments.

3   Adaptive Steerable Orientation Coding

Orientation feature derived by steerable filters is continuous, Fig. 1 (a) shows a typical FKP image and its local feature orientation map is shown in (b). Directly using of the continuous orientation feature for FKP representation and matching needs both considerable storage and significant computational cost. Thus, a quantization method is required for orientation coding. An intuition is to quantize the degree uniformly. Given the quantization value N, the quantized interval is $r_D = 180 / N$. For a continuous degree α, its quantized value is $\alpha_D = [\alpha / r_D]$, where $[\bullet]$ denotes rounding function. Specifically, when N is set as 6, this method degenerates into the competitive coding scheme [9], which has been successfully applied in FKP recognition in [2, 3].

From another perspective, when set $N = 180$, i.e. directly round the real degrees into integer ones, the orientation map can be regarded as an image with 180 gray levels. Then the quantization on a single orientation image can be interpreted as a multilevel image threading process. A key issue for multilevel threading is the determination of multi-thresholds, and histogram based self-adaptive technique is widely used for this task. Fig. 1 (c) shows the histogram of orientation map (b). It should be noticed that $0°$ and $179°$ have only a small difference. However, if we represent it using traditional histogram, we will lose the periodic property of orientation attributes. This problem can be solved by extending the traditional multi-thresholding algorithm into polar coordinate system. Fig. 1 (d) shows the histogram in polar coordinate system, we call it circular histogram. In circular histogram, an angle indicates a certain orientation and a radius is the number of the same orientation.

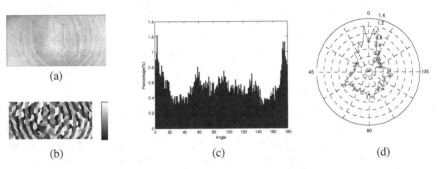

Fig. 1. (a) A typical FKP image from PolyU database and (b) its related local orientation map. Histogram of (b) under (c) Cartesian and (d) polar coordinate system are shown respectively.

Here we extend the traditional multilevel thresholding algorithm based on the Otsu method to circular histogram. The quantization value N is the number of orientation classes, $C_1, C_2, \cdots, C_N$ and $\theta_1, \theta_2, \cdots, \theta_N$ are the corresponding classes and thresholds respectively. Class C_k is defined as $C_k = \{\phi \mid \phi \in (\theta_k, \theta_{k+1}]\}$, where $k \in [1, N-1]$, and C_N is defined as $C_N = \{\phi \mid \phi \in (\theta_N, 179°] \cup [0°, \theta_1]\}$. The circular histogram $h_c(\phi)$ shows the number of occurrences of the orientation ϕ in the orientation map, and normalized histogram is $p(\phi) = h_c(\phi) / S$, with S the size of feature map. For the kth class, statistical properties such as the probability of the class, the mean, and the variance of the class can be calculated as $w_k = \sum_{\phi \in C_k} p(\phi), \mu_k = \sum_{\phi \in C_k} (p(\phi) \cdot \phi / w_k)$ and $\sigma_k^2 = \sum_{\phi \in C_k} (p(\phi) \cdot (\phi - \mu_k)^2 / w_k)$. The optimal thresholds for the method proposed by Otsu are found by minimizing a criterion called within-class variance:

$$[\theta_1^*, \theta_2^* \cdots, \theta_N^*] = \arg\min(\sum_{k=1}^{N} w_k \sigma_k^2). \tag{7}$$

DP-SMAWK algorithm presented in [10] is employed to find the optimal thresholds in $O(180 \cdot N)$ time, and the optimal classes are $C_1^*, C_2^*, \cdots, C_N^*$. For each continuous orientation α in the feature map, its final coded value is given as

$$Code(\alpha) = \mod(\{k \mid [\alpha] \in C_k^*, 1 \le k \le N\}, N). \tag{8}$$

Let P, Q be two generated codes, the angular distance is defined as [11]

$$D(P,Q) = \frac{\sum_{y=0}^{t}\sum_{x=0}^{s} G(P(x, y), Q(x, y))}{(N-1) \cdot s \cdot t}, \tag{9}$$

where $s \times t$ is the size of code, and $G(P(x, y), Q(x, y))$ is defined as

$$G(\bullet) = \begin{cases} \min(P(x, y) - Q(x, y), N - 1 - P(x, y) + Q(x, y)), if\ P(x, y) \geq Q(x, y) \\ \min(Q(x, y) - P(x, y), N - 1 - Q(x, y) + P(x, y)), if\ Q(x, y) > P(x, y) \end{cases}. \tag{10}$$

Obviously, D is between 0 and 1. To overcome imperfect preprocessing, translation of one feature horizontally and vertically then perform the matching again is needed.

4   Experimental Results

In this section, we use the PolyU FKP online database [6] to evaluate the performance of the proposed method. This database consists the left index, left middle, right index and right middle finger from 165 individuals. Each FKP was acquired 12 times during two sessions giving a total of 7920 samples. In our experiments, we took images from the first session as the gallery set and images from the second session as the probe set, each image in probe set was matched against all the images in gallery set.

First, we examine how the number of orientation classes N affects the recognition performance. Another two comparative experiments have also been made by quantizing the orientation uniformly into N parts and making the N - level histogram thresholding using in traditional Cartesian system. N is set as 3, 4, 5, 6, 8, 12 in the experiments, respectively. Table 1 lists the comparison result. For each value of N, the self-adaptive histogram thresholding based method performs better than uniform based one. When thresholding is made under polar coordinate system with $N = 4$, the proposed method gives the best performance with EER=1.221%, and when N grows up, the EER increases simultaneously. The probable reason is that the orientation histogram under polar system is statistically divided in 4 parts. To support this hypothesis, we plot the statistical distribution of orientations of the FKP lines from all the 7920 samples along with their thresholds distribution in Fig. 2 (a), which consists 4 distinct peaks around $0°, 50°, 90°$ and $130°$, and the optimal thresholds separated the peaks into 4 classes clearly around $31°, 70°, 108°$ and $146°$. Thus, four orientation classes is enough to represent the FKP surface lines well using ASOC.

Table 1. EER (%) of different thresholding techniques with different values of N

	3	4	5	6	8	12
Uniform	1.601	1.522	1.487	1.46	1.455	1.422
Cartesian	1.512	1.304	1.247	1.253	1.292	1.413
Polar	1.306	**1.221**	1.249	1.265	1.329	1.446

Then we compare ASOC with CompCode and ImCompCode&MagCode described in [2], and results are represented in table 2. Further comparison of ROC curve with Competitive code is also shown in Fig.2 (b). From the results we can see that our method performs better than other coding based FKP verification methods.

Table 2. Comparison of EER between different methods

Method	EER (%)
CompCode	1.658
ImCompCode&MagCode	1.475
ASOC	**1.221**

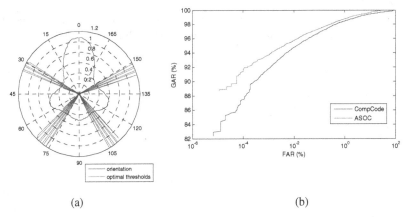

(a)   (b)

Fig. 2. (a) Statistical distribution of orientation and optimal thresholds. (b) ROC curves of CompCode and ASOC

5   Conclusions

In this paper, a novel local orientation extraction method using steerable filters for FKP verification was proposed. Continuous local orientations is extracted using a four order steerable filter, multilevel circular histogram thresholding is presented to discretize the feature map for an efficient and robust FKP matching. The experimental results show that 4 orientation classes are well enough to represent the FKP line feature for recognition. Compared with the state-of-art coding based methods, our method achieves better performance on the PloyU FKP database.

References

1. Woodard, D., Flynn, P.: Finger Surface as a Biometric Identifier. Computer Vision and Image Understanding 100(3), 357–384 (2005)
2. Zhang, L., Zhang, L., Zhang, D., Zhu, H.: Online Finger-knuckle-print Verification for Personal Authentication. Pattern Recognition 43(7), 2560–2571 (2010)

3. Zhang, L., Zhang, L., Zhang, D., Zhu, H.: Ensemble of Local and Global Information for Finger-knuckle-print Recognition. Pattern Recognition 44(9), 1990–1998 (2010)
4. Zhang, L., Zhang, L., Zhang, D., Guo, Z.: Phase Congruency Induced Local Features for Finger-knuckle-print Recognition. Pattern Recognition 45(1), 2522–2531 (2012)
5. Yue, F., Zuo, W., Zhang, D.: ICP Registration using Principal Line and Orientation Features for Palmprint Alignment. In: Proc. ICIP, pp. 3069–3072 (2010)
6. Zhang, L.: PolyU Finger-knuckle-print Database,
   http://www4.comp.polyu.edu.hk/~biometrics/FKP.htm
7. Freeman, W., Adelson, E.: The Design and Use of Steerable Filters. IEEE Trans. Pattern Anal. and Mach. Intell. 13(9), 891–906 (1991)
8. Jacob, M., Unser, M.: Design of Steerable Filters for Feature Detection Using Canny Like Criteria. IEEE Trans. Pattern Anal. and Mach. Intell. 26(8), 1007–1019 (2004)
9. Kong, W., Zhang, D.: Competitive Coding Scheme for Palmprint Verification. In: Proc. ICIP (2004)
10. Luessi, M., Eichmann, M., Schuster, G., Katsaggelos, A.: Framework for Efficient Optimal Multilevel Image Thresholding. Journal of Electronic Imaging 18 (2009)

Nose Localization Based on Subclass Discriminant Analysis

Jiatao Song[1], Lihua Jia[1,2], Gang Xie[2], and Wei Wang[1]

[1] School of Electronic and Information Engineering, Ningbo University of Technology,
Ningbo 315016, P.R. China
[2] College of Information Engineering, Taiyuan University of Technology, Taiyuan 030024,
P.R. China
sjt6612@163.com

Abstract. Nose localization is important for face recognition, face pose recognition, 3D face reconstruction and so on. In this paper, a novel method for nose localization is proposed. Our method includes two Subclass Discriminant Analysis (SDA) based steps. The first step locates nose from the whole face image and some randomly selected image patches are used as negative samples for the training of SDA classifier. The second step refines nose position by using some nose context patches as negative samples. The proposed method detects nose from the whole face image and no prior knowledge about the layout of face components on a face is employed. Experimental results on AR images show that the proposed method can accurately locate nose from face images, and is robust to lighting and facial expression changes.

Keywords: Nose localization, subclass discriminant analysis (SDA), illumination change.

1 Introduction

Nose localization refers to the detection of nose from an image or an image sequence. It is widely used in face pose recognition [1], 3D face reconstruction, head tracking [2] and mouse-free human-computer interaction for the disabled people [3], etc. In the last two decades, nose detection has attracted more and more attention. Xiong, et al. [4] proposed a nose location method by combining the Active Shape Model (ASM) and the Local Binary Pattern (LBP) probability model. Ding, et al. [5] located nose using Subclass Discriminant Analysis (SDA). But their method required two eyes to be firstly detected and a small region below the lower eye lids and between two eye centers are extracted for the localization of nose. In addition, Ren, et al. [6] used GentleBoost algorithm for nose detection.

In this paper, a novel nose localization method based on two SDA based steps is proposed. Our method aims at addressing the problem of nose localization from face images with different illuminations or facial expressions. Compared with Ding's approach [5], our method doesn't use the prior knowledge about the layout of face

D.-S. Huang et al. (Eds.): ICIC 2012, CCIS 304, pp. 231–235, 2012.
© Springer-Verlag Berlin Heidelberg 2012

components on a face. Experimental results on AR face images [7] show that the proposed method achieves high nose localization rate, and is robust to the change of illumination and facial expression.

2   Basic Principle of SDA

Linear Discriminant Analysis (LDA) is only suitable for the classification of single-mode data, i.e. the data of each class is subject to single Gaussian distribution. To resolve the problem of muli-mode data classification, Zhu, et al. [8] proposed a subclass discriminant analysis (SDA) method. The basic idea of SDA is that the data of each class is divided into several subclasses. Each subclass is described by a Gaussian distribution. Then, the target data is linear and separable.

In SDA, the generalized eigenvalue decomposition equation shown in Eq. (1) is used to find the optimal projection direction that best classifies the data.

$$\Sigma_B V = \Sigma_X V \Lambda \tag{1}$$

Where Σ_X is the covariance matrix of the data, V is a matrix whose columns correspond to the discriminant vectors, Λ is a diagonal matrix of corresponding eigenvalue, Σ_B is the between-subclass scatter matrix and can be expressed as:

$$\Sigma_B = \sum_{i=1}^{C-1} \sum_{j=1}^{H_i} \sum_{k=i+1}^{C} \sum_{l=1}^{H_k} p_{ij} p_{kl} (\mu_{ij} - \mu_{kl})(\mu_{ij} - \mu_{kl})^T \tag{2}$$

Where C is the number of the classes, p_{ij} and μ_{ij} are the prior and mean of the j-th subclass of class i, respectively, H_i is the number of subclass divisions of class i. In Ref. [8], two criteria, i.e. the leave-one-out-test criterion and the stability criterion, are defined to find the optimal subclass division, and a nearest neighbor-based algorithm is defined to divide each class into a set of possible subclasses.

3   The Proposed Nose Localization Method

Our method firstly detects face from an input image. After that, a coarse SDA-based nose localization is conducted to find the nose from the whole face image; then the nose location is refined by another SDA-based nose detection step. The main difference between the two SDA-based nose searching steps of the proposed method is the selection of the negative samples for the training of SDA classifiers.

In statistical pattern recognition, both the positive and negative samples should cover as more pattern variation as possible to improve the pattern classification. The main purpose of this work is to precisely locate nose from different lighting and

(a)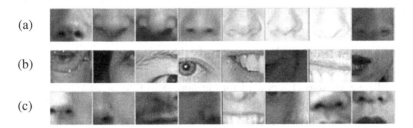

(b)

(c)

Fig. 1. (a) Positive samples; (b) Negative samples for the coarse nose detection; and (c) Negative samples for the fine nose localization

expression conditions, so image patches centered at the nose tip point, but with different illuminations and expressions, just as shown in Fig. 1(a) are selected as the positive samples at both the coarse and the fine nose detection stages of our method. And image patches randomly selected from the entire face region except those centered at nose tip are selected as negative samples for the coarse nose detection, as shown in Fig. 1(b). Obviously, the image patches related to eyes, mouth, chin or other face components are all regarded as negative images and are used to train the SDA classifier for coarse nose detection.

At the nose detection stage of our work, a sliding window with a size of 44×33 pixels slides every 2 pixels across the face image. For each position, the testing region is classified using SDA. After a full sliding period, some nose candidates are found. Nose candidates near image borders are unlikely to be nose, hence deleted. The mean position of the remained nose candidates is regarded as the nose position. Some coarsely detected noses marked with red star are shown in the upper row of Fig. 2.

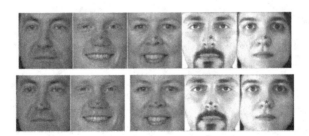

Fig. 2. The coarsely located nose (upper row) and the finely located nose (lower row)

From the upper row of Fig. 2, it can be observed that although nose can be located, the obtained nose location does not always coincide well with the true nose tip and sometimes a disparity exists between them. So in our method, another SDA-based nose localization step is followed to refine the nose position. The second nose searching is limited in a rectangle window centered at the coarsely detected nose position. Some nose context patches proposed by Ding [5], i.e. image patches around the nose and maybe containing part of the nose (as shown in Fig. 1 (c)), are used as negative samples to train SDA classifier. The lower row of Fig. 2 shows the refined noses. Obviously, the nose positions are improved greatly.

4   Experimental Results and Analysis

A subset of AR face database [7] is used for our nose detection experiments. The subset includes 328 images from 26 males and 21 females, with four different expressions (i.e. neutral expression, smile, anger, scream) and three different illuminations (left light on, right light on and both side lights on). Before nose located, face is detected from the original AR images using the well-known AdaBoost algorithm and is normalized to a size of 120×120 pixels. Fig. 3 shows some examples of faces in which noses marked with red star are successfully located. This figure tells that under different illumination and expression conditions, our method can locate noses precisely.

In order to quantitatively evaluate the performance of our nose localization method, nose tips of the AR images are located manually and the results are compared with the automatic detected nose positions, with the disparity between them labeled with DIS. Let r be the width of a nose, in our work, if $|DIS| \leq r/3$, the nose localization is regarded as success. Experimental results show that for the total 328 AR images used, our method achieves a correct nose detection rate of 93.3%, while for the image groups with left light on, right light on and both side lights on, nose location rates reach 97.87%, 100% and 97.87%, respectively, indicating that our method is robust to lighting changes.

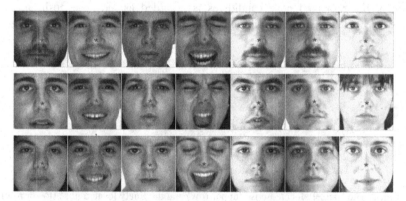

Fig. 3. Correctly located noses of AR images with different lighting and expression (from left to right: neutral, smile, anger, scream, left light on, right light on and both side lights on)

5   Conclusions

In this paper a new nose localization method based on Subclass Discriminant Analysis (SDA) is proposed. Our method includes two SDA-based nose searching steps and no prior knowledge about the layout of face components is used. In the first step, nose is coarsely located from the whole face region; and in the second step, nose position is refined. The main difference between these two steps is the selection of the negative samples used for the training of SDA classifiers. The negative samples used in the first step are some randomly selected image patches from face images, while those used in the second step are some nose context patches. Experimental results on AR images show that our method can achieve high nose localization rates at a high accuracy, and is robust to lighting and facial expression changes.

Acknowledgements. The work described in this paper is partially supported by a project from the National Natural Science Foundation of China (Grant No.60972163), a project from the Natural Science Foundation of Zhejiang Province of China (Grant No.Y1110086), a project from the Natural Science Foundation of Ningbo of China (Grant No.2009A610090), an open project of Zhejiang Provincial Most Important Subject of Information Processing and Automation Technology (Grant No. 201100808), an open project of Zhejiang Provincial Key Laboratory of Information Network Technology(Grant No. 201109) and two projects from the Open Fund of Mobile Network Application Technology Key Laboratory of Zhejiang Province (Grant No. MNATKL2011001, MNATKL2011003).

References

1. Breitenstein, M.D., Kuettel, D., Weise, T., et al.: Real-time Face Pose Estimation from Single Range Images. In: IEEE Conf. on CVPR, pp. 1–8. IEEE Press, New York (2008)
2. Bohme, M., Haker, M., Martinetz, T., Barth, E.: Head Tracking with Combined Face and Nose Detection. In: International Symposium on Signals Circuits and Systems, pp. 1–4. IEEE Press, New York (2009)
3. Gorodnichy, D.O., Roth, G.: Nouse 'Use Your Nose as a Mouse' Perceptual Vision Technology for Hands-Free Games and Interfaces. Image and Vision Computing 22(12), 931–942 (2004)
4. Xiong, T., Xu, L., Wang, K., et al.: Local Binary Pattern Probability Model Based Facial Feature Localization. In: 17th IEEE International Conference on Image Processing, pp. 1425–1428. IEEE Press, New York (2010)
5. Ding, L., Martinez, A.M.: Features versus Context: An Approach for Precise and Detailed Detection and Delineation of Faces and Facial Features. IEEE Transactions on Pattern Analysis and Machine Intelligence 32(11), 2022–2038 (2010)
6. Ren, X., Song, J., Ying, H., Zhu, Y., Qiu, X.: Robust Nose Detection and Tracking Using GentleBoost and Improved Lucas-Kanade Optical Flow Algorithms. In: Huang, D.-S., Heutte, L., Loog, M. (eds.) ICIC 2007. LNCS, vol. 4681, pp. 1240–1246. Springer, Heidelberg (2007)
7. Martinez, A.M., Benavente, R.: The AR Face Database. CVC Technical Report #24 (1998)
8. Zhu, M., Martinez, A.M.: Subclass Discriminant Analysis. IEEE Transactions on Pattern Analysis and Machine Intelligence 28(8), 1274–1286 (2006)

Research on the Interactive Display System Based on Multi-touch Technology

Chang-Qing Yin[1], Bin Chen[2], and Ze-Liang Zhang[1]

[1] School of Software Engineering, Tongji University, Shanghai
[2] School of Electronics and Information, Tongji University, Shanghai
yin_cq@hotmail.com, 76758440@qq.com, chenbin11200@yahoo.com.cn

Abstract. Multi-touch is familiar with more and more people, and be used as a way of human-computer interaction. An interactive system which is based on Frustrated Total Internal Reflection (FTIR) multi-touch technology is designed in this paper to meet people's demand in shows and exhibitions. It is characterized by low cost, high degree of accuracy, and it can show the pictures, videos and have the function of handwriting board. It is applied in different kinds of exhibitions and work situations such as being used as a way to operate design software.

Keywords: FTIR, Multi-touch, Interactive Exhibition, Splice Technology, Multi-screen.

1 Summarization

Since 2007 when Apple Company released IPhone, Multi-touch technology has been familiar with and used by more and more people. As one kind of natural user interface (NUI), Multi-touch substitute for the classical user interface, for it is user-friendly and intuitionistic. People do not need keyboard, mouse or instructions anymore, and it's totally an intuitionistic way in operation.

Based on the touch mode, Multi-touch technology can be divided into two kinds: Capacitive type and IR type[2]. Considering the capacitive type is expensive and with small screen while the IR type can meet any demands in screen size, I designed an IR type multi-touch system based on the FTIR technology[1] in this paper. The system can meet the demand that people can drag, rotate, scale any image, video and handwriting board. We can change the images or videos shown on the screen by editing the CONFIG file. In this way, we can apply the system in any exhibition quickly and meet any special demands.

2 System Design

2.1 Hardware Structure Design

The multi-touch technology is the combination of hardware and software. In the hardware part, we have mainly several hardware structures such as FTIR, ToughtLight,

D.-S. Huang et al. (Eds.): ICIC 2012, CCIS 304, pp. 236–241, 2012.
© Springer-Verlag Berlin Heidelberg 2012

Optical Touch and so on. In this paper, we use the FTIR structure [1] to make sure that the hardware part cost little and we can have high degree of accuracy.

2.2   Software Module Design

The software modules mainly include the touch point recognition module, the touch point sending module and the performance module.

Touch point recognition module: for getting the IR touch points on the screen by IR cameras.

Touch point sending module: We can send the touch point information to the applications or operation system by using TUIO protocol.

Performance module: We can use ActionScript 3.0, openGL and any language we want to develop the performance application.

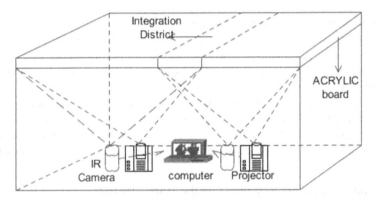

Fig. 1. The global hardware structure

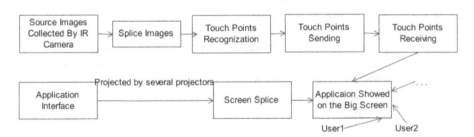

Fig. 2. Software module Structure

3   The Key and Difficulties

3.1   How to Recognize the Touch Point

FITR technology [1]: IR is sent in the ACRYLIC board by IR Led. If the ACRYLIC board is thicker than 8 millimeters, the IR will keep reflexing in the board and never leave the board. This phenomenon is called Total Internal Reflection.[1] If the finger or something reflexible and flexible, such as silica gel stick touch the surface of the board, the total internal reflection will be broken, and the IR will reflexed by the finger and leave the board and caught by the IR camera. The extremely strong light point is the input point.

3.2   Splice of Multi-screen and Multi-camera

Multi-projector and multi-camera should be used and spliced because of the limit of the projector resolution. To having a satisfying user experience, the splice with integration method is a better way that the two adjacent projector will project part of the whole image and show the same content in the integration district. It seems like a big screen, not two detached screens.

3.2.1   Splice of the Camera Video Image

The first step of camera splice is matching the image. We have several ways to match images: the matching technology based on pixel, the matching technology based on transformed domain and the matching technology based on image features and so on.

Meanwhile, in this system, the image is collected by IR camera. Between the finger and the camera, there are board and curtain. We want to focus on the touch point, so that the source image is simple colored and without apparent features. So the methods introduced before cannot be used in this system. So, in this paper, I present a new matching algorithm which is called matching technology based on the matrix district.

3.2.2   Matching Technology Based on the Matrix District

This matching algorithm is designed to help us focus on catching the touch point information and make sure that it is of high degree of accuracy. For easy to explain, we take two IR cameras situation as an example.

As the matching is part of the whole system, it should no occupy a lot of calculation resource. In practice we do not have to match and splice the images which are greatly twisted, and at first, we can adjust the position of the camera in order to calibrate the camera roughly. Thinking about the drag, rotation, scale of image and screen splice will take a lot of computer calculative resource, the camera matching algorithm should be as easy as possible.

We can process the images by binary conversion, and change the binary-conversed image into a matrix. The white pixels are defined as 0, while the black pixels are defined as 1. We can compare the matrix and search the same part. The right part of the matrix from the left camera will match the left part of the matrix from the right camera. If the two parts are totally the same or just a little bit different, this two part are treated as the same image part. According to the matching information, we will translate the images to splice them as a logically full-screen image. The algorithm will be introduced below.

First, we will change the binary-conversed image into a matrix. Then we will have two matrixes(Fig. 3 a).

$$\begin{bmatrix} 0 & 0 & 1 \\ 0 & 1 & 0 \\ 0 & 0 & 0 \\ 1 & 1 & 0 \\ 0 & 0 & 0 \end{bmatrix} \begin{bmatrix} 0 & 1 \\ 0 & 0 \\ 1 & 0 \\ 1 & 0 \\ 1 & 1 \end{bmatrix} \begin{bmatrix} 0 & 1 & 0 & 1 & 1 \\ 0 & 0 & 0 & 1 & 0 \\ 1 & 0 & 1 & 1 & 1 \\ 1 & 1 & 0 & 1 & 0 \\ 1 & 1 & 0 & 0 & 0 \end{bmatrix} \qquad \begin{bmatrix} 0 & 0 & 1 & 0 & 1 & 0 & 1 & 1 \\ 0 & 1 & 0 & 0 & 0 & 0 & 1 & 0 \\ 0 & 0 & 0 & 1 & 0 & 1 & 1 & 1 \\ 1 & 1 & 0 & 1 & 0 & 0 & 1 & 0 \\ 0 & 0 & 0 & 1 & 1 & 0 & 0 & 0 \end{bmatrix}$$

Fig. 3. (a) principle of the matching technology   (b) Mixed matrix

The data in the red box are basically the same, so that the image in the red box is showing the same part of the image. Now we take a 5*5 matrix as an example, however, in practice, there will be a comparison between two 200*480 matrixes. Therefore, basically it will not behave incorrectly in practice. After the matching process, the two matrixes will be spliced into one(Fig. 3 (b)).

This method has the advantage of matching the camera images in short time and high degree of accuracy. Although the image is not clear enough, it also works. The drawback is that we have to adjust the position of camera in advance and the images should not be staggered a lot.

Surely, in addition to this, we also have an easier method. Because the camera image splice does not have to be exactly accurate, we can splice the camera roughly in parallel. It is such a easy way that we just have to input the camera resolution and pixel values. CCV also provide a multi-camera solution. The experiments have proved that this method is feasible.

3.2.3   The Splice of Display Screens
The splice of screen mainly solves the problem in geometric correction and splice of integration region.

3.2.4   Geometric Correction
The projected image will covet a big screen district, so the image will be twisted like a trapezium. So the geometric correction will be done on hardware level, to make the projected image looks like a rectangle.

We can adjust the location of the projector in advance according to the whole screen(ACRYLIC board) size. This is to reduce the calculation pressure, furthermore to prevent the computer crash and slow reaction. The adjustments of the projector mainly include translation motion, rotation, scale and keystone correction. All or part of the adjustment methods can be done for several times, to make the images meet our needs.

3.2.5   Processing the Integration District
As several projectors will show the same pixels in integration district, the integration will brighter than other parts. The brighter parts are called bright band. For making the bright band look as bright as other parts, we can use the edge-blending method

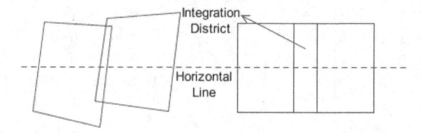

Fig. 4. Geometric Correction

and the alpha mask method. In the former method, we calculate the luminosity function of both projectors, and then reduce the brightness in edges according to the function. In the latter method, we put an alpha mask on the bright band to reduce the brightness.

In this system, we will solve not only the problem in screen splice, but also problems in the use of interactive flash application, such as the touch points coordinates may dislocate in the integration district. Therefore, here we use a special splice method based on Adobe Air technology.

3.2.6   Splice Method Based on Adobe Air Technology

This is essentially an Alpha mask method. While it is different from the splice technology by using OpenGL, it finish the splice job by using latest Flash Air technology. By using Flash Air, we can make the flash file show in different windows and adjust the size of integration district by editing the CONFIG files. We can also use the Alpha mask which already provided by Adobe Flash to reduce the brightness of bright band. It is easy to operate and we can adjust the mask meticulously to have the best effect. Meanwhile, the drawback is that it is not automatically.

Another reason why we use this method is that according to the width of the integration district, we can modify the TUIO protocol to translation the touch point coordinates. The problem that the touch point coordinates in integration district may be dislocated can be resolved by suitable translation of coordinates. The kernel code is shown below:

```
x = Number(node.ARGUMENT[2].@VALUE) *
STAGE.stageWidth+xchange;
```

3.3   Insert the Videos and Operate Them

When we use the Touchlib function, we can find that they are useless in controlling the video object. That is because the video cannot be treated as a container which can support a listener. All the multi-touch operation will control the display objects under the video object. I call this phenomenon as 'perforated window phenomenon'. A low-cost way was found for video controlment. For Adobe Flash can easily make a transparent image, we cover the video object by a transparent image in the same size which is used as a listener container. As soon as there are touch points in the transparent image area and the user try to operate the video (actually the user is operating the transparent image), the video will have the same parameters as the image, including the width, height and angle. We put both the video object and the transparent image into the same Movieclip object, so that we can delete both the transparent image and the video object at the same time. In practice, we did several experiments and proved that this method is feasible and the user can operate the video object easily.

3.4   The Handwriting Board

The handwriting board function is an expanded usage of the point trace. The user can draw or write anything they want on the handwriting board, and save the content.

When there are touch points in the handwriting board area, the line function will be called to draw the lines. At the same time, the system is tracking the point trace and recording any line the user is drawing.

The key point of this module is to operate the handwriting content and the handwriting board at the same time. When we drag the board, we are willing to see the contents are dragged as well. Because the graph object is not the same object as the image object, we have to calculate the location and angle of the handwriting contents so as to make sure it seems like the handwriting board and the contents are operated together. About the save part, we just save the graph object, not the whole handwriting board object to reduce the space expense.

References

1. Jefferson, Y.H.: Low-Cost Multi-Touch Sensing through Frustrated Total Internal Refection. In: UIST 2005 Proceedings of the 18th Annual ACM Symposium on User In-Terface Software and Technology (2005)
2. Zhao, Q.J., Wang, Y.G., Huang, A.Z.: A Multi-touch Desktop System based on FTIR. Computer Engineering 37F(14) (2011)
3. Chi, J.N., Wang, Z.L., Xie, X.Z., Xu, K., Fang, H.L., Xu, Y.Y., Li, Y.: A Survey of Multi-touch Human-computer Interaction Technology. CAAI Transactionson Intelligent Systems 6F(1) (2011)

Very Large-Scale Image Retrieval
Based on Local Features

Chang-Qing Yin, Wei Mao, and Wei Jiang

Tongji University, Shanghai, China
IBM (China) Co. Limited, Shanghai, China
yin_cq@hotmail.com, mwwswswws@hotmail.com, jweish@cn.ibm.com

Abstract. Traditional image retrieval technology is pixel sensitive and with low fault tolerance. To overcome this deficiency, a novel method for large-scale image retrieval is proposed in this paper, which is especially suitable for images with kinds of interferences, such as rotation, pixel lost, watermarks, etc. First, local features of images are extracted to build a visual dictionary with weight, which is a new data structure developed from bag-of-words. In the retrieval process, we look up all the features extracted from the target image in the dictionary and create a single list of weight to get the result. We demonstrate the effectiveness of our approach using a coral image set and online image set on eBay.

Keywords: image retrieval, interference, visual dictionary with weight.

1   Introduction

Image retrieval system is a computer system for browsing, searching and retrieving images form a large database of digital images. According to different purposes, it can be categorized as exact retrieval and fuzzy retrieval. According to different metrics, it can be classified as text-based retrieval, content-based retrieval and retrieval based on a combination of them. In this paper we focus on content-based exact image retrieval (CBIR), which has been developing rapidly in recent years. H. B. Kekre [11] presents a new method using Fourier transform for large database. Wei Bian [12] used Biased Discriminant Euclidean in CBIR creatively. Perronnin, F.[13] proposed a method with compressed Fisher vectors And Douze,M [14] further combined attributes and Fisher vectors for more efficient performance.

Most traditional and common image retrieval methods utilize global features, like color, texture, contours, spatial correlation and so on. However, there are some inherent shortcomings associated with these global-feature based methods. Once the target image has a minor change, a great change will ensue in these features. So such methods are susceptible to interference. Local feature descriptors can serve as solutions for solving such problems. Usually we extract appropriate key points, calculate the descriptor and cluster them via non-supervised learning algorithm. Each clustering center means a visual word. Then, the target image can be expressed as a frequency

D.-S. Huang et al. (Eds.): ICIC 2012, CCIS 304, pp. 242–250, 2012.
© Springer-Verlag Berlin Heidelberg 2012

histogram of visual words. This histogram can replace traditional histograms (color histogram, edge histogram, etc.)

Recently, many scholars have been engaged in improving the algorithm. Farquhar [1] introduced the Gaussian mixture model, in which each Gaussian component looked as a visual word. Jegou [2] added the distance between features and visual words into original formula. Closer the word is to the feature, greater the weight of this word is. All these improvement increase the accuracy of image retrieval, but the computational complexity also grows exponentially at the same time.

It's not difficult to find that, in all above methods, we must encode the local feature of target image to translate it to a single list of visual words. And then we should compare the vector with all images in the image set. As we all know, there are always hundreds of key points in a single image. Therefore it will lead to high dimensions of visual word vector and sharply decrease the efficiency. Assuming that dimensions of visual word vector is N, the number of images in the image set is M, and the complexity of the algorithm will be $O(M \times N)$. Today, with the rapid development of internet, more and more varied images are posted. In such an environment, how to improve the efficiency of the method becomes a serious problem.

2   New Method

Firstly we need to preprocess image set (extracting local feature descriptor, establishing visual dictionary with weight). In retrieval process, the local information of target image will be classified by visual dictionary. After that we get a list of weights rather than words. Sum them, and answer can be found where the maximum weight is.

2.1   Image Set Side

Extract Key Points: In order to deal with pixel interference and enhance robustness, we choose the local features of image instead of some traditional global features (color histogram, edge histogram). Firstly, we must get all key points. Here we use FAST-9[3] [4]. Professor E.Rosten proposed the algorithm in 2005. The main idea is to compare the adjacent pixels on Birmingham Circle of which radius is 3. If there are 9 continuous points on which pixels are greater or smaller than pixel on target point, then we regard the target point as a key point. (Usually the threshold of pixel difference is 30)

Fig. 1. FAST-9

Now we have got hundreds of key points from each image in the image set. Next step is to calculate descriptors. Here we use "Local Gradient Direction" as descriptor which is first used in SIFT [5] method. SIFT is widely used and is outlined by Professor Lowe in 1998. We calculate the gradient in 8 directions according to around 4×4 window in 16×16 sub-area to get the gradient histogram. In this way each key point can generate a 128-dimension feature vector. These vectors are SIFT feature descriptors. Compared to BRISK [6], Ferns [7], ORB [8] and other descriptors proposed recently, SIFT is more suitable because of its great rotate invariance, scale invariance and illumination invariance.

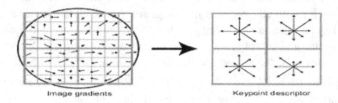

Image gradients   Keypoint descriptor

Fig. 2. SITF descriptor

Generate Visual Dictionary with Weight (VDW):Because of the large number of feature descriptor, it is expensive to generate index for them. Especially for large-scale image set, it is almost impossible. So we propose a novel model, visual dictionary with weight (VDW). The dictionary is composed by a number of visual words (128-Dimension clustering center) and their weights (image serial number contained in corresponding clustering group). We call them Vocabulary Entries (VE).

128D feature descriptor —| Image serial number

Fig. 3. Vocabulary entry in VDW

Assuming that the number of image is M and there are S key points for each image. Then we can get that the number of feature vector is S×M. Now the clustering problem can be described as: cluster S×M vectors (128-Dimension) into K groups and let the sum of the distance between the vector and the cluster center be the smallest. Define d_{ij} as the distance between x_i and x_j:

$$X_i = \{X_{i1}, X_{i2}, ..., X_{i128}\};\ X_j = \{X_{j1}, X_{j2}, ..., X_{j128}\};\ d_{ij} = \sqrt{\sum_{k=1}^{128}(X_{ik} - X_{jk})^2}$$

In this paper, we use an innovative K-Means clustering algorithm. We call it Improved Rapid K-Means (IRKM). During the iteration, we divide the centers into two groups, Static Centers and Dynamic Centers. If the center is static, the belonging points will be removed out of training data. So the size of training data becomes smaller. The time complexity of clustering process can be greatly reduced.

Define: *numThd* is the upper limit of the number of key points in one group; *distThd* is the threshold of distance between clustering center and the points in corresponding group. max *Iter* is the threshold of the maximum iterations; min(i) is the number of key points in group i; $dis(i)$ is the farthest distance between the center and points in group i; *iter* is the current iteration;

IRKM Steps:

1. Randomly pick K key points as clustering center
$$C = \{C_k \mid k = 1, 2 \cdots K\}, 2 \leq K < N \text{ and set } iter = 1;$$
2. If $iter < \max Iter$, jump to step 3, otherwise jump to step 6;
3. Calculate distances between clustering centers and key points. Divide data set according to the result.
4. Find static centers. If the number of key points in corresponding group exceeds the threshold ($\min(i) > numThd$) and the key points are compact enough ($dis(i) > distThd$), we regard C_i as a static center. The entire key points in this kind of group will be removed from data set.
5. Calculate new clustering center, jump to step 2, and set $iter = iter + 1$;
6. Finish and get the final clustering centers.

After that, the number of clustering centers is K, and there are $\dfrac{S \times M}{K}$ key points per group on average. Next step we generate some key-value pairs. Key is the clustering center, and Value is the image serial number contained in corresponding clustering group. Considering search efficiency, we build a KD-tree [9] with the key part. The key-value pairs are called Vocabulary Entries (VE). All these VEs construct a visual dictionary with weight (VDW).

2.2   Target Image Side

When target image is given, first we extract key points from it and calculate descriptors as 2.1.1 stated. Then look up the descriptors in VDW and get the right group for each one. Assuming that we get K descriptors, now we should have K vectors of Value. The next step is to integrate all vectors. A weight table like figure 4 will be generated. Now it's convenient for us to find the maximum weight from it.

According to above model, we can always get an image I' corresponding to target image I. Assuming that there are T key points in target image, the size of image set is M and the maximum weight is W_{max}. Here we need a threshold Per. If $W_{max} > T \times Per$, the Img_{max} corresponding to W_{max} is the right answer and retrieval success, otherwise retrieval fails. The algorithm's time complexity is $O(\log T + M)$.

Table 1. Image weight table

Image	Im g_1	Im g_2	Im g_3	......	Im g_{max}
Weight	W_1	W_2	W_3	......	W_{max}

3   Experiments

In this part, we compared visual dictionary with weight method (VDW) with bag-of-words method [10] (BOW), color histogram based method (CHB) and edge histogram based method (EHB).

3.1   Laboratory Test

The image set we used for testing is COREL, which is widely used in academic area. To show large-scale amount, the entire 9907 images are used as data set. VDW is generated based on all of them.

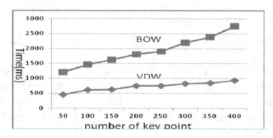

Fig. 4. Comparison in Time-Consuming

Next we pick 80 images with different number of key points. Figure 5 shows the result of time-consuming test used VDW and BOW method. It can be seen clearly from the figure that the average time consumed by VDW is 600ms, while BOD is 2000ms. And time of BOW raises more quickly than VDW as the number of key points grows. Obviously, efficiency of BOD cannot match the practical requirement in case of a large-scale image set anymore.

Again, we randomly selected 200 images from image set and divided them into 4 categories. Add rotation transformation on the first category, pixel interference on the second, edge cutting on the third and remain unchanged on the last one. Samples are given in Figure 7. All these images are treated as target images to test the anti-interference ability of VDW, CHB and EHB.

As Figure 6 shown, the accuracy of all these three methods is close to 100 percent when there is no interference or only rotation interference. When the cutting interference and the pixel interference are added, the VDW method can maintain the correct

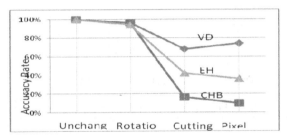

Fig. 5. Algorithm accuracy

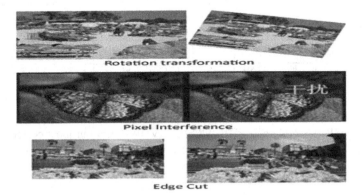

Fig. 6. Three types of interference

rate over 70 percent, at the same time, EHB drops to 35 percent and CHB even drops to 10 percent. From this experiment, it's easy to get the conclusion that VDW's anti-interference ability is stronger than other two global feature algorithms, CHB and EHB.

3.2   Online Test

Now we have such a scenario: eBay is a world-renowned shopping web site. Thousands of items and images will be posted on it every day. But some images are forbidden because of copyright or legal issue. Therefore, we already have a Blacklist image Lib. There are 11579 forbidden images in it. And we also have another 214293 images, which are listed on eBay America Site in the first quarter of 2011. They are target images. The task is ferreting out all forbidden ones among target images. Conceivably seller always add some logo or water print on the images or do some other nauseous transformation to catch buyer's eyes. So there is serious interference. We try to use three different methods to deal with the problem (VDW, CHB and EHB).

Table 2. Online testing result

	CHB	EHB	VDW
Number of result	56	86	458
Correction rate	98.21%	98.83%	70.61%

We also test our method in different categories. We chose Men's Shoes, Toy, Cloth and Digital Camera. Here is the result below. 200 pictures are chosen as training model. Half of them are from forbidden library, half are not.

Table 3. Testing result in different categories

(Toy)	CHB	EHB	VDW	(Cloth)	CHB	EHB	VDW
Number of result	75	87	89	Number of result	62	78	90
Correction rate	87.5%	93.5%	94.5%	Correction rate	81%	89%	95%

(Shoes)	CHB	EHB	VDW	(DC)	CHB	EHB	VDW
Number of result	84	87	94	Number of result	71	65	90
Correction rate	92%	93.5%	97%	Correction rate	85.5%	82.5%	95%

We can find in Figure 8: As to the quantitative aspect, VDW's result is far more than CHB and EHB. Although VDW is 70 percent in terms of correction rate and is lower than CHB (98.21%) and EHB (98.83%), VDW ferret out most correct images. Reviewing those images matched by mistake, we find that Number of their key points is not enough for matching and most of their contents are simplex and monotonous (Figure 11).

Table 4. Result after adding restrictive condition

	VDW	Restrictive VDW
Number of result	458	390
Correction rate	70.61%	85.71%

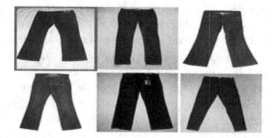

Fig. 7. Examples of mismatch image (query image is in red rectangular box)

To cover this problem we introduction a new minimum threshold φ. If the number of key points is less than φ, we will ignore it in retrieval process. Figure 9 shows the result when φ equal to 50. After adding the restrictive condition, the number of result reduces 68 and correction rate raises 15.1 percent. Figure 12 shows some samples about forbidden images retrieved correctly.

4   Conclusion

This paper proposes a creative algorithm of large-scale image retrieval with interference. We establish a visual dictionary with weights (VDW). The basic element of our method is feature descriptor, rather than image. Experiment shows that this method is much faster than the traditional ones in terms of retrieval speed. So it is suitable to be used in large-scale image retrieval. In the meantime, when target image has interference, our algorithm also shows better noise suppression ability and stronger robustness. Comparing to color-based and edge-based method, more images are ferreted out by VDW and the accuracy is ensured. The following test on eBay site also proves this result.

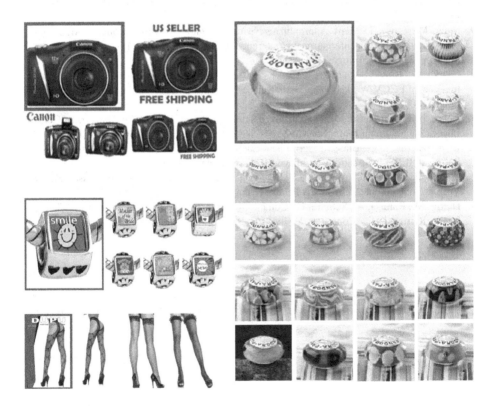

Fig. 8. Examples of retrieval result (query image is in red rectangular box)

Reference

1. Farquhar, J., Szedmak, S., Meng, H., Shawe-Taylor, J.: Improving "Bag-of-keypoints" image categorization. University of Southampton (2005)
2. Jegou, H., Douze, M., Schmid, C.: On the Burstiness of Visual Elements. In: IEEE Conference on Computer Version and Recognition, Miami, FL, USA, pp. 1169–1176 (2009)
3. Edward, R., Drummond, T.: Fusing Points and Lines for High Performance Tracking. In: ICCV, pp. 1508–1515 (2005)
4. Edward, R., Drummond, T.: Machine Learning for High-speed Corner Detection. In: Machine Learning, pp. 1–14 (2006)
5. Lowe, D.: Object Recognition from Scale-invariant Features. In: ICCV, pp. 1150–1157 (1999)
6. Leutenegger, S., Margarita, C., Roland, Y.: Siegwart. BRISK: Binary Robust Invariant Scalable Keypoints. In: ICCV (2011)
7. Anna, B., Andrew, Z., Xavier, M.: Image Classification using Random Forests and Ferns. In: ICCV, pp. 1–8 (2007)
8. Ethan, R., Vincent, R., Kurt, K., Gary, B.: ORB: an Efficient Alternative to SIFT or SURF. In: ICCV (2011)
9. Muja, M., Lowe, D.: Fast Approximate Nearest Neighbours with Automatic Algorithm Configuration. In: 4th International Conference on Computer Vision Theory and Applications, pp. 331–340. Springer, France (2009)
10. Csurka, G., Bray, C., Dance, C., Fan, L.: Visual Categorization with Bags of Keypoints. In: Proc. of ECCV Workshop on Statistical Learning in Computer Vision. Czech Republic, Prague (2004)
11. Kekre, H.B., Dhirendra, M.: Digital Image Search & Retrieval using FFT Sectors of Color Images. International Journal on Computer Science and Engineering, 368–372 (2010)
12. Bian, W., Tao, D.C.: Biased Discriminant Euclidean Embedding for Content-Based Image Retrieval. IEEE Transactions on Image Processing, 545–554 (2010)
13. Perronnin, F., Liu, Y., Sanchez, J.: Large-scale Image Retrieval with Compressed Fisher Vectors. In: Computer Vision and Pattern Recognition (CVPR), pp. 3384–3391 (2010)
14. Douze, M., Ramisa, A., Schmid, C.: Combining Attributes and Fisher Vectors for Efficient Image Retrieval. In: Computer Vision and Pattern Recognition (CVPR), pp. 754–752 (2011)

A Continuous Skeletonization Method
Based on Distance Transform

Ting-Qin Yan[1,2] and Chang-Xiong Zhou[1]

[1] Depart of Electronic Information Engineering, Suzhou Vocational University,
Suzhou, Jiangsu 215104, China
[2] Suzhou Key Lab of Digital Design & Manufacturing Technology, Suzhou,
Jiangsu 215104, China
yantzhen@sohu.com

Abstract. A skeleton extracted by distance map is located at geometrical center, but it is discrete, on the other hand, we can get a continuous skeleton with morphological algorithm, but the skeleton is not located at the geometrical center of the object image. To get a continuous skeleton that is located at geometrical center of the object image, a continuous skeletonization method based on distance transform is proposed in this paper. At first, the distance function is calculated with respect to the object boundary, which is defined as a new indicator for the skeletonization. Then, a thinning algorithm with five deletion templates is given, which can be applied to get a continuous and centered skeleton indicated by distance map. The performance of the proposed algorithm is compared with existing algorithms, experimental results confirm the superiority of our proposed approach.

Keywords: Skeletonization, Distance map, Morphology, Thinning.

1   Introduction

Skeletonization is useful when we are interested not in the size of the pattern but rather in the relative position of the strokes in the pattern. It plays an important role in digital image processing and pattern recognition [1], especially for the analysis and recognition of binary images [2]. It has been widely used in such areas as object representation, data compression, computer vision, and computer animation [3]. Skeletons provide a simple and compact representation of a 2D shape that preserves many of the topological and size characteristics of the original. The process can be viewed as a transformation to transform the width of a binary pattern into just one single pixel. Essentially, such transformation can be achieved by successively removing points or layers of outline from a binary pattern until all the lines or curves are of unit width. The resulting set of lines or curves is called the skeleton of the pattern. As we know, the purpose of skeletonization is to reduce the amount of redundant data embedded in a binary image and to facilitate the extraction of distinctive features from the binary image thereafter. A good skeletonization algorithm should possess the following properties: (1) preserving connectivity of

D.-S. Huang et al. (Eds.): ICIC 2012, CCIS 304, pp. 251–258, 2012.

skeleton, (2) converging to skeleton of unit width, (3) preserving original topology, and (4) locating at the geometrical center of the object image.

Abundant of thinning algorithms have been proposed to obtain a thin-line representation of binary patterns [4]. Most of existing thinning algorithms can be divided into two main types. In the first category also known as "distance transform" [5]. The second category consists of "thinning algorithm" [6] which are constructed by successive removal of outer layers of pixels from an object while retaining any pixel whose removal would alter connectivity or shorten the legs of the skeleton. The aim of the first algorithm is getting distance field with European, chessboard, and so on [7], and the spine of the distance field is taken as the skeleton. Due to the extraction of the spine is difficult, so it is not easy to get a accurate spine. Generally, every point is specified by giving its distance from the nearest boundary point. The skeleton is defined as the set of points whose distance from the nearest boundary is locally maximum. As shown in Fig. 1(a), the position of the skeleton of this method is accurate, but the skeleton is made up of many discrete maximum points, so the skeleton is not a continuous one.

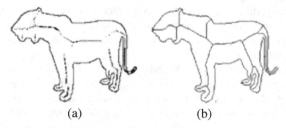

(a)   (b)

Fig. 1. Skeletons Extracted by Distance Transform and Morphological Algorithms (a) Distance Transforms Algorithms, (b) Morphological Algorithms

Skeletonization based on morphological algorithms is the process of peeling off of a pattern as many pixels as possible without affecting the general shape of the pattern. In other words, after pixels have been peeled off, the pattern should still be recognized. There are many algorithms which were designed for this aim. Here we are concerned with one of them namely the Hilditch's algorithm [8]. This consists of performing multiple passes on the pattern and on each pass; the algorithm checks all the pixels and decide to change a pixel from black to white if it satisfies the deleting conditions. This algorithm turned out to be not the perfect algorithm for skeletonization. The result of this algorithm is shown in Fig. 1(b), the skeleton is continuous, but the position of the skeleton is not centered. Other morphological algorithms are just the same as Hilditch's algorithm; the position of the skeleton is not accurate enough.

For taking advantage of morphological algorithms and distance transform, we propose a continuous skeletonization algorithm based on the distance transform. The distance transform of the image is calculated at first, and a distance map will be gotten, then performing our morphological thinning algorithm on the image along the contour of the distance map. The performance of the proposed algorithm is compared with the existing algorithms. The result of this algorithm is centered with respect to morphological algorithms, and it is better than those generated by distance transform algorithms on continuity. Experimental results confirm the superiority of our proposed approach.

2   Distance Transform

The distance transform is a powerful tool in digital image processing. The result of this operation is called distance map. Distance transforms are important preprocessing steps in complex image analysis systems. Operations such as skeletonization, can be relied on accurate distance maps.

The distance transform labels each object element with the distance between this element and the nearest non-object element. For all elements $p \in P$, the algorithm determines

$$t(p) = \min_k \{ d(p, q_k) : t(q_k) = 0 \wedge 0 \le k \le m \}$$ (1)

where $d(p, q_k)$ denotes a metric, and m is the total number of elements in the picture. It follows that $t(p) = 0$, for all non-object elements. Obviously, the values for $t(p)$ depend on the chosen metric. Chessboard is a frequently-used distance metric, and we utilize this metric in our algorithm.

A 3×3 square element is used in chessboard distance transform, just as shown in Fig. 2, taking a point p of object shape p into account; arrange the distance value of 8 neighbours of p as a vector V

$$V = [t(r-1,c), t(r-1,c+1), t(r,c-1),$$
$$t(r,c+1), t(r+1,c-1), t(r+1,c), t(r+1,c+1), t(r-1,c-1)]$$ (2)

− 8	− 1	− 2
− 7	− p	− 3
− 6	− 5	− 4

Fig. 2. Nneighbours vector of pixel p

The distance of pixel p is the minimum of V plus 1

$$t_p(r,c) = \min(V) + 1$$ (3)

The flow chart of the chessboard distance algorithm is shown in Fig. 3.

From the algorithm of chessboard distance transform, we can find that the chessboard distance field have following characteristic:1) the distance value of boundary pixel of object shape is 1, 2) from the boundary of the shape to local maximum point, the distance value increases, 3) the distance value stand for the distance between this element and the nearest non-object element, 4)if a distance value is locally maximum, then the distance value is not smaller than its neighbours', and this point is the centre of a maximal inscribed circle responding. Fig. 5 shows a distance gray-scale map of tiger image, those pixels whose gray are deeper are farther from boundary, and the lighter ones are near the boundary.

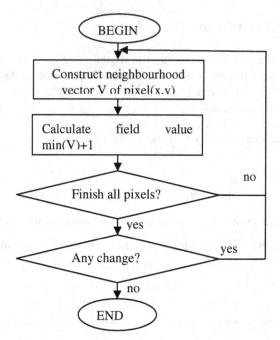

Fig. 3. Flow chart of chessboard distance algorithm

Fig. 4 is an example of chessboard distance field.

0	0	0	0	0	0	0
0	1	1	1	1	1	0
0	1	2	2	2	1	0
0	1	2	3	2	1	0
0	1	2	2	2	1	0
0	1	1	1	1	1	0
0	0	0	0	0	0	0

Fig. 4. Chessboard Distance Field

Fig. 5. Distance gray-scale map of tiger shape

Joining points of equal distance value in Fig. 5, a contour map come into being. The spine of this contour map stands for the right position of skeleton. Because the digital image is discrete, the skeleton gotten is not continuous.

3   Our Computational Scheme

Based on the discussion above, we can find that the data of distance map has a distinctive characteristic. The distance value increases from the boundary to the interior, and the gradient of distance is same at all direction. This is decided by the nature of distance calculating algorithm, every distance value calculated by its neighbours from all direction. Just because of this, the spine of distance map indicates the skeleton position accurately. Related to the continuous property of thinning algorithm, the continuous skeletonization based on distance transform is proposed in this article, the thinning process indicated by the contour of distance field. Two main steps are included in our algorithm.

1) Running the chessboard distance algorithm on the object image, getting the distance field, saving the maximum of distance to variable Max.

2) Selecting 5 deletion templates as in Fig6, changing the pixel that is satisfying these 5 deletion templates and their rotated models into background. Repeating this procedure from the boundary to the interior of given shape by the contour of distance field.

Fig. 6. Five deletion templates

As shown in Fig. 6, the pixel P is the object pixel. The deletion conditions are 1) "1" pixels are continuous in the neighbours of pixel P, 2) the number of "1" pixels is 2 to 6. When these two conditions are satisfied, turn the pixel P into background. The executed procedures as follow:

a) $i = 0$;

b) $i = i + 1$;

c)   Check those pixels whose distance values are i, changing the pixel that is satisfying those deletion templates and their rotated models into background;

d)   If $i < Max$, go to b);

e)   If there is any change for all elements, go to b).

If there is not any change, the iteration procedure is finished.

4   Experiment Results and Analysis

Programming and running our algorithm to extract image skeleton for different kinds of planar shape, the shape of tiger is shown in Fig. 7, and Fig. 7 (a) is the original image(157×514 pixels), the Fig. 7 (b) is the skeleton extracted by our algorithm. Drawing a comparison for experimental results (Fig. 1, Fig. 5 and Fig. 7), conclusion is shown as follow: the position of skeleton in Fig. 1 (a) and Fig. 7 (b) complies with the spine in Fig. 5, which is the set of the ceter of maximal inscribed circle of the given shape, and it is in accord with the definition of skeleton. The skeleton extracted by our algorithm is continuous, as can be observed in Fig. 7 (b), and it preserves the tiger shapes, the processing result of this algorithm is better than distance transform and morphological thinning algorithms.

(a)   (b)

Fig. 7. Skeletonization of Tiger Shape (a) Original shape (b) the skeleton extracted by our algorithm

We also test our algorithm on horse shape; Fig. 8 shows the result of thinning when using our approach in comparison with distance transform and morphological thinning algorithm. (a) is the original shape, (b) is the distance gray-scale map, (c) is the

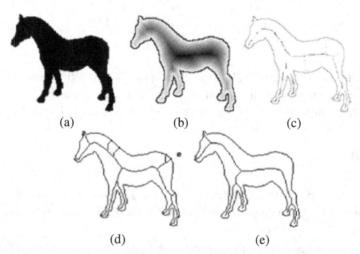

(a)   (b)   (c)

(d)   (e)

Fig. 8. Skeletonization of Horse Shape (a) Original Shape (b) Distance Gray-Scale Map of Tiger Image (c)The Skeleton Extracted by Distance Transform (d) The Skeleton Extracted by Morphological Algorithm (e)The Skeleton Extracted by Our Algorithm

skeleton extracted by distance transform, (d)is the skeleton extracted by morphological algorithm, (e)is the skeleton extracted by our algorithm. A similar conclusion can be drawn as the tiger shape: we can get a continuous and centered skeleton of horse shape, the result of our algorithm (Fig8 (e)) is better than distance transform (Fig8 (c)) and morphological thinning algorithms (Fig. 8 (d)).

A lot of other shapes have been tested on our algorithm, the results of these experiments confirm the universality of the algorithm. As can be observed in Table 1, our algorithm does an excellent job here, it preserves the image shapes. At the same time, the result skeleton is continuous and centered, keep the right angles and interconnections close in terms of the shape to the original picture. The universal performance of this algorithm proved its applications in practice.

Table 1. Results of thinning by our algorithm on different kinds of images

English words	Chinese words	Blood vessel

5   Conclusions

A very large number of algorithms in the skeletonization area have been proposed. Algorithms based on distance transform and morphology were discussed and compared. Short summaries with the available results of these two algorithms were also presented. The main points of view were the result of methodology method is not centered enough, and the result of distance transform is not continuous enough.

We presented a robust and simple method to extract an approximate skeleton for a planar image. The proposed method is based on distance transform and a methodology approach with five new deletion templates. In the first step, the chessboard distance map is calculated, then run the methodology algorithm indicated by the contour in distance map. Many different images have been tested on this method.

The proposed algorithm evolved from distance transform and methodology algorithm introduces its advantages in terms of two important characteristics:centered and continuous. The examples shown in Section 5 for graphical symbols, handwritten words and medical image demonstrate the processing quality of our algorithm. This fact proves the universal character of the algorithm.

Acknowledgements. This research was sponsored by the grants of Natural Science Foundation of China (No.60970058), the grants of Natural Science Foundation of Jiangsu Province of Suzhou Vocational China (No.BK2009131), Suzhou Infrastructure Construction Project of Science and Technology (No.SZS201009), Innovative Team Foundation of Suzhou Vocational University (No.3100125), and Qing Lan Project of Jiangsu Province of China.

References

1. Komala Lakshmi, J., Punithavalli, M.: A Survey on Skeletons in Digital Image Processing. In: Proceedings. 2009 International Conference on Digital Image Processing, ICDIP 2009, pp. 260–269 (2009)
2. Srijeyanthan, K., Thusyanthan, A., Joseph, C.N., et al.: Skeletonization in a Aeal-Time Gesture Recognition System. In: Proceedings of the 2010 5th International Conference on Information and Automation for Sustainability, ICIAfS 2010, pp. 213–218 (2010)
3. Liu, X.X., Dean, M.N., Summers, A.P., et al.: Composite Model of the Shark's Skeleton in Bending: A Novel Architecture for Biomimetic Design of Functional Compression Bias. Materials Science and Engineering C 30(8), 1077–1084 (2010)
4. Rakesh, G., Rajpreet, K.: Skeletonization Algorithm for Numeral Patterns. International Journal of Signal Processing, Image Processing and Pattern Recognition 1(1), 63–72 (2008)
5. Latecki, L.J., Li, Q.N., Bai, X., et al.: Skeletonization Using SSM of the Distance Transform. In: Proceedings - International Conference on Image Processing, ICIP 2007, vol. 5, pp. V349–V352 (2007)
6. Xie, F., Xu, G., Cheng, Y., et al.: Human Body and Posture Recognition System Based on an Improved Thinning Algorithm. IET Image Processing 5(5), 420–428 (2011)
7. Xia, H., Tucker, P.G.: Finite Volume Distance Field Solution Applied to Medial Aaxis Transform. In: 48th AIAA Aerospace Sciences Meeting Including the New Horizons Forum and Aerospace Exposition, vol. 1(82), pp. 114–134 (2010)
8. Naccache, N.J., Shinghal, R.: Investigation Into the Skeletonnization Approach of Hilditch. Source: Pattern Recognition 3(17), 279–284 (1984)

Key-Based Scrambling for Secure Image Communication

Prashan Premaratne[1] and Malin Premaratne[2]

[1] School of Electrical Computer and Telecommunications Engineering,
University of Wollongong, North Wollongong, NSW, Australia
[2] Department of Electrical and Computer Systems Engineering at Monash University,
Victoria, Australia
malin@ieee.org, prashan@uow.edu.au

Abstract. Secure image communication is becoming increasingly important due to theft and manipulation of its content. Law enforcement agents may find it increasingly difficult to stay afloat above the ill intentions of hackers. We have been able to develop an image scrambling algorithm that is very simple to implement but almost impossible to breach with a probability less than $5x10^{-300}$. This is possible due to the fact that a user may purchase or acquire rights for an intended image by specifying a 'key' that can form a sequence of numbers 10 to 100 in length. The content provider uses this sequence as a base in developing another key sequence to scramble the image and transmit it to the user through regular channels such as an email attachment. Since the user is the only party apart from the provider to possess the key for descrambling, any third party will not be able to descramble it successfully as will be shown in this paper.

Keywords: Image scrambling, image communication, image shuffling, key generation.

1 Introduction

Digital images are increasingly sent over networks as documents, commercial items or law enforcement material. Due to the heightened activities of hackers all over the world, these images can easily end up in the hands of unscrupulous third parties who might profit/extort or modify them without the knowledge of the legitimate receiver. To safeguard the image information, research has been carried out in mathematics, cryptology and in information theory over the years. Previously, image watermarking, visual cryptology, information sharing and image scrambling has been proposed to counter image theft. Image scrambling process is an important image encryption method which has been used in watermarking for data hiding. The objective of image scrambling has been to generate a non-intelligible image which prevents human visual system or computer vision system from understanding the true content. An authorized user is empowered to descramble the image using information regarding scrambling method and the variables in order to decipher the image.

Image scrambling has been proposed as a way to mitigate such issues way back in 1960 when the first documented system to do so emerged [1]. Their approach

D.-S. Huang et al. (Eds.): ICIC 2012, CCIS 304, pp. 259–263, 2012.

involved scrambling, concealing or encoding information and unscrambling and decoding the received images using line screens and grids consisting of opaque and transparent lines. Over the years, image scrambling has evolved into two streams; one based on matrix transformation to shift coordinates and another to permuting coordinates of pixels.

Most of the scrambling approaches are based on Arnold Transform or combination of Arnold Transform with other techniques [2-4]. These are also applicable only to equilateral images. If images are not equilateral, then they have to be padded with values to make them equilateral [5]. Since most of these techniques do not use a 'key' that provides additional security, Zhou et.al. proposed Fibonacci P-code based scrambling algorithm which required two parameters to be known by the receiver side to descramble the images [6]. Even though, this is certainly a favorable development over the others, two numbers would not provide adequate protection and the system is very vulnerable to attack.

Others [7-12] have attempted scrambling using random sequences based on chaos or pseudo random number generation based on parameters. Zhou et. al proposed an algorithm using an M-sequence to shuffle image coordinates using two parameter key [13]. The M-sequences is a maximum length sequence that has been used in spread spectrum communications. It is a pseudo random noise sequence. In this approach, the authorized user is given the shift parameter r and the distance parameter p which are used to generate the 2-D M-sequence to descramble the scrambled image.

Gu, et. al. presented an image scrambling algorithm based on chaotic sequences [14]. The chaotic sequence was generated using three parameters and the algorithm typically had to be iterated 100 times to generate the non linear sequence. This introduced high complexity and the resulting scrambled image histogram was modified in the process. Even though these attempts are promising, having one or two parameters controlling the entire pseudorandom sequence generation was very vulnerable to attack.

2 Key Based Scrambling

In image scrambling and descrambling, it is imperative to have simple algorithm to 'shuffle' the pixel values fast and reorder it to reveal the original. However, such simple requirements have most of the time resulted in low-secure solutions. Our approach proposes a solution which provides both simplicity and utmost security using a user defined sequence to safeguard the content.

In our approach, we build a pseudorandom sequence using the user defined 10 to 100 long positive integer value sequence. Since these values are used for image pixel row and column shuffling, the values usually have a lower and an upper limit of 1 and 200. These limits restrict that a small image such as 256x128 will not be shuffled by a value such as 300 in which case, the modulo operations simply will result in switching row value by 44 (300 = 256 +44) rather than 300. This provided sequence is used to generate a longer sequence that is as long as the maximum dimension of the image (length or width). We have few options to generate the longer sequence from the user provided sequence. One option would be to periodically insert the user provided sequence in order to generate the longer sequence. In order to shuffle the image well, we can increment each value of the shorter sequence whenever it is repeated in the longer sequence. This process is illustrated in Fig. 1.

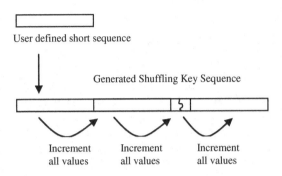

Fig. 1. Key Sequence Generation Using User Provided Key

Once the shuffling order sequence is generated, which is the 'key' in this process, sequence values are read and the rows are switched (if the first value of the sequence is 78, then row 78 of the image is copied into row 1 and row 1 is copied into row 78). Once all rows are switched according to the key sequence, columns are switched using the same sequence. At this stage the amount of scrambling achieved is visually not acceptable as indicated by Figures 2(b). Thus this process is now followed by circular shifting of rows and then the columns using the key sequence. The result is

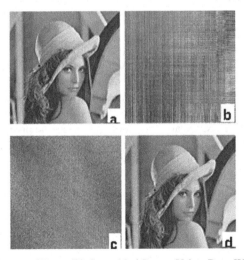

Fig. 2. (a) Original Image of Lena (b) Scrambled Image Using Row-Wise and Column Wise Shuffling. (c) Final Scrambled Image: Result of the Row-Wise Followed by Column Wise Circular Shifting of Image (b). (d) Descrambled Image of (c) Using the Correct Sequence.

visually acceptable and is shown in Fig. 2(c). Table 1 lists the image scrambling process as discussed above. The generated key sequence can again be used by the authorized party to unscramble image by undoing the circular shifting and shuffling. The unscrambled image of Fig.2(c) is shown in Fig. 2(d).

3   Robustness of Our Approach

Since the user defined sequence which can be from 10 to 100 values long positive integers in the range of 1 to 200, statistically, the probability of estimating such a sequence will be $(1/200)^{100} = 5 \times 10^{-300}$. Hence we can conclude that estimating such a sequence to unscramble the image will be practically impossible. Due to this robustness, the user can expect multiple images of different sizes scrambled and communicated by the same content provider. In the event of communication channel or unauthorized party adding noise to the transmitted image, the descrambling process will not be affected.

Table 1. Summary of the proposed scrambling process

Step1	Use the user provided key to generate a key sequence that is of the length of the maximum dimension of the image
Step2	Use the key sequence to switch the rows
Step3	Use the key sequence to switch the columns
Step4	Use the key sequence to circular shift the rows
Step5	Use the key sequence to circular shift the columns

4   Discussion

We have proposed a highly secure yet simple image scrambling algorithm that seems to address most of the concerns of having a random sequence to scramble and descramble an image. Since the sequence generation is not governed by few numbers of parameter as has been reported before [7-12], a sequence that is almost 100 values long will almost be impossible to crack. Since the algorithm does not affect the pixel values of the image, its histogram and the content remain unchanged. Any additive noise will not affect the descrambling process. The algorithm equally applies to color images.

Since the authorized user determines the key, same key can be used multiple times for multiple images when dealing with the same content provider.

References

1. Renesse, R.L.: Hidden and Scrabbled Images- a Review. In: Conference on Optical Security and Counterfeit Deterence Techniques IV, vol. 4677, pp. 333–348. SPIE (2002)
2. Huang, H.: An Image Scrambling Encryption Algorithm Combined Arnold and Chaotic Transform. In: Int. Conf. China Communication, pp. 208–210 (2010)

3. Fang, L., YuKai, W.: Restoring of the Watermarking Image in Arnold Scrambling. In: 2nd International Conference on Signal Processing Systems (ICSPS), pp. 771–774 (2010)

4. Liu, Z., Chen, H., Liu, T., Li, P., Xu, L., Dai, J., Liu, S.: Image Encryption by Us-ing Gyrator Transform and Arnold Transform. Journal of Electronic Imaging 20(1) (2011)

5. Kong, T., Zhang, D.: A New Anti-Arnold Transformation Algorithm. Journal of Software 15(10), 1558–1564 (2004)

6. Zhou, Y., Joyner, V.M., Panetta, K.: Two Fibonacci P-code Based Image Scram-bling Algorithms. Image Processing: Algorithms and Systems VI 6812, 681215, 1–12 (2008)

7. Che, S., Che, Z., Ma, B.: An Improved Image Scrabbling Algorithm. In: Proc. Second Int. Conf. Genetics and Evolutionary Computing, pp. 495–499 (2008)

8. Fridrich, J.: Image Encryption Based on Chaotic Maps. In: Proc. IEEE Conf. Systems, Man, and Cybernetics, pp. 1105–1110 (1997)

9. Yeo, J., Guo, C.: Efficient Hierarchical Chaotic Image Encryption Algorithm and Its VLSI Realisation. In: IEE Proceedings Vision, Image and Signal Processing, vol. 147(2), pp. 167–175 (2000)

10. Liping, S., Zheng, Q., Bo, L., Jun, Q., Huan, L.: Image Scrambling Algorithm Based on Random Shuffling Strategy. In: 3rd IEEE Conference on Industrial Electronics and Applications, vol. 4677, pp. 2278–2283. SPIE (2008)

11. Ville, D., Philips, W., Walle, R., Lemahieu, I.: Image Scrambling Without Band-width Expansion. IEEE Trans. Circ. Sys. Video Tech. 14(6), 892–897 (2004)

12. Liu, S., Sheridan, J.T.: Optical Information Hiding by Combining Image Scrambling Techniques in Fractional Fourier Domains. In: Irish Signal and Systems Conference, pp. 249–254 (2001)

13. Zhou, Y., Panetta, K., Agaian, S.: An Image Scrambling Algorithm Using Parameter Based M-sequence. In: Proc. Seventh Inter. Conf. Mach. Learning and Cybern., pp. 3695–3698 (2008)

14. Gu, G., Han, G.: The Application of Chaos and DWT in Image Scrambling. In: Proceedings of the Fifth International Conference on Machine Learning and Cybernetics, pp. 3729–3373 (2006)

Infrared Face Temperature Normalization in Fourier Domain

Zhihua Xie and Jie Zeng

Key Lab of Optic-Electronic and Communication, Jiangxi Sciences and Technology Normal
University, Nanchang, Jiangxi, 330013
xie_zhihua@yahoo.com.cn

Abstract. This paper proposes a novel temperature normalization method in
Fourier domain, which can lessen the effect on infrared face recognition from
ambient temperature based on the idea of statistical learning in the transform
domain. Firstly, the infrared face images in different ambient temperatures are
transformed to Fourier domain. Secondly, based on statistical theory, the
variances of phase spectrum and amplitude spectrum of the infrared face are used
to describe the extent affected by the ambient temperature. Then, to achieve the
robust information, those parts with big variances in the phase spectrum and
amplitude spectrum are discarded and replaced by corresponding mean parts in
training database. The main idea of this process is that one can set a suitable
threshold for the variance of phase spectrum and amplitude spectrum and find
those characteristic points that should be replaced. Finally, to verify the
effectiveness of our temperature normalization method, the normalized infrared
face can be applied to traditional face recognition system based on classic PCA
method. Experimental results show our normalization method can get stable
information in infrared face and improve the performance of the infrared face
recognition system.

Keywords: discrete fourier transform, infrared face recognition, temperature
normalization, variance.

1   Introduction

Due to its extensive application in identification and security, face recognition has
attracted a great many researchers and became a very active research in computer vision
and biometrics [1-2]. Currently, most researches on face recognition focus on visual
images. The reason is obvious: such sensors are cheap and visual images are widely
used. However, the performance of visual face recognition is usually impacted by
variations both in intrinsic (pose, expression, hairstyle etc) and extrinsic conditions
(illumination, imaging system etc). The infrared radiation which the textures and
structures of the face such as the blood vessels and its distribution emit will be a crucial
element for the formation of the infrared face images. In addition, the coefficients of the
thermal radiation for the faces are obviously different from those for the surrounding
scenes and the faces can be easily distinguished from the scenes [3]. So, to some extent,

D.-S. Huang et al. (Eds.): ICIC 2012, CCIS 304, pp. 264–271, 2012.

the infrared face recognition technology can be used to compensate the defects existing in the visible face recognition technologies because of its advantages of the uniqueness, owning a good anti-interference performance, escaping out of the effect of the visible light, preventing the disguises and frauds and so on[4-6]. Several studies have shown that the use of infrared images can solve limitation of visible-image based face recognition, such as invariance to variations in illumination and robustness to variations in pose [12]. However, there are also some limitations for applying the infrared face recognition technology [4-7]. The variation of the ambient temperature can affect the results of the infrared face recognition with the same way as the variation of the illumination can affect the visible face recognition. The testing infrared face images and the training ones may be inevitably collected at different times. In fact, the faces which are collected at the different times usually own different temperatures. As a result, the performance of the infrared face recognition system will drop in this situation. To lessen the effect of ambient on infrared face recognition, the infrared faces in different ambient temperatures need be preprocessed to retain stable information. This process means temperature normalization. The accurate temperature normalization plays an important role in infrared face recognition [3].

In visible face recognition, a few illumination normalization algorithms are proposed based on frequency domain to lessen the effect of the ambient illumination on the recognition. The reference [8] introduces an illumination normalization algorithm based on the wavelet domain, which converts a face image into the high frequency part and the low frequency part by applying wavelet transform and then process the different frequency elements with different operations. Ju etc[9] proposes an illumination normalization method based on the frequency domain according to analyzing the properties of the phase spectrums and the amplitude spectrums of the face images, which reflects a strong robustness to the variation of the ambient illumination. In addition, the other scholars use the homomorphic filtering to restrain the low frequency elements in order to lessen the effects caused by the variation of the illumination.[10] Inspired by those normalization illumination methods, this paper develops a novel temperature normalization method of infrared face based on transform domain. The main idea of this method is to extract the robust features in phase spectrum and amplitude spectrum of Fourier domain. The main contribution of this paper is that one can set the suitable thresholds both for the variance of phase spectrum and amplitude spectrum to find those characteristic points that are easily variable with the ambient temperature alteration.

2   Discrete Fourier Transform

In this section, we will discuss Fourier Transform. The Fourier Transform of a digital image $f(x, y)$ with resolution of $M \times N$ is defined as:

$$F(u,v) = \frac{1}{\sqrt{MN}} \sum_{x=0}^{M-1} \sum_{y=0}^{N-1} f(x, y) \exp[-j2\pi(\frac{ux}{M} + \frac{vy}{N})] \tag{1}$$

$$u = 0, 1, 2, ..., M-1, v = 0, 1, 2, ..., N-1$$

Its inverse transform is:

$$f(x,y) = \frac{1}{\sqrt{MN}} \sum_{u=0}^{M-1} \sum_{v=0}^{N-1} F(u,v) \exp[j2\pi(\frac{ux}{M} + \frac{vy}{N})]$$ (2)

$$x = 0,1,2,...,M-1, y = 0,1,2,...,N-1$$

A digital image $f(x,y)$ becomes a complex signal after making a Fourier Transform and is described as:

$$F(u,v) = R(u,v) + jI(u,v)$$ (3)

where (u,v) signifies the space position of the space frequency, $F(u,v)$.

The amplitude spectrum $|F(u,v)|$ and the phase spectrum $\phi(u,v)$ of a digital image $f(x,y)$ are defined as:

$$|F(u,v)| = \sqrt{R^2(u,v) + I^2(u,v)}$$ (4)

$$\phi(u,v) = arc \tan \frac{I(u,v)}{R(u,v)}$$ (5)

a) the original face spectrum b)the corresponding amplitude c)the corresponding phase spectrum

Fig. 1. The amplitude spectrum and phase spectrum

3   Temperature Normalization in Fourier Frequency Domain

For instance, there is a testing dataset $\{x_i^{(j)}\}$ which contains c classifications. The ith class contains M infrared face images such as: $x_i^{(1)}, x_i^{(2)},...,x_i^{(j)},...,x_i^{(M)}$. Those are collected in the different ambient temperatures. Each sample of the images is considered as a $m \times n$ matrix. So the variances and mean values of the amplitude coefficients in the amplitude-spectrum matrix $F1$ can respectively comprise a row vector:

$$F1_{(var)} = var(F1') = \left[\left(|F1(1,1)|\right)_{ivar}, \left(|F1(2,1)|\right)_{ivar}, ..., \left(|F1(m \times n,1)|\right)_{ivar} \right]$$ (6)

$$F1_{(mean)} = mean(F1') = \left[\left(|F1(1,1)|\right)_{(imean)}, \left(|F1(2,1)|\right)_{(imean)}, ..., \left(|F1(m \times n,1)|\right)_{(imean)} \right]$$ (7)

The variances and mean values of the phase coefficients in the phase-spectrum matrix $\Phi1$ can respectively comprise a row vector:

$$\Phi1_{(var)} = var(\Phi1') = \left[\left(\phi1(1,1) \right)_{(i\,var)}, \left(\phi1(2,1) \right)_{(i\,var)}, ..., \left(\phi1(m \times n, 1) \right)_{(i\,var)} \right] \qquad (8)$$

$$\Phi1_{(mean)} = mean(\Phi1') = \left[\left(\phi1(1,1) \right)_{(imean)}, \left(\phi1(2,1) \right)_{(imean)}, ..., \left(\phi1(m \times n, 1) \right)_{(imean)} \right] \qquad (9)$$

According to the statistical theory, the ratio $\dfrac{D}{X}$ can reflect the fluctuations of the sample values in the X vector. The higher is the ratio $\dfrac{D}{X}$, the larger is the fluctuation. Conversely, when the ratio $\dfrac{D}{X}$ is lower, the fluctuation is less. Now each element of the vector $F1_{(var)}$ is divided by that of the vector $F1_{(mean)}$ to gain a ratio $\lambda1$. The ratio $\lambda1$ can be used to describe variation of the corresponding amplitude coefficient of the characteristic point in the infrared face images, caused by ambient temperature. With the same way, each element of the vector $\Phi1_{(var)}$ is divided by that of the vector $\Phi1_{(mean)}$ to gain a ratio $\lambda2$. The ratio $\lambda2$ reflects how the corresponding phase coefficients of the characteristic points alter with the ambient temperature variation.

The process of the normalization in this paper can be introduced as follow:

Step one: The suitable threshold $T1$ can be set. Those $\lambda1$ which are higher than threshold $T1$ are unstable information for infrared face recognition in variable ambient temperature.

Step two: In order to normalize the infrared face in Fourier amplitude spectrum, the amplitude coefficients of the characteristic points corresponding to those $\lambda1$ are replaced with the amplitude coefficients of the corresponding characteristic points in the sample-mean image $\overline{x_i}$.

Step three: Considering the phase spectrum, the suitable threshold $T2$ can be set to finds out those $\lambda2$ which are higher than the $T2$, and replaces the phase coefficients of the characteristic points corresponding to these $\lambda2$ with the phase coefficients of the corresponding characteristic points in the sample-mean image $\overline{x_i}$.

Step four: we can get the normalized amplitude spectrum $F2_{(j)}$ and phase spectrum $\Phi2_{(j)}$ of the M testing-sample images. Finally, an inverse Flourier transform is applied to gain the normalized testing-sample image $\widehat{x_i^{(j)}}, j = 1, 2, ..., M$. The M represents the number of the testing samples.

When $\lambda1$ and $\lambda2$ are lower than the thresholds $T1$ and $T2$, there is no replacement to make. How to fix the thresholds will be discussed in following section 4.

4   Experiment Results and Analysis

Due to lacking of a uniform database for the recognition of the infrared face images at present, the database of the infrared face images in this paper is comprised of those images which are collected by the infrared camera named Thermo VisionA4. The database contains the 500 pieces of training-sample images and the 165 pieces of testing-sample images. The original size of the collected infrared face images is the resolution of 240×320. The normalized size of the images becomes the resolution of 80×60. In order to process the data easily the images are transformed into 4800×1 dimensions of the vectors in our experiments.

This experiment will be operated by the following steps. Firstly, this experiment uses the temperature normalization method based on the frequency domain to achieve the normalization of the testing infrared face images. Then the experiment chooses the 400 pieces of images of the first forty persons in the training dataset as the training-sample images. Secondly, the experiment applies the traditional PCA algorithm to extract the features. Furthermore, it chooses the three nearest neighbors classifier to make the judgments considering the complexity of the computation. Finally, the normalized testing infrared face images are used to get recognition results. In order to further demonstrate the fact that this normalization method proposed can be used to improve the performance of the infrared face recognition system, blood perfusion model [11] proposed by Wu et al, is also applied to our experiments.

How to gain the thresholds $T1$ and $T2$ is discussed by the two steps. The first step is to determine $T1$ for the variances of the amplitude spectrum. The 4800 different variances ($\lambda 1$) gotten in this experiment are sorted by an ascending order just like" $\lambda 1'_1, \lambda 1'_2, ..., \lambda 1'_{4800}$ ". Then every time the experiment begins with $\lambda 1'_{4800}$ to replace the amplitude coefficients of the ten characteristic points corresponding to ten $\lambda 1'$ in the testing infrared face images with those of the ten corresponding characteristic points in the sample-mean image $\overline{x_i}$. Finally, the PCA algorithm is used to extract the features. Fig.3 and Fig.4 are the experiment results of replacement of the amplitude spectrums. It can be seen for Fig.3 and Fig.4: (1) When the 650 amplitude coefficients are replaced, the recognition rate is the highest. So the threshold T1 is fixed with the $\lambda 1'_{4150}$, T1= $\lambda 1'_{4150}$ =773.33. (2)In the case that the blood perfusion model is used in the experiment, the 37 amplitude coefficients are replaced to gain the highest

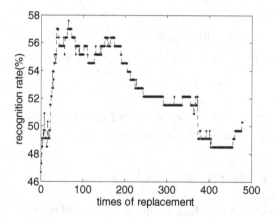

Fig. 2. Recognition rate based on replacement of the amplitude spectrums

recognition rate. As a result, the threshold T1 can be fixed with the $\lambda1'_{4763}$,
T1= $\lambda1'_{4763}$ =0.0735.

The second step is to fix $T2$ for the variances of the phase spectrum. When the
situation that phase coefficients of all the characteristic points vary as the ambient
temperature changes is just considered, the 4800 different $\lambda2$ gotten in this experiment
are sorted by an ascending order just like $\lambda2'_{1}, \lambda2'_{2},...,\lambda2'_{4800}$. The experiment methods
are the same with that of threshold T1. Fig.5 and Fig.6 are the experiment results of
replacement of the phase spectrums. From Fig.5 and Fig.6, we notice: (1) When the
4760 phase coefficients are replaced, the recognition rate is the highest. So the
threshold T2 is fixed with the $\lambda2'_{40}$, T2= $\lambda2'_{40}$ =0.1502. (2) In the case that blood
perfusion model is used in the experiment, the 4730 phase coefficients are replaced to
gain the highest recognition rate. So the threshold T2 can be fixed with the $\lambda2'_{70}$,
T2= $\lambda2'_{70}$ =0.5105.

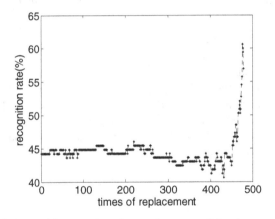

Fig. 3. Recognition rates based on replacement of the phase spectrums

To verify the efficiency of normalization, we use the normalized infrared face
images and the original without normalization for infrared face recognition. Those
normalization methods are introduced as follows: "RPS+T" means the replacement of
the phase spectrum in the thermal infrared face images. "RPS+B" means the
replacement of the phase spectrum in the blood perfusion infrared face images.
"RAS+T" means the replacement of the amplitude spectrum in the thermal infrared
face images. "RAS+B" means the replacement of the amplitude spectrum in the blood
perfusion infrared face images. "RPAS+T" means the replacement of the phase and
amplitude spectrum in the thermal infrared face images. "RPAS+B" means the
replacement of the phase and amplitude spectrum in the blood perfusion infrared face
images. "NN+T" means no normalization in the thermal infrared face images.
"NN+B" means no normalization in the blood perfusion infrared face images.

In our experiments the best recognition rates of the different methods are shown in
the following table.

Table 1. The recognition results of the different methods

Methods	The recognition rate
RPS+T	60.61%
RPS+B	63.64%
RAS+T	57.58%
RAS+B	99.39%
RPAS+T	91.52%
RPAS+B	99.39%
NN+T	44.85%
NN+B	55.76%

From Table 1, compared with the recognition rates without normalization, it is easy to see that the recognition rates after making the normalization are much better in all the methods. Furthermore, the recognition rates are much higher in the blood perfusion infrared face images than in the thermal infrared face images.

Acknowledgement. The main work of this paper is that the testing infrared face images are normalized based on Fourier transform. The more stable information can be gained from the normalized testing images, which can contribute an improvement on the performance of infrared face recognition under different environments. The experiment results demonstrate the novel temperature normalization method is feasible and robust under variable ambient temperatures. In the course of the experiments, the thresholds T1 and T2 are determined by using our experience. So how to get adaptive and automatic thresholds is our further research.

References

1. Pentland, A., Choudhury, T.: Face Recognition for Smart Environments. IEEE Computer 33(2), 50–55 (2000)
2. Wang, Y.: The Principle, Method and Technology of Face Recognition. The Science Press (2010)
3. Li, J.: Research of the Method in the Infrared Images Recognition. Doctoral Dissertation of National University of Defense Technology (2005)
4. Wilde, J., Phillips, P., Jiang, C., Wiener, S.: Comparison of Visible and Infra-Red Imagery for Face Recognition. In: International Conference on Automatic Face and Gesture Recognition, pp. 182–187 (1996)
5. Prokoski, F., Riedel, R., Coffin, J.: Identification of Individuals by Means of Facial Thermography. In: IEEE International Carnahan Conference on Security Technology, pp. 120–125 (1992)
6. Selinger, A., Socolinsky, D.: Appearance-based Facial Recognition Using Visible and Thermal Imagery: a Comparative Study. Technical Report 02-01, Equinox Corporation (2002)
7. Wolff, L., Socolinsky, D., Eveland, C.: Faces Recognition in the Thermal Infrared. Equinox Corporation 43(2), 134–144 (2004)

8. Fan, C., Wang, S., Zhang, F.: Wavelet-based Illumination Normalization Algorithm for Face Recognition. Computer Engineering and Applications 46(6), 174–177 (2010)

9. Ju, S., Zhou, J.: Face Recognition Based on Illumination Normalization in Frequency-Domain. The Transaction of University Electronic Science and Technology of China 38(6), 1021–1025 (2009)

10. Liu, H., Li, J., Jun, M.: Illumination Compensation Based on Multi-method Integration. Journal of System Simulation 13(3), 486–490 (2001)

11. Wu, S.Q., Jiang, L.J., Xie, S.L.: Infrared Face Recognition by Using Blood Perfusion Data Proceeding of Audio and Video based Biometric Person Authentication, pp. 320–328 (2005)

12. Socolinsky, D., Selinger, A.: Comparative Analysis of Face Recognition Performance with Visible and Thermal Infrared Imagery. In: Proceeding of the International Conference on Pattern Recognition, pp. 124–133 (2002)

Faster Computation of Non-zero Invariants from Graph Based Method

Vazeerudeen Abdul Hameed and Siti Mariyam Shamsuddin

Soft Computing Research Group
Faculty of Computer Science and Research Group
Universiti Teknologi Malaysia, Skudai, Johor Bahru
vazeerudeen@yahoo.com, mariyam@utm.my

Abstract. This paper presents a study of geometric moment invariants generated from graph based algorithms. One of the main problems addressed was that the algorithms produced too many graphs that resulted in zero moment invariants. Hence, we propose an algorithm to determine zero moment invariant generating graphs. Induction proof of the steps involved in the algorithm has also been presented with suitable example graphs. It has been found and illustrated with examples that the computational time for identifying non-zero invariants could be largely reduced with the help of our proposed algorithm.

Keywords: computational complexity, geometric moments, image transforms, orthogonal moments, moment invariants.

1   Introduction

Object recognition has long been a vital area of research in the field of Image Processing. Among the several stages of image processing, object recognition by has been a challenging goal for the researchers to accomplish. Numerous methods of object recognition such as edge detection and matching, grey scale matching, geometric hashing, Scale Invariant Feature Transform (SIFT) and Affine Scale Invariant Feature Transform (ASIFT) transforms and others have been proposed. Object recognition via moment invariants has been proving to be successful over the various alternatives due to their invariance to several factors such as image rotation, scaling, translation, horizontal and vertical skew. The moment M_{pq} of an image $f(x, y)$ is defined as

$$M_{pq} = \iint_D P_{pq}(x, y) f(x, y) dx dy \qquad (1)$$

where $r = p + q$ is the order of the moment and $p \geq 0, q \geq 0$ P_{pq} is a polynomial basis function. The polynomial basis function could be orthogonal or non–orthogonal. A number of non–orthogonal polynomial basis functions could be drawn. However in

D.-S. Huang et al. (Eds.): ICIC 2012, CCIS 304, pp. 272–279, 2012.

this paper we discuss about geometric affine moment invariants that are generated from the following function.

$$I(f) = \int_{-\infty}^{\infty} \ldots \int_{-\infty}^{\infty} \prod_{k,j=1}^{r} C_{kj}^{n_{kj}} \bullet \prod_{i=1}^{r} f(x_i, y_i) dx_i dy_i \tag{2}$$

where the cross–product $C_{kj} = x_j y_k - y_k x_j$ involves vertices $(x_k, y_k), (x_j, y_j)$, $(0,0)$, and n_{kj} are non-negative integers. We shall consider only $j > k$, because $C_{kj} = -C_{jk}$ and $C_{kk} = 0$.

2   History of Work on Invariants

2.1   Analysis

Moment invariants have been fundamentally classified into two types namely Orthogonal and Geometric moments. As explained in [1], [2], the orthogonal moments require lower precision computations as against geometric moments to have clear recognition of objects. According to [3] geometric moments are the simplest moment functions. In [4] we find that work over blurred image recognition was also achievable through geometric moments which show that, geometric moments are still reliable.

Complex Zernike moment functions were orthogonal moment invariant functions proposed in 1934. The target image had to be transformed from the cartesian form to polar form as the invariant function was complex. This is evitable from Eq. (3).

$$A_{mn} = \frac{(m+1)}{\Pi} \sum_{x=-\infty}^{\infty} \sum_{y=-\infty}^{\infty} I(x, y)[V_{mn}(x, y)]^*$$

$$V_{mn}(x, y) = V_{mn}(r, \theta) \tag{3}$$

$$= e^{jn\theta} \sum_{s=0}^{s=|m-|n||/2} \frac{(m-s)! r^{m-2s}}{[s![\frac{(m+|n|)}{2} - s]![\frac{m+|n|}{2} - s]!]}$$

Zernike moments are known for the minimum amount of information redundancy. However their invariance is limited to rotation and not scaling or translation.

Legendre moments as in Eq. (4), are orthogonal moment invariant functions, invariant to rotation and scale but variant to rotation unlike Zernike moments.

$$\lambda_{mn} = \frac{(2m+1)(2n+1)}{4} \sum_x \sum_y P_m(x) P_n(y) P_{xy} \tag{4}$$

Seven geometric moment invariant functions were firstly founded by Hu. These invariants were made of second and third order moments as in Eq. (5). The seven moment invariants of Hu were invariant to transformations like rotation, scaling and translation. In [5] the authors proved that the Hu moment invariants were sufficiently invariant to skew transformation based on a quantitative study. J. Flusser and T. Suk explained that there is no general algorithm to extend the Hu moment invariant functions to involve higher order moments [6], [7].

$$I_1 = \eta_{20} + \eta_{02} \qquad\qquad I_2 = (\eta_{20} - \eta_{02})^2 + (2\eta_{11})^2$$
$$I_3 = (\eta_{30} - 3\eta_{12})^2 + (3\eta_{21} - \eta_{03})^2, I_4 = (\eta_{30} + \eta_{12})^2 + (\eta_{21} + \eta_{03})^2$$
$$I_5 = (\eta_{30} - 3\eta_{12})(\eta_{30} + \eta_{12})[(\eta_{30} + \eta_{12})^2 - 3(\eta_{21} + \eta_{03})^2] +$$
$$(3\eta_{21} - \eta_{03})(\eta_{21} + \eta_{03})[3(\eta_{30} + \eta_{12})^2 - (\eta_{21} + \eta_{03})^2] \qquad\qquad (5)$$
$$I_6 = (\eta_{20} - \eta_{02})[(\eta_{30} + \eta_{12})^2 - (\eta_{21} + \eta_{03})^2] + 4\eta_{11}(\eta_{30} + \eta_{12})(\eta_{21} + \eta_{03})$$
$$I_7 = (3\eta_{21} - \eta_{03})(\eta_{30} + \eta_{12})[(\eta_{30} + \eta_{12})^2 - 3(\eta_{21} + \eta_{03})^2]$$
$$-(\eta_{30} - 3\eta_{12})(\eta_{21} + \eta_{03})[3(\eta_{30} + \eta_{12})^2 - (\eta_{21} + \eta_{03})^2]$$

They also found that Hu's invariants I2 and I3 as in (5) are polynomial dependent. They also identified a missing invariant I8 that is of order three as shown in Eq. (6).

$$I_8 = \eta_{11}[(\eta_{30} + \eta_{12})^2 - (\eta_{03} + \eta_{21})^2] - (\eta_{20} - \eta_{02})(\eta_{30} - \eta_{12})(\eta_{03} - \eta_{21}) \qquad\qquad (6)$$

A general method to derive a complete and independent set of invariants that involve higher order moments has been proposed in [10]. J. Flusser and T. Suk have also stated the need for higher order moments in [7], [8] to recognize objects of rotational symmetry. This study discovers the reason for not involving complex moments for object recognition widely thereafter.

2.2   Characteristics of the Graph Algorithm

The graph based algorithm proposed by J. Flusser and T. Suk in [2] is a general method to generate moment invariant functions from graphs. The resulting invariants must still be processed to identify Zero invariants, Identical invariants, Linearly dependent invariants and Polynomial dependent invariants. These are eliminated because they do not contribute much to object recognition. It has also been stated in [2] that, for a weight of 12 or that when graphs were generated with 12 nodes, 2,533,942,752 graphs were generated altogether, of which 2,532,349,394 resulted in zeros. Hence 99.937% of the graphs were zero. There were also 1,575,126 invariants that were equal to other invariants, 2105 invariants were products of other invariants and 14,538 invariants were linearly dependent. Finally 1589 irreducible invariants were found from 2,533,942,752 graphs which is 0.0000627%. These statistics clearly explain us that the algorithms need to be refined in order to ensure that only a vast majority of useful graphs are generated and the remaining graphs are eliminated as early as possible. Similar information has been plotted in Fig. 1 for generating moment functions of order greater than eight.

3   Graph Based Algorithm

The algorithm as proposed by J. Flusser and T. Suk in [2] can be comprehended from an example. Consider a graph of two nodes (x_1, y_1) and (x_2, y_2) connected by two edges as shown in Fig. 1. The algorithm explains us to create a Jacobian matrix for every edge in a given graph and compute the determinant.

Fig. 1. Graph of two nodes connected by a single edge

The resulting determinant of each edge is multiplied. In this example the determinant for each edge connecting nodes 1 and 2 would be $(x_1y_2 - y_1x_2)$. The product of determinants is $(x_1 y_2 - y_1 x_2)^2 = x_1^2 y_2^2 - 2 x_1 y_1 x_2 y_2 + x_2^2 y_1^2$. In every product term in the resulting determinant all the x and y co-ordinates of the same subscript are grouped to form a moment function. In this example we have $x_1^2 = x_2^2 = m_{20}, y_1^2 = y_2^2 = m_{02}, x_1 y_1 = x_2 y_2 = m_{11}$. Substituting the moment functions with the co-ordinates results in $2(m_{20}m_{02} - 2m_{11}^2)$. Hence is the moment invariant function generated by the graph.

4   The Proposed Method

Graphs that are used to generate moment invariants based on the function of Eq. (1) given above have been studied to determine certain characteristics. An algorithm has been devised to determine the zero moment generating graphs. Based upon the characteristics of the moment function generating graphs, they can be classified into three types as discussed below.

4.1   Graphs with All Nodes of Odd and Same Degree

Graphs with all nodes of odd and same degree may result in zero or non–zero invariants.

Euler's theorem 1: The number of odd degree vertices in a graph is always even.

Hence from Euler's theorem, we know that a graph of nodes with all odd and equal degrees will have several pairs of vertices of the same odd degree. We find that for graphs of odd degree n with k nodes $A_1, A_2...A_k$, k being even there would exist invariant terms of the form $m_{n0}m_{0n}$. We start generating all product terms of the form $m_{n0}m_{0n}$. If the sum of such product terms is zero, then the graph would result in a zero. If the sum does not result in a zero we continue to generate the remaining products to determine the complete invariant.

The existence of the term $m_{n0}m_{0n}$ in the invariant can be proved via induction. The degree n is odd and the number of nodes k is even as according to the Euler's theorem. Hence the number of edges in the graph would be $(n*k)/2$ which an even

Fig. 2. Graph of nodes with all vertices of odd degree

number is certain. Every node $A_1...A_k$ appears n times in the cross product function. If a term A_x is chosen from all the $(n*k)/2$ product terms, then there remains $(n*k)/2-n$ terms from which another term A_y may be chosen. Depending upon the number of nodes k, we can find several such combinations of product terms of degree n. Hence there always exists product terms of the form $A_1^n A_2^n...$ where each product term contributes only moments of the form $m_{n0}m_{0n}$.

Example 1:
Let the nodes in Fig. 2 which are 1, 2, 3 and 4 be named as A, B, C and D respectively. The cross product terms in Eq. (2) would form $(A-B)^2(B-C)(C-D)^2(D-A)$

The order of all the nodes is 3 and there are 4 nodes. Then there shall exist $m_{n0}m_{0n}$ moments of the form $m_{30}m_{03}$.

Following the algorithm as described above, we can have the following product terms namely A^3C^3 and B^3D^3 which are both positive and shall not nullify each other. Hence we would have a non–zero invariant. Apparently the invariant for this graph is
$I = 2m_{03}^2 m_{30}^2 - 12m_{03}m_{12}m_{21}m_{30} + 8m_{03}m_{21}^3 + 8m_{12}^3 m_{30} - 6m_{12}^2 m_{21}^2$ which contains
the sum of A^3C^3 and B^3D^3 which is $2m_{03}^2 m_{30}^2$

4.2   Graphs with All Nodes of Even and Same Degree

Graphs having k nodes $A_1, A_2...A_k$ of equal and even degree n may result in two possibilities. They may result in a zero or they may result in an invariant with a pattern. Such non–zero invariants always consist of a term $m_{n/2\,n/2}$. The term shall exist only if the cross product terms C_{kj} are additive in nature. To determine if a graph has a zero invariant, we start generating product terms that only contain moments of the form $m_{n/2\,n/2}$. If the aggregate of such terms is zero, then the graph would result in zero. The pattern of equations as described here can be proved via induction.

The existence of the term $m_{n/2\,n/2}$ in the invariant can be proved easily by induction.

The degree n is even and the number of nodes k may be odd or even. Hence the number of edges in the graph would be $(n*k)/2$ which is certainly an even number.

Every node $A_1...A_k$ appears n times in the cross product function. If a term Ax is chosen from any n/2 terms of the total $(n*k)/2$ product terms then there remains $(n*k)/2 - n/2$ terms from which another term Ay may be chosen. Depending upon the number of nodes k, we can find several such combinations of product terms of degree n/2. Hence there always exists product terms of the form $A_1^{n/2} A_2^{n/2}...$ which contribute only moments of the form $m_{n/2,n/2}$.

Fig. 3. Graph of nodes with all vertices of even degree

Example 2:
Let the nodes in Fig. 3 which are 1, 2, 3 and 4 be named as A, B, C and D respectively. The cross product terms in Eq. (2) would form $(A-B)(B-C)(C-D)(D-A)$

The order of all the nodes is 2 and there are 4 nodes. Then there shall exist $m_{n/2,n/2}$ moments of the form m_{11} and each such product term will have four copies of m_{11} since there are four nodes.From the above expression ABCD is a product term of the form $m_{11} \times m_{11} \times m_{11} \times m_{11}$. There is yet another product term ABCD but it is positive and hence the invariant is non–zero. Apparently the invariant for this graph is $I = 2m_{02}^2 m_{20}^2 - 4m_{02}m_{11}^2 m_{20} + 2m_{11}^4$ which also contains the term 2ABCD which is $2m_{11}^4$

Establishing the cross product expression as in Eq. (2) shall be preferably written as an *Euler's circuit* to enable easier determination of the $m_{n/2,n/2}$ product terms although this is not mandatory.

Euler's theorem 2: A graph of all even order nodes will definitely have an Euler circuit.

4.3   Graphs with Nodes of Different Degrees

An important characteristic of the graphs generated to find moment invariant functions is that the function will always contain the moment of the highest order. If this does not happen then the graph does not serve the process of identifying the invariants of high orders. From this theory we start generating product terms from the nodes of the highest degree in the function (1). If the aggregate of the terms results in a zero then the graph can be eliminated and otherwise the remaining moments are estimated.

Fig. 4. Graph of nodes with vertices of different degrees

Example 3:

Let the nodes in Fig. 4 which are 1, 2, 3, 4, 5 and 6 be named as A, B, C, D, E, and F respectively. The cross product terms in Eq. (2) would form

$$(A - B)\,(C - B)(E - B)\,(C - D)(E - F)$$

The highest order belongs to the node 2 with an order of 3. From above expression we can see the terms $-B3CE$, $-B3DF$ which are terms involving C, E of order 2 and D,F of order 1 respectively and do not nullify each other. We also have B3CF and B3DE which are symmetric but both positive and they do not nullify each other. Apparently the invariant for this graph turns out to be

$$
\begin{aligned}
I\ =\ &2m_{21}m_{01}^3m_{11}m_{20} - m_{30}m_{01}^3m_{11}^2 - m_{12}m_{01}^3m_{20}^2 + 2m_{30}m_{01}^2m_{02}m_{10}m_{11} \\
&- 2m_{21}m_{01}^2m_{02}m_{10}m_{20} - m_{21}m_{01}^2m_{10}m_{11}^2 + m_{03}m_{10}^2m_{10}m_{20}^2 - m_{30}m_{01}m_{02}^2m_{10}^2 \\
&+ 2m_{12}m_{01}m_{02}m_{10}^2m_{20} + m_{12}m_{01}m_{10}^2m_{11}^2 + m_{03}m_{10}^3m_{11}^2 \\
&- 2m_{03}m_{01}m_{10}^2m_{11}m_{20} + m_{21}m_{02}^2m_{10}^3 - 2m_{12}m_{02}m_{10}^3m_{11}
\end{aligned}
$$

In the above invariant we can see that the terms corresponding to B^3CF and B^3DE are additive which is $2m_{30}m_{01}^2m_{02}m_{10}m_{11}$ in the invariant expression. The terms corresponding to $-B^3CE$ which is $-m_{03}m_{01}^3m_{11}^2$ and $-B^3DF$ which is $-m_{30}m_{01}m_{02}^2m_{10}^2$ are singular with no alternatives to nullify these terms

5   Performance Analysis and Discussion

The algorithm proposed in this paper shall improve the speed of generating moment invariants by eliminating the zero invariants at a faster rate. The graph in example 1 utilized 2 out of 64 product terms to ensure non-zero invariant, before the invariant function can be computed. Similarly, example 2 needed 2 out of 8 product terms to ensure that the graph generates non–zero invariant function. In example 3 the graph requires 4 out of 32 product terms to ensure that the graph is non–zero.

We observe that the number of product terms generated to determine a zero generating graph is exponentially smaller than generating all the product terms. Hence we understand that the proposed algorithm improves the process of finding non–zero moment invariant functions.

6   Conclusion

In this paper, we have explained on the importance of geometric moment invariants and their use in various areas of image processing. We have discussed the issues in graph based method that is used to generate geometric moment invariant functions. We have proposed an algorithm whereby we can eliminate the zero invariant producing graphs with reduced computational complexity enabling faster computation of invariants composed of higher order moments.

Acknowledgement. Authors would like to thanks Research Management Centre (RMC) for the research activities and Soft Computing Research Group (SCRG), Universiti Teknologi Malaysia (UTM) for making this study a success. We also like to thank The Ministry of Higher Education (MOHE) and Long Term Research Grant (LRGS).

References

1. Dai, X.B., Zhang, H., Shu, H.Z., Luo, L.M.: Image Recognition by Combined Invariants of Legendre Moment. In: Proc. IEEE International Conference on Information and Automation, pp. 1793–1798 (2010)
2. Flusser, J., Suk, T., Zitová, B.: Moments and Moment Invariants in Pattern Recognition © 2009. John Wiley & Sons, Ltd (2009) ISBN: 978-0-470-69987-4
3. Mukundan, R., Ramakrishnan, K.R.: Moment Functions in Image Analysis: Theory and Applications, p. 9
4. Flusser, J., Suk, T., Saic, S.: Recognition of Blurred Images by the Method of Moments. IEEE Trans. Image Proc. 5, 87–92 (1996)
5. Sivaramakrishna, R., Shashidhar, N.S.: Hu's Moment Invariants: How Invariant are They under Skew and Perspective Transformations? In: Proc. WESCANEX 1997: Communications, Power and Computing Conference, Winnipeg, Man, Canada, pp. 292–295 (1997)
6. Suk, T., Flusser, J.: On the Independence of Rotation Moment Invariants. Pattern Recognition 33, 1405–1410 (2000)
7. Flusser, J., Suk, T.: Rotation Moment Invariants for Recognition of Symmetric Objects. IEEE Trans. Image Proc. 15, 3784–3790 (2006)
8. Suk, T., Flusser, J.: Affine Moment Invariants Generated by Automated Solution of the Equations. In: 19th International Conference on Pattern Recognition, ICPR 2008, pp. 1–4 (2008), doi: 10.1109/ICPR.2008.4761221
9. Shamsuddin, S.M., Sulaiman, M.N., Darus, M.: Invarianceness of Higher Order Centralised Scaled-invariants Undergo Basic Transformations. International Journal of Computer Mathematics 79, 39–48 (2002)
10. Suk, T., Flusser, J.: Affine Moment Invariants Generated by Graph Method. Pattern Recognition 44(9), 2047–2056 (2010)
11. Mu, H.B., Qi, D.W.: Pattern Recognition of Wood Defects Types Based on Hu Invariant Moments. In: 2nd International Congress on Image and Signal Processing, CISP 2009, Tianjin, pp. 1–5 (2009)
12. Zunic, J., Hirota, K., Rosin, P.L.: A Hu Moment Invariant as a Shape Circularitymeasure. Pattern Recognition, 47–57 (2010)
13. Sheela, S.V., Vijaya, P.A.: Non-linear Classification for Iris patterns. In: Proc. Multimedia Computing and Systems (ICMCS), 2011 International Conference Ouarzazate, Morocco, pp. 1–5 (2011)

MutualCascade Method for Pedestrian Detection

Yanwen Chong[1,2], Qingquan Li[1,2], Hulin Kuang[1,2,3], and Chun-Hou Zheng[4]

[1] State Key Laboratory for Information Engineering in Surveying, Mapping and Remote Sensing, Wuhan University, 129 Luoyu Road, Wuhan 430079, China
[2] Engineering Research Center for Spatio-Temporal Data Smart Acquisition and Application, Ministry of Education of China, 129 Luoyu Road, Wuhan 430079, China
[3] School of electronic information, WuHan University, Wuhan 430072, China
[4] College of Electrical Engineering and Automation, Anhui University, Hefei, Anhui 230039, China
{ywchong,qqli,hlkuang,ywchong}@whu.edu.cn

Abstract. An effective and efficient feature selection method based on Gentle Adaboost (GAB) cascade and the Four Direction Feature (FDF), namely, MutualCascade, is proposed in this paper, which can be applied to the pedestrian detection problem in a single image. MutualCascade improves the classic method of cascade to remove irrelevant and redundant features. The mutual correlation coefficient is utilized as a criterion to determine whether a feature should be chosen or not. Experimental results show that the MutualCascade method is more efficient and effective than Voila and Jones' cascade and some other Adaboost-based method, and is comparable with HOG-based methods. It also demonstrates a higher performance compared with the state-of-the-art methods.

Keywords: FDF, GAB, MutualCascade, Pedestrian Detection, Feature Selection.

1 Introduction

Recently, pedestrian detection becomes one of the most interesting and potentially useful challenges for modern engineering [1-2]. Extracting more effective features and developing more powerful learning algorithms have always been the research focus for pedestrian detection problem.

The FDF is a relatively simple feature [3], can extract gradient feature of the pedestrian which is suitable for pedestrian detection.

The cascaded Adaboost (CAdaboost) has been treated as an example of the successful combination of feature selection and learning for rapid pedestrian detection. There is selection redundancy in both the Adaboost stage and the cascade stage. Therefore developing an algorithm that can select the less redundant, uncorrelated feature combination in the cascade stage is very necessary.

A novel, effective and efficient feature selection method based on GAB cascade and FDF, namely, MutualCascade, is proposed in this paper for the pedestrian detection problem in a single image. The mutual correlation coefficient is utilized as a criterion to

D.-S. Huang et al. (Eds.): ICIC 2012, CCIS 304, pp. 280–285, 2012.

determine whether a feature should be chosen or not, in this way, effective and un-correlated features can be selected.

2   The MutualCascade Algorithm

2.1   The Mutual Correlation

Correlation is a well-known similarity measurement between two random variables. The correlation coefficient is invariant to scaling and translation. Hence two features with different variances may have the same correlation coefficient [7]. Denoting a K-dimensional feature vector x_i as

$$x_i = [^1x_i, ..., ^Kx_i]$$ (1)

The mutual correlation for a feature pair x_i and x_j is defined as

$$r_{x_i,x_j} = \frac{\sum_{k=1}^{K} {}^kx_i {}^kx_j - K\overline{x_i}\overline{x_j}}{\sqrt{(\sum_{k=1}^{K} {}^kx_i^2 - K\overline{x_i}^2)(\sum_{k=1}^{K} {}^kx_j^2 - K\overline{x_j}^2)}}$$ (2)

Here $K\overline{x_i} = \sum_{k=1}^{K} {}^kx_i$

We compute the average of the absolute of all mutual correlations. The average R_{avg} can be used as a criterion to judge whether the feature can be selected.

$$R_{avg} = \frac{1}{T}\sum_{i=1}^{T} |r_{x_i,x_{T+1}}|$$ (3)

We define a threshold value Th which is an empirical value fixed by many experiments. We only select the features which meet $R_{avg} \leq Th$.

2.2   The Details of the MutualCascade Algorithm

The MutualCascade method is presented in detail in this section. Given n training samples, $\{(x_1,y_1),(x_2,y_2),...,(x_n,y_n)\}$, where x_i is one training ample, $y_i = \pm 1$ is the sample label. The Gentle Adaboost (GAB) is adopted in this paper. The classification function of the strong classifier $H_n(x)$ is denoted by formula (4).

$$H_n(x) = C(b_1(x), b_2(x), ... b_n(x))$$ (4)

Where $b_t(x) \in R$ is the base classifier corresponding to a selected feature, n is the number of the selected FDF features and $C(\cdot)$ is the classification function which expresses the relationship between the strong classifier and the features selected. Must be noted is that the base classifier in cascade stage is not equal to the weak classifier in Adaboost stage.

Inspired by MutualBoost [6], a novel feature selection method for the GAB cascade, namely, MutualCascade, is proposed in this paper. MutualCascade improves the classic cascade method in three aspects. The details of the MutualCascade algorithm based on the FDF are shown as Algorithm 1.

At the beginning of the GAB training process all features are sorted according to the error rate of each feature from low to high, which makes the following feature selection sequential and more convenient.

What's more, during feature selection we use a new selection mechanism: use mutual correlation coefficient as a criterion to judge whether to add a certain feature. Only when a feature whose average mutual correlation R_{avg} with each feature which has been selected meets $R_{avg} \leq Th$, the feature can be selected. In this way, we can select the more uncorrelated features. If this one cannot meet the condition, try the next one in the rest feature sequence which has not been tried, until the performance meets requirement.

In our proposed algorithm, a new updating mechanism for negative samples is utilized to ensure that the number of the negative samples in any level is the same as the original one during training. In order to select more representative features, we extract the FDF in all kinds of scales and at different locations in training samples, and build a feature pool in advance to make the cascade feature selection to be more convenient. The updating mechanism is as follows: empty the negative samples, we add not only the negative samples which are false positives in the stage, but also negative samples from the optional negative samples library that are false positives after being detected through all former stages.

Algorithm 1. The MutualCascade algorithm
Input: minimum acceptable detection rate, maximum acceptable false positive rate in ith level of the cascade
POS: set of positives
NEG: set of negatives
F_{target}: target overall false positive rate
f   : maximum acceptable false positive rate for each level of cascade
d   : minimum acceptable detection rate for each level of cascade
F(i): false positive rate in ith level of cascade
D(i): detection rate in the ith level of cascade
F_{total}: total false positive rate up to now
Initialize: i=0, D(0)=1.0,F(0)=1.0, F_{total}=1.0
While $F_{total} > F_{target}$

i=i+1 , F(i)=F(i-1) , n_i=0, n_i is the number of feature having been selected, also is the number of base classifier.
While F(i)>f

n_i=n_i+1 , extract n_i features to train a GAB strong classifiers, and test on the validation set to get detection rate DP, the false positive rate FP and the error rate EP.

Decrease the threshold for the classifier until DP>d , record the DP , FP, EP , threshold and the corresponding parameters of features, and F(i)=FP, D(i)=DP.

Sort all the features. Choose the feature with the minimum error rate as the first selected feature, the following features are selected in accordance with the selection mechanism.

End

Save the location, size, number of the feature combination selected and the classifiers, the threshold and other related parameters.

Update the negative samples.

$F_{total}=F_{total}\times F(i)$

End

Output: i-level cascade classifiers.

3   Experiments

3.1   The Computational Cost

By conducting some experiments, we know that the computational cost of one FDF (32*32) is 0.38 seconds, but the computational cost of one HOG (32*32) is 0.139 seconds, the FDF is faster than HOG, besides the number of HOG selected by SVM is more than the number of FDF selected by our method in general, so our method is faster than HOG-based method.

3.2   Comparison with the State Of Arts

We compare the classification results of our method with the state of the art on the INRIA, including HOG+SVM[8], v-HOG+CAdaboost[9], COV+Logitboost[10] and v-HOG+CLML [2] in Fig.1(a). Our method's points on curves in Fig. 1(a) are obtained from different cascade levels of the training processes. The curves of other methods are obtained from their reported results, the same as the following figures. CLML is a new method for pedestrian detection in images proposed in [2]. In the weak classifier learning, the L1-norm minimization learning (LML) and min–max penalty function model were presented. In [10], Tuzel presented a new algorithm to detect humans in still images utilizing covariance matrices as object descriptors and a novel approach for classifying points lying on a Riemannian manifold by incorporating the a priori information about the geometry of the space.

As shown in Fig.1(a), our method reaches a much better performance than the HOG-based results on the INRIA dataset. At the FPPW rate of 0^{-5}, our method achieves 2.5% miss rate which is the lowest among all methods.

In Fig.1(b), we compare the detector performance of our method with those of the state-of-the-art methods on the INRIA, including Shapelet , HOGLBP, PoseInv, VJ method, HOG and FirMine method which are all mentioned in [1].

As shown in Fig.1(b), our method reaches a much better performance than the other Adaboost-based method on the INRIA dataset, besides our method is compara- tive with the HOG method, and a slightly inferior to the HOGLBP method.

In Fig.2(a), we compare the detector performance of our method with those of the state-of-the-art methods on the Caltech.

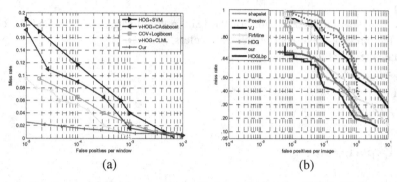

(a)   (b)

Fig. 1. (a) Result comparison of our method with the state of arts on INRIA, (b) Comparison of our method with the state of arts on INRIA test set

From Fig.2(a), we can see that our method is better than other methods which is not HOG-based, is comparative with the HOG method, and only a little inferior to the HOGLBP-based method.

By experiments, we know that the detection time of our method is 6.4 seconds (tested on 480*640 image). The detection time is dependent on the configuration of the computer and the optimization degree. All of our experiments are conducted on Matlab without optimization. If we use C, the time can be decreased. Therefore we cannot say our method has met the need of real-time detection.

3.3   Detection Performance On More Datasets

To demonstrate the detection performance of our method on more test datasets, we choose SDL-A [2], USC-C and INRIA. What shown in Fig.2(b) are the detection results on three datasets: the performance on USC-C is best, and that on SDL is worst with miss rate highest under the same FPPI.

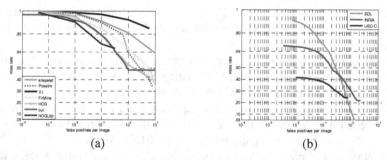

(a)   (b)

Fig. 2. (a) Comparison of our method with the state of arts on Caltech set, (b) Detection results on Sdl, USC-C and INRIA

4 Conclusions

Experimental results show the proposed MutualCascade method is more efficient and more effective than Adaboost-based methods and comparable with HOG-based methods, and can accurately detect upright pedestrians with different postures, under the complex background. But the propsed method is poor in detecting the non-upright pedestrians with shadings or occlusions and in large crowd.

Acknowledgments. This paper was supported by China Postdoctoral Science Foundation, LIESMARS Special Research Funding and the National Natural Science Foundation of China (40721001, 40830530).

References

1. Dollar, P., Wojek, C., Schiele, B., Perona, P.: Pedestrian Detection: an Evaluation of the State of the Art. Submission to IEEE Transactions on Pattern Analysis and Machine Intelligence (2011)
2. Xu, R., Jiao, J.B., Zhang, B.C., Ye, Q.X.: Pedestrian Detection in Images via Cascaded L1-norm Minimization Learning Method. Pattern Recognition 45, 2573–2583 (2012)
3. Soga, M., Hiratsuka, S.: Pedestrian Detection for a Near Infrared Imaging System. In: Proc. the 11th International IEEE Conference on Intelligent Transportation Systems, pp. 12–15 (2008)
4. Viola, P.A., Jones, M.J.: Robust Real-time Face Detection. Intl. Journal of Computer Vision 57(2), 137–154 (2004)
5. Hsu, H.H., Hsieh, C.W.: Feature Selection via Correlation Coefficient Clustering. Journal of Software 5(12), 1371–1377 (2010)
6. Shen, L.L., Bai, L.: MutualBoost Learning for Selecting Gabor Features for Face Recognition. Pattern Recognition Letters 27, 1758–1767 (2006)
7. Haindl, M., Somol, P., Ververidis, D., Kotropoulos, C.: Feature Selection Based on Mutual Correlation. In: Martínez-Trinidad, J.F., Carrasco Ochoa, J.A., Kittler, J. (eds.) CIARP 2006. LNCS, vol. 4225, pp. 569–577. Springer, Heidelberg (2006)
8. Dalal, N., Triggs, B.: Histograms of Oriented Gradients for Human Detection. In: Proceedings of the IEEE Conference on Computer Vision and Pattern Recognition, vol. 1, pp. 886–893 (2005)
9. Zhu, Q., Avidan, S., Yeh, M.C., Cheng, K.T.: Fast Human Detection using a Cascade of Histograms of Oriented Gradients. In: Proceedings of the IEEE Conference on Computer Vision and Pattern Recognition, vol. 2, pp. 1491–1498 (2006)
10. Tuzel, O., Porikli, F., Meer, P.: Human Detection via Classification on Riemannian Riemannian Manifolds. In: Proceedings of the IEEE Conference on Computer Vision and Pattern Recognition, pp. 1–8 (2007)

Super-Resolution Restoration of MMW Image
Using Sparse Representation Based on Couple Dictionaries

Li Shang[1,2], Yan Zhou[1,3], Liu Tao[1], and Zhan-li Sun[4]

[1] Department of Electronic Information Engineering, Suzhou Vocational University,
Suzhou 215104, Jiangsu, China
[2] Department of Automation, University of Science and Technology of China, Anhui 230026,
Hefei, China
[3] School of Electronics and Information Engineering, Soochow University, Suzhou,
Jiangsu 215006, China
[4] College of Electrical Engineering and Automation, Anhui University, Hefei, China
{sl0930,zhy,lt}@jssvc.edu.cn, zhlsun2006@yahoo.com.cn

Abstract. This paper addresses the problem of the super-resolution restoration
of a single millimeter wave image using sparse representation based on couple
dictionary training. Utilizing the coefficients of the sparse representation of
each low-resolution image patch, the high-resolution image patches can be generated, further, the low resolution image can be reconstructed well. The quality
of a restoration MMW image was measured by the relative single noise ratio
(RSNR. Compared with image restoration results of bicubic, experimental results prove that the sparse representation is effective in the super-resolution restoration of MMW.

Keywords: Millimeter wave image, Super-resolution, Image restoration, Sparse
representation, Couple dictionary.

1 Introduction

To obtain the high-resolution MMW image, some super-resolution methods were ex-
plored, such as the approaches of Lucy-Richardson (L-R) [1], maximum a-posteriori
(MAP) under generic image priors [2-3], maximum likelihood estimation (ML) [4] and
bilateral total variation (BTV) [5] and so on. However, the performance of these reconstruction based super-resolution algorithms degrades rapidly when there are not enough
low resolution images to constrain the solution, as in the extreme case of only a single
low-resolution input image [6], so, they were not suitable to process the single MMW
image. While as a strong and reliable model, sparse representation over redundant dictionary has been testified efficiently in super-resolution restoration of a single image
[2, 7-8]. This algorithm can ensure that linear relationships among high-resolution signals can be precisely recovered from their low-dimensional projections. Based on this,
the MMW image super-resolution restoration using sparse representation is discussed in
this paper. Here, the couple dictionaries responding to low- and high-resolution image
patches are learned by using fast sparse coding. The calculated sparse representation

D.-S. Huang et al. (Eds.): ICIC 2012, CCIS 304, pp. 286–291, 2012.
© Springer-Verlag Berlin Heidelberg 2012

adaptively selects the most relevant patches in the dictionary to best represent each patch of the given low-resolution images [2]. Here, using the sparse coefficients of low-resolution image patches and the high-resolution dictionary, the task of MMW image super-resolution can be implemented successfully.

2   Basic Idea of Sparse Representation

Let $D \in \Re^{N \times K}$ be an overcomplete dictionary of K prototype signal-atoms, and suppose a signal $x \in \Re^N$ can be represented as a sparse linear combination of these atoms [8]. Thus, the signal x can be written as $x = Ds$, or approximate $x \approx Ds$, satisfying $\|x - Ds\|_p \le \varepsilon$, where $s \in \Re^K$ is a vector with very few ($<< K$) nonzero entries [8]. This sparsest representation is the solution of either

$$\left(p_{0,\varepsilon}\right) \quad \min_s \|s\|_0 \quad subject \quad to \quad \|x - Ds\|_2 \le \varepsilon \ . \tag{1}$$

where $\|\cdot\|_0$ is the l^0 norm, counting the nonzero entries of a vector.

In practice, only a small set of measurements y of x was observed, which was described as follows:

$$y = Lx = LDs \ . \tag{2}$$

where $L \in \Re^{M \times N}$ with $M < N$ is a projection matrix. In the super-resolution context, x is a high-resolution image (patch), and y is its low-resolution version. If D is overcomplete, the equation $x = Ds$ is underdetermined for the unknown s, and the equation $y = LDs$ is even more dramatically underdetermined [8].

3   Image Super-Resolution from Sparsity

3.1   Two Constraints on Super-Resolution

The goal of the signal-image super-resolution is to recover a higher resolution image X of the same scene from a given low-resolution image Y. To solve this ill-posed problem, two constraints, called Reconstruction constraint and sparsity prior are modeled. Reconstruction constraint requires that the recovered X should be consistent with the input Y with respect to the image observation, and sparsity prior assumes that the high-resolution image patches can be sparsely represented in an appropriately chosen overcomplete dictionary and that their sparse representations can be recovered from the low-resolution observation.

3.2   The Optimized Problem of Sparse Representation

Yang et al proposed the super-resolution image reconstruction method based on sparse representation [8]. In this method, the high- and low-resolution image patches were connected by a dictionary pair, called low-resolution dictionary D_l and high-resolution dictionary D_h. For each input low-resolution patch y, a sparse representation with respect to D_l is found. The corresponding high-resolution patches D_h will be combined according to these coefficients to generate the output high-resolution patch x. Assumed that the high- and low-resolution samples are denoted by X_h and X_l, and considering the matrix form, the object function is written as follows:

$$\{D_h^*, D_l^*, S^*\} = \arg \min_{D_h, D_l, S} \left\{ \|X_h - D_h S\|_2^2 + \|X_l - D_l S\|_2^2 + \beta \|S\|_1 \right\} . \tag{3}$$

where the parameter β balances sparsity of the solution and fidelity of the approximation to y. To guarantee the compatibility between adjacent patches, Yang et al modified the optimization problem of Equation (3), which is written as follows [8]

$$\min_s \left\{ \frac{1}{2} \left\| \begin{bmatrix} Fy \\ \beta x_h \end{bmatrix} - \begin{bmatrix} FD_l \\ \beta PD_h \end{bmatrix} \cdot s \right\|_2^2 + \lambda \|s\|_1 \right\} = \left\{ \frac{1}{2} \|\tilde{D}s - \tilde{y}\|_2^2 + \lambda \|s\|_1 \right\} . \tag{4}$$

where F is a feature extraction operator. The role of F in $\|Fy - FD_l s\|_2^2$ is to provide a perceptually meaningful constraint on how closely the coefficients s must approximate y (here Fy means the low-resolution image patch). The parameter β controls the tradeoff between matching the low-resolution input and finding a high-resolution patch that is compatible with its neighbors. Given the optimal solution s^*, the high-resolution patch can be reconstructed as $x = D_h s^*$, and the patch x is put into the high-resolution image X_0. Using back-projection, the closest image to X_0 that satisfies the reconstruction constraint formula $Y = HX$ is as follows [8]:

$$X^* = \arg \min_X \left\{ \frac{1}{2} \|Y - HX\|^2 + c \|X - X_0\|_2^2 \right\} . \tag{5}$$

3.3   The Couple Dictionary Learning

The individual sparse coding problems in the high- and low-resolution patch spaces are written as follows :

$$\begin{cases} D_h = \arg \min_{D_h, S} \frac{1}{2} \|X_h - D_h S\|_2^2 + \lambda \|S\|_1 \\ D_l = \arg \min_{D_l, S} \frac{1}{2} \|X_l - D_l S\|_2^2 + \lambda \|S\|_1 \end{cases} . \tag{6}$$

Let $X_c = \left[X^h / \sqrt{K_h} ; X^l / \sqrt{K_l} \right]$ and $D_c = \left[D_h / \sqrt{K_h} ; D_l / \sqrt{K_l} \right]$, where K_h and K_l are the dimensions of the high- and low-resolution image patches in vector form, the Equation (6) can be written as

$$\min_{D_h, D_h, S} \| X_c - D_c S \|_2^2 + \lambda \left(\frac{1}{K_h} + \frac{1}{K_l} \right) \| S \|_1 . \tag{7}$$

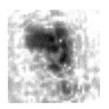

(a) Original image   (b) MMW image

Fig. 1. The original image and its MMW image

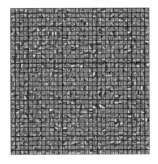
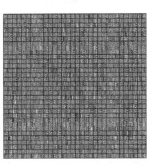

(a) High-resolution dictionary   (b) Low-resolution dictionary

Fig. 2. Couple dictionaries with 1024. (a) High-resolution dictionary. (b) Low-resolution dictionary.

4   Experimental Results and Analysis

In test, the generic natural images with different size were selected as training images, downloaded from benchmark image database. The object of MMW imaging system and its MMW image were shown in Fig.1. In test, the dictionary size is 1024. The length of each atom in the high-resolution dictionary and the low-resolution dictionary is 81 and144. The learned high- and low-resolution dictionary was shown in Fig.2 respectively.

    Utilized the super-resolution image restoration method in Subsection 3, the restoration task of low-resolution images can be implemented, and the restoration results were shown in Fig.3 (a). At the same time, restoration results obtained by the bicubic were shown in Fig.3 (b). However, it is difficult to measure the restored MMW image only with naked eyes. So, the relative single noise ratio (RSNR) and the image bias (denoted by Svar) were used, which are calculated by the following formula:

$$
\begin{cases}
\mathrm{RSNR} = \dfrac{1}{\sqrt{NM}} \left[\sum_{i=1}^{N}\sum_{j=1}^{M} f(i,j) \right] \Big/ \sqrt{\sum_{i=1}^{N}\sum_{j=1}^{M} \left[f(i,j) - \overline{f}(i,j) \right]^2} \\
\mathrm{Svar} = \sqrt{\sum_{i=1}^{N}\sum_{j=1}^{M} \left[f(i,j) - \overline{f}(i,j) \right]^2} \Big/ \sqrt{NM}
\end{cases}
\tag{8}
$$

where $f(i,j)$ denotes an image with the size of $N \times M$, and $\overline{f}(i,j)$ denotes the mean of this image. The values of RSNR and Svar of the MMW image were listed in Table 1. Clearly, the sparse representation method outperforms bicubic method, and this also proved that the former is efficient indeed in restoring the MMW image.

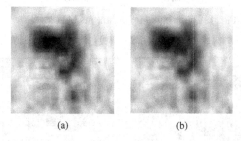

(a)   (b)

Fig. 3. Restoration results obtained by different algorithms. (a) Sparse representation method. (b) Bicubic method.

Table 1. RSNR values of MMW images restored by different methods

Methods	Restoration images		MMW image	
	Svar	RSNR	Svar	RSNR
Sparse representation	7.714	13.630	8.526	12.368
Bicubic	7.756	13.558		

5   Conclusions

In this paper, the super-resolution MMW image reconstruction method using sparse representation based on couple dictionary training is proposed. The learned process of couple dictionaries was implemented by using fast sparse coding algorithm. Utilizing the coefficients of the sparse representation of each low-resolution image patch, the high-resolution image patches can be generated, further, the low resolution image can be reconstructed well. Further, using values of RSNR and image bias (Svar) to measure restored the MMW image, experimental results forcefully testify that the sparse representation is indeed feasible in restoring the super-resolution MMW image.

Acknowledgments. This work was supported by the National Natural Science Foundation of China (No. 60970058), the Natural Science Foundation of Jiangsu Province of China (No. BK2009131), the Innovative Research Team of Suzhou Vocational University (No. 3100125), the "Qing Lan Project" of Jiangsu Province and the Innovative Achievement Foundation of Soochow Vocational University (No.2011SZDCC06).

References

1. Matthias, H., Christoph, S.: Learning Sparse Representations by Non-negative matrix Factorization and Sequential Come Programming. Journal of Machine Learning Research 7, 1385–1407 (2006)
2. Yang, J.C., Wright, J., Huang, T., et al.: Image Super-resolution Via Sparse Representation. IEEE Transactions on Image Processing 19, 2861–2873 (2010)
3. Rubinstein, R., Bruckstein, A.M., Elad, M., et al.: Dictionaries for Sparse Representation Modeling. IEEE Proceedings-Special Issue on Applications of Sparse Representation & Compressive Sensing 98, 1045–1057 (2010)
4. Sundareshan, M.K., Bhattacharjee, S.: Superresolution of Passive Millimeter-Wave Im-ages Using a Combined Maximum-likelihood Optimization and Projection-onto-convex-sets Approach. In: Proc. of SPIE Conf. on Passive Millimeter-wave Imaging Technology, Acrosense 2001, Orlando, FL., USA, vol. 4373, pp. 105–116 (2001)
5. Li, S.Z.: MAP Image Restoration and Segmentation by Constrained Optimization. IEEE Transactions on Image Processing 7, 1730–1735 (2002)
6. Baker, S., Kanade, T.: Limits on Super-resolution and How to Break Them. IEEE Transaction on Pattern Analysis and Machine Intelligence (TPAMI) 24, 1167–1183 (2002)
7. Zeyde, R., Elad, M., Protter, M.: On Single Image Scale-Up Using Sparse-Representations. In: Boissonnat, J.-D., Chenin, P., Cohen, A., Gout, C., Lyche, T., Mazure, M.-L., Schumaker, L. (eds.) Curves and Surfaces 2011. LNCS, vol. 6920, pp. 711–730. Springer, Heidelberg (2012)
8. Yang, J.C., Wright, J., Huang, T., et al.: Image Superresolution Via Sparse Representation of Raw Image Patches. In: Gjessing, S., Chepoi, V. (eds.) ECOOP 1988. LNCS, vol. 322, pp. 1–8. Springer, Heidelberg (1988)

New Structural Similarity Measure
for Image Comparison

Prashan Premaratne and Malin Premaratne[*]

School of Electrical Computer and Telecommunications Engineering,
University of Wollongong, North Wollongong, NSW, Australia
Department of Electrical and Computer Systems Engineering at Monash University,
Victoria, Australia
malin@ieee.org, prashan@uow.edu.au

Abstract. Subjective quality measures based on Human Visual System for images do not agree well with well-known metrics such as Mean Squared Error and Peak Signal to Noise Ratio. Recently, Structural Similarity Measure (SSIM) has received acclaim due to its ability to produce results on a par with Human Visual System. However, experimental results indicate that noise and blur seriously degrade the performance of the SSIM metric. Furthermore, despite SSIM's popularity, it does not provide adequate insight into how it handles 'structural similarity' of images. We propose a structural similarity measure based on approximation level of a given Discrete Wavelet Decomposition that evaluates moment invariants to capture the structural similarity with superior results over SSIM.

Keywords: Image similarity, structural similarity, moment invariants, SSIM, MISM.

1 Introduction

Comparing two images accurately to ascertain whether there is a match or not is essential for many image processing related tasks such as watermarking, compression and content retrieval. Age-old metrics such as Mean Squared Error (MSE) have been used for decades despite its inability to agree with human subjective analysis [1, 2]. Recently, light has been shed on a new metric that seems to agree with Human Visual System [2]. SSIM has been singled out due to its claim of superiority over the existing metrics [3, 4]. However, it has been observed that SSIM does not perform well with blurred images [4]. Since a blurred version of an image essentially contains the same structure, SSIM's inability to measure the structural similarity of blurred images raise an issue as to whether SSIM does truly look for the structural content. From our research, we have concluded that despite SSIM claim of superiority, its ability to compare similar structures is doubtful as will be demonstrated in the Experimental results section. We have developed a new metric that uses some of the concepts exploited by

---

[*] Corresponding author.

D.-S. Huang et al. (Eds.): ICIC 2012, CCIS 304, pp. 292–297, 2012.

SSIM. The new metric demonstrates better performance over SSIM in blurred images and images corrupted by Gaussian and Salt & Pepper noise.

2   Structural Similarity Measure (SSIM)

SSIM attempts to separate the task of similarity measurement of two images into luminance, contrast and structure [2]. Hence, a similarity measure is defined as:

$$SSIM(\mathbf{P_1}, \mathbf{P_2}) = l(\mathbf{P_1}, \mathbf{P_2}) \times c(\mathbf{P_1}, \mathbf{P_2}) \times s(\mathbf{P_1}, \mathbf{P_2}) \tag{1}$$

Where P1 and P2 are the two images being compared and l, c and s stand for luminosity, contrast and similarity measure. μ and σ are mean and standard deviation of the corresponding images and C1, C2 and C3 are constants used for the stability of equations when μ and σ are extremely small. SSIM defines μ, σ, σP1σP2, l, c, s as follows [3]:

$$\mu_{P1} = \frac{1}{M \times N} \sum_{y=0}^{M-1} \sum_{x=0}^{N-1} \mathbf{P_1}(x, y)$$

$$\sigma_{P1} = \sqrt{\frac{1}{(M \times N - 1)} \sum_{y=0}^{M-1} \sum_{x=0}^{N-1} (\mathbf{P_1}(x, y) - \mu_{P1})^2}$$

$$\sigma_{P1}\sigma_{P2} = \frac{1}{M \times N - 1} \sum_{y=0}^{M-1} \sum_{x=0}^{N-1} (\mathbf{P_1}(x, y) - \mu_{P1})(\mathbf{P_2}(x, y) - \mu_{P2})$$

$$l(\mathbf{P_1}, \mathbf{P_2}) = \frac{2\mu_{P1}\mu_{P2} + C_1}{\mu_{P1}^2 + \mu_{P2}^2 C_1}$$

$$c(\mathbf{P_1}, \mathbf{P_2}) = \frac{2\sigma_{P1}\sigma_{P2} + C_2}{\sigma_{P1}^2 + \sigma_{P2}^2 + C_2}$$

$$s(\mathbf{P_1}, \mathbf{P_2}) = \frac{\sigma_{P1P2} + C_3}{\sigma_{P1}\sigma_{P2} + C_3}$$

$$SSIM(\mathbf{P_1}, \mathbf{P_2}) = \frac{(2\mu_{P1}\mu_{P2} + C_1)(\sigma_{P1P2} + C_2)}{(\mu_{P1}^2 + \mu_{P2}^2 C_1)(\sigma_{P1}^2 + \sigma_{P2}^2 + C_2)} \tag{2}$$

(2) has been obtained using (1) when C3 = C2/2   for simplicity. However, it is difficult to understand how s(P1,P2) would represent structure as it is simply a function of cross correlation.

3   Moment Invariant Based Structural Similarity Measure (MISM)

The proposed approach here is very well understood as the approximation level of Discrete Wavelet Decomposition of an image results in revealing the structure of the images. The approximation levels remove detail successively and leave the structure intact even at deeper decomposition levels. At each successive level, structure of an image is maintained while removing the texture and detail. Once the image is reduced to an acceptable level, edge detection can be used to further sharpen the structure of the image. If a metric is produced using this structural information, it will truly capture the structural information and will be a valid measure to evaluate the structural integrity thereby making comparing images more meaningful.

Moment Invariants have been used extensively in identifying shapes or outlay of objects for many years [5, 6]. An image reduced to 16x16 or larger using Wavelet decomposition can be used to generate moment invariants to identify the structural makeup of an image. As our research indicates, matching at two such levels will

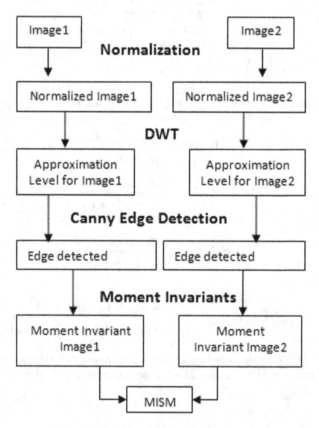

Fig. 1. MISM evaluation using two images

indicate very high similarity for an image undergone blurring or corruption with noise and can be verified visually. Hence the approach complies with Human Visual System and is far superior to MSE estimates.

MISM calculation is outlined in Fig.1. An image is normalized (divided by its own standard deviation) such that the two images being compared have unit standard deviation. An image reduced to an approximation level (usually larger than 16x16) and then edge detected using 'Canny' operator and first moment invariant ($\phi 1$) is calculated for the entire approximation [5]. Then the approximation level is divided into four quadrants and the first and second moments ($\phi i1$, $\phi i2$) are calculated for each

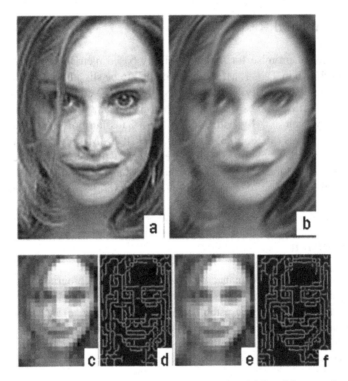

Fig. 2. (a) Original image of Ally, (**b**) Ally with motion blur, (**c**) Level 3 approximation of (**a**), (**d**) Edge detection of (**c**), (**e**) Level 3 approximation of (**b**) and (**f**) Edge detection of (**e**).

Table 1. Comparison of SSIM and MSIM for images

Image	SSIM	MISM
Ally with motion Blur	0.6285	0.8996
Ally with S&P noise	0.6607	0.9315
Ally with Gaussian noise	0.3560	0.9347
Lena	0.1542	0.5525

quadrant. These values are used to calculate the MISM for the entire image using the weights as shown in (3).

$$\text{MISM} = 1 - (0.1\frac{|\phi_1 - \phi_1'|}{\phi_1} + \sum_{i=1}^{4} 0.05\frac{|\phi_{i1} - \phi_{i1}'|}{\phi_{i1}} + \sum_{i=1}^{4} 0.15\frac{|\phi_{i2} - \phi_{i2}'|}{\phi_{i2}}) \quad (3)$$

Here ϕ' indicates the moment invariants of the second image. Fig. 2 indicates clearly that the structure is intact at low decomposition levels despite motion blur. This is also true for images corrupted with noise.

4   Experimental Results

MISM shows lot of promise for image similarity based metrics as well as for image matching. As shown in Tab. 1. MISM is developed to be slightly biased towards similarity rather than dissimilarity. Hence, Lena scores 0.1542 compared with Alice using SSIM where as MISM scores 0.5525. On the other hand, when comparing different versions of Ally such as Ally with motion blur, Gaussian noise and Salt & Pepper noise, SSIM measures 0.6285, 0.3560 and 0.6607. If SSIM truly compares structural similarity as the authors claim [3], all these images with the same structure should record a similar SSIM measure. MISM on the other hand, consistently record, 0.8996, 0.9347 and 0.9315 indicating that the proposed measure is certainly measuring the structural similarity.

5   Conclusion

We have evaluated the performance of the SSIM using the programming code made available by the original authors against our MISM and have demonstrated that image structural similarity can be best established accurately using MISM. In our research, we found that MISM is providing more insight to the image structure opposed to SSIM as it does not represent structure as claimed. MISM is very much comparable to SSIM with similar computer processing time.

References

1. Eskicioglu, A.M.: Quality measurement for monochrome compressed images in the past 25 years. In: Proc. IEEE Int. Conf. Acoustics, Speech, Signal Processing, vol. 4, pp. 1907–1910 (2000)
2. Girod, B.: What's wrong with mean-squared error. In: Digital Images and Human Vision, pp. 207–220. MIT press (1993)
3. Wang, Z., Bovik, A., Sheik, H.R., Simoncelli, E.P.: Image quality assessment: From error visibility to structural similarity. IEEE Trans. Image Process 4, 13(4), 1–14 (2004)

4. Chen, G.H., Yang, C.L., Po, L.M., Xie, S.L.: Edge-based structural similarity for image quality assessment. In: Proc. ICASSP 2006, vol. 2, pp. 933–936 (2006)
5. Premaratne, P., Nguyen, P., Consumer, Q.: electronics control system based on hand gesture moment invariants. IET Computer Vision 1(1), 35–41 (2007)
6. Premaratne, P., Ajaz, S., Premaratne, M.: Hand Gesture Tracking and Recognition System for Control of Consumer Electronics. In: Huang, D.-S., Gan, Y., Gupta, P., Gromiha, M.M. (eds.) ICIC 2011. LNCS (LNAI), vol. 6839, pp. 588–593. Springer, Heidelberg (2012)

Unmanned Aerial Vehicle-Aided Wireless Sensor Network Deployment System for Post-disaster Monitoring

Gurkan Tuna[1], Tarik Veli Mumcu[2], Kayhan Gulez[2],
Vehbi Cagri Gungor[3], and Hayrettin Erturk[4]

[1] Trakya University, Department of Computer Programming, Edirne, Turkey
[2] Yildiz Technical University, Electrical-Electronics Faculty, Control and Automation Eng.
Dept., Istanbul, Turkey
[3] Bahcesehir University, Faculty of Engineering, Department of Computer Engineering,
Istanbul, Turkey
gurkantuna@trakya.edu.tr, cagri.gungor@bahcesehir.edu.tr,
4hayrettinerturk@gmail.com,{tmumcu,gulez}@yildiz.edu.tr

Abstract. This paper presents design strategies of using unmanned aerial vehicles (UAVs) to deploy wireless sensor networks (WSNs) for post-disaster monitoring. Natural disasters are unforeseeable events which cannot be prevented. But some recovery procedures can be followed to minimize their effects. Post-disaster monitoring is important to estimate the effects of disasters, which in turn is used to determine recovery procedures to be followed. We propose an UAV-aided unattended WSN deployment system. The system is a post-disaster solution which can be used anywhere required. In this study, we mainly evaluate the efficiency of localization and navigation performance of the proposed system. Our simulation studies with an AirRobot quadrotor helicopter in Unified System for Automation and Robot Simulation (USARSim) simulation platform show that UAVs can be used to deploy WSNs after disasters to monitor environmental conditions. Future work includes implementing the system using a hexarotor helicopter.

Keywords: wireless sensor networks, unmanned aerial vehicles, localization and navigation systems, Global Positioning System, inertial navigation system, Kalman filter.

1 Introduction

Although natural disasters cannot be prevented, their effects can be minimized through proper warnings and post-disaster recovery procedures. After the disasters monitoring of environmental conditions is a vital process to prevent possible hazardous effects to human health.

Unmanned Aerial Vehicles (UAVs) are used for various civilian and non-civilian tasks including surveillance and reconnaissance operations, monitoring, and aerial photography. Another envisioned use of UAVs is the deployment of wireless sensor networks (WSNs).

D.-S. Huang et al. (Eds.): ICIC 2012, CCIS 304, pp. 298–305, 2012.
© Springer-Verlag Berlin Heidelberg 2012

WSNs are distributed systems of sensor nodes which are interconnected over wireless links [1], [2]. During a deployment phase, sensor nodes can be placed by using different attended/unattended methods such as such as dropping from an aerial vehicle [3], [4], delivering in an artillery shell, or rocket, and placing one by one by either a human or a mobile robot [5], [6], [7], [8]. Deployment phase is the first step of making WSNs operational. In this study, we propose an unattended autonomous WSN deployment system by using an UAV.

Different from existing studies in the literature which mostly explain theoretical background and practical uses of UAV-aided wireless sensor node deployment; in this paper we mainly investigate localization and navigation performance of an UAV responsible for WSN deployment. Since localization and navigation capabilities are the main requirements of all autonomous vehicles, successful implementation of the proposed system depends on these capabilities.

The paper is organized as follows. UAV aided WSN deployment system is explained in Section 2. Simulation studies are given in Section 3. Conclusions of the paper and future work are given in Section 4.

2   Unmanned Aerial Vehicle Aided WSN Deployment

In this study, we propose using UAVs for unattended deployment of wireless sensor nodes. In this system, an UAV follows a predetermined trajectory and drops wireless sensor nodes at predetermined intervals at predetermined locations. Due to several factors a location where a wireless sensor node is dropped for deployment cannot be determined accurately during flight multiple nodes are deployed together. In addition, some nodes may become damaged during deployment. Also communication cannot be established with some nodes since they are out of range. These are common problems in unattended sensor node deployments.

The localization and navigation system plays an important role in the design of the proposed system. It is based on the Kalman Filter (KF). To improve the system's performance we couple Global Positioning System (GPS) receiver and Inertial Navigation System (INS) sensors. Since GPS and INS sensors are common in aerial vehicles, in this study we preferred these sensors. GPS receivers provide absolute information of position and speed, and they do not need information about their previous states to produce a navigation solution [9], GPS signals carry information to determine a GPS receiver's position. The signal is composed of navigation data and a pseudo-random code [10]. GPS receivers cannot be used alone for navigation systems due to the requirement of having an open view of at least four GPS satellites and their low sample rates [10]. The INS consists of an inertial measurement unit (IMU) with an accelerometer and a gyro in addition to a navigation computer. It provides position, velocity and attitude angles. The accelerometer provides a non-gravitational acceleration, and the gyro keeps track of the orientation. Different from GPS receivers, INS systems are not subjected to interferences and reception limitations. But when they are used alone, some drifts are experienced. We combine the advantages of these sensors. An INS sensor keeps the track to the actual position, velocity and attitude with the aid of a GPS receiver. Long term accuracy of the GPS receiver is utilized to reduce the drifts in the INS outputs.

Fig. 1. Using UAVs to deploy WSNs

Centralized architectures designed for GPS-INS integrations generally provide more accurate solutions, but they require intensive computations in addition to requiring to access raw IMU and GPS data. Hence, considering the specifications of the UAV to be used in our field tests, we designed a loosely coupled direct feedback GPS-INS architecture shown in Fig. 2 using the GPS-INS integration architectures in [11] and [12]. The architecture shown in Fig. 2 involves three main steps. These steps are data preprocessing, filtering, and smoothing. This architecture estimates systematic errors in the IMU outputs. To do this it uses observations obtained from the GPS receiver. In case of GPS outages, very common in urban areas, the IMU error estimates obtained with KF based on the previously accumulated GPS data can compensate inertial navigation errors. In Fig. 2, x and y represent position coordinates. $\hat{x}$ and $\hat{y}$ are position estimations. The INS uses $\Delta\theta$ and Δv to calculate a position. Here, $\Delta\theta$ represents incremental angles derived from gyros, and Δv represents incremental velocities derived from accelerometers. The GPS receiver uses s and φ to yield a position. Here, s represents measured range, and φ represents carrier signal phase. C_s^n represents the rotation matrix from sensor to navigation frame.

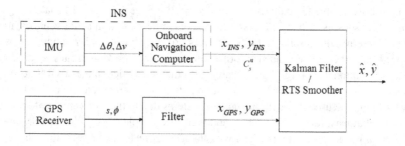

Fig. 2. GPS-INS integration architecture

2.1   Filtering

In the proposed navigation architecture, the observation delivered to the filter is actually the observed error of the inertial navigation, and the filter estimates the errors in this inertial navigation solution. Hence, the inertial navigation equations were linearised, and the filter took on a linear form shown in Fig. 2.

KF is a statistical recursive algorithm which operates recursively in two stages: Prediction and Update [13], [14]. KF provides an estimate of the states, $\hat{x}(k \mid k)$, at time k given all observations up to time k. $\hat{x}(k \mid k-1)$ shows the estimate of the state at time k given information up to time k-1, and is called the prediction. Under the assumption that observation and process noises are zero mean and uncorrelated, KF provides an optimal Minimum Mean Squared Error (MMSE). KF uses a landmark based map and In the prediction stage, the command $u(k)$ and the UAV motion model are utilized to estimate the UAV's location. Then, in the update stage, to update the landmark's position and to refine the estimation of the UAV's location, the new observation $z(k)$ from an exteroceptive sensor is used. Fig. 3 shows the steps of KF based localization and navigation approach.

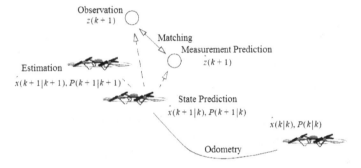

Fig. 3. The steps of KF based localization and navigation

In the GPS-INS integration architecture in Fig. 2, when an observation arrives, the filter estimates the error in the vehicle states. The observation is the observed error of the inertial navigation system. Whenever the GPS receiver provides position and velocity data, the observation error becomes

$$z(k)=\begin{bmatrix} z_{p(k)} \\ z_{v(k)} \end{bmatrix}=\begin{bmatrix} P_{INS}(k) - P_{GPS}(k) \\ V_{INS}(k) - V_{GPS}(k) \end{bmatrix} \tag{1}$$

When position and velocity errors are integrated, the observation model becomes

$$\begin{aligned} z(k)&=\begin{bmatrix} z_{p(k)} \\ z_{v(k)} \end{bmatrix}=\begin{bmatrix} P_{INS}(k) - P_{GPS}(k) \\ V_{INS}(k) - V_{GPS}(k) \end{bmatrix} \\ &=\begin{bmatrix} (P_T(k) + \delta P(k)) - (P_T(k) - v_p(k)) \\ (V_T(k) + \delta V(k)) - (V_T(k) - v_v(k)) \end{bmatrix} \\ &=\begin{bmatrix} \delta P(k) \\ \delta V(k) \end{bmatrix}+\begin{bmatrix} v_p(k) \\ v_V(k) \end{bmatrix} \end{aligned} \tag{2}$$

The observation is the error between the position and velocity obtained from the INS and that of the GPS receiver. The uncertainty in the observation is reflected by the noise of the observation of the GPS receiver. The architecture brings an advantage that tuning the filter is only based on the observation noise matrix.

2.2   Smoothing

Optimal fixed-interval smoothers provide optimal estimates using measurements from a fixed interval. There are several commonly used smoothing algorithms. In this study we preferred The Rauch-Tung-Striebel (RTS) smoother. RTS smoother is a fixed-interval two-pass smoothing algorithm which is commonly used for bridging GPS outages in the post-processing mode. In this algorithm, the standard Kalman estimate and covariance are computed in a forward pass, and then the smoothed quantities are computed in a backward pass.

Forward pass:

$$\hat{x}_{t+1|t} = A\hat{x}_{t|t}$$

$$P_{t+1|t} = AP_{t|t}A^T + Q$$

$$K_{t+1} = P_{t+1|t}C^T\left(CP_{t+1|t}C^T + R\right)^{-1}$$

$$\hat{x}_{t+1|t+1} = \hat{x}_{t+1|t} + K_{t+1}\left(y_{t+1} - C\hat{x}_{t+1|t}\right)$$

$$P_{t+1|t+1} = P_{t+1|t} - K_{t+1}CP_{t+1|t}$$

Backward pass:

$$L_t = P_{t|t}A^T P_{t+1|t}^{-1}$$

$$\hat{x}_{t|T} = \hat{x}_{t|t} + L_t\left(\hat{x}_{t+1|T} - \hat{x}_{t+1|t}\right) \tag{3}$$

$$P_{t|T} = P_{t|t} + L_t(P_{t+1|T} - P_{t+1|t})L_t^T$$

$\hat{x}_{t|T}$ is the optimal estimate of state at time t, $P_{t|T}$ is the measure of uncertainty, and L_t is gain matrix.

3   Performance Evaluations

In this study, we mainly concentrate on the performance of the localization and navigation system. To show the localization and navigation performance of an UAV-aided WSN deployment system, we performed simulation studies by using USARSim and Robot Operating System (ROS). We created a ROS interface to USARSim in Python. USARSim is based on the Unreal Tournament (UT) game engine, and is a simulation of robots and environments. USARSim serves both as a general purpose research tool and as the basis for the RoboCup rescue virtual robot competition [15], [16]. The interface we developed interfaces with the USARSim server, receives input from GPS and INS sensors of the UAV and sends commands to the UAV. We implemented INS and GPS integration by using the KF. Source codes of the simulation application are available upon request.

In our simulation studies, we used an AirRobot [17] autonomous quadrotor helicopter. In USARSim simulation platform, USARBot.AirRobot class is used to represent an AirRobot. Simulated AirRobot is equipped with one tilt-only color camera as the exteroceptive sensor by default. Since the system uses GPS and INS measurements to localize and navigate the AirRobot, we placed a GPS receiver and an INS on it. The GPS sensor finds the current AirRobot position in meters and converts it to latitude and longitude. Since USARSim worlds inherently do not have a GPS coordinate associated with them, we edited the USARBot.ini file and added ZeroZeroLocation inside the GPSSensor section to map a virtual location to a real one. The INS sensor simulates a physical INS sensor by using angular velocities and distance traveled [16]. During localization and navigation simulations we only calculated positional errors from the real trajectory. Positional errors from the East and North are shown in Fig. 5 (a) and Fig. 5 (b). Only first 250 seconds of the simulation are shown in the figures. When calculating the positional errors we compared the filter outputs with the ground truth values.

Fig. 4. The simulated AirRobot

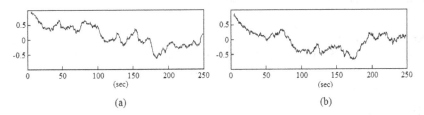

(a)   (b)

Fig. 5. (a) Trajectory Errors - X (in meters), (b) Trajectory Errors −Y (in meters)

Trajectory errors of the simulated UAV are around less than or around 0.5 m for X and Y. These minor deviations can be neglected in UAV-aided WSN deployment system. The results of our simulations show that an UAV can localize and navigate itself successfully during deployment when loaded with a priori map and a waypoint.

In addition to the simulations, we are planning to conduct field tests with an autonomous hexarotor helicopter "Flybox" shown in Fig. 6. The specifications of Flybox can be found in [18]. Since it runs Robot Operating System (ROS) [19] on Ubuntu, we are going to develop our application by using ROS.

Fig. 6. Flybox autonomous hexarotor helicopter

4   Conclusions

This paper focuses on using UAVs to deploy WSNs in case of disasters. Since disasters are mostly unforeseeable events, recovery procedures to minimize the effects of these events need to be planned. Monitoring of the disaster area is important to determining the recovery procedures. Proposed system takes the benefit of UAVs to establish a monitoring system consisted of wireless sensor nodes. Therefore a single UAV team can serve many cities in a small region. The proposed system has a practical use after disasters.

In this study, we specifically address efficiency of the system's localization and navigation aspects. The results of our simulation studies show that an UAV can follow a predetermined trajectory successfully to deploy a WSN for post-disaster monitoring. Future work includes implementing field tests.

Acknowledgement. This research has been supported by Yildiz Technical University Scientific Research Projects Coordination Department. Project Number: 2010-04-02-ODAP01 and Project Number: 2010-04-02-KAP05.

References

1. Akyildiz, I.F., Su, W., Sankarasubramaniam, Y., Cayirci, E.: Wireless Sensor Networks: a Survey. Computer Networks 38(4), 393–422 (2002)
2. Gungor, V.C., Hancke, G.P.: Industrial Wireless Sensor Networks: Challenges, Design Principles, and Technical Approaches. IEEE Transactions on Industrial Electronics 56(10), 4258–4265 (2009)

3. Ollero, A., Bernard, M., Civita, M.L., Hoesel, L.V., Marron, P.J., Lepley, J., Andres, E.D.: AWARE: Platform for Autonomous Self-deploying and Operation of Wireless Sensor-actuator Networks Cooperating with Unmanned Aerial Vehicles. In: Proceedings of the 2007 IEEE International Workshop on Safety, Security and Rescue Robotics, pp. 1–6 (2007)

4. Corke, P., Hrabar, S., Peterson, R., Rus, D., Saripalli, S., Sukhatme, G.: Autonomous Deployment and Repair of a Sensor Network using an Unmanned Aerial Vehicle. In: Proceedings of the 2004 IEEE International Conference on Robotics and Automation (ICRA), pp. 3603–3608 (2004)

5. Wang, Y., Wu, C.H.: Robot-Assisted Sensor Network Deployment and Data Collection. In: Proceedings of the 2007 IEEE International Symposium on Computational Intelligence in Robotics and Automation, pp. 467–472 (2007)

6. Younis, M., Akkaya, K.: Strategies and Techniques for Node Placement in Wireless Sensor Networks: A Survey. Ad Hoc Networks 6(4), 621–655 (2008)

7. Suzuki, T., Kawabata, K., Hada, Y., Tobe, Y.: Deployment of Wireless Sensor Network Using Mobile Robots to Construct an Intelligent Environment in a Multi-Robot Sensor Network. In: Advances in Service Robotics, pp. 315–328 (2008)

8. Suzuki, T., Sugizaki, R., Kawabata, K., Hada, Y., Tobe, Y.: Autonomous Deployment and Restoration of Sensor Network using Mobile Robots. International Journal of Advanced Robotic Systems 7(2), 105–114 (2010)

9. Guivant, J.E., Masson, F.R., Nebot, E.M.: Simultaneous Localization and Map Building Using Natural Features and Absolute Information. Robotics and Autonomous Systems 40(2-3), 79–90 (2002)

10. Huang, J., Tan, H.-S.: A Low-Order DGPS-Based Vehicle Positioning System Under Urban Environment. IEEE Transactions on Mechatronics 11(5), 567–575 (2006)

11. Sukkarieh, S.: Low Cost, High Integrity, Aided Inertial Navigation Systems for Autonomous Land Vehicles. Ph.D. Thesis, University of Sydney (2000)

12. Giremus, A., Doucet, A., Calmettes, V., Tourneret, J.-Y.: A Rao-Blackwellized Particle Filter for INS/GPS Integration. In: Proceedings of the 2004 IEEE International Conference on Acoustics Speech and Signal Processing, pp. 964–967 (2004)

13. Dissanayake, G., Newman, P., Clark, S., Durrant-Whyte, H.F., Csorba, M.: A Solution to the Simultaneous Localization and Map Building (SLAM) Problem. IEEE Transactions on Robotics and Automation 17(3), 229–241 (2001)

14. Thrun, S., Burgard, W., Fox, D.: Probabilistic Robotics. MIT Press, Cambridge (2005)

15. Carpin, S., Lewis, M., Wang, J., Balakirsky, S., Scrapper, C.: USARSim: a Robot Simulator for Research and Education. In: Proceedings of the 2007 IEEE Conference on Robotics and Automation, Roma, pp. 1400–1405 (2007)

16. USARSim (2011), `http://sourceforge.net/apps/mediiki/usarsim/index.php?title=Introduction`

17. AirRobot (2011), `http://www.airrobot.de/`

18. Flybox (2011), `http://www.skybotix.com/pdf/Skotix%20-%20FlyboXScientificFlyerV2.pdf`

19. ROS (2011), `http://www.ros.org/wiki/`

Geometrically Bounded Singularities and Joint Limits Prevention of a Three Dimensional Planar Redundant Manipulator Using Artificial Neural Networks

Samer Yahya[1], Mahmoud Moghavvemi[1,2], and Haider Abbas F. Almurib[3]

[1] Center of Research in Applied Electronics (CRAE),
University of Malaya, 50603 Kuala Lumpur, Malaysia
[2] Faculty of Electrical and Computer Engineering, University of Tehran, Iran
[3] Department of Electrical & Electronic Engineering,
The University of Nottingham Malaysia Campus

Abstract. This paper presents an Artificial Neural Network (ANN) based on the nonlinear dynamical control of a three-dimensional six degrees of freedom planar redundant manipulator. An ANN controller is used for the computation of fast inverse kinematics, and is effective on geometrically bounded singularities and joint limits prevention of redundant manipulators. The radial basis function neural network has been used to estimate the centrifugal and gravitational effects of the joints, when the end-effector follows a desired path.

1 Introduction

In order to take full advantage of the redundancy, various computational schemes have been developed. Most current researchers have utilized the pseudoinverse technique to formulate and resolve the redundancy by considering different optimization criteria, such as joint limits avoidance, singularity avoidance, and obstacle avoidance.

In the last few decades, artificial intelligent control using neural networks has undergone a rapid development to allow the design of a feedback controller for complex systems. Artificial intelligent control has proven to be very powerful techniques in the discipline of systems control, especially when the controlled system is difficult to mathematically model, or has large uncertainties and strong nonlinearities.

Due to the fact that radial basis function neural networks provide a powerful technique for generating multivariate nonlinear mapping, and because of their simple topological structure, the learning algorithm corresponds to the solution of a linear problem, so the training of the network is rapid [1]. In this article, the radial basis function neural networks have been used to estimate the centrifugal and gravitational effects of the joints, while the end-effector is following a desired path.

2 Kinematics of the Manipulator

A manipulator with n joints, whose link position variables are denoted by $\theta=[\theta_1, \theta_2,...,\theta_n]^T$, that are used to control m independent variables of the end-effector, can be

D.-S. Huang et al. (Eds.): ICIC 2012, CCIS 304, pp. 306–312, 2012.
© Springer-Verlag Berlin Heidelberg 2012

described by x=[x_1, x_2,..., x_m]^T ($m \leq 6$), and is described by the following kinematic equation [2]:

$$\dot{x} = J\dot{\theta} \tag{1}$$

If J is singular or rectangular with $m<n$, the vector $\dot{\theta}$ can be computed by the following commonly used method:

$$\dot{\theta} = J^+\dot{x} + (I - J^+J)\dot{\phi} \tag{2}$$

Where J^+ is the Moore-Penrose generalized inverse or pseudoinverse of the Jacobian. If J is fully ranked, the pseudoinverse J^+ is equal to $J^T(JJ^T)^{-1}$. The matrix I is an $n * n$ identity matrix, and $(I - J^+J)$ is the null space projection matrix. Vector $\dot{\phi}$ is an arbitrary joint velocity vector. The first term on the right, $J^+\dot{x}$, is the least-norm joint velocity solution. The second term, $(I - J^+J)\dot{\phi}$, the null space of J, is a homogeneous solution that is orthogonal to $J^+\dot{x}$.

For a desired end-effector trajectory, the homogeneous solution should be appropriately selected to improve the performance of the manipulator by optimizing a performance criterion $H(\theta)$, which is a scalar function of joint angles. In order to optimize $H(\theta)$ using the gradient projection method, the redundancy is resolved by substituting $k\nabla H(\theta)$ for $\dot{\phi}$ in the previous equation and rewriting it as

$$\dot{\theta} = J^+\dot{x} + k(I - J^+J)\nabla H(\theta) \tag{3}$$

Coefficient k is a real scalar constant, and $\nabla H(\theta)$, the gradient vector of $H(\theta)$.

The performance criterion $H(\theta)$ could be used for avoiding singular configurations, joint limits or obstacles [3]. To aid in the planning of motions that avoid singularities, several criteria have been proposed, which in a sense, measure the distance of any given configuration from singularity. Some of them are outlined as [4]:

Max H1(θ) where $H_1 = \sqrt{\det(JJ^T)}$ Manipulability index

Min H2(θ) where $H_2 = \dfrac{\sigma_{max}}{\sigma_{min}}$ Condition number

Another singularity avoidance approach for the planar redundant manipulators is presented in reference [5]. This method considers the angles between the adjacent links to be equal in length. Using this method, the interior singularities can be avoided, due to the fact that the angles between the adjacent links are equals.

All the mentioned singularity avoidance approaches have been tested, and a comparison between all of them is done for different paths using a planar manipulator with a length of links of [19,18,17,16,15] (in cm). The approach of [5] has proven to be very powerful in singularity avoidance; therefore, this approach is used in this work to calculate the inverse kinematics for the manipulator used in the simulation. Figure 1 shows the results of the singularity avoidance indexes values using the approach of ref [5], compared with the other approaches mentioned above.

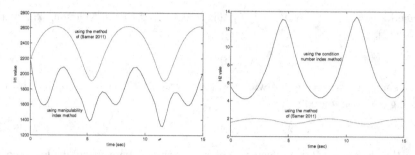

Fig. 1. Singularity avoidance indexes values using different approaches for the path x=14cos(t+3)+15 and y=14sin(t+3)-25

Joint limits avoidance is discussed in this section, as a second advantage for the approach used in this work. An index used in literature for utilizing redundancy to avoid joint limits for any redundant manipulators is considered next. This performance criterion is used in this work, as the joint limits index to calculate how far the manipulator is from its joint limits [2].

$$jl = \sum_{i=1}^{n} \frac{1}{4} \frac{\left(\theta_{i,\max} - \theta_{i,\min}\right)^2}{\left(\theta_{i,\max} - \theta_i\right)\left(\theta_i - \theta_{i,\min}\right)} \tag{4}$$

This index is calculated using the singularity avoidance approaches mentioned for the same cases of Fig.1 using the planar manipulator with length of links [19,18,17,16,15], to check the ability of these approaches for joint limits avoidance. It is considered that all the joints have the ability to move in the range (-170° to 170°), i.e. $\theta_{i,max}$ is (170°) and $\theta_{i,min}$ is (-170°). jl is equal to 1 in the middle of the joint limits, and automatically gives higher weight to the joints nearing their limits, which reaches infinity at the joint bounds. Because the joint limits index has smaller values using our method of ref [5] in fig. 2, this means that our method is proven to be more powerful in joint limits avoidance.

This method has another advantage as well; it reduces the number of motors needed to control the manipulator. In short, this method can be used to build a three dimensional six-degrees of freedom planar manipulator using three motors instead of six, the details of this design is discussed our reference [6].

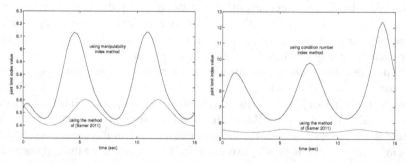

Fig. 2. Joint limits index values using different approaches for the path x=10cos(t+3)+15 and y=10sin(t+3)-25

3   Control of the Manipulator

The manipulator used in this work is a three-dimensional six degrees of freedom planar redundant manipulator. The dynamic motion equations can be written in matrix form as:

$$\tau = M(\theta)\ddot{\theta} + V(\theta,\dot{\theta}) + G(\theta) \tag{5}$$

The first term in this equation is the inertia forces, and the second term represents the Coriolis and centrifugal forces, while the third term gives the gravitational effects. This equation can be handled by the portioned controller scheme as follows:

$$\tau = \alpha\tau' + \beta \tag{6}$$

Where:

$$\alpha = M(\theta) \tag{7}$$

$$\beta = V(\theta,\dot{\theta}) + G(\theta) \tag{8}$$

with the servo law:

$$\tau' = \ddot{\theta}_d + K_v\dot{E} + K_p E \tag{9}$$

Where θ_d is the desired angle of the joint, and:

$$E = \theta_d - \theta \tag{10}$$

and yields:

$$\tau = M(\theta)(\ddot{\theta}_d + K_v\dot{E} + K_p E) \tag{11}$$

Using equation 5 through equation 9, it is shown that a closed-loop system is characterized by the error equation as follow:

$$\ddot{E} + K_v\dot{E} + K_p E = 0 \tag{12}$$

This equation represents the tracking error dynamics, which is stable as long as the derivative gain matrix K_v and the proportional gain matrix K_p are selected as positive definite. It is common to select the gain matrices K_v and K_p as diagonals, so that its stability is ensured as long as all the gains are selected positive. To make the system critically damped (yielding the fastest possible non-oscillatory response), the setting of the control gains is:

$$K_v = 2\sqrt{K_p} \tag{13}$$

As the degree of freedom increases, the computation of the dynamic equations increases as well. The term V takes most of the time comparing with the other terms of equation 5, which leads to difficulties in real time simulation. To make the control model faster, a neural network is used in this work for the computation of the terms $V+G$. The model used in this paper is shown in Fig. 3.

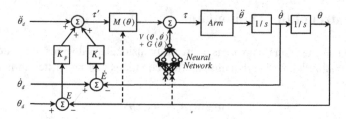

Fig. 3. The control model used in this work. (a) without NN, (b) with NN.

Neural networks (NN), due to their versatile features of learning capability, nonlinear mapping and parallel processing, have gained considerable popularity among the robotic control community. It should be remembered that using the method in [5], θ_3, θ_4, θ_5, and θ_6 are set to be equal. The neural networks model used in this work is a radial basis function neural network, with a mean squared error goal of 0.01 shown in Fig. 4. The MATLAB function 'newrb' is used in our network, as 'newrb' adds neurons to the hidden layer of a radial basis network until it meets the specified mean squared error goal. This network has six input-layer neurons for the current position of the joints of the manipulator $(\theta_1, \theta_2, \theta_3)$, and their velocities are $(\dot{\theta}_1, \dot{\theta}_2, \dot{\theta}_3)$, and six neurons in the output-layer for the centrifugal and gravitational effects of the joints $(V_1 + G_1, V_2 + G_2, V_3 + G_3, V_4 + G_4, V_5 + G_5, V_6 + G_6)$.

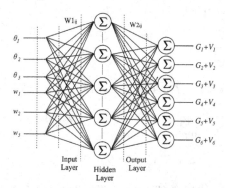

Fig. 4. The neural networks model used in this work

4   Simulation Results

In this paper, simulation studies have been performed on three dimensional six degrees of freedom planar manipulator, with lengths of links are as follows, $l=[19,18,17,16,15]^T$ cm, and the offset d_l is 21 cm, while the masses of links are $m=[1.5,2.26,0.72,0.68,0.64,0.6]^T$ kg. The system is critically damped with a closed-loop stiffness of 36. The desired joint angles path is defined as:

$$\theta_1(t) = -0.5\cos(4t), \quad \theta_2(t) = -\cos(2t)+1, \text{ and } \quad \theta_3(t) = -4\cos(t)+3$$

The model of Fig. 4 has been used to control the joints to follow the desired path. Fig. 5 shows the desired and measured manipulator joints angular positions.

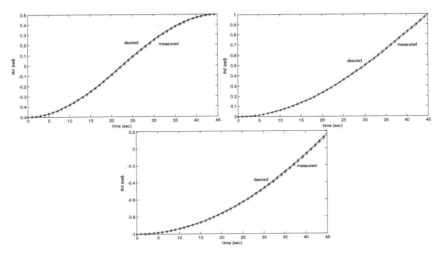

Fig. 5. The joint angular position using the model of Fig. 5

5   Conclusion

In this article, an artificial neural network approach for fast inverse kinematics and efficient singularities and joint limits avoidance for a three dimensional six degrees of freedom planar redundant manipulator has been presented. The radial basis function neural networks have been tested in this work for the control of the robotic manipulator, the results show that the neural networks with the radial basis function rule is very accurate for the manipulator control.

References

1. Zheng-ou, W., Tao, Z.: An Efficient Learning Algorithm for Improving Generalization Performance of Radial Basis Function Neural Networks. Neural Networks 13, 545–553 (2000)
2. Dubey, R.V., Euler, J.A., Babcock, S.M.: Real-Time Implementation of an Optimization Scheme for Seven-Degree-of-Freedom Redundant Manipulators. IEEE Transactions on Robotics and Automation 7(5), 579–588 (1991)
3. Khalil, W., Dombre, E.: Modeling, Identification and Control of Robots. Hermes Penton Ltd. (2002)
4. Samer, Y., Moghavvemi, M., Mohamed, A.F.: A Review of Singularity Avoidance in the Inverse Kinematics of Redundant Robot Manipulators. International Review of Automatic Control 4(5), 807–814 (2011)

5. Samer, Y., Moghavvemi, M., Mohamed, A.F.: Geometrical Approach of Planar Hyper-Redundant Manipulators: Inverse Kinematics, Path Planning and Workspace. Simulation Modelling Practice and Theory 19(1), 406–422 (2011)
6. Samer, Y., Moghavvemi, M., Mohamed, A.F.: Singularity Avoidance of a Six Degree of Freedom Three Dimensional Redundant Planar Manipulator. Computers and Mathematics with Applications (accepted 2012), doi:10.1016/j.camwa.2011.12.073

Float Cascade Method for Pedestrian Detection

Yanwen Chong[1,2], Qingquan Li[1,2], Hulin Kuang[1,2,3], and Chun-Hou Zheng[4]

[1] State Key Laboratory for Information Engineering in Surveying, Mapping and Remote Sensing,
Wuhan University, 129 Luoyu Road, Wuhan 430079, China
{ywchong,qqli,hlkuang}@whu.edu.cn
[2] Engineering Research Center for Spatio-Temporal Data Smart Acquisition and Application,
Ministry of Education of China, 129 Luoyu Road, Wuhan 430079, China
[3] School of Electronic Information, WuHan University , Bayi Road , Wuhan 430072 ,China
[4] College of Electrical Engineering and Automation, Anhui University, Hefei, Anhui 230039,
China
ywchong@whu.edu.cn

Abstract. A novel pedestrian detection method based on the Four Direction Features (FDF), called FloatCascade pedestrian detection, is proposed for the pedestrian detection problem, which can be applied to the pedestrian detection problem in a single image. The FDF can represent pedestrian well, and the computation cost is lower than the HOG's. FloatCascade applies the plus-l-minus-r method to select the effective cascade features to improve the detection performance, where l is fixed by experience, r is a float value which must be lower than l or quite to l. whether add features or not is decided by the detection rate, while whether subtract features or not is decided by error rate. Experimental results show that the MutualCascade method is more effective than Voila and Jones' cascade and some other Adaboost-based method, and is comparable with HOG-based methods. It also demonstrates a higher performance compared with the state-of-the-art methods.

Keywords: FDF, GAB, CAdaboost, FloatCascade, pedestrian detection.

1   Introduction

Recently, pedestrian detection becomes one of the most interesting and potentially useful challenges for modern engineering [1-2]. Extracting more effective features and developing more powerful learning algorithms have always been the research focus for pedestrian detection problem.

The FDF is a relatively simple feature [3], of which the computational complexity is between the Haar feature and HOG feature . The FDF can extract gradient feature of the pedestrian which is suitable for pedestrian detection.

The cascaded Adaboost (CAdaboost) has been treated as an example of the successful combination of feature selection and learning for rapid pedestrian detection. There is selection redundancy in both the Adaboost stage and the cascade stage [4, 5].

D.-S. Huang et al. (Eds.): ICIC 2012, CCIS 304, pp. 313–320, 2012.
© Springer-Verlag Berlin Heidelberg 2012

Therefore developing an algorithm that can select the less redundant features in the cascade stage is very necessary.

A novel wrapper method for FDF feature selection in CAdaboost is proposed in this paper, namely FloatCascade. It uses a kind of plus-l-minus-r [6] method in essence. Compared to the VJ cascade [4], the feature selected in the Floatcascade method is much more effective. The Floatcascade method ensure that the performance of the combination of the feature selected increases monotonically, by the plus-l-minus-r method, i.e. a backtrack mechanism, and can eliminate the redundancy of features to some extent. The thought of Floatcascade and FloatBoost are similar, but the feature selection does not happen in the same stage: in FloatBoost [5] the feature selection happens during the Adaboost stage, while Floatcascade selects features during cascade stage.

2   The FloatCascade Algorithm

Given n training samples, $\{(x_1,y_1),(x_2,y_2),...,(x_n,y_n)\}$, where x_i is one training ample, $y_i=\pm 1$ is the sample label. The Adaboost algorithm adopted in this paper is Gentle Adaboost (GAB). The classification function of the strong classifier $H_n(x)$ in the cascade is denoted by formula (1).

$$H_n(x)=C(b_1(x),b_2(x),...b_n(x)) \tag{1}$$

Where $b_n(x) \in R$ is the base classifier corresponding to a selected feature in cascade stage, n is the number of the selected FDF features and $C(\cdot)$ is the classification function which expresses the relationship between the strong classifier and the features selected.

The different expression form of the same strong classifier can give different guidance for feature selection in Adaboost stage or cascade stage. Formula (1) is used in this paper. The target of our algorithm for feature selection is that the classification performance should increase monotonously with the number of features selected increases.

Inspired by plus-l-minus-r [6], SFFS [7] FloatBoost [5], a new feature selection method, called FloatCascade in CAdaBoost is proposed to select the more effective feature combination. FloatCascade uses a kind of plus-l-minus-r method in essence, here l not only can be changed dynamically, but also can be set to a constant value, r is changed dynamically in accordance with detection performance constraints.

The feature selection of FloatCascade is divided into two steps: feature addition and feature subtraction. The judgment standard for adding features is whether the detection rate increases, and the judgment standard for subtracting features is whether the error rate decreases. Every cascade stage actually aims at getting a strong classifier whose performance meets the requirement through proper features selected.

Suppose that $H_n(x)$ stands for the strong classifier which has selected n features, the new classifier $H_{n+l}(x)$ after adding l features is shown as (3):

$$H_{n+l}(x)=H_n(x) \cup H_l(x)=C(b_1(x),b_2(x),...,b_{n+l}(x)) \qquad (2)$$

Where $H_l(x)$ is composed of l base classifiers which increases the detection rate DP progressively during the process of feature addition one by one. Only when the l feature addition step has been completed, the r feature subtraction step begins. The strong classifier $H_{n+l-r}(x)$ after removing r features is denoted as formula (4).

$$H_{n+l-r}(x)=H_{n+l}(x)-H_r(x)=C(b_1(x),b_2(x),...,b_{n+l-r}(x)) \qquad (3)$$

Where $H_r(x)$ is composed of the base classifiers which meets the demand that the error rate EP can be decreased progressively during the feature subtraction one by one.

The details of the FloatCascade algorithm based on the FDF are shown as Algorithm 1.

At the beginning of the GAB training process all features are sorted from low to high according to the error rate of each feature, which makes the following feature selection sequential and more convenient.

What's more, during feature selection in FloatCascade, a kind of plus-l-minus-r method is adopted in essence. In this way, the more effective features can be selected efficiently. If this one cannot meet the condition, try the next one in the rest feature sequence until the performance meets requirement.

In our proposed algorithm, a new updating mechanism for negative samples is utilized to ensure that the number of the negative samples in any level is the same as the original one during training. In order to provide more discriminative features, we extract the FDF in all kinds of scales and at different locations in training samples, and build a feature pool in advance to make the cascade feature selection to be more convenient. The updating mechanism is as follows: empty the negative samples, we add not only the negative samples which are false positives in the stage, but also negative samples from the optional negative samples library that are false positives after being detected through all former stages.

Algorithm 1. The FloatCascade algorithm

Input: minimum acceptable detection rate, maximum acceptable false positive rate in ith level of the cascade

POS: set of positives

NEG: set of negatives

Ftarget: target overall false positive rate

f   : maximum acccptable false positive rate for each level of cascade

d   : minimum acceptable detection rate for each level of cascade

F(i): false positive rate in ith level of cascade

D(i): detection rate in the ith level of cascade

Ftotal: total false positive rate up to now

n_i : the number of features had been selected, also the number of base classifiers

DP : detection rate

DP(ni): The detection rate of the collection of n_i features

FP :the false positive rate

EP: the error rate

EP(ni): The error rate of the collection of n_i features

$\forall EP(n_i-1)$: The error rate of any n_i-1 feature collection among the n_i features selected.

Initialize: $i=0$, $D(0)=1.0$, $F(0)=1.0$, $F_{total}=1.0$

While $F_{total} > F_{target}$

$i=i+1$, $F(i)=F(i-1)$, $n_i=0$.

While $F(i)>f$

(1) Calculating classification performance

(a) $n_i=n_i+1$, extract n_i features to train a GAB strong classifiers, and test on the validation set to get detection rate DP, the false positive rate FP and the error rate EP.

(b)Decrease the threshold for the classifier until $DP>d$, record the DP , FP, EP , threshold and the corresponding parameters of features, and $F(i)=FP$, $D(i)=DP$.

(c)Sort all features. Choose the feature with the minimum error rate as the first selected feature.

If $F(i) \leq f$ Complete this level.

(2) Adding l features

(a) $n_i=n_i+1$, add a feature in turn according to the error rate order from low to high every time. Training GAB with the n_i features. Record DP(ni), DP (ni-1), EP(ni) and EP (ni-1).

(b) if $DP(ni) \geq DP$ (ni-1)

       Add the feature, record related parameters.

else   Reject the feature, ni=ni-1, continue to select new features. Goto(2)(a)

(c)   until the number of features added has been up to l. Goto3(3)(a)

(3) Subtracting r features

(a) Subtract a feature from the n_i features to get the combination of n_i-1 features every time, train and record related parameters

(b) if $EP(n_i) \leq \forall EP(n_i-1)$

Do not subtract the n_ith feature, update the $F(i)$.

else

Choose the combination of n_i-1 features which owns the lowest error rate, remove the corresponding feature. Update $F(i)$.

(c) if $F(i) \leq f$

. Completed feature selection of this level.

else   Continue to add and delete features. Go to (3)(a)

End

Save the classifiers, and all related parameters of features.

Update the negative samples.

$F_{total}=F_{total} \times F(i)$

End

Output: i-level cascade classifiers.

3   Experiments and Analyses

3.1   Distribution of the Selected Features

In Fig.1, we present the number of the number of FDF at each level. From the Fig.1 we can see the number of FDF at each level is few. By conducting some experiments, we know that the computational cost of one FDF (32*32) is 0.38 seconds, but the computational cost of one HOG (32*32) is 0.139 seconds, the FDF is faster than HOG.

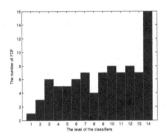

Fig. 1. The number of selected features at each level

From Fig.2, we can find that features selected by our method are multi-scale and sparse; meanwhile, each feature can represent some part of person, such as the head, the legs, the arms and shoulders.

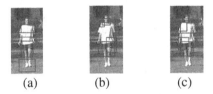

(a)   (b)   (c)

Fig. 2. (a)(b)(c) respectively show features selected in the second,4th and 10level

3.2   Comparison with the State of Arts

We compare the classification results of our method with the state of the art on the INRIA human test set, including HOG+SVM method [8], v-HOG+CAdaboost [9], the COV+Logitboost method [10] and the v-HOG+CLML [2], using miss rate tradeoff False Positives Per Window (FPPW) on a log scale in Fig.3. Our method's points on curves in Fig. 3 are obtained from different cascade levels of the training processes. The curves of other methods are obtained from their reported results.

As shown in Fig.3, our method reaches a much better performance than the HOG-based results on the INRIA dataset. Comparing with others at the FPPW rate of 10-5, our method achieves 2.7% miss rate, which is about 6.3% lower than the

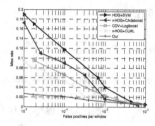

Fig. 3. The result comparison of our method with the state of arts on INRIA test set

v-HOG+CLML method, about 13.3% lower than the HOG+SVM method, about 9.3% lower than Zhu's and about 7.3% lower than Tuzel's.

In Fig. 4 we compare the detector performance of our method with those of the state-of-the-art methods on the INRIA pedestrian test set which are all mentioned in [1]. Our method's points on curves are obtained from detection results on INRIA test set. The curves of other methods are obtained from [1].

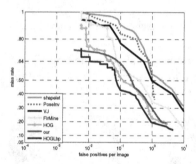

Fig. 4. The comparison of our method with the state of arts on INRIA test set

As shown in Fig. 4, our method reaches a much better performance than the other Adaboost-based method on the INRIA dataset, besides our method is comparable with the HOG method, and a slightly inferior to the HOGLBP method.

From some experiments, we can know that the detection time of our method is 5.8 seconds (tested on a 480*640 image). All of our experiments are conducted on Matlab 2009a without optimization, if we use C, the time can be decreased.

3.3   Detection Performance on More Datasets

To demonstrate the detection performance of our method on more test datasets, we choose SDL-A test set of 140 images [2], USC-C test set of 100 images and INRIA test set of 288 images. What shown in Fig.5 are the detection results on three datasets: the performance on USC-C is best, and that on SDL is worst with miss rate highest under the same FPPI.

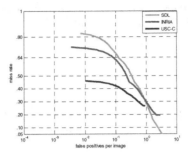

Fig. 5. Detection results on three datasets: Sdl, USC-C and INRIA

3.4   Detection Results Presentation

In Fig.6, some detection results of the FloatCascade classifiers on INRIA test data are presented. From the figure we can find that the FloatCascade classifiers can accurately detect upright pedestrians with different postures, under the complex background.

Fig. 6. Example of detection results of the FloatCascade classifier

4   Conclusion

A novel pedestrian detection method, called FloatCascade pedestrian detection, based on the Four Direction Features is proposed in this paper. FloatCascade, a new cascade method, applies the plus-l-minus-r method to select cascade features, chooses the more effective combination of features which can increase the detection rate and decrease the false positive rate effectively. Experimental results show that the Float
Cascade method can reach much better detection performance using less features than the state-of-the-art CAdaboost methods presented in this paper.

The proposed pedestrian detection method in the paper can accurately detect upright pedestrians with different postures, under the complex background. With the selected proper features and with application of the integral figure theory, the pedestrian detection time is shortened.

There still exists some deficiencies in the method of this paper: Firstly, though the selected features using the FloatCascade method is more effective than the VJ cascade, it is not the optimal combination of features because it does not consider the correlation among the features; Secondly, the method of this paper can detect the upright pedestrians without shading effectively, but is poor in detecting the non-upright pedestrians with shading; Finally, the method of this paper has poor performance for large crowd, which is need to be improved as well.

Acknowledgement. This paper was supported by China Postdoctoral Science Foundation, LIESMARS Special Research Funding and the National Natural Science Foundation of China (40721001, 40830530).

References

1. Dollar, P., Wojek, C., Schiele, B., Perona, P.: Pedestrian Detection: Evaluation of the State of the Art. IEEE Transactions on Pattern Analysis and Machine Intelligence 30(2), 60–80 (2011)
2. Xu, R., Jiao, J., Zhang, B., Ye, Q.: Pedestrian Detection in Images via Cascaded L1 Norm Minimization Learning Method. Pattern Recognition 45(3), 2573–2583 (2012)
3. Soga, M., Hiratsuka, S.: Pedestrian Detection for a Near Infrared Imaging System. In: Proc. the 11th International IEEE Conference on Intelligent Transportation Systems, pp. 12–15 (2008)
4. Viola, P.A., Jones, M.J.: Robust Real-Time Face Detection. Intl. Journal of Computer Vision 57(2), 137–154 (2004)
5. Li, S., Zhang, Z.: FloatBoost Learning and Statistical Face Detection. IEEE Trans. Pattern Analysis and Machine Intelligence 26(9), 1112–1123 (2004)
6. Kittler, J.: Feature Set Search Algorithm. Pattern Recognition in Practice, 41–60 (1980)
7. Pudil, P., Novovicova, J., Choakjarernwanit, N., Kittler, J.: A Comparative Evaluation of Floating Search Methods for Feature Selection. Technical Report VSSP-TR-5/92, University of Surrey, UK (1992)
8. Dalal, N., Triggs, B.: Histograms of Oriented Gradients for Human Detection. In: Proceedings of the IEEE Conference on Computer Vision and Pattern Recognition, vol. 1(3), pp. 886–893 (2005)
9. Zhu, Q., Avidan, S., Yeh, M., Cheng, K.T.: Fast Human Detection Using a Cascade of Histograms of Oriented Gradients. In: Proceedings of the IEEE Conference on Computer Vision and Pattern Recognition, vol. 2(3), pp. 1491–1498 (2006)
10. Tuzel, Q., Porikli, F., Meer, P.: Human Detection via Classification on Riemannian Manifolds. In: Proceedings of the IEEE Conference on Computer Vision and Pattern Recognition, pp. 1–8 (2007)

Particle Filter Based on Multiple Cues Fusion for Pedestrian Tracking

Yanwen Chong[1], Rong Chen[1], Qingquan Li[1], and Chun-Hou Zheng[2]

[1] State Key Laboratory for Information Engineering in Surveying,
Mapping and Remote Sensing, Wuhan University,
129 Luoyu Road, Wuhan 430079, China
{ywchong,chenrong,qqli}@whu.edu.cn
[2] College of Electrical Engineering and Automation,
Anhui University, Hefei, Anhui 230039, China
ywchong@whu.edu.cn

Abstract. A pedestrian tracking algorithm is proposed in this paper which combines color and edge features in particle filter framework to resolve the pedestrian tracking problem in the video set. The color feature tracking work well when the object has low object deformation, scale variation and some rotation, while the edge feature is robust to the target with similar color to its background. In the paper, color histogram (HC) and four direction features (FDF) of the tracking objects is utilized, and experiments demonstrate that pedestrian tracking with multiple features fusion have a good performance even when objects are occluded by other human bodies, shelters or have low discrimination to background.

Keywords: particle filter, tracking, color histogram, four direction features.

1   Introduction

Object tracking plays an important role in intelligent transportation, visual surveillance and public safety. Pedestrian tracking[1,2] is a special tracking problem with more challenges, as a body's movement has great freedom and high degree of nonlinearity, in addition, the body is non-rigid and has complex structure.

Color [3, 4] is a widely used feature for its robust to rotation scale invariant and computationally efficient; color tracking has an excellent job in the given video. Tracking algorithms based on single cue are satisfactory for some certain sequences, but they cannot work well when the brightness changes or target occluded by shelters or other human bodies. In this article we use the method of fusing color histogram and pedestrian contour cues, under condition that ensuring the tracking robustness and accuracy, we used the FDF features to calculate edge feature to reach the real-time pedestrian tracking, which is simpler than the popular HOG[5, 6] feature in calculation.

D.-S. Huang et al. (Eds.): ICIC 2012, CCIS 304, pp. 321–327, 2012.

2   Multiple Cues Algorithm

2.1   Color Cue

Color model[8] is widely used to represent non-rigid moving target for its robustness against deformation, rotation. Let $\{x_i, i = 1...n\}$ be the target candidate, y is centre in the current frame. The likelihood of color features is denoted as:

$$p_{color}(z \mid x) = \frac{1}{\sqrt{2\pi}\sigma_{color}} \exp\left(-\frac{d^2(p_y, q)}{2\sigma_{color}^2}\right) \tag{1}$$

where q is target model, p_y is candidate area, σ_{color} is the variance of color feature

Gaussian distribution, $d(p_y, q) = \sqrt{1 - \rho(\hat{p}(y), \hat{q})}$,and $\rho(\hat{p}(y), \hat{q}) = \sum_{u=1}^{m} \sqrt{\hat{p}_u(y)\hat{q}_u}$

is Bhattacharyya coefficient[10] which is used to measure the similarity between target model and candidate area.

2.2   Edge Cue

FDF feature is a relatively simple feature whose computational complexity is between the Haar feature and the HOG features[11] . The values of the original FDF features are averaged over M×N pixels, the final FDF vector is formed by concatenating the four-direction average gradient[10].

The likelihood of FDF is calculated similar with color, it is defined as (2)

$$p_{FDF}(z \mid x) = \frac{1}{\sqrt{2\pi}\sigma_{FDF}} \exp\left(-\frac{d^2(G, g)}{2\sigma_{FDF}^2}\right) \tag{2}$$

Where G is target model, g is candidate area, σ_{FDF} is the variance of Gaussian distribution, the likelihood function is $d(G, g) = \sqrt{1 - \rho(G, g)}$.

The feature evaluation procedure using particle filter is presented in Table 1.

3   Experiments

In this section, experiments with comparisons are carried out to validate the proposed feature combination algorithm. The implement of our algorithm based on mixed programming of VC and MATLAB, with the computer configuration as follows: Intel Core i3-2100 CPU 3.1HZ, Memory 3G. The experimental videos come from VIVID[13], CAVIAR[14], SDL[15] database.

Table 1. Multiple-cue particle filter algorithm

1. Initiate the confidence of each particle with equal value , where N is the number of particles;
2. For frame k=1, 2, 3, …
2.1 Select particles $x_k^i, i=1,2,\dots,N$ from the set S_{k-1} and propagate each sample from the set S_{k-1} by $S_k = AS_{k-1} + B\omega_{k-1}$
2.2 Update weight of particles
(a) Observe the color distributions and calculate it
(b) Calculate the Bhattacharyya coefficient and likelihood for color feature by Eq. (1)
(c) The likelihood of FDF is calculated similar with color's by Eq. (2);
(d)Calculate the likelihood of each particle using color histogram feature and FDF features as $\left\{ p(z_k \mid x_{k-1}^i) = \alpha p_{color}(z_k \mid x_{k-1}^i) + (1-\alpha) p_{FDF}(z_k \mid x_{k-1}^i) \right\}$, where α . is the weight of the color likelihood.
(e) Get the new value of weight $\omega_k(i) = \omega_{k-1}(i) * p(z_k \mid x_{k-1}^i)$ and normalizing obtain $\omega_k(i)$
2.3 Predict
Estimate the mean state;
2.4 Resampling
3. k=k+1: go to step 2 or end the tracking loop

3.1   Comparison with Single Cue Methods

We first consider a sequence from CARVIA tracking video set where we try to track a person with stripe T-shirt. Throughout the video, the target is occluded by people and walking around with rotation. These different phenomena observed through the video sequence exemplify the tracking effect of our proposed algorithm in the video with occlusion and rotation of the target object.

As the top and bottom of Fig. 1 respectively demonstrate, the HC-based and the FDF-based tracking may lead to inaccurate results due to considering single modalities. When tracking target is occluded, FDF-based method has a bad outcome and when video involves several pedestrians, it lose tracking totally. The color histogram (HC) method has a better performance when occlusion happens, but when tracking target has rotation or there are objects in the background which have similar color to the object of interest, the HC method starts tracking the wrong object. Our proposed method has better tracking results than using only one modality (Fig.1 bottom), tracked person is blocked in 287th frame and it soon recover tracking .In 640th, 730th and 938th frame, the target has continuous rotations about 180 degrees, the combined features method has a good performance for tracking.

In order to quantitatively evaluate the performance of proposed combined feature set, a criterion entitled the relative displacement error rates (DER) is used which is proposed in [7], is defined as (3)

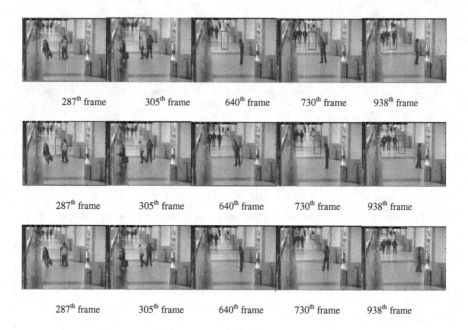

287th frame   305th frame   640th frame   730th frame   938th frame

287th frame   305th frame   640th frame   730th frame   938th frame

287th frame   305th frame   640th frame   730th frame   938th frame

Fig. 1. Top are Results of only FDF-based tracking method. Middle are Results of only color feature tracking method. Bottom are Results of our proposed tracking method based on combined HC and FDF features.

$$DER = \frac{\text{Displacement error between tracked object position and ground-truth}}{\text{Size of the object}} \quad (3)$$

The lower the average DER is, the better the tracking performance will be. The tracking results of HC-based method, FDF-based method and our proposed method are shown in Fig. 2. It can be seen that the DER of our method is lower than that of FDF-based tracking and HC-based tracking in almost the whole tracking process, and the tracking of our proposed method is more stable than the other two methods.

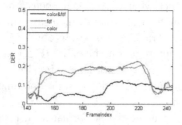

Fig. 2. DER of single cue method and multiple-cue method

3.2   Comparison with other Fusion Methods

In order to further validation our proposed approaches, the comparison is made between [7] and our algorithm. In [7], a combined HOG and HC feature method based on Kalman and particle filter is proposed. There are some quantitative experiments shown in Fig.3 and Fig.4 and the comparison result (the computation of average DER) is shown in Fig.5 qualitatively.

In the experiment shown in Fig. 3, the main challenges of tracking in this video sequence arise from partial occlusions of the object by other pedestrians. It can be seen that our proposed method obtain excellent tracking results. The target pedestrian, marked with red box, is tracked steadily throughout the whole duration and the blue box is the ground-truth.

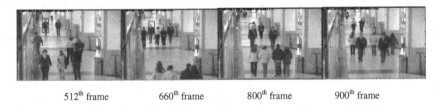

512th frame   660th frame   800th frame   900th frame

Fig. 3. Comparison of ground-truth with blue-rectangle and our tracking value with red-rectangle

The test video in Fig. 4 is from the VIVID set, and the target object is a small red jeep in grassland with the change of background and route, and camera zooming in and out. The Vehicle runs on straight road through the desert, and then turns at the end with long shadows. The tracking method combining FDF and HC cues has a good tracking reflected by the stable bounding box on the object.

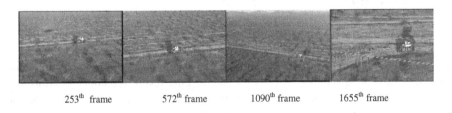

253th frame   572th frame   1090th frame   1655th frame

Fig. 4. Tracking results in changing backgrounds

It can be seen in Fig.5, the DER of three methods are about 0.05-0.15. The black curve which represents HOG and HC based on Kalman Filter has the biggest fluctuations during tracking, though the DER of our tracking algorithm is a little higher than HOG and HC based on Particle Filter tracking method, the curve has a much more stable trend and the tracking result is acceptable. Also FDF features used in our paper to calculate edge feature is simpler than the popular HOG feature in calculation, and the run time is shorter than that of HOG.

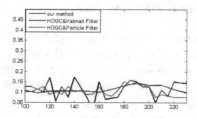

Fig. 5. Comparison of average DER among [16] and our proposed method

The algorithm is also tested on two people tracking in relatively simple environment. In the sequence from CASIA action database, two people are coming from the opposite direction of the road, they meet in the middle of the road and then go on their walking. As shown in Fig.6, in 114th frame the persons meet and in 173th frame they leave apart, the proposed algorithm is robust to occlusion and interference from two people wearing similar colored cloth to accomplish two similar pedestrians tracking task.

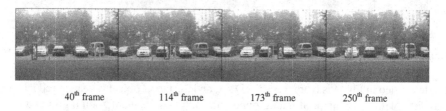

         40th frame   114th frame   173th frame   250th frame

Fig. 6. Two people tracking in relatively simple environment

4   Conclusion

In this article, we combined the HC and FDF cues into the framework of particle filter for pedestrian tracking. FDF feature which is simpler than HOG operator is applied, the run time is greatly reduced. Color is a widely used feature for its robust to rotation scale invariant. The fusing cues method has a good tracking result. It's not difficult to join other features such as motion, infrared brightness with our algorithm based on framework of particle filter to develop tracking algorithms robust to occlusion, brightness changes or similarity between background and target. The next step of our work may involve improving the robustness of algorithm adaptable to the complex environments for both single and multiple targets.

Acknowledgement. This paper was supported by China Postdoctoral Science Foundation, LIESMARS Special Research Funding and the National Natural Science Foundation of China (41071285, 40830530).

References

1. Fen, X., Ming, G.: Pedestrian Tracking Using Particle Filter Algorithm. In: International Conference on Electrical and Control Engineering, pp. 1478–1481 (2010)
2. Geronimo, D., Lopez, A., Angel, D.: Survey of Pedestrian Detection for Advanced Driver Assistance Systems. IEEE Transactions on Pattern Analysis and Machine Intelligence 32(7), 1239–1258 (2010)
3. Collins, R., Liu, Y., Leordeanu, M.: Online Selection of Discriminative Tracking Features. IEEE Transactions on Pattern Analysis and Machine Intelligence 27(10), 1631–1643 (2005)
4. Nummiaro, K., Meier, E., Gool, L.: An Adaptive Color-based Particle Filter. Image and Vision Computing 21(1), 99–110 (2003)
5. Xu, F., Gao, M.: Human Detection and Tracking based on HOG and Particle Filter. In: 3rd International Congress on Image and Signal Processing, pp. 1740–1743 (2011)
6. Niknejad, H., Takahashi, K., Mita, S., McAllester, D.: Embedded Multi-sensors Objects Detection and Tracking for Urban Autonomous Driving. In: IEEE Intelligent Vehicles Symposium, pp. 1128–1135 (2011)
7. Han, H., Ye, Q., Jiao, J.: Combined Feature Evaluation for Adaptive Visual Object Tracking. Computer Vision and Image Understanding 115(1), 69–80 (2011)
8. Comaniciu, D., Ramesh, V., Meer, P.: Kernel-based Object Tracking. IEEE Transaction on Pattern Analysis and Machine Intelligence 25(5), 564–577 (2003)
9. Lin, J.: Divergence Measures Based on the Shannon Entropy. IEEE Transaction Information Theory 25(5), 3–10 (2000)
10. Chong, Y., Li, Q., Kuang, H.: Two-stage Pedestrian Detection Based on Multiple Features and Machine Learning. ACTA Automatica Sinica 38(3), 375–381 (2012)
11. Dalal, N., Triggs, B.: Histograms of Oriented Gradients for Human Detection. In: IEEE Computer Society Conference on Computer Vision and Pattern Recognition, pp. 886–893 (2005)
12. VIVIDTrackingEvaluation, http://vision.cse.psu.edu/data/vividEval/datasets/datasets.html
13. CAVIARTestCaseScenarios, http://groups.inf.ed.ac.uk/vision/CAVIAR/CAVIARDATA1/
14. SDL Data Set, http://coe.gucas.ac.cn/SDL-HomePage/resource.asp

Research on Information Dissemination in Urban Rail Transit Line Network

Quan-Ye Han[1,2], Xiao-Ming Wang[2], and Jian-Wu Dang[2]

[1] Shaanxi Radio & TV University Shaanxi Business College Department of Computing
informatics Shaanxi Xian 710119
[2] Key Laboratory Opto-Electronic Technology and Intelligent Control,
Lanzhou Jiaotong University, Lanzhou 730070
{hqy,Wangxm,Dangjw}@mail.lzjtu.cn

Abstract. Based on the push and pull approach, a kind of adaptive disseminating mechanism is presented, which combines push with pull, by which the system of emergency coordination center in urban rail transit line network can dynamically allocate the available resource between push and pull clients so as to optimize the sending time delay of data chunk in network given their desired currency. The major conclusion is the approach of combined push with pull can fit to stringent coherency requirements information and less stringent coherency requirements information. Also it can fit to information provided according to user's requirements. The approach can better meet the requirement of currency of information on urban rail transit line network.

Keywords: urban rail transit, line network, information dissemination.

1 Introduction

After using the line network operation mode in urban rail transit in China, the topology structure of the total line network system is more complex. The density of passenger flow is larger. The interaction of different station and different line in network is more highlighted. The effect of local problem on operation of total line network is more serious. Emergency coordination center (ECC) is the kernel of operation in the total line network. It undertakes some important tasks including information sharing, operation management, emergency processing and intelligent decision etc. The information flow on urban rail transit line network is shown in Fig.1. Where, LNOMS means line network operation management system. IIN means integrated information network. EPAS means emergency platform application system. ACC means automatic clearing center. "1" means operational supervisor, decision instruction and coordinate linkage. "2" means monitoring information, rescue feedback and information report. "3" means resource scheduling and instruction information. "4" means implementation feedback of information on-site and monitoring information. Among them, some information desired is stringent coherency requirements, such as alarming. Some information desired is less stringent coherency requirements, such as passenger

D.-S. Huang et al. (Eds.): ICIC 2012, CCIS 304, pp. 328–335, 2012.

flow. Also some information is provided according to user's requirement, such as route map about public traffic or video streaming on-site. In order to accurately and timely deal with information in the total line network, Information dissemination mechanism of urban rail transit line network is the key. The main purpose of this paper is to research a kind of information dissemination mechanism, which can fit to urban rail transit line network.

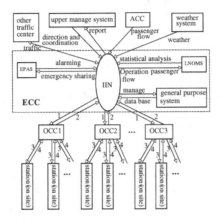

Fig. 1. Information flow on urban rail transit line network

2   Push Disseminating and Pull Disseminating

There are some researches on information dissemination under web situation. An approach of according to round trip time of data chunk to determine the next transfer point among many connected node in network is proposed in [1]. Hybrid architecture of CDN-P2P and Tree-Mesh is reported importantly in [2]. [1-2] are all fit to video streaming. A hardware implementation of quantum-behaved particle swarm optimization algorithm is introduced in [3], by which system can shorten runtime. The tree network structure of disseminating dynamic data on n-node network can yield an $O(\log n)$-approximation time algorithm[4]. [5-7] are all study on live streaming in adaptive networks. Comparing to all of above, the information disseminating of urban rail transit line network has its inherent characteristic on network structure and information flow. In order to illustrate in detail, the following definitions are defined.

Temporal coherency requirement (*TCR*) is defined for interesting data item. The value C of *TCR* denotes the maximum permissible deviation of the cached value from the Server and thus constitutes the user-specified tolerance. Let A_t denote the value of the data item at an agent at time t. Maintaining temporal coherency implies maintaining the inequality (1) for all times t.

$$\| A_t - A_{t-1} \| \le C \tag{1}$$

Time to refresh (*TTR*) is defined to denote the time interval, which is computed by agent to determine the next time it should poll the Server based on the *TCR*, so as to refresh the data item if it has changed in the interim.

Currency is defined as equation (2), the value of $t_1, t_2.....t_n$ denote these durations when user's *TCR* is violated. The value of T denotes the total time for which data was observed by a user.

$$Currency = 1 - \sum_{i=1}^{n} t_i \bigg/ T \qquad Currency \in (0 \ 1] \qquad (2)$$

Communication overheads are defined as the number of messages exchanged between Server and agent. In push approach, the number of messages transferred over the network is equal to the number of pushes. Pull approach requires two messages—request and response—per poll. Clearly, given a certain number of updates received by a client, pull approaches incur larger message overheads. In pull approach, agent polls the Server based on its estimate of how frequently the data is changing. If the data actually changes at a faster rate, then the agent might poll more frequently than necessary. That result a larger load on network.

Flexibility is mainly about the follows: If a Server fails and a user expects the Server to push changes of interest, a user might incorrectly believe that he has temporally coherent data and possibly take some action based on this. On the other hand, if a client explicitly pulls data from a Server, it will soon enough, say at the end of a time period, know about the failure of the Server and take appropriate action.

2.1   Pull

To achieve temporal coherency using pull approach, an agent can compute the *TTR* values based on the rate of change of the data and the user's coherency requirements. Stringent coherency requirements result in a smaller *TTR*, whereas less stringent coherency requirement require less frequent polls to the Server, and hence, a larger *TTR*. Observe that an agent need not pull every change, only those changes that are interesting to the user need to be pulled from the Server. So, the success of the pull technique hinges on the accurate estimation of the *TTR* value. Given a user's coherency requirement, an agent can adaptively vary the *TTR* value based on the rate of change of the data. The *TTR* decreases dynamically when a data starts changing rapidly and increases when a hot data item becomes cold. $TTR_{estimate}$ is computed as equation (3).

$$TTR_{estimate} = TTR_{last} / (|D_{last} - D_{nexttolast}|) \times C \qquad TTR_{min} \leq TTR_{last} \leq TTR_{max} \qquad (3)$$

Where, TTR_{last} denotes the previous time interval, the initial value of which is a random number within $[TTR_{min} \ TTR_{max}]$. $|D_{last} - D_{nexttolast}|$ denotes the difference of interesting data item in last two times. $[TTR_{min} \ TTR_{max}]$ denotes the range within which *TTR* values are bound. C is the value of *TCR*. We can see that $TTR_{estimate}$ ensures that changes which are greater than or equal to C are not missed.

2.2   Push

In push approach, the agent registers with a Server, identifying the data of interest and the associated *TCR*. Whenever the value of data changes, the Server uses the *TCR* value C to determine if the new value should be pushed to the agent, only those changes that are of interest to the user are pushed. Formally, if D_{last} was the last value that was pushed to the agent, then the current value D_p is pushed if and only if $|D_p-D_{last}| \geq C$, $0 \leq last < p$. To achieve this, the Server needs to maintain state information of agent interested in each data, the *TCR* of each agent and the last update sent to that agent. The key advantage of the push approach is that it can meet stringent coherency requirements—since the Server is aware of every change, it can precisely determine what to push and when. It is obvious that the *currency* of push is equal to 1under the condition of the Sever being not fails.

2.3   Experiment of Push Approach and Pull Approach

In experiment, we use real world stock price streams to take the place of information flow in urban rail transit line network as exemplars of dynamic data, which can be obtained from http://www.kitco.com, also which is similar to the information flow on urban rail transit line network, and they mostly are all real-time information flow. The experimental data items were collected at a rate of 2 stock quotes per second. For pull, we used a HTTP web Server with prototype proxy. For push, we used a prototype Server that uses unicast and connection-oriented sockets to push data to proxies. All experiments were done on a local intranet. The pull approach was evaluated using the adaptive *TTR* algorithm with TTR_{min} of 1second and three TTR_{max} values of 10,30,50 seconds. C value of *TCR* is ¥0.06. In contrast, Fig.2 shows that the pull algorithm has *currency* of 70-80%for stringent coherency requirements and its *currency* improves as the coherency requirements become less stringent, while the push approach offers *currency* of 1 in theory.

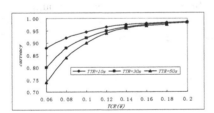
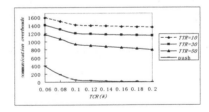

Fig. 2. Effect of varying *TCR* on *currency* for pull

Fig. 3. Effect of varying *TCR* on *communication overheads*

In Fig.3, the push approach incurs small *communication overheads* because only values of interest to a client are transferred over the network. The pull approach imposes a significantly higher overheads and its *communication overheads* decreases as the coherency requirements become less stringent.

It seems push approach can offer high *currency* and decrease the *communication overheads* on network. Push approach has a deadly disadvantage, because the Server maintains crucial state information about the needs of its clients. This state is lost when the Server fails. Consequently, the client's coherency requirements will not be met until the agent detects the failure and re-registers the *TCR* requirements with the Server. We can see the push approach has no *flexibility*. This can be resolved partly by pull approach.

3   Combined Push with Pull Disseminating

The combined push with pull disseminating mechanism is based on the premise that at any given time Server can categorize its clients either as push clients or pull clients and this categorization can change with system dynamics. This categorization is possible since the Server knows the parameters like the number of connections it can handle at a time and can determine the resources it has to devote to push or pull of data dissemination so as to satisfy its current clients. The resources that a Server has to devote for a client connection are sockets, memory, CPU time and bandwidth it has to make available for the connection. The basic ideas of this approach are: allow failures at a Server to be detected early so that clients can switch to pulls, and achieve graceful degradation to such failures. To achieve this, Servers are designed to push data values to push clients when variety of data at the Server equal or larger value C of *TCR* or a certain period of time *TTR* has passed since the last change was forwarded to the clients. This assures, after passage of *TTR* interval the Server is still up and the state of client on the Server is not lost. This ensures that in the worst case, the client remains out of sync with Server never exceeds *TTR*. The purpose of this approach is to set Server's allocation dynamically so as to optimize the resource utilization, minimize the sending time delay (*STD*) of data chunk and the number of clients given their desired *currency*. The adaptive number of pull is adjusted as equation (4). It is an optimizing equation with conditions. The fitness function of optimization is as equation (5). $R_{present}$ is the number of resource on Server at present, N is the number of clients, ξ is the number of pull clients, S is the Socket, C is the CPUtime, M is the Memory, B is the bandwidth. T_{best} is the best *STD* along with the variation of the ξ under a changeless structure of network.

$$R_{present} = R_{push} + R_{pull} \tag{4}$$
$$= (\sum_{i=1}^{N-\xi} S_i, \sum_{i=1}^{N-\xi} C_i, \sum_{i=1}^{N-\xi} M_i, \sum_{i=1}^{N-\xi} B_i) + (\sum_{j=1}^{\xi} S_j, \sum_{j=1}^{\xi} C_j, \sum_{j=1}^{\xi} M_j, \sum_{j=1}^{\xi} B_j)$$

$$T_{best} = \min(T_{best} \quad STD_{present}) \tag{5}$$

The algorithm of combined push with pull disseminating described as follow:

Step1: initialize the size of data chunk, the value of T_{best}, and the iteration.

Step2: Server sort information of data chunk from big to small according to *TCR*.

Step3: initialize clients to push connection and allocate resource order by *TCR*. If (lack of resource) go to step5.

Step4: measure *STD* of data chunk and compute value of fitness function based on equation (5).

Step5: if (lack of resource)

if (certain conditions) then Server adjust clients who can withstand the degraded *currency* from push to pull based on equation (4).

else the request is denied.

else Server adjust peers of pull to push based on equation (4)

Step6: Turn to step4. Until achieve iteration.

Where, certain conditions are bandwidth available, rate of change on data and *TCR*. If bandwidth available to a client is low, then forcing the client to pull will worsen its situation. If the rate of change of data value is low or the *TCR* is high, or those who had originally demanded less than 100% *currency* but had been offered higher *currency* because resources were available, then pull will suffice.

4   Experiment of Combined Push with Pull Disseminating

Using the same data above, the experiments were performed by running the Server on a lightly loaded Linux workstation and simulating clients from four different lightly loaded workstations. There were 56 users on each client machine, each accessing 3-4 data items. The queue size per connection was set to 5 and the total number of connections was set to 25. Fig.4 shows that as the percentage of push connections is increased beyond 65%, request denials increase substantially. At the Server, queues are maintained with each pull connection. When a new pull request is received at the Server and there is no space in the queues, the request is denied. 65% of the connections are allocated for push. about 9 connections are available for pulls – with the potential to have about 44 requests. The 45th request will be denied. Request denials cause an increase in the effective response times for pull clients and overall *currency* of system decreases, as shown in Fig.5, the last portion of the curve clearly brings out

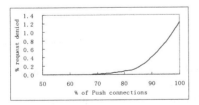
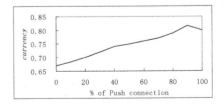

Fig. 4. Effect of% push connections on request denied   **Fig. 5.** Effect of % push connections on *currency*

the *currency* decreases because of resource constraints. That is when request of client access to the Server and the Server resources are unavailable to meet needs of the client, access must be denied.

In Fig.6, The total number of connections was set to 25,35,45. We can see while C=25, the *STD* of data chunk decrease constantly along with the increase of the push sockets.

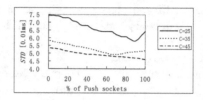

Fig. 6. Effect of % push on *STD* with different C

When ratio of push sockets is about 0.88, the *STD* achieve lowest, later, rising little, because of insufficient resource. When ratio of push sockets lager than 0.88, the request will be deny. This makes the sending of data chunk delayed. Along with the increasing of C, resource becomes sufficient. When C=45, the *STD* decrease slowly with the increase of the push sockets only because the communication overloads is different for push and pull.

5   Conclusion

This paper, based on push and pull approach, a kind of disseminating mechanism is presented, which combines push with pull, by which system of ECC can dynamically allocate resource between push and pull clients so as to optimize *STD* of data chunk given their desired *currency*. The major conclusion is the approach of combined push with pull can fit to stringent coherency requirements and less stringent coherency requirements, also it can fit to information provided according to user's requirements by optimizing the parameter ξ dynamically. The study is mainly bout information disseminating on urban rail transit line network. On which the reasonable network structure is the future work.

References

1. Alessandro, R., Renato, L.C.: Delay-Awareness in Push/Pull Streaming Protocols. Technical Report # DISI-10-012 (January 2010)
2. Huang, S.J., Zhi, H., Wu, J.: Novel Double Hybrid Architecture of Live Video Streaming System. Computer Engineering 37(9), 284–287 (2011)
3. Cai, R., Xu, W.B., Chai, Z.L., Wang, B., Liu, F.: Hardware Implementation and Capability Analysis of Particle Swarm Optimization Algorithm. Computer Engineering 36(4), 166–168 (2010)

4. Chakinala, R.C., Kumarasubramanian, A., Laing, K.A., Manokaran, R., Rangan, C., Pandu, R.R.: Playing Push vs Pull: Models and Algorithms for Disseminating Dynamic Data in Networks. In: SPAA 2006, Cambridge, Massachusetts, USA, July 30–August 2 (2006)

5. Meng, Z., Luo, J.G., Zhao, L., Yang, S.Q.: A Peer-to-Peer Network for Live Media Streaming – Using a Push-Pull Approach. In: MM 2005, Singapore, November 6-11 (2005)

6. Wang, H., Chen, W.T., Liu, Y.: customR2: A Hybrid Push/Pull Scheduling Method with Network Coding in P2P Live Streaming Systems. Journal of Computer Application 30(2), 285–288 (2010)

7. Lu, L.J., Wan, J., Xu, X.H.: Research and Realization of Push and Pull Combined Peer-to-Peer Live System. Computer Engineering 34(8), 240–242 (2008)

Approximation to Linear Algebraic Transition System[*]

Zhiwei Zhang[1,**], Jin-Zhao Wu[2,3], and Hao Yang[1]

[1] Chengdu Institute of Computer Application, Chinese Academy of Sciences, 610041, Chengdu
[2] Guangxi Key Laboratory of Hybrid Computational and IC Design Analysis,
Guangxi University for Nationalities, 530006, Nanning
[3] School of Computer and Information Technology, Beijing Jiaotong University, 100044,
Beijing
Zhangzhiweibest@gmail.com, 415360889@qq.com, wjzcd2011@sina.com

Abstract. We analyze the linear algebraic transition system (LATS) using algebraic theory. For transiting computing of linear algebraic transition system (LATS), we propose a concept of k-times maximum approximate transiting about (B, ε) which B is used to approximating compute for powers of the matrix A of the LATS. ε is maximum absolute error. This method can improve computational speed and conserve memory of computer program which can be modeled by the algebraic transition system. Further more, the theory and its function are verified by a practical example.

Keywords: K-times maximum approximate transiting, linear algebraic transition system, powers of the matrix.

1 Introduction

The definition of algebraic transition system is proposed by Sriram Sankaranarayanan in [12], which is specialized by general transition system, so algebraic transition system is a class of transition system. Transition system [8] is a basic concept in computer system model, which is used to study the real-time systems, hybrid systems .Transition systems, can approach the behavior of the system using symbolic computation. With the development of research for the system, traditional formal methods, which is used for theorem proving, formal verification and model checking, only can reason but not mathematical computer for transition systems. Algebra transition systems avoided the weakness above. It makes that research for transition systems not only can descript the qualitative characters but also the quantitative

[*] This Work is Support by Grants (HCIC201101) of Guangxi Key Laboratory of Hybrid Computational and IC Design Analysis Open Fund, the National Natural Science Foundation of China under Grant No. 60873118 and 60973147, the Natural Science Foundation of Guangxi under Grant No. 2011GXNSFA018154, the Science and Technology Foundation of Guangxi under Grant No. 10169-1, and Guangxi Scientific Research Project No.201012MS274.

[**] Corresponding author.

D.-S. Huang et al. (Eds.): ICIC 2012, CCIS 304, pp. 336–343, 2012.

characters. When we use the computer to investigate an algebra transition system, the values we get from the computer are usually approximating, so it is necessary to investigate an approximating compute method for algebra transition system.

We proposed a method for investigate the approximating algebra transition system of the initial system by giving a concept $(\overset{\sqcup}{S}, \varepsilon)$ to control the error produced. Then we get the maximum k-times approximating transiting under the $(\overset{\sqcup}{S}, \varepsilon)$ by defining k-power approximating of the matrix.

Kinds of methods for the approximations to a matrix, are proposed in papers [2][3][4], and for approximating the action of matrix exponentials are analyzed in the papers [1][5][6][7],For the research of powers of a matrix, convergence is usually analyzed [9][10][11], but it is insignificant for a infinite iterating compute in computer. Here we proposed a condoling method to compute an approximating computer for powers of a matrix, which is used to compute an approximating algebra transition system of the initial system under certain condition.

The paper is organized as follows: in Section 2 we introduce the definition of linear algebraic transition system and norm of matrix. Next we present how we established a method to approximate compute powers of a matrix and approximation to LATS (Section 3) and we use a case to show the application of our theory (Section 4). Finally, In Section 6, we conclude the paper and take a look at the future work.

2   Preliminaries

In this section we introduce some theories of algebra, which are used in our technique, and present our computational model of algebraic transition systems.

2.1   Norm of Matrix

Definition 1. $\|\cdot\|$ is a norm function of matrix $A \in R^{m \times n}$, if $\|A\|$ satisfies following:

1) $\|A\| \geq 0$ ($\|A\| = 0$ if and only if A=0)   ;
2) $\|\alpha A\| = |\alpha| \|A\|$, $\forall \alpha \in R$;
3) $\|A+B\| \leq \|A\| + \|B\|$;
4) $\|AB\| \leq \|A\| \|B\|$;

Proposition 1. let two matrices $A, B \in R^{n \times n}$, $\|\cdot\|$ is a norm function of real matrix, then

$$\| (A^{k} - B^{k}) \| \leq \sum_{i=1}^{k} C_{k} i \| (A - B) \|^{i} \| B \|^{k-i}$$

Especially, let $\| A - B \| = \beta \| B \|$, $\beta \in R$, then the result of above is the form following :

$$\| (A^k - B^k) \| \leq \| B \|^k [(1+\beta)^k - 1]$$

Proof: $\| (A^k - B^k) \| = \| (A - B + B)^k - B^k \|$

When k=1,

$$\| A - B \| = \| B \| [(1+\beta) - 1]$$
$$\leq \| B \| [(1+\beta) - 1]$$

When k =n,

Assume that $\| (A^n - B^n) \| \leq \| B \|^n [(1+\beta)^n - 1]$ holds.

When k=n+1,

$$\| (A^{n+1} - B^{n+1}) \| = \| (A^n A - B^n B) \| =$$

$$\| (A^n (A - B + B) - B^n B) \| = \| A^n (A - B) + (A^n - B^n) B \|$$

$$\leq \beta \| B \| \| A - B + B \|^n + \| B \|^{n+1} [(1+\beta)^n - 1]$$
$$\leq \beta \| B \| (\| A - B \| + \| B \|)^n + \| B \|^{n+1} [(1+\beta)^n - 1]$$
$$= \| B \|^{n+1} [\beta(\beta + 1)^n + (1+\beta)^n - 1]$$
$$= \| B \|^{n+1} [(\beta + 1)^{n+1} - 1]$$

So for each k,

$$\| (A^k - B^k) \| \leq \| B \|^k [(1+\beta)^k - 1] \text{ holds.}$$

Definition 2. σ is defined as absolute error of matrix B about matrix A on $\|\cdot\|$, if $\sigma = \| B - A \|$.where matrices $A, B \in R^{n \times n}$, $\|\cdot\|$ is a norm function of real **matrix.**

2.2   Linear Algebraic Transition System

Definition 3. ATS (algebra transition system) is a 5-tuple $S = (V, Q, q_0, X_0, \Gamma)$, where:

1) V is a finite set of variables over real field;

2) Q is a finite set of locations or states;

3) q_0 is the initial location or initial state;

4) X_0 denotes the initial values of variables over V in q_0;

5) Γ is the set of transitions. Each τ of Γ is a 3-tuple (q, q', f), where $q, q' \in Q$ are the pre-location and post-location, f is a polynomial transition relation over $X \cup X'$, where X, X' are the sets of variables in q, q'. f can be denoted as following :

$$f : \begin{cases} x_1 := f_1(x_1, x_2 \cdots, x_n) \\ \cdots \\ x_n := f_n(x_1, x_2 \cdots, x_n) \end{cases}$$

Let $X = (x_1, x_2 \cdots, x_n)$ denote the set of variables in q, and $X' = (x_1, x_2 \cdots, x_n)$ denote the set of variables in q'.then (1) can be denoted as following :

$X' = F(X)$, if $F(X)$ is linear polynomial $S = (V, Q, q_0, X_0, \Gamma)$ is called linear algebraic transition system. Then f can be denoted as following:

$$f : \begin{cases} x_1 := a_{11}x_1 + a_{22}x_2 \cdots a_{nn}x_n + b_1 \\ \cdots \\ x_n := a_{n1}x_1 + a_{n2}x_2 \cdots + a_{nn}x_n + b_n \end{cases}$$

i.e. $f : X' = AX' + \vec{b}$, where :

$$A = \begin{pmatrix} a_{11} & \cdots & a_{1n} \\ \vdots & \ddots & \vdots \\ a_{n1} & \cdots & a_{nn} \end{pmatrix},$$

$$\vec{b} = (b_1, b_2, \cdots b_n).$$

Moreover, if $\vec{b} = (b_1, b_2, \cdots b_n)^T = \vec{0}$, S is called linear homogeneous algebra transition system .

3   Mathematics Model for LATS

In this section, we simplify LATS to a mathematics model and propose the concept of K-times iterating neighborhood, which is used to approximate compute of linear algebra transition system. Here we only talk about linear transition systems $S = (V, Q, q_0, X_0, \Gamma)$, which satisfy $|\Gamma| = 1$.

Definition 4: B is defined as K-times approximating matrix of A about $(A - B, \varepsilon)$ under norm $\| \cdot \|$, if it satisfies the following expression:

$$\| (A^k - B^k) \| < \varepsilon.$$

Proposition 2: B is K-times approximating matrix of A about $(A - B, \varepsilon)$ under norm $\| \cdot \|$, if the following is satisfied

$$\| B \|^k \| [(1 + \beta)^k - 1] < \varepsilon$$

where $\| A - B \| = \beta \| B \|$.

Proof: From   proposition   1   we   get   the   following:
$$\| (A^k - B^k) \| \leq \| B \|^k [(1 + \beta)^k - 1]$$
Moreover, $\| B \|^k [(1 + \beta)^k - 1] \leq \varepsilon$,
so $\| (A^k - B^k) \| \leq \| B \|^k [(1 + \beta)^k - 1] \leq \varepsilon$,

then B is k-times approximating matrix of A about $(A - B, \varepsilon)$ under norm $\| \cdot \|$.

Proposition 3: B is k-power approximating matrix of A about $(A - B, \varepsilon)$ under norm $\| \cdot \|$, and $\| B \| \geq 1$, then B is j-power approximating matrix of A about $(A - B, \varepsilon)$ under norm $\| \cdot \|$, where $j < k, k \in N$. i.e.:

$$\| (A^k - B^k) \| < \varepsilon, \text{ and } \|B\| > 1, \text{ then for every } 0 < j < k, \ \| (A^j - B^j) \| < \varepsilon.$$

Definition 5: B is defined as maximum k-powers approximate matrix of A about $(A - B, \varepsilon)$ under norm $\| \cdot \|$, if the following are satisfied:

(1) $\|B\| \geq 1$;
(2) $\| (A^k - B^k) \| < \varepsilon$;
(3) $\| (A^{k+1} - B^{k+1}) \| \geq \varepsilon$.

Then we can apply the concept above to investigate homogeneous linear algebra transition system.

Definition 6: Let $S = (V, Q, q_0, X_0, \Gamma)$ and $S^1 = (V, Q, q_0, X_0, \Gamma^1)$ be two homo   linear   algebra   transition   systems. $|\Gamma| = |\Gamma^1| = 1$,then $S^1 = (V, Q, q_0, X_0, \Gamma^1)$ is called as k-times transiting approximating system about $A - A', \varepsilon$) under norm $\| \cdot \|$ of $S = (V, Q, q_0, X_0, \Gamma)$, if and only if for $\tau \in \Gamma$, which can be denoted by $f : X = AX'$, then $\tau^1 \in \Gamma^1$, which can be denoted by $f^0 : X = A'X'$, and $\varepsilon > 0$, following are satisfied:

(1) $\| A' \| \geq 1$;

(2) $\| \Delta X \| = \| (A_i^k - A'^k_i) X_0 \| \leq \varepsilon$;

(3) $\| (A_i^{k+1} - A'^{k+1}_i) X_0 \| > \varepsilon$.

Proposition 4: Let $S = (V, Q, q_0, X_0, \Gamma)$ and $S^1 = (V, Q, q_0, X_0, \Gamma^1)$ be two homogeneous linear algebra transition systems and $|\Gamma| = |\Gamma^1| = 1$ then $S^1 = (V, Q, q_0, X_0, \Gamma^1)$ is k-times transiting approximating system about $(A - A', \varepsilon)$ under norm $\| \cdot \|$ of $S = (V, Q, q_0, X_0, \Gamma)$, if the following are satisfied

  (1) $\| A' \| \geq 1$;

  (2) $\| A' \|^k \| X_0 \| [(1 + \beta)^k - 1] \leq \varepsilon$

  Where $\| A - A' \| = \beta \| A' \|$;

  (3) $\| (A_i^{k+1} - A'^{k+1}_i) X_0 \| > \varepsilon$

Proof:

  $\| \Delta X \| = \| (A_i^k - A'^k_i) X_0 \| \leq \| (A_i^k - A'^k_i) \| \| X_0 \|$ (Definition 1)

  $\leq \| A' \|^k [(1 + \beta)^k - 1] \| X_0 \| \leq \varepsilon$, (proposition 2)

  So $\| \Delta X \| = \| (A_i^k - A'^k_i) X_0 \| \leq \varepsilon$ is   satisfied,   more   over $\| A' \| \geq 1$ and $\| (A_i^{k+1} - A'^{k+1}_i) X_0 \| > \varepsilon$, S^1 is k-times transiting approximating system about $(A - A', \varepsilon)$ under norm $\| \cdot \|$ of S.

  Easily, we can get the following corollaries:

Corollary: Let $S = (V, Q, q_0, X_0, \Gamma)$ and $S^1 = (V, Q, q_0, X_0, \Gamma^1)$ denote two homogeneous linear algebra transition systems, $|\Gamma| = |\Gamma^1| = 1$, if A' ,which satisfies $f^0 \in \Gamma^1 : X = A'X'$,is maximum k-times approximating matrix of A' ,which satisfies $f \in \Gamma : X = AX'$,about $(A - B, \varepsilon)$ under norm $\| \cdot \|$,and $\| X_0 \| \geq 1$,then S^1 is k-times transiting approximating system about $(A - A', \varepsilon)$ under norm $\| \cdot \|$ of S .

  Then we talk about the non-homo linear algebra transition systems like $S = (V, Q, q_0, X_0, \Gamma)$, which satisfies $|\Gamma| = 1$ and $\vec{b} = (b_1, b_2, \cdots b_n)^T \neq \vec{0}$.

Proposition 5: A non-homogeneous linear algebra transition system can be transited to a homogeneous linear algebra transition system.

Proof: let $S = (V, Q, q_0, X_0, \Gamma)$ be a linear algebra transition system, which satisfies $|\Gamma| = 1$, $f \in \Gamma : X = AX' + \vec{b}$, assume $\vec{b_0}$ is one solution of the equation $(A - E)\vec{x} = \vec{b}$, and let $Y = X + \vec{b_0}$, then $f \in \Gamma : X = AX' + \vec{b}$ Can be replaced by $f \in \Gamma : Y = AY'$ where $Y' = X' + \vec{b_0}$.

4   Applications

In this section, we present an application example to show the viability of our approach. We here use Frobenius Norm [13] of matrix, and Euclid Norm of Vector.

Example: A program such as following:

```
Void main () {
Float x1=1, x2=1;
For (i=1, i<6, i++)
```
$$x_1 := x_1 + 1.9999 x_2;$$
$$x_2 := 2.0001 x_1 + 3 x_2;$$
```
Out put x1,x2 ;
Return;
}
```

Let $S = (V, Q, q_0, X_0, \Gamma)$ be a linear homogeneous algebra transition system, $|\Gamma| = \{\tau\}$

$$V = \{x_1, x_2\}, Q = \{q0, q1, q2, q3, q4, q5, q6, q7\}$$

$$A = \begin{pmatrix} 1 & 1.9999 \\ 2.0001 & 3 \end{pmatrix} \text{ and } |\Gamma| = 1, f \in \Gamma : X = AX',$$

$, X_0 = (1,1), S^1 = (V, Q, q_0, X_0, \Gamma^1), f^1 \in \Gamma : X = A'X',$

$$A' = \begin{pmatrix} 1 & 2 \\ 2 & 3 \end{pmatrix}, \quad \| A' \| = 3\sqrt{2} = 4.2426406, \quad \| X_0 \| = \sqrt{2},$$

$$A - A' = \begin{pmatrix} 0 & -0.0001 \\ 0.0001 & 0 \end{pmatrix},$$

$\| A - A' \| = 0.00014142, \quad \beta = \dfrac{\| A - A' \|}{\| A' \|} = 0.00003336$

$\| A' \|^5 \| X_0 \| [(1 + \beta)^5 - 1] = 0.22934911 < 0.8$

$\| A' \|^6 \| X_0 \| [(1 + \beta)^6 - 1] = 1.16767720 > 0.8$

So we can run the program using the approximating transition system in place of initial system if the loop times i<6.

5   Conclusion and Future Work

In this paper, we present a method to approximating compute finite powers of a matrix, which can be used to estimate error for a class of linear algebraic transition system. Obviously, the approximate times k depends on $(A - B , \varepsilon)$ and the norm of matrix used.

In the future work, we will investigate other approximate calculation, for example, we can use Jordan Formal of matrix to the approximation. Also, complexity of the methods and transiting of non-linear algebraic transition system algebraic should be considered.

References

1. Hochbruck, M.: On Krylov Subspace Approximations to the Matrix Exponential Operator. SIAM Journal on Numerical Analysis, 1911–1925 (1994)
2. Frieze, A., Kanna, R.: Fast Monte-Carlo Algorithms For Finding Low-Rank Approximations. Journal of the ACM (JACM), 1025–1041 (2004)
3. Drineas, P., Kannan, R., Mahoney, M.W.: Fast Monte Carlo Algorithms for Matrices III: Computing a Compressed Approximate Matrix Decomposition. SIAM Journal on Computing, 184–206 (2006)
4. Drineas, P., Kannan, R.: Fast Monte Carlo Algorithms for Matrices I: Approximating Matrix Multiplication. SIAM Journal on Computing, 132–157 (2006)
5. Van, J., Eshof, D.: Preconditioning Lanczos Approximations To The Matrix Exponential. SIAM Journal on Scientific Computing, 1438–1457 (2006)
6. Moret, I.: RD-Rational Approximations of The Matrix Exponential. BIT Numerical Mathematics, 595–615 (2004)
7. Zanna, A.: Generalized Polar Decompositions For The Approximation of The Matrix Exponential. SIAM Journal on Matrix Analysis and Applications 23, 840–862 (2002)
8. Manna, Z., Pnueli, A.: Temporal Verification of Reactive Systems: Safety. Springer, New York (1995)
9. Meyer, C.D.: Convergent Powers of a Matrix with Applications to Iterative Methods for Singular Linear Systems. SIAM Journal on Numerical Analysis, 699–712 (1977)
10. Thomason, M.G.: Convergence of Powers of a Fuzzy Matrix. Journal of Mathematical Analysis and Applications, 476–480 (1977)
11. Hashimoto, H.: Convergence Of Powers Of A Fuzzy Transitive Matrix. Fuzzy Sets and Systems, 153–160 (1983)
12. Sriram, S.: Non-linear Loop Invariant Generation using GROBNER Bases. ACM SIGPLAN Notices, 318–329 (2004)
13. Stewart, G.W.: Matrix Perturbation Theory (1990)

Research on Mission Planning of Space-Based Observation Based on Particle Swarm Optimization Algorithm

Bo-quan Li[1,2,3], Xu-zhi Li[2], Hong-fei Wang[2], and Juan Meng[2]

[1] Academy of Opto-Electronics, Chinese Academy of Sciences, Beijing 100094, China
[2] Technology and Engineering Center for Space Utilization, Chinese Academy of Sciences, Beijing 100094, China
[3] Graduate University of Chinese Academy of Sciences, Beijing 100190, China
liboquan010@126.com

Abstract. For big spacecraft has many payloads with complexity constraints and resource-constrained problem, comprehensive analysis of the constraints that the angle between the astronomical observation payload and the sun, the constraints of the operating mode, the platform internal resource constraints and the load side put constraints. The platform internal resource and translate constraints are converted to 01 backpack model, planning and scheduling it through particle swarm optimization algorithm. Verified, in the case of resource-constrained it planning observations of loads at different times to achieve platform for optimal allocation of resources effectively.

Keywords: Space, intelligent, planning, data transmission, multiple payloads.

1 Introduction

Space remote sensing has already been key component of modern society information system. Through multidimensional information of precise image, radiation and scattering of land, ocean, atmosphere and earth system obtained from space, which can make a significant contribution to the issue that geosciences need to resolve. "Space astronomy" is about observation from space, overcome effect of earth's atmosphere on astronomical observation, researching origin and evolvement of overall universe and various spheres include sun. It can obtain some advantages that foundation telescope don't have, because of being above the atmosphere.

It is a heavy work to organize observation effectively, which needs to frame whole thorough observation plan. This observation plan not only optimizes sky choice according to scientific targets, but also needs have the capability to deal with emergency, such as observing the interesting target accurately, observing the target with dissatisfied observation results and the target without observation secondly.

2 Observational Constraints

big spacecraft payload need according to target observation requirement when it is observing, and considers state of sensor synthetically, supply of energy and fuel,

D.-S. Huang et al. (Eds.): ICIC 2012, CCIS 304, pp. 344–351, 2012.

distribution situation of resources such as communications time window of receiving station in ground, optimizing assemble, arranges space work plan reasonably. These observational constraints will be considered as emphasis in study, as follows:

2.1   Constraints of Solar Altitude

Partial observation payloads have definite requirement on sunlight conditions when it observes the target. When payloads are taking observations in progress, they need solar altitude larger than or equal to one minimum which guarantees sunlight conditions the observation needs.

2.2   Constraints of Data Transmission

big spacecraft enter into ground receiving station or visual arc of relay satellite satellite, only open platform data transmission transmitter, let data stored in memory download to ground receiving station. In order to guarantee consistency and categoricalness of data, it is needed for transmission of data payload once observes must be accomplished in once time pulled in station, and it is not permitted that data payload once observes is transported in two or more data transmission segments. [1]

2.3   Constraints of the Operating Mode

Constraints of interior resource include electrical energy and memory space. Payload' work needs electrical energy. Power of platform is a kind of loss-less resource, and the power that is taken up will be released when payload is shut and can continue to be used. [2]

3   Observation Model and Results

3.1   Compute of Observation Priority

In the progress of planning observation activity, it needs to guarantee those tasks possesses superior priority have many executing opportunity. Next concrete achievement introduces installing of priority in detail.

Key coefficient of each payload is given and the magnitude of it is decided by rigorous level for observation condition. The fewer opened time of payload is, and the more higher key coefficient is.

In order to avoid certain target with low weights initialization (namely target with high-frequency of covering in the progress of initialization) can not get opportunity to observe, it needs to make the weights of target be alterable. Weights of certain payload observes one area for i time as follows:

$$w_i = ab(1 - k_{i-1}) \tag{1}$$

Where w is priority of observation, a is key coefficient of payload, b is weights initialization of target and k is percentage of target has covered observation.When target needs untied observation of multiple payloads, priority of untied observation is sum of priority of each payload of untied observation.

3.2   Model of Task Planning

Assuming big spacecraft deploys N observation payload, and key coefficient of each payload is known, constraints of interior resource include electric power source and memory space, external conditions include angle of sight axis and solar vector, and posture conditions of big spacecraft. Electrical energy and memory capacity of big spacecraft, visible situation of ground station of big spacecraft and down transmission rate of data may be achieved according to operation capability of big spacecraft and internal conditions.

Various resources in big spacecraft, such as electric power source is limited, therefore task planning versus payload may boil down to typical issue that resource is limited. Dynamic change of priority of payload: priority of payload is main basis, and the change of priority will influence the results of planning.

Task planning of payload can be handled as approximate knapsack problem (PK). Vasquez made SPOT5 satellite daily task planning to be a mapping of PK, and applied taboo search to solve. [3][4] The advantage of PK is simple form, may show constraints of using level of multiple dimensions resource, and have efficient optimalizing or approximate optimalizing solving arithmetic. [5] But in the practical project, taboo search arithmetic need vast debugging work to get better results. When resource of platform is restricted, planning model is described as: N payloads is given, power of the ith payload is wi, priority of observation is pi, i=1, 2..., n, maximal power is C ; when data transports constraints, n represents number of download task, data size of the ith task is wi, down priority is pi, platform permits down data size is C, it can let total value of materials in knapsack get maximum that making a choice for materials that is put into knapsack, if variable is induced as follows:

$$x_i = \begin{cases} 1, \ material \ i \ is \ put \ into \ knapsack \\ 0, \ on \ the \ contrary \end{cases}, \quad i = 1, 2, ..., n, \tag{2}$$

Then PK can equal to these integer linear planning:

$$\max \quad z = \sum_{i=1}^{n} p_i x_i \tag{3}$$

$$s. \ t. \quad \sum_{i=1}^{n} w_i x_i \tag{4}$$

$$x_i = 0 \ or \ 1, \quad i \in \{1, \ 2, \ ..., \ n\} \tag{5}$$

Firstly, constraints of external conditions of payload is handled, it is decided that whether each payload satisfies constraints conditions of angle versus sun and posture condition. If these conditions can not be satisfied, payload will be shut, otherwise payload will propose corresponding resource requirement to big spacecraft according to itself resource constraints. [6] Because of completion of relay satellite currently, observation data of payload almost transports to ground through relay satellite at any time.

3.3   Arithmetic of Planning

Particle Swarm Optimization (PSO) arithmetic is a novel bionic evolution calculation method, is proposed by Kennedy and Eberhart in 1995[7], principle is very simple, parameters that arithmetic needs is few, it is beneficial for achievement, and velocity of constringency is fast. Assuming in a D-dimensions target search space, m particles consist a community, where the ith particle can be expressed as a D-dimensions vector , i=1, 2,..., m, namely the position of the ith particle in D-dimensions search space is xi, its adaptive value can be calculated by letting xi substitute into a target function, and measure quality of xi according to its adaptive value. Flying velocity of the ith particle is a D-dimensions vector, and is named as. The optimalizing position of the ith particle is searched nowadays is named as, and the optimalizing position of the total particle community is searched nowadays is named as , iterative formula of arithmetic velocity and position is as follows:

$$V_i(t+1) = w \times V_i(t) + c_1 \times rand() \times [P_i - X_i(t)] \\ + c_2 \times rand() \times [P_j - X_i(t)] \tag{6}$$

$$X_i(t+1) = X_i(t) + V_i(t+1) \tag{7}$$

Where c1 and c2 is positive constant and is named as acceleration factor, rand () is random number within region of [0, 1]; w is Inertia factor; t represents certain iteration, Pi is the optimalizing position of particle, and Pj is the optimalizing position of species group. The flow of optimization algorithm of particle swarm is shown as Fig. 1.X in PK is a 0-1 sequence, and position of each particle may be expressed as vector X. The position of particle only expresses feasible solution. Adaptive value function may express as

$$f(X) = \sum_{i=1}^{n} v_i x_i, (\text{ sum of materials in knapsack }) \tag{8}$$

Optimization of particle swarm arithmetic can be expressed as searching X that can let f (X) get maximum.

Velocity in particle swarm is defined as mapping ensemble of materials choice, namely the distance between two positions and is expressed as V, then |V| expresses the number of change velocity include, therefore this velocity can be defined as

$$V = X_1 - X_2 = \{v_i \mid v_i \in \{0,1\}, i = (1,2,\cdots,n)\}, where$$

$$v_i = \begin{cases} 0 : x_{1i} = x_{2i} \\ 1 : x_{1i} \neq x_{2i} \end{cases} \tag{9}$$

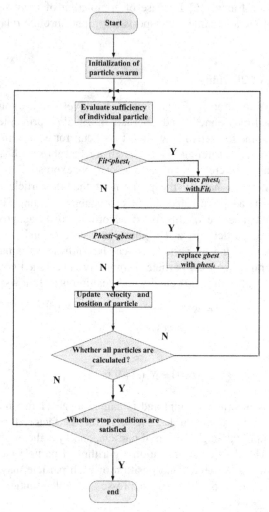

Fig. 1. Flow chart of optimization algorithm of particle swarm

3.4   Simulation of Arithmetic Example

Solve the optimalizing x of payload planning of power of electrical source with single constraint. The form of optimalizing x is one-dimension, each component of vector corresponds to a payload with resource request, the value of component corresponds to work state of payload (1 represents work of payload, and 0 represents close). vector corresponds to a payload with resource request, the value of component corresponds to work state of payload (1 represents work of payload, and 0 represents close).

Time of change of various resource conditions of space is named as judgment hour. Judgment hour make total planning time to divide into several small time periods, and is named as state region. State region is region with half open and half shut and include previous judgment hour. It can be seen that resource conditions of space is only changed in judgment hour and keep unchanged at state region. Assuming the number of observation payload of big spacecraft is N=10, T0, T1 and T2 is judgment hours, [T0-T1) and [T1-T2) is state region. External constraint of each payload, internal constraint and calculation priority is shown as tables, and the maximum power is 500W. EP represents earth observation payload, AP represents astronomical observation payload, EP1 and AP1 represents functions of earth observation and astronomical observation of certain integrative observation payload. The maximum number of iteration is Max=50; acceleration factor c1and c2 is 2, respectively. Inertia factor w is 0.8. Arithmetic run independently for 10 times and selects result with most best value. Each payload planning results in state region [T0-T1) is shown as Table 1.

Table 1. Results of observation payload task planning for example-I

payload	EP1	EP2	EP3	EP4	EP5
Solar altitude angle	Satisfy constraint	Satisfy constraint	Satisfy constraint	Satisfy constraint	Satisfy constraint
Power (W)	125	150	35	40	105
priority	50	33	15	22	40
Planning results	work	work	shut	work	work
payload	AP1	AP2	AP3	AP4	AP5
Angle versus sun	Don't satisfy constraint	Satisfy constraint	Satisfy constraint	Don't satisfy constraint	Satisfy constraint
Power (W)	125	155	60	50	20
priority	20	32	45	11	12
Planning .results	shut	shut	work	shut	work

Start at T1 hour, it is needed that united observation of payload EP1、 EP2、 EP3 versus certain target. Planning results of each payload in region [T1-T2) is shown as Table 2.

Table 2. Results of observation payload task planning for example-II

payload	EP1	EP2	EP3	EP4	EP5
Solar altitude angle	Satisfy constraint	Satisfy constraint	Satisfy constraint	Satisfy constraint	Satisfy constraint
Power (W)	125	150	35	40	105
priority	98(50)	98(33)	98(15)	22	40
Planning results	work	work	work	shut	work
payload	AP1	AP2	AP3	AP4	AP5
Angle versus sun	Don't satisfy constraint	Satisfy constraint	Satisfy constraint	Don't satisfy constraint	Satisfy constraint
Power (W)	125	155	60	50	20
priority	20	32	45	11	12
Planning results	shut	shut	work	shut	work

Then, we use particle swarm arithmetic planning down tasks at certain time with single constraint of platform down condition. The form of solving is also one-dimension vector, and each vector corresponds to a down requirement task, value of component corresponds to down state of task (1 represents download of task, and 0 represents no download of task). Assuming big spacecraft platform has 20 task numbers to download within certain time period, and only 100000M data can be downloaded. The maximum iteration number is Max=100; acceleration factor c1and c2 is 2, respectively. Inertia factor w is 0.7. Arithmetic run independently for 20 times and selects result with best value.

Each task down priority:

v={92,4,43,83,84,68,92,82,6,44,32,18,56,83,25,96,70,48,14,58}

Data number of each task (unit is M):

w={4400,4600,9000,7200,9100,4000,7500,3500,800,5400,7800,4000,7700,1500,6100,1700,7500,2900,7500,6300}

Planning results of down task numbers:

x={1,0,1,1,1,1,1,1,1,1,1,1,1,1,1,1,1,1,0,1,}.

4   Conclusion

This paper takes observation payload on big spacecraft with limited resource for example, plans and dispatches each payload. Through analyzing of characteristic of big spacecraft and payload work constraints, calculate priority of observation, and change the platform constraints to 01 PK, and plan task by using particle swarm methods. This method may deal with various constraints conditions according to situation of platform resource, priority of payload observation, and resource requirement, and plans download data. The results of planning not only ensure payload satisfy various resource constraints, but also can optimize and deploy platform resource coordinating with big spacecraft.

References

1. Guo, Y.H.: The Study on Key Technologies of Multiple Types of Earth Observing Satellites United Scheduling. National University of Defense Technology, Changsha (2009)
2. Xiao, L.: Application Research of Intelligent Algorithm in Planning of Earth Observation Satellite. Center for Space Science and Applied Research, Beijing (2008)
3. Vasquez, M., Hao, J.K.A.: Logic-Constrained" Knapsack Formulation and a Tabu Algorithm for the Daily Photograph Scheduling of an Earth Observation Satellite. Computational Optimization and Applications 20(2), 137–157 (2001)
4. Vasquez, M., Hao, J.K.: Upper Bounds for the SPOT 5 Daily Photograph Scheduling Problem. Journal of Combinatorial Optimization 7, 87–103 (2003)
5. Wang, P., Tan, Y.J.: Mission planning problem for earth observing satellites. Application Research of Computers 25(10), 2893–2897 (2008)
6. Liu, Y., Dai, S.W.: Planning and Scheduling of Payload for Satellite. Aerospace Control 22(5), 73–76 (2004)
7. Kennedy, J., Eberhart, R.C.: Particle swarm optimization. In: Proceedings of IEEE International Conference on Neural Networks, pp. 1942–1948. IEEE Press, Piscataway (1995)

Study of Electron Beam Welding Residual Stresses for Aluminum 99.60

Guifang Guo[1,*], Shiqiong Zhou[2], Li Hao[1], Zeguo Liu[1], and Wang Liang[1]

[1] Information Engineering Department, Tibet University for international, China
[2] Shenzhen Institute of Information Technology, China
{zhuoshiqiong,ggf8053}@163.com

Abstract. Based on measurement and simulation method, this paper studies the effects residual stresses of electron beam welding joints for pure aluminum plate 99.60. The residual stresses were measure by the keyhole method. Moreover, using thermal elastic - plastic theory, and the nonlinear finite element theory, a three - dimensional finite element model using mobile heat source of temperature and stresses field of electron beam welding in pure aluminum is established. The residual stresses distribution of pure aluminum plate in vacuum electron beam welding joint was numerically simulated. The results show that the main residual stress is the longitudinal residual stress, the value of the longitudinal residual stress is much larger than the transverse residual stress. The longitudinal residual stress is tension stress along weld center and the stress peak value appears in the middle of the welded seam; the transversal residual stress is compression stress; the residua l stress in thickness direction is very small. And in the weld center, the maximum value of residual tension stresses is lower than its yield strength. The simulation results about the welded residual stresses are almost identical with the experimental results by measuring.

Keywords: vacuum electron beam welding, welding residual stresses, Nonlinear finite element simulation, the keyhold method, Pure aluminum Al 99.60.

1 Introduction

The welding residual stresses are one of very key factors on the strength and life of welding structure. Therefore, it is very important to the research on the distribution and the influence o f the residual stresses after electron beam welding [1-2]. Electron beam welding has strong penetrating ability, narrow and deep welded seam, small heat affected zone, high welding quality. But the welding process is a dynamic process during high temperature; it is very difficult to use the experimental method to do real time measurement, the numerical simulation method supplies important research means.

The welding residual stresses are produced for non-homogeneous heating and cooling by welding heat resource applied to structure and the uneven plastic flow induces the non-coordination strain of the structure. During the electron beam welding, some certain parts produced very large temperature gradient because of local uneven heating and cooling. The heat expansion of the metal is limited due to the uneven temperature

D.-S. Huang et al. (Eds.): ICIC 2012, CCIS 304, pp. 352–359, 2012.

field during the heating process, so the local compressive plastic yield is formed in the heating zone. But in contrast during cooling, the metallic contraction by compressing is hampered in the plastically deforming area. Then, the welding stress is produced because of the temperature gradient [3-4].

Now, the measuring and testing technique of the welding residual stresses has been not successful in nation and international. Therefore, there is very important significance that the research on the distribution of the residual stress to ensure the safe reliability of the welding structure. So it is urgently to solve key subject, which is accurately know the residual stress distribution rule. One of key factors what affect the strength and life length of the structure is the welding residual stress. The heating mode of electron beam welding is a unique high-energy shock mode; and the residual stress can be reached the high values due to large temperature gradient. So it is very important in theoretical and practical meaning that analysis the formation and development of the residual stress of the pure aluminum by electron beam welding.

In order to prove productivity and quality, the welding process is needed to study in detail. But the welding is a dynamic process, the actual measurement is difficult very much at high temperature by the experimental method, but in contrast the numerical simulation method supply useful research procedure. Numerical simulations of welding processes have been performed since many years [5]. In this paper, the electron beam welding residual stresses of pure aluminum are studied by measurement and simulation in detail.

2   Experimental Processes

2.1   Experimental Materials and Welding Processing Parameters

The specimens were performed in CVE—CW6012 medium voltage electron beam welding machine, which the accelerated voltage is 10~60kV, the vacuum level is -103 Pa. Plates with size 300mm×150mm×2mm and 300mm×150mm×10mm were welded in vacuum along length direction of the plate and a butt-joint was formed respectively. The welding parameters are listed in Table 1[6].

Table 1. Parameters of Electron Beam Welding of Pure Aluminum

Thickness of plate d/mm	Accelerate voltage U/kV	Beam current I_b/mA	Focus current I_f/mA	Welding speed v/mm·min^{-1}
2	55	15	526	500
10	55	76	487	500

2.2   Experimental Measurement by Keyhole Method

The keyhole method which is wide application, high measurement accuracy, and successful measuring technique of half-destructive method was used to measure residual stresses. American test material association ASTM publicated the standard on measuring residual stresses by the keyhole method in 1981, it indicated that the method would be used to industrial practice. The new standard was ASTM E837—99[7-8].

The experimental equipment was JSY003 drilled device made by electric control technology research institute of Anshan City, and the strain gage was YD92B static resistance strain gage. The arrangement of the strain gage is shown in Fig. 1. X direction was defined as parallel to the welded seam direction, and Y direction was defined as vertical to the welded seam direction.

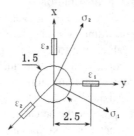

Fig. 1. The Arrangement of the Strain Gaga

In the experiment, the residual stresses of 2mm and 10mm pure aluminum plates were measured respectively. The results are listed in Table 2.

Table 2. Test Results of Residual Stress of Pure Aluminum Joints

Thickness Of plate d (mm)	No.	Distance from weld center d (mm)	Strain ε_1 ($\mu\varepsilon$)	Strain ε_2 ($\mu\varepsilon$)	Strain ε_3 ($\mu\varepsilon$)	Angle β ($°$)	Stress σ_x (MPa)	Stress σ_y (MPa)
	H1	0	-176.0	-166.0	-192.0	31.8	151.0	105.0
	H2	20	-153.0	169.0	-100.0	44.0	-86.4	63.8
2	H3	40	-42.0	-105.0	-153.0	-33.8	-110.0	65.0
	H4	60	-82.0	-35.0	-142.0	25.8	39.0	17.0
	H5	80	-161.0	-170.0	30.0	30.12	29.7	37.5
	J1	0	-143.0	-135.9	-215.0	44.9	125.6	124.3
	J2	20	-171.0	-122.0	-272.0	31.6	175.5	133.9
10	J3	40	-167.0	-120.0	-154.0	-40.5	113.2	110.8
	J4	60	-560.0	-743.0	-740.0	-23.0	-120.8	87.2
	J5	80	-263.0	-105.0	-358.0	38.5	-25.7	60.0

As shown in Table 2, the longitudinal residual stress (σx) is larger than the transverse residual stress (σy) in welded seam. Therefore, the main residual stress of the welded seam is the longitudinal stress for pure aluminum joints. And Table.2 shows that the longitudinal and transverse residual stresses vertical to welded seam in center of plate respectively.

As shown in Table.2, the distribution tendency of the residual stresses of the 2mm and 10mm pure aluminum plates is same in general. However, the residual stress value of 2mm is less than that of 10mm. Because 2mm plate is very thin which induce the postwelding deformation is large very much, so partial residual stress is released.

From Table.2, it can be seen that the longitudinal residual stress σx in welded seam and in the vicinity area is the tensile stress and it is compressive stresses distance from the weld center. But the stress value by means of strain calculation is larger than the yield strength of the material ($\sigma s = 55.7MPa$). One reason is additional stress induce plastic yield during drill hole by keyhole method. Another possible reason is the welding condition and welding parameter has been not successful, then the stress concentration is produced in specimen.

3   Numerical Simulation of Residual Stress of Electron Beam Welding

The welding simulation could be performed to evaluate the influence of the forming residual stresses on the welding distortions using a local/global approach similar to the one commonly employed to access welding distortions of large assembly[9-10]. The numerical simulation of electron beam welding of pure aluminum plate is represented by 10mm pure aluminum plate. To accurately simulate the change of the temperature fields and the stress fields during the electron beam welding, the geometrical symmetry created by the weld path allows half the plate to be modeled.

A three-dimensional finite-element model to calculate welding stresses fields of 10mm pure aluminum 99.60 plates was created in consideration of material nonlinearity [11-12]. During meshing element considering the temperature gradient is

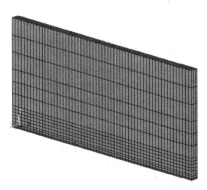

Fig. 2. The finite element model of 10mm Pure aluminum 99.60

large in the adjacent zone of welding heat resource so that the mesh scale is very small in the welded seam and the adjacent zone, and the mesh scale is relatively larger in the base metal zone. Therefore, Non-uniform mesh is divided as shown in Fig.2 in order to ensure the calculation accuracy and saving on computing time.

The electron beam welding heat resource has concentration and moving features, which generate the very large non-homogeneous temperature fields in time and space gradient. Therefore, the residual stresses and deformation in welding are produced. Namely, the welding heat resource is moving, so the stress in same position is varied with time.

The distribution of the longitudinal and the transverse stress of the electron beam welded joint of the pure aluminum Al99.60 along welded seam is given in Fig. 3 and Fig. 4 respectively.

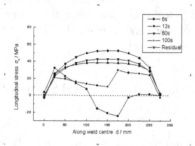

Fig. 3. Longitudinal stresses of Al99.60 welded joint along welded seam

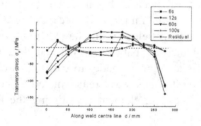

Fig. 4. Transverse stresses of Al99.60 welded joint along welded seam

In Fig. 3 and Fig. 4, it is obviously seen that the longitudinal and the transverse stresses appear two peak values at the place that 20mm from the beginning position and the ending position 20mm. Moreover, they appear symmetrical distribution. As show in Fig. 3 and Fig. 4, the longitudinal residual stress is the tensile stress and the maximum appears on the middle of the weld center line. However, the transverse residual stress may be either the compressive stress or the tensile stress along long welded seam. Meanwhile, the maximum absolute value of residual stress is 0.6—0.8σs. Because the coefficient of heat conductivity of aluminum is very high, so the effect heat expansion on the compressive plastic yield of the material is low. Therefore, the welding residual stress of aluminum is smaller than the steels.

4   Comparison of Measurement and Calculation Results

The comparison of longitudinal and transverse residual stresses of three-dimension finite element calculation results and keyhole method actual measurement results are shown in Fig. 5 and Fig. 6 respectively.

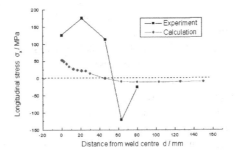

Fig. 5. Comparison of longitudinal residual stresses by calculation and experiment

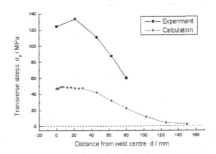

Fig. 6. Comparison of transverse residual stresses by calculation and experiment

From above-mentioned, it is known that the numerical calculation results are basically concordance with the experimental results for the distribution trend of the total welded joint. But the error between the calculation and measurement results is rather large. The main reason is that the premise assumed condition of the finite element is different from real welding. Another important reason is that it is inevitable produce oversize additional machining stress during actual measurement residual stress and the correction of the residual stress has not been correct.

Based on the keyhole method measure residual stress, the error reasons have lot of possibility. For example, the hole position deviation produce error, strain gauge zero drift, strain foil attach quality and sensitivity coefficient error, and additional strain for drilling, and so on. In this paper, the stress value is larger than the yield stress, mainly because of the plastic deformation. In addition, improper welding process caused the stress concentration, this reason also lead to the actual measurement residual stress to reach very high. Anyway, it is indicated that the finite element method and the model developed in this study for simulating the residual stress of electron beam welding is effective.

5   Conclusions

(1) Using the keyhole method, the residual stresses of 2mm and 10mm pure aluminum plates were measured in this study, the main residual stresses of the weld and in the vicinity of the weld were the longitudinal residual stresses.

(2) The longitudinal residual stress is the tension stress along welded seam and has the maximum in the middle of the welded seam. The longitudinal residual stress is quickly decreased from the tensile stress to compressive stress along the line vertical to welded seam. The transverse residual stress may be either the compressive stress or the tensile stress a long welded seam.

(3) Comparing the experimental results and calculating results, the results of numerical calculation were basically concordance with the experimental results.

Acknowledgements. The research is supported by a grant from National Natural Science Foundation of China (No. 51166012).

References

1. Chang, J.M., Tang, W.C.: Finite Element Mode Ling of Heat Transfer and Residual Stress Analysis for Electron Beam Welding. Journal of the Chinese Society of Mechanical Engineers 15(1), 1–10 (1994)
2. Reed, R.C.S., Tone, H.J., Roberts, S.M., et al.: Development and Validation of a Model for the Electron Beam Welding of Aero-Engine Components. Proceedings of the Institution of Mechanical Engineers. Part G: Journal of Aerospace Engineering 211(6), 421–428 (1997)
3. Zhang, J., Dong, P.: Residual Stress in Welded Moment Frames and Implications for Structural Performance. Journal of Structure Engineering 3, 306–315 (2000)
4. Gur, C.H., Tekkaya, A.E., Schuler, W.: Effect of Boundary Conditions and Work Piece Geometry on Residual Stress and Microstructure in Quenching Process. Steel Research 67, 501–506 (1996)
5. Boitout, F., Bergheau, J.M.: The Numerical Simulation of Welding in Europe: Present Capabilities and Future Trends. Trans JWRI 32(1), 197–206 (2003)
6. Li, Y.Y., et al.: Welding Technique and Application. Chemical Industry Press, Beijing (2004)
7. Gu, W.M., (trans.): ATSM E837-81 (American) The Standard Method by Drilling Hole Strain to Measure the Residual Stresses. Journal of Mechanical Strength, 8(1), 40–43 (1985)
8. 《Engineering Material Application Manual》Editorial Commission Compile.: 《Engineering Material Application Manual》. Aluminum Alloy Magnesium Alloy, vol. 3. Standards Press of China, Beijing (2002)
9. Souloumiac, B., Boitout, F., Bergheau, J.M.: A New Local/gLobal Approach for the Modelling of Welded Steel Component distortions. In: Cerjak, H. (ed.) Mathematical Modelling of Weld Phenomena, vol. 6, pp. 573–590. The Institute of Materials, London (2002)

10. Robin, V., Devaux, J., Bhandari, S., Bergheau, J.M.: Modelling of Bimetallic Welds. In: Cerjak, H. (ed.) Mathematical Modelling of Weld Phenomena, vol. 6, pp. 769–791. The Institute of Materials, London (2002)
11. ANSYS Lab-Material Nonlinearity.,
    http://www.asiri.net/courses/meng412/Lab
12. Gallée, S., Bois, C., Vadon, P., Nelias, D.: Forming Residual Stresses Effects on the Electron Beam Welding Distortions of Thick Components. International Journal of Material Forming 1, 367–370 (2008)

Dam Management with Imperfect Models:
Bayesian Model Averaging with and Neural Network Control

Paul J. Darwen

School of Business, James Cook University, Brisbane Campus
349 Queen Street, Brisbane, Queensland, Australia
paul.darwen@jcub.edu.au

Abstract. Dam management is a controversial control problem for two reasons. Firstly, models are (by definition) crudely simplified versions of reality. Secondly, historical rainfall data is limited and noisy. As a result, there is no agreement on the "best" control policy for running a dam. Bayesian model averaging is theoretically a good way to cope with these difficulties, but in practice it degrades under two approximations: discretizing the parameter space, and excluding models with a low probability of being correct. This paper explores the practical aspects of how Bayesian model averaging with a neural network controller can improve dam management and flood control.

1   Introduction

A dam on a river has two functions, to store water for dry times, and to prevent flooding. Unfortunately, these two functions are diametrically opposed:

- To prevent flooding, you should gradually let out all the water from the dam, so that it can catch a future flood.
- To store water for dry times, you should never let out any water.

The dam control problem is stark: how much water should we keep in the dam, and how much should we let out? Currently there is no consensus answer.

Section 3.1 looks at the simple control policy of always letting the water level down to some fixed percentage of the dam's capacity. Section 3.3 considers a more elaborate control policy using a neural network found by expectation maximization, either:

- By finding the single model that best fits historical data (using expectation maximization again), or;
- By finding a whole distribution of plausible models with Bayesian model averaging [2], an approach which is theoretically better [4, page 175] .

This paper explores the practicality of the Bayesian approach. It consumes vastly more computer time, even with two approximations: discretizing the space of models, and deleting models with sufficiently low probability of being correct.

D.-S. Huang et al. (Eds.): ICIC 2012, CCIS 304, pp. 360–366, 2012.

2   A Dam Control Problem

Imagine a river with a dam that has controllable release gates, so the dam's water level can be reduced to any desired level. To calibrate a rainfall model, only 100 years of historical rainfall data are available. For a future 50-year period, the two conflicting aims are to avoid either of these disasters:

- Avoid flooding, when the dam level reaches rises above 100%.
- Avoid running empty, when the dam level reaches 0%.

Evidence suggests that the weather in eastern Australia follows a 5-year cycle of wet and dry, with both shorter- and longer-term cycles to complicate matters [4]. To capture that, this paper makes up a stochastic rainfall function that gives river flow at time t (in months) by taking random samples from a lognormal function with standard deviation $\sigma = 0.1$ and mean μ given by:

$$\mu = \ln(2 + (0.3299928 \times \tanh(3.3 \times \sin(t/9.55))$$
$$+ (0.3345885 \times \tanh(3.4 \times \sin(t/7.00))) \qquad (1)$$
$$+ (0.3354186 \times \tanh(3.5 \times \sin(t/4.15)))$$

Equation 1 has three flood/drought cycles with roughly equal importance, with periods of 4.15, 7, and 9.55 months. The rest is merely to make it more complicated than the simple model described next in Section 2.1.

   To generate 100 years of historical data, running this rainfall function with a particular random number seed gives the historical data shown in Figure 1.

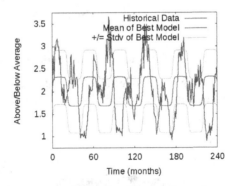

Fig. 1. The first 20 years of the historical data generated by Equation 1, overlaid with the single best-fit model from Equation 2

2.1   A Crude Model

All rainfall models are simpler than the real world, and here the model in Equation 2 is too simple to capture the actual rainfall function in Equation 1. Here, a simple stochastic model has the following form, with mean river flow μ set to:

$$\text{Mean river flow } \mu = 2 + w_0 \times \tanh(4 \times \sin(t/w_1)) \qquad (2)$$

That is, the model assumes a cycle from flood to drought, where the two model parameters are w_0 the amplitude and w_1 the duration of that cycle, and it predicts the river's mean flow at time in months. An example of this model for a particular choice of parameters w_0 and w_1 is in Figure 1.

To give the model a stochastic flavor, the prediction is a random sampling from a normal distribution with mean given by Equation 2 and standard deviation $\sigma = 0.6$. Any negative predictions are set to zero.

2.2   A Control Function

A popular control policy is to set a single parameter, namely how much of the dam's capacity to fill with water, with the unused capacity being a "flood compartment". This policy will be evaluated later in Section 3.1.

A more elaborate controller could be a neural network, and this paper uses the simplest kind: a sigmoid function equivalent to a one-node neural network.

$$\theta (u_0, u_1, x, t) = \frac{1}{1 + e^{u_0 + u_1 x}} \tag{3}$$

The sigmoid function in Equation 3 has bias u_0 and weight u_1, and takes input $x(w_0, w_1, t)$ the water level of the dam at time t as predicted by a model with parameters w_0 and weight w_1 from Equation 2. The sigmoid function θ is the desired water level that the dam should be lowered to. Of course, if the dam's water level is already less than that, then no water need be released.

As a sigmoid function can take an S-shape, the general aim of this controller function is to suggest a lower dam level if wet weather is predicted, and to suggest a higher dam level if dry weather is predicted.

2.3   The Single Best-Fit Model versus Bayesian Model Averaging

A popular approach for finding a controller is to calibrate the model's parameters to the historical data, and then calibrate a controller to that single best-fit model.

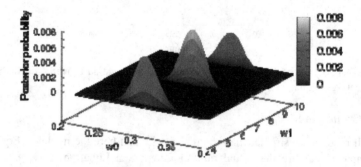

Fig. 2. The probability distribution of plausible models. The single most-probable model is the one at the peak of the highest hill.

To find that single best-fit model, expectation maximization is a popular approach: it finds the model that has the highest probability of being correct, given the data [2]. For the historical data in Figure 1, the most probable model has $w_0=0.32$ and $w_1=6.9964$ in Equation 2. Figure 1 shows this model.

The problem with the best-fit model is that the "highest probability of being correct" often turns out to be disappointingly improbable. With so little historical data, many other models are less probable, but still plausible.

In the Bayesian model averaging approach, the aim is to iterate over all those plausible models to find the probability that the model is correct, given the historical data. Figure 2 shows this probability distribution for our test problem. The highest point in that distribution represents the most probable model, at parameters $w0=0.32$ and $w1=6.9964$. But picking the highest point in the probability distribution (i.e., the best-fit model) ignores all those other less-probable models that are still plausible, throwing away much of the information in the historical data.

In this paper, the problem is not to find the single "best" model, but instead to come up with an adequate controller in spite of the limitations of a too-simple model.

2.4   Two Approximations to Bayesian Model Averaging

Bayesian model averaging is theoretically the better method [4, page 175], but that proof assumes a continuous world. In the messy world of numerical approximations, there are trade-offs. This section describes two approximations.

Firstly, the distribution of models in Figure 2 may look smoothly continuous, but actually uses a discretized grid to step through the parameters of the model. The w_0 axis has step size 0.004 and w_1 has a smaller step size of 0.0012 to capture those narrow sail shapes. These step values were chosen by hand, to be small enough to make Figure 2 smooth.

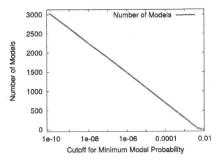

Fig. 3. There are many low-probability models, so this paper uses a cutoff of 10^{-6}, which makes for 1,489 models

Secondly, even with discretized model parameters, there are still a great many models with non-zero probability of being correct. Figure 3 counts how many models there are, as we descend from the peaks of Figure 2. Figure 3 can be extended to the left side without limit, so if you really want every single model with non-*zero* probability of being correct, there is essentially no limit. Rather than enumerate every single model, a reasonable approximation is to use some minimum cutoff, and ignore the low-probability models. From Figure 3, a cutoff of 10^{-6} will take the 1,489 most probable models.

3   Results

3.1   A Fixed Level Is Not a Good Policy

A simple control policy is to gradually release water from the dam until the level is down to some fixed percentage of capacity, so the unused dam space can be a "flood compartment". This section evaluates that kind of policy.

Take the single model that best fits the historical data, and use it to evaluate various fixed levels by doing Monte Carlo simulation of many possible 50-year futures. The peak of the solid line in Figure 4 shows that the single best-fit model predicts a fixed level of 71.65% would be the best water level to keep the dam at, and doing so should prevent disaster (either the dam over-filling, or running empty) with a probability of 99.35% over the next 50 years. Sounds pretty good, if you trust that single best-fit model!

Unfortunately, the dashed line in Figure 4 uses the true, unseen function that generates rainfall (from Equation 1) to evaluate the true probability of success. If you run the dam at a constant water level of 71.65% as suggested by the single best-fit model, then your true probability of success is a lousy 9.4%, much less than the 99.35% that the single best-fit model has led you to believe.

3.2   A Neural Network Controller from the Single Best-Fit Model

Take the single best model (which is the peak of Figure 2), and use it to find the best controller function. That single best model says its best controller should have a success rate of about 98%, which sounds pretty safe.

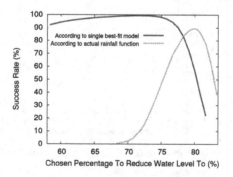

Fig. 4. A simple control policy is to gradually release water to bring the level down to some fixed percentage. Using the single model that best fits the historical data, this shows how well the fixed-level works according to that single best model, and according to the actual, unseen rainfall function. Keeping the water level at 71.65% (as the best-fit model suggests) would give a real success rate of only 9.4%.

Unfortunately, running that controller through 400,000 simulated futures using the true rainfall function gives a true success rate of only 32.3%. The actual success rate is worse because of the simplicity of the model's functional form, and the limited historical data. So for this approach, you have unwittingly doomed your city with a 67.7% chance of disaster some time in the next 50 years, even though your best-fit model predicts only a 2% chance of disaster.

3.3   A Neural Network Controller from Bayesian Model Averaging

Bayesian model averaging generates the whole distribution of models shown in Figure 2. This paper discretizes that distribution and then ignores the low-probability models, as described in Section 2.4.

So here, the best controller is the one that performs best, according to the weighted average of all 1,489 models. The weighting is according to each model's probability of being correct. This approach takes about 1,498 times as much computer time as using the single best-fit model. The best controller should get a success rate of 98%, according to those models, showing that the controller function is not the bottleneck — whatever the model(s), there is a controller which supposedly will have a 98% success rate, according to those models.

Taking that winning controller from Bayesian model averaging, and running it through 400,000 simulated 50-year futures using the true rainfall function gives a true success rate of 45.796%. That's better than the 32.319% from the single best-fit model in Section 3.2, and much better than the lousy 9.4% from using a fixed level back in Section 3.1. These differences are statistically significant.

The single best-fit model gives a controller at the parameters $u_0 = -2.4375$ and $u_1 = 1.546875$. In contrast, the controller from Bayesian model averaging are u0 = -2.83984375 and u1 = 1.9140625, a substantial difference.

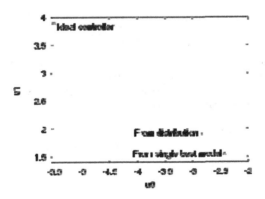

Fig. 5. The two controller functions, one found from the single best model, and the other from a Bayesian distribution of all plausible models, are shown here with the ideal controller, found by using the (usually unseen) function that generates rainfall. The Bayesian approach is closer to the ideal.

Equation 1 describes the (usually unseen) rainfall function. So this section cheats and uses that true function to find the ideal controller: it's at $u0 = -5.5$ and $u1 = +3.9$ and gives a success rate of 98.8% on the true rainfall function. Again, all controllers get about 98% on their choice of models, so it's not controller optimization that matters here. Figure 5 shows all three controllers in parameter space — the Bayesian approach's controller is closer to the ideal.

4   Discussion and Conclusion

Models are merely simplified, abstracted version of the real thing. A more realistic model would have more than the 2 parameters in Equation 2. However, models with many free parameters require more data. Any practical rainfall model cannot have a large number of free parameters, due to the shortage of historical data. This avoids a combinatorial explosion from a high-dimensional space of model parameters. So long as the space of plausible models has reasonably low dimensions, then iterating through that space of models should be feasible for the Bayesian model averaging approach.

In this problem, the complexity of the neural network controller and the algorithm for optimizing that controller were not the bottlenecks that prevent success — in fact, even the simple controller used here was good enough for a 98% success rate. The bottleneck is that the model is too simple. For such models, Bayesian model averaging is a practical way to do dam management and similar control problems.

Acknowledgements. This research was supported by James Cook University's Brisbane campus. The author would like to thank Matthew Fuller and Barrie Russell for invaluable technical support, and Professor Noel Richards for encouragement and support.

References

1. Hoeting, J.A., Madigan, D., Raftery, A.E., Volinsky, C.T.: Bayesian model averaging: A tutorial. Statistical Science 14(4), 382–417 (1999)
2. Jeffreys, H.: Theory of Probability, 1st edn. The International Series of Monographs on Physics. Oxford University Press (1939)
3. Mazzarella, A., Giuliacci, A., Liritzis, I.: On the 60-month cycle of multivariate ENSO index. Theoretical and Applied Climatology 100, 2327 (2010)
4. Mitchell, T.M.: Machine Learning. McGraw-Hill, New York (1997)

Research on Virus Detection Technology Based on Ensemble Neural Network and SVM

Boyun Zhang[1,2], Jianping Yin[2], and Shulin Wang[3]

[1] Department of Computer Science and Technology, Hunan Police Academy,
Changsha, Hunan 410138, China
[2] School of Computer Science, National University of Defense Technology,
Changsha, Hunan 410083, China
[3] School of Computer and Communication, Hunan University, Changsha
410082, China
hnjxzby@yahoo.com.cn

Abstract. Computer viruses have become a serious threat to the information system. In this paper, taken ensemble learning as a guide, automatic virus detection technology is studied, where a novel approach based on the integration of dynamic virus detection and static detection is proposed. The detection system utilizes support vector machine as member classifier for viruses' dynamic behavior modeling, and also uses probabilistic neural network as member classifier for static behavior modeling. Finally, the detection results from all member classifiers are integrated by D-S theory of evidence. Through the combination of heterogeneous classifiers, the accuracy of an ensemble virus detector has been improved.

Keywords: information security, computer viruses, ensemble neural network.

1   Introduction

The constantly increasing virus problems have become one of the greatest threats to information security. The emergence of encryption and metamorphic viruses leads to invalidity of the traditional code scanning method. So the study on new antivirus method is urgently needed. Currently, intelligence and automation of virus detection engine is the research focus. Kephart ct al[1] in IBM Watson research center studied the application of neural network in virus detection, and used it for detection of boot sector viruses, which achieved a good detection effect. However, at that time, only 200 boot sector viruses were detected, which accounted for 5% of the total number of virus samples in IBM virus research center. After that, Arnold et al[2] applied a similar technology in Win32 program detection.

In this paper, taken the statistical learning theory as the guide, automatic virus detection technology has been deeply studied, and a novel method integrated with dynamic virus detection and static detection based on D-S theory of evidence[3] has been put forward. The detection system uses support vector machine as member classifier for viruses' dynamic behavior modeling, and also uses probabilistic neural

D.-S. Huang et al. (Eds.): ICIC 2012, CCIS 304, pp. 367–372, 2012.

network as member classifier for static behavior modeling. At last, heterogeneous classifiers are combined with the use of D-S theory of evidence, which improves the accuracy of the ensemble virus detector.

2   Virus Detection Engine

2.1   System Framework

The virus detection system framework is shown in Figure 1. The system takes the program's dynamic behavior characteristics and static characteristics into account, and extracts two classes of characteristic vectors to represent the pattern of the sample program. One is API function used by the program, and the other is n-gram information extracted in a static way from PE program. The detection engine monitors and also analyzes the program's behaviors, which can effectively detect unknown viruses and various polymorphic viruses. In static analysis process, the method of probability and statistics is adopted to discover implicit information from n-gram[4], which can be used to detect the automatic production machine, compiler and programming environment in virus compilation, or even some programming habits of the program author, and can also effectively prevent counterattacks from the virus author. Member classifiers in this system include Probabilistic Neural Network (PNN) and Support Vector Machine (SVM). Bagging algorithm is used to generate member classifiers involved in ensemble, and the combination method of these member classifiers is based on Dempster-Shafer theory of evidence. In the training process of all member classifiers, the characteristic quantity input to PNN is API function calling information, and that input to SVM is the program's n-gram information, which increases the difference and irrelevance between classifiers.

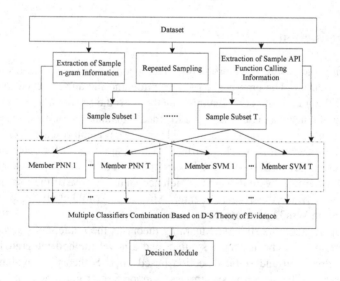

Fig. 1. Virus Detection System Framework

2.2   Generation of Member Classifiers

The commonly used generation methods for an individual member classifier mainly include Boosting and Bagging[5]. From the perspective of time cost in the detection system, we choose Bagging to generate individual member classifiers, for these classifiers generated from this method can be trained in parallel. The specific procedures are as follows:

Given a training set S , a series of training subsets $S_1, S_2, ..., S_T$ can be obtained by repeated sampling. Then, the information gain algorithm is used in each training subset to sort out the static attribute that plays an important role in classification and is input to PNN to turn out the individual member PNN. Meanwhile, the dynamic attribute that plays an important role in classification is sorted out and input to SVM to turn out the individual member SVM classifier.

At last, for the combination of member classifiers, we choose D-S theory of evidence for fusion, and also make a comparison with the results from the voting method.

2.3   Member Classifier Combination Based on D-S Theory of Evidence

As is known to us, whichever type the classifier or whatever its working principle is, in actual modeling, we should do our best to expand the distance between classes. Namely, for a classifier, if it has stronger separability, it has better classification results[6]. Therefore, the distance between classes can be chosen as the evidence probability assignment basis for each member classifier.

N classifiers are considered to be applied in K classification problem, and each class is expressed as θ_k ($k = 1, 2, ..., K$). The recognition framework under D-S theory of evidence is $\Theta = \{\theta_1, \theta_2, ..., \theta_K\}$.

If X_k is the training sample matrix of the class θ_k ($k = 1, 2, ..., K$), the feature matrix extracted from the feature selection modules of different classifiers is recorded as $X_k^{(n)}$. Classifiers can be homogeneous or heterogeneous, and different classifiers have different features space.

To state conveniently, for a classifier, its sample expression in different features spaces can be abstracted to be a modeling function:

$$\Gamma^{(n)}(X_k) = I_k^{(n)} , \quad k = 1, 2, ..., K , \quad n = 1, 2, ..., N . \tag{1}$$

Evidently, based on different principles and methods of classifiers, their modeling functions are different.

For a test sample x, the modeling of each member classifier can be expressed as:

$$\Gamma^{(n)}(x) = \Upsilon^{(n)} , \quad n = 1, 2, ..., N \tag{2}$$

Based on different expressions of a training sample and a test sample, each classifier $e^{(n)}$ can calculate the distance between the test sample and different classes of training samples, which is then normalized and marked as

$$Distance^{(n)}(I_k^{(n)}, \Upsilon^{(n)}), \quad k = 1, 2, ..., K \tag{3}$$

For any classifier $e^{(n)}$, K distance values between classes can be obtained and reorded as:

$$\mathbf{d}^{(n)} = [d_1^{(n)} \ d_2^{(n)} \ ... \ d_K^{(n)}]^T \tag{4}$$

If the classification result of the classifier $e^{(n)}$ for the test sample x is θ_j, its BPA can be calculated based on the following formula:

$$m^{(n)}(\theta_j) = logsig(variance[\mathbf{d}^{(n)}]) \tag{5}$$

in which $variance[\mathbf{d}^{(n)}]$ is the distance variance between classes, and $logsig()$ is an increasing S shaped function which maps variable values to $[0,1]$.

Then, based on Dempster rule, all member classifiers' BPAs are combined:

$$m(\theta_k) = m^{(1)} \oplus m^{(2)} \oplus ... \oplus m^{(N)}(\theta_k) \tag{6}$$

Finally, the decision rule of the combined classifier is:

$$\theta_j = \arg \max_k (m(\theta_k)) \tag{7}$$

3   Experimental Results and Analysis

There is a total of 632 samples in the data set, of which there are 423 normal programs and 209 malicious programs. API calling information of each sample is monitored and recorded in advance in a virtual machine, and meanwhile n-gram information of each sample is extracted[7]. Afterwards, features are selected.

There are two kinds of member classifiers in an ensemble classifier that are SVM and PNN. For the selection of the kernel function and misclassification penalty factor C which are two main parameters of a support vector machine, RBF kernel function is chosen in this article, and the values of C and γ are 2 and 0.015. In PNN, there is only one adjustable parameter that is SPREAD, which thus can be easily determined. The generation of individual members and the training process are seen in Figure 1. In order to improve the efficiency, variables are normalized in training.

In the experiment, we have compared the static virus detection method, dynamic detection method and the integrated detection method of the two in their performance, and the results are shown in Table 1.

Table 1. Detection results of different ensemble classifiers

Ensemble Method	Accuracy (%)	Area Under ROC Curve	Feature
1. Distance Ensemble Based D-S	98.73	0.993	API and n-gram
2. Classwiese Ensemble Based D-S	98.58	0.991	API and n-gram
3.Noneclasswise Ensemble Based D-S	97.31	0.964	API and n-gram
4. Ensemble SVM Based Bagging	96.52	0.921	API
5. Ensemble NN Based IG-Bagging	96.99	0.914	n-gram

Note: 1-probability assignment based on distance measure, D-S ensemble; 2- probability assignment based on recognition performance of a classifier, which has distinguished a classifier's different recognition performance for different classes of samples, D-S ensemble; 3-probability assignment based on recognition performance of a classifier, which hasn't distinguished the difference in a classifier's recognition performance for different classes of samples, D-S ensemble; 4-using Bagging method for SVM ensemble; 5-using IG-Bagging method for PNN ensemble.

From the experimental results we found that whatever ensemble method is used, the accuracy of the detection method that integrates dynamic virus detection and static detection is higher than that of a single detection method. The reason is that the characteristic quantities input to the ensemble classifier are the program's API information and n-gram information, and they are irrelevant, which increases the difference between classifiers to a maximum extent, and thus improves the performance of the detection system.

4   Conclusion

To realize that the dynamic detection and static detection technologies both have their own advantages and disadvantages, in this article, an integrated method of the two detection technologies has been proposed. In the system, member classifiers are heterogeneous essentially, and are not suitable for combination with the traditional voting method, so we use D-S theory of evidence for fusion of the results of different classifiers. The integrated detector has used different classes of characteristic quantities when training member classifiers, which can increase the irrelevance and difference between member classifiers to a great extent. During the combination of member classifiers, the property that a classifier has different classification performance for different classes of samples has been taken into account, so that the detection accuracy of the ensemble classifier has been greatly increased. Meanwhile, we note that for a classifier, during actual modeling, we should do our best to expand the distance between classes. The stronger the separability, the better its classification results are.

In this article, we have also studied the evidence probability assignment method based on a distance measure between classes, which reasonably reflects the influence of each member classifier on the final decision. The experiment shows that this method has good performance.

Acknowledgements. This work was partially supported by the National Natural Science Foundation of China under Grant No.60973153, the Planned Science and Technology Project of Hunan Province.

References

1. Tesauro, G., Kephart, J., Sorkin, G.: Neural Networks for Computer Virus Recognition. IEEE Expert 11, 5–6 (1996)
2. Arnold, W., Tesauro, G.: Automatically Generated Win32 Heuristic Virus Detection. In: Proc. of the 2000 International Virus Bulletin Conference, pp. 51–60 (2000)
3. Barnet, J.A.: Computational Methods for a Mathematical Theory of Evidence. In: Proc. 7th International Conference on Artificial Intelligence, pp. 868–875 (1981)
4. Assaleh, T.A., Cercone, N., Keselj, V., Sweidan, R.: Detection of New Malicious Code Uing n-grams Signatures. In: Proc. of the 2nd Annual Conference on Privacy, Security and Trust, pp. 193–196 (2004)
5. Breiman, L.: Bagging Predictors. Machine Learning 24(2), 123–140 (1996)
6. Schapire, R.E.: The Strength of Weak Learnability. Machine Learning 5(2), 197–227 (1990)
7. Sung, A., Xu, J., Chavez, P., Mukkamala, S.: Static Analyzer for Vicious Executables (SAVE). In: 20th Annual computer Security Applications Conference, pp. 326–334. IEEE Computer Society, Washington, DC (2004)

Enhancing Forecasting Performance of Multivariate Time Series Using New Hybrid Feature Selection

Roselina Sallehuddin, Siti Mariyam Shamsuddin, and Noorfa Haszlinna Mustafa

Soft Computing Research Group, Faculty of Science Computer and Information System, Universiti Teknologi Malaysia, 83010 Skudai, Johor, Malaysia
{Roselina,mariyam,noorfa}@utm.my

Abstract. The aim of this study is to propose a new hybrid feature selection model to improve the performance of multivariate time series (MTS) forecasting under uncertainty situation. This new hybrid model is called cooperative feature selection (CFS) and consists of two different component; GRA Analyzer and ANN Optimizer. The performance of CFS is evaluated on KLSE close price. The statistical analysis of the results shows that CFS has high ability to recognize and remove irrelevant input for obtaining optimum input factors, shortening the learning time and improving forecasting accuracy for vague MTS.

Keywords: GRA Analyzer, ANN Optimizer, Cooperative Feature Selection, Multivariate Time Series, Accuracy.

1 Introduction

The selection of input variables is very important in multivariate time series (MTS) forecasting. Improper selection and redundancy of input factors can lead to instability which will affect the accuracy of forecasting [1]. Generally, FS can be categorized as filter and wrapper method. The filter approach relies on the characteristics of the learning data and selects a subset of feature without considering any learning models. On contrast, the wrapper method employs straightly a learning model to adopt a subset of features. Selection of feature is based on generalization improvement. Thus it increases the computational cost but it has higher of generalization performance [1],[2],[3]. Therefore, hybrid method is employed to take advantage of the filter and wrapper method by complementing each weakness [1], [3].

In a real MTS situation especially in stock market, the environment is usually full of uncertainties and changes occur rapidly, thus future situations must be usually forecasted using limited data available over a short period of time. Therefore forecasting in this situation requires a method that works efficiently with incomplete data. Moreover, there are many input factors that influence the stock price simultaneously and usually these factors such as political events; general economics and trader's expectations are mixed together. As a result, the relationship between the stock prices and the input factors is ambiguous and uncertain. Besides, that knowing the priority of each

D.-S. Huang et al. (Eds.): ICIC 2012, CCIS 304, pp. 373–380, 2012.
© Springer-Verlag Berlin Heidelberg 2012

factor is also beneficial, since it can provide information on the most and least significant factors that influence the forecasting performance.

Although fuzzy methods are suitable for incomplete data situations, their
performance is not always satisfactory [4]. Rough set (RS) theory is also used to
handle uncertainties in time series. However, RS need a large amount of data
especially in attribute reduction step. All data used in RS also need to be coded into
finite several kinds that can lead to poor accuracy performance in MTS [5],[6]. To
overcome Fuzzy and RS limitations, the Grey relational analysis (GRA) which has
being proven to handle problems with small samples and insufficient information
effectively is employed [6]. Since GRA implementation did not utilize any learning
machine in searching the significant factors, it is classified as filter method and lack
of generalization performance. On contrast, the Artificial Neural Network (ANN) is
widely used as wrapper FS [1] but it requires a large amount of data to perform well.
Therefore in this study, GRA and ANN will be adopted as a cooperative feature
selection CFS to pull out the most effective factors when dealing with incomplete
data situations in order to increase forecasting accuracy. Besides that, combination of
both GRA and ANN can take the advantage of the speed of filter and the accuracy of
wrapper [1], [2],[3].

To validate the performance of the CFS, daily Kuala Lumpur stock exchange closing prices with 14 indexes are employed. The experiment results show that the proposed CFS model improves the forecasting performance of MTS. The rest of the
paper is organized as following. In section 2, brief explanation on GRA and ANN as
FS are presented. Section 3 describes the methodology of the proposed CFS. In section 4, the analyses of the experimental results obtained are discussed, and finally
section 5 provides the concluding remarks.

2   Review on GRA and ANN

GRA is a method of analysis, which has been proposed in the Grey system theory and
founded by Professor Deng [5],[6]. The purpose of GRA is to measure the relative
influence of compared series on the reference series. There are three (3) main steps in
GRA such as data normalization, calculating the grey relational coefficient and
calculating grey relational grade. First, data is normalized within [0,1] range using
(1) because the expectancy is the higher-the-better; meaning that the higher GRG
represent the more important input factor.

$$x_i^*(k) = \frac{x_i^0(k) - \min x_i^0(k)}{\max x_i^0(k) - \min x_i^0(k)} . i = 1,...,m; \ k = 1,...,n. . \quad (1)$$

Where m is the number of experimental data items, n is the number of parameters,
$x_i^0(k)$ is the original sequence, $x_i^*(k)$ is the sequence after data pre processing,
$\min x_i^0(k)$ and $\max_i^0(k)$ are the smallest and largest value of $x_i^0(k)$. Then, the
second step is to locate the grey relational coefficient by using (2).

$$\xi_i(k) = \frac{\Delta\min + \zeta\Delta\max}{\Delta_{0,i}(k) + \zeta\Delta\max} \tag{2}$$

Where, $\xi_i(k)$ = grey relational coefficient at any data point (k), Δ_{0i} = deviation sequences of the reference sequence and comparability sequence, $\Delta_{0,i} = \left\|x_0^*(k) - x_i^*(k)\right\|$, $\Delta\min = \min_{\forall j \in i \forall k}\min\left\|x_0^*(k) - x_i^*(k)\right\|$, $\Delta\max = \max_{\forall j \in i \forall k}\max\left\|x_0^*(k) - x_i^*(k)\right\|$, $x_0^*(k)$ = the reference sequence, and $x_i^*(k)$ = the comparative sequence. ζ is known as identification coefficient with $\zeta \in [0,1]$ and normally $\zeta = 0.5$. Finally, to obtain the GRG, the average value of grey relational coefficient is computed.

$$\gamma_i = \frac{1}{n}\sum_{k=1}^{n}\xi_i(k) \tag{3}$$

Where n is the number of the objective function or the reference sequence, $x_0^*(k)$. The GRG; γ_i represents the level of correlation between the reference sequence and the comparability sequence. Based on the calculated value of GRG, the grey relational order based on the size of γ_i is constructed. Each γ_i is ordered to the increasing grey relational coefficient. This derived order then gives the priority list in choosing the series that are closely related to the reference series x_o. Here, the features with the GRG less than 0.6 are excluded from the input list [5].

For ANN, FS can be thought as architecture pruning where input features are pruned rather than hidden neuron or weights. Here, FS is implemented based on some significance measure aiming to remove the less important features. Or in other words, FS is based on the reaction of the cross-validation data set classification error due to the removal of the individual features. The number of feature to be chosen is identified by the significant decrease of the classification accuracy of the test data set when eliminating a feature. Below is feature selection procedure using ANN. Figure 1 shows steps involve in ANN FS. Refer [7] for detail explanation.

3   The Proposed Cooperative Feature Selection Model (CFS)

Figure 2 shows two algorithm phases in CFS; GRA analyzer and ANN optimizer. Each phase is sequentially implemented starting with GRA analyzer followed by ANN optimizer. There are six steps in GRA analyzer algorithm and ten steps in ANN optimizer. Steps (6)–(9) are iterated until the optimum significant IP are obtained. GRA analyzer is used as preprocessing step to examine the relevance between each input factors (IP) and the dependent variables (output). It will rank each IP according to its importance or priority. The GRA analyzer will then examine the relationship between each IP and the dependent variable which is the close price;

i)   Randomly initialize the weights for each member of a set of j=1, . . , L neural networks. For each neural do Steps (ii) – (viii).

ii)   Randomly divide the data set available into Training, Validation and Test data sets

iii) Train the neural network by minimizing the error function and validate the network at each epoch on the validation data set. Equip the network with the weights yielding the minimum validation error.

iv)   Compute the classification accuracy on A_{Tj} for the Test data set.

v)   Identify the feature yielding the smallest drop of classification accuracy for the Test data set when eliminating the feature. Elimination is implemented by setting the value of the feature to zero

vi)   Eliminate the feature

vii) If the actual number of features M>1 go to step (iii)

viii) Record the feature ranking obtained and the test set classification accuracy A_{Tj} achieved using the whole feature set.

ix)   Compute the expected feature ranking and the test set classification accuracy $\hat{A}_T$ by averaging the results obtained from L runs

x)   Eliminate the least salient features according to the expected ranking and execute Step (iii)

xi)   Compute Test data set classification accuracy and drop in the accuracy ΔA when compared to $\hat{A}_T$

xii) If $\Delta A < \Delta A_0$, where ΔA_0 is the acceptable drop in the classification accuracy go to step (x)

xiii) Retain all the remaining and the last removed feature

xiv) Retrain the network with the parsimonious set of features

Fig. 1. ANN Procedure for Feature Selection

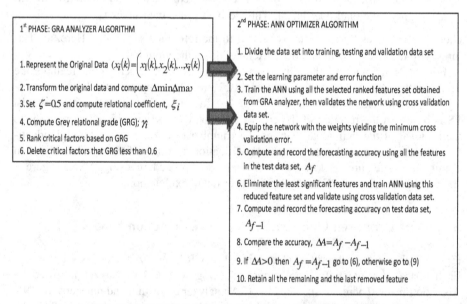

Fig. 2. Algorithm for Cooperative Feature Selection (CFS)

And subsequently rank each IP. Then IP with less priority will be excluded from the list. As recommended by previous studies [4] the IP with GRG values of less than 0.6 are considered as less significant; hence, it can be eliminated from the list of IP.

Finally, these selected IP are fed into ANN optimizer as input. At this point, feature selection is carried out using wrapper method with backward elimination. The backward elimination procedure starts with all available features belonging to the set of selected features. There are three iterative processes involved; testing the ANN accuracy, judging the data and deducing from the data input factors set. The feature with least significant in predictive performance is eliminated until it fulfills the stopping criterion. The output from this phase is the optimum number of IP, which is ranked based on their precedence. These optimum IPs are utilized as input nodes to build the ANN forecaster.

To validate the performance of the proposed CFS model, several experiments are conducted using Kuala Lumpur Stock Exchange (KLSE) closing price. KLSE data contains 200 observations of daily closing price from 4th January 2005 till 21st October 2005 and 14 IP (affecting factors) that influence the movement of KLSE closing price simultaneously. Thus, the relationship among these IPs and closing price becomes ambiguous and uncertain. These IP are Consumer Index, Construction Index, Gold Index, Finance Index, Product Index, Mesdaq Index, Mining Index, Plantation Index, Property Index, Syariah Index, Technology Index, Trading/Service Index, Composite Index and Industrial Index. These data are split into training, validation and testing. To measure the performance of CFS, three statistical tests are used namely, root mean square error (RMSE), mean absolute deviation (MAD) and mean absolute percentage error (MAPE).

4   Results and Analysis of CFS Model

There are two phases of input removal in CFS, first from GRA analyzer and secondly from ANN optimizer. Figure 3 shows the ranking scheme that contains the 14 input for KLSE, which are priorly analyzed by GRA. This ranking scheme is ordered in descending order based on the GRG values. The highest GRG value is ranked at the first ordered (Composite index) followed by the smaller GRG values. The smallest GRG value implied the least important of affecting factors, in this case the property index. Then, the affecting factors that have GRG less than 0.6 is deleted from the ranking scheme [5]. Therefore, Technology index, Construction Index, Mining Index and Property Index that have GRG < 0.6 are excluded from the ranking scheme; only nine input left to be trained further by ANN optimizer for locating optimum significant inputs. From Figure 3, instead of using 14 IPs, only four IPs (Composite, Trading/Service, Syariah and Industrial) are sufficient for predicting the next day KLSE closing price. This information are beneficial to people who are directly involved in stock market trading. These four indexes can be used as indicator for KLSE closing price. The traders can predict the price of the KLSE closing price based on the values of these four indexes. For example, if these indexes are high they may expect the closing price is also high or otherwise. Therefore, this information can assist them in determining the appropriate time to sell or to buy the stocks to maximize their profit.

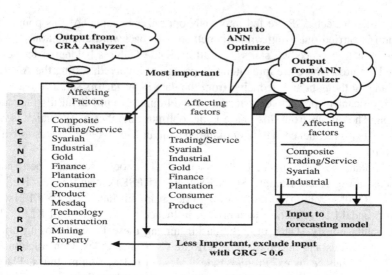

Fig. 3. CFS Implementation on KLSE Close Price

Table1 show the statistical result obtained from GANN, CFS and ANN. GANN represents the network model that trained with input selected from GRA only and ANN represents the neural network that trained without any FS; used all 14 inputs. Table 1 shown that the result obtained from ANN model alone without any FS is the worst compared to GANN and CFS. This indicates that the combination of GRA and ANN has removed the irrelevant factors that cause the instability in the forecasting model that lead to the poor forecasting performance. Besides that, the application of CFS also has successfully simplified the network structures; reduced almost 73% of the input number to be used in ANN forecasting model (14 to 4). Consequently, this simplified network structures shortened the training time to train the network to converge to the optimum solution that is from 65 seconds to 43 seconds and then finally to 12 seconds.

Table 1. Statistical Test for Each Model

Statistical test	GANN	CFS	ANN
Input/ Proc. time	9 inputs/ 43 sec	4 inputs/12 sec	14 inputs/ 65 sec
RMSE	35.92	6.22	44.80
MAD	35.89	6.16	45.11
MAPE	3.75	0.67	4.85
Accuracy	98.75	99.33	98.10

Fig 4 shows the forecasting values produce by each forecasting model. It clearly shown that the forecasted values using CFS is more closely to the actual values. This indicates that the application of CFS can help the ANN to automatically identify the optimum IPs and can minimize the probability of instability occur in forecasting model that lead to poor forecasting performance. Therefore by using the proposed CFS model, the dependency on human expert domain knowledge in determining the optimum IPs is no longer needed. Moreover, the forecasting accuracy of the proposed model also is the highest (99.33%) compared to ANN and GANN. CFS has improved GANN and ANN performance about 0.58% and 1.28% respectively. Table 2 shows the statistic for GANN, CFS and ANN compared to the actual values. It shows that the mean difference, standard deviation, and standard mean error of CFS (6.17) is the lowest compared to GANN and ANN. It indicates that the predicted values yield from CFS is the closest to the actual values as shown in Fig.4.

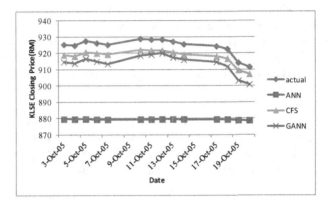

Fig. 4. Comparative Performance Forecasted Values and Actual Data

Moreover, the correlation between actual-CFS is the highest. This result indicates that CFS is better in describing the relationship between the actual and the predicted values of KLSE closing price.

Table 2. Statistic for GANN, CFS and ANN Compared to the Actual

	Paired Difference			
	Mean	Std, Deviation	Std Error Mean	Correlation
Actual - GANN	10.34	0.89	0.24	0.97
Actual-CFS	6.17	0.75	0.20	0.98
Actual- ANN	44.86	4.92	1.31	0.93

While the values obtained from ANN is the worst. This result implies that the forecasting error gained from ANN is the highest since the irrelevant factors used in ANN have degrade the forecasting accuracy. Thus, from the experimental result and statistical analysis, it showed that the proposed model CFS is able to give better result than GANN and ANN and more suitable to be employed as FS in incomplete MTS.

5   Conclusion

This paper discusses the implementation of the proposed cooperative feature selection by hybridizing filter (grey relational analysis-GRA) and wrapper method (ANN with backward strategy). Several experiments have been conducted to investigate the effectiveness of CFS. The results reveal that CFS is generally better in analyzing relationships among input factors and output. Besides improves the forecasting accuracy, CFS is able to identify the most and the least significant input factors by generating a ranking scheme model that listed all the input factors based on priority. Subsequently, it will provide the decision makers with the most and the least dominant factors. This information will assist decision makers on which factor should be emphasized in order to obtain an accurate result. Besides that, CFS can recommend the optimum significant factors without the need to refer to expert domain knowledge. The application of CFS also has simplified the network structure that speed up the training time. This study demonstrates clearly that the proposed CFS has great potential to be an effective and efficient FS tool for improving MTS forecasting performance under uncertainty and can be easily extended to be applied to other multivariate time series problems.

Acknowledgements. The authors first thank the anonymous reviewers for their valuable comments. This study is supported by Fundamental Research Grants Scheme (vot : 4F086) that sponsored by Ministry of Higher Education (MOHE) and Research Management Centre, Universiti Teknologi Malaysia, Skudai, Johor.

References

1. Crone, S.F., Kourentzes, N.: Feature Selection for Time Series Prediction. A Combine Filter & Wrapper Approach for Neural Network. Neurocomputing 73, 1923–1936 (2010)
2. Kabir, M.M., Islam, M.M., Murase, K.: A New Wrapper Feature Selection Ap-proach Using Neural Network. Neurocomputing 73, 3273–3283 (2010)
3. Bu, H., Xia, J.: Hybrid Feature Selection Mechanism Based High Di-mensional Datasets Reduction. Energy Procedia 11, 4973–4978 (2011)
4. Mehdi, K., Seyed, H.R., Mehdi, B.: A New Hybrid ANN and Fuzzy Regression Model for TS forecasting. Fuzzy Sets & Sys. 159, 769–786 (2007)
5. Lin, Y.H., Lee, P.C., Chang, T.P.: Practical Expert Diagnosis Model Based on Grey Relational Analysis Technique. Expert Systems with Applications 36, 1523–1528 (2009)
6. Ip, W.C., Hu, B.Q., Wong, H., Xia, J.: Application of Grey Relational Method to River Environment Quality Evaluation in China. Journal of Hydrology 379, 284–290 (2009)
7. Verikas, A., Bacauskiene, M.: Feature Selection with ANN. Pattern Recognition Letters 23, 1323–1335 (2002)

Porting Contiki Operating System to RIEST2430

Juan Wang, Wei Ma, and Dan Liu

Research Institute of Electronic Science and Technology,
University of Electronic Science and Technology of China, Chengdu, P.R. China
celia_wj@sina.com, mw5945@gmail.com, liudan@uestc.edu.cn

Abstract. Based on the analysis of the structure and elements of Contiki embedded real-time operating system, this paper presents the experience with implementing the transplantation of Contiki to the CC2430-based and low-power RIEST2430 platform. Lastly, we test the function of the porting modules. The test results show that all modules work correctly.

Keywords: WSN, RIEST2430, Contiki OS, porting operating system.

1   Introduction

Wireless Sensor Network (WSN) consists of spatially distributed autonomous sensors to monitor physical or environmental conditions [1]. RIEST2430 is one kind of sensor devices and based on the Chipcon/Texas Instruments CC2430 System-on-chip (SoC) solution. CC2430 has a 2.4GHZ low power RF transceiver which supports ZigBee protocol [2]. Contiki OS is an open source, portable, lightweight and multi-tasking embedded real-time operating system, which has a widespread use in many countries. Compared to other operating system, Contiki OS is more suitable for memory-constrained device [3]. Because of the lacking of support of RIEST2430, it is necessary to research the method of porting the Contiki OS to RIEST2430 platform.

In order to better understand this work, we introduce the RIEST2430 architecture in section 2. Based on the analysis of the structure and hardware-abstract hierarchical on Contiki operating system in section 3, this paper expatiates how to implement the transplantation on the RIEST2430 demo board in section 4. And test the function of the modules in section 5. This paper concludes with a discussion of future work and open issues in section 6.

2   Hardware

RIEST2430 combines a CC2430-based SoC with additional sensing elements, a USB connector, serial communication module, five arrow keys, JTAG debug interface and several LED lights.

CC2430 chip combines an Intel 8051 micro controller (MCU), a 2.4GHZ DSSS RF transceiver, 32/64/128KB of programmable non-volatile flash, 8KB of volatile RAM, Watchdog Timer, Power On Reset, Brown Out Detection and other elements[4]. The

D.-S. Huang et al. (Eds.): ICIC 2012, CCIS 304, pp. 381–386, 2012.

8051 MCU offers performance enhancements while using the same instruction compared to the industry standard 8051.

The memory on CC2430 is separated into four distinct but partially overlapping spaces: DATA, XDATA, SFR and CODE [5]. DATA and XDATA are read/write memory for data and are physically located in the 8KB volatile ram. SFR space is a special register to store data, instruction and stack pointers. The read-only CODE space is used to address flash memory, but it only can address up to 64KB at a time [6]. Technique to expanding CODE space beyond this limit called code banking, which can address more than 64KB spaces for embedded software images.

Serial communication module on RIEST2430 is jointing with UART0 of CC2430. And Serial port is converted to an USB interface through a CH340T chip. Thus the demoboard can be powered over USB. CH340T is jointing with P0.2, P0.3, P0.4 and P0.5, as is shown in figure 1.

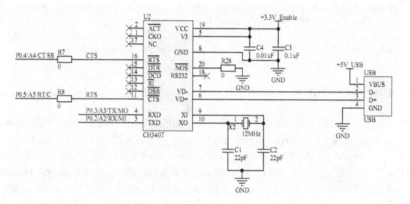

Fig. 1. Schematic of CH340T module

Five arrow keys (include up, down, left, right and middle button) are connected to P0.6 and P0.2 pins. User button is connected to P0.1 pin. Without modifying the I/O definition, this design is also in line with the TI protocol stack design and is compatible with the development of the Z-Stack.

JTAG debug interface provides the access to emulator for online simulation and program download. It is connected to P1.4, P1.5, P1.6, P1.7, P2.1 and P2.4 pins. The power switch can select 3.3V power supply from the debugger through the JTAG interface.

3   Contiki OS

Contiki operating system is developed in C language by Adams Dunkels and is mainly used in embedded system. It only costs very little memory space when executed [7].

Protothreads mechanism and event-driven are two important features of Contiki OS. Protothreads is based on an extremely lightweight thread library without the support of stack. Protothreads are non-preemptable. Therefore, a context switch can only take place on blocking operations [8]. Compared to other operating system which design for WSN, Contiki's each thread only needs ten lines of code and 2B RAM space. As a result, Contiki is more suitable for constrained devices which have limited memory space. And Contiki also support multi-thread.

Event-driven mechanism means that the Contiki kernel is event-driven. The idea of such system is that every execution of a part of the application is a reaction to an event .Every process is related to one kind of event. Process scheduling is based on FIFO algorithm and event scheduling is based on polling algorithm [9].

Alongside its RFC-compliant TCP/IP stack (uIP), Contiki is enhanced to provide support for IPv6 which make it possible to connect Internet on IP layer directly.

4   Porting Contiki OS

Adam Dunkels has provided an Unbuntu-based Integrated Development Environment (IDE) Instant Contiki for Contiki OS developers. However, the Instant Contiki is running in virtual machine. In order to facilitate compiling and debugging, we need to build the development environment and toolchain individually in real Linux environment.

4.1   Development Environment and Toolchain

The visual development tool used in the porting process is Eclipse. Eclipse is a well-known free cross-platform integrated development environment and is primarily used for the development of Java language. So we need install the plugin CDT in order to support C language and add C/C++ perspective to the Eclipse workbench. Contiki source code is imported through the "Standard C the Make Project" option after configuring the Eclipse.

Due to the 8051 MCU's unique characteristics, there are only a handful of toolchains available. The most noteworthy open source solution is the Small Device C Compiler (SDCC) [10]. It can optimize for specific MCU including the global register allocation algorithm and so on. The images of other MCU types can avoid to be compiled by configuring the "device / lib / inc.mk" file and accelerating compilation. SDCC provides debug tools SDCDB. As part of our work, we have solved all compilation and linking errors in the original code.

The following tools are also needed for compilation: gcc, flex, for bison, libboost-graph-dev Python and srecord.

The entire compilation process can be divided into four steps: pre-processing, compilation, linking, generation, as is shown in figure 2.

4.2   Porting the Contiki OS Port

The process of porting Contiki OS is mainly implemented through SFR and I/O port on the MCU to achieve the hardware's adaptation. Therefore the core work is porting board-level peripherals.

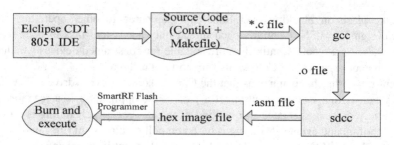

Fig. 2. Process of compilation

The entry function 'main()' of Contiki OS is included in the source file "plat-form\ejoy-cc2430\Contiki-main.c". It handles the initialization for hardware circuit, system processes, network components, watchdog, power management and interrupt. The configuration and control of the CC2430 chip are finished after the initialization of hardware. In fact, this series of initialization process is set to initialize some global variables, SFR and I/O ports.

The system kernel provides support for sensors, IPv6, the DISCO (download pro-gram to external flash), power management, BATMON (battery monitor log program) and watchdog through system service.

At the end of main() function, there is a "while(1)" infinite loop. This loop can be divided into 3 parts: the first part deals with watchdog and events, the second part processes the RF receiver and the third part implements power manager. Event re-sponse is the most important part and it is the kernel of Contiki OS. Pins, serial com-munication module, RF driver and Timer will be introduced in the next part.

Pins. CC2430 total have 21 programmable I/O pins. These pins can be used as usual I/O port or as peripherals I/O port to connect ADC, timers, or USART by setting up a group of SFR register. According to the circuit of RIEST2430 platform, the mainly work is to implement the configuration of peripherals I/O ports of timer, UART0 and LED lights. LED lights are connected to P0.1-P0.4 and are switched by operating the I/O ports.

Serial communication module. CC2430's serial communication module is joint with a CH340T chip to convert serial ports to USB. The USB port connected to PC is recog-nized as serial port after installed the driver. At the end of CC2430, the four pins (RT, CT, TX and RX) of CH340T are connected with UART0.

CC2430 provides serial communication ports by UART0 and UART1. UART mode and SPI mode are both selectable referenced by CC2430's Datasheet. We choose UART mode and use 2-wire and 4-wire mode to enable RXD and TXD ,while RTS and CTS are optional. 2-wire mode multiplex the pins.

RF driver. The structure of RF device driver "radio_driver" is defined in the source file "core/dev/Radio.h" and provides the access of all function points of Radio API calls [11]. The system calls are implemented by filling up these functions. They have to be rewritten in "cpu\cc2430\dev\cc2430_rf.c". RF is controlled by Commands strobes in Datasheet.

In addition to this, when the RF receiver receives data, it will trigger the interrupt and system will startup cc2430_rf_process to deal with these data. This process can be override to meet other requirements.

Timer. CC2430 has 4 timers: Timer1 (16 bits), MAC timer (Timer2), Timer3 (8 bits) and Timer4. MAC timer can provide timer service for IEEE802.15.4 CSMA-CA algorithm and MAC layer. Other three general timers support typical timing/counting function, such as input capture, output compare and PWM function.

The timer interrupt will trigger in the following cases: the counter overflows, capture event or output compare event occurs. An external event can cause CPU interrupts which must meet the following conditions: global interrupt and the corresponding timer interrupt are both enabled. Only when these conditions are met and the corresponding interrupt flag bit is set to true, it will trigger an interrupt.

There are several different timer modules (such as timer, stimer, ctimer, etimer and rtimer) provided by realizing functions clock_init (void) and rtimer_arch_init (void). Timer and stimer only simply detect whether the timer expires. Ctimer is used to call the callback function when timeout. Rtimer can trigger interrupts and schedule real-time tasks.

5   Test and Analysis

Based on the work finished above, we tested the functions of Timer, Serial Communication module, RF module and LED respectively. The test process is as follws:

LED test.To check LED lights and timers' working status, we conduct the test. To control 4 LED lights, timer triggers the event to send a control signal. As a result, the 4 LED lights will turn on or out every 2 second. Test results show that the LED lights and timers are in normal work status.

Serial communication module test. To test the serial communication module, we can use a computer to receive the data from the serial port. We need to connect PC to RIEST 2430's serial port with an USB cable and run serial receiver software on PC to obtain the output from serial port.

The serial communication module and keys test runs by turning on the board and running test cases for serial port and keys. Some data or strings will be received and showed on PC, if UART0 module works effectively.

RF communication test. Switch on two nodes (node1 and node2) and auto-execute point-to-point communication test program which is pre-burn into system image. The nodes will connect by RF radio. LED lights show the connection status by blinking the green one per 2 seconds. If the red LED light is on, we could send message by pressing keys on the node2. Then we can read the connection information strings on PC by serial line. Test results show that the RF radio works properly.

According to the test results above, we have finished the work of porting Contiki OS to RIEST2430 platform successfully.

6   Conclusion

This paper analyzes the porting process of Contiki OS based on RIEST2430 platform. And test the function of the modules. Test results show that the ported modules (pins, serial port module, RF driver, Timer) work correctly.

In the following work, we will focus on the uIP stack and other standards to study the methods of connecting WSN and Internet [12].

Acknowledgement. Thanks for my teacher Liu Dan who supports me finish this paper. Thanks for my classmates and friends and without their help this paper will not be finished. Thanks for my parents and I will love you forever.

References

1. Feng, K., Huang, X., Su, Z.: A Network Management Architecture for 6LoWPAN Network. In: Proceedings of IEEE IC-BNMT 2011, pp. 430–434 (2011)
2. Bruno, L., Franceschinis, M., Pastrone, C., Tomasi, R., Spirito, M.: 6LoWDTN: IPv6-Enabled Delay-Tolerant WSNs for Contiki. In: Distributed Computing in Sensor Systems and Workshops (DCOSS) 2011 International Conference, pp. 1–6 (2011)
3. Chien, T., Chan, H., Huu, T.: A Comparative Study on Operating System for Wireless Sensor Networks. In: International Conference on Advance Computer Science and Information System, pp. 73–78 (2011)
4. A True System on Chip solution for 2.4GHz IEEE 802.15.4/ZigBee. In: CC2430 Data Sheet (2007)
5. System on Chip for 2.4GHz ZigBee/IEEE 802.15.4 with Location Engine. In: CC2431 Data Sheet (2007)
6. Aamodt, K.: CC2431 Location Engine. Texas Instruments Application Note AN042 (2006)
7. Chen, Y., Feng, G.: Using Network Coding to Improve Robustness and Persistence for Data Transmission in Sensor Network. In: 2011 6th International ICST Conference on Communications and Networking, China (2011)
8. He, J., Huang, X.: Incresed Interoperability: Evolution of 6LoWPAN-based Web Application. In: 2011 4th IEEE International Conference on Broadband Network and Multimedia Technology (2011)
9. Kovatsch, M., Duquennoy, S., Dunkels, A.: A Low-Power CoAP for Contiki. In: 2011 Eighth IEEE International Conference on Mobile Ad-Hoc and Sensor Systems, Valencia, Spain, October 17-22 (2011)
10. Sdcc-Small Device C Compiler, http://sdcc.sourceforge.net
11. Hill, J., Szewczyk, R., Woo, A., Hollar, S.: System Architecture Directions for Networked Sensors. In: SIGPLAN Not., pp. 93–104 (2000)
12. Tsiftes, N., Eriksson, J., Dunkels, A.: Poster Abstract: Low-power Wireless IPv6 Routing with ContikiRPL. In: Proceedings of the 9th ACM/IEEE International Conference on Information Processing in Sensor Networks (2010)

A New Approach for Bayesian Classifier Learning Structure via K2 Algorithm

Heni Bouhamed[1], Afif Masmoudi[2], Thierry Lecroq[1], and Ahmed Rebaï[3]

[1] University of Rouen, LITIS EA 4108, 1 rue Thomas Becket,
76821 Mont-Saint-Aignan cedex, France
[2] Department of Mathematics, Faculty of Science of Sfax, Soukra B.P 802 Sfax, Tunisia
[3] Bioinformatics Unit, Centre of Biotechnologie of Sfax, 3018 Sfax, Tunisia
Heni.bouhamed@yahoo.fr, Thierry.lecroq@univ-rouen.fr,
Afif.masmoudi@fss.rnu.tn, Ahmed.rebai@cbs.rnrt.tn

Abstract. It is a well-known fact that the Bayesian Networks' (BNs) use as classifiers in different fields of application has recently witnessed a noticeable growth. Yet, the Naïve Bayes' application, and even the augmented Naïve Bayes', to classifier-structure learning, has been vulnerable to certain limits, which explains the practitioners' resort to other more sophisticated types of algorithms. Consequently, the use of such algorithms has paved the way for raising the problem of super-exponential increase in computational complexity of the Bayesian classifier learning structure, with the increasing number of descriptive variables. In this context, the present work's major objective lies in setting up a further solution whereby a remedy can be conceived for the intricate algorithmic complexity imposed during the learning of Bayesian classifiers' structure with the use of sophisticated algorithms. Noteworthy, the present paper's framework is organized as follows. We start, in the first place, by to propose a novel approach designed to reduce the algorithmic complexity without engendering any loss of information when learning the structure of a Bayesian classifier. We, then, go on to test our approach on a car diagnosis and a Lymphography diagnosis databases. Ultimately, an exposition of our conducted work's interests will be a closing step to this work.

Keywords: Bayesian Classifier, structure learning, classification, clustering, modeling, algorithmic complexity, K2 algorithm.

1   Introduction

It is worth noting that efficient classifiers can be reached through the use of Bayesian networks [1, 2, 3]. In fact, a Bayesian Classifier relative to a problem with p variables is characterized by the distinction of having $p + 1$ nodes. Indeed, all Bayesian classifiers model the fact of belonging to a certain class by means of a discrete node dubbed "class node". This node is discrete and multinomial having k modality. The class node is distinct for not owning a parent node. Regarding the other p variables, which we call descriptive variables, they are denoted X_i (i from 1 to p). The Bayesian classifier with the simplest structure is the Naïve Bayesian Network (RBN) [9], also

D.-S. Huang et al. (Eds.): ICIC 2012, CCIS 304, pp. 387–393, 2012.

called Naïve Bayes classifier. Nevertheless, no correlations between the attributes are taken into account with respect to the Naïve Bayes, where all features contribute to the classification in the same way. The classification node takes advantage of the information provided by each attribute independently of the information provided by other features-still; this may not be optimal for the classification task. Hence, various proposals have been suggested in a bid to enrich the Naive Bayesian Network structure to make it account for correlations between different attributes. In [2], for instance, the authors have proposed a Tree-Augmented Naïve Bayes (TAN) approach to enrich the network structure. According to this approach, a tree structure is applied for the classification to be achieved [20, 5]. The tree structure has the advantage of having a low degree of complexity, along with the ability to avoid over fitting problems. However, it restricts the number of parents, other than the classification node, to exactly one single parent for each node, which turns out to be a strong constraint. So, the resulting structure appears to neglect the case where a variable is correlated with several other variables. Besides, it outlooks the case where a variable is conditionally independent of all other variables within the classification node. In which case, the node representing that variable only needs the class node as a parent. The addition of another parent only adds unnecessary complexity and increases the number of network parameters. Consequently, other authors [4, 5, 6, 28, 8] have proposed the use of more sophisticated methods to overcome these shortcomings, among which are: the use of the K2 algorithms [6, 24, 25, 26, 27, 28, 10, 4], the Genetic Search [7, 4], the Greedy Search [11, 4], the Annealing Simulated [8, 4], the Greedy Hill Climber [7, 4] and the Repeated Hill Climber [7, 4]. Although these algorithms have actually managed to attain performant classifiers, their application has resulted in the frequently and commonly encountered problem of structure-learning computational complexity owing to the increase in the number of descriptive variables.

Hence, a new approach has been proposed through this research work based on a structure learning upstream clustering, which can be jointly used with the K2 algorithms pertinent to the structure learning of Bayesian Classifiers. The envisaged aim behind this framework proposal is to reduce the computational complexity and, consequently, the execution time without engendering a loss of information, in comparison to the use of the classic K2 algorithm.

2   A New Clustering-Based Heuristic: Methodology

The idea lying behind our conceived procedure lies in the rapid super-exponential surge of algorithmic complexity of learning the Bayesian Classifier structure from data [12, 13] with respect to the rise in the number of variables. To remedy this problem, our idea consists in subdividing the variables into subsets (or clusters), by learning the structure of each cluster's separately, while looking for a convenient procedure whereby the different structures could be assembled into a final structure. In this regard, it has been noticed that in the case of a Bayesian classifier learning structure, there exists one single central variable of a global interest called "class" variable. In this respect, we reckon to execute the processing of each cluster's learning structure with the class variable, then, proceed by assembling the different various structures around this class variable as a next step.

2.1   The Variables' Clustering

Regarding our present work, we have chosen to use the K-means algorithm, as it is the most popular and applied in the literature, added to fact that its algorithmic complexity is linear $(O(n))$ [14]. We also propose to use a hierarchical clustering algorithm along with the bootstrap technique to obtain the optimal number of clusters that will be introduced as entries in the K-means algorithm. To note, the databases that will be applied to test our approach, in the experimentation section, consist of categorical variables, and regarding the performance of clustering we will use the toolbox ClustOfVar with the software R [15]. In particular, we will use the variant K-means for categorical variables [16, 17] and the link-likelihood approach [18] (hierarchical clustering algorithm for categorical variables). To assess the stability of all possible partitions, 2 to $p-1$ (where p is the total number of variables) clusters from the hierarchical clustering, we will use a feature called "Stability" (also developed in the ClustOfVar toolbox) based on the "bootstrap" technique. The result is a graph which is then a tool to help to select the number of clusters. The user can be choosing the number K of clusters to the heights of the first increase in the stability.

2.2   Structure Learning

A structure learning has been performed for each cluster of variables including the class variable. The ultimate structure would be the assembling of the n structures obtained from each cluster around the class variable.

We will perform our tests via the K2 algorithm with, as input, the order obtained by applying the algorithm MWST (for the MWST algorithm, the initial node will be the class variable) [21]. In our study case, we would rather try to prove that the joint use of our approach together with the K2 algorithm can be beneficial in reducing the computational complexity without losing information.

Note that in our work, we will use the BNT toolbox [22] running on the Matlab software (2010 version) to apply the MWST and K2 algorithms to structure learning. We will also apply the BNT toolbox for parameters learning and inference.

3   Experimentations Procedures

3.1   Data-Bases

We first test our approach, on a car diagnosis database (Car Diagnosis 2). It has 18 variables, among which is a status variable called "Car starts", the Class variable. The parameters' generating file of this data base is available on the site http://www.norsys.com/downloads/netlib/. According to these parameters, we have been able to generate 10.000 examples, among which 32 have been left aside for the references' testing phase. We also apply our approach to a Lymphography diagnosis database (Lymphography). It is made up of 19 variables, among which is a status variable called "Diagnosis", the Class variable. This lymphography domain has been obtained from the University Medical Centre, Institute of Oncology, Ljubljana, Yugoslavia (available on request on the site http://archive.ics.uci.edu/ml/datasets/Lymphography). Among the *148* instances of data, *32* have been left aside for the references' testing phase.

3.2   Clustering

Regarding the clustering, we are going to use the stability function (bootstrap approach using the mean of corrected rand criterion [19]) of the toolbox ClustOfVar [16] after the application of an hirarchical ascendant algorithm, in order to estimate, approximately, the number of clusters to be entered in the algorithm K-means.

Using the stability graphics, the optimal number of clusters selected, for "Car diagnosis 2" database, has been equal to three.

Using the stability graphics, the optimal number of clusters selected, for "Lymphography" database, has been equal to two.

3.3   The Classical Learning Structure Compared to Our New Heuristic

For the "Car diagnosis 2" database, the execution time has been *3.45* seconds for the classical structure learning of the entire variables. The global execution time of our approach application has been *1.45* seconds (over *1.32* seconds for cluster 1; *0.05* seconds for cluster 2 and *0.09* seconds for cluster 3). The sum of these executions' time (*1.45* seconds) remains significantly inferior to the structure learning of the entire variables simultaneously.

For the "Lymphography" database, the sum of learning structure of "cluster 1" and "cluster 2" executions' time (equal to *1.65* seconds) remains significantly inferior to the structure learning of the entire variables, simultaneously, which equals *2.67* seconds.

3.4   Both Attained Structures' Relevant Inferences and Result Comparisons

Our approach favors the preservation of data for the class variable's sake, we will learn the parameters of the two structures found for each of the databases studied (structure found after learning all the variables simultaneously and structure found after assembling the various structures of the clusters around the class variables). For the class variable, we are going to calculate the probabilities of its different states; given the states of the networks other nodes in respect of the two obtained Bayesian classifiers structures. Thus, a *32* database will be used for experimenting the class variables of both databases. Naturally, the experimentation examples have been excluded during the structures' learning. The statistical significance of difference between the obtained probabilities, with respect to both structures, will be measured via the "Z" test (comparing the two observed means belonging to two different samples) [23].

The two tested Class variables are "Car starts" of the "Car Diagnosis 2" database and "Diagnosis" of the "Lymphography" database. The results are presented in graphs form (See Fig. 1 and Fig. 2) showing the Z-test variation corresponding to each variable studied according to its different possible states.

3.5 Discussion

Based on the achieved experimental results, the pairs of probabilities for the variable "diagnosis" of the "Lymphography" database are identical; the preservation of information has been complete (see Fig. 2). As for the variable "Car Start" of "Car Diagnosis 2" database, the probabilities pairs are very similar but not identical; the hypothesis H_0 has always been rejected, even with very small Z values, not exceeding the value of $|0.46|$, very distant from the threshold of $|1.96|$, as set by the Z test theory (see Fig. 1). It can, therefore, be deduced that the inference results, regarding both of learning structures approaches, are very similar even at eye sight, and without applying any statistical tests to measure the difference's significance. Through our approach, we have managed to reduce, considerably, the algorithmic complexity of the Bayesian classifier structure learning without any significant loss of information.

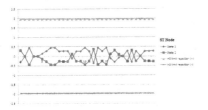

Fig. 1. Z-test variation for the "Car starts" variable

("Car Diagnosis 2" database).

Fig. 2. Z-test variation for the "Diagnosis" variable

("Lymphography" database).

4   Conclusion

Within the scope of the present work, we have set up a new well-defined approach for the Bayesian Classifier structure learning from data-base, so useful that it can be jointly applied with the K2 algorithms in the aim to reduce the computational complexity of this process. we have proved that loss in data turns out to be so negligible that it does not affect the extracted Bayesian classifier stemming results during the inference stage, while saving a great deal of execution time.

References

1. Langley, P., Sage, S.: Induction of Selective Bayesian Classifiers. In: Proceedings of the Tenth Conference on Uncertainty in Artificial Intelligence, pp. 399–406 (1994)
2. Friedman, N., Geiger, D., Goldszmid, M.: Bayesian Network classifiers. In: Machine Learning, pp. 131–163 (1997)

3. Pernkopf, F.: Bayesian Network Classifiers Versus Selective k-NN Classifier. In: Pattern Recognition, pp. 1–10 (2005)
4. Stuart, M., Yulan, H., Kecheng, L.: Choosing the Best Bayesian Classifier: An Empirical Study. IAENG International Journal of Computer Science, 1–10 (2009)
5. Madden, M.G.: A New Bayesian Network Structure for Classification Tasks. In: Irish Conference on Artificial Intelligence & Cognitive Science, pp. 203–208 (2002)
6. Lerner, B., Malka, R.: Investigation of the K2 algorithm in learning Bayesian Network Classifiers. In: Applied Artificial Intelligence, pp. 74–96 (2011)
7. Witten, H.I., Eibe, F.: Data Mining: Practical Machine Learning Tools and Techniques with Java Implementations. Morgan Kaufmann (1999)
8. Kirkpatrick, S., Gelatt, C.D., Vecchi, M.P.: Optimization by Simulated Annealing. Science, 671–681 (1983)
9. Domingos, P., Pazzani, M.: On the Optimality of the Simple Bayesian Classifier under Zero-one Loss. In: Machine Learning, pp. 103–130 (1997)
10. Cooper, G., Hersovits, E.: A Bayesian Method for the Induction of Probabilistic Networks from Data. In: Machine Learning, vol. 9, pp. 309–347 (1992)
11. Spirtes, P., Glymour, C., Scheines, R.: Causation, Prediction, and Search, 2nd edn. MIT Press (2000)
12. Judea, P., Tom, V.: A Theory of Inferred Causation. In: Allen, J., Fikes, R., Sandewall, E. (eds.) KR 1991, Principles of Knowledge Representation and Reasoning, pp. 441–452 (1991)
13. Robinson, R.W.: Counting Unlabeled Acyclic Digraphs. Combinatorial Mathematics 622, 28–43 (1977)
14. Tufféry, S.: Data Mining Et Statistique Décisionnelle: l'intelligence des données, Editions TECHNIP (2010)
15. Jain, A.K.: Data Clustering: 50 years beyond K-means. Pattern Recognition Letters 31, 651–666 (2010)
16. Chavent, M., Kuentz, V., Liquet, B., Saracco, J.: ClustOfVar: an R Package for the Clustering of Variables. In: The R User Conference (2011)
17. Chavent, M., Kuentz, V., Saracco, J.: A Partitioning Method for the Clustering of Categorical Variables. In: Locarek-Junge, H., Weihs, C. (eds.) Proceedings of the IFCS Classification as a Tool for Research. Springer (2009)
18. Lerman, I.C.: Likelihood Linkage Analysis (LLA) Classification Method: An example treated by hand. Biochimie. 75(5), 379–397 (1993)
19. Green, P., Kreiger, A.: A Generalized Rand-Index Method for Consensus Clustering of Separate Partitions of the Same Data Base. Journal of Classification, 63–89 (1999)
20. Chow, C., Liu, C.: Approximating Discrete Probability Distributions with Dependence Trees. IEEE Transactions on Information Theory 14(3), 462–467 (1968)
21. Francois, O., Leray, P.: Evaluation D'algorithmes D'apprentissage de Structure pour les réseaux bayésiens. In: Proceedings of 14ème Congrès Francophone Reconnaissance des Formes et Intelligence Artificielle, pp. 1453–1460 (2004)
22. Murphy, K.: The BayesNet Toolbox for Matlab. In: Computing Science and Statistics: Proceedings of Interface, vol. 33 (2001),
http://www.ai.mit.edu/~murphyk/Software/BNT/bnt.html
23. Sprinthall, R.C.: Basic Statistical Analysis, 7th edn. (2003)
24. Ezawa, K., Singh, M., Norton, S.: Learning Goal Oriented Bayesian Networks for Telecommunications Risk Management. In: Proceedings of the Thirteenth International Conference on Machine Learning, pp. 139–147 (1996)

25. Porwal, A., Carranza, E., Hale, M.: Bayesian Network Classifiers for Mineral Potential Mapping. Computers & Geosciences 32, 1–16 (2006)
26. Malka, R., Lerner, B.: Classification of Fluorescence in Situ Hybridization Images using Belief Networks. Pattern Recognition Letters 25, 1777–1785 (2004)
27. Estevam, R., Hruschka, J., Ebecken, N.: Towards Efficient Variables Ordering for Bayesian Networks Classifier. Data & Knowledge Engineering 63, 258–269 (2007)
28. Carta, J.A., Velázquez, S., Matías, J.M.: Use of Bayesian Networks Classifiers for long-Term Mean Wind Turbine Energy Output Estimation at a Potential Wind Energy Conversion Site. Energy Conversion and Management 52, 1137–1149 (2011)

The Architecture of Internet Software Environment for Creating Teachware with Virtual Reality

Valeria Viktorovna Gribova and Leonid Aleksandrovich Fedorischev

Intelligent System Laboratory, Institute of Automation and Control Processes,
The Far Eastern Branch of Russian Academy of Science
Vladivostok, Russia
gribova@iacp.dvo.ru, fleo1987@mail.ru

Abstract. An architecture of the Internet software environment for creating teachware with virtual reality is presented in the article. Basic components, ontologies, different types of teachware projects, and the scheme of interpretation of projects are considered. Software environment will be used for checking and drilling professional knowledge and skills of students in various fields of knowledge.

Keywords: education, virtual reality, computer simulators, ontologies, teachware, educational software.

1   Introduction

The number and variety of educational software available to schools, universities, and homes has increased over the last several years. One type of them is teachware with virtual reality. Urgency of educational software is well-known and widely discussed in literature [1-3].

There are a lot of tools, special software packages and different technologies simplifying development of teachware with virtual reality at the software market; among them are Virtools, WorldToolKit, Juggler, Delphin, ToolBook, Act3D, Amira, Unity3D, Alternativa3D and others.[4]

However, each teachware with virtual reality is the unique complicated software application (sometimes including special hardware). Teachware development and maintenance is a time consuming process because this type of software is often developed by coding in a programming language and demands the high level of the programmer's qualification.

The aim of this report is to describe the architecture of the Internet software environment, basic components, ontologies, different types of projects, and the process of the interpretation of a project of teachware.

2   Basic Principles of Development of the Internet Software Environment

Key ideas of the Internet software environment are automation of the development of teachware and involvement of not only programmers, but also domain experts and

D.-S. Huang et al. (Eds.): ICIC 2012, CCIS 304, pp. 394–399, 2012.

designers in this process. Implementation of these ideas can be achieved by the use of the ontological approach for automation of professional activity [5, 6].

According to the key ideas, the following principles of software development for creating teachware with virtual reality are proposed [7]:

1. *Development of ontologies for describing a virtual world of teachware.* Ontologies [8] are necessary for developers of teachware (domain experts, designers, and programmers). They can define and modify the structure of a project of teachware in terms of ontologies. Taking into consideration heterogeneity of tasks and different types of developers it is necessary to develop ontologies in accordance with types of developers and their tasks.
2. *Design of a project of teachware in terms of ontologies.* A project of teachware with virtual reality is a concretization of ontologies. It specifies parameters of ontologies and values of their terms.
3. *Support of functioning of teachware by interpretation of its project and generation by it the virtual world.* The interpreter of a project and the generator of a virtual world provides decreasing laboriousness of the development and maintenance of teachware (due to almost entire exclusion of the labour-intensive stage of coding from the life cycle of   teachware).
4. *Implementation of the Internet software environment as a cloudy service, available for users via the Internet.* Using the Internet and the cloud computing technology provides flexibility of control and maintenance of software and expands the quantity of users [9].

3   Architecture of the Internet Software Environment

According to the presented ideas, the Internet software environment comprises some components (see Fig. 1). All the components can be divided into two classes: software components and informational components:

Information components are:

- *ontologies* of teachware with virtual reality;
- a *project or projects* formed using ontologies (a project contains the complete description of   a virtual scene);
- *multi-media data* (figures, 3d-models of the virtual world, and so on);
- *agents* (additional and independent software modules intended for realization some specific functions).

Software components are as follows:

- *Project editor* is the structural editor controlled by ontologies for editing all components of a project. Depending on a downloaded ontology it allows developers to design one of components of a project.
- *Virtual world editor* is the visual editor for designers. The virtual scene is designed using a project formed by the structural editor. After editing the scene by the virtual world editor the updated information is recorded in the project.

- *Agent editor* is the structural editor for creating and modification of agents. Agents are independent modules called by the project interpreter for processing.
- *Interpreter* is a program for processing and analysis of a project and for forming or changing the virtual world of teachware.
- *Client module* is a program for representing a virtual world formed by the interpreter in a browser for users of teachware.

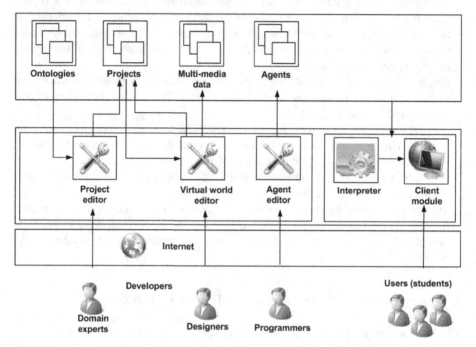

Fig. 1. Architecture of the Internet software environment

4   Ontologies for Creating Teachware with Virtual Reality

Ontologies for creating teachware with virtual reality are described in the [10]:

- *Ontology of objects* describes properties of objects of a virtual scene. Object properties are intended for describing representation, location in a virtual space, relations between objects, and conditions of changing and so on. All objects of a virtual world are divided into elementary and compound; animate and inanimate. In order to display objects in 3d-space it is necessary to use 3d-models (3d-images), textures, 3d-world coordinates. Each object has a set of attributes determining its properties. The attributes can determine characteristics of the whole object as well as characteristics of some states of the object. On this basis there are assigned following classes of objects: Simple Object, Changeable object, Compound Object, and Array.

- *Ontology of actions* describes properties of actions that a student may execute with objects of a virtual scene. Actions can be interactive and instructive; they may have a valuation and representation of results, or change objects. Actions can include different attributes depending on their destination. If an action is to change any objects, the action definition specifies the names of the objects and the states to be changed. If an action is to return the result , the action definition includes attributes describing possible results. The same action can be executed with different objects. So actions are individualized by input parameters.
- *Ontology of a scenario* describes properties of a scenario. It is a chain of actions that a student should execute during his or her work with the program. The scenario can include different type of transitions, branches, cycles, and labels. On the one hand, the scenario is a graph. Nodes of the graph are actions; arcs are transitions from one actions to others. On the other hand, the scenario is a sequence of logical stages. Each stage comprises a subgraph of the graph.. A stage can have parameters for its specification.

Based on ontologies a project describing a set of objects for the virtual scene, actions with objects, and the scenario are designed.

5   Projects of Teachware

Projects of teachware with virtual reality can be divided into two basic types:

1.   Examination of a virtual world.
2.   Execution of training exercises with their checking.

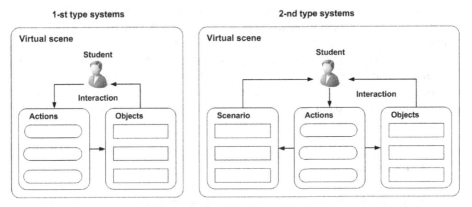

Fig. 2. Two types of projects of teachware

Projects of the first type allow students to carry out different kinds of examination and investigations of the virtual world. In a static virtual world a student can see only locations of objects on the virtual scene. In our case the scene is dynamic and a student can observe results of object interaction in the virtual scene. Results of the interaction are not fixed, they depend on many parameters. There are object attributes, parameters of actions, the current state, and so on.

Projects of the second type allow a student not only to investigate the virtual world, but and to execute training exercises with their checking. It means that the user can interact with any objects of the virtual world, but all actions are recorded and analyzed by the interpreter. If a student makes a mistake the system informs the student and explains what his or her mistakes are. The scenario is intended for describing various possible ways of interaction in the virtual world.

The two types of projects of teachware are shown in Fig. 2.

6   Interpreter

The virtual teachware is formed by the project and is changed during the run-time by the interpreter. The interpreter has different steps depending on the type of the project.

- *Initialization*. This step is intended for forming the virtual scene of teachware: creating objects, adding events, setting initial values of parameters. The initialization involves the following steps: initialization of objects (forming 3D-models, texture overlay), initialization of actions, assignment of connections between objects and actions, assignment of relations among objects, assignment initial states of objects.
- *Action processing*. This step is intended for processing user interaction with the virtual world objects: initialization, identification and launch of actions, alteration of objects, representation of action results and so on. The instructive actions are chosen by the user via the interface. The interactive actions are launched by the user interaction with virtual world objects. One object may be connected with a number of actions, but at the moment the object is connected with the one action. If the object is connected with two or more actions, then the action to be executed at the moment is determined by the current object state. If the current object state is changed, the connection between the action and the object may be changed.
- *Scenario proceeding* (only for projects of the second type). This step provides saving information about executed action, and determination of the next available actions.

7   Conclusions

Features of creating and functioning the Internet software environment for development teachware are described. Characteristics of different types of teachware and their projects based on ontologies are presented. The scheme of interpretation for different types of projects is shown. To date a prototype of the system is realized and experimentally examined, and implementation of a full-function version of the system to be used for creating teachware for various domains is in progress.

Acknowledgements. The research was supported by the Russian Foundation for Basic Research, the project 10-07-00089 and the Far Eastern Branch of Russian Academy of Science, the project 12-I-П15-03.

References

1. Filatova, N.N., Vavilova, N.I.: Design of Multimedia Simulators based on Scenario Models of Knowledge Presentation. Educational Technology S Society 3(4), 193–202 (2000)
2. Gammer, M.D.: Applying of Computer Simulators and Virtual Reality Systems in Educational Process, http://cde.tsogu.ru/publ1/
3. Virtual Reality in Education, http://www.intelin.ru/index.php?p=3
4. Cruz-Neira, C., et al.: An Open Source Platform for Virtual Reality Applications Virtual Reality Applications Center Iowa State University,
   http://oldsite.vrjuggler.org/pub/vrjuggler-aiaa2002.pdf
5. Kleschev, A.S.: The Role of Ontologies in Programming. Part. 1. Analitics. Informational Technologics (10), 42–46 (2008)
6. Kleschev, A.S.: The Role of Ontologies in Programming. Part. 2. Interactive design of informational objects. Informational Technologics (11), 28–33 (2008)
7. Gribova, V.V., Osipenkov, G.N., Sova, S.A.: The Concept of a Tool based on Knowledge for Diagnostic Simulator Development. International Book Series. Human Aspects of Artifical Intelligence (12), 27–33 (2009); Suppl. to the International Journal Information Technologies & Knowledge 32, Sofia, Bulgaria (2009)
8. Kleschev, A.S., Artemyeva, I.L.: The Mathematical Models of Domain Ontologies. Part. 1. The Existing ways to Defining of the "Ontology". Term. NTI. Middle 2(2), 20–26 (2001)
9. Concer T.: Cloud Computing: all as a service. PC Week/RE (32) (638),
   http://www.pcweek.ru/themes/detail.php?ID=112879
10. Gribova, V.V., Petryaeva, M.V., Fedorischev, L.A.: Development of the Virtual World for the Medical Computer Simulator. Distance and Virtual Education (9), 56–66 (2011)

An Efficient Image Database Encryption Algorithm

Kamlesh Tiwari, Ehtesham Akhtar Siddiqui, and Phalguni Gupta

Department of Computer Science and Engineering,
Indian Institute of Technology Kanpur
Kanpur 208016, India
{ktiwari,akhtar,pg}@cse.iitk.ac.in

Abstract. This paper proposes an efficient algorithm to encrypt image database. The proposed algorithm generates a unique key for every image at the time of encryption/decryption to make encryption algorithm robust against attacks. The encrypted image appears chaotic and random; and thereby does not reveal any features of original image. It presents a mechanism for a secure image database transfer over insecure channel. It uses least significant bit insertion method to make the encrypted image visually unsuspicious.

Keywords: Encryption, Decryption, SHA-256, Cryptography, Stenography, Image database.

1   Introduction

Many popular image processing or security systems are image dependent. They acquires substantial number of images in their database over a period of time. Generally such databases are collected by various sources and transmitted to a central repository for storage. As such, the secrecy of these databases is very important because the reliability of overall system deeply rely on the security of transmission and storage of these databases. Traditional cryptographic algorithm are not practically advisable for the image encryption because of the large data size of images which requires much time to directly encrypt/decrypt the image. There is a need to design reliable and fast image encryption algorithm which can ensure the privacy of important biometric or defense related digital images for storage and transmission.

There exists a verity of encryption algorithms to transmit secret images. In [5] a SCAN based methodology for lossless compression and encryption of binary and grayscale images has been presented. It is a formal language based two dimensional spatial accessing method which can efficiently specify and generate a wide range of scanning paths or space filling curves. An efficient mirror like image encryption algorithm which is based on a binary sequence generated from a chaotic system has been proposed in [8]. There exists a digital signature based algorithm in [7] to encrypt an image for secure image transmission. Vector quantization has been used in [2] to design an image cryptosystem. The images are first decomposed into vectors and then are encoded sequentially vector by vector for subsequent use in traditional cryptosystem from commercial applications.

D.-S. Huang et al. (Eds.): ICIC 2012, CCIS 304, pp. 400–407, 2012.

In [3] a method for visual cryptography has been discussed. It uses halftone images to share the secret image. The graylevel visual cryptography method initially converts the graylevel digital image into a halftone image representation and subsequently generates two transparencies of visual cryptography. The characteristics of human vision is used to decrypt the encrypted images. In [9] it is shown to use any existing optical grayscale image encryption methods to encrypt color images. Such images are converted to the indexed image format. The encoding subsystem encodes the image to stationary white noise having dual arbitrary phase masks: first one in the plane of input while another in the plane of Fourier. Decoder recovers the color images by translating back the decrypted indexed images to Red, Green, and Blue format.

This paper presents an efficient image encryption algorithm for image database. It generates a unique key for every encryption/decryption which makes the proposed algorithm robust against attacks. The rest of the paper is organized as follows. Next section describes the proposed encryption approach. Section 3 describes the proposed decryption approach. The experimental results on different images have been analyzed in the next section. Conclusions are presented in the last Section.

2   Encryption

Let there be N_d grayscele or color images in the database. Database images are encrypted one by one in a group of g at a time. The ith image I_i, of dimension $n_i \times m_i$ becomes C_i of size $n_i \times 2m_i$ after encryption. The jth row of image I_i denoted by $R_{i,j}$ is encrypted to $\Lambda_{i,j}$. Image encryption also make use of a publicly known initial image I_0 of dimension $n_0 \times m_0$ and another image I_{test} which is repetitively sent at a fixed interval $t \leq g$.

Let K_E and K_H be two secret private keys of size 1024 bits and 512 bits respectively. The key K_i to encrypt I_i (or to decrypt C_i) is generated with the help of K_E, K_H, g, index of the group currently being encrypted rnd and previous image $Prev_i$ of I_i which is either I_{i-1} when $(i \bmod g) \leq 1$ or I_0 otherwise. Size of K_i is variable and it depends on m_i. The key $K_{i,j}$ for the encryption of $R_{i,j}$ (or decryption of $\Lambda_{i,j}$) is generated using $R_{i,j-1}$, K_i and K_H. Let $P_L^{S,b}$ be L^{th} pseudo-random permutation of integers from 1 to b using initial seed S at first permutation. $P_{i,j}^B$ is the final key obtained from $K_{i,j}$ for encryption/decryption.

2.1   Generating K₁

The key for image I_i is a function of $Prev_i$, K_E, K_H, i, g and rnd. The key K_i is formulated as

$$K_i = P_{size(\eta)}^{K_E,size(\eta)} | P_{size(K_E)}^{\eta,size(K_E)} \tag{1}$$

where η is a pseudo-random bit sequence given by $\eta = H_1|H_2| ... |H_{Z_1}$ with $Z_1 = 2 \times \lceil (m_i/128) \rceil$ and H_1, H_2, ..., H_{Z_1} are hash values given by

$$H_u = SHA(K_H|E_u|K_H) \tag{2}$$

Values of $E_1, E_2, \ldots, E_{Z_1}$ are scrambled bit sequences obtained by applying pseudo-random permutations on $Prev_i$ as

$$E_u = |_{\forall x,y}(P_u^{\psi,8}[prvpixel_{x,y}]) \tag{3}$$

where $prvpixel_{x,y}$ is (x,y) pixel value of $Prev_i$, $P_u^{\psi,8}[prvpixel_{x,y}]$ is the permutation of eight bits of $prvpixel_{x,y}$ according to $P_u^{\psi,8}$ and $|_{\forall x,y}$ is the concatenation in row major form. The value of ψ can be obtained as $\psi = i \times rnd \times S_i$ where S_i is the hash value of K_H concatenated with previous image $Prev_i$ concatenated with K_H, i.e.

$$S_1 = SHA(K_H|Prv_i|K_H) \tag{4}$$

It can be observed from the above construction that even if the cryptanalyst finds S_1 he cannot obtain K_H because SHA-256 is a one-way hash function and determining $\{K_H|Prv_i|K_H\}$ is as complex as breaking SHA-256 [1, 4]. Also, since S_1 is obtained from a secret key K_H, the cryptanalyst cannot predictably fix S_1. Similarly ψ is a linear function of S_1, so its cryptanalysis is as hard as S_1. This in turn implies the hardness of predictably fixing values of E_1, E_2, ..., E_{Z_1}. Deduction of $\{K_H|E_u|K_H\}$ by using the value of H_u is again as complex as breaking SHA-256. Similarly predictably changes in H_1, H_2, ..., H_{Z_1} and η are also not feasible. It is hard to determine K_E and η with known K_i. Therefore, K_i is a secured randomly generated key.

2.2   Generation $K_{i,j}$

The key $K_{i,j}$ is formulated as

$$K_{i,j} = P_{size(\xi)}^{K_i,size(\xi)}|P_{size(K_i)}^{\xi,size(K_i)} \tag{5}$$

where ξ is a pseudo-random bit sequence formulated as $\xi = h_1|h_2|\ldots|h_{Z_2}$ with with $Z_2 = 2 + 6(\lceil(m_i/128)\rceil - 1)$ and h_1, h_2, ..., h_{Z_2} are the 256-bit hash values as

$$h_u = SHA(K_H|e_u|K_H) \tag{6}$$

For row $R_{i,j}$, the values of $e_1, e, \ldots, e_{Z_2}$ are scrambled bit sequences obtained by applying pseudo-random permutations on $R_{i,j-1}$ as

$$e_u = |_{\forall j,y}(P_u^{\delta,8}[prvpixel_{j,y}]) \tag{7}$$

where $prvpixel_{j,y}$ is (j,y) pixel value of $R_{i,j-1}$ and $|_{\forall j,y}$ is the concatenation ranging over all values of y corresponding to $R_{i,j-1}$ and the value of δ is obtained by $\delta = j \times S_2$ where S_2 is the hash value of K_H concatenated with previous row $R_{i,j-1}$ concatenated with K_H as

$$S_2 = SHA(K_H|R_{i,j-1}|K_H) \tag{8}$$

Thus, $K_{i,j}$ is a randomly generated secured key because deducing K_H from known $\backslash S_2$ is as hard as breaking SHA-256. Further, S_2, δ, ξ, $e_1, e, \dots, e_{Z_2}$, h_1, h_2, $\dots$, h_{Z_2} cannot be predictably changed. K_H and e_u are secured against h_u. And K_i and ξ are secured against $K_{i,j}$.

2.3   Generation $K_{i,j}^B$

The key $K_{i,j}^B$ contains $2 \times 8 \times m_i$ bits with equal number of 0-bits and 1-bits. Let $temp\_K_{i,j}$ be the first $2 \times 8 \times m_i$ bits of $K_{i,j}$. Further, assume a and b are the number of ones and number of zeros in $temp\_K_{i,j}$,   respectively. Let $ind_{1,1}$, $ind_{1,2}, \dots, ind_{1,a}$ be the indices or locations of 1 in $temp\_K_{i,j}$. Similarly, let $ind_{0,1}$, $ind_{0,2}, \dots, ind_{0,b}$ be the indices or locations of 0 in $temp\_K_{i,j}$. Without loss of generality assume that $a > b$. With $K_{i,j}$ as a seed $(a-b)/2$ unique natural numbers between 1 and a are generated. Let these numbers be $pos_1, pos_2, \dots, pos_{\frac{(a-b)}{2}}$. Bits of $temp\_K_{i,j}$ are flipped at locations $ind_{0,1}$, ind_{1,pos_1}, $ind_{1,pos_2}, \dots, ind_{1,pos_{(a-b)/2}}$. By this, $temp\_K_{i,j}$ contains $8 \times m_i$ number of ones and zeros each. Finally,

$$K_{i,j}^B = temp\_K_{i,j} \qquad (9)$$

where $size(K_{i,j}^B) = 2 \times 8 \times m_i$ and $K_{i,j}^B$ contains $8 \times m_i$ number of ones and zeros each. Similar procedure can be carried out if $b > a$. We can observe that $K_{i,j}$ is secured against $K_{i,j}^B$ which cannot be predictably changed.

2.4   Image I_i Encryption

For the encryption of the first row $R_{i,1}$ of image I_i to Λ_i, the key $K_{i,1}$ is generated using $R_{i,0}$, K_i and K_H. The key $K_{i,1}$ subsequently generates $K_{i,j}^B$ which gives the location in the encrypted row $\Lambda_{i,1}$ where row $R_{i,1}$ is finally hided. The rest of the bits in $\Lambda_{i,1}$ are random. Similarly, $R_{i,2}$ is encrypted using $K_{i,2}^B$ which is generated using $R_{i,1}$ and other parameters. The rest of the rows of I_i are similarly encrypted to generate rows $\Lambda_{i,1}$, $\Lambda_{i,2}$, $\dots$, Λ_{i,n_i}. Thereafter, the encrypted rows are scrambled using a permutation which is generated using K_i as seed. This scrambling of the encrypted rows serves as an extra security measure and gives the final encrypted image C_i.

Group count g is the number of database images encrypted together. Grouping is done to minimize the propagation of error due to any tampering of images during transmission. Grouping restricts the errors within the group itself. The optimal value of g plays an important role. A large value of g would be used if the channel through which the encrypted images are passed cannot be tampered with. It takes more time for parallel decryption, if any. Again, a small value of g implies faster parallel decryption and can be used if there is a high chance of tampering of encrypted data being sent over a channel. A standard test image I_{test} is sent at a fixed interval $t \leq g$. After decryption of the this particular image, if the image obtained is same as the test image I_{test}, then all images in that particular group till the image I_{test} have been decrypted correctly and there is no tampering of data for that group till the image I_{test}.

2.5 Encryption of Row $R_{i,j}$ Using $K_{i,j}^B$

The process uses key $K_{i,j}^B$ to encrypt $R_{i,j}$ to $\Lambda_{i,j}$ by hiding the data $R_{i,j}$ into various locations of $\Lambda_{i,j}$. These locations are determined using the key $K_{i,j}^B$. These locations are the locations in binary sequence $K_{i,j}^B$ which are set to 1. Since the size($K_{i,j}^B$) = size($\Lambda_{i,j}$) = $2 \times 8 \times m_i$, and number of ones in $K_{i,j}^B$ = size($R_{i,j}$) = $8 \times m_i$, hence we can hide the data of $R_{i,j}$ into the above mentioned locations of $\Lambda_{i,j}$. The rest of the data of $\Lambda_{i,j}$ are random bits. After encrypting all rows of image I_i, we obtain the temporary encrypted image. Rows of this temporary encrypted image is scrambled to obtain the final encrypted image C_i using a permutation generated with K_i as seed.

2.6 Scrambling of Rows

The encrypted rows are permuted using the pseudo random permutation P^{K_i,n_i} which is generated with K_i as seed. This permutation is applied on the rows of the temporary encrypted image $TempC_i$. In other words,

$$new\Lambda_{i,j}\left(P^{K_i,n_i}(j)\right) = \Lambda_{i,j}, \forall j \tag{10}$$

The final encrypted image, C_i is

$$C_i = [new\Lambda_{i,1}, new\Lambda_{i,2}, \dots, new\Lambda_{i,n_i}]^T \tag{11}$$

2.7 Cryptanalysis

The algorithm encrypts row $R_{i,j}$ to $\Lambda_{i,j}$ and then permutes it to the new position whose index is $P^{K_i,n_i}(j)$. This permutation is obtained using K_i as seed. It is very hard to obtain K_i from P^{K_i,n_i}. Now since K_i is itself secure, the reverse is also true i.e. P^{K_i,n_i} cannot be obtained without the knowledge of K_i.

Since P^{K_i,n_i} is a secret permutation therefore, given an image I_i and its encrypted form C_i, the cryptanalyst does not know which $R_{i,j}$ is encrypted to which $\Lambda_{i,j'}$. The only thing that the cryptanalyst can do is to apply Longest Common Subsequence Matching [6] to obtain mapping between $R_{i,j}$, and a $\Lambda_{i,j'}$. Hence, for a particular $R_{i,j}$ the longest common subsequence of $R_{i,j}$ obtained with $new\Lambda_{i,j'}$ for $1 \leq j' \leq n_i$ can always return the maximum length subsequence at a particular j' where new $\Lambda_{i,j'} = \Lambda_{i,j}$. As such the longest common subsequence can be $R_{i,j}$. This process for a particular row is of the order of the number of rows in the image i.e. n_i. Hence, a cryptanalyst can obtain the permutation P^{K_i,n_i} only through an adaptive-chosen-plaintext attack but this permutation $P^{K_{i,n_i}}$ also does not give any information of K_i. Other attacks do not give this permutation away.

Finally, given a particular encrypted row $\Lambda_{i,j}$, it is difficult to obtain $R_{i,j}$ as $8 \times m_i$ bits are already random and the positions where the actual data is hidden are also random because of the secret nature of all keys. In other words, a particular $\Lambda_{i,j}$ can result up to $\binom{16 \times m_i}{8 \times m_i}$ possible positions where the data is hidden. A better brute force would be on the values of $R_{i,j}$ directly which is of the order $2^{8 \times m_i}$. Hence, the process steganographic encryption keeps the value of $R_{i,j}$ also fairly secure so all the permanent keys and generated keys are secure for the complete algorithm.

3   Decryption

Decryption of the first image C_1 requires the knowledge of I_0, K_E and K_H, and K_1. The same permutation used to scramble the rows during encrypteion is used to unscramble the rows of C_1. Subsequently K_1 is used to decrypt C_1 row by row. The key $K_{1,1}$ for the first row $\Lambda_{1,1}$ is generated using the constant $R_{0,1}$, K_1, K_H and other parameters. Since both the algorithms use same parameters to generate $K_{1,1}$, the modified key $K_{1,1}^B$ gives the same location in $\Lambda_{1,1}$ where $R_{1,1}$ is hidden during encryption. Hence $R_{1,1}$ is obtained correctly. Further, $R_{1,1}$ and various other parameters generate the key $K_{1,2}^B$ for decryption of $\Lambda_{1,2}$ to $R_{1,2}$. The same key $K_{1,2}^B$ has been generated by both the algorithms and hence $\Lambda_{1,2}$ is decrypted to $R_{1,2}$. Rest of the rows of C_1 are decrypted the same way to get the original image I_1. The process for decryption of C's to get I's is continued till all images are decrypted. At the ith iteration, K_i is generated using I_{i-1}, obtained from C_{i-1} and is used to get I_i from C_i. Since the encryption is carried out in groups, hence, the images are grouped in the same way for decryption. In every group, g images are decrypted. In the lth group, g grayscale images which are decrypted are $C_{q+1}, C_{q+2}, ..., C_{q+g}$, where the value of $q = g \times (l - 1)$.

3.1   Unscrambling of Rows

A pseudo random permutation with K_i as seed is generated. Since the initial seed is same as that used during the encryption for scrambling of the rows, the same permutation $P^{K_{i,n_i}}$ is generated. The *inverse* of the permutation is applied on the rows of the encrypted image. The same method which is used during the scrambling of rows is applied to generate the same final permutation with K_i as the seed.

3.2 C_i Decryption

The secret key K_H and the generated key K_i for the image C_i along with constant R_{01} are used to decrypt the rows $\Lambda_{i,j}$ to $R_{i,j}$. For the decryption of the first row $\Lambda_{i,1}$ of encrypted image C_i to $R_{i,1}$, the key $K_{i,1}$ is generated using the constant $R_{0,1}$, generated key K_i, secret key K_H and other parameters. This key $K_{i,1}$ is same as the key $K_{i,1}$ generated for encryption of row $R_{i,1}$ to $\Lambda_{i,1}$. Hence, the modified key $K_{i,1}^B$ gives the same locations in $\Lambda_{i,1}$ where $R_{i,1}$ is hidden during encryption. Hence, $R_{i,1}$ is obtained correctly. Further, $R_{i,1}$ and various other parameters generate the key $K_{i,2}^B$ for decryption of $\Lambda_{i,2}$ to $R_{i,2}$ which is same as the key $K_{i,2}^B$ which is used for encryption of $R_{i,2}$ to $\Lambda_{i,2}$. Hence $R_{i,2}$ is also obtained correctly. Rest of the rows of C_i can be decrypted in the same way to get the original image I_i.

3.3   Row $R_{i,j}$ Decryption Using $K_{i,j}^B$

Locations in binary sequence $K_{i,j}^B$ which are set to 1 are used as indicators to obtain the locations of hidden data in $\Lambda_{i,j}$ to get $R_{i,j}$.

4   Results

The proposed technique has been analyzed on a database of 24 color images. To make the encrypted image unsuspicious, it has used a modified version of the *least significant bit insertion* method which does not make significant visible changes in an image. It modifies the last 2/3 bits of each component of a color cover image and hides the relevant data inside these bits. Fig. 1 shows the original and its encrypted images. Images shown in Fig. 2 are obtained with the cover image after using the LSB method to hide the encrypted image of Fig. 1(b).

(a) Example Color Image   (b) Encrypted Color Image

Fig. 1. Input and encrypted image

Assume, cover image considered in Fig. 2(a) is used to embed the encrypted image of Fig. 1(b). The color cover image can be considered as 3 grayscale images I_R, I_G and I_B of R, G and B components. LSB method is used to hide the encrypted image of Fig. 1(b) in these 3 grayscale images and to generate $I_{R'}$, $I_{G'}$ and $I_{B'}$ respectively. Gray scale images $(I_{R'}, I_G, I_B)$, $(I_R, I_{G'}, I_B)$ and $(I_R, I_G, I_{B'})$ are considered to get 3 color images as shown in Fig. 2. One can observe that the appearance of encrypted image in Fig. 1(b) is completely random and does not give away any information about the original image of Fig. 1(a) without decryption with the secret keys K_H and K_E.

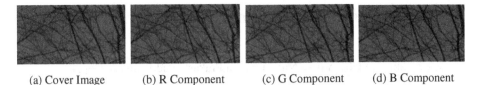

(a) Cover Image   (b) R Component   (c) G Component   (d) B Component

Fig. 2. Cover image and LSB stagnographed image in R, G, B channels

5   Conclusion

This paper has presented an efficient algorithm to encrypt image database. The encrypted images are found to to be random and do not reveal any image characteristics. All images in the database are divided into groups. Images within the group are used to encrypt the subsequent images of the group. Multiplicity of the algorithm without considering the post-processing of the encrypted image is 2.

Acknowledgement. Authors acknowledge the support provided by the Department of Information Technology, Government of India, to carry out this work.

References

1. Aoki, K., Guo, J., Matusiewicz, K., Sasaki, Y., Wang, L.: Preimages for Step-Reduced SHA-2. In: Matsui, M. (ed.) ASIACRYPT 2009. LNCS, vol. 5912, pp. 578–597. Springer, Heidelberg (2009)
2. Chang, C., Hwang, M., Chen, T.: A New Encryption Algorithm for Image Cryptosystems. Journal of Systems and Software 58(2), 83–91 (2001)
3. Hou, Y.: Visual Cryptography for Color Images. Pattern Recognition 36(7), 1619–1629 (2003)
4. Isobe, T., Shibutani, K.: Preimage Attacks on Reduced Tiger and SHA-2. In: Dunkelman, O. (ed.) FSE 2009. LNCS, vol. 5665, pp. 139–155. Springer, Heidelberg (2009)
5. Maniccam, S., Bourbakis, N.: Lossless Compression and Information Hiding in Images. Pattern Recognition 37(3), 475–486 (2004)
6. Paterson, M., Dancik, V.: Longest Common Subsequences. In: Mathematical Foundations of Computer Science, pp. 127–142 (1994)
7. Sinha, A., Singh, K.: A Technique for Image Encryption using Digital Signature. Optics Communications 218(4-6), 229–234 (2003)
8. Yen, J., Guo, J.: A New Chaotic Mirror-like Image Encryption Algorithm and its Vlsi Architecture. In: Pattern Recognition and Image Analysis, vol. 10(2), pp. 236–247 (2000)
9. Zhang, S., Karim, M.: Color Image Encryption using Double Random Phase Encoding. Microwave and Optical Technology Letters 21(5), 318–323 (1999)

Iris Segmentation Using Improved Hough Transform

Amit Bendale, Aditya Nigam, Surya Prakash, and Phalguni Gupta

Department of Computer Science and Engineering, Indian Institute of Technology Kanpur,
Kanpur 208016, India
{bendale,naditya,psurya,pg}@iitk.ac.in

Abstract. This paper presents an efficient iris segmentation algorithm. This paper uses an improved circular Hough transform to detect inner boundary and the circular integro-differential operator to detect the outer boundary of iris from a given eye image. Search space of the standard circular Hough transform is reduced from three dimensions to only one dimension, which is the radius. Local gradient information is used to improve time and efficiency of Hough transform. This algorithm has been tested on the publicly available CASIA 3.0 Interval database consisting of 2639 images of 249 subjects and CASIA 4.0 Lamp database consisting of 16,212 images of 411 subjects. It also provides error categorization for wrong segmentation, as well as a study on parametric influences on error. Parameterized error analysis helps to set parameters intelligently boosting up the segmentation accuracy as high as 99.8% on the Interval database and 99.7% on the Lamp database.

Keywords: Hough Transform, Integro-differential operator, Iris Segmentation, Occlusion, Illumination.

1 Introduction

Applications such as immigration control, aviation security, financial security require reliable identification of people. Biometric identification methods that identify individuals are based on physiological (fingerprint, face, iris, etc.) or behavioral (signature, gait, etc.) characteristics. Currently, major state of the art identification systems are using fingerprint, face, palm, knuckle [8] and iris. Recognition systems which use iris biometric are believed to be very accurate, and hence efforts are being put to improve their accuracy and reliability.

Iris is considered as a donut including colored ring of tissue around the pupil and has a very rich pattern of furrows, ridges, crypts, corona, freckles and pigment spots. These minute details of iris texture are believed to be determined during initial eye development. They are different for different persons and even for the two eyes of same person. Iris is found to be a well-protected and age invariant biometric. Like any other biometric system, iris recognition system mostly proceeds in five major steps: (1) Image acquisition with the help of camera under NIR (near infrared illumination) or visible light, (2) Segmentation to localize the iris, (3) Normalization in which the annular iris region is "unwrapped" from Cartesian to polar coordinates, (4) Feature

D.-S. Huang et al. (Eds.): ICIC 2012, CCIS 304, pp. 408–415, 2012.

extraction from iris texture and finally (5) Matching the iris features robustly. Each step affects overall performance, but segmentation is the most critical step. Wrong segmentation would render the subsequent steps meaningless. Thus, recognition performance of a system can be improved if segmentation is accurate.

Iris recognition using Gabor wavelet [3] is considered to be pioneering and this approach has been deployed widely. Recently, other researchers including Wildes [9], Boles and Boashash [2], Ma et al. [5], [6], and Monro and Zhang [7] have made significant contributions like application of PCA and ICA on iris images for recognition. Li et al. [4] used AdaBoost to learn the detectors of boundaries of iris and then use weighted Hough transform to detect inner and outer boundaries. Though these algorithms are theoretically well-established, but issues like system robustness, speed of enrolment and recognition, and non-cooperative identification remain to be considered. In the proposed segmentation approach, pupil and limbic boundaries are approximated by circles. It first attempts to locate pupil circle using Sobel edge detection on thresholded image and a modified and efficient Hough circular transform [1]. It then detects outer boundary with its center within a small window of pupil center and its perimeter outside the pupil circle within some range, using the robust circular integro-differential operator.

This paper is organized as follows: Section 2 describes the proposed iris segmentation algorithm. This algorithm has been tested on the publicly available CASIA 3.0 Interval and CASIA 4.0 Lamp databases. Experimental results have been analyzed in the next section. It also describes the segmentation error categorization. Conclusions are given in Section 4.

2   Proposed Iris Segmentation

This section discusses the proposed algorithm to segment iris from the eye image. It determines the iris first by localizing the inner boundary which is followed by localization of outer boundary of the iris.

2.1   Iris Inner Boundary Localization

Pupil of the eye can be assumed to be circular and hence is modeled as a dark circular region within the iris. An eye image I is scaled down and thresholded giving a binary image I_t to filter out pupil pixels. This reduces the search space for pupil boundary iris inner boundary) only to the dark pixels in the image. But several types of noise pixels like eyelashes, eyebrows, shadow or specular reflection on the pupil pose severe problems. Morphological flood-filling operator is applied to remove holes from I_t. Hence, specular reflection inside the pupil region and other dark spots caused by eyelashes are removed to give the binary image I_{tf}. Pixels at pupil boundary must be strong edge pixels, hence in order to obtain strong edge pixels, Sobel filters in horizontal as well as in vertical direction are applied on I_{tf} giving the gradient images I_{gh} and I_{gv} respectively. Gradient images I_{gh} and I_{gv} are combined to generate gradient magnitude image I_g as:

$$I_g(x, y) = (I_{gh}^2(x, y) + I_{gv}^2(x, y))^{1/2} \tag{1}$$

Finally, I_g is thresholded based on gradient magnitude with relative threshold of 0.5 to generate binary image I_{gb} having only strong edge pixels. Orientation of edge at any point (x, y) in I_{gb} is obtained using I_{gh} and I_{gv} as:

$$\Theta(x, y) = \tan^{-1}\left(\frac{I_{gv}(x,}{I_{gh}(x,}\right) \tag{2}$$

Standard Hough transform [1] is improved and used on only strong edge pixels represented as "White" in I_{gb} to detect the pupil boundary. Every "White" pixel in I_{gb} is assumed to be on some circle, hence there are two potential pupil center points (c_1^x, c_1^y), and (c_2^x, c_2^y), on opposite sides of tangent to the circle at that point. These potential center points are calculated for different radii using the fact that they lie in the normal direction to the edge orientation $\Theta(x,$ as:

$$c_1^x = x - r * \cos(\Theta(x, y) \tag{3}$$
$$c_1^y = y - r * \sin(\Theta(x, y) \tag{4}$$
$$c_2^x = x + r * \cos(\Theta(x, y) \tag{5}$$
$$c_2^y = y + r * \sin(\Theta(x, y) \tag{6}$$

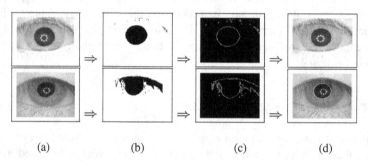

Fig. 1. (a) I (original), (b) I_{tf} (thresholded and filled), (c) I_{gb} (sobel edge), (d) I_{ps} (segmented pupil) images for two iris images

Simple voting strategy is applied to the 3-tuple i.e. pupil center's ordinate, abscissa and radius. A 3-D array A is created for storing the votes for all possible tuples where A(cx, cy, r) represents the number of edge pixels on the circle defined by the pupil center (cx, cy) with radius r. The parameters with maximum value of votes give the coordinates of center and radius of the iris inner boundary. Ties are handled arbitrarily, as they mostly represent the same circle. The algorithm for inner boundary localization is described in Algorithm 1. Proper thresholding is used on the original image I to get the binary image It from which specular reflection is removed to obtain Itf . Sobel edge detection on Itf gives the gradient images Ig, Igh and Igv and the binary edge image Igb with only strong edges. Potential center points (c1x, c1y), and (c2x, c2y) for the "White" points (x, y) in Igb are calculated using equations (3)-(6), with the radii ranging in [prmin, prmin], with the range chosen according to observed sizes of pupil in the database. Votes for these potential centers are incremented and stored in the accumulator array A. The algorithm outputs the required parameters: (cpx, cpy) and pr. Overall time complexity of pupil detection algorithm is $O(S + ER)$, where S is no. of pixels of image, E the number of edge points in Igb, and R is radius range. Steps of pupil segmentation are shown in Figure 1.

Algorithm 1: Pupil Segmentation
Require: Iris image I of dimension m x n, pr_{min}: minimum pupil radius, pr_{max}: maximum pupil radius, t: threshold
Ensure: Pupil center (c_p^x, c_p^y) and pupil radius p_r
1. I_t := threshold(I, t) //generate binary image after thresholding
2. I_{tf} := remove_specular_reflection(I_t) //flood filling
3. I_g, I_{gh}, I_{gv} := Sobel(I_{tf}) //Sobel edge detection
4. I_{gb} := Threshold_Gradient$(I_g, 0.5)$ //choosing strong edge points
5. $A(m$ x n x $pr_{max})$:= 0 //3-D array initialization
6. forall 'White' pixels ε I_{gb}
7.   for $r = pr_{min}$ to pr_{max} do
8.   Calculate $(c_1^x, c_1^y), (c_2^x, c_2^y)$ using equations(3)-(6).
9.   if (c_1^x, c_1^y) is in image I_{gb}'s bounds then
10. $A(c_1^x, c_1^y, r)$:= $A(c_1^x, c_1^y, r)$ +1 //vote casting
11.   end if
12.   if (c_2^x, c_2^y) is in image I_{gb}'s bounds then
13. $A(c_2^x, c_2^y, r)$:= $A(c_2^x, c_2^y, r)$ +1 //vote casting
14.   end if
15.   end for
16.   end for
17. (c_p^x, c_p^y, p_r) := $\text{argmax}_{(i,j,k)} A(i,j,k)$

2.2   Iris Outer Boundary Localization

Inner boundary localization of iris is used to guide the outer boundary localization. The contrast across outer iris boundary is less compared to the inner boundary. Edge detection faces edge-strength thresholding problems. To tackle this problem, the robust circular integro-differential operator [3] is used in a modified manner. This operator sums up pixel intensities over candidate circles and detects maximum change in this sum for neighbour circles per unit perimeter thus indicating presence of circular boundary. The algorithm for outer iris boundary localization is given in Algorithm 2.

In order to localize iris outer boundary, original image I is first smoothened using 2-D radial Gaussian filter to remove stray noise to give I_s. Iris center and pupil center are not necessarily concentric, but are usually close. Using this heuristic to speed up the search, candidate iris centers (c^x, c^y) are searched in W x W window $(W = 15)$ around the pupil center (c_p^x, c_p^y). Each such candidate center and a candidate radius in range (ir_{min}, ir_{max}) can define a circle. The minimum and maximum values of radii are chosen based on the observed sizes of irises from the database, which are almost fixed for a particular acquisition device. Integro-differential operator is applied over only two non-occluded sectors of this circle. Intensity values are summed over the arcs of two sectors defined by $\alpha_{range}= [(-\pi/4, \pi/6)^c \text{ U } (5\pi/6, 5\pi/4)^c]$ instead of the whole circumference. A point on these arcs of circumference of circle with center (c^x, c^y) and radius r can be represented as $(c^x- rsin(\alpha), c^y+rcos(\alpha))$ for $\alpha \in \alpha_{range}$. These sectors are chosen because in these sectors of the iris, occlusion is empirically found to be less compared to other areas of iris, thus facilitating correct localization. The maximum change in this summation and the parameters for it are tracked. This gives us the iris boundary parameters (c_i^x, c_i^y, i_r). Example iris images after localization are shown in Figure 2.

<u>Algorithm 2</u>: Iris Segmentation
<u>Require</u>: Iris image I of dimension m x n, ir_{min}: minimum iris radius, ir_{max}: maximum iris radius, (c_p^x, c_p^y): Pupil center, p_r: pupil radius, W: search window, α_{range}: angular range defining the occlusion free sectors
<u>Ensure</u>: Iris center (c_i^x, c_i^y) and iris radius i_r
1. I_s := GaussSmooth($I, \sigma=0.5, k=3$) //k: kernel size, Gaussian noise removal
2. max_{diff} := 0 //the maximum change in contour summation
3. forall points $(c^x, c^y) \varepsilon W$ x W window around (c_p^x, c_p^y) do
4. $prev_{sum}$:= 0 //previous summation of intensities
5. $start_{flag}$:= True //no circle has yet been summed up
6.   for $r = ir_{min}$ to ir_{max} do
7. c_{sum} := 0
8.   for all α in α_{range} do   //summation in arcs
9. c_{sum} := c_{sum} + $I(c^x - r*sin(\alpha), c^y + r*cos(\alpha))$
10.   end for
11. $diff_{sum}$:= c_{sum} - $prev_{sum}$ //difference of sum
12. $prev_{sum}$:= c_{sum}
13.   if $diff_{sum} > max_{diff}$ and $start_{flag}$!= True then
14. max_{diff} := $diff_{sum}$
15. c_i^x := c^x; c_i^y := c^y; i_r := r; //update parameters
16.   end if
17. $start_{flag}$:= False //a circle has been summed up
18.   end for
19. end for

3   Experimental Results

In order to analyze the proposed iris segmentation algorithm, we have considered the CASIA-Interval and Lamp databases consisting of 2639 images from 249 different subjects and 16,212 images from 411 subjects respectively. The segmentation accuracy using the proposed algorithm is found to be 94.5% on Interval and 94.63% on

Lamp databases. Segmentation parameters for the obtained accuracy for both databases are shown in Table 1.

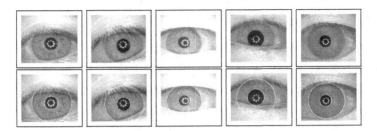

Fig. 2. Correct iris boundary localization

Table 1. Parameter values for CASIA databases

DB	t	pr_{min}	pr_{max}	ir_{min}	ir_{max}	W	α_{range}(radians)
Interval	0.4	20	90	80	130	15	$(-\pi/4,\pi/6)$ U $(5\pi/6, 5\pi/4)$
Lamp	0.1	16	70	65	120	11	$(-\pi/4,0)$ U $(\pi, 4\pi/3)$

An improper segmentation of iris leads to poor recognition. Out of 2639 images of CASIA 3.0 Interval database, we have found 145 segmentation errors and out of 16,212 images of Lamp database, we have got 870 errors. These errors have been critically analyzed and are corrected by adjusting few parameters. This adjustment helps to achieve the accuracy of 99.8% on Interval and 99.7% on Lamp database. Segmentation errors due to occlusion occur because of eyelid and eyelash. In the CASIA Interval database, the proposed algorithm fails to segment iris properly in 4 cases due to eyelid occlusion and in 15 cases due to eyelash occlusion while in the CASIA Lamp database, it fails to segment iris properly in 300 cases due to eyelid occlusion and in 288 cases due to eyelash occlusion. There are 76 cases where iris could not be segmented properly due to noise out of which, there are 71 cases where noise lies on pupil boundary and remaining due to specular reflection in CASIA Interval. Similarly, there are 228 cases where iris could not be segmented properly due to noise out of which, there are 160 cases where noise lies on pupil boundary and remaining due to specular reflection in CASIA Lamp. Illumination also plays a crucial role in getting proper segmented iris. It has been observed that there are 1 bright and 53 dark images in the Lamp database and the proposed algorithm has failed to segment iris from these 54 images. For Interval database, there are 11 bright and 39 dark images. Some images where proposed segmentation has failed are shown in Figure 3.

It has been observed that there are two critical parameters viz. threshold (t) and angular range (α_{range}) which play an important role in proper iris segmentation. Threshold t is relative to the gray-scale range [0,255]. The angular range α_{range} which defines the integration path for outer boundary detection has to be chosen so that it is occlusion free. Experimentally, it is found that variation is needed mostly in the threshold parameter t for correcting various kinds of error on the Interval database as given in Table 2. This table reports the changes in parameters needed to correct the erroneous images of any one sub-category.

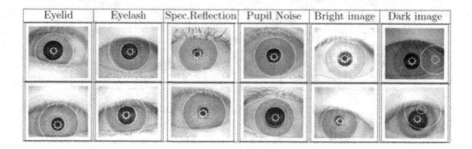

Fig. 3. Types of segmentation errors

It has been observed that there are two critical parameters viz. threshold (t) and angular range (α_{range}) which play an important role in proper iris segmentation. Threshold t is relative to the gray-scale range [0,255]. The angular range α_{range} which defines the integration path for outer boundary detection has to be chosen so that it is occlusion free. Experimentally, it is found that variation is needed mostly in the threshold parameter t for correcting various kinds of error on the Interval database as given in Table 2. This table reports the changes in parameters needed to correct the erroneous images of any one sub-category.

Table 2. Variation in threshold(t) parameter value needed for correct segmentation

Sub-Category	Mean	Minimum	Maximum	Std. Dev
Eyelid	0.39	0.36	0.41	0.022
Eyelash	0.39	0.3	0.43	0.040
Specular Reflection	0.44	0.36	0.5	0.066
Pupil Boundary Noise	0.4	0.26	0.5	0.056
Bright Image	0.46	0.35	0.52	0.060
Dark Image	0.36	0.25	0.51	0.052

Table 3. Parametric variations. (NC: **No Change**, "+": **Increase**, "-" : **Decrease**)

Sub-Category	t	α_{range}
Eyelid	NC	-
Eyelash	-, NC	-
Specular Reflection	+	NC
Pupil Boundary Noise	+, -	NC
Bright Image	+	NC
Dark Image	-	NC

Incorrect inner boundary localization automatically leads to error in outer boundary localization, due to the heuristic of searching outer boundary around inner boundary. In most of the error cases, only threshold parameter is needed to be changed for correction. In general, following the adjustment given in Table 3, parameters t and α_{range} are adjusted to get accurate segmentation. Changes to parameters are intuitive if we look at the error sub-category.

4 Conclusion

This paper has proposed an efficient iris segmentation algorithm. This algorithm makes use of the improved Hough transform using local gradient information to detect inner iris boundary while the outer boundary of iris has been detected with the help of integro-differential operator. It has been tested on CASIA 3.0 Interval database of 2639 images and CASIA 4.0 Lamp database of 16,212 images. It has achieved the accuracy of 94.5% on Interval and 94.63% on Lamp database. However, by tuning few critical parameters, which is needed for specific imaging conditions, segmentation accuracy has been increased up to 99.8% for Interval and 99.7% for Lamp. Thus the proposed algorithm is found to be very accurate and can be considered for iris segmentation. The proposed idea of improved Hough transform can be used to make detection of other shapes like ellipses, etc. efficient by using local gradient information.

Acknowledgement. Authors acknowledge the support provided by the Department of Information Technology, Government of India, to carry out this work.

References

1. Ballard, D.H.: Generalizing the Hough Transform to Detect Arbitrary Shapes. Pattern Recognition 13(2), 111–122 (1981)
2. Boles, W., Boashash, B.: A Human Identification Technique Using Images of the Iris and Wavelet Transform. IEEE Transactions on Signal Processing 46(4), 1185–1188 (1998)
3. Daugman, J.: High Confidence Visual Recognition of Persons by a Test of Statistical Independence. IEEE Transactions on Pattern Analysis and Machine Intelligence 15(11), 1148–1161 (1993)
4. Li, Sun, Tan: Robust Iris Segmentation Based on Learned Boundary Detectors. In: International Conference on Biometrics (2012)
5. Ma, L., Tan, T., Wang, Y., Zhang, D.: Efficient Iris Recognition by Characterizing Key Local Variations. IEEE Transactions on Image Processing 13(6), 739–750 (2004)
6. Ma, L., Tan, T., Wang, Y., Zhang, D.: Personal Identification based on Iris Texture Analysis. IEEE Transactions on Pattern Analysis and Machine Intelligence 25(12), 1519–1533 (2003)
7. Monro, D., Zhang, Z.: An Effective Human Iris Code with Low Complexity. In: IEEE International Conference on Image Processing, ICIP, vol. 3, pp. III-277–III-280. IEEE (2005)
8. Nigam, A., Gupta, P.: Finger Knuckleprint Based Recognition System Using Feature Tracking. In: Sun, Z., Lai, J., Chen, X., Tan, T. (eds.) CCBR 2011. LNCS, vol. 7098, pp. 125–132. Springer, Heidelberg (2011)
9. Wildes, R.: Iris Recognition: an Emerging Biometric Technology. Proceedings of the IEEE 85(9), 1348–1363 (1997)

Enhanced Steganographic Capacity
Using Morphing Technique

Saiful Islam[1], Ekram Khan[2], and Phalguni Gupta[1]

[1] Department of Computer Science and Engineering, Indian Institute of Technology Kanpur,
Kanpur-208 016, India
[2] Department of Electronics Engineering Aligarh Muslim University, Aligarh-202 002, India
{sislam,pg}@cse.iitk.ac.in, ekhan@lycos.com

Abstract. This paper proposes an efficient steganography algorithm which modifies the original F5 algorithm to increase its data hiding capacity. The proposed algorithm uses morphing based technique to embed the message in the same cover image. It embeds message securely and achieves higher embedding efficiency in comparison to the F5 algorithm. The results show that for the test images under consideration, it results up to 80% more embedding capacity as compared to original algorithm for the same cover image.

Keywords: steganography, morphing, transform domain, embedding efficiency.

1   Introduction

Steganography algorithms hide concealed information or messages within carrier medium in such a manner that the existence of the embedded messages in undetectable. The goal of steganography is to avoid drawing suspicion to the transmission of a hidden message [1]. Mostly JPEG image format is used as cover medium for steganographic algorithm as it is one of the most common formats for images [2]. Image steganographic algorithms can be classified on the basis of the domains in which the data is embedded. Embedding is done either in spatial domain or in transform domain. In spatial domain, the most commonly used steganographic algorithm is the least significant bits (LSB) method in which LSB of the cover image is modified according to the secret message. Size of the message that can be embedded is limited to the number of pixel coefficients of the cover image. In [3][4] LSB approach has been extended to hide data in color images. In the transform domain, embedding is done by modifying the Discrete Cosine Transform (DCT) coefficient values. There exist algorithms that modify these DCT coefficients to embed data. F5 algorithm [5] is the most secured algorithm among all well known algorithms but it provides limited steganographic capacity.

In this paper, we propose a novel algorithm based on F5 and image morphing to further enhance steganographic capacity of cover image. The algorithm provides result that shows the number of non-zero DCT coefficients increases considerably for

D.-S. Huang et al. (Eds.): ICIC 2012, CCIS 304, pp. 416–421, 2012.

the same cover image and secret message. It has been observed that number of such coefficients can be increased by 40-50% (on an average) and up to the maximum 80% in some cases through image morphing. The paper is organized as follows: Section 2 briefly reviews background literature. The proposed steganography technique is described in the next section. The simulation results are presented in Section 4 and finally paper is concluded in Section 5.

2   Literature Review

There exist several algorithms to embed data in spatial and transform domains and techniques to detect presence of steganographic data in cover images [6][7]. Detection of presence of message in spatial domain is easier in comparison to that in transform domain. Mostly, visual and statistical attacks are used to detect embedding of messages. Though transform domain provides lesser embedding capacity in comparison to spatial domain but transform domain format is widely used for internet communications. In case of transform domain, mostly embedding is done by modifying LSB of DCT coefficients. Jsteg tool [8] is one of the first algorithms that embed data in the transform domain. It embeds messages in lossy compressed JPEG files. It has a high embedding capacity of 12.8% of the steganogram's size. It is immune to visual attacks but fails against statistical attacks. Outguess algorithm [9] embeds data randomly in DCT coefficients to prevent statistical attacks but it fails against modified Chi Square attack [10]. F5 algorithm tackles weaknesses of Outguess by modifying absolute values of the DCT coefficients instead of flipping its least significant bit.

F5 algorithm is based on F4 [5] with certain enhancements to improve steganographic efficiency. Instead of continuous embedding, F5 employs permutative straddling to distribute the message evenly over the cover image. To prevent attacks, the embedding function uses the carrier medium as regular as possible. Higher embedding efficiency is achieved through matrix encoding as it decreases the necessary number of changes.

Steganographic algorithms are evaluated on the basis of their security and embedding efficiency [1]. Steganographic security implies that embedding of message is undetectable. Most commonly used steganalysis techniques are visual inspection and automated statistical attack. Automated detection of embedding of message can be done through Chi square attack [11]. Embedding efficiency is defined as the average number of secret message bits embedded per unit distortion. Higher the embedding efficiency better is the steganographic algorithm but embedding capacity decreases with increase in efficiency.

3   Proposed Algorithm

The proposed algorithm is a step further towards high capacity steganography. In this algorithm image morphing is used to provide controlled straddling instead of permutative straddling used in F5 algorithm. Purpose of using image morphing is to enhance steganographic capacity by varying degree of morphing on image to increase number of non-zero DCT coefficients so that the message may fit into the cover image. Image metamorphosis, or morphing in short, is commonly referred to as the animated transformation of one digital image to the other [2]. Basically, morphing is achieved by coupling image warping with color interpolation. As the morphing proceeds, the first image (source) is gradually distorted and is faded out, while the second image (target) starts out and is faded in. Thus the whole process consists of warping two images so that they have the same shape and then cross dissolving the resulting images. In this paper, freeware Smart morph software [12] is used to morph cover image. Input to the algorithm is cover image and secret message. The cover image is morphed and then the disparity between the original and the morphed images is computed to locate positions within the image, where message is to be embedded. The block diagram of proposed algorithm is shown in Fig. 1.

The degree of morphing depends on the size of secret message to be embedded. The extraction process is the reverse of the embedding process except the disparity analysis.

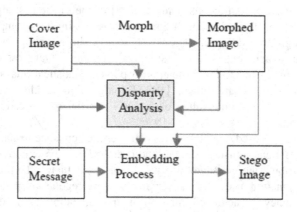

Fig. 1. Block diagram of proposed algorithm

3.1   Embedding Process

Input to the embedding process is cover image and secret message. The embedding algorithm computes number of non-zero DCT in the cover image. If number of nonzero DCT coefficients is less than size of the secret message, then morphing is used to increase number of DCT coefficients in the cover image. During morphing operation intermediate images are created. Any of these intermediate images is used in embedding process. Disparity list of DCT coefficients is computed, it is a list of DCT coefficients which differs in the original and morphed image. Embedding is done at locations provided by the disparity list. Higher embedding efficiency is achieved by embedding k bits of secret message n modifiable bits of coefficients of disparity list. Hence to embed k secret message bits, only one bit of n modifiable bits modified. On the basis of disparity list and secret message size, k is computed [5]. Following are the steps involved to embed the secret message within a cover image.

Step 1: read cover image and count number of non-zero DCT coefficients (say NZ).

Step 2: read secret message and compute data size in bits (say N).

Step 3: while($NZ < N$)

morph the cover image and compute DCT of morphed image and count(NZ).

Step 4: list all non-zero DCT coefficients and compute disparity list.

Step 5: calculate the code word length $n=2^k-1$.

Step 6: embed message using matrix encoding scheme and disparity list in the morphed image.

3.2   Extraction Process

The extraction of secret message, which is the reverse of the embedding process, is performed with the knowledge of cover image, codeword (n,k) and number of morphing iterations performed on it during the embedding process. Following steps are involved in the extraction process:

Step 1: read the original cover image.

Step 2: morph it iteratively same number of times as done in embedding process.

Step 3: compute disparity list of positions where DCT coefficients differ.

Step 4: read the stego image.

Step 5: use code word information (n, k) and disparity list formed to extract the message.

4   Simulation Results

The performance of the algorithm is evaluated using two cover images namely Lady.jpg (531x354 pixels) and Rani.jpg (800x600 pixels) and secret messages of different size are considered for embedding in the cover images. In order to implement the proposed algorithm, freely available SmartMop software is used to perform morphing in the cover image. Similar to F5 algorithm, the proposed algorithm also uses matrix encoding to increase embedding efficiency. The performance of the proposed algorithm is compared with the state-of-art F5 algorithm in term of embedding efficiency, which is function of k only and is the measure of average number of bits embedded per change in code word. In [5], it is defined as $\eta(k)=1+1/(k.2^k-1)$. It should be noted that higher value of η implies higher embedding efficiency.

Table 1 compares the embedding efficiency of the proposed algorithm with F5 algorithm for various combinations of cover and secret images. The first two rows of Table 1 show the embedding of 135000 bits of secret data into Lady.jpg cover image.

Table 1. Comparison of Proposed Algorithm with F5

Cover Image	Algorithm	NZ	Message size	k	n	Embedding efficiency
Lady.jpg	F5	138842	135000	1	2	2
	Proposed	255994	135000	2	3	2.67
Rani.jpg	F5	530024	240000	2	3	2.67
	Proposed	883208	240000	3	7	3.43
Lady.jpg	F5	138842	240000	0	0	-
	Proposed	255994	240000	1	1	2.0

It can be seen that the number of non-zero DCT coefficients in cover image without and with morphology are 138842 and 255994 respectively. Therefore, conventional F5 as well as the proposed algorithm can embed the message in the cover image, but the proposed algorithm has better embedding efficiency as compared to F5. It supports the claim of superiority of the proposed algorithm over traditional F5 algorithm.

The next two rows of Table 1 similarly compare the proposed algorithm with F5 for the secret message of 240000 bits embedded in Rani.jpg cover image. It is seen that F5 algorithm gives 530024 non-zero DCT coefficients for this cover image, which are sufficient enough to hide 240000 bits message resulting in embedding efficiency of 2.67. However, the proposed morphology based algorithm increases the number of non-zero DCT coefficients in the cover image from 530024 to 883208. As the number of non-zero DCT coefficient increases in the morphed cover image which enhances the embedding efficiency to 3.43. So it can be concluded that, although both algorithms can successfully embed the secret message in the given cover image but the embedding efficiency of the proposed algorithm is better than that of F5.

Finally, the last two rows of Table 1 compare the proposed algorithm with F5 for cover image Lady.jpg, and the secret message of 135000 bits. It can be seen from the table that if F5 algorithm is used, only 138842 non-zero DCT coefficients of cover image are available for hiding the secret message, which are not sufficient to embed secret message of 240000 bits in the cover image. However, when morphology based proposed algorithm is applied to the same cover image, the number of non-zero DCT coefficients increases to 255994 which are sufficient enough to embed the secret image having only 24000 bits. Embedding efficiency of 2 is achieved for this case by the proposed algorithm. Therefore, it can be concluded that the proposed algorithm of steganography increases the hiding capacity and the embedding efficiency as compared of the conventional F5 algorithm.

5   Conclusion

In this paper, a novel and efficient steganographic algorithm has been proposed to enhance the embedding capacity. The proposed algorithm is based on F5 algorithm in which permutative straddling of F5 is replaced with morphing based straddling.

Simulation results demonstrate the that proposed algorithm increases the data hiding capacity up to 80% in comparison to F5 algorithm. The data hiding capacity is controllable by controlling the degree of iteration in morphing step.

Acknowledgements. Authors acknowledge the support provided by the Department of Information Technology, Government of India, to carry out this work.

References

1. Cox, I.J., Miller, M.L., Bloom, J.A., Fridrich, J., Kalker, T.: Digital Watermarking and Steganography, 2nd edn. Morgan Kaufmann (2008)
2. Gonzalez, R.C., Woods, R.E.: Digital Image Processing, 2nd edn. Prentice-Hall (2008)
3. Gutub, A.A.: Pixel Indicator Technique for RGB Image Steganography. Journal of Emerging in Web Intelligence 2(1), 56–64 (2010)
4. Bailey, K., Curran, K.: An evaluation of image based steganography methods. Multimedia Tools Appl. 30(1), 55–88 (2006)
5. Westfeld, A.: F5-A Steganographic Algorithm. In: Moskowitz, I.S. (ed.) IH 2001. LNCS, vol. 2137, pp. 289–302. Springer, Heidelberg (2001)
6. Provos, N., Honeyman, P.: Hide and seek: An introduction to steganography. IEEE Security & Privacy 1(3), 32–44 (2003)
7. Fridrich, J.J., Goljan, M., Hogea, D., Soukal, D.: Quantitative steganalysis of digital images: estimating the secret message length. Multimedia Systems 9(3), 288–302 (2003)
8. Westfeld, A., Pfitzmann, A.: Attacks on Steganographic Systems. -Breaking the Steganographic Utilities EzStego, Jsteg, Steganos, and S-Tools and Some Lessons Learned. In: Pfitzmann, A. (ed.) IH 1999. LNCS, vol. 1768, pp. 61–76. Springer, Heidelberg (2000)
9. Provos, N.: Defending against statistical steganalysis. In: 10th USENIX Security Symposium, Washington D.C., pp. 323–335 (2001)
10. Potdar, V.M., Khan, M.A., Chang, E., Ulieru, M., Worthington, P.R.: e-Forensics steganography system for secret information retrieval. Advanced Engineering Informatics 19(3), 235–241 (2005)
11. Stanley, C.: Pairs of Values and the Chi-squared Attack. Master's thesis, Department of Mathematics, Iowa State University (2005)
12. Vinther, M.: Smartmorph (2004), http://meesoft.logicnet.dk

Minutiae Based Geometric Hashing
for Fingerprint Database

J. Umarani[1], J. Viswanathan[2], Aman K. Gupta[1], and Phalguni Gupta[1]

[1] Department of Computer Science and Engineering, Indian Institute of Technology
Kanpur, Kanpur-208 016, India
[2] ARICENT Technologies, Gurgaon, India
{umarani,pg,amankg}@iitk.ac.in, informviswa@gmail.com

Abstract. This paper proposes an efficient indexing technique for fingerprint database using minutiae based geometric hashing. A fixed length feature vector built from each minutia, known as Minutia Binary Pattern, has been suggested for the accurate match at the time of searching. Unlike existing geometric based indexing techniques, the proposed technique inserts each minutia along with the feature vector exactly once into a hash table. As a result, it reduces both computational and memory costs. Since minutiae of all fingerprint images in the database are found to be well distributed into the hash table, no rehashing is required. Experiments over FVC 2004 datasets prove the superiority of the proposed indexing technique against well known geometric based indexing techniques using fingerprints.

Keywords: Fingerprints, Indexing, Identification, Geometric Based Hashing, Minutia Binary Pattern.

1   Introduction

Fingerprint recognition system is used to identify a subject (human) from a large biometric database. One can do this task by searching a query image (henceforth termed as query fingerprint) against all images in the database (henceforth termed as model fingerprints) of the subjects. The process to retrieve each model fingerprint from the database and to compare it against the query fingerprint for a match is computationally inefficient. To make the process computationally efficient there is a need of an efficient indexing technique. There exist few techniques to index the fingerprint database. These techniques can be classified on the basis of the features such as singular points, directional field, local ridge-line orientations, orientation image, minutiae [1], minutiae descriptor [2], multiple features [3] and SIFT features [4]. But most matching algorithms are based on minutiae, so use of minutiae to index the fingerprint database is beneficial in many respects. In [5], geometric features from triplets are used with the help of FLASH (Fast Look up Algorithm for String Homology) hashing technique. Triplets are formed by 3 minutiae and triangles are formed using all possible combinations of minutiae. In this technique, angles formed by each triangle are used as index. The technique proposed in [6] also uses geometric features from minutiae

D.-S. Huang et al. (Eds.): ICIC 2012, CCIS 304, pp. 422–427, 2012.

triplets where the triplet features are maximum length of three sides, median and minimum angles, triangle handedness, type, direction and ridge count minutiae density. Since triangles are formed using all possible minutiae, there are large number of possible triangles which increase both memory and computational cost. A fast and robust projective matching for fingerprints has been proposed in [7]. It performs a fast match using a Geometric Hashing. However, geometric hashing may not be suitable because of its computational time and memory requirement which uses $n \times^n C_2$ bases pairs. In [8], geometric features from Delaunay triangles formed on the minutiae are used for indexing the fingerprints, instead of all possible combination of triangles. However, the major issue with Delaunay triangulation is that it is more sensitive to noise and distortion. For example, if some minutiae are missed or added (spurious minutiae), the structure of Delaunay triangulation gets seriously affected. Hence, this technique requires high quality of fingerprint images. This paper presents an efficient indexing technique which uses invariant spatial (distance) and directional (angle) information to index each minutia into a hash table. The technique is invariant to translation and rotation. It can be conveniently represented by a hash table containing spatial and directional information. Each minutia can be uniquely identified by its distance and angle information from its core point C and is inserted exactly once into a hash table. As a result, it eliminates multiple entries of same minutia into a hash table. So the proposed technique effectively removes the use of all possible triangles used in [6] and bases pairs in [7]; thus it reduces memory and computational complexity.

The rest of the paper is organized as follows. Feature extraction from a fingerprint image is discussed in the next section. Section 3 is discusses the proposed indexing technique while searching strategy is discussed in next section. Experimental results are analyzed in Section 5. Conclusions are given in the last section.

2   Feature Extraction

Features are extracted with the help of a series of steps such as core point detection, minutiae detection and minutia binary pattern construction. Singular point detection is defined as the point with maximum curvature of convex ridges. The singular points (SPs) are the discontinuities in the directional field [9] of a fingerprint image.   There exist two types of SPs, core and delta. A core is the uppermost point of the innermost curving ridge and a delta is a point where three ridge flows meet. Many images can have more than one core point. In that case, the top most core point is used. If a core point does not exist in an image, we use high curvature point as reference point. In our experiment, core point is marked manually to minimize the error rate. Let $C = (x_c, y_c, \alpha_c)$ be the core point, detected manually where (x_c, y_c) denote the coordinates and α_c is the direction of the core point. Next, minutiae points are detected by tracing the ridges. Ridges are represented by a list of points. Two types of ridge points which are considered in our study are bifurcation and termination. Bifurcation is associated with three ridges while termination is the ridge end point. Let $M = \{m^1, m^2,..., m^o\}$ be the detected minutiae from each model fingerprint image. Each minutia m^i is a 4-tuple $(x_m^i, y_m^i, \alpha_m^i, T_m^i)$ denoting their coordinates, direction and type (bifurcation or ridge end point), respectively. A representation of feature vector built from each minutia, called Minutia Binary Pattern (MBP), is constructed for the accurate match at the time of searching. Representation of MBP associates a local structure to each minutia (m^i) and is represented by 3 X 3 neighborhood of square window W whose base is centered at minutiae location (x_m^i, y_m^i) and it is aligned according to the minutiae direction α_m^i. Each cell is a small square window and can be uniquely identified by two indices (a, b), both a and b lying between 1 and 3, denote its position in the square window. For each minutia, m^i, binary pattern is constructed by accumulating the binary values in the cells (a,b) of 3 X 3 square window W associated with m^i starting from its direction α_m^i Thus,

$$MBP = \{ m^i \in M; W(a,b); 1 \le (a, b) \le 3 \}$$

where $W(a,b)$ is a binary value associated with cell (a,b) of 3 X 3 square window W and M is model fingerprint. An advantage of the MBP representation is that the value of each cell can be stored as a bit with a negligible loss of accuracy. Such a bit-based representation is particularly well suited for accurate match at the time of searching. Also, the computation of fixed length MBP value is very simple, fast and reduces storage cost.

3   Indexing

A query fingerprint may be translated or rotated relative to its respective model fingerprint in the database. Invariant spatial (distance) and directional (angle) information can be used to handle translation and rotation that are present in a fingerprint image. The proposed indexing technique is built using invariant distance and angle from core point C of each minutia of a model fingerprint. The technique encodes spatial (distance) and directional (angle) relationship between core point and each minutia which can be conveniently represented as a 2-D hash table whose rows and columns are related to the spatial (distance) and directional (angle) information respectively. In order to get the two indexing elements (spatial and directional) associated with each minutia, a convex hull $Conv_{Hull}(M, \Omega)$ is obtained by considering all minutiae in M by adding Ω offset pixels from the original convex hull. Then a circle with center at (x_c, y_c) and radius R is drawn where R is the farthest point lying on the convex hull and (x_c, y_c) are the coordinates of the core point. This circle is divided into several sectors, each having 5° of difference. Let N_M and N_S be the number of minutiae and number of sectors of a modal fingerprint image. Note that in a fingerprint image, number of sectors is fixed while number of minutiae is varied. For each minutia mi lying in a sector S^j, the Euclidean distance, $D^i(m^i, C)$, between m^i and the core point C, is calculated as

$$INT(D^i(m^i, C)) = \sqrt{(x_m^i - x_c)^2 + (y_m^i - y_c)^2}$$

Each minutia m^i can be uniquely identified by its distance $D^i(m^i, C)$ and sector number $S^j(m^i, C)$ from the core point C. $D^i(m^i, C)$ is the spatial contribution of minutia m^i from the core point C while $S^j(m^i, C)$ is the directional contribution of minutia m^i that lies in sector S^j from C. These two invariant information are used as indexing element to insert each minutiae of a model fingerprint along with $(M^i_{id}, MBP^i, \alpha^i)$ in hash table H where M^i_{id}, MBP^i and α^i are the model fingerprint identity, minutiae binary pattern and direction of a minutia m^i respectively.

4   Searching

During *searching*, index generated by each query minutia is used to map the same index in the hash table and vote for all (M_{id}, MBP) pairs under this index I. It can be noted that due to noise present in the fingerprint images, the minutiae of the different images of the same model may be shifted or missed. In such cases, to improve the recognition performance, it is considered the minutiae not only from its mapped bin but also from its nearest bins of size $k \times k$. For each query fingerprint minutia vote is casted and model fingerprints are sorted based on their votes and the top t models are considered as best matches.

5   Experimental Results

Most of the well known techniques for fingerprint indexing have been evaluated on FVC 2004 dataset [11]. In our experiment, DB2 and DB3 are used to evaluate the performance of the proposed indexing technique.

— FVC 2004 DB2: Second FVC 2004 dataset contains 800 fingerprints from 100 fingers (8 impressions per finger) captured using the optical sensor "U.are.U 4000" by Digital Persona and size of image is 328 x 364 at 500 dpi.
— FVC 2004 DB3: Third FVC 2004 dataset contains 800 fingerprints from 100 fingers (8 impressions per finger) captured using thermal sweeping sensor "FingerChip FCD4B14CB" by Atmel and size of image is 300 × 480 at 512 dpi.

To determine the performance of the proposed indexing technique, two measures, namely, *Hit Rate* and *Penetration Rate* are used. A query is regarded as *hit* if the true fingerprint is contained in the candidate list. The *Hit Rate* is the ratio of the correct queries to all queries. The *Penetration Rate* is the ratio of the size of the candidate list to the size of the whole database. Minutiae obtained from all model fingerprints are indexed using a single hash table. At the time of *searching*, it uses the indexed hash table to retrieve the set of model fingerprint identities M_{id} that are similar to the query fingerprint image. Each minutia m^j of the query fingerprint image is mapped to the hash table. Let it be mapped to the bin b of the hash table. Instead of considering only the bth bin, it considers $k \times k$ neighboring bins to determine the *Hit Rate*. Fig. 1 shows *Hit Rate* against *Penetration Rate* for top *10* best matches of the proposed indexing technique.

In order to evaluate accuracy and efficiency, the proposed indexing technique has been compared with techniques presented in [6],[8]. All these techniques are evaluated on a Quad-Core (2×2.83 GHz) workstation with 3.23 GB RAM. In all these cases, comparisons are done on FVC 2004 datasets. Memory and computational cost of all these techniques are shown in Table 1. One can observe that the proposed technique is efficient with respect to the memory and computational cost.

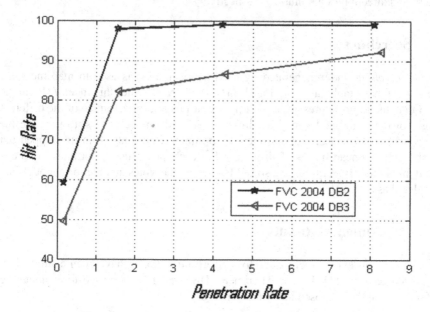

Fig. 1. Hit Rate against Penetration Rate for DB2 and DB3

Table 1. Comparison Table

Data Set	Memory Cost in MB			Computational Cost					
				Hash Table Entries			Query Time in Sec [1]		
	[6]	[8]	Proposed	[6]	[8]	Proposed	[6]	[8]	Proposed
DB2	1095	18.5	5.2	76764	447	2623	234.5	6.0	7.5
DB3	680	22.1	6.4	47465	5471	3124	265.8	6.7	8.0

6   Conclusion

This paper has proposed minutiae based geometric hashing technique to index the fingerprint database. Also, we have proposed minutia binary pattern (MBP) representation of feature vector of fixed length which is bit oriented coding, simple but very effective for the accurate search. The proposed technique performs indexing and searching in one pass with linear complexity. Unlike other geometric based indexing techniques, it inserts each minutia exactly once into a hash table. It effectively removes the use of all possible triangles proposed in [6] and bases pairs proposed in [7];

---

[1] Query time includes feature extraction, searching and matching.

thus it reduces memory and computational complexity. Extensive experiments over FVC 2004 databases show the effectiveness of the proposed indexing technique with respect to well known geometric based indexing techniques [6][8].

Acknowledgements. Authors acknowledge the support provided by the Department of Information Technology, Government of India, to carry out this work.

References

1. Raffaele, C., Matteo, F., Davide, M.: Fingerprint Indexing Based on Minutia Cylinder-Code. IEEE Transactions on Pattern Analysis and Machine Intelligence 33(5), 1051–1057 (2011)
2. Feng, J.: Combining Minutiae Descriptors for Fingerprint Matching. Pattern Recognition 41(1), 342–352 (2008)
3. Boer, J.D., Bazen, A.M., Gerez, S.H.: Indexing Fingerprint Databases Based on Multiple Features. In: Proc. of the 12th Annual Workshop on Circuits, Systems and Signal Processing, pp. 300–306 (2001)
4. Shuai, X., Zhang, C., Hao, P.: Fingerprint Indexing Based on Composite Set of Reduced SIFT Features. In: Proc. of International Conference on Pattern Recognition, pp. 1–4 (2008)
5. Germain, R., Califano, A., Colville, S.: Fingerprint Matching Using Transformation Parameter Clustering. IEEE Computational Science and Engineering 4(4), 42–49 (1997)
6. Bhanu, B., Tan, X.: Fingerprint Indexing Based on Novel Features of Minutiae Triplets. IEEE Transactions on Pattern Analysis and Machine Intelligence 25(5), 616–622 (2003)
7. Boro, R., Roy, S.D.: Fast and Robust Projective Matching for Fingerprints Using Geometric Hashing. In: Proc. of the 4th Indian Conference on Computer Vision, Graphics and Image Processing, pp. 681–686 (2004)
8. Bebis, G., Deaconu, T., Georgiopoulos, M.: Fingerprint Identification using Delaunay Triangulation. In: Proc. of IEEE International Conference on Intelligence, Information, and Systems, pp. 452–459 (1999)
9. Bazen, A., Gerez, S.: Extraction of Singular Points From Directional Fields of Fingerprints. In: Proc. of The Annual CTIT Workshop on Mobile Communications, pp. 41–44 (2001)
10. Maio, D., Maltoni, D., Cappelli, R., Wayman, J.L., Jain, A.K.: FVC2004: Third Fingerprint Verification Competition. In: Zhang, D., Jain, A.K. (eds.) ICBA 2004. LNCS, vol. 3072, pp. 1–7. Springer, Heidelberg (2004)

A Tracking Controller Using RBFNs
for Closed-Chain Robotic Manipulators

Tien Dung Le[1], Hee-Jun Kang[2,*], and Young-Soo Suh[2]

[1] Graduate School of Electrical Engineering, University of Ulsan, Ulsan, South Korea
[2] School of Electrical Engineering, University of Ulsan, Ulsan, South Korea
dung.letien@gmail.com, {hjkang,yssuh}@ulsan.ac.kr

Abstract. Tracking control of closed-chain robotic manipulators has posed a challenging and difficult task due to the complicated dynamic model, the presence of multi closed-loop chains and singularities. This paper presents a novel tracking controller using radial basic function networks (RBFNs) for closed-chain robotic manipulators. The dynamic model of a general closed-chain robotic manipulator is presented in the presence of structured and unstructured uncertainties. In order to compensate the uncertainties, the RBFNs are used. An adaptation law is proposed to adjust on-line the output weights of the RBFNs. The validity of the proposed controller is shown by computer simulations of a five-bar planar parallel manipulator.

Keywords: Closed kinematic chains, Dynamic computation, Tracking control, Radial basic function network, On-line tuning.

1 Introduction

Closed-chain robotic manipulators have potential advantages in terms of stiffness, accuracy and high speed. They have wide applications such as flight simulators, photonics alignment, pick and place operation.

Motion control of closed-chain robotic manipulators has attracted many researchers to study its potential performance. The proportional derivative (PD) controller proposed in [1, 2], the nonlinear PD controller proposed in [3], and the synchronization controller reported in [4] belong to the error based control methods of closed-chain manipulators. These controllers are simple and easy to implement but do not deliver good performance because the full dynamic of closed-chain manipulators is not compensated. Some other advanced controllers belong to model based control strategy were proposed such as the computed torque controller [5, 6], the model-based iterative learning controller [2] and the nonlinear adaptive controller [7]. However, it is very difficult to obtain a precise dynamic model of the closed-chain manipulators because of the complex structure.

---

[*] Corresponding author.

D.-S. Huang et al. (Eds.): ICIC 2012, CCIS 304, pp. 428–434, 2012.

The RBFN is functionally equivalent to the T-S model of fuzzy system [8]. Therefore, it is widely used in control of dynamic systems. Adaptive tracking controllers using RBFN for open chain manipulators were proposed in [9-11]. In these controllers, the RBFNs were used to learn both dynamic model and uncertainties of robot. Although these controllers show good result, it is difficult to apply to tracking control of closed-chain manipulators for the large size of the RBFNs and the enormous number of calculations.

In this paper, we propose a new adaptive control scheme for tracking control of closed-chain manipulators using radial basic function networks. The rest of the paper is organized as follows. In section 2, the dynamic model of general closed-chain robotic manipulator is formulated in the active join space. The proposed adaptive tracking controller using RBFNs is presented in section 3. A five-bar planar robotic manipulator with planned trajectory is simulated to verify the validity of the proposed controller as given in section 4. Finally, a conclusion is reached in section 5.

2   Dynamic Modeling

We consider a general closed-chain robotic manipulator consisting of a number of serial kinematic chains formed by rigid links and joints. Let N_a be the number of active joints, $q_a \in R^{Na}$ the actuated joint angle vector, $\tau_a \in R^{Na}$ the actuated torques vector, N_p the number of passive joints, $q_p \in R^{Np}$ the passive joint angle vector. The active joints are actuated by actuators while the passive joints are free to move.

The dynamic model of the general closed-chain robotic manipulator in the active joint space is expressed as the following:

$$\hat{M}_a \ddot{q}_a + \hat{C}_a \dot{q}_a + \hat{G}_a + F_a = \tau_a \tag{1}$$

where $\hat{M}_a \in R^{Na \times Na}$ is the inertia matrix, $\hat{C}_a \in R^{Na \times Na}$ is the Coriolis and centrifugal force matrix, $\hat{G}_a \in R^{Na}$ is the gravity force vector and $F_a \in R^{Na}$ is the friction force vector of the origin closed-chain robotic manipulators in the active joint space. Note that the effect of friction forces on the passive joints is often much smaller than on the active joints. Thus, in order to simplify the dynamic model, only the friction forces on the active joints are considered.

The dynamic model (1) have the following properties which were proven in [12]:

Property 1: $\hat{M}_a$ is symmetric and positive definite.

Property 2: $(\dot{\hat{M}}_a - 2\hat{C}_a)$ is skew-symmetric.

In practice, due to the presence of the highly nonlinear uncertainties, the exact dynamic model of closed-chain robotic manipulators will never be known. If the modeling errors caused by the uncertainties are bounded, we can express the actual dynamic model of closed-chain manipulators as follows:

$$\hat{M}_a \ddot{q}_a + \hat{C}_a \dot{q}_a + \hat{G}_a + \Delta\tau_a = \tau_a \tag{2}$$

in which $\Delta\tau_a = \Delta M_a\ddot{q}_a + \Delta C_a\dot{q}_a + \Delta G_a + F_a$ is the vector of the unknown uncertainties of the closed-chain manipulator; ΔM_a, ΔC_a, and ΔG_a are the bounded modeling errors.

3 Proposed Tracking Controller

Given a desired trajectory $q_{da} \in R^{N_a}$ of the closed-chain manipulator, the tracking error is defined as:

$$e = q_a - q_{da} \tag{3}$$

The filter tracking error is:

$$r = \dot{e} + \Lambda e = \dot{q}_a - \dot{q}_{ar} \tag{4}$$

where $\Lambda = \Lambda^T > 0$ is a design parameter matrix; and $\dot{q}_{ar} = \dot{q}_{da} - \Lambda e$ is defined as the reference velocity vector.

The proposed tracking controller for closed-chain robotic manipulators is expressed as the following:

$$\tau_a = \hat{M}_a\ddot{q}_{ar} + \hat{C}_a\dot{q}_{ar} + \hat{G}_a + f_{RBFN} - Ksign(r) \tag{5}$$

where K is diagonal and positive matrix, and f_{RBFN} is a vector of a set of RBFNs for compensating the system uncertainties $\Delta\tau_a$ which is defined as:

$$f_{RBFN} = [f_1, f_2, ..., f_{N_a}]^T = \left[W_1^T\varphi_1(x_1), W_2^T\varphi_2(x_2), ..., W_{N_a}^T\varphi_{N_a}(x_{N_a})\right]^T \tag{6}$$

In the equation (6), each f_i is a RBFN and x_i is the input vector, W_i is the ouput weights vector and $\varphi_i(x_i)$ is a set of radial basis function defined as:

$$\varphi_i(x_i) = [\phi_{i1}(x_i), \phi_{i2}(x_i), ..., \phi_{iL}(x_i)]^T, \quad i = 1, .., N_a \tag{7}$$

where L is the number of the kernel units in each RBFN, and the radial basis function $\phi_{ij}(x_i)$ is chosen to be the Gaussian function:

$$\phi_{ij}(x_i) = \exp\left(-\|x_i - c_{ij}\|^2 / 2\sigma_{ij}^2\right), \quad i = 1, ..., N_a; j = 1, ..., L \tag{8}$$

in which c_{ij} and σ_{ij} are the center and the variance of the jth kernel unit of RBFN i.

The input vector x_i of each RBFN is used as:

$$x_i = [e_i, \dot{e}_i]^T, \quad i = 1, ..., N_a \tag{9}$$

where e_i and $\dot{e}_i$ are respectively the tracking error and derivative of tracking error of each active joint of the robot.

For tuning the output weights of the RBFNs, we propose an adaptation tuning law which is expressed as the following:

$$\dot{W}_i = -\Gamma_i\varphi_i(x_i)r_i - \Gamma_i|r_i|W_i \tag{10}$$

where Γ_i are diagonal, symmetric, and positive constant matrices ($i = 1, ..., N_a$).

The signum function $sign(r)$ in the controller (5) may cause chattering in the control input. The most common method so-called *"boundary layer method"* (BLM) [13] can be used to overcome this problem. Based on this method, the control input can be smoothed replacing $sign(r)$ with a saturation function which is defined by:

$$sat\left(\frac{r}{\delta}\right) = \begin{cases} r/\delta & if \ |r| \le \delta \\ sign(r/\delta) & if \ |r| > \delta \end{cases} \tag{11}$$

where δ is the boundary layer thickness.

4   Simulation and Results

To verify the effectiveness of the proposed controller, computer simulation was conducted for trajectory tracking control of a five-bar planar robotic manipulator which is described in Figure 2. The robotic manipulator has $N_a = 2$ active joints, $N_p = 3$ passive joints. The active joints are actuated by actuators while the passive joints are free to move.

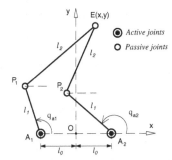

Fig. 1. The five-bar planar manipulator

Simulation studies were conducted on Matlab-Simulink and the mechanical of the five-bar planar manipulator was built on SimMechanics toolbox following the method presented in [14]. The simulations were carried out with respect to the case when the five-bar manipulator tracks a line on XY plane. The comparisons between the performance of a robust controller and the proposed controller were performed.

The link parameters of the five-bar manipulators are $l_1 = 0.102$m, $l_2 = 0.18$m, $l_0 = 0.066$m, $m_1 = 0.8$kg, $m_2 = 1.2$kg, $I_{z1} = 0.0013$kgm^2, $I_{z2} = 0.0027$kgm^2, $l_{c1} = 0.055$m, $l_{c2} = 0.091$m in which l_0, l_1, l_2 are the link lengths; m_1, m_2 are the masses; I_{zi1}, I_{zi2} are the inertias tensor of links of serial chain i; l_{c1}, l_{c2} are the distances from the joints to the center of mass for each link of the five-bar manipulator.

Figure 2 shows the results of tracking of robot. The parameters of the robust controller were set to be: $K_1 = K_2 = 3$, $\delta_1 = \delta_2 = 0.2$. In the proposed controller, these parameters were set to the same values, and all the initial values of the output weights of the RBFNs were set to be: $W_i(0) = 0.1 \times I$. The learning rate matrix was set to be: $\Gamma_l = 4.10^{-3} \times I$. The centers of the RBF networks are $c_{xij} = c_{yij} = [-0.5, -0.25, 0,$

$0.25, 0.5]^T$. And the variances of kernel units in the hidden layer are $\sigma_{ij} = 0.1$, $i = 1,2, j = 1,...,25$. These parameters were obtained by trial and error method.

The tracking error curves of the end-effector on X-direction and Y-direction are showed in the Figure 3. It can be seen that the tracking accuracy of the proposed controller is better than that of the robust controller.

Figure 4 shows the control input of the proposed controller. It can be seen that the chattering phenomenon often caused by the signum function is avoided.

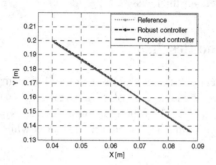

Fig. 2. The linear trajectory of tracking control

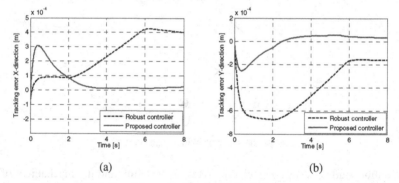

(a)   (b)

Fig. 3. Tracking error of the end-effector: (a) X-direction and (b) Y-direction

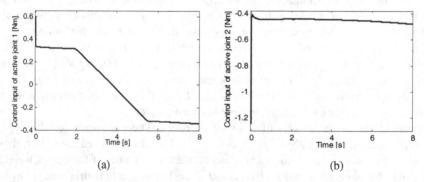

(a)   (b)

Fig. 4. Control input of the proposed controller: (a) Active joint 1 and (b) Active joint 2

It could be concluded from the above-mentioned simulation results that the proposed controller is of high efficiency for the tracking control of the closed-chain robotic manipulators.

5   Conclusion

In this paper, a novel adaptive tracking controller using RBF networks is proposed for closed-chain robotic manipulators. The analysis and simulation results have shown that the RBFNs can adaptively compensate the highly nonlinear uncertainties of closed-chain robotic manipulators. The adaptation tuning law for the output weights allows the RBFNs to be tuned online during the trajectory tracking control of closed-chain manipulators without any offline training phase. In the simulation example, the proposed adaptive tracking controller is applied to a five-bar planar parallel manipulator. The simulations results demonstrate the effectiveness of the proposed controller in trajectory tracking control.

Acknowledgement. This work was supported by the Ministry of Knowledge Economy under the Human Resources Development Program for Convergence Robot Specialists and under Industrial Core Technology Project.

References

1. Ghorbel, F.H., et al.: Modeling and Set Point Control of Closed-chain Mechanisms: Theory and Experiment. IEEE Transactions on Control Systems Technology 8 (2000)
2. Abdellatif, H., Heimann, B.: Advanced Model-Based Control of a 6-DOF Hexapod Robot: A Case Study. IEEE/ASME Transactions on Mechatronics 15 (2010)
3. Ouyang, P.R., et al.: Nonlinear PD Control for Trajectory Tracking with Consideration of the Design for Control Methodology. In: Proceedings IEEE International Conference on Robotics and Automation, ICRA 2002, vol. 4, pp. 4126–4131 (2002)
4. Lu, R., et al.: Trajectory Tracking Control for a 3-DOF Planar Parallel Manipulator Using the Convex Synchronized Control Method. IEEE Transactions on Control Systems Technology 16, 613–623 (2008)
5. Paccot, F., et al.: A Vision-based Computed Torque Control for Parallel Kinematic Machines. In: IEEE International Conference on Robotics and Automation, ICRA 2008, pp. 1556–1561 (2008)
6. Shang, W.W., et al.: Dynamic Model based Nonlinear Tracking Control of a Planar Parallel Manipulator. Nonlinear Dynamics 60, 597–606 (2010)
7. Shang, W., Cong, S.: Nonlinear Adaptive Task Space Control for a 2-DOF Redundantly Actuated Parallel Manipulator. Nonlinear Dynamics 59, 61–72 (2010)
8. Hunt, K.J., et al.: Extending the Functional Equivalence of Radial Basis Function Networks and Fuzzy Inference Systems. IEEE Transactions on Neural Networks 7 (1996)
9. Jung, L.M., Kiu, C.Y.: An Adaptive Neurocontroller Using RBFN for Robot Manipulators. IEEE Transactions on Industrial Electronics 51, 711–717 (2004)
10. Shuzhi, S.G., et al.: Adaptive Neural Network Control of Robot Manipulators in Task Space. IEEE Transactions on Industrial Electronics 44, 746–752 (1997)

11. Sun, F.C., et al.: Neural Adaptive Tracking Controller for Robot Manipulators with Unknown Dynamics. In: IEE Proceedings-Control Theory and Applications, vol. 147 (2000)
12. Hui, C., et al.: Dynamics and Control of Redundantly Actuated Parallel Manipulators. IEEE/ASME Transactions on Mechatronics 8, 483–491 (2003)
13. Slotine, J.J.E., Li, W.: Applied Nonliner Control. Prentice-Hall (1991)
14. Tien, D.L., et al.: Robot manipulator modeling in Matlab-SimMechanics with PD control and online gravity compensation. In: 2010 International Forum on Strategic Technology (IFOST), pp. 446–449 (2010)

Enhancing 3D Scene Models Based on Automatic Context Analysis and Optimization Algorithm

My-Ha Le, Andrey Vavilin, and Kang-Hyun Jo

Graduated School of Electrical Engineering, University of Ulsan, Ulsan, Korea
{lemyha,andy}@islab.ulsan.ac.kr, acejo@ulsan.ac.kr

Abstract. This paper proposes a method for enhancing accuracy of scene model. The main contributions are threefold: first, the contex of the scene images are analyzed. Some objects which may have negative effect should be removed. For instance, the sky often appears as backgroud and moving objects appear in most of scene images. They are also one of reasons that causes the outliers. Second, the global rotations of images are computed based on correspondence between pair-wise images. These constraints are fed to the point clouds generation procedure. Third, in contrast with using only canonical bundle adjustment which yields unstable structure in small baseline geometry and local minima, the proposed method utilized known-rotation framework to compute the initial guess for bundle adjustment process. The patch-based multi-view stereopsis is applied to upgrade the reconstructed structure. The simulation results demonstrate the accuracy of structures by this method from scene images in outdoor environment.

Keywords: context analysis, SIFT, correspondence, RANSAC, global rotation estimation, convex optimization, PMVS.

1 Introduction

3D reconstruction or modeling of scene is one of important process in various applications of virtual environment, scene planning and navigation of autonomous mobile robot. Some progress has been made in the 3D reconstruction which is obtained during the last few decades but still there is no methods satisfy the requirement of high accurate as well as stable with different kind of dataset. Also, some of them needed a large amount of work done by hand or apparatus, such as laser radar, and airborne light detection and ranging. They are usually expensive and require much more time for data acquisition.

In recent years many well known algorithms have been developed for 3D reconstruction and motion estimation, which can roughly be devised into several categories, namely methods using bundle adjustment (BA) [1], methods based on factorization [2-4] and hierarchical methods [5-6]. In the first group, multi-view structure from motion start by estimating the geometry of two views. These structure will be used to estimate the pose of the adjacent camera. The quality of the reconstruction depend heavily on the initial structure of first pair cameras [7], [8].

D.-S. Huang et al. (Eds.): ICIC 2012, CCIS 304, pp. 435–440, 2012.

Another disadvantage of this method is the drift problem [9]. The expensive computation and acummulate errors increase in iterative process of adding new camera of this sequence method. In the second group, the missing data and sensitivily to outliers is the main problem. It is well studied by some author groups, e.g. in [4]. In the third group, the input images will be arrange in the hierarchical tree and they are processed from root to the top.

Without using any addition electro-manegtic device out of monocular camera, this proposed method overcomes some disadvantages mentioned above. The flow chart of the proposed method is described in figure 1. Using perspective camera, images are acquired from objects of the scene with complecated objects and structure. The problem of reconstruction from scene images are how to detect and remove outliers as well as optimize the results with highest accuracy. One of the outlier problems causes by un-necessary objects appear in image and distorsion. So, the pre-process named scene analysic should be perform. Remark that, in most of outdoor image the sky and cloud often appear as image background and humans, cars...etc appear as moving objects. Here, solution is proposed for removing those kind of object [10], [11]. In the next step, the robust method for global camera rotation estimation based on pair-wise constraint will be perform. In order to find the robust constrains of images, SIFT algorithm [12] is applied to find invariant feature and matching for each pair of views in combinatorial form. The global camera rotation are computed according to graph-based sampling scheme [13]. After obtaining camera rotation matrix in global cordinate, high accuracy point clouds will be generate by applying known rotation frame work[14]. Instead of using only canonical BA which may gain unstable structure of crictical geometry configuration and traped in local minima, the result of known-rotation framework are treat as initial guess for BA process. This ideal is inspired from the orginal approach as proposed in [15]. However, the model is haven't created completely. The dense upgradding process is needed. Here, the patch based multiview stereopsis method (PMVS) [16] is applied to create the final dense scene model.

This paper is organized into 6 sections. The next section describes the pre-process: context analysic of scene images. Section 3 presents global camera rotation method. Section 4 presents scene model generation.Also, PMVS method is briefly introduced. The Experiments are showed in section 5. Finally, paper is finished with conclusions and point out future works discussion in section 6.

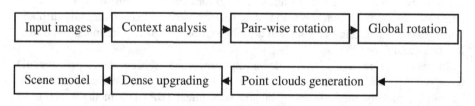

Fig. 1. General proposed scheme

2   Context Analysis

Main purpose of this step is to remove objects which may have negative effect for scene reconstruction process from the further processing. Natural objects such as sky, clouds are difficult for 3D model reconstruction and may cause inconsistence in reconstructed scene due to false matching between points from different frames. To overcome this problem, a context analysis is used. In this work, we consider a scene consist of three semantic layers: first layer contains sky and clouds information, second layer contain buildings, ground and trees, and last layer contains moving objects. Objects of different layers separated into classes as follows.

- Layer 1: *sky, clouds.*
- Layer 2: *building, grass, trees, road and pavement etc.*
- Layer 3: *cars, trucks, humans etc.*

The proposed method of scene analysis consists of two steps: first, system is trained to select optimal feature subset for separating buildings from other objects based on set of labeled images. On the second step, these features are used to remove unwanted objects form the input images.

Filtering process is based on recursive segmentation of image into rectangular blocks which are classified according to the features selected on the training step. Blocks which could not be classified with a high probability are separated into four sub-blocks and process repeats. Process stops after all blocks bigger than predefined minimum size are classified. Isolated unclassified blocks and blocks belonged to unwanted classes are filtered out. More details on proposed context analysis could be found at [10], [11].

3   Rotation Registration

In this section, a short description of global camera rotation registration is presented. First, the local pair-wise constraints are computed based on invariant feature matching after outliers removing, here, SIFT feature and RANSAC algorithm is applied. Second, robust rotation averaging method as proposed in [13] is utilized. The results proclaim that graph-based sampling scheme efficiently removes outliers in the individual relative motions. The main idea is presented as follow: given the relative rotation R_{ij}, how to find a robust method to compute a set of all camera rotations R_k in the global coordinate, e. g,

$$R_i = R_{ij}R_j \tag{1}$$

4   Scene Model Generation

Triangulation with known rotation consistency will be recast as quasi-convex optimization problem in this process [14]. Also, some author groups proposed methods using L_∞-norm combined L_1-norm [17] instead of L_2-norm in minimizing the residual and back-projection error. It is easy to figure out that solving the L_2-norm for more than two cameras is a hard non-convex problem. These results are treated as initial guess and fed into BA process. For dense structure upgrading, in recent years, PMVS is considered as state of the art of multi-view stereopsis modeling method and it is applied in this paper. The seed points or initial spare point cloud of this algorithm are generate from previous step.

5   Experiments

The simulation results are presented to evaluate effectiveness of proposed method. The main objects are medium scale scenes in outdoor environment. The dataset images are acquired by digital perspective camera (Casio EX-Z90) which may causes distortion in large view. The results were simulated on Intel(R) Core(TM) i5 CPU 750@2.67 GHz with 3GB RAM under Matlab environment and MOSEK toolbox [18]. The scene composed by three statues stand in front of three pillars located on campus square and 30 images of size [2048x1536] were used. The result of scene model after dense upgrading is showed in figure 2. Here, figure 2(b) is the dense upgrading without context analysis in pre-process step. It is easy to see that the outliers appear in this model (points from sky region). In contrast, the result consists of pre-process (see figure 2(c)) show the better model without outlier. In the second experiment, the images were taken in large scale scene. The number of image in this simulation is 322 of size [2048x1536]. The results are showed in figure 3.

| (a) | (b) | (c) |

Fig. 2. Dense model. (a) is one of 30 input images. (b) is the model without pre-process. (c) is the model include context analysis in pre-process.

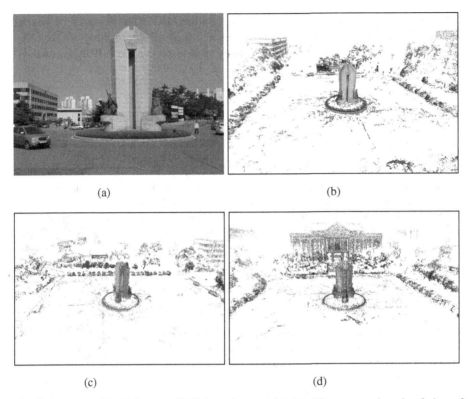

(a)   (b)

(c)   (d)

Fig. 3. Dense model. (a) is one of 322 input images. (b), (c), (d) are several angle of view of scene model.

6   Conclusions

Outdoor scene reconstruction from multiple views based on context analysis and known-rotation frame work combined with BA method is presented on this paper. Some advantage points were pointed out through our experiments. First, the pre-process was performed to remove unnecessary objects which often generate outliers. Second, the method avoids only using BA which often causes unstable structures in critical geometry configuration. Moreover, BA algorithm used L_2-norm which may trap in local minima. Instead, the convex optimization combined with BA utilizing known-rotation frame work creates robust initial guess for next structure generation process. Third, in the global camera rotation estimation, graph-based sampling scheme according to RANSAC yields robust estimation results. Our future woks focus on the comparison of this method with L_1 combined L_∞-norm. It is expected to improve this method for Omni-directional camera in outdoor scene. The lasting target of this method is real time and accuracy visual SLAM.

Acknowledgement. This work was supported by the MKE (The Ministry of Knowledge Economy), Korea, under the Human Resources Development Program for Convergence Robot Specialists support program supervised by the NIPA(National IT Industry Promotion Agency) (NIPA-2010-C7000-1001-0007).

References

1. Mclauchlan, P., Hartley, R.: Bundle Adjustment – a Modern Synthesis (2000)
2. Tomasi, C., Kanade, T.: Shape and Motion from Image Streams under Orthography: a Factorization Method. Int. Journal of Computer Vision (1992)
3. Sturm, P., Triggs, B.: A Factorization Based Algorithm for Multi-image Projective Structure and Motion. In: European Conf. on Computer Vision (1996)
4. Tardif, J.P., Bartoli, A.: Algorithms for Batch Matrix Factorization with Application to Structure from Motion. In: Conf. Computer Vision and Patern Recognition (2007)
5. Nister, D.: Reconstruction from Uncalibrated Sequences with a Hierarchy of Trifocal Tesors. In: European Conf. on Computer Vision (2000)
6. Farenzena, M., Fusiello, A.: Improving the Efficiency of Hierarchical Structure-and-motion. In: Conf. Computer Vision and Pattern Recognition (2010)
7. Thormaehlen, T., Broszio, H.: Keyframe Selection for Camera Motion and Structure Estimation from Multiple Views. In: European Conf. on Computer Vision (2004)
8. Torr, P., Zisserman, A.: The Problem of Degeneracy in Structure and Motion Recovery from Uncalibrated Image Sequences. Int. Journal of Computer Vision (1999)
9. Cornelis, K., Verbiest, F.: Drift Detection and Removal for Sequential Structure from Motion Algorithms. IEEE Transactions on Pattern Analysis and Machine Intelligence (2004)
10. Vavilin, A., Jo, K.-H., Jeong, M.-H., Ha, J.-E., Kang, D.-J.: Automatic Context Analysis for Image Classification and Retrieval. In: Huang, D.-S., Gan, Y., Bevilacqua, V., Figueroa, J.C. (eds.) ICIC 2011. LNCS, vol. 6838, pp. 377–382. Springer, Heidelberg (2011)
11. Andrey, V., Le, M.: Optimal Feature Subset Selection for Urban Scenes Understanding. In: URAI (2010)
12. Lowe, D.: Distinctive Image Features from Scale-Invariant Interest Points. International Journal of Computer Vision 60(2), 91–110 (2004)
13. Boyd, S., Vandenberghe, L.: Convex Optimization. Cambridge University Press (2004)
14. Kahl, F.: Multiple View Geometry under the L∞-norm. IEEE Transations on Pattern Analysis and Machine Intelligence (2008)
15. Olsson, C., Eriksson, A.: Outlier Removal using Duality. In: IEEE Conference on Computer Vision and Pattern Recognition (2010)
16. Furukawa, Y.: Accurate, Dense, and Robust Multi-View Stereopsis. IEEE Transactions on Pattern Analysis and Machine Intelligence (2009)
17. Dalalyan, A.: L1-penalized Robust Estimation for a Class of Inverse Problems Arising in Multiview Geometry. In: Neural Information Processing Systems (2009)
18. The MOSEK Optimization Toolbox for MATLAB Manual, http://www.mosek.com

Inference of Target Gene Regulation via miRNAs during Cell Senescence by Using the MiRaGE Server

Y.-h. Taguchi

Department of Physics, Chuo University, 1-13-27 Kasuga,Bukyo-ku, Tokyo 112-8551, Japan
tag@granular.com

Abstract. miRNAs have recently been shown to play a key role in cell senescence, by downregulating target genes.Thus, inference of those miRNAs that critically downregulate target genes is important. However, inference of target gene regulation by miRNAs is difficult and is often achieved simply by investigating significant upregulation during cell senescence. Here, we inferred the regulation of target genes by miRNAs, using the recently developed MiRaGE server, together with the change in miRNA expression during fibroblast IMR90 cell senescence.We revealed that the simultaneous consideration of 2 criteria, the up(down)regulation and the down(up)regulatiion of target genes, yields more feasible miRNA, i.e., those that are most frequently reported to be down/upregulated and/or to possess biological backgrounds that induce cell senescence. Thus, when analyzing miRNAs that critically contribute to cell senescence, it is important to consider the level of target gene regulation, simultaneously with the change in miRNA expression.

Keywords: Bioinformatics, miRNA, target gene, expression regulation, cell senescence.

1 Introduction

MiRNAs are small non-coding RNAs, which play important roles in a variety of biological processes. miRNAs negatively regulate the expression of specific target genes at the post-transcriptonal level [1]. A single miRNA has the potential to regulate hundreds of mRNAs, and therefore it is conceivable that miRNAs are important regulatory molecules in complex biological processes such as aging and cancer. miRNAs were recently reported to play a critical role in the control of cell senescence [2]. Neverthless, effective experimental procedures to directly evaluate target gene regulation by miRNAs have not yet been developed. Target genes themselves are often computationally predicted [3], and are therefore usually considered to include a relatively large number of false positives. The restricted accuracy of the target gene prediction means that critical miRNAs for cell senescence are usually selected from among those miRNAs showing high expression in senescent cells, without considering target gene expression [4].

Hackl et al. [5] reported that some miRNAs, including members of the miRNA17-92 cluster, were significantly downregulated during cell senescence. This was the first

D.-S. Huang et al. (Eds.): ICIC 2012, CCIS 304, pp. 441–446, 2012.

indication of the biological importance of miRNAs not upregulated during cell senescence. More recently, Wang et al. [6] demonstrated the induction of cell senescence, following the suppression of downregulated miRNAs. Thus, miRNAs may contribute to the progress of cell senescence progression, even when they are not expressed in senescent cells. Using next generation sequencing (NGS) Dhahbi et al. [7] identified many more miRNAs up/downregulated during cell senescence than were previously shown to exist by means of microarray analysis. This ability of NGS to detect such a large number of up/downregulated miRNAs generates the following questions. If the number of up/downregulated miRNAs is in the hundreds, which miRNA is the most important? Moreover, is the induction of cell senescence dependent on the up/downregulation of most of these hundreds of miRNAs?

Dhahbi et al. [7] demonstrated that a set of genes targeted by up/downregulated miRNAs is biologically informative. However, the importance of individual miRNAs during cell senescence remains to be elucidated.

Here, we propose a procedure for ranking miRNAs based not only on fold changes during cell senescence, but also on criticality during cell senescence: This ranking of miRNAs based upon the level of target gene regulation facilitates the detection of "important" miRNAs among hundreds of up/downregulated miRNAs.

2   Materials and Methods

2.1   mRNA Expression

mRNA expression profiles during fibroblast cell senescence (accession numbers GSE19018 and GSE15919) were downloaded from the gene expression omnibus (GEO). GSE19018 and GSE15919 represent IMR90 cell lines MRC5 cell lines, respectively.

2.2   Inference of Target Gene Expression via the MiRaGE Server

The target gene regulation by miRNAs was inferred by the MiRaGE server [8], Gene expression in young samples was taken to be unit, while that in senescent samples was considered to be $\exp(x_g)$, where x_g is gene expression transformed by principal component analysis (PCA) and linear discriminant analysis (LDA). The 1st PC obtained by PCA is used to discriminate diseases/cancers from health control. Then projection of each miRNA to discriminant function is used as x_g. The values were then uploaded to the MiRaGE server. All options other than "Select the conservation of miRNA", which was taken to be "all", are defaults.

2.3   miRNA Expression Extraction from Sequencing Data

Fastq files of GSE27404 were downloaded. The young (senescent) sample was the IMR90 cell line at population doubling (PD) 14 (34). The fastq files obtained were treated by miRDeep2 [9].

2.4   Coincidence of miRNA Rankings between the IMR90 and MRC5 Cell Lines, Based upon P-Values

We checked for a significant coincidence between the miRNA rankings for the IMR90 cell lines and MRC5 cell lines. P-values were computed via binomial distribution, $P(x, N, \frac{N}{N_{all}})$, where the number of common miRNAs is greater than x, when N represents the number of top-ranked miRNAs considered for each of the cell lines and N_{all} represents the total number of miRNAs considered.

2.5   Correlation Coefficients between the Senescence-Associated miRNA Expression Change and the Rejection Probability for Target Gene Regulation

The miRNA expression in young cells was subtracted from the miRNA expression in senescent cells. The resulting senescence-associated miRNA expression changes were compared with the rejection probability for target gene regulation, obtained using the MiRaGE server. The miRNA was excluded from the analysis when the miRDeep2 scores in young cells and senescent cells were less than the threshold value. The miRNA was also ignored when the rejection probability for target gene regulation was not significant, i.e., not less than 0.05. Pearson's correlation coefficients and associated P-values were computed between the miRNA expression changes and the rejection probabilities for target gene regulation, for a series of threshold values: none, 0, 1, 10, ..., 10^4.

3   Results

First, we attributed a P-value to each miRNA via the MiRaGE server [8]. The P-values, i.e., the rejection probabilities of target gene regulation, are measures of the likelihood of target gene up/downregulation, if each miRNA does not regulate target genes. Thus, smaller P-values indicate more plausible target gene regulation by each miRNA. Statistical validation revealed that top-ranked miRNAs were often common between IMR90 and MRC5 cell lines ($P < 10^{-10}$).

Given that these 2 rankings were obtained from 2 different experiments for the distinct cell lines, this remarkable coincidence indicates the validity of our bioinformatic analysis. To our knowledge, this is the rst report of common miRNAs regulating target gene expression in 2 distinct cell lines.

Next we calculated the correlation coefficients between the P-values obtained, and the senescence-associated miRNA expression changes for IMR90 cell lines computed according to the NGS data of Dhahbi et al. [7]. We revealed that the P-values associated with the correlation coefficients were often significant (typically $P < 10^{-2}$).

Thus, we concluded that the senescence-associated miRNA expression changes match the rejection probabilities of target gene regulation. To our knowledge, this is the first report of a significant correlation between individual miRNA expression and target gene expression during cell senescence.

4   Discussion

We have successfully demonstrated that inference of target gene regulation is coincident with miRNA expression changes during cell senescence. Here, we will confirm the validity of our inference when selecting critical miRNAs during cell senescence.

Table 1. miRNAs downregulated during cell senescence. If the rejection probability for target gene upgulation is not signi cant, i.e., not less than 0.05, the miRNA is omitted. RFC: reciprocal fold change during cell senescence (larger values indicate upregulation in young cells). NMRC: normalized mature read count such that summation over all over miRNAs is taken to be unit. SCORE: miRDeep2 score. P-value: the rejection probabilities for target gene upregulation during cell senescence (smaller values indicate more plausible target gene upregulation in senescent cells), computed using the t test implemented in the MiRaGE server. Q-value: FDR correced P-value (BH-criterion).

miRNA	Senescent		Young		P-value	Q-value	RFC
	NMRC	SCORE	NMRC	SCORE			
hsa-miR-143-5p	1.4E-04	7.4E+03	5.9E-04	2.4E+04	1.9E-02	2.1E-02	4.2E+00
hsa-miR-155-5p	1.3E-04	0.0E+00	1.3E-03	7.3E+03	2.3E-02	2.3E-02	1.0E+01
hsa-miR-16-5p	3.5E-05	0.0E+00	3.6E-04	2.0E+03	1.6E-03	5.5E-03	1.0E+01
hsa-miR-199a-3p	3.1E-02	1.6E+05	8.3E-02	4.6E+05	1.5E-02	2.1E-02	2.7E+00
hsa-miR-199b-3p	3.1E-02	1.6E+05	8.3E-02	4.6E+05	1.5E-02	2.1E-02	2.7E+00
hsa-miR-214-3p	1.6E-04	0.0E+00	2.0E-04	1.1E+03	6.9E-03	1.4E-02	1.3E+00
hsa-miR-27a-5p	3.8E-06	5.1E+03	6.6E-06	2.8E+03	1.7E-04	1.7E-03	1.7E+00
hsa-miR-423-3p	3.5E-04	3.7E+04	7.1E-04	3.6E+04	3.3E-03	8.3E-03	2.0E+00
hsa-miR-424-5p	1.7E-04	2.2E+03	6.3E-04	7.0E+03	1.6E-03	5.5E-03	3.6E+00
hsa-miR-503	9.7E-04	5.0E+03	2.0E-03	1.1E+04	1.7E-02	2.1E-02	2.1E+00

Table 1 and 2 list those miRNAs that are down(up)regulated during cell senescence, together with their corresponding target genes that are up(down)regulated.

Thus, if the miRNA is down(up)regulated during cell senescence, the rejection probability of the corresponding target genes being up(down)regulated should be small. The threshold miRDeep2 score is taken to be 103, such that the P −value associated with the correlation coefficient is at a minimum.

Our findings regarding most of the miRNAs listed in Tables 1 and 2 have experimentally been validated (e.g. Table S2 [5]). Moreover, it is likely that supporting evidence will soon be available for the remaining miRNAs, because new ndings are reported on a frequent basis.

Finally, it is important to recognize that not all miRNAs undergo more than 2 fold changes. This suggests that, not only fold changes, but also target gene regulations, should be considered when further investigating the correlation between miRNA expression and target gene expression during cell senescence.

Table 2. miRNAs upregulated during the cell senescence. FC: fold change during cell senescence (larger values indicate upregulation in senescent cells). P -value: the rejection probabilities for target gene downregulation during cell senescence (smaller values indicate more plausible target gene downregulation in senescent cells), computed using the t test implemented in the MiRaGE server. Q-value: FDR corrected P-value (BH-criterion). Other notations are the same as in Table 1.

miRNA	Senescent		Young		P-value	Q-value	FC
	NMRC	SCORE	NMRC	SCORE			
hsa-let-7a-5p	1.7E-01	4.5E+05	1.4E-01	4.4E+05	3.2E-05	1.3E-04	1.2E+00
hsa-let-7c	8.8E-02	0.0E+00	8.7E-02	1.3E+04	3.2E-05	1.3E-04	1.0E+00
hsa-let-7e-5p	9.2E-02	1.2E+05	7.3E-02	6.4E+04	3.2E-05	1.3E-04	1.3E+00
hsa-let-7f-5p	1.5E-01	3.6E+05	1.3E-01	3.5E+05	3.2E-05	1.3E-04	1.1E+00
hsa-let-7i-5p	1.7E-02	8.7E+04	1.2E-02	6.5E+04	3.2E-05	1.3E-04	1.5E+00
hsa-miR-10a-3p	5.0E-05	1.9E+04	4.9E-05	2.0E+04	2.8E-09	9.0E-08	1.0E+00
hsa-miR-125a-5p	6.0E-04	3.1E+03	3.1E-04	1.8E+03	2.4E-02	2.8E-02	1.9E+00
hsa-miR-125b-5p	3.0E-03	1.6E+04	1.9E-03	1.1E+04	2.4E-02	2.8E-02	1.6E+00
hsa-miR-136-5p	2.1E-04	1.3E+03	2.1E-04	1.3E+03	3.0E-06	4.7E-05	1.0E+00
hsa-miR-154-3p	2.5E-04	1.5E+03	2.3E-04	1.4E+03	2.0E-02	2.7E-02	1.1E+00
hsa-miR-154-5p	3.0E-05	1.5E+03	2.5E-05	1.4E+03	4.5E-02	4.6E-02	1.2E+00
hsa-miR-181a-5p	5.1E-03	2.6E+04	4.2E-03	2.4E+04	7.5E-04	1.4E-03	1.2E+00
hsa-miR-181b-5p	5.9E-03	2.8E+04	3.6E-03	1.6E+04	7.5E-04	1.4E-03	1.6E+00
hsa-miR-181d	4.7E-03	0.0E+00	3.0E-03	5.4E+03	7.5E-04	1.4E-03	1.5E+00
hsa-miR-193a-5p	5.1E-04	3.0E+03	3.1E-04	2.6E+03	4.8E-04	1.4E-03	1.6E+00
hsa-miR-221-3p	7.7E-02	3.9E+05	4.8E-02	2.7E+05	7.6E-04	1.4E-03	1.6E+00
hsa-miR-23a-3p	3.3E-03	1.6E+04	1.7E-03	9.0E+03	4.6E-02	4.6E-02	1.9E+00
hsa-miR-23b-3p	3.1E-03	3.5E+03	1.6E-03	2.9E+03	4.6E-02	4.6E-02	1.9E+00
hsa-miR-30a-3p	2.6E-03	5.1E+04	1.1E-03	1.8E+04	6.5E-04	1.4E-03	2.5E+00
hsa-miR-30d-3p	7.0E-06	4.2E+03	4.2E-06	8.4E+03	6.5E-04	1.4E-03	1.7E+00
hsa-miR-30e-3p	2.0E-03	2.5E+03	9.3E-04	3.2E+03	6.5E-04	1.4E-03	2.2E+00
hsa-miR-323b-3p	2.0E-04	1.0E+03	4.9E-05	0.0E+00	7.1E-04	1.4E-03	4.0E+00
hsa-miR-323b-5p	1.3E-06	1.0E+03	3.7E-07	0.0E+00	2.3E-02	2.8E-02	3.5E+00
hsa-miR-369-3p	2.8E-03	1.5E+04	9.6E-04	5.6E+03	1.7E-02	2.4E-02	2.9E+00
hsa-miR-369-5p	9.7E-05	1.5E+04	5.5E-05	5.6E+03	1.3E-02	1.9E-02	1.8E+00
hsa-miR-382-5p	1.3E-03	7.3E+03	1.0E-03	6.5E+03	3.7E-03	5.9E-03	1.3E+00
hsa-miR-409-3p	6.0E-04	0.0E+00	4.9E-04	3.7E+03	2.2E-02	2.8E-02	1.2E+00
hsa-miR-485-3p	5.6E-04	7.0E+03	5.0E-04	5.3E+03	1.9F-02	2.6E-02	1.1E+00
hsa-miR-493-5p	2.7E-04	2.6E+03	8.8E-05	1.1E+03	1.7E-03	2.9E-03	3.0E+00
hsa-miR-494	4.4E-04	2.2E+03	2.1E-04	1.2E+03	2.8E-02	3.1E-02	2.1E+00
hsa-miR-495	2.7E-03	1.4E+04	1.3E-03	7.2E+03	4.6E-04	1.4E-03	2.1E+00
hsa-miR-98	3.8E-04	1.5E+03	1.9E-04	0.0E+00	3.2E-05	1.3E-04	2.0E+00

5   Conclusion

We propose that inference of target gene regulation by miRNAs, together with the miRNA expression change during cell senescence, should be used to estimate critical miRNAs during cell senescence. Liang et al. [10] reported that miRNA expression does not always reflect miRNA activities. Thus, when selecting critical miRNAs, it is insu cient to only consider the miRNA expression change. Our strategy of screening candidate miRNAs by simultaneously considering target gene regulation and miRNA expression of particular value when using NGS to measure miRNA expression, In comparison with microarray analysis, NGS facilities the detection of more subtle changes during cell senescence, and yields more candidates for critical miRNAs

Acknowledgements. This research was supported by KAKENHI (2, 3300357).

References

1. Ghildiyal, M., Zamore, P.D.: Small silencing RNAs: an expanding universe. Nat. Rev. Genet., 1094–108 (2009)
2. Laferty-Whyte, K., Cairney, C.J., Jamieson, N.B., Oien, K.A., Keith, W.N.: Pathway Analysis of Senescence-associated MiRNA Targets Reveals Common Processes to Different Senescence Induction Mechanisms. Biochim. Biophys. Acta 1792, 341–352 (2009)
3. Barbato, C., Arisi, I., Frizzo, M.E., Brandi, R., Da Sacco, L., Masotti, A.: Computational Challenges in MiRNA Target Predictions: to be or not to be a True Target? J. Biomed. Biotechnol. 2009, 803069 (2009)
4. Feliciano, A., Sanchez-Sendra, B., Kondoh, H., Lleonart, M.E.: MicroRNAs Regulate Key Effector Pathways of Senescence. J. Aging. Res., 205378 (2011)
5. Hackl, M., Brunner, S., Fortschegger, K., Schreiner, C., Micutkova, L., Mück, C., Laschober, G.T., Lepperdinger, G., Sampson, N., Berger, P., Herndler-Brandstetter, D., Wieser, M., Kühnel, H., Strasser, A., Rinnerthaler, M., Breitenbach, M., Mildner, M., Eckhart, L., Tschachler, E., Trost, A., Bauer, J.W., Papak, C., Trajanoski, Z., Scheideler, M., Grillari-Voglauer, R., Grubeck-Loebenstein, B., Jansen-Dürr, P., Grillari, J.: miR-17, miR-19b, miR-20a, and miR-106a are downregulated in human aging. Aging Cell 9, 291–296 (2010)
6. Wang, M., Cheng, Z., Tian, T., Chen, J., Dou, F., Guo, M., Cong, Y.S.: Differential Expression of Oncogenic MiRNAs in Proliferating and Senescent Human Fibroblasts. Mol. Cell. Biochem. 352, 27–279 (2011)
7. Dhahbi, J.M., Atamna, H., Boffelli, D., Magis, W., Spindler, S.R., Martin, D.I.: Deep Sequencing Reveals Novel MicroRNAs and Regulation of MicroRNA Expression During Cell Senescence. PLoS ONE 6, e20509 (2011)
8. Yoshizawa, M., Taguchi, Y.-h., Yasuda, J.: Inference of Gene Regulation Via MiRNAs During ES Cell Differentiation Using MiRaGE Method. Int. J. Mol. Sci. 12, 9265–9276 (2011)
9. Friedländer, M.R., Mackowiak, S.D., Li, N., Chen, W., Rajewsky, N.: MiRDeep2 Accurately Identifies Known and Hundreds of Novel MicroRNA Genes in Seven Animal Clades. Nucleic Acids Res. 40, 37–52 (2012)
10. Liang, Z., Zhou, H., Zheng, H., Wu, J.: Expression Levels of MicroRNAs are not Associated with Their Regulatory Activities. Biol. Direct 6, 43 (2011)

Sequence Analysis and Discrimination of Amyloid and Non-amyloid Peptides

M. Michael Gromiha[1], A. Mary Thangakani[2], Sandeep Kumar[3], and D. Velmurugan[2]

[1] Department of Biotechnology, Indian Institute of Technology Madras,
Chennai 600 036, Tamilnadu, India
[2] Department of Crystallography and Biophysics, University of Madras,
Chennai 600025, Tamilnadu, India
[3] Biotherapeutics Pharmaceutical Sciences, Pfizer Inc., MC6S,
575 Maryville Centre Drive, St. Louis, MO 63141, USA
gromiha@iitm.ac.in

Abstract. The main cause of several neurodegenerative diseases such as Alzhemier, Parkinson and spongiform encephalopathies is the formation of amyloid fibrils in proteins. The systematic analysis of amyloid and non-amyloid sequences provide deep insights on the preference of amino acid residues at different locations of amyloid and non-amyloid peptides. In this work, we have systematically analyzed 139 amyloid and 168 non-amyloid hexapeptides and revealed the preference of residues at six different positions. We observed that Glu, Ile, Ser, Thr and Val are dominant at positions six, five, one, two and three, respectively in amyloid peptides. In non-amyloids, similar trend is noticed for few residues whereas the residues Ala in position 2, Asn in position 4, Gly in position 6 etc, showed different trends to that of amyloids. Utilizing the positional preference of 20 amino acid residues, we devised a statistical method for discriminating amlyloids and non-amyloids, which showed an accuracy of 89% and 54%, respectively. Further, we have examined various machine learning techniques, and a method based on Random Forest showed an overall accuracy of 99.7% and 83% using self-consistent and 10-fold cross-validation, respectively using the positional preference of amyloids and non-amyloids along with three selected amino acid properties.

Keywords: amino acid composition, discrimination, machine learning, statistical methods, amyloids, amino acid properties.

1   Introduction

Aggregation is a process, which prevents proper folding of proteins and it is necessary for all organisms to overcome aggregation for maintaining their native states. The aggregation of proteins causes several neurogenerative human diseases including Parkinson disease and Alzheimer disease. Given the importance of amyloid fibril formation in different areas of biology, it is important to elucidate the mechanisms for aggregation as well as to identify the probability of peptides to form aggregation.

D.-S. Huang et al. (Eds.): ICIC 2012, CCIS 304, pp. 447–452, 2012.
© Springer-Verlag Berlin Heidelberg 2012

Several experimental studies have been carried out to understand the molecular determinants of aggregation, mutational effects as well as the influence of hydrophobic residues for promoting aggregation [1-5].

On the other hand, several computer approaches have been put forward to understand the mechanism of aggregation, aggregation strategies for mesophilic and thermophilic proteins and for predicting amyloid prone peptides [6-9]. These methods are mainly based on amino acid properties, such as hydrophobicity, charge distribution, propensity of β-strands etc., empirical potentials, structure based analysis and so on [7-9]. In addition, the merits and shortcomings of different methods developed for identifying amyloid peptides have been extensively reviewed [10,11].

In this work, we have systematically analyzed the amino acid composition of amyloid and non-amyloid peptides and specifically, the preference of residues at different positions in hexapeptides. We observed that the residues, Glu, Ile, Ser, Thr and Val showed specific preferences in amyloids at positions 6, 5, 1, 2 and 3, respectively. In non-amyloids, similar trend is noticed for few residues whereas the residues Ala in position 2, Asn in position 4, Gly in position 6 etc, showed different trends to that of amyloids. Further, we developed statistical methods and machine learning techniques for discriminating amyloid and non-amyloid peptides using positional preference of amino acid residues and amino acid properties. Our method could discriminate the amyloid and non-amyloid peptides with an accuracy of 99.7% and 82.7% using self-consistent and 10-fold cross-validation methods, respectively.

2   Materials and Methods

2.1   Datasets

We have developed a dataset, which contains 139 amyloid and 168 non-amyloid hexapeptides, which have been often used in experiments to grow amyloid-fibrils [9, 12].These data have been collected from the careful search on the literature. The datasets are available from the corresponding author upon request.

2.2   Computation of Amino Acid Composition

The amino acid composition for the set of amyloids and non-amyloids at different positions has been computed using the number of amino acids of each type and the total number of residues in their respective positions. It is defined as [13]:

$$\text{Comp}(i,j) = \Sigma\ n_{ij}/N_j \qquad (1)$$

where i and j stands   for the 20 amino acid residues and six positions, n_{ij} is the number of residues of each type i at position j and N is the total number of residues at position j.

2.3   Discrimination of Amyloid and Non-amyloid Peptides Using Statistical Methods and Machine Learning Techniques

We formulated a statistical method for discriminating amyloid and non-amyloid peptides using the preference of residues at six different positions. For each peptide, we calculated the total preference using the preference of amyloid and non-amyloid peptides at different positions. The peptide is assigned as amyloid if the total value is higher with amyloid preference than non-amyloid preference and vice-versa. In addition, we have analyzed several machine learning techniques implemented in WEKA program [14] for discriminating amyloids and non-amyloids. The details of all the methods are available in our earlier articles [15].

2.4   Assessment of Predictive Ability

The performance of the methods were assessed with self-consistency, 5-fold, 10-fold and 20-fold cross-validation tests. We have used different measures, such as sensitivity, specificity and accuracy, to assess the performance of discriminating amyloids and non-amyloids. The term sensitivity shows the correct prediction of amyloids, specificity is the correct prediction of non-amyloids and accuracy indicates the overall assessment. These terms are defined as follows:

$$Sensitivity = TP/(TP+FN)$$

$$Specificity = TN/(TN+FP)$$

$$Accuracy = (TP+TN)/(TP+TN+FP+FN),$$

where, TP, FP, TN and FN refer to the number of true positives, false positives, true negatives and false negatives, respectively.

3   Results and Discussion

3.1   Preference of Residues at Six Different Positions of Amyloid and Non-amyloid Hexapeptides

The amino acid compositions at six positions of amyloid forming hexapeptides are shown in **Figure 1a**. We observed that specific residues are preferred at some positions. Especially, Glu prefers to accommodate at position 6 compared with other positions as well as other amino acid residues; Ile is dominant in positions 4 and 5 and the difference is highly significant; position 1 is accommodated by Ser; Thr and Val showed their preference at positions 2 and 3, respectively. The dissection of amino acid composition based on different positions is very helpful to discriminate amyloid and non-amyloid peptides.

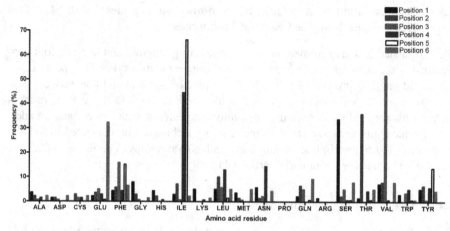

Fig. 1. Preference of amino acid residue at six different positions of amyloid forming hexapeptides

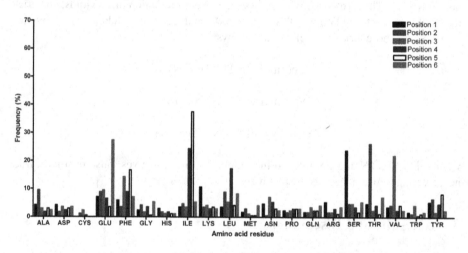

Fig. 2. Preference of amino acid residue at six different positions of non-amyloids

The general analysis of non-amyloids showed that the highest frequency of occurrence of amino acid is less than 40% (Figure 1b) whereas it is about 70% in the case of amyloids (Figure 1a). Specifically, Ser prefers position 1; Ala and Thr show high preference at position 2; Val in position 3; Ile and Leu in position 4; Phe and Ile in position 5, and Gln in position 6. Although some of the features are similar to amyloids and non-amyloids the occurrence of several amino acids are different from each other. For example, Ala in position 2, Asn in position 4, Gly in position 6 and so on. These differences are helpful for discriminating amyloids and non-amyloids.

3.2   Discrimination of Amyloid and Non-amyloid Peptides Using Statistical Methods

We developed a statistical method for discriminating amyloid and non-amyloid peptides using the preference of residues at six different positions (section 2.3). This method showed that an accuracy of 89% (123/139) to detect amyloid peptides whereas non-amyloids are discriminated with an accuracy of 54%. The poor performance of non-amyloid is due to the point mutation of specific residues in a hexapeptide STVVIE, and a difference of one single residue is not properly taken into account with the preference using statistical methods. In order to improve the performance, we utilized several machine learning techniques (see below).

3.3   Discrimination of Amyloid and Non-amyloid Peptides Using Machine Learning Techniques

We have utilized several machine learning techniques for discriminating amyloids and non-amyloids. We noticed that the input samples have been successfully modeled using Random forest with an accuracy of 99.7%. The method has been tested with 10-fold cross-validation and we obtained an accuracy of 82.1% using position specific preference of amino acid residues. The combination of these preferences with three amino acid properties, hydrophobicity, isoelectric point and long-range non-bonded energy improved the accuracy up to 82.74%; the sensitivity and specificity are 81.3% and 83.9%, respectively. We tested the method with 5-fold, 10-fold and 20-fold cross-validations and the accuracies are 80%, 82.7% and 81.1%, respectively.

4   Conclusions

We have systematically analyzed the characteristic features of amino acid residues at different positions of amyloid and non-amyloid hexapeptides and the results showed specific preferences of residues in these two classes; We have utilized the positional preference of residues along with amino acid properties to discriminate amyloids and non-amyloids using statistical methods and machine learning techniques. The statistical method showed an accuracy of 89% and 54%, respectively for identifying the amyloids and non-amyloids. Further, different machine learning techniques have been utilized for discrimination, which showed an accuracy of 99% and 83%, using self-consistency and 10-fold cross-validation tests, respectively.

Acknowledgement. This research was partially supported by Indian Institute of Technology Madras research grant to MMG (BIO/10-11/540/NFSC/MICH). AMT and DV thank the Bioinformatics Facility of University of Madras for computational facilities. SK acknowledges his discussions with Drs. Satish Singh and Patrick Buck.

References

1. Wurth, C., Guimard, N.K., Hecht, M.H.: Mutations that Reduce Aggregation of the Alzheimer's Aβ42 Peptide: an Unbiased Search for the Sequence Determinants of Aβ Amyloidogenesis. J. Mol. Biol. 319(3), 1279–1290 (2004)

2. Groot, N.S., Aviles, F.X., Vendrell, J., Ventura, S.: Mutagenesis of the Central Hydrophobic Cluster in Aβ42 Alzheimer's Peptide. Side-chain Properties Correlate with Aggregation Propensities. FEBS J. 273, 658–668 (2006)
3. Kim, W., Hecht, M.H.: Generic Hydrophobic Residues are Sufficient to Promote Aggregation of the Alzheimer's Aβ42 Peptide. Proc. Natl. Acad. Sci. USA 103(4), 15824–15829 (2003)
4. Luheshi, L.M.: Systematic in Vivo Analysis of the Intrinsic Determinants of Amyloid β Pathogenicity. PLoS Biol. 5(11), e290 (2007)
5. Winkelmann, J., Calloni, G., Campioni, S., Mannini, B., Taddei, N., Chiti, F.: Low-level Expression of a Folding-incompetent Protein in Escherichia Coli: Search for the Molecular Determinants of Protein Aggregation in Vivo. J. Mol. Biol. 398, 600–613 (2010)
6. Thangakani, A.M., Kumar, S., Velmurugan, D., Gromiha, M.M.: How do Thermophilic Proteins Resist Aggregation? Proteins 80, 1003–1015 (2012)
7. Fernandez-Escamilla, A.M., Rousseau, F.: Prediction of Sequence-dependent and Mutational Effects on the Aggregation of Peptides and Proteins. Nat. Biotechnol. 22, 1302–1306 (2004)
8. Conchillo-Solé, O., Avilés, F.X., Vendrell, J., Daura, X., Ventura, S.: AGGRESCAN: a Server for the Prediction and Evaluation of "Hot Spots" of Aggregation in Polypeptides. BMC Bioinformatics 8(3), 65 (2007)
9. Maurer-Stroh, S.: Exploring the Sequence Determinants of Amyloid Structure Using Position-specific Scoring Matrices. Nat. Methods 7, 237–242 (2010)
10. Agrawal, N.J., Kumar, S., Helk, B., Singh, S.K., Trout, B.L.: Aggregation in Protein-based Biotherapeutics: Computational Studies and Tools to Identify Aggregation-prone Regions. J. Pharm. Sci. 100(12), 5081–5095 (2010)
11. Belli, M., Ramazzotti, M., Chiti, F.: Prediction of Amyloid Aggregation in Vivo. EMBO Rep. 12(7), 657–663 (2011)
12. Lopez de la Paz, M., Serrano, L.: Sequence Determinants of Amyloid Fibril Formation. Proc. Natl. Acad. Sci. 101, 87–92 (2004)
13. Gromiha, M.M., Suwa, M.: A Simple Statistical Method for Discriminating Outer Membrane Proteins with Better Accuracy. Bioinformatics 21, 961–968 (2004)
14. Witten, I.H., Frank, E.: Data Mining: Practical Machine Learning Tools and Techniques, 2nd edn., San Francisco (2005)
15. Gromiha, M.M., Suwa, M.: Discrimination of Outer Membrane Proteins Using Machine Learning Algorithms. Proteins 63, 1031–1037 (2006)

Fast DNA Sequence Clustering
Based on Longest Common Subsequence

Youhei Namiki, Takashi Ishida, and Yutaka Akiyama

Department of Computer Science, Graduate School of Information Science and Engineering,
Tokyo Institute of Technology
{y_namiki,t.ishida,akiyama}@bi.cs.titech.ac.jp

Abstract. With recent improvements in sequencing throughput, huge numbers
of genomes can now be sequenced rapidly. However, data analysis methods
have not kept up, making it difficult to process the vast amounts of sequence
data now available. Thus, there is a strong demand for a faster sequence clustering algorithm. We developed a new fast DNA sequence clustering method
called LCS-HIT based on the popular CD-HIT program. The proposed method
employs a novel filtering technique based on the longest common subsequence
to identify similar sequence pairs. This filtering technique affords a considerable speed-up over CD-HIT without loss of sensitivity. For a dataset with two
million DNA sequences, our method was about 7.1, 4.4 and 2.5 times faster
than CD-HIT for 100, 150, and 400 bases, respectively.

Keywords: longest common subsequence, DNA sequence clustering, next
generation sequencer.

1 Introduction

Recent progresses in DNA sequencing have enabled us to amass huge amounts of
genomic data in a short time. While current sequencers produce relatively short sequences ($\sim$ 150 bases), the number of such sequences is quite huge (10 million $\sim$).
However, these vast amounts of data require a considerable amount of time for analysis. This necessitates a shift in focus from sequencing throughput to the computational
speed of algorithms for sequence data analysis. Sequence clustering is a data mining
method that aims to identify similar sequence groups in huge DNA and amino acid
sequence datasets. The two main objectives of sequence clustering are as follows:
first, to reduce the size of the dataset by identifying representatives for each cluster
and removing redundant sequences; and second, to find sequence patterns that appear
in the dataset by checking cluster sizes (the number of members). Generally, clustering algorithms require $O(N^2)$ time for N sequences, making it difficult to scale them to
large datasets. However, several algorithms have been developed for more efficient
sequence clustering[1][2].

Among these, CD-HIT[3] is now one of the most widely used sequence clustering
tools. CD-HIT is used on public databases such as Uniprot and PDB to remove

D.-S. Huang et al. (Eds.): ICIC 2012, CCIS 304, pp. 453–460, 2012.

redundant sequences. It clusters sequences on the basis of sequence identity between pairs and can deal with large datasets in a relatively short time by relying on an approximate clustering approach and short word filtering. Short word filtering greatly decreases the burden of the sequence alignment calculation by identifying similar sequences on the basis of matches between short subsequences. However, although this filtering scheme is very computationally efficient, it is too rough to exclude many dissimilar sequence pairs. Thus, even this well-known tool requires at least a couple of days to cluster 10 million sequences. And given the potential of the next generation of sequencers, it is clear that further speed-up is necessary.

Here we present a faster and more accurate clustering system named LCS-HIT. We introduce a novel filtering technique to select similar sequence pairs on the basis of the longest common subsequence (LCS) before the sequence alignment process. This approach is much faster than sequence alignment and stricter than short word filtering. Thus, our clustering algorithm achieves a significant speedup over CD-HIT without compromising on clustering accuracy.

2   Methods

2.1   Algorithm

Our sequence clustering method consists of several parts, and operates according to the following sequence of steps:

1. Let Q be the set of sequences to be clustered and $R=\emptyset$ be the set of existing cluster representatives.
2. For each $q \in Q$,
   (a) Compare q and R by using the short word table, and find the set $R_{q,k} (\subseteq R)$, the subset of representatives with $\geq t$ common k-mers (partial sequences of k nucleotides) with q (**short word filtering**).
   (b) For each q and each $r \in R_{q,k}$,
      (i) Compute the length of the longest common subsequence $LLCS(q, r)$ between q and r. If $LLCS(q, r)$ is above a certain threshold, save the pair as a candidate similar sequence pair that may belong to the same cluster. Otherwise q and r are considered to belong to different clusters (**LCS filtering**).
      (ii) A For each saved sequence pair q and r, compute the optimal sequence alignment using affine gap penalties and the sequence identity between q and r. If the sequence identity is greater than or equal to the threshold s, then q and r are considered to belong to the same cluster, and q is added to r's cluster (the cluster representative is not updated). Otherwise they are considered to belong to different clusters.

(c) If q does not belong to any existing cluster, then create a new cluster whose member and representative is q. q is also registered in the short word table, and let $R \leftarrow R \cup q$.

An optimal alignment must be computed when checking whether a pair of sequences belongs to the same cluster. However, the time complexity of computing an optimal alignment is $O(mn)$ by dynamic programming, where m and n are the lengths of the two sequences. This is very slow, making it unrealistic to attempt to compute alignments for all combinations of sequences. Additionally, the number of sequence pairs with a sequence identity less than the threshold s is much more than the number of similar sequence pairs with a sequence identity above the threshold. Thus, our method filters similar sequence pairs by a faster method in advance, and prunes the comparison set of dissimilar pairs. As a result, the number of alignment computations dramatically decreases, and the whole clustering process can be completed in a reasonable length of time. In the following sections, we describe the two filtering methods, short word filtering and the proposed LCS filtering. When a new cluster is created, the first assigned sequence is selected as the representative for its cluster. Representatives of existing clusters are not updated even if new sequences are added to the clusters. This means that the clustering result depends on the order of input sequences, while the computational cost in comparing an input sequence with the cluster representative can be significantly reduced. Our clustering method is largely based on CD-HIT and retains many similarities. However, there are two main differences; our method employs a new filtering process (LCS filtering) after short word filtering and different filtering criteria are used for short word filtering.

2.2   Filtering Similar Sequence Pairs Based on the Longest Common Subsequence

Short word filtering can process large amounts of sequence data in little time because of the low computational complexity. It is thus suitable for filtering large sequence datasets. However, the filtering is rough: many dissimilar sequence pairs, i.e., with sequence identity less than the threshold s, pass through the short word filter. Thus, the subsequent sequence alignment process will be hampered and the overall computation time for clustering will be prolonged. Instead, it is necessary to introduce a fast and accurate filtering process that follows the rough, short word filtering stage.

Here, we introduce a new filtering method that relies on the relation between the length of the LCS and the sequence identity. Although the computational cost for determining the LCS is generally not negligible, we can use a bit-parallel algorithm to accelerate its calculation and avoid the bottleneck.

The Longest Common Subsequence

Let a subsequence be created by picking up elements from a main sequence while preserving their relative order. The LCS is the longest common subsequence among all possible common subsequences. For example, "TAGC" is the LCS of

"ATCAGTC" and "CTAGAC." Finding the LCS of a sequence pair is equivalent to aligning the two sequences in order to maximize the number of the matched elements.

The Length of the Longest Common Subsequence

The LCS of two sequences $X = (x_1, x_2, ..., x_m)$ and $Y = (y_1, y_2, ..., y_n)$ can be computed as follows:

Let $X_i = (x_1, x_2, ..., x_i)(0 \leq i \leq m)$ and $Y_i = (y_1, y_2, ..., y_j)(0 \leq j \leq n)$; and let $LLCS(X, Y)$ be the length of the LCS between X and Y. Then,

$$LLCS(X_i, Y_j) = \begin{cases} 0 & (\text{if } i = 0 \text{ or } j = 0) \\ LLCS(X_{i-1}, Yj-1) + 1 & (\text{if } x_i = y_j) \\ \max(LLCS(X_i, Y_{j-1}), LLCS(X_{i-1}, Y_j)) & (\text{if } x_i \neq y_j) \end{cases}$$

Generally, $LLCS(X, Y)$ can be computed by dynamic programming, which has $O(mn)$ time complexity.

LCS Filtering for Similar Sequence Pairs

The length of the LCS of a sequence pair, $LLCS(X, Y)$, equals the number of matches in the sequence alignment that maximizes matches between the two sequences. Suppose the sequence X is longer than or of equal length to $Y(m \geq n)$. The sequence identity of a sequence pair equals the number of matches in the alignment that maximizes the alignment score for the two sequences divided by the shorter sequence length n.

From this, the following relationship holds between the length of the LCS and the sequence identity.

$$\frac{LLCS(X, Y)}{n} \geq \text{Sequence identity} \tag{1}$$

This means that the ratio of $LLCS(X, Y)$ to the sequence length n equals the upper bound of the sequence identity of the two sequences. By using this relation, dissimilar sequence pairs whose sequence identity is less than the threshold s can be pruned by checking whether $LLCS(X, Y)/n$ is greater than s before computing the sequence identity.

LCS filtering has two advantages. First, LCS filtering can be performed with the threshold of sequence identity s as the filtering criterion and does not need new heuristic thresholds. Second, sequence pairs with sequence identity greater than the given threshold s always pass LCS filtering (no false negatives) since $LLCS(X, Y)/n$ is always larger than the sequence identity. Thus, LCS filtering can be considered a suitable filtering process to follow the short word filter and precede the alignment computation.

Fast Bitparallel LLCS computation

As described above, by using $LLCS(X, Y)$ we can filter similar sequence pairs with higher accuracy than that of the short word filter. However, the time complexity of $LLCS(X, Y)$ computation by dynamic programming is $O(mn)$, which is too large.

Nevertheless, there are several bit-parallel LCS-length computation algorithms whose time complexity is almost $O(n)$, and by using them we can compute $LLCS(X,Y)$ in a reasonable amount of time[4][5]. We use the most efficient of Hyyro's bit-parallel algorithms to reduce the computation time for $LLCS(X,Y)$.

Here, b_i denotes i repetitions of bit b. With this notation, we can write $1111 = 1^4$ and $0011100 = 0^2 1^3 0^2$. Additionally, let Σ be the set of alphabets that appear in X and Y, and let $\sigma = |\Sigma|$ be the number of alphabets.

Let $ComputePM(X)$ be defined as in Fig. 1(A), where "|" denotes the bitwise OR operation. $ComputePM(X)$ sets the corresponding positions of bits of PM (position matrix) for each nucleotide in the sequence X. With this $ComputePM(X)$, $LLCS(X, Y)$ can be computed as shown in Fig. 1(B). In the figure, "&" denotes the bitwise AND operation, and + and - denote arithmetic addition and subtraction of integers, respectively. These operations will require carries and borrows between adjacent bits.

The time complexity of $ComputePM(X)$ is, $O(\sigma \lceil m/w \rceil + m)$ and that of $LLCS$ is $O(\sigma \lceil m/w \rceil n)$, where w is the bit-length of a variable used for storing sequence data. Therefore, we can see that the computation of $ComputePM(X)$ and $LLCS(X, Y)$ is much faster than dynamic programming and also faster than the alignment computation.

(A)

$ComputePM(X)$
1: **for** $\lambda \in \Sigma$ **do**
2:    $PM_\lambda \leftarrow 0^m$
3: **end for**
4: **for** $i \in 1...m$ **do**
5:    $PM_{X_i} \leftarrow PM_{X_i} \mid 0^{m-i}10^{i-1}$
6: **end for**

(B)

$LLCS(X,Y)$
1: $ComputePM(X)$
2: $V' \leftarrow 1^m$
3: **for** $j \in 1...n$ **do**
4:    $U \leftarrow V' \ \& \ PM_{Y_j}$
5:    $V' \leftarrow (V' + U) \mid (V' - U)$
6: **end for**
7: Return the number of unset bits in V'

Fig. 1. (A) Computation of $ComputePM(X)$ and (B) Computation of $LLCS(X, Y)$ by bit-parallel algorithm

2.3   Modification of Short Word Filtering

Short word filtering is a fast filtering method to find similar sequence pairs between existing cluster representatives and a query sequence. It checks for the number of common k-mers (partial sequences of k nucleotides) between the two to find a match. The main idea behind this method is that a pair of similar sequences with high sequence identity must have short identical words. The value k should be decided according to the length of the query sequences and the threshold of sequence identity. The short word filter is used in CD-HIT, but in the proposed method, we use different filtering criteria to accommodate the subsequent LCS filter. In short word filtering, k-mers in the representatives are indexed in an index table (short word table) in advance, so cluster representatives with specific k-mers can be filtered quickly.

As mentioned, the short word filter used in our method enumerates every kth k-mer of cluster representatives and all k-mers of the query sequences. By contrast, CD-HIT's short word filter enumerates all the k-mers of the cluster representatives and query sequences. There are mainly two advantages of enumerating and registering every kth k-mer instead of all the k-mers. The first is that the size of the short word table in main memory is reduced to about $1/k$. And second is that the computation time necessary for searching cluster representatives in the short word table is also reduced since the number of the entries decreases to about $1/k$.

On the other hand, there are several possible demerits. Since our short word filter uses a lower threshold t than that of CD-HIT, it is possible that the number of dissimilar sequence pairs may increase because of coincidental partial matches between sequences. Also, short word filtering fails to find a common k-mer between similar sequences if mismatches and gaps between a cluster representative and query sequence appear at equal intervals.

However, the first demerit can be addressed by introducing a fast and more accurate filtering process after the short word filter and before the alignment process. Our method uses LCS filtering for this purpose. The second demerit occurs very rarely, since DNA sequences are not random sequences, and it can be considered as a rare case that mismatches and gaps in a sequence pair appear at equal intervals even when their sequence identity meets the threshold s.

3   Implementation

We implemented our clustering method in C++ and compared its efficiency with that of CD-HIT.

3.1   Performance Evaluation

For this evaluation, we used two different types of datasets of short reads. One type comprised artificial datasets including short reads generated by the MetaSim software[6] from the *Bacillus amyloliquefaciens* genome sequence. The datasets included reads of fixed length. We used two million sequences with three different patterns of sequence lengths (100, 150, and 400 bases). The other comprised real sequencing data for metagenomic samples obtained by Roche's 454 and Illumina/Solexa. The 454 dataset includes 34,719 reads of length from 41 to 629 bases, and the Illumina dataset includes 6,822,944 reads with lengths from 60 to 75 bases.

We set the thresholds and parameters as follows: the threshold of sequence identity s was 0.9, the length of short word k was 9, the threshold of the number of common k-mers t was 1 (for 100 bases and 150 bases) and 4 (for 400 bases). We ran the clustering programs on a workstation running SUSE Linux 10 with a single-core AMD Opteron processor (2.8 GHz) and 32 GB of memory.

3.2   Results and Discussion

Tables 1 show the computation times of the clustering processes for the artificial sequencing datasets. Performance ratios of our method are shown in the parentheses.

These results clearly show that our method was faster in all cases. For set with two million DNA sequences, our method was about 7.1, 4.4, and 2.5 times faster than CD-HIT for 100, 150, and 400 bases, respectively. While the speed-up was large for shorter sequences, longer sequence lengths tended to see less improvement with the proposed algorithm. One of the reasons for this is that the longer are the sequences, there greater is the number of cases where sequence pairs with sequence identity less than the threshold have $LLCS(X,Y)/n$ larger than the threshold. This is because there is more room to make an alignment with sufficient matches by using many gaps in a longer sequence pair. Thus, both our method and CD-HIT suffer the same increases in computational time for increases in sequence length. We think this problem might be solved by considering gaps in LCS alignments and compensating the LCS score.

Table 2 shows the number of clusters generated by each method. Although there is no large difference between the clustering results, CD-HIT sometimes does not properly cluster similar sequence pairs that our method could correctly assign. The short word filter in CD-HIT is too strict and even similar sequence pairs sometimes fail to pass through. However, our modified short word filter is relatively loose, allowing more non-similar sequence pairs pass. Nevertheless, almost all similar sequence pairs pass through our filter.

We also applied our method to real sequencing datasets, Roche's 454 and Illumina/Solexa reads, as shown in Table 3. Our method outperformed CD-HIT for both datasets, but did especially well for Illumina/Solexa. This is because the length of the Illumina/Solexa reads is shorter.

Table 1. Computation time for each sequence length (2 million sequences)

	100 bases		150 bases		400 bases	
CD-HIT	2h11m47s		2h17m56s		2h50m38s	
Our method	18m42s	(7.1)	31m41s	(4.4)	1h7m26s	(2.5)

Table 2. Number of clusters (2 million sequences)

	100 bases	150 bases	400 bases
CD-HIT	1,242,054	1,015,466	493,384
Our method	1,185,704	970,419	480,201

Table 3. Computation time for real sequencing datasets

	454		Illumina/Solexa	
CD-HIT	2m47s		27h2m5s	
Our method	44s	(3.8)	3h44m31s	(7.4)

4   Conclusion

We developed the LCS-HIT fast clustering algorithm for DNA sequences, which employs a new filtering scheme that is based on the longest common subsequence (LCS). This filtering scheme allows accurate pruning of dissimilar sequence pairs that are not be discarded by the short word filter alone. Thus, it accelerates the clustering process as a whole. For two million DNA sequences, our method was about 7.1, 4.4, and 2.5 times faster than CD-HIT for 100, 150, and 400 bases, respectively.

Acknowledgement. This research was supported in part by the HPCI STRATEGIC PROGRAM in Computational Life Science and Application in Drug Discovery and Medical Development by MEXTof Japan, Cancer Research Development Funding by the National Cancer Center of Japan.

References

1. Altschul, S.F., Gish, W., Miller, W., Myers, E.W., Lipman, D.J.: Basic Local Alignment Search Tool. Journal of Molecular Biology 215, 403–410 (1990)
2. Li, W., Jaroszewski, L., Godzik, A.: Clustering of Highly Homologous Sequences to Reduce the Size of Large Protein Databases. Bioinformatics (Oxford, England) 17, 282–283 (2001)
3. Li, W., Godzik, A.: Cd-hit: a Fast Program for Clustering and Comparing Large Sets of Protein or Nucleotide Sequences. Bioinformatics (Oxford, England) 22, 1658–1659 (2006)
4. Crochemore, M., Iliopoulos, C.S., Pinzon, Y.J., Reid, J.F.: A Fast and Practical Bit-vector Algorithm for the Longest Common Subsequence Problem. Information Processing Letters 80, 279–285 (2001)
5. Hyyro, H.: Bit-Parallel LCS-length Computation Revisited. In: Proc. 15th Australasian Workshop on Combinatorial Algorithms (AWOCA 2004), pp. 16–27 (2004)
6. Richter, D.C., Ott, F., Auch, A.F., Schmid, R., Huson, D.H.: MetaSim: a Sequencing Simulator for Genomics and Metagenomics. PloS One 3, e3373 (2008)

A Diversity-Guided Hybrid Particle Swarm Optimization

Fei Han and Qing Liu

School of Computer Science and Telecommunication Engineering, Jiangsu University,
Zhenjiang, Jiangsu, 212013, China
hanfei@ujs.edu.cn, qingjing_03@126.com

Abstract. As an evolutionary computing technique, particle swarm optimization (PSO) has good global search ability, but the swarm loses its diversity easily and thus leads to premature convergence. In this paper, a diversity-guided hybrid PSO based on gradient search is proposed to improve the search ability of the swarm. The standard PSO is firstly used to search the solution till the swarm loses its diversity. Then, the search process turns to a new PSO which the particles update their velocities with their gradient directions and repel each other to improve the swarm diversity. The experiment results show that the proposed algorithm has better convergence performance than some classical PSOs.

Keywords: particle swarm optimization, diversity, gradient search.

1 Introduction

As a global search algorithm, PSO is a population-based stochastic optimization technique developed by Kennedy and Eberhart [1,2]. Since PSO is easy to implement without complex evolutionary operations compared with genetic algorithm (GA) [3,4], it has been widely used in many fields such as power system optimization, process control, dynamic optimization, adaptive control and electromagnetic optimization [5,6]. Although PSO has shown good performance in solving many test as well as real life optimization problems, it suffers from the problem of premature convergence like most of the stochastic search techniques, particularly in multimodal optimization problems [6].

Low diversity may lead to the particles in the swarm be trapped into local minima, which is called premature convergence. Many improved PSOs were proposed to overcome this disadvantage, such as passive PSO [7], CPSO [8,9], attractive and repulsive PSO (ARPSO) [10], fuzzy PSO [11], and gradient-based PSO (GPSO) [6].

Although random search such as standard PSO converges faster than GA, it is easy to converge to local minima because of losing the diversity of the swarm. On the other hand, some improved PSOs such as passive PSO, CPSO and ARPSO, may improve their search ability, but they require more time to find the best solution.

In this paper, an improved hybrid particle swarm optimization called DGHPSOGS is proposed to overcome the problem of premature convergence. The improved method takes advantages of random search and deterministic search. When the diversity

D.-S. Huang et al. (Eds.): ICIC 2012, CCIS 304, pp. 461–466, 2012.

value of the swarm is below a predetermined threshold, the proposed diversity-guided PSO based on gradient search called DGPSOGS is used to perform search. On the other hand, the particles update their positions by the standard PSO as the diversity value of the swarm is greater than the threshold. In the hybrid method, the stand PSO is used to perform stochastic search by attracting the particles and the DGPSOGS is used to perform deterministic search as well as repel the particles to keep the diversity of the swarm in a reasonable range. Therefore, the hybrid algorithm can decrease the likelihood of premature convergence with a reasonable convergence rate.

2   Particle Swarm Optimization

PSO is an evolutionary computation technique in searching for the best solution by simulating the movement of birds in a flocking [1,2]. The population of the birds is called flock or swarm, and the members of the population are particles. Each particle represents a possible solution to the optimizing problem. During each iteration, each particle flies independently in its own direction which guided by its own previous best position as well as the global best position of all the particles. Assume that the dimension of the search space is D, and the swarm is $S=(X_1, X_2, X_3, ..., X_{Np})$; each particle represents a position in the D dimension; the position of the i-th particle in the search space can be denoted as $X_i=(x_{i1}, x_{i2}, ..., x_{iD})$, i=1, 2, ..., Np, where Np is the number of all particles. The best position of the i-th particle being searched until now is called *pbest* which is expressed as $P_i=(p_{i1}, p_{i2}, ..., p_{iD})$. The best position of the all particles are called *gbest* which is denoted as $P_g= (p_{g1}, p_{g2}, ..., p_{gD})$. The velocity of the i-th particle is expressed as $V_i= (v_{i1}, v_{i2}, ..., v_{iD})$. According to the literatures [1,2], the basic PSO was described as:

$$V_i(t+1)=V_i(t)+c1*rand()*(P_i(t)-X_i(t))+c2*rand()*(P_g(t)-X_i(t)) \tag{1}$$

$$X_i(t+1) = X_i(t)+V_i(t+1) \tag{2}$$

where $c1$, $c2$ are the acceleration constants with positive values; $rand()$ is a random number ranged from 0 to 1.

In order to obtain better performance, adaptive particle swarm optimization (APSO) algorithm was proposed [12], and the corresponding velocity update of particles was denoted as follows:

$$V_i(t+1)=W(t)*V_i(t)+c1*rand()*(P_i(t)-X_i(t))+c2*rand()*(P_g(t)-X_i(t)) \tag{3}$$

where $W(t)$ can be computed by the following equation:

$$W(t) = W_{max}-t*(W_{max}-W_{min})/N_{pso} \tag{4}$$

In Eq.(4), W_{max}, W_{min} and N_{pso} are the initial inertial weight, the final inertial weight and the maximum iterations, respectively.

3   The Proposed Hybrid Algorithm

First of all, a diversity-guided PSO combing with gradient search (DGPSOGS) is proposed in this study. Since the negative gradient always points in the direction of steepest decrease in the fitness function, the nearest local minimum (maybe global minimum) will be reached eventually. However, in the case of a fitness function with a single minimum, the gradient descent algorithm converges faster than stochastic search algorithms because stochastic search algorithms waste computational effort doing a random search. For many minima, the gradient descent algorithm will con-verge to the local minimum nearest to the starting point [6]. When the swarm is trapped into the local minimum, the swarm will lose its diversity. In order to make the swarm jump out of the local minimum, the particles in the swarm should be repelled each other and thus improve the diversity of the swarm. For quickly searching the global minimum as well as avoiding being trapped into local minimum, the particle velocity update equation in DGPSOGS is proposed as follows:

$$V_i(t+1) = W(t)*V_i(t) + c1*rand()*(\frac{-\frac{\partial f(X_i(t))}{\partial X_i(t)}}{\left\| -\frac{\partial f(X_i(t))}{\partial X_i(t)} \right\|}) - c2*rand()*\frac{(P_g(t) - X_i(t))}{diversity(t) + \xi} \tag{5}$$

where $f()$ is the fitness function; ξ is a predetermined small positive number for fear that the denominator is equal to zero. The second term on the right side of Eq.(5) guides the particles to search in the negative gradient direction. The third term on the right side of Eq.(5) is inversely proportional to the diversity of the swarm, $diversity(t)$. The smaller is the diversity of the swarm, the bigger is the value of the third term, which results into the particles repelling each other more greatly and improving the diversity of the swarm.

Then, the proposed hybrid method (DGHPSOGS) combines random search and semi-deterministic search to improve its search ability. The standard PSO is firstly used to perform random search till the diversity value of the swarm is less than a pre-determined threshold, d. When the swarm loses its diversity, the DGPSOGS algo-rithm is used to perform semi-deterministic search.

4   Experiment Results

In this section, the performance of the proposed hybrid PSO algorithm is compared with the standard PSO, CPSO and ARPSO in the De Jong test suite of benchmark optimization problems. The problems provide common challenges that an evolutio-nary computation algorithm is expected to face, such as multiple local minima and flat regions surrounding global minimum. Table 1 shows the test functions used in the experiments. The Sphere and Ellipsoid functions both are convex and unimodal. The Rosenbrock function has a single global minimum located in a long narrow parabolic shaped flat valley and tests the ability of an optimization algorithm to navigate flat regions with small gradients. The Rastrigin function is highly multimodal and tests the ability of an optimization algorithm to escape from local minima.

Table 1. Test functions used for comparison of DGHPSOGS with other PSOs

Test function	Equation	Search space
Sphere (F1)	$\sum_{1}^{n} x_i^2$	$(-100,100)^n$
Ellipsoid (F2)	$\sum_{1}^{n} i x_i^2$	$(-100,100)^n$
Rosenbrock (F3)	$\sum_{i=1}^{n-1}(100(x_{i+1}-x_i^2)^2+(1-x_i)^2)$	$(-100,100)^n$
Rastrigin (F4)	$10n + \sum_{i=1}^{n}(x_i^2 - 10\cos(2\pi x_i))$	$(-100,100)^n$

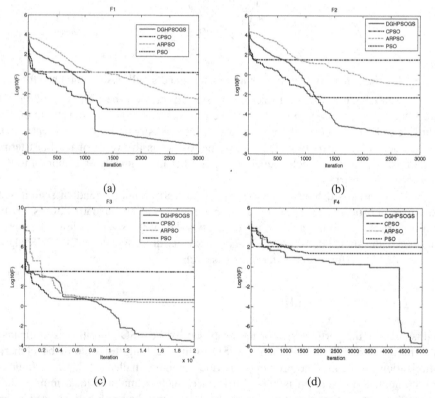

Fig. 1. Best solution versus iteration number for the four test functions by using four PSOs (a) Sphere (b) Ellipsoid (c) Rosenbrock (d) Rastrigin

The population size for all PSOs is 20 in all experiments. And the acceleration constants $c1$ and $c2$ for PSO and ARPSO both are set as 2.0. The constants $c1$ and $c2$ are 2.05 in CPSO. In the proposed algorithm, $c1$ and $c2$ both are 2.1.. The inertia weight w starting at 0.9 and ending at 0.4 is set for all PSOs according to the literature [12]. All the results shown in this paper are the mean values of 20 trails.

The Sphere and Ellipsoid test functions are unimodal, convex and differitiable test functions without flat regions. Fig.1 (a) and (b) show that the gradient descent algorithm such as DGHPSOGS performs better than stochastic search algorithms (PSO, ARPSO and CPSO). CPSO and PSO converge to local minima at near 100 and 1200 iterations, respectively, both for the two functions. Although ARPSO does not converge to local minimum, it also does not converge to global minimum at 3000 iterations for the two functions. The DGHPSOGS converges to global minimum at nearly 1500 iterations for the two functions. Fig. 1 (c) shows the performance of the four PSOs for the Rosenbrock test function which has flat regions. Form Fig.1(c), PSO, CPSO and ARPSO lose global search ability early because of random search, which shows that the swarm is trapped into local minimum. The proposed hybrid PSO converges more accurately than other PSOs. Fig.1.(d) shows the performance of the four PSOs for the multimodal Rastrigin test function. This test function has steep gradients throughout the solution space. Similarly, the DGHPSOGS converges signif-icantly faster to a better solution than other PSOs. Although the gradient descent por-tion of the DGHPSOGS uses gradient information to accurately find local minima, it can jump out of the local minima by improving the diversity of the swarm.

Table 2 shows mean best solution for the four test functions by using four PSOs. It can be found that the proposed algorithm has better convergence accuracy than other PSOs in all cases except on the Rastrigin function with 30 dimensions.

Table 2. Mean best solution for the four test functions by using four PSOs

Test function	Dimension	PSO	ARPSO	CPSO	DGHPSOGS
		Mean best solution			
Sphere (F1)	10	2.7886e-004	0.0033	1.6423	1.2643e-008
	20	0.2212	0.3756	1.1103e+003	2.5164e-007
	30	0.2056	11.0210	4.4263e+003	2.6444e-007
Ellipsoid (F2)	10	0.0051	0.1122	33.4223	3.3717e-007
	20	2.9059	66.7240	5.9418e+003	7.9255e-006
	30	135.6027	6.1134e+003	3.3328e+004	1.5574e-005
Rosenbrock (F3)	10	4.7326	2.7268	1.4624e+004	4.5016e-004
	20	21.5091	191.1912	1.5924e+005	5.1551e-004
	30	65.0592	352.6755	1.2969e+006	0.0055
Rastrigin (F4)	10	0.0271	79.4817	107.5419	9.3668e-006
	20	3.2919	14.9138	433.1537	2.9506
	30	4.1096	40.5797	3.1820e+003	25.5679

5   Conclusions

In order to improve the search ability, a hybrid PSO combing random search with semi-deterministic search was proposed in this paper. In the hybrid PSO, the search alternated from the standard PSO to DGPSOGS according the diversity value of the swarm. The standard PSO led the swarm to converge to local minima. The DGPSOGS kept the diversity of the swarm adaptively as well as search in the negative gradient direction, which increased the likelihood of find the global minima with faster convergence rate. The experiment results were given to verify that the proposed hybrid algorithms had better convergence performance with faster convergence rate than PSO, CPSO and ARPSO.

Acknowledgement. This work was supported by the National Natural Science Foundation of China (No.60702056) Natural Science Foundation of Jiangsu Province (No.BK2009197) and the Initial Foundation of Science Research of Jiangsu University (No.07JDG033).

References

1. Kennedy, J., Eberhart, R.C.: Particle Swarm Optimization. In: IEEE International Conference on Neural Networks, vol. 4, pp. 1942–1948 (1995)
2. Eberhart, R.C., Kennedy, J.: A New Optimizer Using Particle Swarm Theory. In: Proceedings of the Sixth International Symposium on Micro Machines and Human Science, pp. 39–43 (1995)
3. Grosan, C., Abraham, A.: A Novel Global Optimization Technique for High Dimensional Functions. International Journal of Intelligent Systems 24(4), 421–440 (2009)
4. Goldberg, D.: Genetic Algorithms in Search, Optimization, and Machine Learning. Addison-Wesley, Reading (1989)
5. Del valle Y., Venayagamoorthy, G.K., Mohagheghi, S.: Particle Swarm Optimization : Basic Concepts, Variants and Applications in Power Systems. IEEE Transactions on Evolutionary Computation 12, 171–195 (2008)
6. Mathew, M.: A New Gradient Based Particle Swarm Optimization Algorithm for Accurate Computation of Global Minimum. Applied Soft Computing 12(1), 353–359 (2012)
7. He, S., Wu, Q.H., Wen, J.Y.: A Particle Swarm Optimizer with Passive Congregation. Biosystems 78, 135–147 (2004)
8. Clerc, M.: The Swarm and the Queen: towards a Deterministic and Adaptive Particle Swarm Optimization. In: Proc. 1999 Congress on Evolutionary Computation, Washington, DC, pp. 1951–1957 (1999)
9. Corne, D., Dorigo, M., Glover, F.: New Ideas in Optimization, pp. 379–387 (1999)
10. Riget, J., Vesterstrom, J.S.: A diversity-guided Particle Swarm Optimizer - the ArPSO. EVAlife Technical report (2002)
11. Shi, Y., Eberhary, R.C.: Fuzzy Adaptive Particle Swarm Optimization. Evolutionary Computation 1(3), 101–106 (2001)
12. Shi, Y., Eberhart, R.C.: A Modified Particle Swarm Optimizer. Computational Intelligence 6(1), 69–73 (1998)

A Voting Procedure Supported by a Neural Validity Classifier for Optic Disk Detection

Leonarda Carnimeo, Anna Cinzia Benedetto, and Giuseppe Mastronardi

Dept. of Electrical and Electronic Engineering, Politecnico di Bari,
Via G. Re David n. 200, 70125 Bari Italy
{Carnimeo,mastrona}@poliba.it

Abstract. In this work a Voting Procedure supported by a Neural Validity Classifier for assuring a correct localization of the reference point of optic disk in retinal imaging is proposed. A multiple procedure with multiple resulting points is briefly described. A Neural Network behaving as a Validity Classifier of regular/abnormal solutions is then synthesized to validate the adequacy of the resulting midpoints as candidate reference points. A Voting Procedure, supported by the synthesized Neural Validity Classifier, is successively performed, by comparing only candidate pixels classified as valid ones. In this way, the most suitable and reliable candidate can be voted to be adopted as the reference point of OD in successive retinal analyses.

Keywords: Retinal Image Analysis, Computer Aided Diagnosis, Optic Disc Detection, Neural Classifier.

1 Introduction

Over the last years significant improvements in image processing for ophthalmology were introduced [1-8]. Retinal imaging is an important modality to document both the health of human eyes and their biometric features [1]. Recent advances in automated diagnostic systems actually enable eye doctors to perform a large number of screening exams for frequent diseases, such as diabetes or glaucoma [1-3]. On this proposal, precise information about the Optic Disk (OD) reveals necessary to examine the severity of some diseases, since changes in the OD often indicate a pathologic progression [4 - 6]. Diagnostic systems of analysis are usually based on the detection of an optic disc Region of Interest (ROI), which is a subset of the image domain important for each retinal analysis [3], [5]. In detail, a properly extracted ROI provides a smaller image containing the most diagnostic information and is less time-consuming when processed [3]. Thus, in retinal imaging the localization of the OD, in terms of position of its middle point and radius, has to be the best possible, being OD viewed as the main reference when analyzing every anatomic/pathologic retinal detail and the detection of a unique reference middle point C as a key step in automatic extraction of retinal anatomic features [3-5]. In order to adequately use information about the disc, a region that includes the optic disc but also its surrounding part has to be extracted. Only considering also chromatic characteristics of the retina it is possible to derive a

D.-S. Huang et al. (Eds.): ICIC 2012, CCIS 304, pp. 467–474, 2012.

complete description of the disc. For this purpose, it is necessary to cut a portion of the image centered on the evaluated reference point, which is at most equal to the 11% of the size of the original image [3]. Unfortunately, drawbacks arise for the existence of different determinations of C for each selected evaluation procedure. In [5] candidate centers C_k are computed using more procedures, but the presence of artifacts and bright fringes on original retinal images can cause significant mistakes for some candidate pixel. In [6] an interesting geometrical technique for fusing information collected about more candidate centers is presented, but this technique is not adequate in the case of diseased retina. A validation process of candidate pixels seems to be necessary to guarantee reliability to the final adopted reference point of OD. In [7] a neural approach is suggested to extract retinal features also in the presence of noisy data. Taking into account all these considerations, in this work a Voting Procedure supported by an effective Neural Validity Classifier is presented to assure an adequate localization of the reference point C of OD. A multiple procedure with multiple solutions, obtained applying three different procedures, is firstly introduced and briefly described. An effective Neural Network behaving as a Classifier of regular/abnormal cases is then synthesized to validate the reliability of the obtained pixels as candidate reference points C_k. A Voting Procedure supported by the synthesized Neural Validity Classifier is finally developed to compare only valid candidate points and determine the most suitable one to be adopted as the middle reference point C of OD in successive retinal processing.

2   A Multiple Procedure for Determining Candidate References

The optic disc appears as the brightest region in human fundus oculi images. Thus, the maximum variation of gray level values usually occurs within the optic disc. A multiple procedure to detect probable midpoints $C_k(i,j)$ of OD is herein applied to fundus oculi images, based on the contemporary implementation of the following techniques

- Maximum Difference Evaluation Technique
- Maximum Local Variance Method
- Maximum Gray-Level Pixel Procedure

Each procedure aims at obtaining its own candidate pixel as a reasonable reference midpoint of the OD to be successively validated by an effective Neural Validity Classifier and compared with other candidates via a Voting Procedure as shown in Fig.1.

2.1   Maximum Difference Evaluation Procedure

In the Maximum Difference Evaluation procedure the maximum gray level value in each retinal image is focused and the corresponding pixel is selected as the candidate midpoint in the Optic Disk. More in detail, a median filter is firstly applied to the original image I_g in order to remove non-significant gray level values caused by acquisition noise. Then, the evaluation of maximum difference between gray level values of pixels for each column and for each row in the obtained image is computed, as well as the coordinates of all corresponding pixels. The candidate midpoint $C_1(i,j)$ is obtained as the pixel having coordinates with average values.

2.2   Maximum Local Variance Method

The Maximum Local Variance Method estimates features of the optic disc in each image $I_g(i,j)$ from a statistic point of view by considering the corresponding statistical variance image $I_{var}(i,j)$. A green optimal thresholding based on variance magnitudes is subsequently performed [10] to segment images $I_g(i,j)$. In the same way, $I_b(i,j)$ can be segmented by separating its brighter pixels with respect to its darker ones, after performing a blue optimal thresholding on the basis of image histograms. Then, segmented images on the two channels can be compared to select the highest variance pixels on image $I_g(i,j)$, which coincide with the highest brightness pixels on image $I_b(i,j)$. After an adequate smoothing process, the candidate pixel $C_2(i,j)$ for this method is selected as the average point of the area containing coincident pixels in image $I(i,j)$.

2.3   Maximum Gray-Level Pixel Technique

Although the optic disc is usually the brightest area in a retinal image I_g, the pixel with the highest gray level value could be located not inside the OD. It could be positioned in a noisy area of image I_g, or inside other small bright regions, if a retinopathy is present. In order to smooth out these distractors, in this procedure each image $I_g(i,j)$ is FFT-transformed into the frequency domain and then filtered by a Gaussian low-pass filter as in [5]. The required midpoint $C_3(i,j)$ is the maximum gray-level pixel in the filtered image after returning into the image spatial domain.

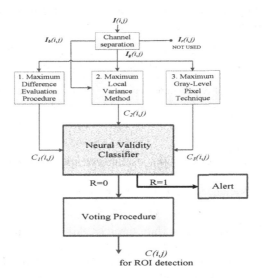

Fig. 1. Block diagram of the proposed Retinal Imaging System

3   A Neural Validity Classifier for a Retinal Voting Procedure

Candidate pixels $C_k(i,j)$, $k=1,..3$, have now to be compared each other in order to individuate the final pixel that will be assumed as the reference pixel $C(i,j)$ of OD, before a subsequent ROI extraction. For the sake of comprehension, in Fig. 2 a selected example of a retinal image $I(i,j)$ is reported together with a zoomed image of the area containing its OD with evaluated candidate midpoints $C_k(i,j)$ in various colours.

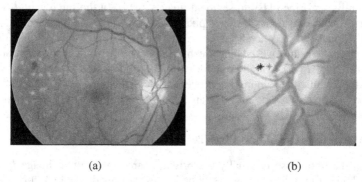

(a)   (b)

Fig. 2. (a) Retinal Image $I(i,j)$; (b) Zoomed image of OD with candidate midpoints $C_k(i,j)$

The final reference point of OD will be individuated through a Voting Procedure based on the coordinates of pixels $C_k(i,j)$, $k=1,..3$, and of the centroid $O(i,j)$ among them [5, 6], that is to say, their average point. For this purpose, it has to be given a sort of measure of the *closeness* between pixels. As reported in [11], the closeness can be evaluated with respect to one fifth of the image as the maximum estimation of the diameter of the optic disk. Possible cases to be considered are:

a) *If*   all OD candidate pixels are *close to* the centroid $O(i,j)$
   Then   the selected midpoint $C(i,j)$ is the centroid itself

b) *If*   only two candidates C_k are *close to* the centroid $O(i,j)$
   Then   the selected $C(i,j)$ is the average point between the closest pixels
   C_k

c) *If*   any other case
   Then   the selected $C(i,j)$ is the candidate pixel obtained with the
   Maximum
                 Variance Procedure in the retinal imaging system.

In so far as the authors are aware, the Maximum Variance Procedure has been considered as a very reliable method [5]. Unfortunately, this procedure seems to collapse when retinal images showing bright fringes or other acquisition errors are considered as shown in Fig.3, causing a severe failure in the subsequent Voting Procedure It can be noted that the white candidate pixel C_k is not in the OD area in the selected retina. This could become a severe drawback. A system able to validate the identification of the three pixels $C_k(i,j)$ before determining the reference point C reveals necessary. For this reason, a neural validity classifier for candidate pixels $C_k(i,j)$, is synthesized able to classify both regular cases and abnormal ones. It has to be noted that a case can be called *abnormal* when computed pixels $C_k(i,j)$, or even only one of them, are not close to each other in the retinal image, as in Fig.3.

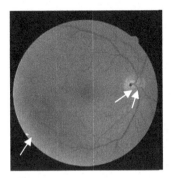

Fig. 3. Selected image affected by bright fringes with the three Candidate pixels $C_k(i,j)$

If the neural validity check is passed, candidate pixels $C_k(i,j)$ can be adopted and successively considered in the Voting Procedure to localize the reference point $C(i,j$ of the OD. Otherwise an Alert is provided by the Neural Classifier.

4 Synthesis of the Neural Validity Classifier

In the synthesis of the dedicated neural network, a variety of images has to be considered: images in which the optic disc is clearly highlighted, images with features similar to the optic disc, like exudates, and images with bright fringes caused by patient's movement during acquisition. In this study images taken from the publicly available DRIVE database have been used [9], together with colour fundus images collected by eye doctors from a local Ophthalmology Hospital.

The approach provides three points for every image, in terms of three couples of coordinates. The geometric centroid $O(i,j)$ among them is estimated together with its distances to each point. The proposed neural system takes into account the distances of the three candidates from their centroid to provide the classification of previously described cases. For experimental reasons, the method has been tested on 80 images. For every image under investigation, inputs submitted to the neural network (NN) are given by the three cited distances, composing a (3x80)-dimension input matrix. An adequate output for the NN has to return R_{exp} =0 for *Regular cases* and R_{exp}=1 for abnormal ones. Then, the neural network can be synthesized. In this work an MLP neural network has been designed, with 3 input neurons, 2 hidden neurons and 1 output neuron. Gradient descent method with momentum error backpropagation was specified as the learning method with a learning rate $l_r = 0,5$ and a transfer function given by

$$f(x) = \tan sig(x) = \frac{2}{(1+e^{-2x})-1}$$

The training behaviour has been analyzed using a Mean Squared Error function $E(w)$ as shown in fig. 5. The neural network has been trained until the relationship between each input and each output was recognized. The pattern of errors on training set and validation set with increasing epochs was analysed and training was stopped when $E(w)$ reached its minimum value in the validation phase as reported in Fig.4.

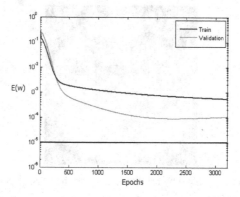

Fig. 4. Errors on training set and validation set

In the following figures the behaviour of the synthesized network after training can be observed, where computed output classification Results R are identified with red circles, and the corresponding expected Results R_{exp} are indicated by blue asterisks. Simulations on the complete data set and on a validation set of 15 images are reported in Fig.5 and in Fig.6, respectively.

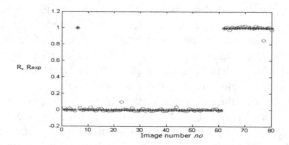

Fig. 5. Behaviour of the synthesized network after training using the complete data set

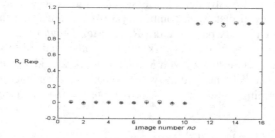

Fig. 6. Behaviour of the synthesized network by considering a validation set of 15 images

The Neural Network performances have been evaluated using the Root Mean Square Error (RMSE) as

$$\text{RMSE} = \sqrt{\frac{\sum_{i=1}^{n} (R_{\exp} - R)^2}{n_o}}$$

In the test phase 20 unknown cases were submitted to the NN and it was noticed that the synthesized Neural Validity Classifier reveals able to correctly classify submitted cases, thus satisfactorily supporting the subsequent Voting Procedure.

5   Conclusions

In this work a validation methodology for guaranteeing correctness to OD positioning in retinal imaging was presented. A multiple procedure for determining more candidate centers was involved. A Neural Validity Classifier was synthesized to assure the validity of computed centres, which could be affected by errors caused by artifacts and bright fringe on retinal images. Then, valid candidates have been compared through a Voting Procedure in order to determine which pixel could be considered as the best centre of OD. Obtained results reveal satisfactory and show that the proposed approach offers a reliable and robust solution, since the choice of a Neural Classifier for supporting the Voting Procedure avoids some fatal errors.

References

1. Abramoff, M.D., Garvin, M.K., Sonka, M.: Retinal Imaging and image Analysis. IEEE Reviews in Biomedical Eng. 3, 169–208 (2010)
2. Bevilacqua, V., Carnimeo, L., Mastronardi, G., Santarcangelo, V., Scaramuzzi, R.: On the Comparison of NN-Based Architectures for Diabetic Damage Detection in Retinal Images. J. of Circuits, Systems & Computers 18(8), 1369–1380 (2009)
3. Zhang, Z., Lee, B., Liu, J., Wong, D., Tan, N., Lim, J., Yin, F., Huang, W., Li, H., Wong, T.: Optic Disc Region of Interest Localization in Fundus Image for Glaucoma Detection in ARGALI. In: 5th IEEE Conf. on Industrial Electronics & Appl., New York, pp. 1686–1689 (2010)
4. Sekhar, S., Al-Nuaimy, W., Nandi, A.K.: Automated Localization of Retinal Optic Disk Using Hough Transform. In: 5th IEEE Int. Symposium on Biomedical Imaging: from Nano to Macro, pp. 1577–1580. IEEE Press, New York (2008)
5. Aquino, A., Gegúndez-Arias, M.E., Marín, D.: Detecting the Optic Disc Boundary in Digital Fundus Images Using Morphological, edge detection and feature extraction techniques. IEEE Trans. on Medical Imaging 29(11), 1860–1869 (2010)
6. Harangi, B., Qureshi, R.J., Csutak, A., Peto, T., Hajadu, A.: Automatic Detection of the Optic Disc Using Majority Voting in a Collection of Optic Disc Detectors. In: IEEE Int. Symp. on Biom. Imaging from Nano to Macro, pp. 1329–1332. IEEE Press, New York (2010)
7. Carnimeo, L., Bevilacqua, V., Cariello, L., Mastronardi, G.: Retinal Vessel Extraction by a Combined Neural Network–Wavelet Enhancement Method. In: Huang, D.-S., Jo, K.-H., Lee, H.-H., Kang, H.-J., Bevilacqua, V. (eds.) ICIC 2009. LNCS (LNAI), vol. 5755, pp. 1106–1116. Springer, Heidelberg (2009)

8. Bevilacqua, V., Mastronardi, G., Colaninno, A., D'Addabbo, A.: Retina Images using Genetic Algorithm and Maximum Likelihood Method. In: Int. Conf. on Advances in Computer Science and Technology. IASTED Press, US Virgin Island (2004)
9. Niemeijer, M., Staal, J.J., van Ginneken, B., Loog, M., Abramoff, M.D.: DRIVE Retinal Database from Comparative Study of Retinal Vessel Segmentation Methods on a New Publicly Available Database,
   http://www.isi.uu.nl/Research/Databases/DRIVE/
10. Otsu, N.: A Threshold Selection Method from Gray-scale Histogram. IEEE Trans. on SMC 9(1), 62–66 (1979)
11. Li, H., Chutatape, O.: Automatic Location of Optic Disc in Retinal Images. In: IEEE Int. Conf. on Image Processing, pp. 837–840. IEEE Press, New York (2001)

Using Artificial Neural Networks for Closed Loop Control of a Hydraulic Prosthesis for a Human Elbow

Vitoantonio Bevilacqua[1], Mariagrazia Dotoli[1], Mario Massimo Foglia[2], Francesco Acciani[1], Giacomo Tattoli[1], and Marcello Valori[2]

[1] Dipartimento di Elettrotecnica ed Elettronica, Politecnico di Bari, Italy
[2] Dipartimento di Ingegneria Meccanica e Gestionale, Politecnico di Bari, Italy
{Bevilacqua,dotoli,mm.foglia}@poliba.it,
francesco8899@gmail.com, {TATTOLIG_84,valmarce}@libero.it

Abstract. We address control of a hydraulic prosthesis for human elbow, a problem in which it is essential to obtain quick simulation results to appreciate the system dynamic. The forward kinematics problem for a prosthesis developed at Politecnico di Bari is solved using artificial neural networks as an effective and simple method to solve the problem in real time and limit computations. We show the method effectiveness designing two PID regulators that control the arm thanks to the neural computation of the forward kinematics.

1 Introduction

The topic of actuated prostheses for human use is one of the most important branches of biorobotics. Nowadays, several solutions are available in the related literature to model and simulate the work of articulations in limb prostheses: choices concern both the mechanisms typology and energy supply. The research group of Politecnico di Bari chose to develop a parallel simplified "Stewart platform like" mechanism. A wire transmission links the floating platform to three hydraulic cylinders [1]. The device uses two cylindrical elementary hinges to connect forearm and arm, three hydraulic actuators placed on the upper arm to reduce moving masses. These actuators are classified into main ones (frontally placed) and a secondary one (rear placed). Each frontal actuator is linked with two wires, one towards front forearm and the other towards the rear part of the forearm. These two actuators are responsible of the positioning of the floating platform, connected to the forearm. The rear piston brings a pulley that forces another wire connected with the forearm. This particular parallel geometry is characterized by the analytical indetermination of the forward kinematics problem, in spite of the solution of the inverse one. Indeed, the configuration required to the linear actuators for each position of the floating platform, and consequently their law of motion, is easily obtained analytically using rotation matrices with the required orientation angles. However, it is not possible to univocally determine the configuration of the mobile platform starting from the actuators' elongations. In fact, the direct kinematic problem consists in finding the postures of the moving platform for a given set of connecting wires lengths. The formulation of closed relations generates highly non linear equations with multiple solutions [2]. In the literature different numerical methods have been studied to determine in real time the solution of the problem, such as the Stewart platform. In this paper, the problem is solved using

D.-S. Huang et al. (Eds.): ICIC 2012, CCIS 304, pp. 475–480, 2012.

artificial neural networks as an effective and simple method to obtain in real time the solution of the forward kinematic problem without an excessive computational effort [4]. The approach is applied to the hydraulic prosthesis developed by the research group [1] and we show the method effectiveness designing two PID regulators to control the arm by the neural computation of the forward kinematics.

2   The Innovative Elbow Prosthetic Device

Figure 1 shows a scheme of the prosthesis: upper/lower hinges allows respectively flexion/extension and pronation/supination. The two forearm movements are actuated by the coordinate motion of two hydraulic cylinders. Flexible synthetic ropes transmit motion to the platform, give stiffness to the mechanism in all direction during motion, and take advantage of the third cylinder. The device is based on a parallel mechanism, in which motion along the required DOF is obtained acting on the lengths of links L1 and L2 connecting B1-P1 and B2-P2 (Fig. 1). Points B1/2 are also connected to the fixed base, the terminal part of the humerus, whereas P1/2 are part of the floating platform, connected to the forearm. The orientation of the floating platform toward the fixed frame is ruled by the rotation matrix:

$$[\mathbf{R}_{\varphi,\theta}] = \begin{bmatrix} \cos[\theta] & -\sin[\theta] & 0 \\ \sin[\theta]\cos[\phi] & \cos[\theta]\cos[\phi] & -\sin[\phi] \\ \sin[\theta]\sin[\phi] & \cos[\theta]\sin[\phi] & \cos[\phi] \end{bmatrix} \tag{1}$$

where the range of motion is $\theta \in [-70°,70°]$ and $\varphi \in [0,90°]$.

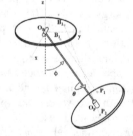

Fig. 1. The 3D kinematic scheme of the parallel mechanism of the hydraulic prosthesis

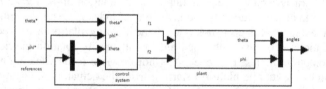

Fig. 2. A scheme of the global hydraulic prosthesis system

The analytical solution of the inverse kinematic problem, which corresponds to determine the relations L1=f1(φ,θ), L2=f2(φ,θ), is easily obtained by the relation:

$$[\mathbf{Links}] = [\mathbf{R}_{\varphi,\theta}][\mathbf{Plat}] - [\mathbf{Base}] \tag{2}$$

in which the 3x2 matrix [Links] represents the components of L1 and L2 in one column for each length among the global frame. Moreover, [Plat] and [Base] respectively represent the coordinates of the mobile platform and of the fixed upper base. More details about the hydraulic prosthesis architecture are available in [1].

3   The Model Description

The system is composed of three fundamental blocks containing the main components (see Fig. 2): the references block, the control system block, and the plant block. Feedback is used to compare the output values and of angles with the current input values. The references block provides the target values θ^* and φ^*. Since the actuation is provided by managing the elongations of the hydraulic pistons, the control system block in Fig. 2 performs a variables conversion to produce in output the error relative to the elongations, evaluated as the difference between the reference signal and the feedback: $errorl_1 = l_1 - l_1^*$ and $errorl_2 = l_2 - l_2^*$, where l1 and l2 are the elongations and l1* and l2* represent their reference values. The control block includes two PID controllers, each associated to an error signal, i.e., to a hydraulic piston. This block provides the variable implementation that has the purpose of controlling the duty cycle of each electronic valve of the pistons to control its elongation. The signals that represent the duty cycle are called f1 and f2 and are the outputs of the control system block in Fig. 2. The next block in Fig. 2 represents the plant modeling the prosthesis. This block includes the artificial neural network to solve the forward kinematic problem discussed in Section 1. Obviously, it is important to have a good precision of the neural network in order to avoid the error to propagate through the feedback signal, thus worsening the action of the controller.

4   Solving the Kinematic Problem by Neural Networks

An Artificial Neural Network (ANN) is an information processing paradigm that is inspired by the way in which the biological nervous systems processes information. The key element of this paradigm is the structure of the information processing system, which is composed of a large number of highly interconnected processing elements (neurons) that cooperate to solve specific problems. All connections among neurons are characterized by numeric values (weights) that are updated during the training. Let us call n the number of input layer neurons, m the number of output layer neurons, N1 the number of neurons in the lth layer and ok the output of the kth neuron of the lth layer. Then the computation by each neuron is [3]:

$$net_k^l = \sum_{l=1}^{N_{l-1}} w_{kj}^l o_j^{l-1} \tag{3}$$

$$o_k^l = f(net_k^l) \tag{4}$$

where net_k^l is the weighted sum of the k neurons of the lth layer, w_{kj}^l is the weight by which the same neuron multiplies output o_j^{l-1} of the jth neuron of the previous layer and f(.) is a nonlinear bounded function. The ANN is trained by supervised learning: in the training phase the network processes all the input-output pairs given by the user, learning how to associate a particular input to a specific output and trying to extend the information also to cases that do not belong to the training set. Any pair of data in the training set is presented to the system a quantity of time determined by the user a priori. The input dataset is preprocessed by normalizing variables to have a uniform distribution, with data normalized in range [0-1].

The ANN is used to find the correspondence of a pair of non-linear algebraic functions that represents the elongations of the two pistons each as a function of two angles θ* and φ* by (2). Using these two relations we obtain all the values of elongations l1 and l2 with respect to the angles θ and φ. The ANN is used for solving the kinematic problem. Indeed, in the system model the variation of the elongations of the pistons is continuous, hence it is essential for the proper functioning of the prosthesis model that the ANN features a good generalization propriety, as well as associativity propriety. In other words, the ANN purpose is to obtain the inverse relation, so as to have the possibility of obtaining values of θ and φ from the network, by entering as an input the values of the elongations of the pistons l1 and l2.

The first step for implementing the ANN is deciding which type of network is suitable for solving the problem. After testing different kinds of solutions, we picked a two-layer error back-propagation ANN. In particular, we chose error back-propagation since it tends to give good responses when processing inputs that it has never processed before [3]. In fact, a new input will lead to an output that is similar to the correct input used in training similar to the one presented to the network.

Table 1. Types and parameters of the chosen neural network

Type	Training function	Output layer function	Hidden layer function	Epoch	Neurons	Performance	Performance function	Pre-processing function
Cascade-forward	Levenberg-Marquardt	Purelin	tansig	406	10	3.16	mse	mapminmax

Table 2. The relative error by the ANN and MATLAB *solve* solutions

Elongations (mm)		Correct Degrees		Relative error by the ANN		Relative error by the *solve* MATLAB function	
L_1	L_2	θ	φ	E_θ	E_φ	E_θ	E_φ
34.97	15.63	45	60	0.0002	0.0001	0.1240	-0.0158
17.03	11.81	13	82	-0.0004	0.0008	0.0606	-0.0204
40.14	56.76	-43	25	-0.0017	0.0013	0.1420	0.0146
34.09	33.63	1	50	-0.0328	-0.0001	0.1008	-0.0126
69.03	54.16	50	1	0.0024	0.0289	0.1655	-0.2860

Obviously, the network generalizes the solution, so we can train it using a representative set of input and target pairs. We use a vector of inputs and outputs uniformly distributed over the working range of the prosthesis, to have the best generalization performance. Due to the generalization propriety, we trained the network with few examples, saving computation time during the training. After different configurations, we obtained a 30 neurons first layer. The output layer contains 2 neurons, one for each DOF of the prosthesis, and each uses the purelin MATLAB transfer function, because its output can be any value in the range [-5, 69.98]. The hidden layer uses the tansig function. For the training, we use an input data set containing a vector of 12,831 pairs of elements that are divided randomly in a quantity equal to 60% for the train set, 20% for the test set and validation set and for backpropagation weight. The bias learning function is learngdm. The performance function is the normalized mean squared error performance function (mse):

$$F = mse = \frac{1}{N}\sum_{i=1}^{N}(e_i)^2 = \frac{1}{N}\sum_{i=1}^{N}(t_i - a_i)^2 \tag{5}$$

The ranges of θ and φ are respectively [-70, 70] and [0,90] degrees. Since the mechanical system has a low sensitivity, it was possible to construct the input vectors in steps of 1° and calculate the vector of elongations of the pistons from the algebraic relations. This vector is the input vector, called P, of the neural network while the vector containing all possible combinations of the angles θ and φ is the target vector. The size of these two vectors is two rows and 12,831 columns. After a test with several neural networks topologies and training algorithms, The best balance between speed of training of the neural network and accuracy is achieved with the network in Table I.

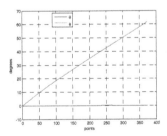

Fig. 3. Test of generalization of the ANN

Comparing the results of the simulation using our network and the values of angles obtained by using the inverse-kinematic formula, we can show that the error is minimal (see Table II). In addition, the computation time required by Matlab to invert the function using the solve command is so high to make it unfeasible. Another important aspect to consider is the generalization performance. As we can see, presenting input values which were not used for training, we still have a good performance, obtaining the correct values of outputs (see Fig. 3).

5   Conclusions

We present a novel approach for calculating the forward kinematics of a hydraulic prosthesis based on Artificial Neural Networks (ANN). The process is highly nonlinear and as such difficult to model and control, but using an ANN allows to solve the problem in real time. The procedure is innovative since it allows designers to test, by means of a robust trial and error procedure, the system behavior. In addition, it allows achieving good performance like closed-form solutions. Moreover, even if the procedure requires time for training, after that the ANN response requires a short computation time. The proposed technique leads to straightforwardly design the control scheme in real time. Future research will address limiting the required energy to move the prosthesis by employing genetic algorithms.

References

1. Foglia, M.M., Valori, M.: A wired actuated elbow for human prosthesis. UPB Scientific Bullettin, Series D: Mechanical Engineering 73(2), 49–58 (2011)
2. Huang, X.G., He, G.P.: New and efficient method for the direct kinematic solution of the general planar Stewart platform. In: IEEE International Conference on Automation and Logistics, Shenyang, China, vol. 5 (2009)
3. Haykin, S.: Neural Networks: A Comprehensive Foundation, 2nd edn. (1998)
4. Lee, H.S., Han, M.-C.: The estimation for forward kinematic solution of Stewart platform using the neural network. In: International Conference on Intelligent Robots and Systems, vol. 1, pp. 501–506 (1999)

Real Coded Feature Selection Integrated
with Self-adaptive Differential Evolution Algorithm

Zhigang Shang, Zhihui Li, and Jing Liang

School of Electrical Engineering, Zhengzhou University
zhigang_shang@zzu.edu.cn

Abstract. The current optimization algorithms for feature selection are mostly based on binary coded swarm intelligence algorithms. A novel real coded optimization algorithm which using the weighted distance metric is proposed in this paper, integrated with the self-adaptive differential evolution algorithm in order to self-adapting control parameter. The optimal real weight vector of all features is expected to be found to maximize the multi-class margin, and a criterion to select feature based on the optimal weight vector is given. This method is tested by classifying the breast impedance feature from UCI breast tissue dataset, and result indicates it is helpful to improve classification capability and generalized capability.

Keywords: feature selection, real coded, self-adaptive differential evolution, weighted distance metric, multi-class margin.

1   Introduction

Feature selection is the classic problem in the domain of pattern classification and machine learning, and it means selecting a subset of d features from a set of D features ($d < D$) based on some optimization criterion. A great number of feature selection methods have been introduced in the last decades, typically including filter, wrapper and embedded approaches. In order to discover the most informative and least redundant subset of features among the whole set, the 'space search' strategies to select features is important to each approach. Exhaustive search is the simplest way, which finds the best feature subset by evaluating all possible subsets, but it will bring the overwhelming computational cost. Swarm intelligence algorithms have attracted a lot of attention to avoid this prohibitive complexity since last decade. As a representative, the genetic algorithm (GA) is biologically inspired and has a great deal of potential in scientific and engineering optimization problems. Furthermore, GA is naturally applicable to feature selection since the problem has an exponential search space. Many literatures were published that have shown advantages of the GA for feature selection [1]. Binary coded Swarm optimization (PSO) now is used to solve the problems of feature selection. Ant colony optimization (ACO) is another promising approach to solve the combinatorial optimization problems and has been widely utilized in feature selection [2,3].

D.-S. Huang et al. (Eds.): ICIC 2012, CCIS 304, pp. 481–488, 2012.

The current swarm intelligence optimization algorithms for feature selection are mostly based on binary coded mode in which one feature will be used or deleted before evaluating the optimization objective function. This mode is too rigid to lose the complementary information between features. It is feasible to take the contribution of each feature for classifying as the normalized weight vector, and we can use real coded optimization algorithm to get the optimal or sub-optimal feature weights, which will keep all the data points within the same class close while separating all the data points from different classes. In the optimization process, features weights are adjusted adaptively for each training point to reflect the importance of features in determining its class label, and finally we can set a threshold of weights vector to determine which features should be selected in classifying or embed the weights information into K Nearest Neighbor (KNN) classifier, which heavily rely on the distance metric for the input data patterns [4].

As a simple but very competitive and powerful form of evolutionary computing, Differential Evolution (DE) is a popular real coded optimization algorithm and there are a great deal of variants of the basic algorithm with improved performance since its inception in 1995. In DE, there are two special control parameters need to be determine, including the mutation scale factor F and the crossover ratio Cr. The global optimum searching capability and the convergence speed of DE are very sensitive to the choice of these parameters. In order to tune the control parameters F and Cr self-adaptively, a typical and well used method is SaDE algorithm proposed by Qin [5], in which both the trial vector generation strategies and their associated control parameters are gradually self-adapted by learning from their previous experiences of generating promising solutions.

In this paper, we create the optimal objective function based on the global distance metric learning, and transfer the traditional binary coded mode for selecting optimum feature set into the real coded mode by optimizing weight vector. The self-adaptive differential evolution algorithm SaDE is used to search the optimal solution. This method is tested finally by classifying the breast impedance feature from UCI breast tissue dataset. The rest of this paper is organized as follows: The method we proposed is introduced in detail in Section 2, and the test experiment and result of feature selection by using the UCI breast tissue dataset is described in Section 3. At last, discussion and conclusion are given in Section 4.

2   Methods

2.1   Weighted Distance Metric and Class Margin

For a given collection of pair of similar and dissimilar points in supervised learning, a good distance metric will keep all the data pairs in the same class close while separating those in the different classes. In N-dimension feature space, the weighted distance function between the two points x and y can be calculated by following equation:

$$d_A^2(x, y) = \|x - y\|_A^2 = (x - y)^T A(x - y) \tag{1}$$

Where A is the weight matrix, superscript T means transposition operation

In order to learn a distance metric A for the input space of data from training data, the criterion to evaluate classification performance of A could be created using class margin. Given a distance function, the two nearest neighbors of each sample X_n could be found, one from the same class (called nearest hit or NH) and the other from the different class (called nearest miss or NM). The class margin of X_n is defined as

$$CM = d_A^2(X_n, NM_{X_n}) / d_A^2(X_n, NH_{X_n}) \tag{2}$$

Clearly, distance metric A will be better if CM is larger, that means the larger between-class distance and the small within-class distance.

2.2   Optimization Objective Function

To avoid neglecting the correlate and complementary information among the various features, the global muti-class margin is defined as:

$$M_{mc} = \min(CM_{\min}^1, \cdots, CM_{\min}^i, \cdots, CM_{\min}^c) \tag{3}$$

Where superscript i means the ith class in totally C classes, and $CM_{\min}^i$ is the minimum class margin   from all points in the same class i.

The Optimization Objective Function can be given as:

$$Max\{\min(CM_{\min}^1, \cdots, CM_{\min}^i, \cdots, CM_{\min}^c)\} \tag{4}$$
$$st. \text{ } A \geq 0,$$

2.3   Differential Evolution Algorithm

For a real parameter single-objective optimization question, parameter X can be represented as a vector $X = [x_1, x_2, \cdots, x_d]^T$ in D-dimension parameter space. The original DE algorithm is described in detail as follows:

- The Population

$$P_{x,g} = (X_{i,G}), i = 0,1,\cdots Np-1, G = 0,1,\cdots,G_{\max}$$
$$X_{i,g} = (x_{j,i,G}), j = 0,1,\cdots D-1 \tag{5}$$

Where Np denotes the number of population vectors, G defines the generation counter, and D the dimensionality.

- Population Initialization

$$x_{j,i,0} = rand_j[0,1) * (b_{j,U} - b_{j,L}) + b_{j,L} \tag{6}$$

where bL and bU indicate the lower and upper bounds of the parameter vectors.
- Mutation Operation

For each target vector $X_{i,G}$ at generation G, an associated mutant vector $V_{i,G}$ can usually be generated by using one of the following strategies:

"DE/rand/1": $V_{i,G} = X_{r1,G} + F(X_{r2,G} - X_{r3,G})$
"DE/best/1": $V_{i,G} = X_{best,G} + F \cdot (X_{r1,G} - X_{r2,G})$
"DE/current to best/1": $V_{i,G} = X_{i,G} + F \cdot (X_{bset,G} - X_{i,G}) + F \cdot (X_{r1,G} - X_{r2,G})$
"DE/best/2": $V_{i,G} = X_{best,G} + F \cdot (X_{r1,G} - X_{r2,G}) + F \cdot (X_{r3,G} - X_{r4,G})$
"DE/rand/2": $V_{i,G} = X_{r1G} + F \cdot (X_{r2,G} - X_{r3,G}) + F \cdot (X_{r4,G} - X_{r5,G})$

$$\tag{7}$$

Where indices $r1, r2, r3, r4, r5$ are random and mutually different integers generated in the range [1, Np], which should also be different from the current trial vector's index i. F is the mutation scale factor and $X_{best,G}$ is the individual vector with best fitness value in the population at current generation G.

- Crossover Operation

The binominal crossover operation is applied to each pair of the generated mutant vector $V_{i,G}$ and its corresponding target vector $X_{i,G}$ to generate a trial vector $U_{i,G}$:

$$U_{i,G} = (u_{j,i,G}) = \begin{cases} v_{j,i,G} & if\,(rand_j[0,1) \le Cr) \\ x_{j,i,G} & otherwise \end{cases} \tag{8}$$

Where Cr is the crossover ratio.
- Selection Operation

DE uses simple one-to-one survivor selection where the trial vector $U_{i,G}$ competes against the target vector $X_{i,G}$. The vector with the best fitness value survives into the next generation $G+1$.

$$X_{i,G+1} = \begin{cases} U_{i,G} & if\,\,f(U_{i,G}) \le f(X_{i,G}) \\ X_{i,G} & otherwise \end{cases} \tag{9}$$

2.4   SaDE

SaDE use a probability p to select one mutation strategy from several available ones and apply it to the current population, then the mutation scale factor F and the crossover ratio Cr are sampled respectively from the normal distribution with specified mean and variance. Scheme of SaDE are summarized as follows [5]:

- Mutation strategies self-adaptation

SaDE selects mutation strategies "DE/rand/1" and "DE/current to best/1" in Eq. (7) as candidates, and produces the trial vector based on:

$$V_{i,G} = \begin{cases} X_{r1,G} + F(X_{r2,G} - X_{r3,G}), & if\,(rand[0,1) \le p) \\ X_{i,G} + F(X_{bset,G} - X_{i,G}) + F(X_{r1,G} - X_{r2,G}), & otherwise \end{cases} \tag{10}$$

After evaluation of all offspring, the number of offspring successfully entering the next generation while generated by above two strategies are recorded as ns_1 and ns_2

respectively, and the numbers of offspring discarded are recorded as nf_1 and nf_2. Those two pairs of numbers are accumulated within a specified number of generations. Then, the probability p is updated as:

$$p = \frac{ns_1 \cdot (ns_2 + nf_2)}{ns_2 \cdot (ns_1 + nf_1) + ns_1 \cdot (ns_2 + nf_2)} \tag{11}$$

- Mmutation scale factor F self-adaptation
  In SaDE, F is set to:

$$F_i = N_i(0.5, 0.3) \tag{12}$$

where $N_i(0.5, 0.3)$ denotes a Gaussian random number with mean 0.5 and standard deviation 0.3.
- Crossover ratio Cr self-adaptation
  SaDE allocates a Cr_i for each individuals according to:

$$Cr_i = N_i(Cr_m, 0.1) \tag{13}$$

These Cr values for all individuals remain the same for several generations During every generation, the Cr values associated with offspring successfully entering the next generation are recorded in an array Cr_{rec} which length is N_s. After a specified number of generations, Cr_m will be updated:

$$Cr_m = \frac{1}{N_s} \sum_{k=1}^{Ns} Cr_{rec}(k) \tag{14}$$

2.5   Feature Selection Integrated with SaDE

To find the optimal or sub-optimal feature weights which keep all the data points within the same class close, a N-dimension real vector $X = [x_1, x_2, \cdots, x_d]^T$ which range in $[0,1]$ is normalized and is made diagonal to form the distance metric matrix A:

$$A = \begin{bmatrix} w_1 & \cdots & 0 \\ \vdots & \ddots & \vdots \\ 0 & \cdots & w_d \end{bmatrix}, \quad w_i = \frac{x_i}{\sum_{k=1}^{d} x_k} \tag{15}$$

To calculate the objective function Eq.(4), the Eq.(1)-(3) will be used in term of A. SaDE is used to apply optimization to guarantee features weights are adjusted adaptively. When the weight vector representing contribution of each feature for classifying is achieved, features should be selected according to the following criterion:

$$\frac{\displaystyle\sum_{k=1}^{j} W_k}{\displaystyle\sum_{k=1}^{d} W_k} \geq 90\% \tag{16}$$

Where W is the vector formed by sorting w with descending order, so the former j features are selected when their cumulative sum over 0.9.

3   Experiment and Result

The UCI Breast Tissue Data Set is used to test the result of feature selection. This Dataset provides 106 instances, which including 9 impedance measurements features of breast tissue and 1 class attribute [6]. The dataset can be used for predicting the classification of either the original 6 classes or of 4 classes by merging together the fibro-adenoma, mastopathy and glandular classes whose discrimination is not important. For simplify, we use the merged together 4 classes as class label for corresponding sample. For the convenience of denotation and comparison, we use the feature index to substitute name of original impedance features showed as Table.1

Table 1. Substitution of original impedance features

Name	I0	PA500	HFS	DA	Area	A/DA	Max IP	DR	P
Index	F1	F2	F3	F4	F5	F6	F7	F8	F9

We use the K-fold(K=5) cross validation method to get the robust result. For each training and test dataset, SaDE algorithm is run ten times and its best performance in all round are treated as feature selection result. All the algorithms are implemented using Matlab 7.1 and executed on the computer with Intel Pentium® 4 CPU and 2 Gb of RAM memory. For SaDE, the population size and maximum number of function evaluations are set to be the same. The maximum number of function evaluations is set to 200 and the population size is 45.

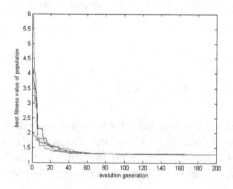

Fig. 1. The convergence curve of SaDE

Fig.1 shows the convergence speed curve of SaDE in 5 different data partition for cross-validation. It indicates the fitness value (the reciprocal of global multi-class margin) will be convergent after about 100 generation no matter whatever dataset.

Table.2 gives the optimal feature weights and final result of feature selection according to the criterion (Eq.16), for 5 different data partition for cross-validation. It indicates the weight based on distance metric learning is sensitive to the data, but the complementary information is preserved and the redundant relationship is eliminated between features.

Table 2. The weight of features and   the selected feature subset

F1	F2	F3	F4	F5	F6	F7	F8	F9	Selected subset
0.4012	0.2306	0.2511	0.0093	0.0000	0.1040	0.0027	0.0010	0.0001	[F1, F2, F3, F6]
0.5020	0.0152	0.2847	0.0062	0.0000	0.0005	0.1376	0.0536	0.0001	[F1, F3, F7]
0.0058	0.2077	0.3380	0.0398	0.0000	0.0029	0.3386	0.0649	0.0023	[F2, F3, F7, F8]
0.3225	0.2068	0.2004	0.0182	0.0000	0.2333	0.0034	0.0104	0.0051	[F1, F2, F3, F6]
0.0771	0.2534	0.2691	0.2613	0.0000	0.0060	0.1000	0.0330	0.0001	[F1, F2, F3, F4, F7]

Form Table.2, we can choose [F1,F2,F3,F4,F6] as the final feature subset considering the high correlation between F1 and F9, F4 and F8, that make the classifier has robust and good performance at different data environment. According to the result of using the classification correction rate of naïve Bayesian   classifier and exhaustive searching, there are not only one result that the features subset which has the smaller features number but high correction rate, such as   [F4,F6,F9],[F6,F8,F9], [F5,F6,F7,F8,F9] and so on.

4   Discussion and Conclusion

This paper presented a new SaDE based feature selection algorithm utilizing both SaDE and maximize multi-classes margin. The proposed method was tested and compared with the result of exhaustive searching, which embedded in the wrapper feature selection method. The former has a quantified weight to every feature to evaluate their contribution to classification and the result has a good robust, while the latter have need more computation resource and the result highly depends on the used training set.

Although the test result shows the feature selection with the algorithm we proposed is feasible and effective, It is should noted here we only use the linear weighted idea. For applying it to the more complex problem, this algorithm is further extended to the nonlinear case integrated by using kernel method. In the future, more experiment results will be investigated to evaluate its efficacy compared to other conventional approaches, especially when handling large training data with high dimensions. Feature selection also can be handled as Multi-objective Optimization, and recently the Multi-swarm PSO which also real coded are emerging [7,8], we will try to integrated our method with these Multi-objective Optimization method to select feature subset.

Acknowledgement. This paper is supported by National Natural Science Foundation of China (Grant NO. 60905039,71001072).

References

1. Liu, H.: Evolving Feature Selection. IEEE Intell. Syst. 20(3), 64–76 (2005)
2. Huang, H., Xie, H., Gup, J.: Ant Colony Optimization-based Feature Selection Method for Surface Electromyography Signals Classification. Computers in Biology and Medicine 42(2), 30–38 (2012)
3. Zhang, J., Zhan, Z.: Evolutionary Computation Meets Machine Learning: A Survey. Computational Intelligence Magazine 6(4), 68–75 (2011)
4. Jin, R., Wang, S., Zhou, Y.: Regularized Distance Metric Learning: Theory and Algorithm. In: Proc. 22nd Advances in Neural Information Processing Systems (2009)
5. Qin, A.K., Huang, V.L., Suganthan, P.N.: Differential Evolution Algorithm With Strategy Adaptation for Global Numerical Optimization. Evolutionary Computation 13(2), 398–417 (2009)
6. Lin, J.: Divergence Measures Based on the Shannon Entropy. IEEE Transaction Information Theory 25(5), 3–10 (2000)
7. Niu, B., Xue, B., Li, L., Chai, Y.: Symbiotic Multi-swarm PSO for Portfolio Optimization. In: Huang, D.-S., Jo, K.-H., Lee, H.-H., Kang, H.-J., Bevilacqua, V. (eds.) ICIC 2009. LNCS, vol. 5755, pp. 776–784. Springer, Heidelberg (2009)
8. Niu, B., Wang, H., Tan, L.J., Xu, J.: Multi-objective Optimization Using BFO Algorithm. Lecture Notes in Bioinformatics, pp. 582–587 (2011)

Optimization Based on Bacterial Colony Foraging

Wei Liu[1,2], Yunlong Zhu[1], Ben Niu[3], and Hanning Chen[1]

[1] Laboratory of Information Service and Intelligent Control, Shenyang Institute of Automation, Chinese Academy of Sciences, Liaoning, Shenyang, 110016, China
[2] Jilin Normal University, Jilin, Siping, 136000, China
[3] College of Management, Shenzhen University, Shenzhen, 518060, China
Chenhanning@sia.cn

Abstract. This paper proposes a novel bacterial colony foraging (BCF) algorithm for complex optimization problems. The proposed BCF extend original bacterial foraging algorithm to adaptive and cooperative mode by combining bacterial chemotaxis, cell-to-cell communication, and a self-adaptive foraging strategy. The cell-to-cell communication enables the historical search experience sharing among the bacterial colony that can significantly improve convergence. With the self-adaptive strategy, each bacterium can be characterized by focused and deeper exploitation of the promising regions and wider exploration of other regions of the search space. In the experiments, the proposed algorithm is benchmarked against four state-of-the-art reference algorithms using a set of classical test functions.

Keywords: bacterial colony, cell-to-cell communication, chemotaxis, self-adaptive, optimization.

1 Introduction

In recent years, the computational models of chemotaxis (i.e. the bacterial foraging behavior) have attracted more and more attention, due to its research potential in engineering applications. A few models have been developed to mimic bacterial foraging behavior and have been applied for solving some practical problems[1-3]. Among them, bacterial foraging optimization (BFO) is a successful population-based numerical optimization algorithm that mimics the foraging behavior of E. coli bacteria3. Until now, BFO has been applied to some engineering problems, such as optimal control[4], optimal power flow[5], color image enhancement[6], and machine learning[7]. However, experimentation with complex and multimodal benchmark functions reveals that the BFO algorithm possesses a poor convergence behavior and its performance heavily decreases with the growth of search space dimensionality and problem complexity.

This paper aims to demonstrate convincingly that the self-adaptive and communication approaches are both effective strategies and can be utilized to help scaling up the performance of bacterial foraging algorithms for solving complex optimization problems with high dimensionality. That is, this paper extend the classical BFO to a

D.-S. Huang et al. (Eds.): ICIC 2012, CCIS 304, pp. 489–494, 2012.

novel bacterial colony foraging (BCF) optimization model by applying two enhanced manipulated steps, namely a cell-to-cell communication and a self-adaptive foraging strategy t in nature. In the proposed BCF model, each artificial bacterium can climb the nutrient gradient based on not only its own experience but also the knowledge of the others; also, each bacterium can strike a balance between the exploration and the exploitation of the search space during its evolution, by adaptively tuning the magnitude of its chemotactic step size.

Experiments were performed to evaluate the performance of the proposed algorithm. The test-suit contains five classical benchmark functions, namely the Sphere, Rosenbrock, Ackley, Rastrigrin, and Griewank functions. The proposed BCF algorithm has been compared with its classical counterpart, the classical BFO algorithm, the very popular swarm-intelligence algorithm known as PSO[8], a hybrid optimization technique that synergistically couples BFOA with PSO that called BSO[9], and a standard real-coded genetic algorithm (GA)[10] over the test suite with respect to the statistical performance measures of solution quality and convergence speed.

The rest of the paper is organized as follows. In Section 2, the proposed BCF algorithm will be introduced and its implementation details will be given. In Section 3, the experiment studies of the proposed BCF and the other algorithms are presented with descriptions of the benchmark functions, experimental settings, and experimental results. Finally, conclusions are drawn in Section 4.

2   The Bacterial Colony Foraging Algorithm

This work extends the classical BFO to a self-adaptive and cooperative optimization model by constructing the following processes:

2.1   Self-adaptation

Here each bacterium in the colony has to permanently maintain an appropriate balance between "Exploration" and "Exploitation" states by varying its own run-length unit adaptively. The criteria that determine the adjustment of individual run-length unit and the entrance into one of the states are defined as following:

Criterion-1: if the bacterium discovers a promising domain, the run-length unit of this bacterium is adapted to a smaller one.

Criterion-2: if the bacterium's current fitness is unchanged for a number K_u (user-defined) of consecutive generations, then augment this bacterium's run-length unit and this bacterium enters the Exploration state.

This self-adaptive strategy is given in pseudocode in Table 1. Where t is the current generation number, $C_i(t)$ is the current run-length unit of the ith bacterium, $\varepsilon_i(t)$ is the required precision in the current generation of the ith bacterium, λ is the run-length unit decreasing parameter that is a user-defined constant, $C^{initial}$ and $\varepsilon^{initial}$ are the initialized run-length unit and the precision goal respectively.

Table 1. The dynamic self-adaptive strategy

1: **FOR** (each bacterium i) **IN   PARALLEL**
2:     **IF** (*Criterion-1*) **then** //*exploitation*
3:         $C_i(t+1) = C_i(t) / \lambda$;
4:         $\varepsilon_i^i(t+1) = \varepsilon_i^i(t) / \lambda$;
5:     **ELSE IF** (*Criterion-2*) **then**   //*exploration*
6:         $C_i(t+1) = C^{initial}$;
7:         $\varepsilon_i^i(t+1) = \varepsilon^{initial}$;
8:     **ELSE**
9:         $C_i(t+1) = C_i(t)$;
10:         $\varepsilon_i^i(t+1) = \varepsilon_i^i(t)$;
11:     **END IF**
12: **END FOR IN PARALLEL**

2.2   Cell-to-cell Communication

In BCF model, when a bacterial turns, its choice of a new direction should not be governed by a probability distribution, while be dominated by the information combination of itself and its colony members. Accordingly, we introduce an additional direction component D_i to each bacterium. Then in the BCF algorithm, at the tth iteration the direction is computed as:

$$D_i(t) = kD_i(t-1) + \phi_1 R_1 \|X_{p_i} - X_i(t-1)\| + \phi_2 R_2 \|X_{s_i} - X_i(t-1)\| \qquad (1)$$

where k is the weight for the previous direction of the ith bacterium, which represents how the bacterium trusts its own status at present location, X_{p_i} is the best position where this bacterium had been, X_{s_i} is the overall global best position ever achieved by the bacterial colony, $\|X_{p_i} - X_i(t-1)\|$ and $\|X_{s_i} - X_i(t-1)\|$ are both unit vectors for indicating the directions only, ϕ_1 and ϕ_2 are the learning rates that control the influence levels of cognitive and social components to make different swimming directions, R_1 and R_2 are random numbers uniformly distributed in [0, 1].

2.3   Enhanced Chemotaxis

Then in each chemotactic step, the self-adaptive chemotactic step-size C_i controls the swim amplitude taken by the ith bacterium towards a desired direction, which is specified by the cell-to-cell communication based tumble direction D_i:

$$X_i(t) = X_i(t-1) + C_i(t-1)D_i(t-1) \qquad (2)$$

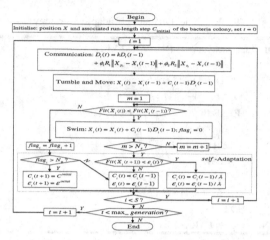

Fig. 1. Flowchart of the BCF algorithm

The flowchart of the BCF algorithm is illustrated in Fig. 1, where S is the colony size, t is the chemotactic generation counter from 1 to max-generation, i is the bacterium's ID counter from 1 to S, X_i is the position of the ith bacterium, N_s is the maximum number of steps for a single activity of swim, $flag_i$ is the number of generations that the ith bacterium has not improved its own fitness.

3   Experimental Result

3.1   Benchmarks

In order to fully evaluate the performance of BCF on complex optimization problems, we have employed a carefully chosen set of benchmark functions that including Sphere, Rosenbrock, Ackley, Rastrigrin and Griewank functions. The mathematical formulations of these five functions can be referred to the literature [9].

3.2   Settings

To fully evaluate the performance of the proposed BCF algorithm, four successful nature-inspired optimization algorithms were used for comparison, namely the canonical particle swarm optimization (PSO), the bacterial foraging optimization (BFO), the bacteria swarm optimization (BSO) and the standard genetic algorithm with elitism (GA).

In all experiments in this section, the values of the population size used in each algorithm were chosen to be the same as 50. The other specific parameters of algorithms are given below:

PSO Settings: For canonical PSO, the learning rates c_1 and c_2 are both 2.05, the constriction factor $\chi=0.729$, and the global communication topology is used.

Table 2. Performance of all algorithms on classical test suite. In bold are the best results

Functions		BCF	BFO	PSO	BSO	GA
Sphere	Mean	**6.0662e-051**	22.3747	3.5030e-045	8.3078e-004	0.0239
	Std	**1.3192e-050**	6.1294	1.5613e-044	1.6060e-004	0.0433
Rosenbrock	Mean	**0.2559**	2.5276	3.5233	4.7843	501.0495
	Std	**0.1357**	1.0547	2.1613	2.2227	611.4213
Ackley	Mean	**4.3249**	44.9659	6.4175	4.8253	8.5194
	Std	**2.5722**	10.0562	4.1900	1.6043	2.8877
Rastrigrin	Mean	**0.0742**	129.2755	0.0841	0.0913	0.3875
	Std	**0.0325**	25.2335	0.0380	0.0438	0.2018
Griewank	Mean	**0.0025**	9.4676	0.0518	2.5098	2.0553
	Std	**6.3156**	1.2219	0.1176	0.2565	1.2341

BFO Settings: For the classical BFO algorithm, we take $C=0.1$ and $P_{ed}=0.25$, which is the standard set of these two parameter values as recommended in [3]. We set $N_c=200$ or 100 for classical and composition functions respectively, $N_s=4$, $N_{re}=5$ and $N_{ed}=2$.

BSO Settings: The BSO algorithm, referred to as the bacterial swarm optimization, performs local search through the chemotactic movement operation of BFO whereas the global search over the entire search space is accomplished by a social-only PSO operator. Parametric setup for the algorithm was kept exactly same as described in [9].

GA Settings: Single point crossover operation with the rate of 0.8 was employed. Mutation operation restores genetic diversity lost during the application of reproduction and crossover. Mutation rate in the experiment was set to be 0.01.

BCF Settings: For the proposed BCF algorithm, the initialized run-length unit $C^{initial}$ was set to be 1% of the search space, the initial precision goal $\varepsilon^{initial}=100$, the generation limit for jumping out of local optima $K_u=20$, and the run-length unit decreasing parameter $\lambda=10$.

3.3   Results

Table 2 presents the mean and stand deviations of the 30 runs of the five involved algorithms on the classical test suite. From Table 2, the proposed BCF achieved significantly better results than all the other algorithms. It should be noted that BCF is the fastest one for finding good results within relatively few generations. For example, BCF can consistently found the minimum of multimodal functions within relatively fewer generations, while the other algorithms generated poorer results on them. On Griewank function, the BCF algorithm yielded similar results to the PSO, BSO and GA, while still achieved significantly better performance than the original BFO algorithm.

4   Conclusions

In order to apply bacterial foraging inspired algorithms to solve complex optimization problems efficiently and effectively, we have proposed a new bacterial colony foraging algorithm (BCF). The proposed BCF combines several optimal foraging approaches such as: bacterial chemotaxis, cell-to-cell communication based cooperation, and a self-adaptive foraging strategy. This combination successfully cast bacterial foraging algorithm into the adaptive and cooperative fashion. An extensive performance analysis has been provided. Results show the proposed algorithm outperformed four state-of-the-art nature inspired algorithms on a classical test suite that totally including five mathematical functions.

Acknowledgment. This work was supported in part by the National Natural Science Foundation of China under Grant Nos.61105067 and 61174164.

References

1. Bremermann, H.J., Anderson, R.W.: An Alternative to Back-propagation: a Simple Rule of Synaptic Modification for Neural Net Training and Memory. Technical Report PAM-483, Center for Pure and Applied Mathematics, University of California (1990)
2. Müeller, S., Marchetto, J., Airaghi, S., Koumoutsakos, P.: Optimization on Bacterial Chemotaxis. IEEE Trans. on Evolutionary Computation 6(1), 16–29 (2002)
3. Passino, K.M.: Biomimicry of Bacterial Foraging for Distributed Optimization and Control. IEEE Control System Magazine 22(3) (2002)
4. Su, T., Chen, G., Cheng, J.: Fuzzy PID Controller Design Using Synchronous Bacterial Foraging Optimization. In: Proceedings of 3rd International Conference on Information Sciences and Interaction Sciences, pp. 639–642 (2010)
5. Tang, W.J., Li, M.S., Wu, Q.H., Saunders, J.R.: Bacterial Foraging Algorithm for Optimal Power Flow in Dynamic Environments. IEEE Transactions on Circuits and Systems I 55(8), 2433–2442 (2008)
6. Hanmandlu, M., Verma, O.P., Kumar, N.K., Kulkarni, M.: A Novel Optimal Fuzzy System for Color Image Enhancement Using Bacterial Foraging. IEEE Transactions on Instrumentation and Measurement 58(8), 2867–2879 (2009)
7. Kim, D., Nair, S.B.: Novel Emotion Engine for Robot and Its Parameter Tuning by Bacterial Foraging. In: Proceedings of 5th International Symposium on Applied Computational Intelligence and Informatics, pp. 23–28 (2009)
8. Kennedy, J.: The Particle Swarm as Collaborative Sampling of the Search Space. Advances in Complex Systems 10, 191–213 (2007)
9. Biswas, A., Dasgupta, S., Abraham, A.: Synergy of PSO and Bacterial Foraging Optimization - A Comparative Study on Numerical Benchmarks. In: Proceeding of Innovations in Hybrid Intelligent Systems, pp. 255–263 (2008)
10. Sumathi, S., Hamsapriya, T., Surekha, P.: Evolutionary Intelligence: An Introduction to Theory and Applications with Matlab. Springer (2008)

Differential Evolution Based on Fitness Euclidean-Distance Ratio for Multimodal Optimization

Jing Liang[1], Boyang Qu[2], Mao Xiaobo[1], and Tiejun Chen[1]

[1] School of Electrical Engineering, Zhengzhou Univerisity, Zhengzhou, China
{liangjing,mail-mxb,tchen}@zzu.edu.cn
[2] School of Electric and Information Engineering,
Zhongyuan University of Technology, Zhengzhou, China
e070088@e.ntu.edu.sg

Abstract. In this paper, fitness euclidean-distance ratio (FER) is incorprated into differential evolution to solve multimodal optimization problems. The prime target of multi-modal optimization is to finding multiple global and local optima of a problem in one single run. Though variants of differential evolution (DE) are highly effective in locating single global optimum, few DE algorithms perform well when solving multi-optima problems. This work uses the FER technique to enhance the DE's ability of locating and maintaining multiple peaks. The proposed algorithm is tested on a number of benchmark test function and the experimental results show that the proposed simple algorithm performs better comparing with a number of state-of-the-art multimodal optimization approaches.

Keywords: multimodal optimization, niching algorithm, differential evolution, fitness euclidean-distance ratio.

1 Introduction

In real world optimization, many engineering problems can be classified as multimodal optimization problems. The problems are often desirable to locate not only one global optimum but also severl global or local optimal solutions and then to choose the most appropriate solution on the basis of practical issues. In recent years, evolutionary algorithms (EAs) have been proven to be effective in solving optimization problems [1-4]. However orignal EAs are often not suitable to solve multi-modal optimization problems. To overcome this problem, various methods that know as niching techniques have been successfully incorprated into different EAs to solve multi-modal optimization problems.

Niching refers to the method of finding and preserving multiple small stable groups. Many niching methods have been proposed over the past few decades, including crowding [5], restricted toumament selection [6], fitness sharing [7], speciation [8], etc. [9-11]. Differential evoltuion (DE) is a simple yet effective global optimization technique. Various niching methods are combined with DE to handle multi-modal optimization problems. In this paper, a fitness euclidean-ration based

D.-S. Huang et al. (Eds.): ICIC 2012, CCIS 304, pp. 495–500, 2012.

differential evolution is proposed and comopared with a number of popular niching algorithms on a set of commonly used multi-modal test functions.

The remainder of this paper is structured as follows. Section 2 gives a brief overview of differential evolution and the FER methods. In section 3, the proposed differential evolution based on fitness Euclidean-distance ration is introduced. Experimental setup and results are present in section 4. Finally, the paper is concluded in section 5.

2   Differential Evolution and Fitness Eulidean-Distance Ratio

Differential evolution (DE) was first proposed by Storn and Price in 1995 [12]. DE is a powerful and efficient evolutionary algorithm in solving global optimization problem. DE generates offspring by using differences of randomly sampled pairs of individual vectors from the population. Similar to other algorithm, DE is also a population based searching algorithm. The offspring compete with their parents inside the population and the winner will be kept as parents for next generation. Four main steps are involved in DE known as, initialization, mutation, recombination and selection. In the mutation operation, DE/rand/1 strategy which is commonly used is employed in this paper:

$$\text{DE/rand/1:} \qquad\qquad v_p = x_{r1} + F \cdot (x_{r2} - x_{r3}) \qquad\qquad (1)$$

where r_1 to r_3 are mutually different integers randomly generated in the range [1, NP (population size)], F is the scale factor used to scale differential vectors. x_{best} is the solution with the best fitness value in the current population.

The crossover operation is applied to each pair of the generated mutant vector and its corresponding parent vector using the following equations:

$$u_{p,d} = \begin{cases} v_{p,d} & \text{if } rand_d \leq CR \text{ or } d = d_{rand} \\ x_{p,d} & \text{otherwise} \end{cases} \qquad\qquad (2)$$

where up is the offspring vector. CR is the crossover rate which is a user-specified constant in the range of [0, 1].

Fitness Eulidean-distance ration was first introduced by Li [13] to solve multi-modal optimizaiton problems. The technique was incorprated into Particle Swam Optimizaiton (PSO) to push the particles moving towards its "fittest-and-closest" neighbors *nbest*.

The *nbest* for i^{th} particle was selected as the neighborhood personal best with the largest Fitness-Euclidean distance Ratio (FER) and the FER value is calculated as :

$$FER_{(j,i)} = \alpha \cdot \frac{f(p_j) - f(p_i)}{\|p_j - p_i\|} \qquad\qquad (3)$$

Where p_j and p_i are the personal best of the jth and i^{th} particle respectively. $\alpha = \frac{\|s\|}{f(p_g) - f(p_w)}$ is a scaling factor. $\|s\|$ is the size of the search space, which is estimated by its diagonal distance $\sqrt{\sum_{k=1}^{d}(x_k^u - x_k^l)^2}$ (where x_k^u and x_k^l are the upper and lower bounds of the *kth* dimension of the search space). p_w is the worst-fit particle in the current population.

Recently, Qu et al. [14]proposed a current based fitness Euclidean-distance ration particle swarm optimizer which selected the neighborhood best with respect to the current particle position. The proposed method further improves the performance of the original FERPSO.

3   Differential Evolution Based on Fitness Eulidean-Distance Ratio

In the standard differntial evolution, x_{r1} to x_{r5} are randomly chosen from the whole population. While the individual which are far from x_i cannot represent the properties of the local landscape of x_i, this operator is not suitable for the multi-modal optimization. Thus in the proposed differential evolution based on fitness Euclidean-distance ratio (FERDE), the fittest-and-closest individuals are chosen as x_{r1} to x_{r5} to generate the offspring u_i. Considering the scaling factor α is a constant value for the current population and does not affect the sorting of FER values, it is omitted in the proposed algorithm to decrease the computational complexity.

$$FER_{(j,i)} = \frac{f(p_j) - f(p_i)}{\|p_j - p_i\|} \tag{4}$$

In conventional DE, the offspring compete with its parent, whereas in Crowding-DE[5], the fitness value of an offspring is compared with that of the nearest individual in the current population and the fitter one will be kept for following generation. This strategy discourages the population converge to a single optimum and makes DE performs better when solving multi-modal optimization problems. In the new proposed algorithm, this strategy is kept.

The steps of FERDE algorithm is presented as below:

- Step 1: Initialization.
        Randomly generate *NP* number of initial trial solutions.
- Step 2: Generating new population
        For each target vector x_i :
    1)   Calculate FER values with the whole population
    2)   Choose x_{r1} to x_{r3} randomly from the top n individuals according to FER values (n is set to 5 in the experiments).
    3)   Produce an offspring u_i using the standard DE.
    4)   Calculate the Euclidean distance of u_i to the other individuals in the DE population.
    5)   Compare the fitness of u_i with the most similar individual and replace it if the u_i has a better fitness value.
- Step 3: Stop if a termination criterion is satisfied. Otherwise go to Step 2.

4   Experimental Results

To assess the performance of the proposed algorithm, eight commonly used multi-modal optimization benchmark test functions with different characteristics are used. The details of these test functions are shown in Table 1.

Table 1. Test functions

Test Function	Number of Peaks	Dimension	Level of Accuracy
F1: Two-peak trap[15]	2	1	0.05
F2: Central Two-Peak Trap[15]	2	1	0.05
F3: Five-uneven-peak trap[16]	5	1	0.05
F4: Equal Maxima [17]	5	1	1e-6
F5: Decreasing Maxima[17]	5	1	1e-6
F6: Uneven Maxima[17]	5	1	1e-6
F7: Himmelblau's function[17]	4	2	0.0005
F8: Six-hump camel back[18]	2	2	1e-6

FERDE and other four different state-of-art multi-modal optimization algorithms: CDE [5], SDE [21], SPSO [22], FERPSO [22], are examined in this conducted experiment. The population size is set to 50 for all five algorithms and the maximal number of function evaluations is set to 100,000. The DE parameters used in this work are as follow: F=0.9, CR=0.1. All performances are calculated and averaged over 25 independent runs to deal with the effect due to the random initialization.

A level of accuracy needs to be specified in order to assess the performance of different algorithms. An optimum is considered to be found if there exists a solution in the population within the tolerated distance to that optimum. When doing the comparison, following to criteria are used:

1. Success Rate: (The percentage of runs in which all global peaks are successfully located).
2. Average number of peaks found

In this experiment, Matlab R2008a is used as the programming language. The configurations of the computer are Intel Pentium® 4 CPU, 4 Gb of memory.

Success rates with ranks (inside the bracket) of the compared algorithms are listed in Table 2. Total ranks (summation of all the individual ranks) are listed in the last row of the table. The best algorithm of each test function is highlighted in boldface. As can be seen from these results, FERDE performs the best over the compared algorithms. Compare with CDE, FERDE almost improve all the test function except for F1 and F2 which both of the algorithms are able to get 100 percent success rate.

Beside success rate, number of optima found is another important criterion to access multi-modal optimization algorithms, especially on challenging functions. The average number of peaks found are listed in Table 3. From the results, although the success rates of the five algorithms are all not 100% on the two test functions, F3 and F5, FERDE still achieves the higher average number of peaks.

Table 2. Success rate

Test Function	FERDE	CDE	SDE	SPSO	FERPSO
F1	**100**(1)	**100**(1)	84(3)	44(5)	64(4)
F2	**100**(1)	**100**(1)	68(5)	72(4)	88(3)
F3	**88**(1)	44(2)	4(3)	0(4.5)	0(4.5)
F4	**100**(1)	28(5)	72(4)	88(2)	84(3)
F5	**100**(1)	48(3)	0(4.5)	**100**(1)	0(4.5)
F6	**100**(1)	28(5)	60(4)	92(3)	**100**(1)
F7	**92**(1)	0(4.5)	72(2.5)	0(4.5)	72(2.5)
F8	**100**(1)	0(4.5)	**100**(1)	0(4.5)	96(3)
Total Rank	**8**	26	27	28.5	25.5

Table 3. Average number of peaks found

Test Function	FERDE	CDE	SDE	SPSO	FERPSO
F1	**2**(1)	**2**(1)	1.84(3)	1.44(5)	1.48(4)
F2	**2**(1)	**2**(1)	1.68(3)	1.72(2)	1.88(1)
F3	**4.88**(1)	4.44(2)	3.04(4)	3.08(3)	0.64(5)
F4	**5**(1)	3.84(5)	4.72(4)	4.88(2)	4.84(3)
F5	**5**(1)	4.28(3)	1.52(4)	**5**(1)	1(5)
F6	**5**(1)	3.96(5)	4.6(4)	4.92(3)	**5**(1)
F7	**3.92**(1)	0.32(5)	3.72(2)	0.84(4)	3.68(3)
F8	**2**(1)	0.04(5)	**2**(1)	0.08(4)	1.96(3)
Total Rank	**8**	27	25	24	25

5   Conclusions

This paper proposed a differential evolution based on fitness Euclidean-distance ratio (FERDE), which combined CDE with fitness Euclidean-distance ratio. Different from the previous DE algorithms for multi-modal optimization, in the novel algorithm, the mutant vectors are chosen from the individuals with higher fitness Euclidean-distance ratio values. In this way, the local information is exploited better and the diversity which is important for multi-modal optimization is kept. The experiments are conducted on eight benchmark functions and the results show that the novel algorithms performs best comparing with other four state-of-art algorithms.

In the furture work, FERDE with more strategies will be tested. And self-adaptive parameters will be combined into this algorithm to improve its performance and make it easier to be used in the real world optimization problems.

Acknowledgments. This research is partially supported by National Natural Science Foundation of China (Grant NO. 60905039) and Postdoctoral Science Foundation of China (Grants 20100480859).

References

1. Price, K., Storn, R.: Differential Evolution: a Practical Approach to Global Optimization. Springer (2005)
2. Kennedy, J., Eberhart, R.C.: Particle swarm optimization. In: Proceedings of IEEE International Conference on Neural Networks, pp. 1942–1948 (1995)
3. Qu, B.Y., Gouthanan, P., Suganthan, P.N.: Dynamic Grouping Crowding Differential Evolution with Ensemble of Parameters for Multi-modal Optimization. In: Panigrahi, B.K., Das, S., Suganthan, P.N., Dash, S.S. (eds.) SEMCCO 2010. LNCS, vol. 6466, pp. 19–28. Springer, Heidelberg (2010)
4. Qu, B.Y.: Multi-Objective Evolutionary Algorithms on the Summation of Normalized Objectives and Diversified Selection. Information Sciences 180(17), 3170–3181 (2010)
5. Thomsen, R.: Multimodal Optimization Using Crowding-based Differential Evolution. In: CEC 2004, pp. 1382–1389 (2004)
6. Harik, G.R.: Finding Multimodal Solutions Using Restricted Tournament Selection. In: The 6th International Conference on Genetic Algorithms, pp. 24–31 (1995)
7. Goldberg, D.E.: Genetic Algorithms with Sharing for Multimodal Function Optimization. In: The 2nd International Conference on Genetic Algorithms, pp. 41–49 (1987)
8. Li, X.: Adaptively Choosing Neighbourhood Bests Using Species in a Particle Swarm Optimizer for Multimodal Function Optimization. In: Deb, K., Tari, Z. (eds.) GECCO 2004. LNCS, vol. 3102, pp. 105–116. Springer, Heidelberg (2004)
9. Qu, B.: Niching Particle Swarm Optimization with Local Search for Multi-modal Optimization. Information Sciences 180(17), 323–334 (2011)
10. Liang, J.J., Qu, B.Y., Ma, S.T., Suganthan, P.N.: Memetic Fitness Euclidean-Distance Particle Swarm Optimization for Multi Modal Optimization. In: Huang, D.-S., Gan, Y., Premaratne, P., Han, K. (eds.) ICIC 2011. LNCS, vol. 6840, pp. 378–385. Springer, Heidelberg (2012)
11. Qu, B.Y., Suganthan, P.N.: Modified Species-based Differential Evolution with Self-adaptive Radius for Multi-modal Optimization. In: ICCP (2010)
12. Storn, R., Price, K.V.: Differential Evolution-A Simple and Efficient Heuristic for Global Optimization over Continuous Spaces. Journal of Global Optimization 11(3), 341–359 (1995)
13. Li, X.: A Multimodal Particle Swarm Optimizer on Fitness Euclidean-distance Ration. In: GECCO, pp. 78–85 (2007)
14. Qu, B.Y.: Current Based Fitness Euclidean-distance Ratio Particle Swarm Optimizer for Multi-modal Optimization. In: NaBIC (2010)
15. Ackley, D.: An Empirical Study of Bit Vector Function Optimization Genetic Algorithms Simulated Annealing, London, U.K. Pitman (1987)
16. Li, J.P., Balazs, M.E.: Species Conserving Genetic Algorithm for Multimodal Function Optimization. Evol. Comput. 10(3), 207–234 (2002)
17. Deb, K.: Genetic Algorithms in Multimodal Function Optimization, the Clearing house for Genetic Algorithms. M.S thesis and Rep. 89002, Univ. Alabama, Tuscaloosa (1989)
18. Michalewicz, Z.: Genetic Algorithms + Data Structures = Evolution Programs. Springer, New York (1996)
19. Li, X.: Efficient Differential Evolution Using Speciation for Multimodal Function Optimization. In: Proceedings of the Conference on Genetic and Evolutionary Computation, Washington DC, USA, pp. 873–880 (2005)
20. Li, X.: Niching without Niching Parameters: Particle Swarm Optimization Using a Ring Topology. IEEE Transactions on Evolutionary Computation 14(3), 123–134 (2010)

Bacterial Colony Optimization:
Principles and Foundations

Ben Niu[1,2,3] and Hong Wang[1]

[1] College of Management, Shenzhen University, Shenzhen 518060, China
[2] Hefei Institute of Intelligent Machines, Chinese Academy of Sciences, Hefei 230031, China
[3] Institute for Cultural Industries, Shenzhen University, Shenzhen 518060, China
drniuben@gmail.com

Abstract. In this paper we proposes a new optimization algorithm—Bacterial Colony Optimization (BCO) which formulates the bacterial behavior model in a new way. The model is based on the principle of artificial bacterial behavior, including Chemotaxis, Communication, Elimination, Reproduction and Migration. The Chemotaxis and Communication are spread over the whole optimization process while other behaviors are implemented only when their relevant conditions are reached. Experiment results have proved a high efficiency searching capability of the new proposed artificial bacterial colony.

Keywords: Bacterial Colony Optimization (BCO), artificial bacterial behavior, optional communication.

1   Introduction

Motivated by evolution of nature, heuristic search algorithms can be classified as: evolutionary programming algorithms [1], genetic algorithms [2], evolutionary algorithms [3] and so on. Other heuristic approaches simulate the behavior of natural organisms include algorithms like particle swarm optimization algorithms [4, 13], artificial bee algorithms [5], ant colony algorithms [6], etc.

Two well-known study based on bacterial behavior heuristic algorithm (BFA and BC) are proposed by by Passino[7] and Muller [8] respectively. Those two papers broadened the bacterial optimization area with a new horizon. Since then, a growing number of researchers who paid great attention to this field began to divert their concentrations on this new algorithm and extended the concept to algorithms such as Fast Bacterial Swarming Algorithm (FBSA) [9], Bacterial Foraging Algorithm (BFA). Except the new proposed algorithms, improvements of bacterial foraging optimization (BFO) were considered by investigators. Some of the key models involve the discussion of chemotaxis step length [10, 11], and its variance to solve multiobjective problems [12]. Those researches on bacterial foraging optimization suggested that predicting and controlling the dynamical behavior of microbial colonies might have profound implications in reality.

D.-S. Huang et al. (Eds.): ICIC 2012, CCIS 304, pp. 501–506, 2012.
© Springer-Verlag Berlin Heidelberg 2012

However, most of those bacterial based algorithms considered little about the bacterial behavior as swarm intelligence. All individuals of the colony are independent; they seek for nutrition by their own random orientation without any exchange of information with others. What made the situation worse is complicated nature of the original algorithms. Long period of time has been spent on random chemotaxis.

To deal with the aforementioned problems, we proposed a new optimization algorithm—Bacterial Colony Optimization (BCO) to formulate bacteria's behavior in the swarm intelligence way.

The rest of the paper is organized as follows: Section 2 describes the basic behavior of artificial bacteria, and their corresponding models are proposed in Section 3. Section 4 presents the results of the simulation studies, followed by the conclusion in Section.

2   The Behavior of Artificial Bacteria

The basic behavior of bacteria can be simply divided into five parts: Chemotaxis, Elimination, Reproduction, Migration and Communication. Firstly, bacteria swim by rotating whip-like flagella driven by a reversible motor embedded in the cell wall (Fig. 1. a). As environment changed, the fittest individuals will survive while the poorer ones will be eliminate. After a while, the existing bacteria generate new offsprings (Fig. 1. b).

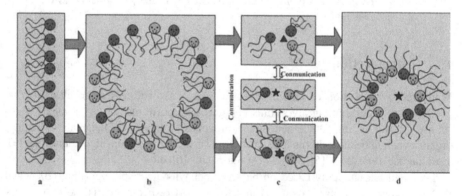

Fig. 1. Bacterial behavior mechanism

With the depletion of nutrition and increasing of population, the resources can no longer hold the bacteria population. Some individuals may choose to migrate to a new area with better nutrition supply (Fig. 1. c). During the searching for a new habitat, information sharing and self experience are both essential (Fig. 1. c). In the algorithms, this phenomenon is reflected by chemotaxis with communication throughout the optimization process. Reproduction, Elimination and Migration are optimizing strategies merged to the Chemotaxis and Communication until the optimal process finishing (Fig. 1. d).

3   Bacterial Colony Optimization Principle

As described aboved, the behavior of artificial bacteria in this paper include five parts, but those behaviors are continuous, mingle and amalgamate. Therefore, their corresponding models can be divided into four smaller models: Chemotaxis & Communication model, Reproduction model, Elimination model, and Migration model. The overall model of bacterial lifecycle is represented in Fig. 2.

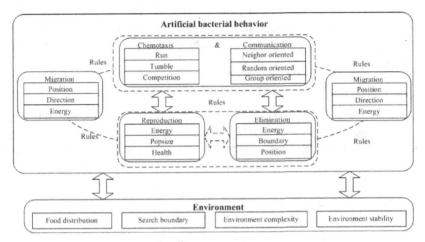

Fig. 2. The overall model

3.1   Chemotaxis and Communication Model

Chemotaxis is accompanied with communication in the whole optimization process. Bacteria run and tumble in the competitive environment. However, they also have to offer their information to the colony in exchange of overall information which would guide them in direction and ways of movement. Bacterial chemotaxis is directed by three elements: group information, personal previous information and a random direction. All three factors conduct bacteria running and tumbling toward optimum. Bacterium runs or tumbles with communication process can be formulated as:

$$Poistion_i(T) = Poistion_i(T-1) + R_i * (Ru_{Infor}) + R\Delta(i) \tag{1}$$

$$Poistion_i(T) = Poistion_i(T-1) + R_i * (Tumb_{Infor}) + R\Delta(i) \tag{2}$$

3.2   Elimination and Reproduction Model

Each bacterium is marked with an energy degree based on its search capability. The higher level of energy indicates a better performance of bacterium. The level of energy decides the probability of elimination and reproduction. Distribution of bacterial energy degree was sorted and analyze and then used as a criterion to judge the qualification of the bacteria. The details are summarized by equation 3-5.

If $L_i > L_{given}$, and $i \in healthy$, then $i \in Candidate_{repr}$ (3)

If $L_i < L_{given}$, and $i \in healthy$, then $i \in Candidate_{eli}$ (4)

If $i \in unhealthy$, then $i \in Candidate_{eli}$ (5)

3.3   Migration Model

Naturally, bacteria could pursue more nutrition aby migration. In optimization aspect, migration can avoid local optimum within some distance. Especially, migration of artificial bacteria in BCO is not based on a certain given probability; it depends on a given condition. When condition is fulfilled, bacterium would migrate to a new random place, as described by equation 6.

$$Poistion_i(T) = rand*(ub-lb)+lb$$ (6)

where: $rand \in [0,1]$, ub and lb are the upper and lower boundary. Bacterium has no need to migrate will search for nutrition continuously as it was. Migration in BCO algorithm is influenced by average energy degree, individual similarity, and chemotaxis efficiency. These factors altogether make up the migration condition.

4   Simulation Studies

To measure the performance of bacteria in new model, simulation studies have conducted in a vary environment with nutrient-noxious distribution. The nutrient distribution of environment at t=0 is set by the function presented by Passino [8].

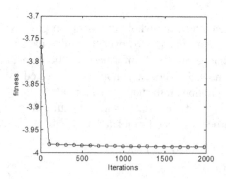

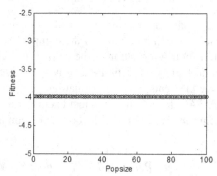

Fig. 3. The average fitness values obtained with iterations

Fig. 4. The final optimal function values of each individual

From Fig. 3, we are able to conclude that the new proposed optimization algorithm can find optimum at a high speed. When a relative optimum was found, the strategy was changed so that more time would be spent on local searching. The final fitness value of each bacteria have been showed in Fig. 4. From Fig. 4, we know that all of the bacteria have found the optimum at the end of 2000 runs.

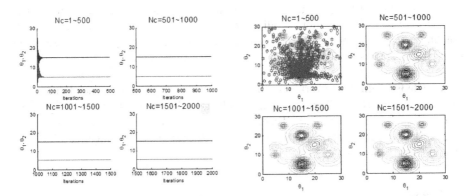

Fig. 5. 2-D position with the iteration process

Fig. 6. The process of finding the optimum

Fig. 5. and 6. suggest that the position of the bacterial group change with the chemotaxis process from two dimensions. In BCO, bacterial chemotaxis time equals to running frequency. Chemotaxis goes along with entire optimization process. What the figures inform us is that bacteria can search for optimum quickly with the help of communication. Most individuals can even find the optimum in the first 500 runs.

Fig. 7. pictures the single bacterium chemotaxis process when chemotaxis ranges between 1 to 100. Optimum can be quickly achieved with our proposed method. In the first 25 steps, the bacterium had already entered into optimum region. There after, it changed the strategy to local search. Fig. 8. presents the whole procedure in one figure, it reveals the fact that the bacterium has find the optimum after 100 runs.

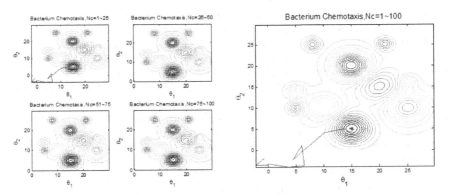

Fig. 7. Single bacterium finds the optimum when chemotaxis ranges between 1~100

Fig. 8. Optimal process of one bacterium when chemotaxis ranges between 1 ~ 100

5   Conclusions

In this paper, a new optimization algorithm based on artificial bacteria is proposed. The bacteria are treated with agent with swarm intelligence. The communication capability is one of the reflections of the group intelligence. Additionally, reproduction, elimination and migration are all optimization strategies to be realized as certain conditions fulfilled. The results show that artificial bacteria have quick response to the complicated environment and can find the optimum in short time.

Acknowledgement. This work is supported by National Natural Science Foundation of China (Grant No.71001072), China Postdoctoral Science Foundation (Grant No. 20100480705), Science and Technology Project of Shenzhen (Grant No. JC201005280492A) , The Natural Science Foundation of Guangdong Province (Grant no. 9451806001002294).

References

1. Tan, Q., He, Q., Zhao, W.Z.: An Improved FCMBP Fuzzy Clustering Method Based on Evolutionary Programming. Computers & Mathematics with Applications 6(4), 1129–1144 (2010)
2. Vasconcelos, J.A., Ramirez, J.A., Takahashi, R.H.C., Saldanha, R.R.: Improvements in Genetic Algorithms. IEEE Transactions on Magnetics 37(5), 3414–3417 (2001)
3. Akbari, R., Ziarati, K.: A Multilevel Evolutionary Algorithm for Optimizing Numerical Functions. International Journal of Industrial Engineering Computations 2, 419–430 (2011)
4. Kennedy, J., Eberhart, R.: Particle Swarm Optimization. In: Proceedings of International Conference on Neural Networks, vol. 4(3), pp. 1942–1948 (1995)
5. Karaboga, D., Akay, B.: A Comparative Study of Artificial Bee Colony Algorithm. Applied Mathematics and Computation 214, 108–132 (2009)
6. Dorigo, M., Birattari, M., Stutzle, T.: Ant Colony Optimization. Computational Intelligence Magazine 1(4), 28–39 (2006)
7. Passino, K.M.: Biomimicry of Bacterial Foraging for Distributed Optimization and Control. IEEE Control Systems Magazine 22(3), 52–67 (2002)
8. Muller, S.D., Marchetto, J., Airaghi, S., Koumoutsakos, P.: Optimization Based on Bacterial Chemotaxis. IEEE Transactions on Evolutionary Computation 6(1), 16–30 (2002)
9. Chu, Y., Mi, H., Liao, H.L., Zhen, J., Wu, Q.H.: A Fast Bacterial Swarming Algorithm for High-Dimensional Function Optimization. In: IEEE Congress on Evolutionary Computation (CEC), pp. 3135–3140 (2008)
10. Niu, B., Fan, Y., Wang, H.: Novel Bacterial Foraging Optimization with Time-varying Chemotaxis Step. International Journal of Artifical Intelligence 7, 257–273 (2011)
11. Niu, B., Wang, H., Tan, L.J., Li, L.: Improved BFO with Adaptive Chemotaxis Step for Global Optimization. In: International Conference on Computational Intelligence and Security (CIS), pp. 76–80 (2011)
12. Niu, B., Wang, H., Tan, L.J., Xu, J.: Multi-Objective Optimization Using BFO Algorithm. In: Huang, D.-S., Gan, Y., Premaratne, P., Han, K. (eds.) ICIC 2011. LNCS, vol. 6840, pp. 582–587. Springer, Heidelberg (2012)
13. Niu, B., Xue, B., Li, L., Chai, Y.: Symbiotic Multi-swarm PSO for Portfolio Optimization. In: Huang, D.-S., Jo, K.-H., Lee, H.-H., Kang, H.-J., Bevilacqua, V. (eds.) ICIC 2009. LNCS, vol. 5755, pp. 776–784. Springer, Heidelberg (2009)

Author Index